ENGLISH SPANISH
SPANISH ENGLISH
WORD TO WORD
DICTIONARY

Martha Arturo Sánchez
Féquière Vilsaint
Orlando Figueredo

EDUCA VISION

English Spanish
Spanish English Word to Word Dictionary

Authors: Martha Arturo Sánchez, Féquière Vilsaint, and
                Orlando Figueredo
Cover design: Nathalie Jean-Baptiste

For information, please contact:

Educa Vision Inc.,
7550 NW 47th Avenue,
Coconut Creek, FL 33073
Telephone: 954 968-7433.
E-mail: educa@aol.com.
Web: www.educavision.com

ISBN: 1-58432-484-8

DEDICATION

This book is dedicated to the teachers who throughout this project assisted us with patience. They helped develop this dictionary into a compre-hensive ressource.

PREFACE

The English Spanish Dictionary is a practical instrument to help both English and Spanish learners of the other language to improve their language skills and clarify issues of orthography. It contains 27,000 word entries and expressions, many with multiple meanings.

We depart dramatically from our previous edition first by using a word frequency list of the English language to select frequent entries in common English communication. Second, we added special vocabulary from school content fields such as social sciences, physical sciences, biological sciences, mathematics, language arts, etc. The result is a comprehensive list of English entries with Spanish equivalents in all areas covered in school curricula.

We wish to thank the teachers from Florida, New York, Texas, and California for testing several drafts of the manuscript and for sending useful feedback.

Special thanks to: Nelda Gallardo, Neale Pruisner, Maude Heurtelou, Andrea DeCastro, Simone Alvarado, Anne Valérie Dorsainvil, Vanessa Adam, Nathalie Jean Baptiste, Olivia Blobaum, Paula Lafitola, Greg and Gilda Simeone, Joanna Koontz, Margaret Abbott, Elvira Wald, and Susana Ramirez.

Féquière Vilsaint
Educa Vision
May 2008

LIST OF ABREVIATIONS

	English	**Spanish**
a.	adjective	adjetivo
adv.	adverb	adverbio
art.	article	artículo
conj.	conjunction	conjunción
interj.	interjection	interjección
n.	name	nombre
pos.	possessive adjective	adjetivo posesivo
prep.	preposition	preposición
pron.	pronoun	pronombre
v.	verb	verbo

SECTION ONE

English Spanish

A

a: un; una
a priori: *adv.* a priori
abaca: *n.* abacá
aback: *adv.* detrás; atrás
abacus: *n.* ábaco
abalone: *n.* abalone
abandonment: *n.* abandono
abash: *v.* avergonzar
abate: *v.* suprimir; disminuir; reducir
abatement: *n.* supresión; rebaja
Abbe condenser: condensador de Abbe
abbess: *n.* abadesa
abbey: *n.* abadía; monasterio
abbot: *n.* abad; prior
abbreviate: *v.* abreviar; abreviatura
abbreviation: abreviación; abreviatura
ABC-book: *n.* abecedario
abdicate: *v.* renunciar
abdomen: *n.* abdomen; vientre; estómago
abdominal: *adj.* abdominal
abdominal pain: cólicos abdominales
abdominal tap: paracentesis
abduct: *v.* raptar; secuestrar; abducir
abduction: *n.* abducción
abductor: *n.* abductor
aberrant: *adj.* aberrante
abeyance: *n.* suspensión
abhor: *v.* aborrecer
abhorrence: *n.* aborrecimiento
abhorrent: aborrecible
ability: habilidad; capacidad
abiotic factor: factor abiótico
abjure: *v.* abjurar
ablative: *adj.* Ablativo
ablaze: *adj.* Brillante
able: *adj.* hábil; capaz
ablution: *n.* ablución; lavado
abnegation: *n.* abnegación

abnormal: *adj.* Anormal
abnormality: *n.* anormalidad
abode: *n.* domicilio; hogar
abolish: *v.* abolir; angular
abolition: *n.* abolición
abomination: *n.* abominación
aboriginal: 1. *adj.* nativo; 2. *n.* nativo
abort: *v.* abortar
abortion: *n.* aborto
abortionist: *n.* abortista
abortive: *adj.* abortivo
abound: *v.* abundar
about: 1. *adv.* alrededor de; sobre; 2. *prep.* sobre
above: 1. *adj.* antedicho; 2. *n.* antedicho; 3. *prep.* sobre; 4. *adv.* arriba
abracadabra!: interj. ¡abracadabra!
Abraham: Abrahán
abrasion: *n.* abrasión
abrasive: *adj.* abrasivo
abreast: *adv.* al lado (uno de otro); de frente
abridge: *v.* abreviar; simplificar
abrogate: *v.* abrogar; revocar; rescindir
abrogation: *n.* revocación; rescisión
abrupt: *adj.* abrupto
abscess: *n.* absceso
abscissa: *n.* abscisa
abscond: *v.* evadirse
absence: *n.* inasistencia; ausencia
absent: *adj.* ausente
absentee: *n.* ausente
absentee landlord: absentista
absenteeism: *n.* absentismo; ausentismo
absinthe: *n.* absenta
absolute: *adj.* absoluto; pleno
absolute acceptance: aceptación absoluta
absolute age: edad absoluta
absolute brightness: magnitud

absoluta
absolute chemical potential:
potencial químico absoluto
absolute error: error absoluto
absolute estate: propiedad plena
absolute guarantee: garantía
completa
absolute purchase: compra de
derecho pleno
absolute sale: venta incondicional
absolute temperature: temperatura
absoluta
absolute title: título de propiedad
plena
absolute value: valor absoluto
absolute zero: cero absoluto
absolution: *n.* absolución
absolutism: *n.* absolutismo
absolve: *v.* perdonar
absorb: *v.* absorber
absorbance: *n.* absorbencia
absorbed concentration:
concentración absorbida
absorbed dose: dosis absorbida
absorbing: *adj.* absorbente
absorbent: *n.* absorbente
absorption: *n.* absorción
absorption coefficient: coeficiente
de absorción
absorption factor: factor de
absorción
absorption merger: fusión por
absorción
absorption spectrum: espectro de
absorción
absorbency factor: factor de
absorbencia
abstain: *v.* abstenerse
abstainer: *n.* abstencionista
abstention: *n.* abstención
abstinence: *n.* abstinencia
abstract: *adj.* abstracto; *n.* resumen;
sumario; extracto
abstract: *v.* resumir

abstract of account: extracto de
cuenta; resumen de cuenta
abstraction: *n.* abstracción
absurd: *adj.* absurdo
abundant: *adj.* abundante
abuse: *n.* abuso
abuse: *v.* maltratar; abusar de
abutment: *n.* linde; confín
abysm: *n.* abismo
abyssal plain: llanura abismal
acacia: *n.* acacia
academe: *n.* mundo académico
academic: *adj.* académico
academician: *adj.* académico
academy: *n.* academia
acanthus: *n.* acanto
acarido: *n.* acaro
accede: *v.* acceder
accelerate: *v.* acelerar; adelantar
accelerated: *adj.* acelerado
accelerated depreciation:
amortización acelerada
accelerated maturity: vencimiento
adelantado
acceleration: *n.* aceleración;
adelantamiento
acceleration clause: cláusula que
permite la cancelación anticipada
accelerator: *n.* acelerador
accent: 1. *n.* acento; 2. *v.* acentuar
accentuation: *n.* acentuación
accept: *v.* aceptar
acceptable: *adj.* aceptable
acceptance: *n.* aceptación
acceptance credit: crédito
respaldado por una aceptación
acceptance dealer: corredor de
aceptaciones
acceptance market: mercado de
aceptaciones
acceptance sampling: muestreo de
aceptación
accepted: *adj.* aceptado
accepted bill: letra aceptada

acceptor: *n.* aceptante; aceptador
acceptor site: centro aceptor
access: *n.* acceso
access time: tiempo de acceso
accession: *n.* accesión
accessory: *n.* accesorio
accident: *n.* accidente
accident benefit: indemnización por accidente
accident indemnification: indemnización por accidente
accident insurance: seguro de accidentes
accident prevention: prevención de accidentes
accident victim: accidentado
accidental: *n.* accidental
acclaim: *n.* aclamación
acclamation: *n.* aclamación
acclivity: *n.* rampa
accolade: *n.* acolada
accommodate: *v.* acomodar
accommodation: *n.* acomodación
accommodation acceptance: aceptación de favor
accommodation bill: letra de deferencia
accommodation bill of lading: conocimiento de favor
accommodation draft: giro de favor
accommodation endorsement: aval; endoso de favor
accommodation paper: pagaré de favor
accompaniment: *n.* acompañamiento
accompanist: *n.* acompañante
accompany: *v.* acompañar
accomplice: *n.* cómplice
accomplish: *v.* realizar
accord: 1. *n.* acuerdo; 2. *v.* concordar
according: *prep.* según
accordion: *n.* acordeón
accordionist: *n.* acordeonista

account: *n.* cuenta
account balance: saldo de la cuenta
account director: director de cuenta
account dividend: dividendo a cuenta
account due: cuenta vencida
account executive: ejecutivo de cuenta
account heading: nombre de la cuenta
account holder: titular de una cuenta
account in guarantee: cuenta en garantía
account manager: director de cuenta
account number: número de cuenta
account overdrawn: cuenta sobregirada
account overdue: cuenta vencida
account payable: cuenta a pagar
account payee: pagadero sólo al beneficiario
account receivable: activo exigible
accountability: *n.* responsabilidad
accountancy: *n.* contabilidad
accountancy book: libro de contabilidad
accountancy chief: jefe de contaduría
accountancy director: director de contabilidad
accountancy manager: gerente de contabilidad
accountant: *n.* contable; contador
accounting: *n.* contabilidad
accounting adjustment: ajuste contable
accounting convention: práctica contable
accounting data: documentación contable
accounting documents: documentación contable
accounting entry: apunte contable
accounting office: oficina de

contabilidad
accounting period: período contable
accounting plan: plan contable
accounting policy: política contable
accounting principles: principios de contabilidad
accounting profit: beneficio contable
accounting record: registro contable
accounting standard: norma contable
accounting statements: estados contables
accounting system: sistema contable
accounting valuation: valuación contable
accounting value: valor contable
accounting year: ejercicio contable
accreditation: *n.* acreditación
accredited: *adj.* acreditado
accredited school: escuela acreditada
accretion: *n.* acrecentamiento
accrual: *n.* acumulación
accruals and prepayments: *n.* acumulación y pago por adelantado
accrue: *v.* acumular; devengar
accrued: *adj.* acumulado; devengado
accrued asset: *n* activo devengado
accrued benefits: beneficios acumulados
accrued dividend: dividendo acumulado
accrued expense: gasto acumulado
accrued income: ingresos acumulados
accrued interest: interés acumulado
accrued liability: pasivo devengado
accrued tax: impuesto devengado
acculturation: *n.* aculturación
accumulate: *v.* acumular
accumulated depreciation: depreciación acumulada
accumulated profit: ganancia acumulada

accumulation: *n.* acumulación
accumulative: *adj.* acumulable
accuracy: *n.* exactitud; precisión
accurate: *adj.* exacto; preciso
accusation: *n.* acusación
accusative: *adj.* Acusativo
accused: *adj.* acusado
accuser: *n.* acusador
ace: *n.* as; uno; unidad
acephalous: *adj.* Acéfalo
acerb: *adj.* Acerbo
acerola: *n.* acerola
acetaminophen: *n.* acetaminofen
acetate: *n.* acetato
ache: *n.* dolor continuo
achieve: *v.* lograr; alcanzar; cumplir
Achilles' tendon: tendón de Aquiles
achromatic condenser: condensador acromático
achromatopsia: *n.* acromatopsia
acid: *n.* ácido; *adj.* ácido
acid phosphatase: fosfataza ácida
acid rain: lluvia ácida
acid test: prueba ácida
acid test ratio: índice de liquidez ácida
acid-base balance: equilibrio acidobásico
acidic: *adj.* sabor ácido
acidic taste: sabor ácido
acidity: *n.* acidez
acidosis: *n.* acidosis
acknowledge: *n.* acusar recibo
acknowledge receipt: acusar recibo
acknowledgement: reconocimiento; confirmación
acne: *n.* acné
acolyte: *n.* acólito
aconite: *n.* acónito
acorn: *n.* bellota
acoustic: *adj.* acústico
acoustical: *adj.* acústico
acoustics: *n.* acústica

acquaint: *v.* informar
acquiesce: *v.* asentir
acquiescence: *n.* consentimiento; aquiescencia
acquire: *v.* adquirir; obtener; conseguir
acquisition: *n.* adquisición
acquisition cost: coste de adquisición
acquisition price: valor de adquisición
acquittance: *n.* quitanza
acre: *n.* acre
acreage: *n.* medida en acres
acrid: *adj.* acre
acrimony: *n.* acrimonia
acrobat: *n.* acróbata; sonámbulo
acrobatic: *adj.* acrobático
acrobatics: *n.* acrobacia
acromegaly: *n.* acromegalia
acronym: *n.* acrónimo; sigla
acrostic: *n.* acróstico
across: *adv.* a través
acrostic: *adj.* acróstico
acrylic: *adj.* acrílico
act: *n.* ley; decreto; acto
act of bankruptcy: suspensión de pagos
act of God: fuerza mayor
act of incorporation: escritura de constitución
acting: *n.* actuación
acting president: presidente interino
actinic: *adj.* actínico
action: *n.* acción
activation energy: energía de activación
activator: *n.* activador
active: *adj.* activo; en funciones
active debt: deuda efectiva
active immunity: inmunidad activa
active member: miembro activo
active partner: socio activo
active site: centro activo

active transport: transporte activo
actively: *adv.* activamente
activism: *n.* activismo
activist: *n.* activista
activity: *n.* actividad
activity coefficient: coeficiente de actividad
activity rate: tasa de actividad
activity ratio: coeficiente de actividad
actor: *n.* actor
actors union: sindicato de actores
actress: *n.* actriz
actual: *adj.* real; verdadero
actual depreciation: depreciación real
actual loss: pérdida efectiva
actual possession: posesión real
actual salary: salario real
actual value: valor real
actual weight: peso real
actuarial: *adj.* actuarial
actuary: *n.* actuario
acuity: *n.* acuidad
acupuncture: *n.* acupuntura
acute: *adj.* agudo; perspicaz
acute angle: ángulo agudo
acute triangle: triangulo acutángulo
acyclic: *adj.* acíclico
ad: *n.* anuncio; aviso
ad honorem: ad honorem
ad infinitum: *adv.* ad infinitum
ad valorem: ad valorem
adage: *n.* adagio
adagio: *n.* adagio
Adam's apple: nuez de Adán
adapt: *v.* adaptar
adaptability: *n.* adaptabilidad; facilidad
adaptable: *adj.* adaptable
adaptation: *n.* adaptación
adapter: *n.* adaptador
adaptive: *adj.* adaptable
adaptive radiation: radiación

adaptable
add: *v.* sumar; adicionar; agregar; añadir
add up: totalizar; sumar el total
added value: valor añadido
addend: *n.* sumando
addendum: *n.* addenda; anexo
addict: *n.* adicto; -a
addicted: *adj.* aficionado
addiction: *n.* adicción
adding machine: máquina de sumar
Addis Ababa: Addis-Abeba
addition: *n.* adición; suma
addition mutation: mutación por adición
addition property of equality: propiedad de igualdad en la suma
additive: *adj.* aditivo
additive identity: identidad de la suma; identidad aditiva
additive inverse: sumando inverso; inverso aditivo
addle: *v.* vaciar
address: *n.* dirección; domicilio
addressee: *n.* destinatario; consignatario
addresser: *n.* remitente
addressing machine: máquina rotuladora
adduce: *v.* aducir
adduction: *n.* aducción
adductor: *n.* aductor
Aden: Adén
adenectomy: *n.* adenectomía
adenine: *n.* adenina
adenitis: *n.* adenitis
adenoids: *n.* adenoides
adenopathy: *n.* adenopatía
adenosine: *n.* adenosina
adenovirus: *n.* adenovirus
adept: *adj.* Experto
adequate: *adj.* suficiente; adecuado; justo
adequate compensation: indemnización justa
adhere: *v.* adherir (se)
adherence assay: ensayo de adherencia
adhesive: *n.* adhesivo
adhesive (tape): *n.* adhesivo
adieu: *n.* adiós
adipose: *adj.* adiposo
adiposity: *n.* adiposidad
adjacent: *adj.* adyacente
adjacent angles: ángulos adyacentes
adjectival: *adj.* adjetival
adjective: *n.* adjetivo
adjourn: *v.* retrasar; aplazar
adjournment: *n.* aplazamiento
adjudge: *v.* decretar
adjudicate: *v.* adjudicar
adjudication: *n.* adjudicación
adjudication of bankruptcy: declaración de quiebra
adjunct: *adj.* adjunto
adjure: *v.* implorar
adjust: *v.* ajustar; liquidar
adjustable: *adj.* adaptable
adjusted rate: tasa ajustada
adjuster: *n.* ajustador
adjustment: *n.* ajuste; liquidación
adjustment clause: cláusula de ajuste
adjustment entry: asiento de ajuste
adjustment of accounts: liquidación de cuentas
adjustor: *n.* liquidador
adjutant: *n.* ayudante
administer: *n.* administrar
administered price: precio administrado
administrate: *v.* administrar; dirigir
administration: *n.* administración; gestión
administration board: consejo de administración
administration cost: coste de administración

administration expense: gasto de administración
administration office: oficina de administración
administrative: *adj.* administrativo
administrator: *n.* administrador (a)
admirable: *adj.* admirable
admiral: *n.* almirante
admiralty: 1. *s.* almirantazgo; 2. *adj.* concerniente al mar
admiralty law: derecho de navegación
admiration: *n.* admiración
admire: *v.* admirar
admirer: *n.* admirador
admissible: *adj.* admisible; computable
admissible asset: activo admisible; activo computable
admission: *n.* admisión; alta; entrada; recaudación
admissions tax: impuesto sobre las entradas
admittance: *n.* admisión
admitted: *adj.* admitido
admixture: *n.* mezcla
admonish: 1. *v.* advertir; 2. *n.* ruido
admonition: *n.* admonición; amonestación
adnexa: *n.* anexos
ado: *n.* ruido
adobe: *n.* adobe
adolescence: *n.* adolescencia
adolescent: *adj.* adolescente
adolescent: *n.* adolescente
adopted: *adj.* adoptado
adoption: *n.* adopción
adoptive: *adj.* adoptivo
adorable: *adj.* adorable
adoration: *n.* adoración
adore: *v.* adorar; idolatrar
adorn: *v.* adornar
adornment: *n.* adorno
adrenal: *adj.* adrenal

adrenal cortex: corteza suprarrenal
adrenal gland: glándula suprarrenal
adrenaline: *n.* adrenalina
Adriatic: Adriático
adrift: *adv.* a la deriva
adroit: *adj.* hábil; diestro
adsorption: *n.* adsorción
adsorption chromatography: cromatografía de adsorción
adulation: *n.* adulación
adulator: *n.* adulador
adult: 1. *adj.* adulto; 2. *n.* adulto
adulterant: *n.* sustancia adulterante
adulterated: *adj.* adulterado
adultery: *n.* adulterio
adulthood: *n.* edad adulta
advance: 1. *v.* anticipar; adelantar; 2. *n.* anticipo
advance (film): *vt.* avanzar
advance filing: reclamación por adelantado
advance payment: pago adelantado
advanced: *adj.* avanzado
advanced letter of credit: carta de crédito anticipada
advancing: *adj.* progresivo
advantage: *n.* ventaja
Advent: *n.* Adviento
Adventist: *n.* adventista
adventure: *n.* aventura
adventure: *v.* aventurar
adventurer: *n.* aventurero
adventurous: *adj.* aventurero
adverb: *n.* adverbio
adverbial: *adj.* adverbial
adversary: *n.* adversario
adverse: *adj.* adverso; contrario
adverse balance: saldo negativo
adverse claim: solicitud adversa
adverse possession: prescripción adquisitiva
adverse title: título obtenido por prescripción adquisitiva
adversity: *n.* adversidad

advert: *v.* aludir
advertise: *v.* anunciar; publicitar
advertisement: *n.* publicidad; anuncio
advertisement song: canto de anuncio
advertiser: *n.* anunciante; publicista
advertising: 1. *n.* publicidad; 2. *adj.* publicitario
advertising agency: agencia de publicidad
advertising campaign: campaña de publicidad
advertising cost: costo de publicidad
advertising department: departamento de publicidad
advertising director: director de publicidad
advertising expense: gasto de publicidad
advertising literature: literatura publicitaria
advertising manager: director de publicidad
advertising media: medios de publicidad
advertising plan: plan publicitario
advertising rate: tarifa de publicidad
advice: *n.* consejo; aviso
advise: *v.* asesorar; aconsejar; avisar
adviser, advisor: *n.* consultor; asesor
advisory: *adj.* consultivo
advisory board: consejo consultivo
advisory committee: comisión consultiva
advocacy group: grupos de presión
advocate: *n.* abogado
Aegean: Egeo
Aeneid: *n.* Eneída
aerate: *v.* airear; ventilar
aeration: *n.* aeración
aeria: *adj.* aéreo
aerial map: aerómapa
aerial photo: aerófoto

aerobic: *adj.* aeróbico
aerobics: *n.* aeróbica
aerodrome: *n.* aeródromo
aerodynamics: *n.* aerodinámica
aerogenic: *adj.* aerogénico
aerogram: *n.* aerograma
aerology: *n.* aerología
aeromancy: *n.* aeromancia
aeromedicine: *n.* aerómedicina
aeronautical: *adj.* aeronáutico
aeronautics: *n.* aeronáutica
aerosol: *n.* aerosol
aerospace: *n.* espacio
aerosphere: *n.* aerosfera
aerostat: *n.* aeróstato
aerotolerant: *adj.* aerótolerante
aesthete; esthete: *n.* esteta
aesthetics; esthetics: *n.* estético
aetiology: *n.* etiología
afar: *adv.* lejos
affability: *n.* afabilidad
affair: *n.* asunto; aventura
affect: *v.* afectar; impresionar
affectation: *n.* afectación
affection: *n.* afección; afecto
afferent: *adj.* aferente
affidavit: *n.* affidávit; declaración; declaración jurada
affiliate: *n.* afiliado
affiliate: *v.* afiliar; adoptar
affiliated: *adj.* afiliado
affiliated company: compañía afiliada
affiliation: *n.* afiliación; afiliada
affinity: *n.* afinidad
affinity constant: constante de afinidad
affirm: *v.* afirmar
affirmative: *adj.* afirmativo
affirmative warranty: garantía escrita
affix: *n.* afijo
afflict: *v.* afligir
affliction: *n.* aflicción

affluence: *n.* afluencia
afford: *v.* tener (dinero; etc.)
affranchise: *v.* emancipar
affreighter: *n.* fletador
affreightment: *n.* fletamento
affright: *v.* aterrar
affront: *n.* afrenta
Afghan: 1. *adj.* afgano; 2. *n.* Afgano
Afghanistan: Afganistán
afoot: *adv.* a pie; en marcha
afraid: *adj.* espantado (a); asustado (a)
afresh: *adv.* otra vez; de nuevo
Africa: África
African: *adj.* africano; -a
African: *n.* africano; (a)
African-American: africanoamericano
Africanist: *n.* africanista
Afrikaans: *n.* Africaanos
Afro: *n.* afro
Afro-Asiatic: *adj.* afroasiático
after: 1. *adj.* siguiente; 2. *adv.* después; 3. *prep.* según; 4. *conj.* después que
afternoon: 1. *n.* tarde
after-sales service: servicio de posventa
aftershock: *n.* replica
again: *adv.* de nuevo; otra vez; además
against: *prep.* contra; cerca de
agar: *n.* agar; gelatina
agar diffusion test: prueba de difusión en agar
agar; agar-agar: *n.* agar; agar-agar
agarose: *n.* agarosa
agate: *n.* ágata
agave: *n.* agave
age: 1. *n.* edad; antigüedad; 2. *v.* clasificar según antigüedad
aged account: cuenta vencida
aged; blind; disabled: *adj.* anciano; ciego; o incapacitado

ageing of accounts: envejecimiento de cuentas
agency: *n.* agencia; representación
agenda: *n.* agenda; orden del día
agent: *n.* agente; representante
agglutination: *n.* aglutinación
agglutinative: *adj.* aglutinante
aggrandize: *v.* agrandar; engrandecer
aggravate: *v.* agravar
aggravated (assault): *adj.* con agravante
aggregate: 1. *v.* acumular; 2. *adj.* acumulado
aggregate demand: demanda agregada
aggression: *n.* agresión; agresividad
aggressor: *n.* agresor
aggrieve: *v.* afligir
aghast: *adj.* horrorizado
agile: *adj.* ágil; hábil
agility: *n.* agilidad
aging: 1. *n.* senescencia; 2. *adj.* senescente
aging: envejecimiento
agio: *n.* agio
agitate: *v.* agitar; hacer campana
agitation: *n.* agitación
agitated: *adj.* agitado
agitator: *n.* agitador
agnosticism: *n.* agnosticismo
ago: *adv.* hace; ha; pasado; long time ago hace mucho tiempo
agony: *n.* agonía; angustia
agraphia: *n.* agrafia
agrarian: *adj.* agrario
agreable: *adj.* agradable
agree: *v.* acordar; convenir
agree to notify: estar de acuerdo en notificar
agreeable: *adj.* agradable
agreed: *adj.* convenido
agreement: *n.* acuerdo; convenio
agricultural: *adj.* agrario; agrícola
agricultural bank: banco agrario

agricultural commodity: producto agrícola
agricultural concern: explotación agrícola
agricultural economy: economía agrícola
agricultural engineer: ingeniero agrónomo
agricultural equipment: equipo agrícola
agricultural labor: trabajo agrícola
agricultural produce: producto agrícola
agriculture: *n.* agricultura
agronomist: *n.* agrónomo; -a
agronomy: *n.* agronomía
aground: 1. *adj.* varado; encallado; 2. *adv.* varado
aha!: intj. ¡ajá!
ahead: *adv.* delante; al frente
ahem!: intj. ¡ejem!
ahoy!: intj. ¡ahó!
aid: *n.* auxilio; ayuda
aid: *v.* ayudar
aide: *n.* ayudante
AIDS: SIDA
ail: *v.* inquietar; sufrir
aileron: *n.* alerón
ailing: *adj.* enfermizo; achacoso
ailment: *n.* enfermedad; achaque
aim: *n.* puntería
air: *n.* aire
air brake: freno de aire
air conditioner: acondicionador de aire
air conditioning: aire acondicionado
air consignment: transporte aéreo
air consignment note: conocimiento aéreo
air freight: flete aéreo; transporte aéreo
air industry: industria aeronáutica
air mail: correo aéreo; carta por avión

air mass: masa de aire
air out: *vt.* airear
air pressure: presión de aire
air rate: tarifa aérea
air resistance: resistencia del aire
air taxi: *n.* aerotaxi
air transport: transporte aéreo
air waybill: carta de porte aéreo
airborne transmission: transmisión aérea
airbrush: *n.* aerógrafo
airing: *n.* ventilación
airless: *adj.* sin aire
airline: *n.* línea aérea; aerolínea
airliner: *n.* aeronave
airmail: *n.* correo aéreo
airplane: *n.* aeroplano
airport: *n.* aeropuerto
airstrip: *n.* pista
airtight: *adj.* hermético
airway: *n.* vía aérea; línea aérea
airway bill of lading: conocimiento aéreo
aisle: *n.* pasillo
ajar: *adj.* entreabierto; entornado
akin: *adj.* emparentado; semejante
Akkadian: *n.* acadio
alabaster: *n.* alabastro
aladdin: *n.* aladino
alalia: *n.* alalia
alanine: *n.* alanina
alarm: *n.* alarma
alarmed: *adj.* alarmado
alarmist: *n.* alarmista
alas: interj. ay!; ay de mi!
alb: *n.* alba
albacore: *n.* albacora
Albania: Albania
Albanian: *adj.* albanés; -esa
albeit: *conj.* aunque; bien que
albinism: *n.* albinismo
album: *n.* álbum
albumen: *n.* albumen
albumin: *n.* albúmina

alchemy: *n.* alquimia
alcohol: *n.* alcohol
alcohol and drug use: uso de alcohol y drogas
alcohol oxidase: alcohol-oxidasa
alcoholic: *adj.* alcohólico
alcoholism: *n.* alcoholismo; problema de alcoholismo
alcove: *n.* alcoba
alderman: *n.* concejal
aldosterone: *n.* aldosterona
ale: *n.* cerveza inglesa
aleph: *n.* taberna
alert: *n.* alerta
Aleutian: *adj.* Aleutiano; na
Alexandria: Alejandría
alexandrine: *adj.* alejandrino
alexia: *n.* alexia
alfalfa: *n.* alfalfa
alga: *n.* alga
algebra: *n.* álgebra
algebraic: *adj.* algebraico
algebraic expression: expresión algebraica
Algeria: Argelia
Algerian: *adj.* argelino; -a
Algiers: Argel
algin: *n.* algina
algorithm: *n.* algoritmo
alias: *n.* alias
alibi: *n.* coartada
alien: *n.* extranjero; alienígena
alien corporation: empresa extranjera
alien lawfully admitted: extranjero legalmente admitido
alien registration card: tarjeta de residencia
alien status: estado legal de extranjero
alienate: *v.* alienar
alienation: *n.* alienación
alight: *v.* apearse; bajar
align: *v.* alinear

alignment: *n.* alineación
alike: *adj.* semejante; parecido; igual
aliment: 1. *n.* alimento; 2. *v.* alimentar
alimentary: *adj.* alimenticio
alimony: *n.* manutención; alimentos
aliquot: *n.* alícuota
alive: *adj.* vivo; activo
alkali metal: metal alcalino
alkaline: *adj.* alcalino
alkaline earth metal: metal alcalinotérreo
alkalinity: *n.* alcalinidad
alkalosis: *n.* alcalosis
all: 1. *adj.* ind. todo; todos; todo el; todos los; 2. *pron.* el todo; todos
Allah: Alá
allay: *v.* aliviar; calmar; mitigar
allegiance: *n.* lealtad; fidelidad
allegory: *n.* alegoría
allegretto: *adv.* alegreto
allegro: *adv.* alegro
allele: *n.* alelo
allelotype: *n.* alelótipo
allemande: *n.* alemana
allergen: *n.* alérgeno
allergies: *n.* alergias
allergist: *n.* alergista
allergy: *n.* alergia
alleviate: *v.* aliviar
alleviation: *n.* alivio
alley: *n.* callejón; callejuela
alligator: *n.* aligator; cocodrilo americano
alliteration: *n.* aliteración
allocate: *v.* asignar; aplicar; afectar; asignar
allocated: *adj.* asignado; afecto
allocated profit: beneficio asignado; ganancia asignada
allocation: *n.* asignación; aplicación
allocation of resources: asignación de recursos
allopathy: *n.* alopatía

allonge: *n.* pliego
allopath: *n.* alópata
allopathy: *n.* alopatía
allot: *v.* asignar; distribuir
allotment: *n.* asignación; dotación
allotrope: *n.* forma alotrópica
allotrope: *adj.* alotrópico (a)
allow: *v.* permitir; asignar; conceder; dejar
allowable: *adj.* tolerable
allowance: *n.* asignación; permiso
allowance letter: carta de aprobación
allowed depreciation: depreciación permitida
alloy: 1. *n.* aleación; 2. *v.* alear; ligar
allozyme: *n.* aloenzima
allude: *v.* aludir
allure: *v.* seducir; atraer
allusion: *n.* alusión
alluvial fan: abanico aluvial
ally: *n.* aliado
almanac: *n.* almanaque
almighty: *adj.* todopoderoso
almond: *n.* almendra
almond tree: almendro
almost: *adv.* casi
alms: *n.* limosna; caridad
aloe: *n.* áloe; aloe
aloft: *adv.* arriba; en alto
alone: *adj.* solo
along: 1. *prep.* a lo largo de; 2. *adv.* a lo largo
alongside: *prep.* junto a
aloof: 1. *adj.* reservado; 2. *adv.* lejos; a distancia
aloud: *adv.* alto
alpaca: *n.* alpaca
alpha: *n.* alfa
alpha particle: partícula alfa
alphabet: *n.* alfabeto
alphabetical: *adj.* alfabético
alphabetical order: orden alfabético
alpha-fetoprotein: alfa fetoproteína
alphanumeric: *adj.* alfanumérico

alpine: *adj.* alpestre; alpino
alpinism: *n.* alpinismo
alpinist: *n.* alpinista
Alps: Alpes
already: *adv.* ya
Alsace: Alsacia
Alsatian: *adj.* alsaciano; -a
also: *adv.* también; además
alta: *adj.* alta
Altaic: *adj.* altaico
altar: *v.* altar
alter: *v.* modificar/alterar
alter: *v.* alterar
alter ego: álter ego
alteration: *n.* alteración
altercation: *n.* altercado
altered cheque: cheque alterado
alternate: *adj.* alterno; suplente
alternate member: miembro suplente
alternating: *adj.* alterno; alternante
alternating current: corriente alterna
alternative: *adj.* alternativo
alternative pathway: vía alternativa
alternator: *n.* alternador
although: *conj.* aunque; a pesar de que
altimeter: *n.* altímetro
altimetry: *n.* altimetría
altitude: *n.* altura; altitud
alto: *adj.* contralto; alto
altogether: *adv.* enteramente; por completo
altruism: *n.* altruismo
altruist: *n.* altruista
altruistic: *n.* altruista
aluminum: *n.* aluminio
alveoli: *n.* alvéolos
alveolus: *n.* alvéolo
always: *adv.* siempre; en todo tiempo
Alzheimer's disease: enfermedad de Alzheimer
AM: AM

amalgamate: *v.* fusionar; amalgamar
amalgamation: *n.* fusión; consolidación
amaranth: *n.* amaranto
amaryllis: *n.* amarilis
amass: *v.* amasar
amateur: *n.* amateur
amateur: *adj.* amateur
amaze: *v.* asombrar; pasmar
Amazon: Amazonas
ambassador: *n.* embajador
ambassadorship: *n.* embajada
amber: *adj.* ambarino
amber codon: codón ámbar
amber mutation: mutación ámbar
ambiance: *n.* ambiente
ambidextrous: *adj.* ambidextro
ambiguous: *adj.* ambiguo
ambition: *n.* ambición
ambitious: *adj.* ambicioso
ambivalence: *n.* ambivalencia
amblyopia: *n.* ambliopía
ambrosia: *n.* ambrosia
ambulance: *n.* ambulancia
ambulance driver: ambulanciero
ambulatory: *adj.* ambulatorio
ambush: *n.* emboscada
amebae: *n.* ameba
amelioration: *n.* mejora; reforma
amen!: *intj.* ¡amén!
amend: *v.* enmendar; corregir
amended birth certificate: certificado de nacimiento enmendado
amendment: *n.* enmienda
amenity: *n.* amenidad
amenorrhea; amenorrea: *n.* amenorrea
America: América
American: 1. *adj.* americano; (a); 2. *n.* americano (a)
Americanism: *n.* americanismo
Americanization: *n.* americanización
amethyst: *n.* amatista

ametropia: *n.* ametropía
Amharic: *n.* amhárico
amiability: *n.* amabilidad
amiable: *adj.* amable
amicable: *adj.* amigable
amid: *prep.* en medio de; rodeado por
amidst: *prep.* en medio de
amino acid: amino ácido
amiss: *adv.* erradamente; impropiamente
amity: *n.* amistad
Amman: Amán
ammeter: *n.* amperímetro
ammoniemia: concentración de amonio en plasma
ammonium: *n.* amonio
ammunition: *n.* munición
amnesia: *n.* amnesia
amnesiac; amnesic: *adj.* amnésico
amnestied person: amnistiado
amnesty: *n.* amnistía
amniocentesis: *n.* amniocentesis
amniotic: *adj.* amniótico (a)
amniotic egg: huevo amniótico
amniotic fluid: líquido amniótico
amniotic sac: saco amniótico
among: *prep.* entre
amongst: *prep.* entre; en medio de
amorality: *n.* amoralidad
amorphous solid: sólido amorfo
amortizable: *adj.* amortizable
amortization: *n.* amortización; depreciación
amortization schedule: tabla de amortización
amortize: *v.* amortizar; depreciar
amortized bond: bono amortizado
amortized share: acción amortizada
amortization: *n.* amortización
amount: 1. *n.* importe; suma
amount: *n.* cantidad
amount of substance: cantidad de sustancia

amount payable: importe a pagar
amount receivable: importe a cobrar
amp: *n.* amperio
amperage: *n.* amperaje
ampere: *n.* amperio
amperometry: *n.* amperimetría
amphetamines: *n.* anfetamina
amphibian: *n.* anfibio
amphibious: *adj.* anfibio
amphioxus: *n.* anfioxo
amphitheater: *n.* anfiteatro
amphoteric: *adj.* anfótero
ampicillin: *n.* ampicilina
ample: *adj.* amplio
ampleness: *n.* amplitud
amplification: *n.* ampliación
amplifier: *n.* amplificador
amplify: *v.* amplificar
amplitude: *n.* amplitud
amplitude modulation: amplitud modulada
amply: *adv.* ampliamente; abundantemente
ampoule: *n.* ampolla; ampolleta
ampulla: *n.* ampolla
amputate: *v.* amputar; cortar
amputation: *n.* amputación
amputee: *n.* amputado; -a
amulet: *n.* amuleto
amuse: *v.* divertir; entretener
amusing: *adj.* divertido; entretenido
amylase: *n.* amilasa
an: art. ind. un; una
anabaptism: *n.* anabaptismo
anabaptist: *n.* anabaptista
anabolic steroids: esteroides anabólicos
anabolism: *n.* anabolismo
anachronism: *n.* anacronismo
anaconda: *n.* anaconda
anacrusis: *n.* anacrusis
anaerobe: *n.* anaerobio
anaerobic bacilli: bacilo anaerobio
anaerobic chamber: cámara

anaeróbica
anaerobic culture: cultivo para anaerobios
anaerogenic: *n.* anaerogénico
anagram: *n.* anagrama
anal: *adj.* anal
anal itching: picazón del ano
anal mucus: muco anal
anal sex: sexo anal coito anal
analeptic: *adj.* analéptico
analgesia: *n.* analgesia
analgesic: *adj.* analgésico
analogue: *n.* análogo
analog signal: serial analógica
analogue: *adj.* analógico; análogo
analogue computer: computadora análoga
analyze: *v.* analizar
analyzer: *n.* analizador
analysis: *n.* análisis
analysis of accounts: análisis de cuentas
analysis of financial condition: análisis del estado financiero
analyst: *n.* analista
analytic: *adj.* analítico
analytic geometry: geometría analítica
analytical: *adj.* analítico
analytical chemistry: química analítica
analytical control: control analítico
analytical curve: curva analítica
analytical function: función analítica
analytical instrument: instrumento analítico
analytical intercomparison: intercomparación analítica
analytical interference: interferencia analítica
analytical interferent: interferente analítico
analytical method: método analítico

analytical portion: porción analítica
analytical procedure: procedimiento analítico
analytical process: proceso analítico
analytical radiochemistry: radioquímica analítica
analytical range: intervalo analítico
analytical run: serie analítica
analytical specificity: especificidad analítica
analytical system: sistema analítico
analytics: *n.* analítica
analyze: *v.* analizar
analyzer: *n.* analizador
anapest: *n.* anapesto
anaphora: *n.* angora; anáfora
anaphrodisiac: *adj.* anafrodisíaco
anaphylaxis: *n.* anafilaxis
anarchism: *n.* anarquismo
anarchist: *n.* anarquista
anarchy: *n.* anarquía
anathema: *n.* anatema
anatomy: *n.* anatomía
ancestral: *adj.* ancestral; hereditario
anchor: *n.* ancla; ancora; anclaje
anchorage: *n.* fondeadero; tarifa portuaria; anclaje; ancladero
anchovy: *n.* ancho; a
ancient: *adj.* antiguo
ancient deed: título antiguo
ancillary: *n.* complementario; accesorio; subordinado
and: *conj.* y; e
Andalusia: Andalucía
andalusia: *n.* andalucía
Andalusian: *adj.* andaluz (a)
andalusian: *n.* andaluz
andante: *adv.* andante
Andes: Andes
androgen: *n.* andrógeno
androgens: *n.* hormonas masculinas
android: *n.* androide
androstenedione: *n.* androstenodiona

anecdote: *n.* anécdota
anecdote collection: anecdotario
anemia: *n.* anemia
anemometer: *n.* anemómetro
anemone: *n.* anémona
aneroid barometer: barómetro aneroide
anesthesia: *n.* anestesia
anesthesiologist: *n.* anestesiólogo
anesthesiology: *n.* anestesiología
anesthetic: *adj.* anestésico
anesthetist: *n.* anestetista
aneuploidy: *n.* aneuploidía
aneurysm; aneurism: *n.* aneurisma
anew: *adv.* nuevamente; de nuevo
angel: *n.* ángel
angelfish: *n.* angelote
anger: 1. *n.* ira; cólera; *v.* enfurecer; irritar
angina: *n.* angina
angiogram: *n.* angioscopio; angiograma
angiography: *n.* angiografía
angioma: *n.* angioma
angioplasty: *n.* angioplastía
angiosperm: *n.* angiosperma
angiotensin: *n.* angiotensina
angle: *n.* ángulo
angle beam: la viga angular
angle iron: angular
angle of rotation: ángulo de rotación
angle valve: la válvula angular
angler: *n.* pescador de cana
Anglican: *adj.* anglicano
Anglican: *adj.* anglicano; -a
Anglicanism: *n.* anglicanismo
Anglicism: *n.* anglicismo
Anglo-Saxon: anglosajón
Angola: Angola
Angolan: 1. *adj.* angoleño; (a); 2. *n.* Angolano (a)
angora: *n.* angora
angrily: *adv.* airadamente
angry: *adj.* enojado (a)

Anguilla: anguila
anguish: *n.* angustia; congoja; tormento; ansia.
anguished: *adj.* angustiado
angular: *adj.* angular
anhydrosis: *n.* anhidrosis
annihilate: *v.* aniquilar; destruir
anil: *n.* añil
animadversion: *n.* animadversión
animadvert: *v.* advertir; observar
animal: *adj.* animal
animal: *n.* animal
animalism: *n.* animalismo
animate: *adj.* animado
animation: *n.* animación
animator: *n.* animador (a)
animism: *n.* animismo
animosity: *n.* animosidad
anise: *n.* anís
anisette: *n.* licor de anís
ankle: *n.* tobillo; talón
ankylosis: *n.* anquilosis
annalist: *adj.* analista
annelid anopheles: anofeles anélido
annex: *n.* anexo
anniversary: *n.* aniversario
annotation: *n.* anotación
annotator: *n.* anotador (a)
announce: *v.* anunciar; avisar; pregonar
announcement: *n.* anuncio
announcer: *n.* anunciador (a)
annoy: *v.* molestar; fastidiar
annoying: *adj.* molesto; engorroso
annual: *adj.* anual; anuario
annual allowance: anualidad; asignación anual
annual audit: auditoria anual
annual earnings test: límite anual de ganancias
annual general meeting: asamblea anual
annual interest rate: tasa de interés anual

annual leave: vacaciones anuales
annual meeting: reunión anual
annual payment: pago anual; anualidad
annual rate: tasa anual
annual report: informe anual
annual report of earnings: informe anual de ganancias
annuary: *n.* anuario
annuitant: *n.* pensionista
annuity: *n.* anualidad
annuity bond: bono sin vencimiento
annuity certain: anualidad incondicional
annuity holder: beneficiario de una renta vitalicia
annuity payable: anualidad a pagar
annul: *v.* anular; invalidar
annulment: *n.* anulación; revocación
anode: *n.* ánodo
anodyne: *adj.* anodino
anofeles: *n.* anofeles
anoint: *v.* consagrar
anomalous: *adj.* anómalo
anomaly: *n.* anomalía
anon: *prep.* pronto
anonymity: *n.* anonimato
anonymous: *adj.* anónimo
anorexia: *n.* anorexia
anorexic: *adj.* anoréxico
anosmia: *n.* anosmia
another: *pron.* uno mas
anoxemia; anoxia: *n.* anoxemia; anoxia
answer: *v.* contestar
answer: *n.* respuesta
answering service: servicio de mensajes
ant: *n.* hormiga
antacid: *adj.* antiácido
antagonism: *n.* antagonismo
antagonist: *n.* antagonista
Antarctic: *adj.* antártico
Antarctica: Antártica

antebellum: antes de la guerra civil
antecedent: *adj.* antecedente
antedate: *v.* antedatar
antelope: *n.* antílope; gacela
antemeridian: *adj.* antemeridiano
antenna: *n.* antena
anterior: *adj.* anterior
anteroom: *n.* antesala
anthelmintic: *adj.* antihelmíntico
anthem: *n.* himno
anthology: *n.* antología
anthrax: *n.* ántrax
anthropoid: *adj.* antropoide
anthropological: *adj.* antropológico
anthropology: *n.* antropología
anthropometry: *n.* antropometría
anti aircraft: antiaéreo
anti virus: ante virus
anti-antibody: anticuerpo
antiantitoxin: *n.* antitoxina
antiarrhythmic: *adj.* antiarrítmico
antibacterial: *adj.* antibacteriano; antibactérico
antiballistic: *adj.* antibalístico
antibiogram: *n.* antibiograma
antibiotic: *n.* antibiótico
antibody: *n.* anticuerpo
antic: *adj.* extraño
anticipation: *n.* anticipación; previsión
anticipatory: *adj.* anticipador
anticlimax: *n.* anticlímax
anticline: *adj.* anticlinal
anticoagulant: *adj.* anticoagulante
anticoding strand: cadena intranscrita
anticodon: *n.* anticodón
anticommunist: *n.* anticomunista
anticonvulsant: *adj.* anticonvulsionante
anti-corrosive: resistente a la corrosión
anticyclone: *n.* anticiclón
antidepressant: *adj.* antidepresivo

antiderivative: *n.* antiderivada
antidifferentiation: *n.* antidiferenciación
antidiuretic hormone: hormona antidiurética
antidote: *n.* antídoto
antifreeze: *n.* anticongelante
antifungal: *adj.* antimicótico
antifungal agent: agente antimicótico
antigen: *n.* antígeno
antigenic determinant: determinante antigénico
antihero: *n.* antihéroe
antihistamine: *n.* antihistamínico
antihypertensive: *adj.* antihipertensivo
Antilles: Antillas
antilogarithm: *n.* antilogaritmo
antimalarial: *adj.* antipalúdico
anti-microbial: *adj.* antimicrobiano
anti-microsomal antibody: anticuerpo antimicrosómico
anti-militarist: *n.* antimilitarista
anti-missile: antiproyectil
antimonopoly: 1. *n.* antimonopolio; 2. *adj.* antimonopólico
antimonopoly law: ley antimonopólica
antinode: *adj.* antinodo
antioxidant: *n.* antioxidante
antiparkinson agent: agente antiparkinsoniano
antipathetic: *adj.* antipático
antipathy: *n.* antipatía
antiperspirant: *adj.* antisudoral
antiperspirant: *adj.* antisudoral
antiphonal: *adj.* antifonal
antipodes: *n.* antípodas
antipoison: *n.* contraveneno
antipsychotic: *adj.* antipsicótico
antipyretic: *adj.* antipirético
antipyretic agent: medicina para bajar la fiebre; antipirético

antique: *adj.* antiguo; anticuado
antique shop: anticuario
antiques: *n.* antigüedades
anti-Semitism: *n.* antisemitismo
antisense strand: cadena antisentido
antisepsis: *n.* antisepsia
antiseptic: *adj.* antiséptico (a)
antiserum: *n.* antisuero
antiserum avidity: avidez de un antisuero
antislavery: *n.* antiesclavitud
antisocial: *adj.* antisocial
antispasmodic: *adj.* antiespasmódico
antistatic: *adj.* antiestático
antisubmarine: *n.* antisubmarino
antitermination: *n.* antiterminación
antithesis: *n.* antítesis
antitoxin: *n.* antitoxina
antitrust: *n.* antimonopólico
antitrust law: ley antimonopólica
antitussive: *adj.* antitusígeno
antiviral: *adj.* antiviral
antler: *n.* cuerno
antonym: *n.* antónimo
anus: *n.* ano
anxiety: *n.* ansiedad
anxious (eager): *adj.* ansioso
any: *adj. indef.* algún; (o); (a)
any time: alguna vez
anybody: *pron.* cualquiera; alguno
anyhow: *adv.* de cualquier modo
anyone: *pron.* cualquiera; alguno
anything: *pron.* indef. algo; alguna cosa
anyway: *adv.* de cualquier modo
anywhere: *adv.* dondequiera
anywise: *adv.* de cualquier modo
aorta: *n.* aorta
apace: *adv.* aprisa
apartheid: *n.* apartheid
apartment: *n.* apartamento; piso
apartment hotel: apartotel
apathy: *n.* apatía
ape: *n.* (zool.) mono

Apennines: Apeninos
aperiodic: *adj.* aperiódico
aperitif: *n.* aperitivo
aperture: *n.* apertura
apex: *n.* ápice
aphaeresis: *n.* aféresis
aphasia: *n.* afasia
aphasic: *adj.* afásico; -a
aphonia: *n.* afonía
aphorism: *n.* aforismo
aphrodisiac: *adj.* afrodisíaco
apiculture: *n.* apicultura
apiece: *adv.* cada uno; por cabeza
aplasia: *n.* aplasia
aplomb: *adj.* aplomo
apnea: *n.* apnea
apogee: *n.* apogeo
apoli-poprotein: apolipoproteína
apologetics: *n.* apologética
apologist: *n.* apologista
apoplexy: *n.* apoplejía
apoptosis: *n.* apoptosis
apostasy: *n.* apostasía
apostle: *n.* apóstol
apostrophe: *n.* apóstrofe
apothegm: *n.* apotegma
apothem: *n.* apotema
apotheosis: *n.* apoteosis
Appalachia: los Apalaches
Appalachians: Apalaches
appalling: *adj.* espantoso
apparatus: *n.* aparato
apparel: *n.* vestuario
apparent: *adj.* aparente
apparent brightness: magnitud aparente
apparition: *n.* aparición
appeal: 1. *n.* apelación; recurso; 2. *v.* apelar
appeal: *n.* apelación; suplica
appeal rights: derechos de apelación
appeals council: consejo de apelaciones
appear: *vi.* aparecer

appearance: *n.* aparición; apariencia
appease: *v.* apaciguar
appellant: *n.* apelante
append: *v.* añadir
appendage: *n.* apéndice
appendectomy: *n.* apendectomía
appendicitis: *n.* apendicitis
appendix: *n.* apéndice
appertain: intr. pertenecer
appetite: *n.* apetito
applaud: *v.* aplaudir
applause: *n.* aplauso
apple: *n.* manzana
appliance: *n.* dispositivo; instrumento
applicant: *n.* aspirante; solicitante; candidato
application: *n.* aplicación
application blank: formulario de solicitud
application form: formulario de solicitud
application of funds: aplicación de fondos
application of resources: aplicación de recursos
applications package: paquete de aplicación
applicator: *n.* aplicador
applied: *adj.* aplicado
applique: *n.* aplicación
apply: *v.* aplicar
appoggiatura: *n.* apoyatura
appoint: *v.* nombrar; designar
appointed: *adj.* nominado; designado
appointer: que nombra o designa
appointment: *n.* cita; designación; compromiso
apportion: *v.* asignar; repartir; prorratear
apportionment: *n.* asignación
apposite: *adj.* oportuno
appositive: *adj.* apositivo

appraising: *adj.* apreciativo
appraisal: *n.* evaluación
appraisal value: valor de tasación
appraise: *v.* tasar; valorar; evaluar
appraiser: *n.* tasador; valuador
appreciable: *adj.* apreciable
appreciate: *v.* apreciar; valorar
appreciation: *n.* apreciación; valorización
apprehend: *v.* aprehender
apprehension: *n.* aprensión
apprehensive: *adj.* aprensivo; aprehensivo
apprentice: *n.* aprendiz
apprenticeship: *n.* aprendizaje
apprise: *v.* informar
approach: 1. *n.* enfoque; 2. *vi.* acercarse; 3 *vt.* acercar
approach: *n.* acercamiento; entrada
approaching: *adj.* próximo; cercano
approbation: *n.* aprobación
appropriate: *adj.* apropiado
appropriate: 1. *v.* apropiar; 2. *adj.* apropiado
appropriation: *n.* asignación; dotación
appropriation of profits: asignación de ganancias
approval: *n.* aprobación
approve: *v.* aprobar
approved school: escuela aprobada
approximate: *adj.* aproximado
approximate: *v.* aproximar
approximation: *n.* aproximación
appurtenance: *n.* pertenencia
apricot: *n.* albaricoque
April: *n.* abril
apron: *n.* delantal
apse: *n.* ábside
apt: *adj.* apto
aptitude: *n.* aptitud
aquaculture: *n.* acuacultura
aqueduct: *n.* acueducto
aquamarine: *n.* aguamarina

aquanaut: *n.* acuanauta
aquaplane: *n.* acuaplano
aquarelle: *n.* acuarela
aquarium: *n.* acuario
aquatic: *adj.* acuático
aquatics: *n.* deportes acuáticos
aquatint: *n.* acuatinta
aqueous: *adj.* acuoso
aquifer: *adj.* acuífero
aquiline: *n.* aguileño; aquilino
aquiline: *adj.* aquilino
Arab: *adj.* árabe
arabesque: *adj.* arabesco
arabesque: *n.* arabesco
Arabia: Arabia
Arabian: *n.* Arábigo
Arabic: *adj.* arábigo; árabe
Arabic expression: arabismo
arabinose: *n.* arabinosa
Arabist: *n.* arabista
arable: *adj.* arable
arachnid: *n.* arácnido
Aragon: Aragón
Aramaic: *n.* arameo
arbiter: *n.* árbitro
arbitrage: *n.* arbitraje
arbitrariness: *n.* arbitrariedad
arbitrary standard: patrón
arbitrario
arbitration: *n.* arbitración; arbitraje
arbitration clause: cláusula de
arbitración
arbitrator: *n.* árbitro
arbovirus: *n.* arbovirus
arc: *n.* arco; arco eléctrico
arc length: longitud de arco
arcade: *n.* arcada
Arcadia: Arcadia
Arcadian: *adj.* arcadio
Arcadian: *adj.* arcadio
arcane: *adj.* arcano
arch: *n.* arco
arch: *adj.* astuto; travieso
archaic: *adj.* arcaico

archbishop: *n.* arzobispo
archdeacon: *n.* archidiácono
archdiocese: *n.* archidiócesis;
arquidiócesis
archduchess: *n.* archiduquesa
archduke: *n.* archiduque
arched: *adj.* arqueado
archeology: *n.* arqueología
archer: *n.* arquero
archery: *n.* tiro de arco
Archetype: *n.* arquetipo
Archimedes' principle: principio de
Arquímedes
archipelago: *n.* archipiélago
architect: *n.* arquitecto
architectura: *n.* arquitectura
architectural: *adj.* arquitectónico
Architrave: *n.* arquitrabe
archive: 1. *n.* archivo; 2. *v.* archivar
archives npl: *n.* archivo
archivist: *n.* archivero
archlike: *adj.* en forma de arco
archpriest: *n.* arcipreste
archway: *n.* arcada; pasaje
abovedado
arcing: *n.* el arqueo
Arctic: *adj.* ártico
ardent: *adj.* ardiente
ardor: *n.* ardor
arduous: *adj.* arduo
area: *n.* área
area code: código de área
area director: director de área
area graph: gráfico de áreas
area manager: gerente de área
area representative: representante
de área
area sampling: muestreo por áreas
arena: *n.* arena
areola: *n.* areola; areola
Argentina: Argentina
Argentine; Argentinean: *adj.*
argentino
Argentinian: *n.* argentinismo

arginase: *n.* arginasa
arginine: *n.* arginina
arginine amidinase: arginasa
argipressin: *n.* argipresina
argonaut: *n.* argonauta
argot: *n.* argot
argue: *v.* debatir; argumentar
arguer: *n.* argumentador (a)
argument: *n.* argumento
argumentation: *n.* argumentación
aria: *n.* aria
arid: *adj.* árido
aridity: *n.* aridez
Aries: *n.* aries
arise: *n.* surge
arise: *v.* levantarse; sublevarse
aristocracy: *n.* aristocracia
aristocrat: *adj.* aristócrata
Aristotelian: *n.* aristotélico
aristotelianism: *n.* aristotelismo
arithmetic: *adj.* aritmético; (a)
arithmetic: *n.* aritmética
arithmetic average: promedio aritmético
arithmetic mean: media aritmética
arithmetic progression: progresión aritmética
arithmetic series: serie aritmética
ark: *n.* arca
arm: *n.* brazo
armada: *n.* armada
armadillo: *n.* armadillo
armament: *n.* armamento; fuerzas militares
armature: *n.* armadura; armazón
Armenia: Armenia
Armenian: 1. *adj.* armenio; (a); 2. *n.* armenio (a)
armistice: *n.* armisticio
armless: *adj.* manco
armor: *n.* armadura
armorial: *adj.* heráldico
armory: *n.* armería
arms: *n.* armamento; armas; milicia; brazos
arms industry: industria de armamentos
army: 1. *n.* (pl. -mies) ejercito; 2. *adj.* militar
aroma: *n.* aroma
aromatherapy: *n.* aromaterapia
around: *prep.* alrededor
arouse: *v.* despertar; mover
arpeggio: *n.* arpegio
arraign: *v.* acusar
arrange: *v.* arreglar; disponer
arrangement: *n.* arreglo
arranger: *n.* arreglista
array: *n.* orden; batalla; adorno
arrears: *n.* mora; retraso
arrest: *n.* arresto; detención; prisión
arrhythmia: *n.* arritmia
arrive: *v.* llegar; tener éxito
arrogance: *n.* arrogancia
arrogate: *v.* arrogar
arrow: *n.* flecha
arsenal: *n.* arsenal
arsenic: *n.* arsénico
arsenic: *adj.* arsénico
arson: *n.* incendio premeditado; provocado
art: *n.* artes
art deco: art deco
arteriogram: *n.* arteriógrama
arteriography: *n.* arteriografía
arteriosclerosis: *n.* arteriosclerosis
artery: *n.* arteria
artesian: *n.* pozo artesiano
artesian well: pozo artesiano
artful: *adj.* ingenioso; artificial
arthralgia: *n.* artralgia
arthritis: *n.* artritis
arthrocentesis: *n.* artrocentesis
arthrogram: *n.* artrograma
arthroplasty: *n.* artroplastia
arthropod: *adj.* artrópodo
arthroscope: *adj.* artroscopio
arthroscopy: *n.* artroscopia

article: *n.* artículo
article writer: articulista
articles of association: contrato de asociación
articles of incorporation: escritura de constitución
articles of partnership: contrato de asociación
articulate: *adj.* articulado
articulation: *n.* articulación
articulatory: *adj.* articulatorio
artificial: *adj.* artificial
artificial insemination: inseminación artificial
artificial intelligence: inteligencia artificial
artificial person: persona de existencia ideal
artificial respiration: *n.* respiración artificial
artificial sweetener: azúcar artificial
artificiality: *n.* falta de naturalidad
artillery: *n.* artillería
artilleryman: *n.* artillero
artisan: *n.* artesano; -a
artist: *n.* artista
artistry: *n.* talento artístico
artless: *adj.* sencillo
arts and crafts: artes y oficios
Aruba: Aruba
Aryan: *adj.* ario
arylsulfatase: *n.* arilsulfatasa
as: *conj.* como; a semejanza de; según
asbestos: *n.* asbesto
asbestos-free: sin asbesto
asbestosis: *n.* asbestosis
ascend: *v.* subir
ascending: *adj.* ascendente
ascent: *n.* ascensión; promoción
ascertain: *v.* averiguar
asceticism: *n.* ascetismo
ASCII: ASCII
ascitic fluid: líquido ascítico

ascorbate: *adj.* ascorbato
ascorbic (acid): *adj.* ascórbico
ascorbic acid: ácido ascórbico
asepsis: *n.* asepsia
aseptic: *adj.* aséptico
asexual reproduction: reproducción asexual
ash: *n.* ceniza
Ashkenazi: *n.* askenazita
Ashkenazi: *adj.* askenazita
ashore: *adv.* en tierra; a tierra
ash-tray: cenicero
Asia: Asia
Asia Minor: Asia Menor
Asian: 1. *adj.* asiático; (a); 2. *n.* asiático
ask: *v.* preguntar
ask for: *v.* pedir
asking price: precio inicial; precio de oferta
associative of addition: la asociatividad de la adición
associative of multiplication: la asociatividad de la multiplicación
asp: *n.* áspid
asparaginase: *n.* asparraginasa
asparagines: *n.* asparragina
asparagus: *n.* espárrago
aspartate: *n.* aspartato
aspartic acid: ácido aspártico
aspect: *n.* aspecto
asphalt: *n.* asfalto
asphyxia; asphyxiation: *n.* asfixia
asphyxiation: *n.* asfixia
aspiration: *n.* aspiración; anhelo; punción articular
aspirator: *n.* aspirador
aspire: *v.* aspirar; pretender
aspirin: *n.* aspirina
ass: *n.* asno
assail: *v.* asaltar
assailant: *n.* asaltante
assassin: *n.* asesino; -a
assassination: *n.* asesinato

assault: *n.* asalto
assay: *n.* ensayo; valoración
assemblage: *n.* ensamblaje; asamblea
assemble: *v.* armar; ensamblar
assembler: *n.* ensamblador
assembler (language): *n.* ensamblador
assembly: *n.* asamblea; montaje
assembly hall: sala de sesiones
assembly line: línea de montaje
assembly plant: planta de montaje
assembly room: sala de reuniones
assemblyman: *n.* asambleísto
assemblywoman: *n.* asambleísta
assent: *n.* asentimiento; asenso; aprobación
assert: *v.* afirmar
assertion: *n.* aserción; aserto
assess: *v.* evaluar; tasar; gravar
assessed valuation: valoración catastral
assessed value: valor de tasación; valor catastral
assessment: *n.* evaluación; tasación
assessment centre: centro de evaluación
assessment electrocardiogram: electrocardiograma
assets: *n.* bienes; activo
assign: *v.* asignar
assign number: asignar número
assigned value: valor asignado
assignment: *n.* asignación
assimilation: *n.* asimilación
assimilation test: prueba de asimilación
assist: *v.* asistir
assisted living: ayuda ocasional
assistant: *n.* ayudante; adjunto; auxiliar
associate: *n.* asociado
associate member: miembro no numerario
association: *n.* asociación

associative property of addition: propiedad asociativa de la suma
associative property of multiplication: propiedad asociativa de la multiplicación
assonance: *n.* asonancia
assort: *v.* ordenar
assortative mating: apareamiento concordante
assortment: *n.* surtido
assuage: *v.* aliviar
assume: *v.* asumir; imaginarse
assuming: *adj.* presumido
assumption: supuesto
Assumption: Asunción
assumption (duties): *n.* asunción
assurance: *n.* convencimiento
assure: *v.* asegurar; garantizar
Assyrian: 1. *adj.* asirio (a); 2. *n.* asirio (a)
astatic: *adj.* astático; inestable
aster: *n.* aster
astern: *adv.* a popa
asteroid: *n.* asteroides
asteroid belt: cinturón de asteroides
asthenia: *n.* astenia
asthenosphere: *n.* astenosfera
asthma: *n.* asma
asthmatic: *adj.* asmático; -a
astigmatism: *n.* astigmatismo
astir: *adv.* en movimiento
astonish: *v.* asombrar
astonishing: *adj.* asombroso
astound: *v.* pasmar
astrakhan: *n.* astracán
astral: *adj.* astral
astray: *adv.* por mal camino
astringent: *adj.* astringente
astrodome: *n.* astródomo
astrologer: *n.* astrólogo
astrology: *n.* astrología
astronaut: *n.* astronauta
astronautics: *n.* astronáutica
astronomer: *n.* astrónomo

astronomical: *adj.* astronómico
astronomy: *n.* astronomía
astrophysics: *n.* astrofísica
astuteness: *n.* astucia
asylee: *n.* asilado
asylum: *n.* asilo
asymmetry: *n.* asimetría
asymptomatic: *adj.* asintomático
asymptote: *n.* asíntota
asynchronous: *adj.* asíncrono
at: en
at rest: en reposo
ataxia: *n.* ataxia
atchoo!: intj. ¡achís!
atheism: *n.* ateísmo
Athenian: *adj.* ateniense
Athens: Atenas
atheroma: *n.* ateroma
atherosclerosis: *n.* aterosclerosis
athlete: *n.* atleta
athlete's foot: *n.* pie de atleta
athletics: *n.* atletismo
Atlantic: Atlántico
atlas: *n.* atlas
atmosphere: *n.* atmósfera
atoll: *n.* atolón
atom: *n.* átomo
atomic: *adj.* atómico
atomic absorption: espectrometría de absorción atómica
atomic mass: masa atómica
atomic mass constant: constante de masa atómica
atomic mass unit: unidad de masa atómica
atomic number: número atómico
atomic weight: peso atómico
atomicity: *n.* atomicidad
atomism: *n.* atomismo
atomizer: *n.* atomizador
atonality: *n.* atonalidad
atone: *v.* expiar; reparar
atonement: *n.* expiación
atonic: *adj.* atónico

atrium: *n.* atrio; aurícula
atrocious: *adj.* atroz
atrocity: *n.* atrocidad
atrophy: *n.* atrofia
atropism: *n.* atropismo
attach: *v.* atar; conectar; pegar
attachment: *n.* conexión
attack: *n.* ataque
attacker: *n.* atacador; atacante
attain: *v.* lograr
attainder: *n.* pérdida de derechos civiles
attainment of age: cumplimiento de edad
attempt: *n.* tentativa; atentado
attend: *v.* atender; asistir
attending school: asistiendo a la escuela
attention!: intj. ¡atención!
attentive: *adj.* atento
attenuance: *n.* atenuancia
attenuate: *v.* atenuar
attenuating: *adj.* atenuante
attest: *v.* atestiguar
attestation: *n.* atestación; atestado
attestor: *n.* testigo
attic: 1. a. ático; 2. *n.* ático
attire: 1. *n.* atavío; 2. *v.* ataviar
attitude: *n.* actitud
attorney: *n.* abogado; procurador
attorney fees: honorarios para abogado
attraction: *n.* atracción
attractive: *adj.* atractivo; atrayente
attrat: *v.* atraer; ganarse
attributable: *adj.* atribuible; atribuida
attribute: *n.* atributo
attributive: *adj.* atributivo
attrition: *n.* atrición
attune: *v.* afinar
atypical: *adj.* atípico
auburn: *adj.* pardo; rojizo
audacious: *adj.* audaz

audacity: *n.* audacia
audible: *adj.* audible
audience: *n.* audiencia; auditorio
audience participation:
participación del público
audio: *n.* audio
audio system: el audio
audio frequency: *n.* audiofrecuencia
audiogram: *n.* audiograma
audiologist: *n.* audiólogo; -a
audiology: *n.* audiología
audiometer: *n.* audiómetro
audiometry: *n.* audiometría
audiovisual: *adj.* audiovisual
audir: 1. *n.* intervención; 2. *v.*
intervenir
audit: *n.* auditoria
audition: *n.* audición
auditor: *n.* auditor; oyente
auditorium: *n.* auditorio
auditory: *n.* auditivo
auger: *n.* barrenador mecánico
augment: *v.* aumentar
augmentative: *adj.* aumentativo
augmented: *adj.* aumentado
augur: *v.* augur
augury: *n.* augurio
August: *n.* agosto
Augustinian: *adj.* agustino
aunt: *n.* tía
aura: *n.* aura
aureomycin: *n.* aureomicina
auricle: *n.* aurícula
aurora *n.* aurora
auscultation: *n.* auscultación
auspices: *n.* auspicios
austere: *adj.* austero
austerity: *n.* austeridad
Australasia: Austrolasia
Australasian: *adj.* australasiático
Australia: Australia
Australian: *adj.* australiano; -a
Austria: Austria
Austrian: 1. *adj.* austriaco; (a); 2. *n.*
austriaco (a)
Austro-Asiatic: *adj.* austroasiático
Austronesian: *adj.* austronesio
autarchy: *n.* autarquía
authentic: *adj.* auténtico
authenticate: *v.* autorizar; autenticar;
legalizar
author: *n.* autor
authoritarian: *adj.* autoritario
authoritarianism: *n.* autoritarismo
authority: autoridad; autorización
authorize: *v.* autorizar
authorized health agency: agencia
autorizada de salud
authorized representative:
representante autorizado
autism: *n.* autismo
auto; automobile: *n.* auto; automóvil
auto-antibody: autoanticuerpo
autobiography: *n.* autobiografía
autoclave: *n.* autoclave
autocracy: *n.* autocracia
autocrat: *n.* autócrata
autogenous: *adj.* autógeno
autograph: *n.* autógrafo
autogyro: *n.* autogiro
autoharp: *n.* autoarpa
autoimmune: *n.* autoinmune autoinmune
autoimmune: *adj.* autoinmuno
autointoxication: *n.*
autointoxicación
automatic enrollment: inscripción
automática
automatic entitlement: derecho
automático
automatic increase: aumento
automático
automatic recomputation:
recomputación automática
automatic weapon: arma automática
automation: *n.* automación;
automatización
automaton: *n.* autómata

automobile: *n.* automóvil
automotive: *n.* automotor; automotriz
autonomic: *adj.* autónomo

autonomic nervous system: sistema nervioso autónomo
autonomous: *adj.* autónomo; (a)
autonomy: *n.* autonomía
autopsy: *n.* autopsia
autoradiograph: *n.* autoradiografía
autotroph: *n.* autótrofo
autumn: *n.* otoño
autumnal: *adj.* otoñal
auxiliaries: *n.* tropas auxiliares
auxiliary: *adj.* auxiliar
auxin: *n.* auxina
auxotroph: *n.* auxótrofo
avail: 1. *n.* provecho; 2. *v.* beneficiar
availability of funds: disponibilidad de fondos
available: *adj.* disponible
available assets: activo disponible
avalanche: *n.* avalancha
avant-garde: *n.* vanguardia
avarice: *n.* avaricia
avatar: *n.* avatar
avenge: *v.* vengar
avenger: *n.* vengador
avenue: *n.* avenida; alameda
aver: *v.* afirmar
average: *n.* promedio
average speed: velocidad media
averse: *adj.* adverso; contrario
aversion: *n.* aversión
avert: *v.* desviar; impedir
avian: *adj.* ave
Avian pox: viruela aviaria (Poxvirus avium)
aviary: *n.* pajarera
aviation: *n.* aviación
aviculture: *n.* avicultura
avid: *adj.* ávido
avidity: *n.* avidez

Avignon: Aviñón
avionics: *n.* aviónica
avitaminosis: *n.* avitaminosis
Avogadro constant: constante de Avogadro
Avogadro number: número de Avogadro
avoid: *v.* evitar
avoidable: *adj.* evitable
avow: *v.* admitir; declarar
avulsion: *n.* avulsión
await: *v.* aguardar; esperar
awaken: *v.* . i. despertar
award: *n.* adjudicación; premio
award certificate: certificado de adjudicación
award letter: carta de aprobación
away: *adj.* ausente
awe: *n.* miedo; asombro
awesome: *adj.* imponente
awhile: *adv.* algún tiempo
awn: *n.* arista
axe: *n.* hacha
axerol: *n.* retinol
axerophtal: *n.* retinal
axilla: *n.* axila
axiom: *n.* axioma
axis: *n.* eje
axolote: *n.* olote
axon: *n.* axón
ay!: *intj.* ¡ay!
azalea: *n.* azalea
Azerbaijan: *n.* azerbaijano
Azerbaijani: *adj.* azerbaiyàni
azimuth: *n.* acimut; azimut
azlocillin: *n.* azlocilina
Azores: Azores
azotemia: *n.* concentración de urea en plasma
aztreonam: *n.* aztreonam
azure: *n.* azul

B

B cell: célula B
babble: 1. *n.* charla; 2. *v.* hablar por los codos
babe: *n.* nene; criatura
babe; baby: *n.* bebé
babirusa; babiroussa: *n.* babirusa
baboon: *n.* babuino
baby: 1. *n.* nene; bebé 2. *adj.* infantil
baby sitter: niñera
babyish: *adj.* infantil; pueril
Babylonian: 1. *adj.* babilonio (a); 2. *n.* babilonio (a)
bacampicillin: *n.* bacampicilina
baccalaureate: *n.* bachillerato
baccarat: *n.* bacará
bachelor: *n.* bachiller; diplomado; licenciado
bachelor of accountancy: bachiller en contabilidad
bachelor of arts: licenciado en artes
bachelor of business: licenciado en administración
bachelor of commerce: licenciado comercial
bachelor of science: licenciado en ciencias
bacillus: *n.* bacilo
bacitracin: *n.* bacitracina
back: 1. *adj.* atrasado; 2. *v.* respaldar
back: *adv.* atrás; detrás
back office: sección de una empresa
back order: orden pendiente
back pain: dolor de la espalda
back pay: pago retroactivo
back street: callejón
back tax: impuesto vencido
back up: *n.* apoyo; copia de seguridad
back-end cost: costo de salida

back-end load: recargo por reembolso anticipado
backgammon: *n.* back gamón
background: *n.* antecedentes; fondo
background music: música de fondo
backing: *n.* apoyo
backshop: *n.* trastienda
backup: *n.* copia de seguridad
backward: 1. *adj.* atrasado; 2. *adv.* atrás
bacon: *n.* tocino
bacteremia: *n.* bacteremia
bacteria: *n.* bacterias
bacterial: *adj.* bacteriano
bacterial cast: cilindro bacteriano
bacterial luciferase: alcanal-monooxigenasa
bactericidal: *n.* bactericida
bactericide: *n.* bactericida
bacteriological: *adj.* bacteriológico
bacteriology: *n.* bacteriología
bacteriophage: *n.* bacteriófago
bacteriostatic: *adj.* bacteriostático
bacterium: *n.* bacteria
bacteriuria: *n.* bacteriuria
bad: *adj.* malo; falso
bad account: cuenta incobrable
bad credit: crédito incobrable
bad debt: deuda incobrable
bad debtor: deudor incobrable
bad faith: mala fe
bad loan: préstamo incobrable
bad money: dinero falso
bad taste: sabor desagradable
bad title: título imperfecto
badge: *n.* insignia; divisa
badminton: *n.* bádminton
baffle: *n.* confusión
bag: 1. *n.* saco; rodillera; 2. *v.* embolsar
bagatelle: *n.* bagatela
baggage: *n.* bagaje; equipaje
Baghdad: Bagdad
bagpipe: *n.* gaita

bah!: intj. ¡bah!
Bahai: *n.* bahai
Bahaism: *n.* bahaísmo
Bahamas: Bahamas
Bahamian: *adj.* bahameño; -a;
bahamés; -esa
Bahamian: 1. *adj.* bahameño; (a); 2.
n. bahameño (a)
Bahrain: Bahrein
bail: *n.* fianza
bail: *v.* dar fianza (por uno)
bailiff: *n.* alguacil; corchete
bait: 1. *n.* carnada; 2. *v.* cebar
baize: *n.* bayeta
bake: *v.* hornear
baked: *adj.* horneado[a]
Baker: *n.* panadero
balalaika: *n.* balalaica
balance: *n.* balanza; equilibrio
balance: *v.* balancear
balance due: saldo deudor; saldo a
pagar
balance forward: saldo transportado
del último
balance in hand: saldo disponible
balance of payments: balanza de
pagos
balance of trade: balanza comercial
balance outstanding: saldo
pendiente
balance per books: saldo según
libros
balance sheet report: reporte del
balance general
balanced (diet): *adj.* balanceado
balanced forces: fuerzas
equilibradas
balancing: *n.* equilibrio
balboa: *n.* balboa
balcony: *n.* balcón; galería
bald: *adj.* calvo; desnudo
bale: *v.* embalar; empaquetar
Balearics: Baleares
Bali: Balí

Balinese: 1. *adj.* balines; (esa); 2. *n.*
balines; (esa)
balk: 1. *n.* obstáculo; 2. *v.* evitar
Balkan: 1. *adj.* balcánico; (a); 2. *n.*
balcánico; (a)
Balkan: *n.* balcánico
Balkans: *n.* Balcanes
ball: *n.* bola; baile
ballad: *n.* balada
ballerina: *n.* bailarina
ballet: *n.* ballet
balletomane: *n.* aficionado al ballet
ballistic: *adj.* balístico
balloon: *n.* balón
ballot: *n.* balota; papeleta
ballroom: *n.* salón de baile
balm: *n.* bálsamo
balmy: *adj.* balsámico
balneotherapy: *n.* balneoterapia
balsa: *n.* balsa
balsam: *n.* balsamina
Baltic: 1. *adj.* báltico; (a); 2. *n.*
Báltico
balustrade: *n.* balaustrada
bamboo: *n.* bambú
ban: *n.* prohibición; desterrar
banality: *n.* banalidad
banana: *n.* banana
banana plantation: bananar
band: *n.* banda; cuadrilla
bandage: *n.* venda; vendaje
banded: *adj.* vendado; fajado
banding pattern: diagrama de
bandas
bandit: *n.* bandido
banditry: *n.* bandidaje
bandoleer; bandolier: *n.* bandolera
bandwidth: *n.* amplitud de banda;
ancho de banda
bane: *n.* azote; castigo
bang: 1. *n.* detonación; golpazo; 2.
adv. de repente
Bangkok: Bangkok
Bangladesh: Bangladesh

Bangladeshi: 1. *adj.* bangladesi; 2. *n.* bangladesi
bangle: *n.* ajorca; pulsera
banish: *v.* desterrar
banjo: *n.* banjo
bank: *n.* banco
bank: 1. *n.* banco; 2. *adj.* bancario
bank: *n.* banca
bank acceptance: aceptación bancaria
bank account: cuenta bancaria
bank balance: saldo bancario
bank bill: aceptación bancaria
bank book: libreta de banco
bank charge: cargo bancario
bank cheque: cheque bancario
bank clearing: compensación bancaria
bank clerk: empleado bancario
bank commission: comisión bancaria
bank credit: crédito bancario
bank debit: débito bancario
bank debt: deuda bancaria
bank deposit: depósito bancario
bank discount: descuento bancario
bank draft: giro bancario
bank endorsement: endoso bancario
bank expense: gasto bancario
bank fee: comisión bancaria
bank guarantee: garantía bancaria
bank order: orden bancaria
bank overdraft: sobregiro bancario
bank rate: tipo de interés bancario
bank reconciliation: conciliación bancaria
bank reserve: reserva bancaria
bank share: acción bancaria
bank statement: estado de cuenta; extracto bancario
bank transfer: transferencia bancaria
banker: *n.* banquero
banking: banca; relativo a los bancos

banking center: centro bancario
banking company: sociedad bancaria
banking house: casa bancaria; institución bancaria
banking system: sistema bancario
bankrupt: *adj.* insolvente; fallido
bankruptcy: *n.* bancarrota; quiebra
bankruptcy law: ley de quiebra (bancarrota)
bankruptcy proceedings: juicio de quiebra
banner: *n.* bandera
banquet: *n.* banquete
banquette: *n.* banqueta
bantam: 1. *n.* Pequeño; 2. *adj.* diminuto
Bantu: *adj.* bantú
banyan: *adj.* baniano
baobab: *n.* baobab
baptism: *n.* bautismo; bautizo
baptismal certificate: certificado de bautismo
Baptist: *n.* bautista
baptistery; baptistry: *n.* baptisterio; bautisterio
baptizer: *n.* bautista
bar: *n.* asociación de abogados; barra ; reja
bar association: colegio de abogados
bar chart: gráfico de barras
bar graph: grafica de barras
bar mitzvah: bar mitzvah
Barbadian: *adj.* barbadense
Barbados: Barbados
barbarian: *adj.* bárbaro
barbarism: *n.* barbarismo
Barbary: Berbería
barbecue: *n.* barbacoa
barbed: *adj.* armado de púas; punzante
barber: *n.* barbero; -a
barbershop: *n.* barbería
barbiturate: *adj.* barbiturato

barbituric acid: ácido barbitúrico
barbiturism: *n.* barbiturismo
barcarole; barcarolle: *n.* barcarola
Barcelona: Barcelona
bard: *adj.* bardo (a)
bare: *adj.* desnudo
barefoot: *adj.* descalzo
bareness: *n.* desnudez
bargain: *n.* negocio; trato
bargain: *v.* regatear; pactar
bargain counter: mostrador de rebajas
bargain department: sección de rebajas o saldos
bargain price: precio de liquidación
bargain sale: liquidación; realización
baritone: *n.* barítono
barium enema: enema de bario
barium swallow: trago de bario
bark: *n.* corteza; ladrido; tos
barker: *n.* labrador; descortezador
barmaid: *n.* camarera
barman: *n.* camarero
barn: *n.* granero; pajar
barogram: *n.* barograma
barograph: *n.* barógrafo
barometer: *n.* barómetro
baron: *n.* barón
baroness: *n.* baronesa
baronet: *n.* baronet
barony: *n.* baronía
baroque: *n.* barroco
barracks: *n.* barraca
barracuda: *n.* barracuda
barrage: *n.* presa de embalse
barratry: *n.* demanda fraudulenta
barred: *adj.* barreteado
barrel: *n.* barril; tonel; cañón
barrel organ: organillo
barren: *adj.* estéril; árido; seco; improductivo
barren investment: inversión improductiva

barricade: *n.* barricada
barring: *prep.* excepto; salvo
barrio: *n.* barrio
barrister: *n.* abogado; procurador
barter: *n.* permuta; cambio; trueque
barter: *v.* permutar
Barton's bacillus: Bartonella bacilliformis
basalt: *n.* basalto
base: *n.* base
base: *v.* basar; fundar
base index: índice base
base of a parallelogram: base de un paralelogramo
base of a power: base de una potencia
base of a solid: base de un cuerpo geométrico
base of a triangle: base de un triangulo
base pairing: apareamiento de bases
base pay: salario básico; sueldo básico
base price: precio base
base quantity: magnitud de base
base rate: tipo de interés básico; tasa básica
base tax: impuesto básico
base unit: unidad de base (de medida)
base value: valor base
baseball: *n.* béisbol; baseball
baseball (object): *n.* pelota de béisbol
baseball fan: beisbolista; aficionado al béisbol
base-isolated building: edificio de base aislada
baseless: *adj.* infundado; sin base
baseline: *n.* línea de base; situación basal
bases of a trapezoid: bases de un trapecio
bashful: *adj.* vergonzoso; tímido

basic: *adj.* básico
basic commodity: artículo de primera necesidad
Basic English: *n.* Inglés básico
basic salary: salario básico; sueldo básico
basicity: *n.* basicidad
basilica: *n.* basílica
basin: *n.* palangana; vasija
basis: *n.* base; fundamento
bask: *v.* asolear; calentar
basketball: *n.* básquetbol
basophil: *n.* basófilo
basophilocyte: *n.* basofilocito
Basque: *n.* vascuence; vasco
bas-relief: *n.* bajorrelieve
bass: 1. *adj.* bajo; 2. *n.* bajo
bass: *adj.* bajo
basset hound: basset
basso: *n.* bajo
basso profundo: bajo profundo
bassoon: *n.* bajón
bassoonist: *n.* bajonista
basting: *n.* baste
bastion: *n.* bastión; baluarte
bat: *n.* palo; raqueta; bate
bat: *n.* bate
bat mitzvah: bat mitzvah
batch: *n.* cochura; hornada
batch cost: coste por lotes
batch culture: cultivo discontinuo
batch operation: operación por grupos
batch processing: procesamiento por lotes
batch production: producción por lotes
bathe: *v.* bañarse
bathing: *n.* baño
batholith: *n.* batolito
bathroom: *n.* cuarto de baño
bathtub: *n.* bañera
batiste: *n.* batista
baton: *n.* batuta

batroxobin: *n.* batroxobina
battalion: *n.* batallón
batter: *n.* bateador
battery: *n.* batería; pila
batting: *n.* bateo
battle: *n.* batalla
battle: *v.* batallar con
baud: *n.* baudio
Bavaria: Baviera
Bavarian: *adj.* bávaro; -a
bawdy: *adj.* obsceno
bawl: *n.* voces
bawl: *v.* vocear
bay: *n.* bahía; ladrido
bayonet: *n.* bayoneta
Bayonne: Bayona
bazaar; bazar: *n.* bazar
beach: *n.* playa; costa
Bead: *n.* cuenta; perla
beagle: *n.* sabueso
beam: 1. *n.* viga; rayo; 2. *v.* emitir
beans: *n.* frijoles
Bear: 1. *n.* bajista; 2. *adj.* bajista;
Bear: *v.* devengar; rendir
Bear interest: rendir interés
Bear market: mercado bajista
bearer: *n.* tenedor; portador
bearer bond: bono al portador
bearer cheque: cheque al portador
bearer deposit: depósito transferible
bearer instrument: instrumento al portador
bearer note: pagaré al portador
bearer paper: efectos al portador
bearer security: título al portador
bearer share: acción al portador
bearing: *n.* porte; conducción
beast: *n.* bestia; animal
beast of burden: bestia de carga
beat: *vt.* batir
beater: *n.* batidora
beatification: *n.* beatificación
beating: *n.* paliza
beatnik (obs): *n.* beatnik

beauteous: *adj.* bello
beautification: *n.* beatificación
beautiful: *adj.* hermoso
beautify: *v.* embellecer; hermosear
beauty salon: salón de belleza
becalm: *v.* serenar; calmar
because: *conj.* porque; a causa de
bechamel: *n.* bechamel; besamel
beckon: *v.* hacer señas
become: *v.* convenir; volverse
become effective: entrar en vigor
becquerel: *n.* becquerelio
bed: *n.* cama; lecho
bedeck: *v.* adornar
bedew: *v.* rociar
bedlam: *n.* confusión; manicomio
bedrock: *n.* lecho rocoso
bedroom: *n.* dormitorio
bedspread: *n.* sobrecama
bee: *n.* abeja
beef: *n.* carne de vaca
beefsteak: *n.* biftec; bistec
beep: *n.* bip
beer: *n.* cerveza
beet: *n.* remolacha
beetle: *n.* escarabajo
befall: *v.* acontecer
befit: *v.* convenir; venir bien
befog: *v.* oscurecer; confundir
befool: *v.* engañar
before: *prep.* delante de; *adv.* antes de
before taxes: antes de impuestos
befriend: *v.* amparar
beg: *v.* solicitar; mendigar
beget: *v.* engendrar; originar
beggar: *n.* mendigo
begging: *adj.* mendigante
begin: *v.* empezar; comenzar
beginner: *n.* principiante
beginning: *n.* principio
beginning of the year: apertura del ejercicio
begonia: *n.* begonia

begrudge: *v.* envidiar
behave: *v.* actuar
behavior: *n.* comportamiento
behead: *v.* decapitar
behind: *prep.* detrás
behold: *v.* mirar; contemplar; observar
beholden: *adj.* obligado
behoof: *n.* provecho; beneficio
behove: *v.* incumbir; tocar
beige: *adj.* beige
Beijing: Beijing
bekiss: *v.* cubrir de besos
bel canto: bel canto; canto bello
belabor: *v.* maltratar
belfry: *n.* campanario
Belgian: *adj.* belga
Belgium: Bélgica
Belgrade: Belgrado
belief: *n.* creencia
believe: *v.* creer
belittle: *v.* despreciar
Belize: Belice
Belizean: 1. *adj.* beliceño; (a); 2. *n.* beliceño (a)
bell: *n.* campana; timbre
belladonna: *n.* belladona
belles-lettres: *n.* bellas letras
bellicose: *n.* belicoso
belligerent: *n.* beligerante
belligerence: *n.* beligerancia
belligerent: *adj.* beligerante
bellow: *n.* bramido
bellow: *v.* gritar
belly: *n.* vientre; abdomen
belong: *v.* pertenecer
belongings: *n.* pertenencias
beloved: *adj.* amado
below: 1. *adv.* abajo; 2. *prep.* debajo de
belt: *n.* cinturón
belt conveyor: cinta transportadora
beluga: *n.* beluga
bemean: *v.* empequeñecer

bemoan: *v.* deplorar; lamentar
bemuse: *v.* aturdir; confundir
bench: *n.* banco; asiento
benchmark: *n.* parámetro de
referencia
benchmarking: comparación de
parámetros o estándares
bend: *n.* curva
bend: *v.* doblar; encorvar
Benedictine: *n.* benedictino
benediction: *n.* bendición
benefactor: *n.* benefactor
benefice: *n.* beneficio
beneficial: *adj.* benéfico
beneficial association: sociedad de
beneficencia
beneficial interest: interés
beneficioso
beneficial owner: usufructuario
beneficiary: *n.* beneficiario;
asignatario
beneficiary's behalf: en nombre del
beneficiario
bend: *n.* curva
benefit: *n.* beneficio
benefit amount: cantidad de
beneficio
benefit estimate: presupuesto de
beneficio
benefit increase: aumento de
beneficio
benefit payments: pagos de
beneficios
benefit period: período de beneficios
benefit plan: plan de beneficios
benefit society: asociación benéfica
benefit statement: declaración de
beneficios
Benelux: *n.* benelux
benevolence: *n.* benevolencia
benevolent: *n.* benévolo; caritativo
benevolent association: asociación
de beneficencia
benevolent fund: fondo de

beneficencia
benevolent institution: institución
de beneficencia
Bengal: Bengala
Bengali: *n.* bengalí
Bengali; Bengalese: *adj.* bengalí
benighted: *adj.* sorprendido por la
noche
benign: *adj.* benigno
bent: 1. *adj.* encorvado; doblado; 2.
n. pliegue; inclinación
benthos: *n.* bentos
bentiromide: *n.* bentiromida
benumb: *v.* entorpecer
Benzedrine: *n.* bencedrina
benzidine test: determinación de
sangre en heces
benzocaine: *n.* benzocaine
bequeath: *v.* legar
bequest: *adj.* legado
berate: *v.* reñir
Berber: *n.* bereber
bereave: *v.* despojar
beret: *n.* boina
bergamot: *n.* bergamota
beriberi: *n.* beriberi
Berlin: Berlín
Berliner: *n.* berlinés; -esa
Bermuda: Bermudas
Bermudian: *adj.* bermudeño; -a
Bern; Berne: Berna
Bernoulli's principle: principio de
Bernoulli
berry: *n.* baya
berth: *n.* atracadero; litera;
berth: *v.* atracar
beset: *v.* asediar; acosar
beside: 1. *adv.* cerca; 2. *prep.* junto a
besides: 1. *adv.* además; 2. *prep.*
excepto
besmirch: *v.* ensuciar
bespatter: *v.* salpicar
bespeak: *v.* apalabrar; demostrar
best: 1. *adj.* superior; 2. *adv.* lo

mejor
bestiality: *n*. bestialidad
bestir: *v*. mover
bestow: *v*. otorgar; conferir
bestowal: *n*. donativo
best-seller: *n*. éxito de ventas
bet: *n*. apuesta
bet: *v*. apostar
beta: *n*. beta
beta particle: Particula beta
betel: *n*. betel
betray: *v*. traicionar
betroth: *v*. desposar
betrothal: *n*. noviazgo
betrothed: 1. *adj*. prometido; 2. *n*. prometido
better: 1. *adj*. mejor; 2. *adv*. mas
better: *v*. mejorar
betting: *n*. apuesta
between: *adv*. en medio
between-day imprecision: imprecisión interdiaria
between-run imprecision: imprecisión interserial
bevel: *n*. bisel
beverage: *n*. bebida
bevy: *n*. bandada; grupo (de personas)
bewail: *v*. lamentar
beware: *v*. guardarse de; precaverse
bewilder: *v*. extraviar
bewitch: *v*. hechizar
beyond: 1. *adv*. lejos; 2. *prep*. detrás
Bhagavad-Gita: Bhagavad-Gita
Bhutan: Bután
Bhutanese: *adj*. butanés; -esa
bias: *n*. parcialidad; prejuicio
biased sample: muestra parcial
Bible: *n*. Biblia
biblical: *adj*. bíblico
bibliographer: *n*. bibliógrafo; -a
bibliography: *n*. bibliografía
bibliomaniac: *adj*. bibliómano
bibliophile: *n*. bibliófilo; -a

bicameral: *adj*. bicameral
bicarbonate: *n*. bicarbonato
bicentenary: *adj*. bicentenario
biceps: *n*. bíceps
bicuspid: *adj*. bicúspide
bicycle: *n*. bicicleta
bid: *n*. oferta
bid: *v*. ofertar; ordenar
bid bond: caución de licitación
bidding: *n*. oferta; licitación
bidding conditions: pliego de licitación
bidding price: precio de oferta
bidding specifications: condiciones de licitación
bide: *v*. esperar; soportar
bidet: *n*. bidé; bidet
biennial: 1. *adj*. bienal; 2. *n*. planta bienal
bier: *n*. féretro
bifocal: *adj*. bifocal
bifocals: *n*. lentes bifocales
bifurcation: *n*. bifurcación
big: *adj*. grande; engreído; *adv*. con jactancia
Big Bang: Big Bang
bigamist: *n*. bígamo
bigamous marriage: matrimonio bígamo
bigamy: *n*. bigamia
bight: *n*. ensenada
bignonia: *n*. bignonia
bigot: *n*. fanático
bike: *n*. bici
bikini: *n*. bikini
bilateral: *adj*. bilateral
bilateral contract: contrato bilateral
bilateral symmetry: simetría bilateral
bilateral trade: intercambio bilateral
bile: *n*. bilis
bile acid: ácido biliar
bilharzias: *n*. bilharziosis
bilingual: *adj*. bilingüe

bilingual secretary: secretaria bilingüe
bilirubin: *n.* bilirrubina
bilirubin ester: bilirrubina esterificada
bilirubin non-esterified: bilirrubina no esterificada
bill: *n.* billete; factura; cuenta
bill: *v.* facturar
bill book: libreta de facturas
bill for collection: factura a cobrar
bill of debit: pagaré
bill of entry: declaración de importación
bill of exchange: letra de cambio
bill of health: certificado de salud
bill of lading: conocimiento de embarque
bill of materials: lista de materiales
bill of sale: contrato de compraventa
bill on hand: letra en cartera
bill overhang: gancho del pico
bill payable: factura a pagar
bill receivable: factura a cobrar
billboard: *n.* cartelera
billiard: *n.* billar
billing: *n.* facturación
billing price: precio de factura
billing statement: cuenta de cobro; factura
billing system: sistema de facturación
billion: *n.* billón
billionth: *adj.* billonésimo
binary: *adj.* binario
binary code: código binario
binary digit: dígito binario
binary fission: fisión binaria
binary star: estrella binaria
binary system: sistema binario
bind: *n.* lazo; ligadura
binding: *n.* ligadura; encuadernación
binding capacity: capacidad enlazante

binding site: centro de unión
bingo: *n.* bingo
bingo!: intj. ¡bingo!
binocular: *adj.* binocular
binoculars: *n.* binoculares
binomial: 1. *adj.* binomial; 2. *n.* binomio
binomial nomenclature: nomenclatura binaria
binomial theorem: teorema binomial
bioacoustics: *n.* bioacústica
bioactive: *adj.* bioactivo
bioassay: *n.* bioensayo; bioanálisis
bioastronautics: *n.* bioastronáutica
bioavailability: *n.* biodisponibilidad
biocatalyst: *n.* biocatalizador
biochemical profile: perfil bioquímico
biochemical quantity: magnitud bioquímica
biochemistry: *n.* bioquímica
bioclimatology: *n.* bioclimatología
biodegradable: *adj.* biodegradable
biodiversity: *n.* biodiversidad
bioecology: *n.* bioecología
bioelectronics: *n.* bioelectrónica
bioengineering: *n.* bioingeniería
biofeedback: *n.* bioreacción
biogeography: *n.* biogeografía
biographer: *n.* biógrafo; -a
biographical: *adj.* biográfico
biography: *n.* biografía
biological: *adj.* biológico
biological chemistry: bioquímica
biological control: control biológico
biological fluid: líquido biológico
biological half-life: semivida biológica
biological plausibility: verosimilitud biológica
biological quantity: magnitud biológica
biological variability: variabilidad

biológica
biological variation: variación biológica
biologicals: *n.* productos biológicos
biology: *n.* biología
bioluminescence: *n.* bioluminiscencia
biomass: *n.* biomasa
biomass fuel: combustible de biomasa
biome: *n.* bioma
biomechanics: *n.* biomecánica
biomedical: *adj.* biomédico
biomedicine: *n.* biomedicina
biometrics: *n.* biometría
biometry: *n.* biometría
bionics: *n.* biónica
biophysics: *n.* biofísica
biopsy: *n.* biopsia
biorhythm: *n.* biorritmo
biosafety: *n.* bioseguridad
bioscopy: *n.* biscopía
biosensor: *n.* biosensor
biosphere: *n.* biosfera
biotechnology: *n.* biotecnología
biotherapy: *n.* bioterapia
biotic factor: factor biótico
biotin: *n.* biotina
biotinidase: *n.* biotinidasa
biotinylation: *n.* biotinilación
biotype: *n.* biotipo
biotyping: *n.* biotipificación
biped: *adj.* bípedo
biplane: *n.* biplano
bird: *n.* ave; pájaro
birth: *n.* nacimiento
birth control: anticonceptivos
birth control pill: píldoras anticonceptivas
birth rate: tasa de natalidad
birthmark: *n.* marca de nacimiento
biscuit: *n.* bizcocho
bisect: *v.* dividir en dos partes iguales

bisection: *n.* bisección
bisector: *n.* bisector; bisectriz
bisexual: *adj.* bisexual
bishop: *n.* obispo
bishopric: *n.* obispado
bison: *n.* bisonte
bit: *n.* trozo; pedazo
bitch: *n.* perra; bruja
bite: *n.* mordedura; picadura
bite: *v.* morder; picar
bitter: 1. *adj.* amargo; 2. *n.* amargura
bitter: *n.* sabor amargo
bitter taste: sabor amargo
bitumen: *n.* betun
biuret: *n.* biuret
bivalve: *n.* bivalvo
biweekly: *adj.* quincenal
black: *adj.* negro; oscuro
black coffee: café negro
black hole: agujero negro
black list: lista negra
black lung disease: enfermedad pulmonar minera
black magic: magia negra
black market: mercado negro
black money: dinero negro
black numbers: cuenta con saldo a favor
black paper: el papel negro
black stool: heces negras
blackboard: *n.* pizarra
blacken: *v.* ennegrecer
blackjack: *n.* pirata; cachiporra
blackmail: *n.* chantaje
black-out: lagunas mentales
blacksmith: *n.* herrero
bladder: *n.* vejiga
blade: *n.* hoja; cuchilla
blah; blah; blah!: *intj.* ¡bla; bla; bla!
blame: *n.* culpa
blame: *v.* acusar
blanch: *n.* blanco
blanch: *v.* desteñir; blanquear
bland: *adj.* blando

blank: 1. *n.* formulario en blanco; 2. *adj.* blanco
blank: *adj.* blanco
blank check: cheque en blanco
blank date: fecha en blanco
blank endorsement: endoso en blanco
blank form: formulario en blanco
blank paper: papel en blanco
blank signature: firma en blanco
blank value: valor del blanco
blanket: *v.* cubrir
blanket: *n.* manta
blanket insurance: seguro contra todo riesgo
blanket mortgage: hipoteca colectiva
blasphemy: *n.* blasfemia
blasphemy: *n.* blasfemia
blast: *n.* ráfaga
blasted: *adj.* arruinado
blastoconidium: *n.* blastoconidio
blather: *n.* charla
blather: *v.* charlar
blaze: *n.* llama; incendio
blazer: *n.* chaqueta deportiva
blazer: *n.* blazer
blazing: en llamas
blazon: *n.* blasón
blazon: *v.* adornar
bleak: *adj.* sombrío; triste
bleed: *v.* sangrar; desangrar
bleeding tendency: tendencia a sangrar
bleeding time: tiempo de sangría
blend: *n.* mezcla
blend: *v.* mezclar
blepharoptosis: *n.* blefaroptosis
blind: *adj.* ciego; oscuro
blind spots: manchas negras
blindfold: 1. *adj.* vendado; 2. *n.* venda
blindfold: *v.* vendar
blindness: *n.* ceguera

blister: *n.* ampolla; herida
blithe (ful): *adj.* gozoso; alegre; jovial
blizzard: *n.* ventisca
block: *n.* bloque; bloqueo
block: *v.* bloquear
block wall: el muro de bloque
blockade: *n.* bloqueo
blocked: *adj.* cerrado
blocked account: cuenta bloqueada
blocked currency: moneda bloqueada
blocked funds: fondos bloqueados
blockhead: *n.* necio
blockhouse: *n.* fortaleza
blocking: *n.* bloqueo
blond: 1. *adj.* rubio; 2. *n.* rubio
blood: *n.* sangre
blood agar: agar-sangre
blood clots: coágulos
blood clotting test: análisis de la coagulación de la sangre
blood count: hemograma
blood culture: hemocultivo
blood film: extensión sanguínea
blood gas: gasometría
blood pressure: presión arterial; presión de sangre
blood test: prueba de sangre
blood transfusion: transfusión de sangre
blood type: tipo de sangre; grupo sanguíneo
blood vessel: *n.* vaso sanguíneo
blood-streaked: manchas de sangre
bloody: *adj.* sangriento
bloody stools: heces con sangre
blossom: *n.* flor; brote
blossom: *v.* florecer
blot: *n.* transferencia (por adsorción)
blouse: *n.* blusa
blouse (long): *n.* blusón
blow: *n.* soplo; golpe
blow pipe: soplete

blower: *n.* sopladora
bludgeon: *n.* palo; estaca
blue: *adj.* azul
blue chip: acción de empresa sólida y estable
blue-collar worker: trabajador manual
blueprint: *n.* plano; copia impresa
blues: *n.* blues; trizteza
blue-sky law: ley de reglamentación bursátil
bluffing: *n.* fanfarronada
bluffness: *n.* rudeza
bluish color: morado
blunder: *n.* disparate
blunt end: extremo romo
bluntly: *adv.* sin rodeos
blur: *n.* mancha
blurred: *adj.* vista nublada
blurred vision: vista nublada
boa: *n.* boa
board: *n.* consejo; . bordo; tabla; plancha
board: *v.* embarcar
board meeting: reunión de consejeros
board of audit: consejo de revisión
board of directors: consejo de administración
board of governors: junta directiva
board of trustees: junta de fideicomisarios
board wage: pago con alojamiento y comida
boarding: *n.* embarque
boarding card: tarjeta de embarque
boarding house: casa de huéspedes
boardroom: *n.* sala del consejo
boat: *n.* bote; barco
boating: *n.* paseo en bote
bobbin: *n.* bobina
bobcat: *n.* bobcat
bodied: *adj.* corpóreo; incorpóreo
body: *n.* cuerpo; organismo

body fluid: líquido biológico
body of rules: normativa; conjunto de reglas
body of shareholders: accionistas
body of the estate: cuerpo de estado
body weight: masa corporal
body-builder: entrenador
bodyguard: *n.* guardaespaldas
bog: *n.* pantano
bog: *v.* atascarse
boggle: *v.* dudar
Bogota: Bogotá
Bohemia: Bohemia
Bohemian: *adj.* bohemio; -a
boil: *n.* ebullición
boiled: *adj.* hervido; a
boiler: *n.* caldera
boiling: *n.* ebullición
boiling point: punto de ebullición
boisterous: *adj.* ruidoso
bold: *adj.* osado; atrevido
boldness: *n.* osadía
bolero: *n.* bolero
Bolivar: *n.* bolívar
Bolivia: Bolivia
Bolivian: *adj.* boliviano; -a
Bologna: Bolonia
Bolognese: *n.* boloñesa
bolshevism: *n.* bolchevismo
bolster: *n.* almohadón
bolster: *v.* apoyar
bolt: *n.* perno
bomb: *n.* bomba
bombard: *v.* bombardear; asediar
bombardier: *n.* bombardero
bombastic: *adj.* bombástico
bomber: *n.* bombardero
bombing: *n.* bombardeo
bona-fide: auténtico; genuino
bonbon: *n.* bombón
bond: *n.* bono; fianza
bond: *v.* adherir; hipotecar
bond issue: emisión de bonos
bond market: mercado de bonos

bond note: certificado de depósito
bond of indemnity: fianza de indemnización
bondage: *n.* cautiverio
bonded: *adj.* en depósito
bonded creditor: acreedor en caución
bonded debt: deuda garantizada
bonded goods: mercancía en caución
bonded warehouse: almacén de aduana
bondholder: *n.* tenedor de bonos
bonding company: compañía de fianzas
bondsman: *n.* garante
bone: *n.* hueso; espina
bone density: densidad de huesos; densidad ósea
bone marrow: médula ósea
bone marrow biopsy: biopsia de la medula ósea
boneless: *adj.* sin hueso
bone-marrow biopsy: biopsia de la médula ósea
bonfire: *n.* hoguera
bongo: *n.* bongó; bongo
bonito: *adj.* bonito
bonnet: *n.* gorra; capó
bonnet: *v.* cubrir
bonny: 1. *n.* bonito; hermoso; 2. *adj.* huesudo
bonsai: *n.* bonsái
bonus: *n.* bonificación; prima
bonus payment: paga extra; gratificación
boo: *vt.* abuchear
boo!: *intj.* ¡bú!
boob: *n.* bobo; -a
booby-prize: premio de consolación
boogie-woogie: bugui-bugui
boo-hoo!: *intj.* ¡buuah!
book: *n.* libro
book: *v.* inscribir; anotar
book audit: auditoria de libros

book balance: saldo según libros
book debt: deuda registrada
book in: dar de alta
book inventory: existencias según libros
book loss: pérdida contable
book of accounts: libro contable
book out: dar de baja; eliminar de libros
book profit: ganancia contable
book shop: *n.* librería
book value: valor según libros
booking: *n.* reserva
bookkeeper: *n.* tenedor de libros
bookkeeping: contabilidad
bookkeeping entry: asiento
booklet: *n.* folleto
bookseller: *n.* librero
bookshelf: *n.* librero
bookstall: *n.* puesto para venta de libros
boom: *n.* boom; estampido; prosperidad
boost: *n.* alza
boot: *n.* bota; botín
bootee: *n.* botita
booth: *n.* quiosco; cabina
booty: *n.* botín
bop: *n.* bop
border: *n.* frontera
border: *v.* limitar
bore: *n.* barreno
bore: *v.* calar; taladrar; agujerear
bored: *adj.* aburrido; deprimido
boredom: *n.* aburrimiento
boring: *adj.* aburrido; aburridor
born: *adj.* nacido
Borneo: Borneo
borough: *n.* villa; barrio
borrow: *v.* tomar prestado
borrowed capital: capital ajeno; capital adeudado
borrowed funds: fondos ajenos; fondos adeudados

borrower: *n.* prestatario
borrowing: *n.* préstamo
borrowing limit: límite de endeudamiento
borrowing operation: operación de toma de préstamo
borrowing rate: tipo de interés pasivo
borrowing ratio: índice de endeudamiento
Bosnia: Bosnia
Bosnian: *adj.* bosnio; -a
bosom: *n.* seno; pecho
Bosphorus: Bósforo
boss: *n.* jefe
boss: *v.* regentar; dominar
botanist: *n.* botanista; botánico
botany: *n.* botánica
both: *adj.* ambos
bother: *n.* incomodidad
bother: *v.* incomodar; molestar
Bothnia: *n.* Botnia
Botswana: Botsuana
Botswanan: *adj.* botsuano; -a
bottle: *n.* botella
bottle: *v.* embotellar
bottleneck: *n.* cuello de botella; embotellamiento
bottle-opener: *n.* abrebotellas
bottom line: consecuencia final; resultado económico
botulism: *n.* botulismo
bougainvillea: *n.* buganvilla
bough: *n.* rama
bouillabaisse: *n.* bullabesa
boulder: *n.* guijarro
boulevard: *n.* bulevar
bound: 1. *n.* salto adj; 2. *adj.* atado; obligado
boundary: *n.* límite
bounder: *n.* vulgar
boundless: *adj.* ilimitado
bounteous: *adj.* generoso
bounty: *n.* generosidad

bouquet: *n.* bouquet; buqué
bourgeois: *n.* burgués
bourgeoisie: *n.* burguesía
bourrée: *n.* bourrée
bourse: *n.* bolsa; lonja
boustrophedon: *n.* bustrófedon
boutique: *n.* boutique; tienda
bovine: *n.* bovino
bow: *n.* inclinación; reverencia
bower: *n.* glorieta; músico de arco
bowie-knife: *n.* cuchillo de monte
bowl: *n.* taza; sopero; plato
bowler: *n.* jugador de bolos
bowline: *n.* bolina
bowling: *n.* bolos
bowling alley: bowling
bow-wow: guau-guau
box: *n.* caja; arca; secuencia
box: *v.* embalar; boxear
box camera: cámara de cajón
box scheme: sistema de financiación y venta
box-and-whisker plot: diagrama de limas y bloques
boxer: *n.* boxeador; bóxer
boxing: *n.* boxeo
boy: *n.* muchacho; chico
boycott: *n.* boicot; boicoteo
boycott: *v.* boicotear
Boyle's law: ley de Boyle
bra: *n.* sostén
brace: *n.* refuerzo
bracelet: *n.* brazalete
braces (dental): *n.* frenos; ganchos dentales
bracket: *n.* escuadra
bracket: *v.* apuntalar; asegurar
bradikinin: *n.* bradicinina
bradycardia: *n.* bradicardia
braggart: 1. *adj.* fanfarrón; 2. *n.* fanfarrón
Brahma: Brahma
Brahman; Brahmin: *n.* brahmán; brahmín

Brahmanism: *n.* brahmanismo
braid: *n.* trenza
brain: *n.* cerebro; encéfalo; inteligencia
brain scan: centellograma del cerebro
brain stem: tronco encefálico
brainstorming: *n.* lluvia de ideas
brain-wave: *n.* idea luminosa
braise: *v.* dorar
brake: *n.* freno; matorral
branch: 1. *n.* rama; sucursal; 2. *adj.* sucursal; dependiente
branch: *v.* ramificarse
branch director: director de sucursal
branch manager: gerente de sucursal
branch migration: prolongación del apareamiento
branch office: sucursal; oficina
branch sucursal: agencia; oficina; división
branching tree: árbol ramificado
brand: *n.* marca
brand awareness: conocimiento de marca
brand leader: producto líder; marca líder
brand loyalty: fidelidad a una marca
brand name: marca; marca registrada
brand new: completamente nuevo
branded: *adj.* de marca reconocida
branded good: producto de marca reconocida
brand-new: *adj.* flamante
brandy: *n.* coñac; brandy
brass: *n.* latón
brassard: *n.* brazal
bravado: *n.* bravata
brave: 1. *adj.* bravo; airoso; 2. *n.* valiente
brave: *v.* desafiar; retar
bravery: *n.* bravura; valentía

bravo!: intj. ¡bravo!
brawn: *n.* músculo
braze: *n.* soldadura
brazen: *adj.* bronceado
brazier: *n.* brasero
Brazil: Brasil
Brazilian: 1. *adj.* brasileño; (a); 2. *n.* brasileño (a)
breach: *n.* abertura
bread: *n.* pan
bread winner: proveedor de la familia
breadth: 1. *n.* anchura; 2. *adv.* a lo ancho
break: *n.* interrupción; cambio repentino
break: *v.* romper; quebrar
break and reunion model: modelo de rotura y reunión
break dancing: tipo de danza; breakdance
break even: llegar al punto de equilibrio
breakable: *adj.* frágil
breakdown: *n.* demoler
breaker: *n.* triturador
break-even point: punto de equilibrio; punto muerto
break-even rate: tasa de equilibrio
breakfast: *n.* desayuno
break-up value: valor proporcional
bream: *n.* besugo
breast: *n.* seno; pecho
breast examination: examen del seno
breasts: pechos senos pezones
breath: *n.* respiración
breathe: *v.* respirar
breathing difficulty in: dificultad respiratoria
breathing test: examen respiratorio
breathlessness: *n.* falta de respiración
breech: *n.* trasero

breed: *n.* raza
breed: *v.* reproducirse; criarse
breeder: *n.* criador
breeding: *n.* reproducción; cría
breeding performance: desempeño reproductivo
breeding season: estación reproductiva
breeding success: éxito reproductivo
breeding system: sistema reproductivo
breeze: *n.* brisa
breezy: *adj.* airoso; ligero
brethren: *n.* pl. hermanos
Breton: *n.* bretón; -a
breve: 1. *n.* breve; 2. *adj.* breve
breviary: *n.* breviario
brew: *n.* mezcla
brew: *v.* fabricar cerveza
bribe: *n.* soborno
bribe: *v.* sobornar
bribery: *adj.* soborno
bridal: 1. *n.* boda; 2. *adj.* nupcial;
bride: *n.* novia
bridegroom: *n.* novio
bridesmaid: *n.* madrina de boda
bridge: *n.* puente
bridge loan: préstamo puente
brie: *n.* brie
brief: 1. *adj.* breve; 2. *n.* resumen
briefcase: *n.* maletín; portafolios
briefless: *adj.* sin clientela
brigade: *n.* brigada
brigadier: *n.* brigadier
brigand: *n.* bandolero
bright: *adj.* brillante; transparente
brightfield microscopy: microscopio de campo claro
brilliant: *adj.* brillante; genial
brilliantine: *n.* brillantina
brim: *n.* borde; ala
brimstone: *n.* azufre
brindle: *adj.* jaspeado; rayado
bring: *v.* traer; traer; llevar

bringing up: *n.* educación
briny: *n.* salmuera
brio: *n.* brío
brioche: *n.* brioche
brisk: *n.* vivo
brisk: *v.* avivar; animar
Britain: Bretaña
British: *adj.* británico
British Virgin Island: Islas Vírgenes Británicas
Brittany: Bretaña
brittle: *adj.* quebradizo
broch: *n.* folleto
broad: *adj.* ancho; comprensivo
broadband: *n.* banda ancha
broadcast: 1. *n.* difusión; 2. *adv.* por todas panes
broadcast: *v.* difundir; radiar
broadish: *adj.* algo ancho
broadly: *adv.* anchamente
brocade: *adj.* brocado
broccoli: *n.* brécol; brócoli
brochure: *n.* folleto
broil: *n.* asar a la parrilla
broiled: *adj.* asado (a) al fuego
broiler: *n.* parrilla
broke: *adj.* sin blanca
broken: *adj.* quebrado; interrumpido
broken account: cuenta inactiva
broken bone: fracturas
broker: *n.* comisionista; corredor
brokerage: *n.* corretaje
brokerage fee: comisión de corretaje
brome: *n.* bromo
bromeliad: *n.* broméela; bromeliácea
bromide: *n.* bromuro
bromocriptine: *n.* bromocriptina
bronchi: *n.* bronquios
bronchia: *n.* bronquios
bronchial brushing: raspado bronquial
bronchial lavage: lavado bronquial
bronchiole: *n.* bronquíolo
bronchitis: *n.* bronquitis

bronchodilator: *n.* broncodilatador
bronchoscope: *n.* broncoscopio
bronchoscopy: *n.* broncoscopia
bronco: *n.* potro; caballo salvaje
bronze: *n.* bronce
bronze: *v.* broncear
brooch: *n.* broche
brood: *n.* cría
brood: *v.* incubar; empollar
brook: *n.* arroyo
brook: *v.* sufrir
broom: *n.* escoba
broth: *n.* caldo
brother: *n.* hermano
brother-in-law: cuñado
brotherlike: *adj.* fraternal
brought forward: trasladado de una página; columna
brow: *n.* frente; ceja
browbeat: *v.* intimidar; desconcertar
browless: *adj.* descarado
brown: 1. *adj.* moreno; 2. *n.* pardo
brown: *v.* ponerse
brown shirt: camisa parda
browse: *v.* corner; pacer
browser: *n.* navegador
brrr!: *intj.* ¡brrr!
brucellosis: *n.* brucelosis
Bruges: Brujas
bruise: *n.* magulladura; moretón
bruise: *v.* magullar
brush: *n.* cepillo; pincel
brush: *n.* brocha
brushstroke: *n.* brochazo
brushwood: *n.* matorral
brusque: *adj.* brusco
brusqueness: *n.* brusquedad
Brussels: Bruselas
brutal: *adj.* brutal
brutal; brutish: *adj.* brutal
brutality: *n.* brutalidad
brute: *n.* bruto
bryony: *n.* brionia
bryophyte: *n.* briofita

bryozoan: *adj.* briozoario
bubble: *n.* burbuja
bubbler: *n.* engañador
bubbly: *adj.* espumoso
bubo: *n.* bubón; buba
bubonic plague: *n.* peste bubónica
buccal: *adj.* bucal
Bucharest: Bucarest
buck: *n.* dólar
bucket: *n.* cubo; balde
bucolic: *adj.* bucólico
bud: *n.* capullo
bud: *v.* injertar
Budapest: Budapest
Buddha: Buda
Buddhism: *n.* budismo
Buddhist: *n.* budista
budding: *n.* gemación; en capullo
budge: *v.* mover
budget: *n.* presupuesto; mochilla
budget: *v.* presupuestar
budget allowance: asignación presupuestaria
budget control: control presupuestario
budget deficit: déficit presupuestario
budget law: ley de presupuestos
budgetary: *adj.* presupuestario
buff: *n.* ante; color de ante
buffalo: *n.* búfalo
buffer: *n.* cojinete; tampón
buffer capacity: capacidad tamponadora
buffet: *n.* buffet; bufé; bofetada
buffet: *v.* abofetear
buffoon: *n.* bufón
buffoonery: *n.* bufonería
buffy: *adj.* anteado
buffy-coat: capa leucocitaria
bug: *n.* chinche; bicho
bugle: *n.* clarín; corneta; bugle
build: *n.* estructura
build: *v.* construir
builder: *n.* arquitecto; constructor

building: *n.* construcción; edificio; obra
building code: código de edificación
building company: empresa constructora
building permit: permiso de edificación
built-in: incorporado
Bulgaria: Bulgaria
Bulgarian: *adj.* búlgaro; -a
bulimia: *n.* bulimia
bulk: *n.* volumen; granel
bulk: *v.* abultar
bulk cargo: cargamento a granel
bulk up: comprar en grandes cantidades
bull: 1. *adj.* robusto; 2. *n.* bula; toro; alcista
bull: *v.* elevar el precio
bull market: mercado alcista
bull terrier: bulterrier
bulldog: *n.* buldog; mastin; revolver de gran calibre
bulldozer: *n.* buldózer
bullet: *n.* bala; viñeta
bulletin: *n.* boletín
bulletin board: cartelera
bullfight: *n.* corrida de toros
bullfighter: *n.* torero
bullion lingotes: oro en barras
bullish: *n.* alcista con tendencia a aumentar
bullring: *n.* plaza de toros; redondel
bully: 1. *n.* matón; 2. *adj.* magnífico
bully: *v.* intimidar; bravear
bulwart: *n.* baluarte; fortaleza
bum: *n.* nalgas
bumblebee: *n.* abejorro
bump: *n.* batacazo; golpe
bumper: *n.* tope; parachoques
bun: *n.* bollo; mono
bunch: 1. *n.* manojo; racimo
bunch: *v.* agrupar
bundle: *n.* bulto

bundle: *v.* atar
bungalow: *n.* bungalow
bunk: *n.* tarima; litera; camastro
bunk: *v.* dormir en tarima
bunker: *n.* bunker; carbonera
bunker: *n.* búnker
bunny: *n.* conejito
Bunsen burner: mechero Bunsen
buoy: *n.* boya
buoyant force: fuerza de flotación
burden: *n.* carga; estribillo; gasto
burden: *v.* cargar
bureau: *n.* cómoda; oficina
bureau of vital statistics: registro demográfico
bureaucracy: *n.* burocracia
bureaucrat: *n.* burócrata
bureaucratic: *adj.* burocrático
burette: *n.* bureta
burg: *n.* pueblo; ciudad
Burgandy: Borgoña
burglar: *n.* ladrón
burglar alarm: alarma antirrobo
Burgundian: *adj.* borgoñón; -ona
burgundian: *adj.* borgoñón
Burgundy: *n.* Borgoña
burial: *n.* entierro
burial expenses: gastos de funeral
burial plot: panteón
burlap: *n.* lona
burlesque: *adj.* burlesco
Burmese: *n.* birmano
burn: *n.* quemadura
burn: *v.* quemar; cocer
burned: *adj.* quemado
burning: *n.* ardor; quemante
burro: *n.* burro
burrow: *n.* madriguera
bursitis: *n.* bursitis
burst: *n.* explosión; reventón
burst: *v.* reventar
Burundi: Burundi
Burundian: *adj.* burundés; -esa
bury: *v.* enterrar

bury: *n.* sepultar
bus; autobus: *n.* bus; autobús
bush: *n.* arbusto
bush hammer: el martillo para texturizar
bushy: *adj.* espeso; lanudo
business: *n.* negocio; asunto; comercio; oficio
business address: domicilio comercial
business administration: administración de empresas
business agent: agente comercial; administrador
business agreement: convenio de negocios; trato comercial
business angel: ángel; inversor particular
business association: asociación empresarial
business card: tarjeta comercial; tarjeta de negocios
business center: centro de negocios
business circle: círculo empresarial
business class: clase de negocios
business college: escuela de negocios
business connections: relaciones comerciales
business contract: contrato comercial
business corporation: sociedad comercial
business cycle: ciclo económico
business day: día laborable; día hábil
business deal: convenio de negocios
business document: documento comercial
business enterprise: empresa comercial
business establishment: establecimiento comercial
business expense: gasto profesional
business graduate: licenciado en ciencias empresariales
business hours: horario de oficina
business interruption: interrupción de la actividad empresarial
business journal: boletín económico
business law: derecho comercial
business license: licencia comercial
business manager: director ejecutivo
business name: razón social
business papers: efectos comerciales
business park: parque de negocios
business portal: portal de negocios
business relations: relaciones comerciales
business school: escuela de comercio; escuela de negocios
business suit: traje formal
business trust: asociación voluntaria
business year: ejercicio económico
businessman: *n.* hombre de negocios
businesswoman: *n.* mujer de negocios; empresaria
bust: *n.* busto
bust: *n.* busto; pecho de mujer
bust: *v.* arruinar
busy: *adj.* ocupado
busy: *v.* ocupar
busy signal: señal de ocupado
but: 1. *n.* objeción; 2. *adv.* solo; 3. *prep.* excepto; 4. *conj.* pero
butcher: *n.* carnicero
butcher: *v.* matar
butler: *n.* mayordomo
butt: *n.* culata; colilla
butted: *adj.* bien pegado
butter: *n.* mantequilla
butterfly: *n.* mariposa
butterfly valve: la válvula de mariposa
buttocks: *n.* glúteos
button: *n.* botón
button dealer: botonero
button shop: botonería

buttonhole: *n.* ojal
buttress: *n.* contrafuerte
buxom: *adj.* rollizo
buy: *n.* compra
buy: *v.* comprar
buyer: *n.* comprador
buying market: mercado comprador
buying order: orden de compra
buying price: precio de compra
buying rate: porcentaje de cambio
comprador
buyout: *n.* compra de todos los
activos
buzz: *n.* susurro
by: *prep.* por; de; para; cerca de
Byelorus; Bielorus: Bielorrusia
Byelorussian: *adj.* bielorruso; -a
bygone: *adj.* pasado
by-laws: estatuto
bypass: *n.* bypass
bypass: *v.* evitar
bypass switch: el interruptor de
derivación
by-product: subproducto; producto
secundario
bystander: *n.* espectador;
circunstantes
byte: *n.* byte
Byzantine: *adj.* bizantino

C

C. E. O (chief executive officer):
director general
c. o. (carried over): *v.* trasladar; n.
transportación a un periodo
c/p: (carriage paid): porte pagado
ca: *n.* símbolo del elemento calcio
cab: *n.* taxímetro
cabal: *n.* cábala
cabal: *v.* tramar
cabalist: *n.* cabalista
cabaret: *n.* cabaret
cabbage: *n.* col
cabernet: *n.* cabernet
cabin: *n.* cabaña
cabinet: *n.* gabinete; vitrina;
escaparate
cabinet secretaries: secretarios de
gabinete
cabinet-maker: el ebanista
cable: *n.* cable
cablegram: *n.* cablegrama
cabotage: *n.* cabotaje
cacao: *n.* cacao
cachalot: *n.* cachalote
cache: *n.* cache; escondidos
cache: *v.* esconder
cachet: *n.* sello
cachexia: *n.* caquexia
cacophony: *n.* cacofonía
cactus: *n.* cactus; cacto
cadastre: *n.* catastro
cadaver: *n.* cadáver
caddish: *adj.* mal educado
caddy: *n.* bote; lata
cadence: *n.* cadencia
cadet: *n.* cadete
cadre: *n.* cuadro

caduceus: *n.* caduceo
Caesarean section: *n.* cesárea
caesura: *n.* censura
cafe; café: *n.* café
cafeteria: *n.* cafetería
caffeine: *n.* cafeína
caffeinism: *n.* cafeinismo
caftan: *n.* caftán
cage: *n.* jaula; cárcel
cage: *v.* enjaular
caiman: *n.* caimán
Cairo: El Cairo
caisson: *n.* cajón
cake: *n.* torta; pastelillo
calabash: *n.* calabacero; calabaza
calaboose: *n.* calabozo
caladium: *n.* caladio
calamine (lotion): *n.* calamina
calamity: *n.* calamidad
calcemia: *n.* concentración de calcio en plasma
calcidiol: *n.* calcidiol
calcifediol: *n.* calcidiol
calciferol: *n.* ercalciol
calcification: *n.* calcificación
calciol: *n.* calciol
calcitonin: *n.* calcitonina
calcitriol: *n.* calcitriol
calcium: *n.* calcio
calcium ion: ion calcio
calciuria: *n.* concentración de calcio en orina
calculability: *n.* calculabilidad
calculate: *v.* calcular
calculated (risk): *adj.* calculado
calculating: *n.* calculador; maquina calculadora
calculation: *n.* cálculo; cómputo
calculator: *n.* calculadora; calculista
calculus: *n.* cálculo
calcutta: *n.* Calcuta
caldera: *n.* caldera
caldron: *n.* calderón
calefacient: *n.* calefaciente

calendar: 1. *n.* calendario; 2. *adj.* calendario
calendar day: día corrido.
calendar year: año calendario; año civil
calender: *n.* calandria
calendula: *n.* caléndula
calf: *n.* pantorrilla
caliber: *adj.* calibre
calibrated flask: matraz aforado
calibrated loop: asa calibrada
calibrated pipet: pipeta calibrada
calibration: *n.* calibración
calibration bench: banco de calibración
calibration curve: curva de calibración
calibration function: función de calibración
calibration material: material de calibración
calibration standard: patrón de calibración
calibrator: *n.* calibrador
calico: *n.* calicó
caliphate: *n.* califato
calisthenics: *n.* calistenia
calyx: *n.* cáliz
call: *n.* llamada; opción de compra
call: *v.* llamar; convocar
call blocking: bloqueo de llamadas
call center: central de llamadas
call loan: préstamo a la vista
call money: dinero a corto plazo
call option: opción de compra
call price: precio de recuperación
call rate: tipo de interés a corto plazo
callable: *adj.* rescatable; recuperable
callable capital: capital subscripto
callable stock: acción recuperable
called-up: capital exigido
calligrapher: *n.* calígrafo; -a
calligraphy: *n.* caligrafía
calling: *n.* profesión; vocación

callow: *adj.* joven
callowness: *n.* inexperiencia
callus: *n.* callo
calm: *adj.* calma
calmative: *adj.* calmante
calmness: *n.* calma
calomel: *n.* calomelanos; calomel
calorie: *n.* caloría
calorimeter: *n.* calorímetro
calque: *n.* calco
calumniate: *v.* calumniar
calumny: *n.* calumnia
Calvinism: *n.* calvinismo
Calvinist: *n.* calvinista
calypso: *n.* calipso
camaraderie: *n.* camaradería
cambium: *n.* cambium
Cambodia: Camboya
Cambodian: *adj.* camboyano; -a
cambric: *n.* cambray
camcorder: *n.* camcórder
camel: *n.* camello
camellia: *n.* camelia
camembert: *n.* camembert
cameo: *n.* camafeo
camera: la cámara
camera: *n.* cámara
cameraman: *n.* cameraman; camarógrafo
Cameron: Camerón
Cameroonian: *adj.* camerunés; -esa
camisole: *n.* camiseta de mujer
camouflage: *n.* camuflaje; disfraz
camp; encampment: *n.* campamento
campaign: *n.* campaña
campanile: *n.* campanario
campanula: *n.* campanula
camper: *n.* campista
camphor: *n.* alcanfor
camphor ice: cerato de alcanfor
camphorated oil: aceite alcanforado
camping: *n.* camping
campus: *n.* campo
Canada: Canadá

Canadian: *adj.* canadiense
canal: *n.* canal
canalization: *n.* canalización
canape: *n.* canapé
Canarian: *adj.* canario; -a
Canaries: Canarias
canary: *n.* canario
canary-yellow: amarillo canario
canasta: *n.* canasta
canavanase: *n.* arginasa
canaveral: *n.* cañaveral
cancan: *n.* cancán
cancel: *v.* cancelar; anular; prescindir
cancelable: *adj.* prescindible
cancellation: *n.* cancelación; anulación
cancelled: *adj.* cancelado; anulado
cancelled cheque: cheque anulado
cancer: *n.* cáncer
candela: *n.* candela
candelabrum: *n.* candelabro
candidate: *n.* candidato; aspirante; postulante
candle: *n.* candela; vela
candlestick: *n.* candelero
candy: *n.* bombón; dulce
cane: *n.* bastón
canine: 1. tooth: *n.* canino; diente *n.* colmillo; 2. *adj.* canino
canister: *n.* bote; frasco
canker: *n.* llaga; úlcera
canned goods: conservas
cannibal: *adj.* caníbal
cannibalism: *n.* canibalismo
cannon: *n.* cañón
cannoneer: *n.* cafionero
cannula: *n.* cánula
canny: *adj.* astuto
canoe: *n.* canoa
canoeing: *n.* canotaje
canoeist: *n.* canoero
canon: *n.* canónigo; canon
canonization: *n.* canonización
canopy: *n.* bóveda arbórea

cant: 1. *n.* canto; esquina; 2. *adj.* inclinado
cant: *v.* inclinar; invertir
cantabile: *adj.* cantabile
cantabile: *n.* cantábile
cantaloupe: *n.* cantalupo
cantata: *n.* cantata
canteen: *n.* cantina
canto: *n.* canto
Canton: Cantón
Cantonese: *adj.* cantones; -esa
cantor: *n.* cantor
canvas: *n.* escrutinio; investigación
canyon: *n.* cañón
caoutchouc: *n.* caucho
cap: *n.* remate
capable: *adj.* capaza; competente
capacious: *adj.* espacioso; capaz
capacitance: *n.* capacitancia
capacitor: *n.* capacitor
capacity: *n.* capacidad
capacity cost: coste a capacidad plena
cape: *n.* cabo; capa
capella: *n.* capela
capillary: *n.* capilar
capital: 1. *n.* capital; . 2. *adj.* capital; magnífico
capital account: cuenta patrimonial
capital asset: activo fijo
capital drain: fuga de capitales
capital flight: fuga de capitales
capital flow: flujo de capital
capital gain: beneficio de inversiones
capital good: bien de capital
capital letter: letra capital
capital levy: impuesto al capital
capital liability: pasivo consolidado
capital market: mercado de capitales
capital movement: movimiento de capitales
capital reserve: reserva de capital

capital stock: acción de capital
capital structure: estructura del capital
capital surplus: excedente de capital
capital tax: impuesto al capital
capital turnover: rotación del capital
capitalization: *n.* capitalización
capitalization unit: partida capitalizable
capitalize: *v.* capitalizar
capitalized profit: beneficio capitalizado
capitalism: *n.* capitalismo
capitalist: *n.* capitalista
capitation: *n.* capitación
capitol (building): *n.* capitolio
capitulation: *n.* capitulación
capivating: *adj.* fascinante
capneic incubation: incubación capneica
capnophilic: *adj.* capnofílico
capon: *n.* capón
capped: *adj.* colorado
cappuccino: *n.* capuchino
capriccio: *n.* capricho
caprice: *n.* capricho
capricious: *adj.* caprichoso
capriciousness: *n.* capricho
Capricorn: *n.* capricornio
capsid: *n.* cápsida
capsize: *v.* volcar
capsule: *n.* cápsula
captain: *n.* capitán
captaincy: *n.* capitanía
captious: *adj.* criticón; insidioso
captivate: *v.* cautivar
captivating: *n.* cautivador
captive: *adj.* cautivo
captive breeding: reproducción en cautiverio
captivity: *n.* cautiverio; cautividad
captor: *n.* captor
captor; capturer: *n.* capturador
capture: *v.* capturar

capuchin: *n.* capuchino
car: *n.* coche; carro; automóvil
car dealer: concesionario de automóviles
car insurance: seguro de automóvil
car title: título de automóvil
carabao: *n.* carabao
Caracas: Caracas
caracul; karakul: *n.* caracul; karakul
carafe: *n.* garrafa
caramel: *n.* caramelo
carat: *n.* quilate
caravan: *n.* caravana
caravel: *n.* carabela
caraway: *n.* alcaravea
carbenicillin: *n.* carbenicilina
carbide: *n.* carburo
carbine: *n.* carabina
carbohydrate: *n.* carbohidrato
carbon: *n.* carbón; carbono
carbon copy: copia carbónica
carbon dioxide: dióxido de carbono
carbon film: película de carbono
carbon monoxide: monóxido de carbono
carbon paper: papel carbónico; papel carbón
carbonated: *adj.* carbonatado
carbonic anhydrase: anidro-carbonato
carboxyl group: grupo carboxilo
carbuncle (ruby): *n.* carbúnculo; carbunclo
carburetor: *n.* carburador
carcass: *n.* cadáver (de animal)
carcinoembryonic antigen: antígeno carcinoembrionario
carcinogen: *n.* agente cancerígeno; carcinógeno
carcinogenic: *adj.* carcinogénico
carcinoma: *n.* carcinoma
card: *n.* tarjeta; ficha; carta
cardamom: *n.* cardamomo
cardboard: *n.* cartón

cardiac: *adj.* cateterismo cardiaco
cardiac arrest: ataque cardiaco
cardiac catheterization: cateterismo cardiaco
cardiac muscle: músculo cardiaco
cardigan: *n.* cárdigan
cardinal: *adj.* cardinal
cardinal point: punto cardinal
cardiography: *n.* cardiografía
cardiologist: *n.* cardiólogo
cardiology: *n.* cardiología
cardiomegaly: *n.* cardiomegalia
cardiopulmonary: *adj.* cardiopulmonar
cardiotonic: *adj.* cardiotónico
cardiovascular: *adj.* cardiovascular
cardiovascular: *adj.* cardiovascular
cardiovascular system: sistema cardiovascular
cardiovascular-respiratory systems: sistemas cardiovascular y de respiración
care and welfare: cuidado y bienestar
careen: *n.* carena
careen: *v.* carenar
career: *n.* carrera
careful: *adj.* cuidado
careless: *adj.* descuidado
caress: *n.* caricia
caress: *v.* acariciar
caretaker: *n.* cuidador de paciente; vigilante; conserje
cargo: *n.* carga; cargamento
Caribbean: Caribe
caribou: *n.* caribú
caricature: *n.* caricatura
caricaturist: *n.* caricaturista
carillon: *n.* carillón
Carmelite: *n.* carmelita
carminative: *adj.* carminativo
carmine: *n.* carmín
carnage: *n.* carnicería
carnation: *n.* clavel

carnelian: *n.* carniola; cornalina
carnival: *n.* carnaval
carnivore: *n.* carnívoro
carnivorous: *adj.* carnívoro; carnicero
carol: *n.* canción
carol: *v.* cantar villancicos
carom: *n.* carambola
carotene: *n.* caroteno
carotene oxidase: lipoxigenasa
carotenoid: *adj.* carotenoide
carotenoid pigments: pigmentos carotenoides
carousal: *n.* festín
carouse: *n.* juerga
carouse: *v.* juerguear; emborracharse
carousel: *n.* carrusel
carp: *n.* carpa
carp: *v.* censurar; criticar
carp: *n.* carpa
carpal: *adj.* carpiano
Carpathians: Carpatos
carpenter: *n.* carpintero
carpentry: *n.* carpintería
carpet: *n.* alfombra
carpet roller: el rodillo para alfombras
carpet stretcher: el estirador de alfombras
carport: *n.* cochera
carpus: *n.* carpo
carriage: *n.* carruaje; transporte
carriage forward: porte a pagar por el destinatario
carriage-free: franco de porte
carrier: *n.* agencia (compañía); portador
carrier-culture: cultivo portador
carrion: *n.* carroña
carrot: *n.* zanahoria
carroty: *adj.* pelirrojo
carrousel: *n.* carrusel
carry: *v.* llevar; cargar; transportar
carry back: transportar al lugar de

origen
carry forward: transportar; trasladar
carry insurance: poseer seguro
carry over: transportar; trasladar
carrying capacity: capacidad de carga
carry-over: importe traspasado
cart: *n.* carreta
cart: *v.* acarrear
cartage: *n.* transporte
cartel: *n.* cartel
carter: *n.* carretero
Cartesian: *adj.* cartesiano
Cartesian: *n.* cartesiano; -a
cartilage: *n.* cartílago
cartload: *n.* carretada
cartographer: *n.* cartógrafo
cartography: *n.* cartografía
cartridge: *n.* cartucho
carve: *v.* tallar
cascade: *n.* cascada
case: *n.* caso
casein: *n.* caseína
casement: *n.* puerta; ventana
casement window: la ventana a bisagra
cash: *n.* contado; metálico; caja
cash: *v.* cobrar; realizar
cash account: cuenta de caja
cash and banks: activo disponible
cash assets: activos disponibles; disponibilidades
cash audit: auditoria de caja
cash balance: saldo de caja
cash benefits: beneficios en efectivo
cash box: caja; caja donde se guarda el dinero
cash card: tarjeta de débito
cash count: arqueo de caja
cash cow: fuente estable de ingresos
cash deficit: déficit de caja
cash desk: caja
cash discount: descuento por pago en efectivo

cash dispenser: cajero automático
cash dividend: dividendo en efectivo
cash entry: asiento de caja
cash flow: flujo de fondos
cash machine: cajero automático
cash movement: movimiento de caja
cash on delivery: pago contra entrega
cash on hand: activo disponible
cash order: orden de caja
cash payment: pago en efectivo
cash position: posición de caja; encaje
cash price: precio de contado
cash purchase: compra al contado
cash ratio: coeficiente de caja
cash register: caja registradora
cash reserve: reserva de efectivo; reserva de caja
cash resources: recursos de caja
cash sale: venta al contado
cash shortage: faltante de caja
cash value: valor efectivo
cash wages: salario en efectivo
cashbook: *n.* libro de caja
cashier: *n.* cajero
cashier: *v.* destituir
cashier check: cheque de caja
cashmere: *n.* cachemira
casing: *n.* cubierta
casino: *n.* casino
cask: *n.* tonel; cuba
casket: *n.* ataúd
Caspian: Caspio
casserole: *n.* cacerola
cassette: *n.* cassete; casete
cassette mechanism: mecanismo de casete
cassock: *n.* sotana
cast: *n.* vaciado; yeso; echada; forma
cast: *v.* fundir; echar
castanet: *n.* castañeta; castañuela
castaway: 1. *n.* naufrago; 2. *adj.* abandonado

caste: *n.* casta
Castile: Castilla
Castilian: *n.* castellano
Castilian: *adj.* castellano; -a
casting: *n.* fundición
casting shop: taller de fundición
cast-iron: *n.* hierro fundido (colado)
castle: *n.* castillo
castor: *n.* castor
castor oil: aceite de ricino
castration: *n.* castración
casuist: *n.* casuista
cat: *n.* gato
cat scan: tomografía computada
catabolism: *n.* catabolismo
cataclysm: *n.* cataclismo
catacombs: *n.* catacumbas
catafalque: *n.* catafalco
Catalan: *n.* catalán
Catalan; Catalonian: *adj.* catalán; -lana
catalase: *n.* catalasa
catalase test: prueba de la catalasa
catalepsy: *n.* catalepsia
catalog: *n.* catálogo
catalog: *v.* catalogar
cataloger: *n.* catalogador
cataloger; cataloguer: *n.* catalogador (a)
cataloging; cataloguing: *n.* catalogación.
catalogue: *n.* catálogo
Catalonia: Cataluña
catalpa: *n.* catalpa
catalyst: *n.* catalizador; catalítico
catalytic activity: actividad catalítica
catalytic activity rate: caudal de actividad catalítica
catalytic centre: centro catalítico
catalytic concentration: concentración catalítica
catalytic content: contenido catalítico
catalytic converter: catalizador

catalytic flow rate: caudal catalítico
catalytic fraction: fracción catalítica
catalytic rate: caudal catalítico
catamaran: *n.* catamarán
cataphasia: *n.* catafasia
catapult: *n.* catapulta
cataract: *n.* catarata
catarrh: *n.* catarro
catastrophe: *n.* catástrofe
catastrophic: *adj.* catastrófico
catastrophic coverage: protección contra catástrofe
catastrophic illness: enfermedad catastrófica
catatonia: *n.* catatonía
catch: *v.* coger; agarrar; sujetar
catch drain: cuneta
catching: *adj.* contagioso; seductor
catechism: *n.* catecismo
catechumen: *n.* catecúmeno
catecholamine: *n.* catecolamina
categoric: *adj.* categórico
category: *n.* categoría
cater: *v.* abastecer; proveer
catgut: *n.* catgut
catharsis: *n.* catarsis
cathedral: *n.* catedral
catheter: *n.* catéter
catheterization; cardiac: cateterismo cardiaco
cathode: *n.* cátodo
catholic: *adj.* católico
Catholicism: *n.* catolicismo
cattle: *n.* ganado; hacienda
cattle farm: hacienda; estancia
cattle market: mercado de ganado
Cattle ranch: hacienda; rancho de ganado
cattleya: *n.* catleya
Caucasian: *adj.* caucasiano; caucásico
Caucasoid: *n.* caucasoide
Caucasus: Cáucaso
caudal: *adj.* caudal

cauf: *n.* vivero de peces
cauliflower: *n.* coliflor
Caulk: *v.* calafatear
causality: *n.* causalidad
causation: *n.* causalidad; etiología
causative: *adj.* causativo
Cause: *n.* causa; origen
causeway: *n.* calzada
cauterization: *n.* cauterización
cautery: *n.* cauterio
cautious: *adj.* cauteloso; cauto
cava: *n.* cava
cavalcade: *n.* cabalgata
cavalier: *n.* caballero; galán
cavalry: *n.* caballería
cavalryman: *n.* soldado de caballería
cave: *n.* cueva
cave: *v.* hundirse
cavern: *n.* caverna
caviar: *n.* caviar
cavity: *n.* cavidad; (dental) *n.* carie
cay: *n.* cayo
cayenne: *n.* cayena
Cayman Islands: Islas Caimanes
Caymans: Caimanes
CD (abrev. de "compact disk"): disco compacto
CD-ROM: CD-ROM
CEA: antígeno carcinoembrionario
cease: *v.* cesar; parar
cease-fire: cese del fuego
cecils: *n.* albóndigas de carne
cedar: *n.* cedro
cede: *v.* ceder
cedilla: *n.* cedilla
cefaclor: *n.* cefaclor
cefadroxil: *n.* cefadroxilo
cefalexin: *n.* cefalexina
cefaloridine: *n.* cefaloridina
cefamandole: *n.* cefamandol
cefazolin: *n.* cefazolina
cefixime: *n.* cefixima
cefmenoxime: *n.* cefmenoxima
cefmetazole: *n.* cefmetazol

cefonicid: *n.* cefonicido
cefoperazone: *n.* cefoperazona
cefotaxime: *n.* cefotaxima
cefotetan: *n.* cefotetano
cefoxitin: *n.* cefoxitina
cefradine: *n.* cefradina
cefsulodin: *n.* cefsulodina
ceftazidime: *n.* ceftazidima
ceftizoxime: *n.* ceftizoxima
ceftriaxone: *n.* ceftriaxona
cefuroxime: *n.* cefuroxima
ceiba: *n.* ceiba
ceiling: *n.* límite; techo
ceiling price: precio máximo; precio límite
celebrate: *v.* celebrar
celebrated: *adj.* célebre; famoso
celebration: *n.* celebración
celebrity: *n.* celebridad
celerity: *n.* celeridad
celesta: *n.* celesta
celestial: *adj.* celestial
celibacy: *n.* celibato; soltería
celioscopy: *n.* celioscopia
cell: *n.* célula; celda
cell count: concentración de células
cell culture: cultivo celular
cell cycle: ciclo celular
cell line: línea celular
cell membrane: membrana celular
cell phone: teléfono celular
cell theory: teoría celular
cell wall: pared celular
cellar: *n.* sótano; bodega
cellist: *n.* chelista; violonchelista
cello: *n.* chelo; violonchelo
cellobiase: *n.* glucosidasa
cellophane: *n.* celofán
cellular telephone: teléfono celular
cellulase: *n.* celulaza
cellulitis: *n.* celulitis
celluloid: *n.* celuloide
cellulose: *n.* celulosa
Celsius: Celsio

Celsius scale: escala Celsius
Celsius temperature: temperatura Celsius
celtic: *n.* celta
cement: *n.* cemento
cement: *v.* revestir de cemento
cementation: *n.* cementación
cementite: *n.* cementita
cementum: *n.* cemento
cemetery: *n.* cementerio
cenotaph: *n.* cenotafio
censor: *n.* censor
censorship: *n.* censura
census: *n.* censo
census bureau: oficina del censo
cent: *n.* centavo
centenary: 1. *n.* centenario; 2. *adj.* centenario
centennial: *adj.* centenario
center: *n.* centro
center: *v.* centrar; concentrar
center of a circle: centro de un circulo
center of rotation: centro de rotación
centesimal: *adj.* centésimo
centesimo: *n.* centésimo
centigrade: *adj.* centígrado
centigram: *n.* centigramo
centiliter: *n.* centilitro
centime: *n.* céntimo
centimeter: *n.* centímetro
central: *adj.* central
Central America: Centroamérica
Central American: centroamericano; (a)
central bank: banco central
central market: mercado central
central nervous system: sistema nervioso central
central office: oficina central
central processing unit (CPU): unidad central de procesamiento (CPU)

Central Standard Time: hora central
centralize: *v.* centralizar
centralized management: administración centralizada
centralized: *adj.* centralizado
centrifugal force: fuerza centrífuga
centrifugal radius: radio centrífugo
centrifugation: *n.* centrifugación
centrifuge: *n.* centrífuga
centripetal force: fuerza centripeta
centrist: *n.* centrista
centurion: *n.* centurión
century: *n.* centuria
cephalalgia: *n.* cefalalgia; cefalea
cephalexin: *n.* cefalexina
cephalic: *adj.* cefálico
cephalic index: índice cefálico
cephalopod: *n.* cefalópodo
cephaloridine: *n.* cefaloridina
cephradine: *n.* cefradina
ceramicist: *n.* ceramista
ceramics: *n.* cerámica
ceramidase: *n.* ceramidasa
cereal: *n.* cereal
cereal: 1. *adj.* cereal; 2. *n.* cereal
cerebellum: *n.* cerebelo
cerebral palsy: parálisis cerebral
cerebrospinal: *adj.* cerebroespinal
cerebrum: *n.* cerebro
ceremonial: *adj.* ceremonial
ceremony: *n.* ceremonia
cerise: *adj.* (color) cereza
certain: *adj.* cierto; positivo
certainty: *n.* certeza; certidumbre
certificate: *n.* certificado
certificate of damage: certificado de averías
certificate of deposit: certificado de depósito
certificate of incorporation: certificado de constitución
certificate of indebtedness: certificado de deuda

certificate of insurance: certificado de seguros
certificate of manufacture: certificado de fabricación
certificate of origin: certificado de origen
certificate of ownership: certificado de propiedad
certificate of quality: certificado de calidad
certificate value: valor certificado
certification: *n.* certificación
certified: *adj.* certificado
certified accountant: contable titulado
certified check: cheque certificado
certified copy: copia certificada
Certified Public Accountant: contador público
certify: *v.* certificar
certifying accountant: contador certificado
certifying of payments: certificación de pagos
ceruloplasmin: *n.* ferroxidasa
cerumen: *n.* cerumen
cervical mucus: moco cervical
cervical pool: contenido cervical
cervicitis: *n.* cervicitis
cervix: *n.* cerviz; cuello uterino
cessation: *n.* cesación; paro
cessation of disability: suspensión de incapacidad
cession: *n.* cesión; traspaso
cesspool: *n.* pozo negro
cestode: *n.* cestodo
cha-cha-cha: *n.* cha-cha-chá
chaconne: *n.* chacona
chafe: *n.* frotamiento
chafe: *v.* frotar
chaffer: *n.* regateo
chaffer: *v.* regatear; burlarse
chagrin: *n.* pesadumbre; disgusto
chagrin: *v.* disgustar

chain: *n.* cadena
chain: *v.* encadenar
chain reaction: reacción en cadena
chain rule: regla en cadena
chain store: tienda de una cadena
chain terminator: finalizador de cadena
chair: *n.* silla
chairman: *n.* presidente; coordinador
chairmanship: *n.* presidencia
chairperson: *n.* presidente; coordinador
chairwoman: *n.* presidenta; presidenta de una asamblea
chalet: *n.* chalé; chalet
chalice: *n.* cáliz
chalk: *n.* yeso; tiza
challenge: *n.* desafió
challenge: *v.* desafiar; exigir
chamber: *n.* cámara; alcoba
chamber music: música de cámara
chamber of commerce: cámara de comercio
chamber of industry: cámara de la industria
chamber orchestra: orquesta de cámara
chamberlain: *n.* chambelán
chamber-maid: *n.* camarera; doncella
chameleon: *n.* camaleón
chamois: *n.* (Zool.) gamuza; ante
champagne: *n.* champán; champaña
champion: 1. *adj.* campeón; 2. *n.* campeón
championship: *n.* campeonato
chancellery: *n.* cancillería
chancellor: *n.* canciller
chancre: *n.* chancro
chancroid: *n.* chancroide
change: *n.* cambio; dinero
change: *v.* cambiar; cambiarse
change of state: cambio de estado
changeful: *adj.* cambiante; voluble

changeless: *adj.* inmutable
channel: *n.* canal
channel: *v.* canalizar
channel-lock pliers: los alicates ajustables
chant: *n.* canto; canción
chant: *v.* cantar
chantry: *n.* capilla
chaos: *n.* caos
chap: *n.* muchacho; mozo
chap: *v.* agrietar
chapel: *n.* capilla; ermita
chaperon: *n.* señora o señorita de compania
chaperon: *v.* acompañar
chaperonine: *n.* chaperonina
chaplain: *n.* capellán
chapter
chapter: *n.* capítulo
chapter: *v.* carbonizarse
character: *n.* carácter
characteristic: *n.* característica
characterization: *n.* caracterización
charades: *n.* charadas
charcoal: *n.* carbón vegetal
charge: *n.* carga; cargo; precio
charge: *v.* cobrar; cargar; debitar
charge number: número de carga
charge sale: venta a crédito; venta a cuenta
chargeable: *adj.* imputable en cuenta
charger: *n.* cargador; caballo de batalla
chariot: *n.* carroza; carro militar
charisma: *n.* carisma
charitable: *adj.* benéfico; caritativo
charitable institution: institución de caridad
charitable organization: organización de caridad
charity: *n.* caridad; institución de caridad
charlatan: *n.* charlatán (a)
Charles's law: ley de Charles

charmer: *n.* hechicero
chart: *n.* carta; gráfico; cuadro; tabla
chart of accounts: plan de cuentas
charter: *n.* contrato; chárter; carta
charter: *v.* fletar
charter member: miembro fundador
charter of the company: escritura de constitución
charter party: carta de fletamento
chartered accountant: contable titulado
chartered company: sociedad anónima
charterer: *n.* fletador
charwoman: *n.* criada; asistenta
chary: *adj.* cuidadoso; económico
chase: *n.* caza; encaje
chase: *v.* cazar; perseguir
chasm: *n.* hendidura
chassis: *n.* chasis
chaste: *adj.* casto
chasten: *v.* castigar
chastise: *v.* castigar
chat: *n.* conversación
chat: *v.* charlar
chattel: *n.* bien mueble; prenda
chattel bond: bono prendario
chattel credit: crédito prendario
chattel creditor: acreedor prendario
chattel debt: deuda prendaría
chattel mortgage: prenda; préstamo
chattel security: título prendario
chauffeur: *n.* chofer
chauvinist: *n.* chovinista
chayote: *n.* chayote; cayote
cheap: *adj.* barato
cheapen: *v.* abaratar
cheat: *n.* trampa; engaño
cheat: *v.* encanar; estafar
check: *n.* cheque; jaque
check: *v.* revisar; averiguar; verificar; cotejar; chequear; marcar
check book: libreta de cheques; chequera

check card: tarjeta de banco
check clearing: compensación de cheques
check in: facturar; inscribirse
check list: lista de comprobación
check out: retirarse; darse de baja
check stub: talón de cheque; talonario
check valve: la válvula de antiretorno
checkers: *n.* juego de damas
checkgirl: *n.* guardar
checking account: cuenta corriente o cuenta de cheque
checkmate: *n.* jaque y mate
checkup: *n.* chequeo
cheek: *n.* mejilla
cheeky: *adj.* descarado
cheer: *n.* alegría; aplauso
cheese: *n.* queso
cheetah: *n.* chita
chef: *n.* chef; jefe
chelation: *n.* quelación
chemical: 1. *n.* producto químico; 2. *adj.* químico
chemical analysis: análisis químico
chemical bond: enlace químico
chemical bondenlace: unión química
chemical change: cambio químico
chemical digestion: digestión química
chemical energy: energía química
chemical equation: ecuación química
chemical formula: fórmula química
chemical industry: industria química
chemical pathology: patología clínica
chemical potential: potencial químico
chemical property: propiedad química

chemical reaction: reacción química
chemical rock: roca química
chemical symbol: símbolo químico
chemical weathering: desgaste químico
chemist: *n.* químico; farmacéutico
chemistry: *n.* química
chemometrics: *n.* quimiometría
chemotherapeutics: *n.* quimioterapéutica
chemotherapy: *n.* quimioterapia
cheque: *adj.* cheque
Cherokee: *adj.* cheroquí
cherry: *n.* cereza
cherry orchard: cerezal
cherry wood: la madera de cerezo
cherub: *n.* querubín
chess: *n.* ajedrez
chessboard: *n.* tablero de ajedrez
chest: *n.* tórax; pecho
Chest pain: dolor de pecho
Chest x-ray: radiografía del tórax
chestnut: 1. *adj.* castaño; marrón; 2. *n.* castaño
cheviot: *n.* cheviot
Chew: *n.* mascadura
Chew: *v.* mascar
chewing tobacco: rape; mascar tabaco
chewing-gum: *n.* chicle
chi: *n.* ji
chianti: *n.* quianti
chiasma: *n.* quiasma
chicanery: *n.* embuste
chicken: *n.* pollo; polluelo
chicken pox: varicela
chicken wire: el alambre de gallinero; el mallazo
chickory: *n.* achicoria
chickpea: *n.* garbanzo
chicle: *n.* chicle
chief: 1. *adj.* principal; 2. *n.* jefe; caudillo
chief executive: director general

chief financial officer: director financiero
chief operations: director de operaciones
chief technical: director técnico
chiffon: *n.* chiffón; gasa
child: *n.* niño; hijo
child labor: trabajo infantil
child support: mantenimiento de hijos
childhood: *n.* niñez
childhood illnesses: enfermedades de la niñez
children: nov; hijos
Chile: Chile
Chilean: *adj.* chileno; -a
chili; chilli: *n.* chile
chill: 1. *adj.* frió; reservado; 2. *n.* frialdad
chill: *v.* enfriar; desanimar
chilly: *adj.* frió
chimney: *n.* chimenea
chimney flue: el conducto de humo en la chimenea
chimpanzee: *n.* chimpanco
chin: n mentó; barbilla
China: La China
china closet: chinero
Chinatown: *n.* barrio chino
Chinese: *n.* chino
Chinese: *adj.* chino; -a
Chinese: *adj.* chinesco
Chinese puzzle: problema complicadísimo
Chink: *n.* grieta
Chink: *v.* hender; rajarse
chintz: *n.* chintz; chinz
chip: *n.* chip; astilla
chip: *v.* cortar
chipboard: *n.* aglomerado
chipped: *adj.* mellado
chiromancer: *adj.* quiromántico
chiromancy: *n.* quiromancia
chiropodist: *n.* quiropodista

chiropody: *n.* quiropedia
chiropractor: *n.* quiropráctico
chisel: *n.* cincel
chit: *n.* chiquillo
chit: *v.* quitar los brotes
chitinase: *n.* quitinasa
chitodextrinase: *n.* quitinasa
chiton: *n.* quitón
chlamydia: *n.* clamidia
chlamydospore: *n.* clamidospora
chloramphenicol: *n.* cloranfenicol
chlorhexidine: *n.* clorhexidina
chloride: *n.* cloruro
chlorination: *n.* clorinación
chlorine: *n.* cloro
chloroform: *n.* cloroformo
chlorophyll: *n.* clorofila
chlorophyte: *n.* clorofita
chloroplast: *n.* cloroplasto
chlorpheniramine: *n.* clorfenamina
chlorpromazine: *n.* clorpromazina
chock-full: *adj.* colmado
chocolate: 1. (color) *adj.* chocolate;
2. *n.* chocolate
choice: *n.* elección
choir: *n.* coro
choirmaster: *n.* director de coro
cholangiogram: *n.* colangiograma
cholecalciferol: *n.* calciol
cholecystectomy: *n.* colecistectomía
cholecystokinin: *n.* pancreozimina
cholera: *n.* cólera
cholesterol: *n.* colesterol
cholesterolemia: *n.* concentración de
colesterol en plasma
cholic acid: ácido cólico
choline kinase: colina-cinasa
choline oxidase: colina-oxidasa
cholinesterase: *n.* colinesterasa
chondroma: *n.* condroma
choo-choo: *n.* chu-cu-chu (cu)
choose: *v.* elegir; optar
chop: *v.* tajar
chop suey: chop suey

chopper: *n.* hacha
chorale: *n.* coral
chord: *n.* acorde; cuerda
chordate: *n.* cordado
chore: *n.* tarea
chorea: *n.* corea
choreographer: *n.* coreógrafo
choreography: *n.* coreografía
chorister: *n.* corista
chorus: *n.* coro
chow mein: chow mein
Christ: *n.* Cristo
christen: *n.* cronista
christen: *v.* bautizar
Christian: *adj.* cristiano
Christian: *n.* cristiano; -a
Christianity: *n.* cristiandad
Christianize: *v.* cristianizar;
acristianizar
chromatic: *adj.* cromático
chromatogram: *n.* cromatograma
chromatograph: *n.* cromatógrafo
chromatography: *n.* cromatografía
chrome: *n.* cromo
chromophore: *n.* cromóforo
chromosome: *n.* cromosoma
chromosome analysis: análisis
cromosómico
chromosome banding: bandeo
cromosómico
chromosphere: *n.* cromosfera
chronic: *adj.* crónico
chronicle: *n.* crónica
chronicler: *n.* cronista
chronological: *adj.* cronológico
chronology: *n.* cronología
chronometer: *n.* cronómetro
chronometry: *n.* cronometría
chronoscope: *n.* cronoscopio
chrysanthemum: *n.* crisantemo
chummy: *adj.* íntimo
chunk: *n.* pedazo grueso de algo
chunky: *adj.* rechoncho
church: *n.* iglesia

churchyard: *n.* cementerio
chutney: *n.* chutney
chyle: *n.* quilo
chyme: *n.* quimo
chymotrypsin: *n.* quimotripsina
cianocobalamin: *n.* cianocobalamina
ciao!: intj. ¡chao!
cicatrix: *n.* cicatriz
cicerone: *n.* cicerone
ciclosporin: *n.* ciclosporina
cider: *n.* sidra
cigar: *n.* cigarro
cigarette: *n.* cigarrillo
cilia: *n.* cilios
cinchona: *n.* chinchona
cinder: *n.* ceniza
cinder cone: cono de escoria
cinema: *n.* cine
cinema buff: cinéfilo
cinema industry: industria cinematográfica
cinemascope: *n.* cinemascope
Cinemascope: CinemaScope
cinematographer: *n.* cinematógrafo
cinematography: *n.* cinematografía
cinerama: *n.* cinerama
cineraria: *n.* cineraria
cingulum: *n.* cíngulo
cinquefoil: *n.* quinquefolio
cipher: *n.* cifra; cero
circadian: *adj.* circadiano
circadian (rhythm): *adj.* circadiano
circadian rhythm: ritmo circadiano
circle: *n.* círculo
circle graph: grafica circular
circuit: *n.* circuito
circuit board: el tablero de circuitos
circuit breaker: interruptor de circuito
circuit tester: el probador de circuitos
circular: 1. *n.* circular; 2. *adj.* circular
circular saw: la sierra circular

circulate: *v.* circular
circulating: *adj.* circulante
circulating antibody: anticuerpo circulante
circulating asset: activo flotante
circulating medium: circulante monetario
circulation: *n.* circulación
circulatory: *adj.* circulatorio
circumcision: *n.* circuncisión
circumference: *n.* circunferencia
circumflex: *adj.* circunflejo
circumlocution: *n.* circunlocución
circumnavigation: *n.* circunnavegación
circumscribed: *adj.* circunscrito
circumspection: *n.* circunspección
circumstance: *n.* circunstancia
circumvent: *v.* embaucar
circus: *n.* circo; redondel; arena
cirrhosis: *n.* cirrosis
cirrhosis of the liver: cirrosis del hígado
cirrocumulus: *n.* cirrocúmulo
cirrostratus: *n.* cirrostrato
cirrus: *n.* cirro
cistern: *n.* cisterna
cistron: *n.* cistrón
citadel: *n.* ciudadela
citation: *n.* citación
cite: *v.* citar; advertir
citizen: 1. *adj.* ciudadano; 2. *n.* ciudadano
citizenship: *n.* ciudadanía
citrate: *n.* citrato
citric acid: ácido cítrico; citrato
citron: *n.* cidro
citronella: *n.* citronela
citrulline: *n.* citrulina
citrus: *n.* cítrico
citrus grove: huerta de cítricos
city: *n.* ciudad
city centre: centro urbano
city council: consejo municipal

city hall: ayuntamiento; municipalidad
city market: mercado municipal
civet: *n.* civeto
civic-mindedness: civismo; civilidad
civics: *n.* educación cívica
civil: *adj.* civil
civil code: código civil
civil corporation: sociedad de derecho civil
civil disability: incapacidad civil
civil disobedience: desobediencia civil
civil law: derecho civil; ley civil
civil liability: responsabilidad civil
civil registry: registro civil
civil rights: derechos civiles
civil servant: funcionario público
civil service: servicio público
civil status: estado civil
civil suit: juicio civil
civil year: año civil
civilian: 1. *adj.* civil; 2. *n.* hombre civil; paisano
civility: *n.* cortesía; atención
civilization: *n.* civilización
clack: 1. *n.* ruido agudo y corto
clack: *v.* repiquetear
claim: 1. *n.* reclamo
claim: *v.* reclamar
claim number: número de reclamo
claimant: *n.* reclamante
clairvoyance: *n.* clarividencia
clairvoyant: 1. *adj.* clarividente; 2. *n.* clarividente
clamber: *v.* trepar
clammy: *adj.* frío; húmedo
clamor: *n.* clamor
clamour: *n.* alboroto
clamour: *v.* gritar
clamp: *n.* empalmadura; tornillo de banco
clan: *n.* clan; familia
clang: *n.* sonido metálico

clap: *n.* aplauso
clap: *v.* aplaudir
clapboard: *n.* tablilla
claque: *n.* claque
claret: *n.* clarete
clarification: *n.* aclaración
clarify: *v.* clarificar
clarinet: *n.* clarinete
clarinetist: *n.* clarinete; clarinetista
clarion: *n.* clarín
clash: *n.* choque
clash: *v.* chocar; golpear
clasp: *n.* broche; hebilla
clasp: *v.* abrochar
class: *n.* clase
class: *n.* clase; categoría
class: *v.* clasificar
classical: *adj.* clásico (a)
classical pathway: vía clásica
classicism: *n.* clasicismo
classicist: *n.* clasicista
classification: *n.* clasificación
classification of accounts: clasificación de cuentas
classified: *adj.* clasificado
classified advertisement: anuncio clasificado
classify: *v.* clasificar
classmate: *n.* compañero de clase
clastic rock: roca clástica
claudication: *n.* claudicación
clause: *n.* cláusula; artículo
claustrophobia: *n.* claustrofobia
clavichord: *n.* clavicordio
clavicle: *n.* clavícula
claw: *n.* una
claw: *v.* agarrar; arañar
clay: *n.* arcilla; greda
clay-colored: heces de color de arcilla
clay-colored stools: heces de color de arcilla
clean: *adj.* limpio; perfecto
clean acceptance: aceptación

incondicional
cleaning agent: liquido limpiador
clean-out: el registro
clean-out stop: el tapón de limpieza
clear: *adj.* claro; limpio
clean: *v.* liquidar; vender saldos;
liberar
clear a debt: cancelar una deuda
clear customs: pasar aduanas
clearance: *n.* depuración; realización
clearance sale: liquidación
clearance value: valor de liquidación
clear-cut: tala total
clear-cutting: tala total
clearing: *n.* compensación; (en
forestaría) claridad
clearing account: cuenta puente
clearing bank: banco de
compensación
clearing house: cámara de
compensación
clearing of decimals: supresión de
decimales
clearness: *n.* claridad
cleavage: *n.* escisión; exfoliacion
clef: *n.* clave
cleft: *n.* llave; clave (mus.)
clematis: *n.* clemátide
clemency: *n.* clemencia
clement: *adj.* clemente
clench: *n.* agarro
clench: *v.* agarrar; remachar
clepsydra: *n.* clepsidra
clergy: *n.* clero
clergyman: *n.* clérigo; sacerdote
clergywoman: *n.* clériga
cleric: 1. *adj.* clérigo; 2. *n.* clérigo
clerical work: trabajo administrativo
clericalism: *n.* clericalismo
clerk: *n.* empleado; empleado
administrativo
clever: *adj.* inteligente; diestro; hábil
cliche: *n.* cliché
click: *n.* clic; selección

click: *v.* pulsar; hacer click
client: *n.* cliente
clientele: *n.* clientela
climacteric: 1. *n.* climaterio; 2. *adj.*
climaterio
climate: *n.* clima
climatologist: *n.* climatólogo; -a
climatologist: *adj.* climatólogo
climatology: *n.* climatología
climax: *n.* clímax; crisis
climb: *n.* subida
climb: *v.* trepar; subir
clinic: *n.* clínica
clinical analysis: análisis clínico
clinical assay: ensayo clínico
clinical records: registros; récord
clinical toxicology: toxicología
clínica
clinician: *n.* clínico; -a
clip: *n.* clip
clip-on (earrings): *n.* de clip
clipping: 1. *adj.* rápido; 2. *n.* recorte
clique: *n.* pandilla; corrillo
clitoris: *n.* clítoris
cloak: *n.* capa; manto
cloak: *v.* disimular
cloakroom: *n.* guardarropa
clock: *n.* reloj
clock radio: radiodespertador
clockmaker: *n.* relojero
clod: *n.* terrón
clog: *n.* obstáculo; zueco
cloisonne: *n.* cloisonné
cloister: *n.* claustro
cloister: *v.* enclaustrar
clone: *n.* clon
clonidine: *n.* clonidina
cloning: *n.* clonación
clonus: *n.* clonus; clono
close: *v.* cerrar; cesar; clausurar
closed: *adj.* cerrado
closed chapter: asunto concluido
closed circulatory system: sistema
circulatorio cerrado

closed corporation: compañía propietaria
closed economy: economía cerrada
closed session: sesión a puertas cerradas
closed system: sistema cerrado
closed-circuit: por circuito cerrado
closeness: *n.* cercanía
closing: *n.* conclusión; clausura
closing balance: saldo final; balance de cierre
closing date: fecha de cierre
closing entry: asiento de cierre
closing inventory: existencia final
closing price: precio final
closure: *n.* cierre; clausura
clot: *n.* coágulo
clot: *v.* coagularse
cloth: *n.* lienzo; patio; vestidos
cloud: *n.* nube
cloud: *v.* anublar
cloud seeding: siembra de nubes
cloudless: *adj.* sin nubes
cloudy urine: orina turbia
clove: *n.* clavo
clover: *n.* trébol
clown: *n.* payaso
clown: *v.* hacer el payaso
cloxacillin: *n.* cloxacilina
cloy: *v.* empalagar
club: *n.* club
clue: *n.* guía; pista
clump: *n.* mata; grupo
clumsy: *adj.* tosco
cluster: *n.* racimo; enjambre; grupo
cluster: *v.* agrupar
clustering: *n.* agrupación
clutter: *n.* confusión
clutter: *v.* alborotar
cnidarian: *n.* cnidario
coach: *n.* preceptor
coach: *v.* dar clases particulares
coachman: *n.* cochero
co-administrate: coadministrar

coagglutination test: prueba de la coaglutinación
coagulase test: prueba de la coagulasa
coagulation: *n.* coagulación
coagulum: *n.* coágulo
coal: *n.* carbón
coal: *v.* proveer de carbón
coalescence: *n.* coalescencia
coalition: *n.* coalición
co-applicant: *n.* co-solicitante
coast: *n.* costa
coast: *v.* costear; navegar en cabotaje
coastal: *adj.* costero
coastguard: *n.* guardacostas
coasting trade: cabotaje
coat: *n.* chaqueta
coauthor: *n.* coautor
coaxial: *adj.* coaxial
cobalamin: *n.* cobalamina
cobble: *n.* guijarro
coble: *v.* empedrar; remendar
cobol: *n.* cobol
cobra: *n.* cobra
coca: *n.* coca
coca plantation: cocal
cocaine: *n.* cocaína
coccus: *n.* coco
coccyx: *n.* cóccix
cochlea: *n.* cóclea
cock: *n.* grifo
cockatoo: *n.* cacatúa
cocker spaniel: cocker
cockle: *n.* almeja
cockpit: *n.* cabina
cockroach: *n.* cucaracha
cocksure: *adj.* confiado
cocktail: *n.* cóctel
cocktail shaker: coctelera
cocoa: *n.* cacao
coconut: *n.* coco
coconut plantation: cocotal
cocreditor: *n.* coacreedor
cod: *n.* abadejo; bacalao

coda: *n.* coda
coddle: *v.* mimar
code: *n.* código
code of accounts: código de cuentas
code of commerce: código de comercio
codebtor: *n.* codeudor
codeine: *n.* codeína
codex: *n.* códice
codicil: *adj.* codicilo
codification: *n.* codificación
codifier: *n.* codificador
codify: *v.* codificar
coding strand: cadena transcrita
codominance: *n.* codominancia
codon: *n.* codón
codon bias: preferencia codónica
coeducational: *adj.* coeducacional
coefficient: *n.* coeficiente
coenzyme: *n.* coenzima
coercion: *n.* coerción
coercive: *adj.* coercitivo
coexistence: *n.* coexistencia
cofactor: *n.* cofactor
coffee: 1. *adj.* (color) café; 2. *n.* café
coffee bar: *n.* cafetín
coffee grower: cafetero; cafetalero
coffee merchant: cafetero
coffee plantation: cafetal
coffee tree: cafeto
coffeepot: *n.* cafetera
coffeepot; coffee maker: cafetera
coffin: *n.* ataúd
cog: *n.* diente
cogent: *adj.* fuerte
cogitate: *v.* meditar
cognac: *n.* coñac
cognate: *adj.* cognado
cognate: *adj.* semejante; pariente
cognate sequence: secuencia consanguínea
cohabit: *v.* cohabitar
cohabitation: *n.* cohabitación
coherence: *n.* coherencia

coherent: *adj.* coherente
cohesive end: extremo cohesivo
cohort: *n.* cómplice; aliado
coif: *n.* cofia
coiffure: *n.* peinado; tocado
coil: *n.* rosca; rollo
coil: *v.* enrollar
coin: *n.* moneda
coin: *v.* acuñar
coin money: acuñar moneda
coincide: *v.* coincidir
coiner: *n.* monedero; acuñador
coinsurance: *n.* seguro suplementario
coinsurance clause: cláusula de co-seguro
coinsure: *v.* coasegurar
coinsurer: *n.* coasegurador
coke: *n.* coca-cola
cola: *n.* cola
colander: *n.* colador
colchicum: *n.* colchisina
cold: *adj.* frío; indiferente
cold industry: industria frigorífica
cold intolerance: intolerancia al frío
Cold sweat: sudor frío
Cold-sensitive mutant: mutante criolábil
coleus: *n.* coleo
Colic: 1. *n.* cólico; 2. *adj.* cólico
coliform: *adj.* coliforme
coliseum: *n.* coliseo
colistin: *n.* colistina
colitis: *n.* colitis
collaboration: *n.* colaboración
collaborationist: *n.* colaboracionista
collaborator: *n.* colaborador
collaborate: *v.* colaborar
collage: *n.* colage
collagen: *n.* colágena
collapse: *n.* colapso
collar: *n.* cuello; collar
collaspe: *n.* hundimiento
collapse: *v.* aplastar

collateral: 1. a colateral; adicional;
2. *n.* garantía
collateral: *adj.* colateral
collateral assurance: garantía
colateral
collateral commodity: mercadería
como garantía
collateral guarantee: garantía
colateral
collateral loan: préstamo con
garantía
collateral note: pagaré con garantía
collateral security: garantía colateral
collateral signature: aval
colleague: *n.* colega
collect: *v.* colectionar; cobrar;
recaudar; colectar
collectible: *adj.* cobrable; cobradero
collectible debt: deuda cobrable
collection: *n.* colección; cobro;
cobranza
collection at source: retención de
impuestos en origen
collection draft: letra al cobro
collection fee: comisión de cobro
collection in advance: cobro
anticipado
collective: *adj.* colectivo
collective bargaining: negociación
colectiva
collective contract: contrato
colectivo
collective farm: granja colectiva
collectivism: *n.* colectivismo
collector: *n.* cobrador; coleccionista
collector of customs: cobrador de
aduanas
college: *n.* colegio
collide: *v.* chocar
collie: *n.* collie; perro
colliery: *n.* mina de carbón
cauliflower: *n.* coliflor
collinear: *adj.* colineal
collision: *n.* colisión

collocate: *v.* colocar
collocation: *n.* colocación
colloid: *adj.* coloide
colloidal: *adj.* coloidal
colloquial: *adj.* familiar; coloquial
colloquialism: *n.* expresión coloquial
colloquium: *n.* coloquio
colloquy: *n.* coloquio
collusion: *n.* confabulación
Cologne: Colonia
cologne: *n.* colonia
Colombia: Colombia
Colombian: *adj.* colombiano; -a
colon: *n.* colón
colonel: *n.* coronel
colonial: *adj.* colonial
colonist: *n.* colono
colonizer: *n.* colonizador
colonnade: *n.* columnata
colonoscopy: *n.* colonoscopia
colony: *n.* colonia
colophon: *n.* colofón
color: *n.* color
color: *v.* colorear
color of law: apariencia legal
color scheme: combinación de color
colorant: *n.* colorante
coloration: *n.* coloración
coloratura: *n.* coloratura
colored: *adj.* colorado
colorful: *adj.* lleno de colorido
coloring: *n.* coloración; colorido
colorist: *n.* colorista
colorless: *adj.* incoloro
colossal: *adj.* colosal
colostomy: *n.* colostomía
colostrum: *n.* calostro
color monitor: monitor de color
colposcopy: *n.* colposcopia
colt: *n.* potro; revólver
Columbus: Colón
column: *n.* columna
column chart: gráfico de columnas
column chromatography:

cromatografía en columna
column packing: relleno de la
columna
column system: sistema tabular
columnist: *n.* columnista
coma: *n.* coma
comanage: *v.* coadministrar;
codirigir
comb: *n.* peine
comb: *v.* peinar; romper
combat: *n.* combate
combat: *v.* combatir
combat fatigue: fatiga de combate
combatant: *n.* combatiente
combative: *adj.* combativo
combination: *n.* combinación
combination lock: *n.* cerradura de
combinación
combination pill: píldora combinada
combine: *vt.* combinar (se)
combined: *adj.* combinado
combined check: cheque combinado
combustion: *n.* combustión
comedian: *n.* comediante
comedy: *n.* comedia
comely: *adj.* gracioso
come-off: *n.* salida
comestibles: *n.* comestibles
comet: *n.* cometa
comfort: *n.* confort
comfort: *v.* confortar
comfort letter: carta de
recomendación
comfortable: *adj.* cómodo (a);
confortable
comic: *adj.* cómico
comic book: libros comicos
comics; comic strip: *n.* tira cómica
coming: 1. *adj.* venidero; 2. *n.*
advenimiento
comma: *n.* coma
command: *n.* mandato
command: *v.* mandar; ordenar
command post (area): comandancia

commandant: *n.* comandante
commanding: *adj.* poderoso;
autorizado
commando: *n.* comando
commemorate: *v.* conmemorar;
celebrar
commence: *v.* comenzar
commend: *v.* alabar
commensal: *adj.* comensal
commensalism: *n.* comensalismo
comment: *n.* comentario
comment: *v.* comentar
commentary: *n.* comentario
commentator: *n.* comentarista
commerce: *n.* comercio
commercial: *adj.* comercial
commercial acceptance: aceptación
comercial
commercial activity: actividad
comercial
commercial address: domicilio
comercial
commercial agent: agente comercial
commercial area: área comercial
commercial association: sociedad
mercantil
commercial bank: banco comercial
commercial banking: banca
comercial
commercial bond: bono comercial
commercial break: pausa
publicitaria
commercial business: firma
comercial
commercial centre: centro
comercial
commercial chain: cadena comercial
commercial code: código de
comercio
commercial college: escuela de
comercio
commercial contract: contrato
comercial
commercial corporation: sociedad

comercial
commercial debt: deuda comercial
commercial department: departamento comercial
commercial director: director comercial
commercial district: distrito comercial
commercial expense: gasto comercial
commercial firm: firma de comercio
commercial house: firma comercial
commercial invoice: factura comercial
commercial law: derecho comercial; ley comercial
commercial letter of credit: carta de crédito comercial
commercial literature: literatura comercial
commercial manager: director comercial
commercial name: denominación comercial
commercial note: pagaré comercial
commercial paper: documento comercial
commercial policy: política comercial
commercial school: escuela comercial
commercial sector: sector comercial
commercial set: documentos de embarque
commercial trade: intercambio comercial
commercial traveler: viandante comercial
commercial usage: práctica comercial
commercial vehicle: vehículo comercial
commercial year: año comercial
commercialize: *v.* comercializar

commercialism: *n.* comercialismo
commercialization: *n.* comercialización
commiserate: *v.* compadecer
commiseration: *n.* conmiseración
commissariat: *n.* comisariato
commissary: *n.* comisario
commission: *n.* comisión
commission agent: comisionista
commissioner: *n.* comisionado
commit: *v.* confiar; cometer
commitment: *n.* compromiso; obligación
committee: *n.* comité; comisión; consejo
commode (chest): *n.* cómoda
commodious: *adj.* cómodo; holgado
commodities: *n.* mercancías; mercaderías
commodities exchange: bolsa de comercio
commodity: *n.* mercancía; mercadería; producto
commodity futures: mercancía futura
commodore: *adj.* comodoro
common: *adj.* común; habitual
common average: promedio simple
common carrier: empresa de transporte público
common creditor: acreedor ordinario
common denominator: denominador común
common factor: factor común
common market: mercado común
common multiple: múltiplo común
common ownership: condominio
common share: acción ordinaria
common-law marriage: matrimonio consensual
commotion: *n.* conmoción
communal: *adj.* comunal
communicable: *adj.* comunicable;

contagioso; transmisible
communicate: *v.* comunicar; contagiar
communication: *n.* comunicación
communication theory: *n.* comunicología
communications: *n.* comunicaciones
communications department: departamento de comunicaciones
communications director: director de comunicaciones
communications manager: director de comunicaciones
communicative: *adj.* comunicativo
communion: *n.* comunión
communique: *adj.* comunicado
communiqué: *n.* comunicado
communism: *n.* comunismo
communist: 1. *adj.* comunista; 2. *n.* comunista
community: *n.* comunidad
community centre: centro de la comunidad
community charge: gasto comunitario
community expense: gasto comunitario
community income: renta pro indiviso
community property: propiedad comunitaria
community rules: reglamento de copropiedad
commutation: *n.* conmutación
commutative property of addition: propiedad conmutativa de la suma.
commutative property of multiplication: propiedad conmutativa de la multiplicación
commutator: *n.* conmutador
commuting allowance: dietas de desplazamiento
commuting expenses: gastos de desplazamiento

compact: 1. *adj.* compacto; 2. *n.* coche compacto
compact: *v.* comprimir; apretar
compact bone: hueso compacto
compact disk: disco compacto
compaction: *n.* compactación
compaigner: *n.* veterano
companies act: ley de sociedades
companion: *n.* compañero
companionship: *n.* compañerismo
company: *n.* compañía; sociedad; firma
company law: ley de sociedades
company tax: impuesto a las sociedades
company union: sindicato de la empresa
comparative: *adj.* comparativo
comparative advantage: ventaja comparativa
comparative advertising: publicidad comparativa
comparative cost: coste comparativo
comparative method: método comparativo
comparatively: *adv.* relativamente
compare: *v.* comparar; cotejar
comparison: *n.* comparación
compartment: *n.* compartimiento
compass: *n.* compás
compass: *v.* circundar
compassion: *n.* compasión
compassionate: *adj.* compasivo
compatible: *adj.* compatible
compatible numbers: números compatibles
compatriot: *n.* compatriota
compeer: *n.* compañero; colega
compendium: *n.* compendio
compensate: *v.* compensar; indemnizar
compensation: *n.* compensación; indemnización
compete: *v.* competir; rivalizar

competency: *n.* competencia
competent: *adj.* competente
competition: *n.* competencia
competitive: *adj.* competitivo
competitor: *n.* competidor
compilation: *n.* compilación;
recopilación
compile: *v.* compilar; recopilar
compiler: *n.* compilador; recopilador
complain: *v.* quejarse; lamentarse
complaint: *n.* demanda; queja
complement: *n.* complemento
complementary: *adj.*
complementario
complementary angles: ángulos
complementarlos
complementary colors: colores
complementarios
complementary events: sucesos
complementarlos
complete: *adj.* completo
complete: *v.* finalizar; completar
complete metamorphosis:
metamorfosis completa
completion: *n.* terminación;
ejecución
complex: 1. *adj.* complejo; 2. *n.*
complejo
complex analysis: el análisis
complejo
complex carbohydrate:
carbohidrato complejo
complex number: número complejo
complex variable: variable compleja
complexion: *n.* complexión; estado
complexity: *n.* complejidad
compliance: *n.* cumplimiento;
acatamiento
compliance code: código de
cumplimiento obligatorio
compliant: *adj.* condescendiente;
dócil
complicate: *v.* complicar; embrollar
complication: *n.* complicación

complicity: *n.* complicidad
compliment: *n.* cumplido; alabanza
comply with: cumplir con
component: 1. *adj.* componente; 2.
n. componente
comportment: *n.* conducta
compose: *v.* componer; redactar
composer: *n.* compositor; autor
composite: 1. *adj.* compuesto; mixto;
2. *n.* material compuesto
composite index: índice compuesto
composite number: número
compuesto
composite volcano: volcán
compuesto
composition: *n.* composición
compost: *n.* fertilizante
composure: *n.* compostura
compote: *n.* compota
compound: 1. *adj.* combinado; 2. *n.*
compuesto
compound: *v.* combinar; componer
compound entry: asiento compuesto
compound fraction: fracción
compuesta
compound index: índice combinado
compound interest: interés
compuesto
compound machine: máquina
compuesta
compound number: número
complejo
compound rate: índice combinado
comprehensive: *adj.* general; global
compress: *n.* compresa
compress: *v.* comprimir
compression: *n.* compresión
compressor: *n.* compresor
comprise: *v.* comprender; abarcar
comptroller auditor: contralor
comptrollership: *n.* auditoria;
contraloría
compulsive: *adj.* compulsivo
compunction: *n.* arrepentimiento

computable: *adj.* admisible; computable
computation: *n.* cálculo; cómputo; computación
compute: *v.* calcular; computar
computer: *n.* computadora
computer game: juego de computadora
computer language: lenguaje de computación
computer network: red de computadoras
computer program: programa de computación
computer programmer: programador de computadoras
computerized: *adj.* informatizado; computadorizado
computing: *n.* informática; computación
comrade: *n.* camarada
comradeship: *n.* camaradería
concatemer: *n.* concatémero
concave: *adj.* cóncavo
concave lens: lente cóncava
concave mirror: espejo cóncavo
conceal: *v.* encubrir; esconder
concealed asset: activo oculto
concealed damage: vicio oculto
concealed loss: pérdida oculta
concealed reserve: reserva oculta
concealment: encubrimiento
concede: *v.* conceder
conceit: *n.* orgullo; concepto
concentrate: *n.* concentrado
concentrate: 1. *adj.* concentrado; 2. *n.* sustancia
concentrate: *v.* concentrar
concentrated solution: solución concentrada
concentration: *n.* concentración
concentration camp: campo de concentración
concentration gradient: gradiente

de concentración
concentric: *adj.* concéntrico
concept: *n.* concepto
conception: *n.* concepción
concern: *n.* explotación; negocio
concern: *vt.* concernir
concerning: *prep.* concerniente a; sobre
concert: *n.* concierto
concert: *v.* concertar; ajustar
concert artist: concertista
concert hall: sala de conciertos
concertina: *n.* concertina
concertmaster: *n.* concertino
concerto: *n.* concierto
concession: *n.* concesión
concessionaire: *n.* concesionario
concessive: *adj.* concesivo
conch: *n.* concha
conciliate: *v.* conciliar; granjear
conciliation: *n.* conciliación
conciliator: *n.* conciliador
conciliatory: *adj.* conciliador
concise: *adj.* conciso
conclave: *n.* cónclave
conclude: *v.* concluir; acabar; decidir
conclusion: *n.* conclusión
conclusive: *adj.* concluyente
concoct: *v.* confeccionar; tramar
concord: *n.* concordia
concordance: *n.* concordancia
concordat: *n.* concordato
concrete: 1. *adj.* concreto; 2. *n.* hormigón; concreto
concubinage: *n.* concubinato
concur: *v.* concurrir; acordarse
concurrent: *adj.* concurrente
concurrent obligation: obligación mancomunada
concussion: *n.* concusión
condemn: *v.* condenar; expropiar
condemnation: *n.* condena; expropiación
condensation: *n.* condensación

condense: *v.* condensar; abreviar
condensed milk: leche condensada
condensed soup: sopa condensada
condenser: *n.* condensador
condescend: *v.* dignarse
condescending: *adj.*
condescendiente
condescension: *n.* condescendencia
condiment: *n.* condimento
condition: *n.* condición; calidad;
situación
conditional: *adj.* condicional
conditional acceptance: aceptación
condicional
conditional deed: dominio
condicionado
conditional endorsement: endoso
condicional
conditional sale: venta condicional
conditioner: *n.* acondicionador
conditioning: *n.* condicionamiento
condole: *v.* condolerse; deplorar
condolence: *n.* condolencia
condom: *n.* condón; preservativo
condominium: *n.* condominio
condonation: *n.* condonación
condone: *v.* condonar
condor: *n.* cóndor
conduct: *v.* conducir; dirigir
conductance: *n.* conductancia
conduction: *n.* conducción
conductivity: *n.* conductividad
conductometry: *n.* conductimetría
conductor: *n.* conductor
conduit: *n.* conducto
cone: *n.* cono
confection: *n.* confección
confection: *v.* confeccionar
confederacy: *n.* confederación
confederation: *n.* confederación
confer: *v.* conferenciar; tratar
conference: *n.* conferencia;
congreso; reunión
confess: *v.* confiar

confession: *n.* confesión
confessional: *adj.* confesionario
confessor: *n.* confesor
confetti: *n.* confeti
confidant: *adj.* confidente
confidence: *n.* confianza
confident: 1. *adj.* seguro; 2. *n.*
confidente
confidential: *adj.* confidencial
confidentiality: *n.* confidencialidad
configurate: *v.* configurar
configuration: *n.* configuración
confine: *n.* límite
confine: *v.* confinar; limitar
confinement: *n.* confinamiento
confirm: *v.* confirmar
confirmation: *n.* confirmación
confirmation request: solicitud de
confirmación
confirmatory test: prueba
confirmatoria
confirmed check: cheque
confirmado
confiscate: *v.* confiscar
confiscation: *n.* confiscación
conflagration: *n.* conflagración
conflict: *n.* conflicto
conflict: *v.* combatir
conflict of interest: conflicto de
intereses
confluence: *n.* confluencia
conform: *v.* conformar
conformist: *n.* conformista
conformity: *n.* conformidad
confound: *v.* confundir; desconcertar
confounded: *adj.* maldito
confront: *v.* confrontar con; hacer
frente a
confrontation: *n.* confrontación
Confucianism: *n.* confucianismo
confucianist: *n.* confucianista
Confucianist: *n.* confucianista;
confuciano
Confucius: *n.* Confucio

confuse: *v.* confundir; desconcertar
confused: *adj.* confundido (a)
confusion: *n.* confusión
confutable: *adj.* refutable
confute: *v.* refutar; anular
conga: *n.* conga
congenital: *adj.* congénito
congenital defects: defectos congénitos; defectos del nacimiento
congenital illnesses: defectos congénitos
conger: *n.* congrio
congest: *v.* congestionar
congestion: *n.* congestión
conglomerate: *adj.* conglomerado
conglomerate: *v.* conglomerar
Congo: Congo
congratulate: *v.* congratular; felicitar
congratulations: *n.* congratulaciones
congregate: *v.* congregar; reunir; congregarse
congregate: *v.* congregarse
congregation: *n.* congregación
congregationalism: *n.* congregacionalismo
Congregationalist: *n.* congregacionalista
congress: *n.* congreso; asamblea; (U. S.) parlamento
congressman: *n.* congresista
congruence: *n.* congruencia
congruent: *adj.* congruente
congruent angles: ángulos congruentes
congruent figures: figuras congruentes
congruent sides: lados congruentes
conic: *n.* sección cónica
conic section: la sección cónica
conifer: *n.* confiera
coniferous: *adj.* conífero
coniferous tree: árbol conífero
conjecture: *n.* conjetura
conjecture: *v.* conjeturar

conjoin: *v.* juntar; asociar
conjugal: *adj.* conyugal
conjugate: *v.* conjugar
conjunction: *n.* conjunción
conjunctive: *adj.* conjuntivo
conjunctivitis: *n.* conjuntivitis
conjure: *v.* conjurar; abjurar
connect: *v.* conectar; unir
connection: *n.* conexión
connection box: la caja de empalmes
connective: *adj.* conectivo
connective tissue: tejido conectivo
connector: *n.* conector; conectador
connivance: *n.* connivencia
connive: *v.* fingir; hacer la vista gorda
connoisseur: *n.* conocedor (a)
connotative: *adj.* connotativo
connubial: *adj.* connubial
conquer: *v.* e intr. conquistar; ganar.
conqueror: *n.* conquistador
conquest: *n.* conquista
consanguinity: *n.* consanguinidad
conscience: *n.* conciencia
conscienceless: *adj.* sin conciencia
conscientious: *adj.* concienzudo; responsable
conscious: *adj.* consciente
consciousness: *n.* conciencia
conscrate: *v.* consagrar; dedicar
conscribe: *v.* reclutar
conscript: *n.* conscripto
consecration: *n.* consagración
consecutive: *adj.* consecutivo
consensus: *n.* consenso
consensus sequence: secuencia de consenso
consensus value: valor consensual
consent: *n.* consentimiento; acuerdo
consequence: *n.* consecuencia
consequent: *adj.* consiguiente; lógico
conservation: *n.* conservación
conservation of charge:

conservación de la carga eléctrica
conservation of mass: conservación de la masa
conservation plowing: arada de conservación
conservationist: *n.* conservacionista
conservatism: *n.* conservatismo
conservative: *n.* conservador
conservatory: *adj.* conservatorio
conservatory: *n.* conservatorio
conserve: *n.* conserva
conserve: *v.* conservar
conserved funds: fondos conservados
consider: *v.* considerar; examinar
considerable: *adj.* considerable
considerate: *adj.* considerado
consign: *v.* consignar; enviar
consignation: *n.* consignación
consignee: *n.* consignatario
consignment: *n.* consignación
consignment sale: venta en consignación
consignor: *n.* consignador; remitente
consist: *v.* consistir
consistency: *n.* consistencia
consistory: *n.* consistorio
consolation: *n.* consuelo
console: *n.* consola
console: *v.* consolar; confortar
consoler: *n.* consolador
consolidate: *v.* consolidar; fusionar
consolidated debt: deuda consolidada
consolidated statement: estado consolidado
consolidation: *n.* consolidación
consomme: *n.* consomé
consonance: *n.* consonancia
consonant: *n.* consonante
consort: *n.* consorte
consort: *v.* asociar; casar
consortium: *n.* consorcio
conspicuity: *n.* claridad

conspiracy: *n.* conspiración
conspirator: *n.* conspirador
conspire: *v.* maquinar; tramar
constable: *n.* guardián; alguacil
constabulary: *n.* comisaría; policía
constant: *adj.* constante
constant charge: cargo constante
constant cost: coste constante
constant expense: gasto constante
constant money: moneda constante
constant term: término constante
constellation: *n.* constelación
consternation: *n.* consternación
constipated: *adj.* estreñido; a
constipation: *n.* estreñimiento
constituent: *adj.* constitutivo
constitute: *v.* constituir; componer
constitution: *n.* constitución
constitutional: *adj.* constitucional
constrain: *v.* constreñir; restringir
constraint: *n.* limitante; restricción
constrict: *v.* apretar; constreñir
constriction: *n.* constricción
constrictor: *n.* constrictor
construct: *n.* construccion
construct: *v.* construir; edificar
construction: *n.* construcción
construction contract: contrato de construcción
construction industry: industria de la construcción
construction work: trabajo de construcción
construction worker: obrero de la construcción
constructive: *adj.* constructivo; implícito
constructive acceptance: aceptación implícita
constructive conversion: apropiación implícita
constructive force: fuerza constructiva
constructive fraud: fraude presunto

constructive interference:
interferencia constructiva
constructive payment: pago
implícito
constructivism: *n.* constructivismo
constructivist: *n.* constructivista
constructor: *n.* constructor
construe: *v.* interpretar; construir
consul: *n.* cónsul
consular: *n.* consular
consular charge: gasto consular
consular fee: tarifa consular
consular invoice: factura consular
consulate: *n.* consulado
consulship: *n.* consulado
consult: *v.* consumar; considerar
consultancy: *n.* asesoría
consultant: *n.* consultor
consultation: *n.* consulta;
consultación
consultative examination: examen
consultativo
consulting: *n.* consultoría
consulting board: comisión
consultiva
consulting committee: comisión
consultiva
consulting physician: médico
consultor
consumable fungible: bien
consumible
consume: *v.* consumir; acabar
consumer: *n.* consumidor
consumer credit: crédito de
consumo
consumer durable: bien de consume
duradero
consumer good: bien de consumo
consumer price: precio al
consumidor
consumer price index: índice de
precios al consumidor
consumer protection: protección al
consumidor

consumer society: sociedad de
consumo
consumer spending: gasto en bienes
de consumo
consumer survey: encuesta de
consumo
consumer tax: impuesto al
consumidor
consumerism: *n.* consumismo
consummate: *adj.* consumado
consummate: *v.* consumar
consumption: *n.* consumo;
consunción
consumption tax: impuesto al
consumo
contact: *n.* contacto
contact: *v.* contactar
contact lenses: lentes de contacto
contact plate: la placa de contacto
contagion: *n.* contagio;
contaminación
contagious: *adj.* contagioso
contain: *v.* contener
container: *n.* contenedor; envase;
recipiente
contaminant: *n.* contaminador;
contaminante
contaminated: *adj.* contaminado
contamination: *n.* contaminación
contemn: *v.* desacatar; despreciar
contemplate: *v.* contemplar; meditar
contemplation: *n.* contemplación
contemporary: *adj.* contemporáneo
contempt: *n.* descato; desprecio
contemptuous: *adj.* desdeñoso;
despectivo
contend: *v.* sostener
contender: *n.* contendiente
content; contented: *adj.* contento
contented: *adj.* contento
contentment: *n.* contento
content: *n.* contenido
contest: *n.* concurso
contest: *v.* competir

contextual: *adj.* del contexto
contiguous: *adj.* contiguo
continent: *n.* continente
continental: *adj.* continental
continental air mass: masa de aire continental
continental climate: clima continental
continental drift: deriva continental
continental glacier: glaciar continental
continental shelf: plataforma continental
continental slope: talud continental
contingency: *n.* contingencia
contingent: *n.* contingente
contingent annuity: anualidad condicional
contingent dividend: dividendo condicional
contingent liability: pasivo eventual
continual; continuous: *adj.* continuo
continuance: *n.* continuidad
continuance of eligibility: continuación de elegibilidad
continue: *v.* continuar; seguir; durar
continuing disability: incapacidad continua
continuity: *n.* continuidad
continuous: *adj.* continuo
continuous function: la función continua
continuous method: método continuo
continuous shift: turno continuo
contortionist: *n.* contorsionista
contour: *n.* contorno; perímetro
contour feather: pluma remera
contour interval: intervalo entre curvas de nivel
contour line: curva de nivel
contour plowing: arada en contorno
contra-account: contrapartida
contraband: *n.* contrabando

contrabass: *n.* contrabajo
contrabassoon: *n.* contrabajón
contraception: *n.* contracepción; anticoncepción
contraceptive: *adj.* contraceptivo; anticonceptivo
contraceptive patch: parche anticonceptivo
contraceptive ring: anillo anticonceptivo
contract: *n.* contrato
contract: *v.* contratar; contraer
contract of sale: contrato de venta
contractile vacuole: vacuola contráctil
contracting: *n.* contratación
contracting party: parte contratante
contraction: *n.* contracción
contractor: *n.* contratista
contractual: *adj.* contractual
contradict: *v.* contradecir
contradiction: *n.* contradicción
contraindication: *n.* contraindicación
contralto: *n.* contralto
contrapuntal: *adj.* de contrapunto
contrary: *adj.* contrario
contrast: *n.* contraste
contrast: *v.* contrastar
contrastive: *adj.* contrastivo
contravene: *v.* contravenir
contredance: *n.* contradanza
contribute: *v.* contribuir; poner
contribution: *n.* contribución; aporte
contributive pension: pensión contributiva
contributor: *n.* contribuyente
contributory: *adj.* contributivo
contriet: *adj.* contrito; arrepentido
contrition: *n.* contrición
contrive: *v.* inventar; gestionar
control: *n.* control
control: *v.* controlar
control account: cuenta de control

control board: tablero de control
control box: la caja de control
control code: código de control
control group: grupo de control
control joint: la junta de control
control material: material de control
control panel: tablero de control; panel de control
control rod: varilla de control
control room: sala de control
control unit: unidad de control
controlled: *adj.* controlado
controlled economy: economía dirigida
controlled experiment: experimento controlado
controlled price: precio controlado
controlled rate: tipo regulado
controller: *n.* inspector; controlador
controllership: *n.* auditoria; contraloría
controlling: *n.* determinante
controlling committee: consejo de vigilancia
controlling company: sociedad determinante
controlling interest: interés dominante
controversy: *n.* controversia; disputa
controvert: *v.* controvertir; disputar
contumacious: *adj.* contumaz
contumacy: *n.* contumacia
contusion: *n.* contusión
conundrum: *n.* adivinanza; rompecabezas
convalesce: *v.* convalecer
convalescence: *n.* convalecencia
convalescent: *adj.* convaleciente
convalescent home: casa de convalecencia
convalescent serum: suero de convaleciente
convection: *n.* convección
convection current: corriente de

convección
convection zone: zona de convección
convene: *v.* convocar; convenir; juntarse
convenience: *n.* comodidad; conveniencia
convenience items: artículos de conveniencia
convenor: *n.* coordinador
convent: *n.* convento
convention: *n.* convención; congreso; asamblea
conventional: *adj.* convencional
conventioneer: *n.* convencionista
converge: *v.* convergir
convergence: *n.* convergencia
convergent: *adj.* convergente
convergent boundary: borde convergente
conversant: *adj.* versado; entendido
conversation: *n.* conversación
conversationalist: *n.* conversador
converse: 1. *adj.* contrario; inverso; reciproco; 2. *n.* conversación
conversion: *n.* conversión; transformación
convert: *v.* convertir; canjear
converter: *n.* convertidor
convertible: *adj.* convertible; canjeable
convertible currency: moneda convertible
convertible debenture: obligación convertible
convertible security: título convertible
convertible share: acción convertible
convertible sofa: sofá-cama
convex: *adj.* convexo
convex lens: lente convexa
convex mirror: espejo convexo
convey: *v.* transportar; conducir

conveyance: *n.* transporte; cesión; traspaso
conveyer: *n.* transportador
conveyer belt: cinta transportadora
conveyor: la cinta transportadora
convict: *adj.* convicto
convict: *v.* probar la culpabilidad
conviction: *n.* convicción
convince: *v.* satisfacer
convivial: *adj.* jovial; sociable
convocation: *n.* convocatoria
convoke: *v.* convocar; citar
convulse: *v.* convulsionar; agitar
convulsion: *n.* convulsión
cook: *n.* cocinero (a)
cook: *v.* cocinar
cooker: *n.* cocina
cookie: *n.* pastelito de dulce
cool: *adj.* fresco; sereno
cool: *v.* enfriar
cooperate: *v.* cooperar
cooperation: *n.* cooperación
cooperative: *n.* cooperativa
cooperative bank: banco cooperativo
cooperative society: sociedad cooperativa
coordinate: *n.* coordenada
coordinate: *adj.* coordinado
coordinate: 1. *adj.* coordenado; (a); 2. *n.* coordenada
coordinate: *v.* coordinar
coordinate grid: cuadricula de coordenadas
coordinate plane: plano de coordenadas
coordinate system: sistema coordenado
coordinating: *adj.* coordinante
coordination: *n.* coordinación
coordinator: *n.* coordinador
co-owner: *n.* copropietario
co-ownership: *n.* copropiedad
Copenhagen: Copenhague

cophouse: *n.* caseta de herramientas
copier: *n.* fotocopiadora; copista
copilot: *n.* copiloto
coping saw: la sierra de arco
copious: *adj.* copioso
copiousness: *n.* abundancia
coplanar: *adj.* coplanario
copper: 1. *adj.* cobrizo; (color) cobre; 2. *n.* cobre
copper: *v.* cubrir o forrar con cobre
coppery: *adj.* cobrizo
copra: *n.* copra
coprolalia: *n.* coprolalia
copse: *n.* matorral
Coptic: *n.* Copto; -a
copula: *n.* cópula
copulate: *v.* unir; juntar
copulative: *adj.* copulativo
copy: *n.* copia; duplicado
copy: *v.* copiar
copy testing: prueba de texto
copybook: libro copiador; cuaderno
copyist: *n.* copista
copyright: *n.* derechos de autor
copywriter: *n.* redactor; redactor publicitario
coral: *n.* coral
coral reef: arrecife de coral
corbel: *n.* saledizo
cord: *n.* cordón; cordel; cuerda
cordial: *adj.* cordial
cordiality: *n.* cordialidad
cordless: *adj.* inalámbrico
cordless drill: el taladro portátil
Cordoba: *n.* córdoba
cordon: *n.* cordón
Cordova: Córdoba
Cordovan: *adj.* cordobés; -esa
core: *n.* centro; núcleo
core: *v.* quitar el corazón o centro
core business: negocio principal
Corfu: Corfú
Corian: la corrían
coriander: *n.* cilandro

Corinthian: *adj.* corintio
Coriolis effect: efecto de Coriolis
cork: *n.* corcho; tapa
cork oak: alcornoque
corkscrew: *n.* sacacorchos
corn: *n.* maíz
cornea: *n.* córnea
corned beef: carne de vaca en conserva
corner: *n.* ángulo; la esquina
corner: *v.* monopolizar; acaparar
cornering: *n.* monopolización; acaparamiento
cornet: *n.* corneta
cornetist: *n.* corneta
cornice: la cornisa
Cornish: *n.* córnico
cornu: *adj.* corno
Cornwall: Cornualles
corollary: *n.* corolario
coronary: 1. *adj.* coronario; 2. *n.* coronario
coronary artery: arteria coronaria
coronation: *n.* coronación
coronet: *n.* corona
corporal: *n.* corporal
corporate: *adj.* corporativo; colectivo
corporate address: sede de la sociedad
corporate asset: activo de la sociedad
corporate banking: banca mayorista
corporate books: libros de la sociedad
corporate capital: capital de la sociedad
corporate charter: acta de constitución
corporate debt: deuda de la sociedad
corporate enterprise: sociedad anónima
corporate image: imagen de la empresa
corporate law: derecho de sociedades
corporate liability: pasivo de la sociedad
corporate loan: préstamo a una sociedad
corporate name: razón social
corporate property: propiedad social
corporate purpose: objeto de la sociedad
corporate seal: sello de la sociedad
corporate share: acción de sociedad anónima
corporate shareholder: empresa accionista
corporate signature: firma social
corporate tax: impuesto a las sociedades
corporate trust: fideicomiso de sociedad anónima
corporate year: ejercicio social
corporation: *n.* sociedad; corporación
corporation charter: escritura de constitución
corporation law: ley de sociedades
corporation tax: impuesto a las sociedades
corporative: *adj.* corporativo
corporeal: *adj.* corpóreo
corps: *n.* cuerpo
corps de ballet: cuerpo de baile
corpse: *n.* cadáver
corpulence: *n.* corpulencia
corpulence: *n.* corpulencia
corpulent: *adj.* corpulento
corpus: *n.* cuerpo
corpus callosum: *n.* cuerpo calloso
corral: *adj.* corral
correct: *adj.* correcto
correct: *v.* corregir
correction: *n.* corrección

correction factor: factor de corrección
corrective: *adj.* correctivo
correctness: *n.* corrección
correlation: *n.* correlación
correlative: *adj.* correlativo
correspond: *v.* corresponder; escribirse
correspondence: *n.* correspondencia
correspondent: *adj.* correspondiente
corresponding angles: ángulos correspondientes
corresponding parts: elementos correspondientes
corridor: *n.* corredor
corroborate: *v.* corroborar; confirmar
corroboration: *n.* corroboración
corroborator: *n.* corroborante
corrode: *v.* morder
corrosion: *n.* corrosión
corrosive: *adj.* corrosivo
corrugated steel: el acero corrugado
corrupt: *adj.* corrupto; corrompido
corrupt: *vt.* corromper
corrupter: *n.* corruptor
corruption: *n.* corrupción
corsair: *n.* corsario
corselet: *n.* coselete
corset: *n.* corsé
Corsica: Córcega
Corsican: *adj.* corso; -a
cortege; cortêge: *n.* cortejo
cortex: *n.* corteza
corticosteroid: *n.* corticosteroide
corticosterone: *n.* corticosterona
cortisol: *n.* cortisol
cortisone: *n.* cortisona
coruscate: *v.* brillar; relampaguear
corvette: *n.* corbeta
coryza: *n.* coriza
cos end: extremo cos
cos site: centro cos
cosecant: *n.* cosecante

cosignatory: *n.* cosignatario
co-signature: firma conjunta
co-signer: *n.* cofirmante
cosine: *n.* coseno
cosmetic: *adj.* cosmético
cosmetologist: *n.* cosmetólogo
cosmetology: *n.* cosmetología; cosmética
cosmic background radiation: radiación cósmica de fondo
cosmid: *n.* cósmico
cosmogony: *n.* cosmogonía
cosmography: *n.* cosmografía
cosmology: *n.* cosmología
cosmonaut: *n.* cosmonauta
cosmopolitan: *n.* cosmopolita
cosmopolite: *n.* cosmopolita
cosmos: *n.* cosmos
cost: *n.* costo; costo
cost: *v.* costar; valer
cost accounting: contabilidad de costes
cost allocation: asignación de costes
cost and freight: costo y flete
cost apportionment: asignación de costos
cost calculation: cálculo de costos
cost centre: centro de costos
cost control: control de costos
cost curve: curva de costos
cost economy: economía de costos
cost evaluation: evaluación de costos
cost flow: flujo de costos
cost free: sin costos; sin cargo; sin gastos
cost inflation: inflación de costos
cost insurance and freight: costo; seguro y flete
cost of delivery: costo de entrega
cost of issue: costo de emisión
cost of living: costo de vida
cost of money: precio del dinero
cost of sales: costo de ventas

cost price: precio de costo
cost saving: economía de costos
cost structure: estructura de costos
cost; insurance and freight: costo;
seguro y flete
Costa Rica: Costa Rica
Costa Rican: *adj.* costarricense;
costarriqueño; -a
costal: *adj.* costal
cost-benefit analysis: análisis de
costo-beneficio
costing: costeo; cálculo de costos
costless: *adj.* de balde; gratis
costume: *n.* traje
cosy: *adj.* confortable
cot: *n.* catre; choza
cotangent: *n.* cotangente
co-tenant: coinquilino
coterie: *n.* grupo; cofradía
cotillion: *n.* cotillón
cottage: *n.* cabaña; casa de campo
cottager: *n.* veraneante; morador de
una choza
cotton: *n.* algodón
cotton wool: algodón
cotyledon: *n.* cotiledón
couch: el sofá
cough: *n.* tos
cough: *v.* toser
Cough syrup: remedio Para la tos
coulomb: *n.* culombio
coulometry: *n.* culombimetría
council: *n.* consejo; concilio; junta
council: *n.* concejo
councilor: *n.* concejal; consejero
councilman: *n.* concejal
councilwoman: *n.* concejala
counsel: *n.* consejo
counsel: *v.* asesorar; aconsejar
counseling services: servicios de
asesoramiento
counselor: *n.* consejero
count: *n.* cuenta; arqueo
count: *v.* contar; arquear

countable: *adj.* contable
countenance: *n.* semblante;
serenidad
counter: 1. *adj.* contrario; 2. *n.*
contador; mostrador
counter: *v.* oponerse a; devolver (un
golpe)
counter check: cheque de mostrador
counter-attack: contra-ataque
counterbid: *n.* contraoferta
counterbid: *v.* contraofertar
counterclockwise: contra las agujas
del reloj
counterculture: *n.* contracultura
counterentry: *n.* contrapartida
counterespionage: *n.*
contraespionaje
counterfeit: 1. *adj.* falso; 2. *n.*
falsificación
counterfeit: *v.* falsificar
counterfeit money: moneda falsa
counterfoil: *n.* talón (cheque)
counter-intelligence:
contrainteligencia
counterirritant: *n.* contrairritante
counter-offensive: contraofensiva
counter-offer: *n.* contraoferta
counter-offer: *v.* contraofertar
counterpane: *n.* cubrecama
counterpart: *n.* copia; duplicado
counterpoint: *n.* contrapunto
counterproductive: *adj.*
contraproducente
Counter-Reformation:
Contrarreforma
countersign: *n.* contraseña; consigna
countersign: *v.* refrendar
counter-signature: segunda firma
counterspy: *n.* contraespía
counterstain: *n.* contracoloración
countertop: la cubierta del
mostrador
countertranscript: *n.*
contratranscrito

counterweight: *n.* contrapeso
countess: *n.* condesa
counting chamber: cámara de recuento
counting principle: principio de conteo
countless: *adj.* incontable
country: *n.* país; patria
county: *n.* condado; partido; provincia
coup: *n.* golpe; jugada brillante
coupe: *n.* cupé
couple: *n.* matrimonio
couple: *v.* juntar
coupler: *n.* acoplador
couplet: *n.* copla
coupling: *n.* acoplamiento
coupon: *n.* cupón; talón
courage: *n.* coraje; valor
course: *n.* hilera; curso
court: *n.* corte
court: *v.* cortejar
court cost: costa judicial
court martial: *n.* consejo de guerra
court of appeal: tribunal de apelación
court of bankruptcy: tribunal de quiebras
court of justice: sala de justicia
court order: orden judicial
court proceeding: procedimiento judicial
court tribunal: juzgado
courteous: *adj.* cortés
courtesy: *n.* cortesía
courting: *n.* cortejo
courtship: *n.* cortejo
courtship behavior: comportamiento de cortejo; comportamiento
courtyard: *n.* patio
couscous: *n.* couscous
cousin: *n.* primo; prima
covalent bond: enlace covalente

covariance: *n.* covariancia
covenant: *n.* convenio; pacto
covenant: *v.* pactar
cover: *n.* cubierta
coverage: *n.* cobertura; protección
covered: *adj.* cubierto
covering: *n.* cubierta; techado
covert: *n.* escondrijo; asilo
covet: *v.* codiciar
cow: *n.* vaca
cow: *v.* acobardar
coward: 1. *adj.* cobarde; gallina; 2. *n.* gallina
coward: *n.* cobarde
cowardice: *n.* cobardía
cowardly: *adj.* cobarde; *adv.* cobardemente
cowboy: *n.* cowboy; vaquero
cower: *v.* agacharse
coxcomb: *n.* fanfarrón
coxswain: *n.* timonel; patrón
coy: *adj.* recatado
coy: *v.* acariciar; halagar
coyote: *n.* coyote
crack: *n.* grieta; crac
crack: *v.* agrietar; agrietarse
cracked: *adj.* agrietado
cracker: *n.* galleta
crackle: *n.* crujido
crackle: *v.* crujir
cradle: *n.* cuna
cradle: *v.* acunar
craft: *n.* arte; artesanía
craftsman: *n.* artesano
crafty: 1. *adj.* astuto; pícaro
crag: *n.* peñasco
Crakow: Cracovia
cram: *v.* embutir; hartar
cramp: 1. *adj.* apretado; 2. *n.* grapa; calambre
cramp: *v.* engrapar; apretar
crane: *n.* grúa
cranial nerves: nervios craneales
craniotomy: *n.* craniotomía

cranium: *n.* cráneo
crank: 1. *adj.* inestable; 2. *n.* biela
crank: *v.* acodar
craps: *n.* estupidez
crapulence: *n.* crápula
crash: *n.* quiebra; hendidura
crash: *v.* quebrar
crash course: curso intensivo
crash program: programa intensivo
crass: *adj.* craso
crater: *n.* cráter
crave: *v.* ansiar; suplicar
crawl: *n.* marcha lenta; arrastre
crawl: *v.* trepar; arrastrarse
Crawling sensation: algo se arrastra por su piel
crayon: *n.* lápiz
crayon: *v.* dibujar a lápiz
craze: *n.* moda; locura
craze: *v.* enloquecer
crazy: *adj.* loco; insensato
cream: *n.* crema
creamery: *n.* mantequería; lechería
creamy: *adj.* cremoso
crease: *n.* arruga
crease: *v.* arrugar; plegarse
create: *v.* crear; criar; causar
creatinase: *n.* creatinasa
creatine: *n.* creatina
creatine kinase: creatin-quinasa
creatininase: *n.* creatininasa
creatinine: *n.* creatinina
creatinine clearance: depuración de creatinina
creation: *n.* creación
creationism: *n.* creacionismo
creative: *adj.* creativo
creativity: *n.* creatividad
creator: *n.* creador
Creator: *n.* Creador
credibility: *n.* credibilidad
credible: *adj.* creíble
credit: *n.* crédito
credit: *v.* abonar

credit account: cuenta de crédito
credit advice: aviso de crédito
credit analysis: análisis de créditos
credit analyst: analista de créditos
credit balance: saldo acreedor
credit bank: banco de crédito
credit broker: intermediario financiero
credit card: tarjeta de crédito
credit department: departamento de créditos
credit director: director de créditos
credit entry: asiento de crédito
credit institution: entidad de crédito
credit instrument: instrumento de crédito
credit limit: límite de crédito
credit line: línea de crédito
credit manager: director de créditos
credit memorandum: nota de abono
credit note: nota de abono
credit portfolio: cartera de créditos
credit purchase: compra a crédito
credit rating: calificación crediticia
credit report: informe crediticio
credit restriction: restricción crediticia
credit risk: riesgo crediticio
credit sale: venta a crédito
credit union: cooperativa de crédito
creditable: *adj.* honorable
creditor: *n.* acreedor
creditworthiness: *n.* solvencia
creditworthy: *adj.* solvente
credo; creed: *n.* credo
creed: *n.* credo
creek: *n.* arroyo
creeping sensation: algo se arrastra por su piel
cremate: *v.* incinerar
cremation: *n.* cremación
crematorium: *n.* crematorio
Creole: *n.* criollo
Creole: 1. a criollo; 2. *n.* criollo

creosote: *n.* creosota
crepe: *n.* crepé; crespón
crepe; crêpe: *n.* crepa
crepitation: *n.* crepitación
crescendo: *n.* crescendo
crest: *n.* cresta
crest: *v.* encrestarse
crestfallen: *adj.* cabizbajo
Cretan: *adj.* cretense
Crete: Creta
cretin: *adj.* cretino
cretinism: *n.* cretinismo
cretonne: *n.* cretona
crevice: *n.* grieta
crew: *n.* equipo
crew leader: jefe de cuadrilla
crib: *n.* pesebre; cuna
crick: *n.* calambre
cricket: *n.* críquet; grillo
crier: *n.* pregonero
crime: *n.* delito; crimen
crime: *n.* crimen
Crimea: Crimea
criminal: *adj.* criminal
criminalist: *n.* criminalista
criminologist: *n.* criminalista
criminology: *n.* criminología
crinoline: *n.* crinolina
cripple: 1. *adj.* lisiado; 2. *n.* lisiado
cripple: *v.* lisiar; baldar
crippled: *adj.* lisiado; impedido
crisis: *n.* crisis
crisp: *adj.* frágil
crisp: *v.* encrespar
criterion: *n.* criterio
critic: *n.* crítico; -a
critical: *adj.* crítico
critical mass: masa crítica
critical night length: longitud nocturna crítica
critical point: el punto crítico
critical-path method: método del camino crítico
criticize: *v.* criticar; censurar

criticism: *n.* crítica
critique: *n.* crítica
croak: *n.* graznido
Croat; Croatian: *adj.* croata
Croatia: Croacia
crochet: *n.* crochet; croché
crockery: *n.* loza
crocodile: *n.* cocodrilo
crocus: *n.* croco
croissant: *n.* croissant
cro-magnon: cromañón
crook: *n.* gancho
crook: *v.* encorvar
crooked: *adj.* encorvado
crop: *n.* cultivo; cosecha; buche (de ave)
crop insurance: seguro de cosechas
crop rotation: rotación de cultivos
crop sharing: reparto de cosecha
croquet: *n.* croquet
croquette: *n.* croqueta
crosier: *n.* cayado
cross: 1. *adj.* cruzado; 2. *n.* cruz; cruce
cross: *v.* cruzar; contrariar
cross examination: interrogar
cross products: productos cruzados
cross products property: propiedad de los productos cruzados
cross reaction: reacción cruzada
cross refer: referir
cross section: muestra representativa
cross-bar: travesaño
crossbred: *adj.* cruzado
cross-country: cross-country
crosscurrent: contracorriente
crossed check: cheque cruzado
cross-examine: interrogar rigurosamente
crossing: *n.* cruce; travesía; crucero
crossing-over: entrecruzamiento
crossover: *n.* cruzamiento
crossover fixation: fijación entrecruzada

crossroad: *n.* encrucijada
crosswise: *adv.* en cruz; al través
crossword: *n.* crucigrama
crossword puzzle: crucigrama
croton: *n.* croto
crouch: *n.* grajo
crouch: *v.* agacharse; rebajarse
croup: *n.* crup
croupier: *n.* crupié; crupier
crouton: *n.* crutón
crowbar: *n.* palanca
crowd: *n.* gentío
crowd: *v.* apilar
crown: *n.* corona; coronilla
crown prince: príncipe heredero
crowning: *n.* coronación
crucial: *adj.* crucial
crucifix: *n.* crucifijo
crude oil: petróleo crudo
cruel: *adj.* cruel
cruelty: *n.* crueldad
cruise: *n.* crucero
cruise: *v.* navegar
cruise missile: misil de crucero
crumb: *n.* miga; pan rallado
crumble: *v.* desmenuzar;
desmoronarse
crumpet: *n.* bollo blando
crunch: *v.* mascar
crusade: *n.* cruzada
Crusade: *n.* cruzada
crush: *n.* estrujadura
crush: *v.* estrujar; aplastar
crust: *n.* corteza
crustacean: *n.* crustáceo
crutches: *n.* muletas
cruzeiro: *n.* cruzeiro
cry: *n.* grito; lamento
cryoanesthesia: *n.* crioanestesia
cryobiology: *n.* criobiología
cryogen: *n.* criógeno
cryogenics: *n.* criogenia
cryoglobulin: *n.* crioglobulina
cryoprecipitable protein: proteína

crioprecipitable
cryosurgery: *n.* criocirugía
crypt: *n.* cripta
cryptic: *adj.* críptico
cryptical: *adj.* secreto; escondido
cryptogam: *n.* criptogama
cryptogram: *n.* criptograma
cryptographer: *n.* criptógrafo
cryptography: *n.* criptografía;
criptograma
crystal: 1. *n.* cristal; 2. *adj.* cristal
crystal ball: bola de cristal
crystalline solid: sólido cristalino
crystallization: *n.* cristalización
crystallography: *n.* cristalografía
crystaloid: *adj.* cristaloide
CT: computada
cub: *n.* cachorro; ballenato
Cuba: Cuba
Cuban: *adj.* cubano; -a
Cubanism: *n.* cubanismo
cube: *n.* cubo
cube: *v.* cubicar
cubed: *adj.* elevado al cubo
cubic: *adj.* cúbico
cubic centimeter: centímetro cúbico
cubicle: *n.* cubículo
cubism: *n.* cubismo
cubist: *n.* cubista
cuckoo: *n.* cuco
cuddle: *n.* abrazo cariñoso
cuddle: *v.* abrazar con cariño
cue: *n.* puntal; apunte
cue ball: bola blanca
cuff: *n.* bofetada
cuff: *v.* abofetear
culdocentesis: *n.* culdocentesis
culinary: *adj.* culinario
cull: *v.* entresacar
culmination: *n.* culminación
culpability: *n.* culpabilidad
culprit: *adj.* culpable
cult: *n.* culto; secta
cultivate: *v.* cultivar

cultivation: *n.* cultivo
cultivator: *n.* cultivador (a)
culture: *n.* cultura; cultivo
culture: *v.* cultivar; educar
culture medium: medio de cultivo
culture shock: choque de culturas
cultured: *adj.* cultivado
cum laude: cum laude
cumin: *n.* comino
cumulate: *v.* acumular
cumulative: *adj.* acumulativo; cumulativo
cumulative letter of credit: carta de crédito acumulativa
cumulative share: acción acumulativa
cumulonimbus: *n.* cumulonimbo
cumulus: *n.* cúmulo
cuneiform: *adj.* cuneiforme
cunning: 1. *adj.* mafioso; 2. *n.* astucia
cup: *n.* copa; taza
cupboard: *n.* aparador
cupidity: *n.* codicia
curable: *adj.* curable
Curacao: Curazao
curare: *n.* curare
curate: *n.* cura
curb: *n.* freno
curd: *n.* cuajada
curd: *v.* cuajar
cure: *n.* cura; remedio
cure: *v.* curar; remediar
cure-all: *n.* curalotodo
curette: *n.* cureta
curettage: *n.* curetaje; raspado
curfew: *n.* toque de queda
curing: *n.* curación
curio: *n.* curiosidad
curiosity: *n.* curiosidad
curious: *adj.* curioso
curling: *n.* ensortijamiento; abarquillamiento
curling: *n.* tenacillas

currant: *n.* uva pasa de corinto
currency: *n.* moneda corriente
currency depreciation: depreciación monetaria
currency devaluation: devaluación monetaria
currency divisa: moneda
currency flight: fuga de divisas
currency flow: flujo de divisas
currency market: mercado de divisas
current: 1. *n.* corriente; 2. *adj.* corriente
current: *adj.* corriente
current account: cuenta corriente
current asset: activo corriente
current debt: deuda corriente
current expense: gasto corriente
current investment: inversión corriente
current liabilities: pasivo exigible; pasivo corriente
current liquidity: liquidez corriente
current market value: valor actual en el mercado
current maturity: vencimiento a corto plazo
current money: moneda corriente
current price: precio corriente
current rate: interés actual
current receivable: cuenta a cobrar a corto plazo
current year: año actual
curriculum: *n.* currículo; plan de estudios
curriculum vitae: curriculum vitae
curry: condimento de origen indio; curry; cari
curse: n maleficio
curse: *v.* maldecir
cursive script: cursiva
cursor: *n.* cursor
cursory: *adj.* superficial; hecho de pasada

curt: *adj.* corto; conciso
curtail: *v.* acortar; reducir
curtain: *n.* cortina
curtain: *v.* poner cortinas
curvature: *n.* curvatura
curve: 1. *adj.* curvo; 2. *n.* curva
curve: *v.* encorvar
curved: *adj.* curvo
curvilinear: *adj.* curvilíneo
cushion: *n.* cojín; almohadón
cusp: *n.* cúspide
custard: *n.* natillas
custodial care: cuidado custodial
custodian: *n.* guardián
custodian account: cuenta de custodia
custody: *n.* custodia; in custodia en prisión
custody account: cuenta de custodia
custody fee: comisión de custodia
custody security: título en custodia
custom: *n.* costumbre; hábito; aduana
customary: *adj.* habitual; común
customer: *n.* cliente
customer training: formación para clientes
customhouse; customs house: aduana; edificio de la aduana
customize: *v.* construir
custom-made: hecho a medida; hecho por encargo
customs: *n.* aduana; derechos de aduana
customs agent: transitario; agente de aduanas
customs broker: despachante de aduana; agente de aduana
customs certificate: certificado de aduana
customs clearance: despacho de aduana
customs collector: recaudador de aduana

customs court: tribunal de aduanas
customs declaration: declaración de aduana
customs duties: derecho de aduana
customs exempt: exento de derechos aduaneros
customs exemption: exención de derechos aduaneros
customs forwarder: transitario
customs free: libre de aduana
customs inspector: inspector de aduana
customs officer: oficial de aduana
customs quota: cuota de aduana
customs receipts: recibos de aduana
customs regulations: reglamento de aduana
customs tariff: tarifa de aduana
customs union: sindicato de trabajadores de aduana
cut: *n.* corte; rebaja
cut: *v.* cortar; rebajar
cuticle: *n.* cutícula
cutis: *n.* cutis
cut-off point: valor discriminante
cut-off rate: tasa de equilibrio
cut-price: de precio reducido; con descuento
cutting enzyme: enzima cortadora
cutting sequence: secuencia de corte
cyanosis: *n.* cianosis
cybernetic: *adj.* cibernético
cybernetics: *n.* cibernética
cyberspace: *n.* espacio cibernético; ciberespacio
cybrid: *adj.* cíbrido
cycad: *n.* cicadacea
cyclamen: *n.* ciclamen; ciclamino
cycle: *n.* ciclo
cyclic: *adj.* cíclico
cyclical: *adj.* cíclico
cycling: *n.* ciclismo
cyclist: *n.* ciclista
cycloid: *adj.* cicloide

cyclone: *n.* ciclón
cyclorama: *n.* ciclorama
cyclosporin: *n.* ciclosporina
cyclosporine: *n.* ciclosporina
cyclotron: *n.* ciclotrón
cylinder: *n.* cilindro
cylinder capacity: cilindrada
cylindrical: *adj.* cilíndrico
cylindruria: *n.* cilindruria
cymbal: *n.* címbalo
cynic: *n.* cínico; -a
cynical: *adj.* cínico
cynicism: *n.* cinismo
cypress: *n.* ciprés
Cypriot: *adj.* chipriota
Cyprus: Chipre
Cyrillic: *adj.* cirílico
cyst: *n.* quiste
cystectomy: *n.* ciscectomía
cysteine: *n.* cisteína
cystic fibrosis: fibrosis cística
cystine: *n.* cistina
cystitis: *n.* cistitis
cystocele: *n.* ciscocele
cystoscope: *n.* ciscoscopio
cystoscopy: *n.* ciscoscopia
cytidine: *n.* citidina
cytochemistry: *n.* citoquímica
cytochrome: *n.* citocromo
cytogenetics: *n.* citogenética
cytokinesis: *n.* citocinesis
cytology: *n.* citología
cytometry: *n.* citometría
cytopathic effect: efecto citopático
cytopathology: *n.* citopatología
cytoplasm: *n.* citoplasma
cytosine: *n.* citosina
Czech: *n.* checo
Czech: *adj.* checo; -a
Czech Republic: Republica Checa

D

dab: *n.* golpecito
dab: *v.* golpear
dabble: *v.* salpicar; rociar
dacron: *n.* dacrón
dactyl: *n.* dáctilo
dactylography: *n.* dactilografía
dad: *n.* papá
dadaism: *n.* dadaísmo
dado: *n.* dado
daft: *adj.* chiflado; tonto; bobo
dagger: *n.* daga
daguerreotype: *n.* daguerrotipo
dahlia: *n.* dalia
daily: 1. *adj.* diario; 2. *adv.*
diariamente
daily maintenance: manutención
diaria
daily report: parte diario; informe
diario
daintiness: *n.* dolosina
daiquiri: *n.* daikiri; daiquiri
dairy: 1. *adj.* lácteo; 2. *n.* granja
lechera
dairy farm: granja lechera
dairy product: producto lácteo
dais: *n.* estrado
dalai lama: dalai lama
dale: *n.* valle; cañada
daltonism: *n.* daltonismo
dam: *n.* pantano\
dam: *v.* embalsar
damage: *n.* daño; siniestro
damage: *v.* dañar; averiar
Damascus: Damasco
damask: *n.* damasco
dame: *n.* dama; ama
damn: *v.* condenar
damp: *adj.* húmedo; humedad;
damp: *v.* humedecer; abatir;

desanimar
damsel: *n.* señorita
dance: *n.* danza
dancer: *n.* danzante
danger: *n.* peligro
danger: *v.* colgar
Danish: *n.* danés; dinamarqués
Danube: Danubio
danza: *n.* danza
dapper: *adj.* aseado
Dardanelles: Dardanelos
daring: 1. *adj.* atrevido; 2. *n.* atrevimiento
dark energy: energía negra
dark matter: materia negra
darken: *v.* oscurecer
darkness: *n.* oscuridad
darling: 1. *adj.* querido; 2. *n.* amor
darnel: *n.* cizaña
dart: *n.* dardo
dart: *v.* lanzar
dash: *n.* colisión
dash: *v.* lanzar
data: *n.* datos; información
data bank: banco de datos
data base: base de datos
data center: centro de datos
data processing: procesamiento de datos
data processor: procesador de datos
data protection: protección de datos
data transmission: transmisión de datos
database: *n.* base de datos
date: fecha; cita
date: *v.* datar; poner
date of delivery: fecha de entrega
date of issue: fecha de emisión
date of record: fecha de registro
date palm: datilera
dated security: título a plazo; título a fecha
dateline: *n.* data
dative: *adj.* dativo

datum: *n.* dato
datura: *n.* datura
daughter: *n.* hija
daughter-in-law: nuera
daunt: *v.* espantar
dawdle: *v.* malgastar
dawn: *n.* amanecer
day: *n.* día
day labor: trabajo a jornal
day laborer: jornalero
day of grace: día de gracia
day off: día libre
day rate: tarifa por día; paga por día
day shift: turno diurno
day wage: jornal; jornada
day-book: libro diario
daylight: *n.* luz del día
day-neutral plant: planta de día neutro
days of the week: días de la semana
daytime: *adv.* día
dazzle: *v.* deslumbrar
de facto: de facto; de hecho
deacon: *n.* diácono
deaconess: *n.* diaconisa
deaconry: *n.* diaconado; diaconato
dead: *adj.* muerto; inactivo
dead account: cuenta inactiva
dead load: carga muerta
dead rent: alquiler fijo
dead time: tiempo improductivo
dead toll: tabla de mortandad
dead tonnage: tonelaje de carga
dead weight: peso muerto
dead/out of service: fuera de servicio
deadline: *n.* vencimiento
deadlock: *v.* estancar
deaf: *adj.* sordo
deafen: *v.* ensordecer
deafness: *n.* sordera
deal: *n.* trato; convenio
deal: *v.* traficar; tratar
dealer: *n.* traficante; vendedor

dealer network: red de distribuidores
dealership: *n.* concesión
dealing: *n.* tráfico; comercio
dean: *n.* decano
dear: *adj.* querido; costoso
dearth: *n.* escasez
death: *n.* muerte
death benefit: indemnización por muerte
death certificate: certificado de defunción
death duty: impuesto de sucesión
death indemnification: indemnización por muerte
death rate: tasa de mortalidad
death tax: impuesto de sucesión
debacle: *n.* debacle
debar: *v.* excluir; prohibir
debark: *v.* desembarcar
debase: *v.* rebajar; degradar
debate: *n.* debate
debauch: *n.* libertinaje
debauch: *v.* seducir
debenture: *n.* bono de deuda
debilitate: *v.* debilitar
debilitating: *adj.* debilitante
debility: *n.* debilidad
debit: n débito; cargo; debe
debit: *v.* debitar; cargar; adeudar
debit advice: aviso de débito
debit balance: saldo deudor
debit card: tarjeta de débito
debit limit: límite de endeudamiento
debit note: nota de débito
debouch: *v.* desembocar
debris: *n.* ruinas; escombros
debt: *n.* deuda
debt collector: cobrador
debt due: deuda exigible
debt of record: deuda registrada
debt receivable: deuda exigible
debt service: servicio de una deuda
debtor: *n.* deudor

debunk: *v.* desbaratar
debutante: *n.* debutante
decade: *n.* década; decenio; acacia
decadent: *adj.* decadente
decadic absorbance: absorbancia decimal
decadic attenuance: atenuancia decimal
decaffeinated: *adj.* descafeinado
decagon: *n.* decágono
decalcification: *n.* descalcificación
decameter: *n.* decámetro
decamp: *v.* largarse
decanter: *n.* decantador; garrafa
decapitalization: *n.* descapitalización
decapitalize: *v.* descapitalizar
decapitation: *n.* decapitación
decathlon: *n.* decatlón
decay: *n.* podredumbre
decay: *v.* pudrir
decay constant: constante de desintegración
decayed tooth: diente dañado
decease: *n.* deceso
decease: *v.* fallecer
deceased: difunto; finado; fallecido
deceit: *n.* engaño
deceleration: *n.* deceleración
December: *n.* diciembre
decency: *n.* decencia
decennial: *n.* aniversario decenal
decennial: *adj.* decenal
decennium: *n.* decenio
decent: *adj.* decente
decentralization: *n.* descentralización
decentralize: *v.* descentralizar
decentralized company: empresa descentralizada
decentralized management: administración. descentralizada
decentralized office: oficina descentralizada

deceptive: *adj.* engañoso
decibel (dB): *n.* decibel (dB)
decide: *v.* decidir
decidua: *n.* decidua
deciduous (tree): *adj.* deciduo
deciduous tree: árbol caducifolio
decigram: *n.* decigramo
deciliter: *n.* decilitro
decimal: 1. *adj.* decimal; 2. *n.* decimal
decimal currency: moneda de sistema decimal
decimal digit: dígito decimal
decimal fraction: fracción decimal
decimal place: posición decimal
decimal point: punto decimal
decimal system: sistema decimal
decimeter: *n.* decímetro
decipher: *v.* descifrar
decipherer: *n.* descifrador; -a
decipherment: *n.* descifre
decision: *n.* decisión
decision making: toma de decisiones
decision taking: toma de decisiones
decking screws: los tornillos de terraza
declaim: *v.* declamar
declaimer: *n.* declamador (a)
declamation: *n.* declamación
declaration: *n.* declaración; manifestación
declaration of assets: manifestación de bienes
declaration of bankruptcy: declaración de quiebra
declarative: *adj.* declarativo
declaratory: *adj.* declaratorio
declare: *v.* declarar; confesar
declared capital: capital declarado
declared income: ingresos declarados
declared profit: ganancia declarada
declared value: valor declarado
declension: *n.* declinación

declivity: *n.* declive
decode: *v.* descodificar; descifrar
decoder: *n.* decodificador; descodificador
decolorization: *n.* descoloramiento
decolorizer: *n.* decolorante
decompose: *v.* descomponer
decomposer: *n.* descomponedor
decomposition: *n.* descomposición
decompression: *n.* descompresión
decongestant: *n.* descongestivo
decontamination: *n.* descontaminación
decor: *n.* decorado
decorate: *v.* decorar
decorated: decorado
decoration: *n.* decoración
decorative: *adj.* decorativo
decorator: *n.* decorador
decorum: *n.* decoro
Decoy: 1. *n.* reclamo
decoy: *v.* atraer
decrease: *n.* disminución; baja
decrease: *v.* disminuir; decrementar
decreasing: decreciente
decreasing-charge: depreciación-amortización
decree: *n.* decreto; ley
decree: *v.* decretar
decrement: *n.* decremento
decrepit: *adj.* caduco
decrepitude: *n.* decrepitud
decrescendo: *adj.* decrescendo
decrown: *v.* destronar
decry: *v.* desacreditar
dedicate: *v.* dedicar
dedicated: *adj.* dedicado
dedication: *n.* dedicación; dedicatoria
dedication: *n.* dedicación
deduce: *v.* deducir
deduct: *v.* restar; deducir
deductible: *n.* deducible
deductible expense: gasto deducible

deduction: *n.* deducción; rebaja
deed: *n.* hecho; proeza
deed escritura: título de propiedad
deed of arrangement: concordato
deed of assignment: escritura de cesión
deed of conveyance: escritura de traspaso
deed of partnership: contrato de sociedad
deed of sale: escritura de venta
deem: *v.* atribuir; pensar; considerar
deemable income: ingreso atribuible
deemed child: hijo atribuido
deemed income: ingreso atribuido
deep: *adj.* profundo; serio; absorto
deep breath: respiración profunda
deepen: *v.* profundizar
deep-freeze: *n.* congeladora
deep-freeze: *v.* congelar
deeply: *adv.* profundamente
deep-ocean trench: fosa oceánica profunda
deer: *n.* ciervo
deface: *v.* desfigurar
defalcate: *v.* desfalcar
defalcation: *n.* desfalco
defamation: *n.* difamación
defame: *v.* difamar
defamer: *n.* difamador
default: *n.* incomparecencia; mora
default: *v.* no comparecer; faltar al pago
default value: valor por defecto
defeat: *n.* derrota; anulación
defeat: *v.* derrotar; vencer
defecation: *n.* defecación
defect: *adj.* defecto
defection: *n.* defección
defective: *adj.* defectivo
defective phage: fago defectuoso
defend: *v.* defender
defender: *n.* defensor
defense: *n.* defensa

defer: *v.* diferir; remitir
deference: *n.* deferencia
deferential: *adj.* deferente
deferment: *n.* aplazamiento; diferimiento
deferral: *n.* aplazamiento
deferred: *adj.* diferido; aplazado
deferred asset: activo diferido
deferred charge: cargo diferido
deferred collection: cobro diferido
deferred compensation: compensación diferida
deferred credit: crédito diferido
deferred expense: gasto diferido
deferred liability: pasivo diferido
deferred payment: pago diferido; pago a plazo
deferred share: acción diferida
deferred tax: impuesto diferido
defiance: *n.* desafió; reto
defiant: *adj.* desafiante
defibrillation: *n.* desfibrilación
deficiency: *n.* deficiencia; déficit
deficient: *adj.* deficiente
deficit: *n.* déficit
defile: *v.* manchar; deshonra
define: *v.* definir
definite: *adj.* definido
definite integral: integral definida
definition: *n.* definición
definitive: *adj.* definitivo
definitive host: huésped definitivo
definitive measurement procedure: procedimiento de medida definitivo
definitive method: método definitivo
definitive value: valor definitivo
deflate: *v.* desinflar
deflation: *n.* deflación
deflect: *v.* desviar
deflection: *n.* deflexión
deflower: *v.* violar
deforest: *v.* talar bosques
deforestation: *n.* deforestación

deform: *v.* deformar
deformity: *n.* deformidad
defraud: *v.* defraudar; estafar
defraudation: *n.* defraudación; fraude; estafa
defrauder: *n.* defraudador
defray: *v.* costear
defrost: *v.* deshelar
defroster: el descongelador
deft: *n.* ágil; hábil
defunct: *adj.* difunto
defy: *v.* desafiar; despreciar
degenerate: *v.* degenerar
degenerate: *adj.* degenerado; -a
degeneration: *n.* degeneración
degenerative: *adj.* degenerativo
degradation: *n.* degradación
degrade: *v.* degradar
degree: *n.* grado; categoría
degree of dissociation: grado de disociación
dehumidifier: *n.* deshumedecedor
dehydration: *n.* deshidratación
deicide (god killing): *n.* deicidio
deification: *n.* deificación
deism: *n.* deísmo
deity: *n.* deidad; divinidad
deject: *v.* abatir
delay: *n.* atraso; demora; retraso
delay: *v.* retrasar; atrasar; dilatar; aplazar
delayed: *adj.* atrasado; retrasado
delayed birth certificate: acta de nacimiento demorada
delayed retirement credits: créditos por jubilación demorada
delegate: *n.* delegado
delegate: *v.* delegar
delegation: *n.* delegación
delete: *v.* borrar; suprimir
deleterious mutation: mutación deletérea
deletion: *n.* borrón
delft: *n.* pieza de cerámica estilo deft

deliberate: *v.* reflexionar
deliberation: *n.* deliberación
delicate: *adj.* delicado; fino; educado; enfermizo
delicious: *adj.* delicioso
delight: *n.* deleite
delight: *v.* deleitar; encantar
delimitation: *n.* delimitación
delimiter: *n.* símbolo delimitador
delineation: *n.* delineación
delinquency: *n.* delincuencia
delinquency interest: interés por mora
delinquent: *adj.* delincuente; moroso
delinquent debtor: deudor moroso
delirium: *n.* delirio
delirium tremens: delirium tremens
deliver: *v.* remitir; enviar; expedir
delivery: *n.* remesa; envío; expedición
delivery cost: costo de entrega
delivery date: fecha de entrega
delivery fee: costo de entrega; tarifa por entrega
delivery note: albarán; nota de entrega
delivery order: orden de entrega
delivery period: plazo de entrega
delivery price: precio de entrega
delivery time: horario de entrega
delivery truck: camión de reparto
delivery van: furgoneta de reparto
dell: *n.* hondonada
delphinium: *n.* delfinio
delta: *n.* delta
deltoid: *n.* deltoides
delude: *v.* engañar
deluge: *n.* diluvio; inundación
deluxe: *adj.* de lujo
delve: *v.* cavar; ahondar
demagogue: *adj.* demagogo
demand: *n.* demanda
demand: *v.* demandar
demand curve: curva de demanda

demand deposit: depósito exigible
demand draft: giro exigible
demand inflation: inflación de demanda
demand letter of credit: carta de crédito a la vista
demand liability: obligación exigible
demand loan: préstamo exigible
demand note: pagaré exigible
demandable: *adj.* exigible
demarcation: *n.* demarcación
demean: *v.* rebajar
dementia: *n.* demencia
demerit: *adj.* demérito
demilitarization: *n.* desmilitarización
demise: *n.* muerte; transmisión de la corona
demit: *v.* dimitir; renunciar
demobilization: *n.* desmovilización
democracy: *n.* democracia
democrat: *n.* demócrata
demographer: *n.* demógrafo
demography: *n.* demografía
demolish: *v.* demoler
demon: 1. *n.* demonio; 2. *adj.* endemoniado
demonetization: *n.* desmonetización
demonetize: *v.* desmonetizar
demonism: *n.* demonismo
demonology: *n.* demonología
demonstrate: *v.* demostrar
demonstrated: *adj.* demostrado
demonstration: *n.* demostración; manifestación
demonstrative: *adj.* demostrativo
demonstrator: *n.* demostrador; expositor
demoralization: *n.* desmoralización
demoralize: *v.* desmoralizar
demote: *v.* degradar
demount: *v.* desmontar
demur: *n.* demora; objeción

demur: *v.* aplazar
den: *n.* caverna; antro
denarius: *n.* denario
denationalization: *n.* desnacionalización
denationalize: *v.* desnacionalizar
denaturation: *n.* desnaturalización
dendochronology: *n.* dendocronología
dendrite: *n.* dendrita
dendrology: *n.* dendrología
dengue: *n.* dengue
denial: *n.* negación
denial letter: carta de denegación
denial notice: aviso de denegación
denigrating: *adj.* denigrante
denigration: *n.* denigración
denigrator: *n.* denigrador; denigrante
denizen: *n.* habitante
Denmark: Dinamarca
denominate: *v.* denominar
denomination: *n.* denominación; valor
denominator: *n.* denominador
denotative: *adj.* denotativo
denote: *v.* indicar; significar
denounce: *v.* denunciar; amenazar
densitometer: *n.* densitómetro
density: *n.* densidad
dent: *n.* hueco
dent: *v.* abollar; mellar
dental: *adj.* dental
dental care: cuidado dental
dental cavity: diente cariado
dented: *adj.* abollado
dentine: *n.* dentina
dentist: *n.* dentista
denture: *n.* dentadura
denude: *v.* desnudar
denunciate: *v.* denunciar
denunciation: *n.* denuncia; denunciación
deny: *v.* negar; contradecir

deodorant: 1. *n.* desodorante;
2. *adj.* desodorante
deoxyadenosine: *n.* desoxiadenosina
deoxyribonucleic: *adj.*
desoxirribonucleico
depart: *v.* dejar; abandonar
departed: 1. *n.* difunto; 2. *adj.*
difunto
department: *n.* departamento
department director: director de
departamento
department manager: director de
departamento
department stores: grandes tiendas
depend: *v.* depender; colgar
dependent: 1. *n.* dependiente; 2. *adj.*
dependiente
dependency: *n.* dependencia
dependency and support:
dependencia y mantenimiento
dependent events: sucesos
dependientes
dependents benefit: asignación por
dependientes
depict: *v.* pintar; representar;
describir
depilate: *v.* depilar
depilation: *n.* depilación
depilatory: *adj.* depilatorio
depilatory: *n.* depilatorio
depletable asset: activo agotable;
activo consumible
deplete: *v.* agotar
depleted: *adj.* agotado
depletion: *n.* agotamiento;
reducción; disminución
deplorable: *adj.* deplorable
deplore: *v.* deplorar
deploy: *v.* desplegar
deponent: *n.* deponente
Depo-Provera shot: inyección de
Depo-Provera
depo-provera shot: inyección de
depo-provera

depopulate: *v.* despoblar
deport: *v.* deportar
deportation: *n.* deportación
deportee: *n.* deportado
deportment: *n.* comportamiento;
conducta
depose: *v.* deponer
deposit: *n.* depósito; ingreso
deposit: *v.* ingresar; depositar
deposit account: cuenta de ahorro a
plazo fijo
deposit certificate: certificado de
depósito
deposit in escrow: depósito en
garantía
deposit slip: comprobante de
depósito
depositary: *n.* depositario
depositary bond: fianza de depósito
deposition: *n.* deposición
depositor: *n.* depositante
depot: *n.* almacén; depósito
deprave: *v.* corromper; adulterar
depraved: *adj.* depravado
depravity: *n.* depravación
deprecate: *v.* desaprobar; censurar
depreciable: *adj.* depreciable;
amortizable
depreciable asset: activo
depreciable; activo amortizable
depreciate: *v.* depreciar; amortizar
depreciated value: valor depreciado
depreciation: *n.* depreciación;
desvalorización; . amortización
depreciation allowance: previsión
para depreciación
depreciation base: base de
depreciación
depreciation fund: fondo para
depreciación
depreciation period: período de
amortización
depreciation policy: política de
depreciación

depreciation rate: tasa de depreciación
depreciation reserve: reserva para amortizaciones
depreciation schedule: tabla de amortización
depreciation value: valor depreciable
depress: *v.* deprimir; abatir
depressant: *n.* sustancia depresora
depressed: *adj.* deprimido
depression: *n.* depresión
depressor: *n.* depresor
deprivation: *n.* privación; deshabituación
deprive: *v.* privar; despojar
depth: *n.* profundidad
depurate: *v.* depurar
deputy: *n.* delegado; suplente; diputado
deputy commissioner: comisionado adjunto
derby: *n.* derby
derepression: *n.* derepresión
deride: *v.* ridiculizar
derisory: *adj.* irrisorio
derivative: *n.* derivada
derive: *v.* derivar
derived demand: demanda indirecta
derived quantity: magnitud derivada
derived unit: unidad derivada
derm: *n.* dermis
dermatitis: *n.* dermatitis
dermatologist: especialista en la piel
dermatologist: *n.* dermatólogo; especialista de la piel
dermatology: *n.* dermatología
dermatophyte: *n.* dermatofito
dermis: *n.* dermis
derrail: *v.* descarrilar
derrick: *n.* derrick; grúa
dervish: *n.* derviche
desalinization: *n.* desalinización
descend: *v.* descender

descending: *adj.* descendente
descent: *n.* descenso
descrate: *v.* profanar; violar
describe: *v.* describir; explicar
description: *n.* descripción
description sheet: hoja de descripción
descriptor: *n.* descriptor
descry: *v.* descubrir; divisar
desensitization: *n.* desensibilización
desensitizer: *n.* desensibilizador
desert: *n.* desierto
deserter: *n.* desertor
desertion: *n.* deserción
desert-like: desértico
deserve: *v.* merecer; tener merecimientos
design: *n.* diseño
design: *v.* diseñar
designate: *adj.* designado
designate: *v.* designar
designated driver: conductor designado
designation: *n.* designación
designer: *n.* diseñador; disefiador; dibujante; proyectista
desire: *n.* deseo
desire: *v.* desear; ambicionar
desist: *v.* desistir
desk: *n.* escritorio; pupitre
desk copy: ejemplar de trabajo
desk work: trabajo de oficina
desolate: *adj.* desolado
desolate: *v.* desolar; arrasar
desolation: *n.* desolación
despair: *n.* desesperación
despair: *v.* desesperar
desperation: *n.* desesperación
despairins: *adj.* desesperado; desesperante
desperate: *adj.* desesperado
despicable: *adj.* despreciable
despise: *v.* despreciar
despite: *n.* insulto

despoil: *v.* despojar
despond: *n.* abatimiento
despond: *v.* abatirse
despot: *n.* déspota
despotic: *n.* despótico
dessert: *n.* postre
destabilizing protein: proteína desestabilizadora
destalinization: *n.* desestalinización
destination: *n.* destino
destine: *v.* destinar; designar
destiny: *n.* destino
destitute: *adj.* indigente
destroy: *v.* destruir; invalidar
destroyer: *n.* destructor
destruct: *v.* destrucción deliberada
destructive: *adj.* destructor
destructive force: fuerza destructiva
destructive interference: interferencia destructiva
desultory: *adj.* intermitente; discontinuo
detach: *v.* separar; destacar
detachment: *n.* destacamento; separación
detail: *n.* detalle
detail: *v.* detallar
detailed: *adj.* detallado
detain: *v.* detener
detainee: *n.* detenido
detainer: *n.* detentador
detect: *v.* descubrir; detectar
detectability: *n.* detectabilidad
detection: *n.* detección
detection limit: límite de detección
detective: *n.* detective
detective novel: novela policial
detector: *n.* detector
detention: *n.* detención
detergent: *n.* detergente
deteriorate: *v.* deteriorar
deterioration: *n.* deterioro
determinant: *n.* determinante
determination: *n.* determinación

determine: *v.* determinar
determined period of time: período de tiempo determinado
determiner: *n.* determinativo
determinism: *n.* determinismo
detest: *v.* detestar
detestable: *adj.* detestable
detestation: *n.* detestación
dethrone: *v.* destronar
detonate: *v.* detonar; estallar
detour: *n.* rodeo
detour: *v.* desviar
detoxification: *n.* desintoxicación
detract: *v.* apartar; menguar
detractor: *n.* detractor
detriment: *n.* detrimento
deuce: *n.* dos
deuced: *adj.* diabólico
devaluate: *v.* devaluar
devaluation: *n.* devaluación; desvalorización
devalue: *v.* devaluar; desvalorizar
devastate: *v.* devastar
devastation: *n.* devastación
develop: *v.* desarrollar; urbanizar
developer: *n.* empresario constructor
developing: en desarrollo
developing country: país en desarrollo
development: *n.* desarrollo; urbanización
development agency: agencia de desarrollo
development bond: bono de fomento
development department: departamento de desarrollo
development director: director de desarrollo
development expense: gasto de desarrollo
development manager: gerente de desarrollo
developmental: *adj.* de desarrollo

deviance: *n.* desviación
deviate: *v.* desviar
deviation: *n.* desviación
device: *n.* dispositivo; artificio; aparato
devil: *n.* demonio; diablo
devise: *n.* legado; donación
devise: *v.* proyectar; legar; inventar
devolve: *v.* transmitir
devote: *v.* dedicar
devoted: *adj.* devoto
devour: *v.* devorar
devout: *adj.* devoto; piadoso
dew: *n.* rocío
dew: *v.* rociar
dew point: punto de rocio; punto de condensación
dexterity: *n.* destreza
dexterous: *adj.* diestro
dextrose: *n.* dextrosa
diabetes: *n.* diabetes
diabetic: *adj.* diabético; -a
diabolic: *adj.* diabólico
diabolism: *n.* diabolismo
diachronic: *adj.* diacrónico
diacritic: *n.* signo diacrítico
diadem: *n.* diadema
diagnose: *v.* diagnosticar
diagnosis: *n.* diagnóstico; diagnosis
diagnostic: *adj.* diagnóstico
diagnostic program: programa de diagnóstico
diagnostic test: prueba; examen
diagonal: *adj.* diagonal
diagram: *n.* diagrama
diakinesis: *n.* diacinesis
dial: *n.* dial
dial tone: tono de marcar/discar
dialect: *n.* dialecto
dialectal: *adj.* dialectal
dialectician: *n.* dialéctico; -a
dialectics: *n.* dialéctica
dialectology: *n.* dialectología
dialogue: *n.* diálogo

dialog writer: dialoguista
dialogue: *n.* dialogo
dialogue: *v.* dialogar
dialysis: *n.* diálisis
diameter: *n.* diámetro
diameter of a circle: diámetro de un círculo
diamond: *n.* diamante
diamond cutter: diamantista
diapason: *n.* diapasón
diaphragm: *n.* diafragma
diarist: *n.* diarista
diarrhea: *n.* diarrea
diary: *n.* diario
diary agenda: diario
diaspora: *n.* diáspora
diastase: *n.* diastasa
diastole: *n.* diástole
diathermy: *n.* diatermia
diatom: *n.* diatomea
diatomic molecule: molécula diatomica
diatonic: *adj.* diatónico
diatribe: *n.* diatriba
dice: *n.* dados
dichotomy: *n.* dicotomía
dictate: *v.* dictar; mandar
dictates (of fashion): *n.* dictados
dictation: *n.* dictado
dictator: *n.* dictador
dictatorial: *adj.* dictatorial
dictatorship: *n.* dictadura
diction: *n.* dicción; lenguaje
dictionary: *n.* diccionario
dictum: *n.* dictamen; sentencia
dicyclomine: *n.* dicicloverina
didactic: *adj.* didáctico
didactics: *n.* didáctica
dice: *n.* dado
die: *v.* morir; acabar
dielectric: *adj.* dieléctrico
dieresis: *n.* diéresis
diesel: *n.* diesel
diet: *n.* régimen; dieta

dietary: *adj.* dietético
dietetics: *n.* dietética
diethylpropion: *n.* anfepramona
dietician: *n.* dietista
differ: *v.* diferir
difference: *n.* diferencia
difference of cubes: la diferencia de cubos
difference of squares: la diferencia de cuadrados
difference scale: escala de diferencias
different: *adj.* diferente
differentiation medium: medio de diferenciación
differential: *n.* diferencial
differential: 1. *n.* diferencial; 2. *adj.* diferencial
differential calculus: cálculo diferencial
differential count: recuento diferencial
differential diagnosis: diagnóstico diferencial
differential equation: ecuación diferencial
differential geometry: geometría diferencial
differential rate: tarifa diferencial
differentiation: *n.* diferenciación
difficult: *adj.* difícil
difficult in hearing: dificultad para oír
difficulty: *n.* dificultad
difficulty in breathing: dificultad respiratoria
diffidence: *n.* timidez
diffraction: *n.* difracción
diffraction grating: red de difracción
diffuse: *adj.* difuso
diffuse: *v.* difundir; extender
diffuse reflection: reflexión difusa
diffusion: *n.* difusión

diffusion coefficient: coeficiente de difusión
dig: *v.* cavar; escudriñar
digest: *v.* digerir; asimilar
digestion: *n.* digestión
digestion: *n.* digestión
digestive: *adj.* digestivo
digestive biscuit: galleta integral
digit: *n.* dígito
digital: *adj.* digital
digital cable: el cable digital
digital computer: computadora digital
digital signal: señal digital
digital technology: tecnología digital
digitalization: *n.* digitalización
digitalize: *v.* digitalizar
digitation: *n.* digitalización
digitize: *v.* digitalizar
digitizer: *n.* digitalizador
digitizing: digitalizar
digitoxin: *n.* digitoxina
dignified: *adj.* digno
dignitary: *adj.* dignatario
dignity: *n.* dignidad
digraph: *n.* dígrafo
digress: *v.* divagar
digression: *n.* digresión
dike: *n.* dique
dilapidate: *v.* dilapidar
dilatation: *n.* dilatación
dilatation and curettage: dilatación y legrado
dilate: *v.* dilatar
dilation: *n.* dilatación
dilator: *n.* dilator
dilatory: *adj.* dilatorio
dilemma: *n.* dilema
dilettante: *n.* diletante
diligence: *n.* diligencia
diligent: *adj.* diligente
dill: *n.* eneldo
diluent: *adj.* diluyente
dilute: *adj.* oscuro

dilute: *v.* diluir
dilute solution: solución diluida
diluted: *adj.* diluido
diluted share: acción diluida
diluter: *adj.* diluidor
dilution: *n.* dilución
dimension: *n.* dimensión
dimensional metrology: metrología dimensional
dimensionless quantity: magnitud adimensional
dimeter: *n.* dímetro
diminish: *v.* disminuir; mermar; decrecer
diminished: *adj.* disminuido
diminishing: decreciente; que disminuye
diminishing asset: activo consumible
diminishing profit: beneficio decreciente
diminishing returns: rendimiento decreciente
diminuendo: *adv.* diminuyendo
diminution: *n.* disminución
diminutive: *adj.* diminutivo
dimmer switch: el interruptor con regulador/el potenciómetro
dimorphic fungi: hongo dimórfico
dynamic: *adj.* dinámico
dinar: *v.* dinar
ding-dong: *n.* din don
dingo: *n.* dingo
dining hall: refectorio
dining room: comedor
dining room table: mesa de comedor
dinner: *n.* comida; cena
dinner time: hora de cenar
dint: *n.* golpe
dint: *v.* abollar
diocese: *n.* diócesis
diode: *n.* diodo
diopter: *n.* dioptría

diorama: *n.* diorama
dip: *n.* baño
dip: *v.* sumergir
diphtheria: *n.* difteria
diphtheroide: *n.* difteroide
diplex: *adj.* diplex; díplex
diploid: *n.* diploide
diploma: *n.* diploma; título
diplomacy: *n.* diplomacia
diplomat: *n.* diplomático
diplomat: *n.* diplomada; -a
diplopia: *n.* diplopía
diplotene: *n.* diplotena
dipole: *n.* dipolo
dipsomaniac: *n.* dipsómano; -a
dipstick: *n.* tira reactiva
diptych: *n.* díptico
dipyrone: *n.* metamizol
direct: *adj.* directo
direct: *v.* dirigir; administrar
direct advertising: publicidad directa
direct consumption: consumo directo
direct conversion: apropiación directa
direct cost: coste directo
direct current: corriente directa
direct debit: débito directo; cargo en cuenta
direct deposit: depósito directo
direct dial: discado directo
direct discourse: estilo directo
direct expense: gasto directo
direct interest: interés directo
direct labor: mano de obra directa
direct loss: pérdida efectiva
direct marketing: comercialización directa; venta directa
direct object: complemento directo
direct rate: tasa directa; tipo de interés directo
direct repeat: repetición directa
direct sale: venta directa

direct sampling: muestreo directo
direct tax: impuesto directo
direct wet mount: preparación en fresco
directed mutagenesis: mutagénesis dirigida
direction: *n.* dirección
directional: *adj.* direccional
directive: 1. *n.* orden; directiva; 2. *adj.* directivo
directly proportional: directamente proporcional
directness: *n.* franqueza
director: *n.* director
director general: ejecutivo en jefe; gerente general
directory: *n.* directorio
directrix: *n.* directriz
dirigible: *adj.* dirigible
dirt: *n.* polvo
dirty: *adj.* sucio
disability: *n.* incapacidad; impedimento
disability benefit: indemnización por discapacidad
disability freeze: período de incapacidad inactivo
disability indemnification: indemnización por discapacidad
disability insurance: seguro de incapacidad
disability pay: indemnización por discapacidad
disability pension: pensión por invalidez
disable: *adj.* incapacitado
disable: *v.* inhabilitar
disabled: *adj.* discapacitado; incapacitado; inválido
disaccord: *n.* desacuerdo
disadvantage: *n.* desventaja
disadvantage: *v.* dañar
disaffection: *n.* desafecto
disagree: *v.* disentir

disagreeable: *adj.* desagradable
disagreement: *n.* discrepancia
disallow: *v.* denegar
disallowance: *n.* denegación
disappear: *v.* desaparecer
disappearance: *n.* desaparición
disappoint: *v.* decepcionar; defraudar
disapproval: *n.* desaprobación
disapprove: *v.* desaprobar; rechazar
disarm: *v.* desarmar
disarmament: *n.* desarme
disaster: *n.* desastre; calamidad
disavow: *v.* negar; repudiar
disband: *v.* desbandar; disolver
disbelief: *n.* incredulidad
disburse: *v.* desembolsar
disbursement: *n.* desembolso; erogación; egreso
discard: *n.* descarte
discard: *v.* descartar; despedir
discern: *v.* discernir
discernment: *n.* discernimiento
discharge: *n.* descarga
discharge: *n.* descarga; liberación
discharge: *v.* despedir; liberar
discharger: *n.* descargador
disciple: *n.* discípulo
discipline: *n.* disciplina
discipline: *v.* disciplinar; educar
disciplined: *adj.* disciplinado
disc-jockey: *n.* disc-jockey
disclaimer: *n.* advertencia
disclose: *v.* descubrir; revelar
disclosure of information: revelación de información
discoloration: *n.* decoloración; descoloramiento
discolored: *adj.* descolorido
discomfit: *v.* derrotar
discompose: *v.* descomponer; agitar
disconcert: *v.* desconcertar; confundir
disconcerted: *adj.* desconcertado

disconnect: *v.* desunir; desconectar
disconsolate: *adj.* desconsolado
discontent: *n.* descontento
discontented: *adj.* descontento
discontinuity: *n.* discontinuidad
discord: *n.* discordia
discordant: *adj.* discordante; discorde
discotheque: *n.* discoteca
discount: *n.* descuento; rebaja
discount: *v.* descontar; rebajar
discount market: mercado de descuentos
discount pending: descuento pendiente
discount rate: tasa de descuento
discount store: tienda de descuento
discountable: *adj.* descontable
discounted bill: letra descontada
discounted paper: documento descontado
discourse: *n.* discurso
discourse: *n.* discurso
discourse: *v.* discursear
discourse analysis: *n.* análisis del discurso
discourteous: *adj.* descortés
discourtesy: *n.* descortesía
discover: *v.* descubrir
discoverer: *n.* descubridor
discovery: *n.* descubrimiento
discredit: *n.* descrédito; deshonra
discredit: *v.* desacreditar
discreet: *adj.* discreto
discrepancy: *n.* discrepancia
discrete: *adj.* discreto
discrete flow: flujo discreto
discrete transport: transporte discreto
discretion: *n.* discreción
discriminate: *n.* discriminar; distinguir
discrimination: *n.* discriminación
discrimination threshold: umbral

discriminante
discus: *n.* disco
discus thrower: discóbolo
discuss: *v.* discutir; debatir
discussion: *n.* discusión
disdain: *n.* desprecio; desdén
disdain: *v.* despreciar
disdainful: *adj.* desdeñoso
disease: *n.* enfermedad
disease: *v.* enfermar
disembark: *v.* desembarcar
disenchantment: *n.* desencanto
disentangle: *v.* desenredar
disfigure: *v.* desfigurar
disfigurement: *n.* desfiguración
disgrace: *n.* deshonra
disgrace: *v.* deshonrar; desacreditar
disguise: *n.* disfraz; máscara
disguise: *v.* disfrazar
disgust: *n.* repugnancia
disgust: *v.* repugnar
dish: *n.* plato; vasija
dish: *v.* servir en un plato
dishearten: *v.* abatir
dishonesty: *n.* deshonestidad
dishonor: *n.* deshonra
dishonor: *v.* deshonrar
dishonorable: *adj.* deshonroso
dishonor: *n.* faltar al pago
dishonored check: cheque rechazado
dishwasher: *n.* lavaplatos
disillusion: *n.* desilusión
disincline: *v.* desinclinar; indisponer
disinfect: *v.* desinfectar
disinfectant: *adj.* desinfectante
disinfection: *n.* desinfección
disinherit: *v.* desheredar
disintegrate: *v.* desintegrar; disgregar
disintegration constant: constante de desintegración
disjoint: *v.* desunir; desarticular; dislocar

disjoint events: sucesos disjuntos
disjunction: *n.* disyunción
disjunctive: *adj.* disyuntivo
disk: *n.* disco
disk drive: unidad de disco; disquetera
diskette: disquete; disco flexible
dislike: *n.* aversión; antipatía
dislike: *v.* no gustar
dislocate: *v.* dislocar
dislocation: *n.* dislocación
dislodge: *v.* desalojar
disloyal: *adj.* desleal
disloyalty: *n.* deslealtad
dismal: *adj.* triste; tétrico
dismantle: *v.* desmantelar; desarmar
dismay: *n.* desmayo
dismay: *v.* desanimar
dismember: *v.* desmembrar
dismemberment: *n.* desmembramiento
dismiss: *v.* despedir
dismissal: *n.* despido
dismount: *v.* desmontar
disobedient: *adj.* desobediente
disobey: *v.* desobedecer
disopyramide: *n.* disopiramida
disorder: *n.* alteración; trastorno
disorder: *v.* desordenar
disorganization: *n.* desorganización
disorganize: *v.* desorganizar
disorganized: *adj.* desorganizado
disorientation: *n.* desorientación
disoriented: *adj.* desorientado
disown: *v.* repudiar
disparage: *v.* menospreciar; desacreditar
disparity: *n.* disparidad
dispase: *n.* aeromonolisina
dispatch: *n.* despacho; expedición
dispatch: *v.* despachar
dispatch note: nota de envío
dispatch notice: aviso de envío
dispensary: *n.* dispensario

dispensation: *n.* dispensa
dispense: *v.* dispensar; distribuir
dispenser: *n.* dispensador
dispersal: *n.* dispersión
disperse: *v.* dispersar; disgregar; intr. dispersarse.
dispersed repeat: repetición dispersa
dispersion: *n.* dispersión
dispirit: *v.* desalentar
displace: *v.* dislocar
displaced person: desplazado
displacement: *n.* desplazamiento
displacement analysis: análisis por desplazamiento
display: *n.* exhibición; despliegue; ostentación
display: *v.* exhibir; mostrar; desplegar
display: *n.* exposicion
display window: escaparate; vidriera
displeasing: *adj.* desagradable
displeasure: *n.* desplacer
disport: *n.* diversión
disport: *v.* divertir
disposable: *n.* desechable
disposable income: salario después de restar impuestos y deducciones
disposable product: producto desechable
dispose: *v.* disponer; componer; mover.
disposition: *n.* disposición; índole; genio.
dispossess: *v.* desahuciar; desalojar
dispossessing proceedings: juicio de desahucio
dispossession: *n.* desahucio; desalojo; desposeimiento
disproof: *n.* refutación.
disproportionate: *adj.* desproporcionado
disproportionate: *adj.* desproporcionado
disprove: *v.* refutar

disputant: *n.* disputador
dispute: *n.* disputa; querella
dispute: *v.* discutir; pelear
disputer: *n.* disputador
disqualification: *n.* descalificación
disqualify: *v.* descalificar
disquiet: *n.* inquietud
disquiet: *v.* inquietar
disquiet; disquietude: *n.* inquietud
disquisition: *n.* disquisición
disregard: *n.* desatención; desaire
disregard: *v.* desatender
disrepair: *n.* desconcierto; malestado
disrespect: *n.* falta de respeto
disrespect: *v.* desacatar; desairar
disrespectful: *adj.* irrespetuoso
disrupt: *v.* romper
dissatisfaction: *n.* insatisfacción; descontento
dissatisfied: *adj.* insatisfecho
dissect: *v.* disecar; analizar
dissection: *n.* disección
dissemble: *v.* disimular; esconder
disseminate: *v.* diseminar; propagar.
dissemination: *n.* diseminación
dissemination: *n.* diseminación
dissension: *n.* disensión
dissent: *n.* disenso
dissenter; dissident: *n.* disidente
dissert: *v.* disertar
dissertation: *n.* disertación
disservice: deservicio
dissidence: *n.* disidencia
dissimilarity: *n.* disimilitud
dissimulate: *v.* disimular
dissipate: *v.* disipar; desaparecer; disiparse
dissociate: *v.* disociar; i*n.* disociarse
dissociation constant: constante de disociación
dissolute: *adj.* disoluto
dissolution: *n.* disolución; liquidación
dissolve: *v.* disolver; liquidar

dissonance: *n.* disonancia
dissonant: *adj.* disonante
dissuade: *v.* disuadir
dissuasion: *n.* disuasión
dissymmetrical: *adj.* disimétrico
dissymmetry: *n.* disimetría
distance: *n.* distancia
distance sampling: muestreo de distancia
distant: *adj.* distante; indiferente
distasteful: *adj.* desagradable
distaste: *n.* disgusto
distension; distention: *n.* distensión
distich: *n.* dístico
distil: *v.* destilar
distilled: *adj.* destilado
distiller: *n.* destilador
distillery: *n.* destilería
distinction: *n.* distinción
distinguish: *v.* distinguir; percibir
distinguished: *adj.* distinguido
distort: *v.* torcer; deformar; distorsionar
distortion: *n.* distorsión
distract: *v.* distraer
distracted: *adj.* distraído
distraction: *n.* distracción
distress: *n.* pena; peligro
distress: *v.* apenar
distressed: *adj.* angustiado
distribute: *v.* distribuir; repartir
distributed profit: beneficio distribuido
distributing company: empresa distribuidora
distribution: *n.* distribución; reparto; repartición
distribution board: el tablero auxiliar
distribution center: centro de distribución
distribution channel: canal de distribución
distribution coefficient: coeficiente

de distribución
distribution constant: constante de distribución
distribution cost: coste de distribución
distribution network: red de distribución
distribution of profits: distribución de ganancias
distribution pipe: la tubería de derivación
distributive: *adj.* distributivo
distributive law: ley distributiva
distributive property: propiedad distributiva
distributor: *n.* distribuidor; repartidor
district: *n.* distrito
district attorney fiscal: fiscal de distrito
district manager: gerente de distrito; gerente regional
distrust: *n.* desconfianza
distrust: *v.* desconfiar
distrustfulness: *n.* desconfianza; sospecha
disturb: *v.* turbar; trastornar; interrumpir
disturbance: *n.* disturbios
disunite: *v.* desunir; desunirse
disunity: *n.* desunión
disuse: *n.* desuso
disuse: *v.* desusar
diteh: *n.* zanja; acequia; cuenta
diuresis: *n.* diuresis
diuretic: *n.* diurético
diva: *n.* diva
divagate: *v.* divagar
divan: *n.* diván
diver: *n.* buzo; nadador
diverge: *v.* divergir
divergence: *n.* divergencia
divergent: *adj.* divergente
divergent boundary: borde

divergente
divergent promoter: promotor divergente
diversified: *adj.* diversificado
diversion: *n.* diversión
diversity: *n.* diversidad
divert: *v.* divertir; desviar
diverticulitis: *n.* diverticulitis
diverticulum: *n.* divertículo
divertimento: *n.* divertimento
divest: *v.* desnudar
divestment: *n.* desinversión
divide: *n.* divisoria
divide: *v.* dividir
divided by: dividido por; dividido entre (prep)
dividend: *n.* dividendo
dividend coupon: cupón de dividendo
dividend in kind: dividendo en especie
dividend payable: dividendo a pagar
dividend warrant: cupón
divider: *n.* divisor
divination: *n.* adivinación
divine: 1. *n.* teólogo; 2. *adj.* divino
divinity: *n.* divinidad
divisibility: *n.* divisibilidad
divisible: *adj.* divisible
division: *n.* división
division director: director de división
division manager: gerente de división
division of labor: división del trabajo
division of tasks: división de tareas
division property of equality: propiedad de igualdad en la división
divisor: *n.* divisor
divorce: *n.* divorcio
divorce: *v.* divorciar
divot: *n.* dicotiledónea
divulge: *v.* divulgar

dizziness: n mareo
DNA: ADN
DNA amplification: amplificación de DNA
DNA damage: lesión del DNA
DNA fingerprint: Huella genética de identificación
DNA fingerprinting: Huellas dactilares genéticas; dactiloscópica genética
DNA ligase (ATP): DNA-ligasa (ATP)
DNA ligase (NAD+): DNA-ligasa (NAD+)
DNA melting: fusión del DNA
DNA mutagenic repair: reparación mutágena del DNA
DNA packaging: empaquetamiento del DNA
DNA repair: reparación del DNA
DNA restriction: restricción del DNA
DNA sequence polymorphism: polimorfismo de una secuencia de DNA
DNA topoisomerase: DNA-topoisomerasa
do: *n.* droga; narcótico
do: *v.* drogarse
docile: *adj.* dócil
docility: n docilidad
dock: 1. *n.* muelle; dársena
dock: *v.* atracar
dock duty: arancel portuario
dock receipt: guía de muelle; resguardo de muelle
dock warrant: resguardo de muelle; conocimiento de almacén
dockage: *n.* derecho de atraque
docker: *n.* trabajador del muelle; descargador
dockyard: *n.* astillero; arsenal
doctor: *n.* doctor; médico
doctoral: *adj.* doctoral

doctorate: *n.* doctorado
doctor's office: consultorio médico
doctrine: *n.* doctrina
docudrama: *n.* docudrama
document: *n.* documento
document: *v.* documentar
documentary: *n.* documental
documentary bill: letra documentaria
documentary credit: crédito documentario
documentary debt: deuda documentaria
documentary letter of credit: carta de crédito documentaria
documentary loan: préstamo documentario
documentation: documentación
documented: *adj.* documentado
dodder: *v.* temblar; tambalearse
dodecahedron: *n.* dodecaedro
dodge: *n.* regate; movimiento rápido
dodge: *v.* regatear; evitar; evadir
doer: *n.* actor; agente
dogfish: *n.* cazón; perro
dogma: *n.* dogma
dogmatic: *adj.* dogmático
dogmatist: *n.* dogmatista
dole: *n.* desempleo
doleful: *adj.* dolorido
doll: *n.* muñeca
doll: *v.* engalanar
dollar: *n.* dólar
dolly: *n.* muñequita
dolphin: *n.* delfín
domain: *n.* dominio; propiedad; zona
domain of a function: dominio de una función
dome: *n.* cúpula; domo
domestic: 1. *n.* doméstico; 2. *adj.* nacional; doméstico; interno
domestic appliance: electrodoméstico
domestic bill: letra sobre el interior

domestic commerce: comercio interior
domestic commodity: producto del país; fruto del país
domestic competition: competencia interna; consumo nacional
domestic corporation: compañía local; nacional
domestic income: renta interna
domestic market: mercado interno; mercado doméstico
domestic services: servicios domésticos
domestic trade: comercio interior; comercio nacional
domestic workers: trabajadores domésticos
domesticate: *v.* domesticar; amansar.
domesticity: *n.* domesticidad
domicile: *n.* domicilio
domicile: *v.* domiciliar
dominant: 1. *n.* dominante; 2. *adj.* dominante
dominant allele: alelo dominante
domination: *n.* dominación
domineer: *v.* intr. dominar
domineering: *adj.* dominante
Dominica: Dominica
Dominican: *adj.* dominicano; -a
Dominican: *n.* dominico
Dominican Republic: República Dominicana
dominion: *n.* dominio; señorío
domino: *n.* dominó
donate: *v.* donar
donation: *n.* donación; donativo
done: *adj.* hecho; terminado; cansado
donkey: *n.* burro; asno.
donor: *n.* donador; donante
donor site: centro donador
doom: 1. *n.* destino; suerte; ruina
doom: *v.* condenar a muerte; desahuciar
door: *n.* puerta

door bolt: cerrojo
doorkeeper: *n.* portero
doorway: *n.* portal
dopamine: *n.* dopamina
Doppler effect: efecto Doppler
doric: *adj.* dórico
dormancy: *n.* dormicion; letargo
dormant: *adj.* durmiente; inactivo
dormant account: cuenta inactiva
dormant partner: socio secreto
dormitory: *n.* dormitorio
dorsal: *adj.* dorsal
dosage effect: efecto de la dosis
dose: *n.* dosis
dose: *v.* dosificar
dose equivalent: dosis equivalente
dose-effect curve: curva de dosis y respuesta
dosimeter: *n.* dosímetro
dosimetry: *n.* dosimetría
dossier: *n.* expediente
dot blot: transferencia en mancha
dot with: poner trocitos encima
dot-matrix printer: impresor matricial
dotted: *adj.* punteado
double: *adj.* doble
double: *vt.* doblar
double bar graph: gráfica de doble barra
double bond: enlace doble
double creditor: acreedor de dos gravámenes
double diffusion test: prueba de doble difusión
double entry: partida doble
double helix: doble hélice
double standard: bimetalismo
double strand: cadena doble
double taxation: doble tributación; doble gravamen
double vision: visión doble
double-minute: minicromosoma
double-rounded tail: cola

doblemente redondeada
double-strand break repair: reparación por recombinación
doubloon: *n.* doblon
doubly-labeled water: agua isotópica
doubt: *n.* duda
doubtful: *adj.* dudoso
doubtful debtor: deudor moroso
doubtful title: título dudoso; título incierto
doubtless: *adj.* indudable
douche: *n.* ducha
dough: *n.* masa; pasta.
doughnut: *n.* dona; donut
dour: *adj.* adusto; terco
douse: *v.* zambullir (se)
dove: *n.* paloma
down: *prep.* abajo
down feather: plumón
down mutation: mutación lentificadora
down payment: paga y señal; pago a cuenta
down time: tiempo inactivo; tiempo muerto
downfall: *n.* caída; ruina; descenso
download: *v.* copiar información de un proveedor remoto
download (computer): copiar; descargar
downpour: *n.* aguacero
down-promoter mutation: mutación lentificadora
downright: *adj.* absoluto
Down's syndrome: síndrome de Down
downstream: en dirección de la corriente
dowry: *n.* dote
doxology: *n.* doxología
doxycycline: *n.* doxiciclina
doze: *n.* sueño ligero
doze: *v.* dormitar

dozen: *n.* docena
dracaena: *n.* drago
drachma: *n.* dracma
draft: 1. n letra; letra de cambio
draft: *v.* realizar en borrador
draft card: tarjeta de reclutamiento
draft contract: antecontrato; contrato en borrador
draftsman: *n.* delineante
drag: *n.* rastra; rastreo
drag: *v.* arrastrar
drain: *v.* escurrir
drainage: *n.* drenaje
dram: *n.* dracma
drama: *n.* drama
dramatic: *adj.* dramático
dramatics: *n.* arte dramático
dramatist: *n.* dramaturgo
dramatist: *n.* dramaturgo; -a
dramatization: *n.* dramatización
dramaturge: *n.* dramaturgo
drape: *v.* cubrir; adornar
drar: *n.* ticero
draught: *n.* esquema; borrador
draught: *v.* realizar en borrador
draw: *n.* empate; arrastre; tracción
drawback: *n.* retención; desventaja; reintegro; reembolso
drawback certificate: certificado de reintegro
drawbridge: *n.* puente levadizo
drawee: *n.* librado; girado
drawer: *n.* librador; girador; cajón
drawing: *n.* dibujo; sorteo (en la lotería)
drawing account: cuenta de extracciones
drawing board: tablero de dibujo
drawn bond: bono amortizado; bono pagado
drawn check: cheque librado
drawn librado: girado
dread: 1. *n.* horror; temor; 2. *adj.* espantoso; terrible

dread: *v.* temer
dream: *n.* sueño
dreary: *adj.* triste; sombrío
dredge: *n.* draga
dredge: *v.* dragar; excavar
dredger: *n.* draga
drench: *n.* mojadura
drench: *v.* mojar; saturar
dress: *n.* vestido; traje; hábito
dress: *v.* vestir de etiqueta; ataviar; peinar
dress: *vt.* aderezar
dressed crab: cangrejo preparado
dressing: *n.* aliño; aderezo
dribble: *n.* gota; drible
dribble: *v.* gotear; driblar
dribbling: *n.* goteo al terminar
drift: *n.* deriva; corriente
drill: *n.* dril; taladro
drink: *n.* bebida
drink: *v.* beber
drinking: *n.* acción de beber
drinking problem: problema de alcoholismo
drip: *n.* goteo
drip: *v.* gotear; destilar
drive: *n.* calzada para coches; paseo en coche
driver: *n.* conductor; chofer
driver's license: licencia de conducir
drizzle: *n.* llovizna
droll: *adj.* raro; cómico
dromedary: *n.* dromedario
drone: *n.* zángano
drop: *n.* gota; pendiente; cuesta
drop-down list: lista desplegable
drop-out (school): *v.* abandonar
drop-out years: años descartados
dropper: *n.* cuentagotas
dross: *n.* escoria
drought: *n.* sequía
drove: *n.* manada; rebaño
drown: *v.* apagar; anegar; ahogar (se)
drudge: *n.* yunque

drudge: *v.* abrumar de trabajo
drudgery: *n.* afán; trabajo penoso
drug: *n.* droga; fármaco
drug abuse: abuso de drogas
drug addict: adicto a drogas; drogadicto
drug addiction: adicción a drogas; drogadicción
druggist: *n.* droguero; droguista
drugstore: *n.* droguería
drum: *n.* tambor; cilindro
drumstick: *n.* palillo de tambor
drumstick (chicken): *n.* muslo de pollo
drunk: *adj.* borracho; embriagado
drunken: *adj.* borracho; embriagado
druse: *n.* druso
dry: *v.* secar
dry cleaning: limpieza en seco
dry cell: celda seta
dry chemistry: química en fase sólida
dry medium: medio seco
dry trust: fideicomiso pasivo
dryer: la secadora
drying: *adj.* secado
dryness: *n.* sequedad
drywall: *n.* enyesado
drywall compound: la masilla premezclada
drywall hammer: el martillo para enyesado
drywall nails: los clavos para enyesado
drywall screws: los tornillos para enyesado
drywall spackle: el relleno/el mastique para el enyesado
drywall tape: la cinta adhesiva para enyesado
drywaller: *n.* yesero
dual: *adj.* dual
dualism: *n.* dualismo
duality: *n.* dualidad

dub: *n.* jugador; retoque de tambor
dub: *v.* titular
Dublin: Dublín
Dubliner: *n.* dublinés; -esa
ducat: *adj.* ducado
duchess: *n.* duquesa
duchy: *adj.* ducado
duck: *n.* pato; querida
duck: *v.* agachar; zambullir
duct: *n.* conducto
duct tape: la cinta adhesiva
ductile: *adj.* ductil
dudgeon: *n.* resentimiento; enojo
due: *adj.* debido; pagadero.
due at sight: pagadero a la vista
due bill: pagaré
due date: fecha de vencimiento
due on demand: pagadero a la vista
due process of law: debido proceso de ley
duel: 1. *n.* duelo; 2. *adj.* duelo
duel: *v.* combatir en el duelo
duelist: *n.* duelista
dues: *n.* cuota
duet: *n.* dueto
duke: *n.* duque
dukedom: *adj.* ducado
dulcet: *adj.* dulce
dulcet: *n.* dulce
dulcimer: *n.* dúlcemele
dull: *n.* romo
dumb: *adj.* mudo
dummy: *adj.* sustituto; testaferro
dummy shareholder: accionista testaferro
dump truck: el camión volquete
dumpster: *n.* basurero grande
dune: *n.* duna
Dunkirk: Dunquerque
duo: *n.* dúo
duodecimal: *adj.* duodecimal
duodenum: *n.* duodeno
duple: *adj.* doble
duplex: *n.* duplex

duplicate: *adj.* duplicado
duplicate claim: reclamación duplicada
duplication: *n.* duplicación
duplicator: *n.* duplicador
duplicity: *n.* duplicidad
durable: *adj.* durable; duradero
durable good: producto duradero
durable medical equipment: equipo médico duradero
duration: *n.* duración
during: *prep.* durante
dusk: 1. *n.* crepúsculo; 2. *adj.* oscuro
dust: *n.* polvo; cenizas
dust bowl: cuenca del polvo
dustpan: *n.* pala de recoger basura
dutiful: *adj.* obediente
duty: *n.* obligación
duty arancel: derecho; impuesto
duty drawback: reintegro de derechos
dwell: *v.* vivir
dwelling: *n.* vivienda
dwindle: *v.* disminuir
dyad: *n.* díada
dye: *n.* tinte; matiz
dying: *n.* muerte
dynamic: *adj.* dinámico
dynamics: *n.* dinámica
dynamism: *n.* dinamismo
dynamite: *n.* dinamita
dynamo: *n.* dínamo
dynamometer: *n.* dinamómetro
dynamotor: *n.* dinamotor
dynasty: *n.* dinastía
dynatron: *n.* dinatrón
dyne: *n.* dina
dynode: *n.* dinodo
dysentery: *n.* disentería
dysfunction: *n.* disfunción
dyslexia: *n.* dislexia
dyspepsia: *n.* dispepsia
dysphasia: *n.* disfagia
dyspnea; dyspnoea: *n.* disnea

dystrophy: *n.* distrofia
dysuria: *n.* disuria

E

each: *adj.* cada; cada uno
eager: *adj.* ansioso; anhelante
eagle: *n.* águila
ear: *n.* oído; oreja
ear canal: canal auditivo
ear drum: tímpano
earache: *n.* dolor del oído
earliness: *n.* prontitud
early: 1. *adj.* temprano; antiguo; 2.
adv. temprano; al principio
early closure: cancelación anticipada
early retirement: jubilación
anticipada
early-stage capital: financiación
inicial
earn: *v.* ganar; percibir; devengar
earned income: ingreso de trabajo
earned interest: interés devengado
earned profit: beneficio de
operaciones
earned surplus: beneficio
acumulado
earning asset: capital productivo
earnings: *n.* beneficio; ingresos;
ganancia
earnings record: registro de
ganancias
earnings test: límite de ganancias
earplugs: *n.* tapones del oído
earring: *n.* pendiente
earth: *n.* tierra; mundo
Earth science: ciencia de la Tierra
Earth science: ciencia de la tierra

earthquake: terremoto
earthquake: *n.* terremoto
ease: 1. *n.* alivio; comodidad; 2. *v.*
tranquilizar; facilitar
easement: *n.* servidumbre
east: *n.* este
east bound: con rumbo al este
eastbound: *adv.* con rumbo al este
Easter: *n.* Pascua de Resurrección;
Semana Santa
easterly: *adv.* del este
eastern: *adj.* del este; oriental
Eastern Hemisphere: hemisferio
oriental
Eastern time: *n.* hora oficial del Este
Easterner: *n.* habitante del este
easternmost: *adv.* más al este
eastward: *adv.* hacia el este
eastward: *adj.* hacia el este
easy: *adj.* fácil; acomodado
eatable: *adj.* comestible
eathemware: *n.* loza de barro
eaves: *n.* alero
eavesdrop: *n.* gotera
eavesdrop: *v.* escuchar detrás de las
puertas
ebb-tide: *n.* marea menguante
ebony: *n.* ébano
Ebro: Ebro
e-business: empresa basada en
Internet
eccentric: *adj.* excéntrico
eccentricity: *n.* excentricidad
ecclesiastic: *adj.* eclesiástico
echelon: *n.* escalón
echidna: *n.* equidna
echinoderm: *n.* equinodermo
echo: *n.* eco
echo: *v.* resonar
echocardiogram: *n.* ecocardiograma
echolalia: *n.* ecolalia
echolocation: *n.* ecolocación
eclectic: *adj.* ecléctico
eclecticism: *n.* eclecticismo

eclipse: *n.* eclipse
eclipsing binary: eclipse binario
ecology: *n.* ecología
e-commerce: comercio electrónico
econometrics: *n.* econometría
economic: *adj.* económico
economic activity: actividad económica
economic aid: ayuda económica
economic cost: costo económico
economic cycle: ciclo económico
economic good: bien económico
economic indicator: indicador económico
economic information: información económica
economic journal: boletín económico
economic life: vida útil
economic policy: política económica
economic support: apoyo económico
economic unit: unidad económica
economic value: valor económico
economic year: año económico
economical: *adj.* económico; de bajo costo
economics: *n.* economía
economies of scale: economías de escala
economist: *n.* economista
economize: *v.* economizar; ahorrar
economy: *n.* economía
economy class: clase económica
ecosystem: *n.* ecosistema
Ecstasy: Éxtasis
ecstasy: *n.* éxtasis
ectomorph: *n.* ectomorfo
ectoparasite: *n.* ectoparásito
ectopia: *n.* ectopia
ectoplasm: *n.* ectoplasma
ectotherm: *n.* ectodermo
Ecuador: Ecuador
Ecuadorian: *adj.* ecuatoriano; -a

ecumenism: *n.* ecumenismo
ecur: *v.* volver a ocurrir; repetirse
eczema: *n.* eczema
edelweiss: *n.* edelweiss
edema: *n.* edema
edge: *n.* filo; borde; margen
edge: *v.* afilar; ribetear
edge of a solid: arista de un cuerpo geométrico
edge trim: el reborde
edible: 1. *n.* comestible; 2. *adj.* comestible
edict: *n.* edicto
edification: *n.* edificación
edifice: *n.* edificio
Edinburgh: Edimburgo
edit: *v.* corregir; redactar
editing: *n.* corrección; redacción; edición
editor: *n.* editor
editorial: *n.* editorial
editorial writer: editorialista
educate: *v.* educar; formar
education: *n.* educación
educational: *adj.* educativo
educational advertising: publicidad educativa
educational grant: beca
educator: *n.* educador
efface: *v.* borrar
effect: *n.* efecto; documento; bien
effective: *adj.* efectivo
effective concentration: concentración eficaz
effective date: fecha efectiva
effective debt: deuda efectiva; deuda real
effective demand: demanda real
effective loss: pérdida efectiva; pérdida real
effective price: precio real
effective rate: tipo de interés efectivo; tasa efectiva
effector: *n.* efector

effectual: *adj.* eficaz
effeminate: *adj.* afeminado
effeminate: *v.* afeminar
efferent: *adj.* eferente
effervescence: *n.* efervescencia
effervescent: *adj.* efervescente
efficiency: *n.* eficiencia
efficient: *adj.* eficiente
effluent: n. residuales
effort: *n.* esfuerzo; empeño
effusion: *n.* efusión
effusive: *adj.* efusivo
eflectance: *n.* eflectancia
egalitarian: *adj.* igualitario
egg: *n.* huevo; óvulo
egg cup: huevera
egg plant: berenjena
egg timer: reloj de arena
egg white: clara de huevo
egg yolk: yema de huevo
eggnog: *n.* ponche de huevo
egocentric: *adj.* egocéntrico
egocentrism: *n.* egocentrismo
egoism: *n.* egoísmo
egoistic: *n.* egoísta
egotism: *n.* egotismo
egotist: *n.* egotista
Egypt: Egipto
Egyptian: *adj.* egipcio; -a
eh?: *intj.* ¿eh?
eiderdown: *n.* edredón
eiderdown (quilt): *n.* edredón
eight: ocho
eighteen: *adj.* dieciocho
eighth: *adj.* octavo
eighty: ochenta
either: 1. *pron.* cualquiera; 2. *adv.* tampoco
ejaculation: *n.* eyaculación
eject: *v.* expulsar
ejection: *n.* eyección
ejector: *n.* eyector
eke: *v.* aumentar con dificultad
El Nino: El Niño

El Salvador: El Salvador
elaborate: *v.* elaborar
elaborate: *adj.* elaborado
elaboration: *n.* elaboración
elapse: *v.* pasar
elapsed time: tiempo transcurrido
elapsed years: años transcurridos
elastic: *adj.* elástico
elastic potential energy: energía elástica potencial
elasticity: *n.* elasticidad
elate: *v.* regocijar
Elba: Elba
elbow: *n.* codo
elbow pipe: el codo de cuarenta y cinco grados
elder: 1. *adj.* mayor; 2. *n.* mayor; anciano
elder-down: *n.* edredón
elect: *v.* elegir
election: *n.* elección
elector: *n.* elector
electorate: *adj.* electorado
electric: *adj.* eléctrico
electric capacitance: capacidad eléctrica
electric charge: carga eléctrica
electric circuit: circuito eléctrico
electric conductance: conductancia eléctrica
electric conductivity: conductividad eléctrica
electric current: corriente eléctrica
electric current density: densidad de corriente eléctrica
electric field: campo eléctrico
electric field strength: fuerza del campo eléctrico
electric force: fuerza eléctrica
electric generador: generador eléctrico
electric mobility: movilidad eléctrica
electric motor: motor eléctrico

electric resistance: resistencia eléctrica
Electrical: *adj.* eléctrico
electrical energy: energía eléctrica
Electrician: *n.* electricista
Electricity: *n.* electricidad
Electrification: *n.* electrificación
Electrify: *v.* electrizar; electrificar
Electroblotting: *n.* electrotransferencia por absorción
Electrocardiogram: *n.* electrocardiograma
Electrocardiograph: *n.* electrocardiógrafo
electrochemical cell: celda electroquímica
Electrochemistry: *n.* electroquímica
Electrocution: *n.* electrocución
Electrode: *n.* electrodo
electrode potencial: potencial de electrodo
electrodialysis: *n.* electrodiálisis
electrodynamics: *n.* electrodinámica
electrodynamometer: *n.* electrodinamómetro
electroencephalogram: *n.* electroencefalograma
electroencephalograph: *n.* electroencefalógrafo
electro-endosmosis: elctroendósmosis
electroerosion: *n.* electroerosión
electrogravimetry: *n.* electrogravimetría
electrokaryotipe: *n.* electro cariotipo
electrokinetics: *n.* electrocinética
electrolysis: *n.* electrólisis
electrolyte: *n.* electrolito
electromagnet: *n.* electroimán
electromagnetic energy: energía electromagnética
electromagnetic induction: inducción electromagnética
electromagnetic radiation:

radiación electromagnética
electromagnetic spectrum: espectro electromagnético
electromagnetic wave: ondas electromagnéticas
electromagnetism: *n.* electromagnetismo
electromechanical: *adj.* electromecánico
electrometer: *n.* electrómetro
electromotive force: fuerza electromotriz
electromyography: *n.* electro miografía
electrón: *n.* electrón
electrón dot diagram: diagrama de puntos de electrones
electrón microscope: microscopio electrónico
electrón microscopy: microscopio electrónica
electronegative: *adj.* electronegativo
electronic: *adj.* electrónico
electronic comerse: comercio electrónico
electronic data interchange: intercambio electrónico de datos
electronic data processing: procesamiento electrónico de datos
electronic funds transfer: transferencia electrónica de fondos
electronic industry: industria electrónica
electronic mail: correo electrónico
electronic newsletter: noticiero electrónico
electronic signal: senal electrónica
electronics: *n.* electrónica
electronvolt: *n.* electronvoltio
electrophoresis: *n.* electroforesis
electrophoretic karyotipe: cariotipo electroforético
electrophoretic mobility: movilidad electroforética

electroporation: *n.* electroporación
electropositive: *adj.* electropositivo
electropulsation: *n.* electropulsación
electroscope: *n.* electroscopio
electroshock: *n.* electrochoque
electrosurgery: *n.* electro cirugía
electrotechnology: *n.* electrotecnia
electrotherapy: *n.* electroterapia
electrothermics: *n.* electrotermia
electrotonus: *n.* electrotono
eleemosynary corporation: sociedad de beneficencia
elegante: *n.* elegancia
elegant: *adj.* elegante
elegy: *n.* elegía
element: *n.* elemento
elementary: *adj.* elemental
elementary charge: carga elemental
elements: *n.* elementos
elephant: *n.* elefante
elephantiasis: *n.* elefantiasis
elephantine: *adj.* elefantino
elevate: *v.* elevar
elevated railroad: ferrocarril elevado
elevation: *n.* elevación
elevator: *n.* elevador
eleven: once
elf: *n.* elfo
elicit: *v.* sacar
eligibility: *n.* elegibilidad
eligible: *adj.* elegible
eligible individual: individuo elegible
eligible paper: efectos negociables; documentos negociables
eliminate: *v.* eliminar
elimination: *n.* eliminación
elitism: *n.* elitismo
elixir: *n.* elíxir
elk: *n.* alce
ellipse: *n.* elipse
ellipsoid: *n.* elipsoide
elliptic: *adj.* elíptico

elliptical: *adj.* elíptico
elliptical galaxy: galaxia elíptica
elocution: *n.* elocución
elongation: *n.* elongación
elope: *v.* escaparse
eloquent: *adj.* elocuente
else: *adj.* otro; diferente
elude: *v.* burlar
elucidation: *n.* elucidación
elusive: *adj.* inaprensible
elution chromatography: cromatografía de elución
elution curve: curva de elución
e-mail: correo electrónico
emancipation: *n.* emancipación
emancipator: *n.* emancipador
embalm: *v.* embalsamar
embalmer: *n.* embalsamador (a)
embalmer: *n.* embalsamador
embalming: *n.* embalsamamiento
embargo: *n.* embargo
embark: *v.* embarcar
embarrass: *v.* desconcertar
embarrassing: *adj.* vergonzoso; desconcertante
embassy: *n.* embajada
embellish: *v.* embellecer
embezzle: *v.* malversar; estafar; desfalcar
embezzlement: *n.* malversación; fraude; desfalco
embitter: *v.* amargar
emblem: *n.* emblema
emblem: 2. *v.* simbolizar
embolism: *n.* embolia
embolus: *n.* émbolo
embosom: *v.* abrigar; proteger
embrace: *n.* abrazo
embrace: *v.* abrazar
embroidery: *v.* bordado
embryo: *n.* embrión
embryologist: *n.* embriólogo; -a
embryology: *n.* embriología
emendation: *n.* enmienda

emerald: *n.* esmeralda
emerald: *adj.* esmeraldino
emerald: *n.* esmeralda
emerge: *v.* emerger
emergence: *n.* afloramiento;
emergencia
emergency: *n.* emergencia; urgencia
emergency fund: fondo para
contingencias
emergency laboratory: laboratorio
de urgencias
emergency room: sala de
emergencia
emergency service: servicio de
emergencia
emeritus: *adj.* emérito
emetic: *adj.* emético
emigrate: *v.* emigrar
emigration: *n.* emigración
emigre: *adj.* emigrado
eminence: *n.* eminencia
emirate: *adj.* emirato
emission: *n.* emisión
emit: *v.* emitir
emittance: *n.* emitancia
emmetropia: *n.* emetropía
emollient: 1. *n.* emoliente; 2. *n.*
emoliente
emolument: *n.* emolumento;
honorario; retribución
emotion: *n.* emoción
emotional: *adj.* emocional
emotional assessment: evaluación
emocional
emperor: *n.* emperador
emphasize: *v.* acentuar
emphatic: *adj.* enfático
emphysema: *n.* enfisema
empire: *n.* imperio
empiricism: *n.* empirismo
empiricist: *n.* empírico; -a
emplacement: *n.* emplazamiento
employ: *n.* empleo
employ: *v.* emplear

employee: *n.* empleado
employees' association: asociación
de empleados
employees' trade union: sindicato
de empleados
employer: *n.* empleador; patrón
employers' association: asociación
patronal
employment: *n.* empleo; ocupación
employment act: ley laboral
employment agency: agencia de
colocaciones
employment contract: contrato de
trabajo
employment history: datos
ocupacionales
employment office: oficina de
empleos
employment rate: tasa de empleo
employment relationship: relación
de empleo
employment support: ayuda de
empleo
emporium: *n.* emporio
empower: *n.* otorgar poder o
autorización
empress: *n.* emperatriz
emptiness: *n.* vacío
empty: *adj.* vacío
empty: *v.* vaciar
empyema: *n.* empiema; supuración
emu: *n.* emù
emulator: emulador
emulsifier: *n.* emulsor
emulsion: *n.* emulsión
enable: *v.* capacitar; permitir
enact: *v.* decretar; establecer
enactment: *n.* promulgación
enamel: *n.* esmalte
enamour: *v.* enamorar
encage: *v.* enjaular
encampment: *n.* campamento
encapsidation: *n.* encapsidación
encase: *v.* encerrar

encephalitis: *n.* encefalitis
encephalomyelitis: *n.* encéfalo
mielitis
encephalon: *n.* encéfalo
enchanter; enchantress: *n.*
encantador
enchanting: encantador
enchantment: *n.* encantamiento;
encanto
enchilada: *n.* enchilada
encircle: *v.* cercar
enclave: *n.* enclave
enclitic: *adj.* enclítico
enclose: *v.* incluir
enclosed: *adj.* untado
enclosure: *n.* contenido
encode: *n.* codificar
encomium: *n.* encomio
encore: *n.* bis; repetición
encounter: *n.* encuentro
encourage: *v.* animar; alentar;
exhortar
encroach: *v.* invadir
encrypt: *v.* cifrar; codificar
encryption: *n.* cifrado; codificado
encumber: *v.* gravar; afectar;
embarazar
encumbrance: *n.* gravamen;
afectación
encyclical: *n.* encíclica
encyclopedia: *n.* enciclopedia
encyclopedist: *n.* enciclopedista
end: *n.* fin; final
end balance: saldo final
end consumer: consumidor final
end inventory: inventario de cierre
end of period: cierre del ejercicio
end product: producto final
end to end: de punta a punta
endanger: *v.* poner en peligro
endangered species: especie en
peligro de extinción
endeavor: *n.* esfuerzo
endeavor: *v.* tratar de; procurar

endemic: *adj.* endémico
ending: *n.* final; terminacion
endive: *n.* endibia; endivia
end-labeling: marcaje terminal
endocarditis: *n.* endocarditis
endocardium: *n.* endocardio
endocervical mucus: moco
endocervical
endocrine: *adj.* endocrino
endocrine gland: glándula endocrina
endocrine system: sistema
endocrino
endocrinologist: *n.* endocrinólogo
endocrinology: *n.* endocrinología
endoenzyme: *n.* endoenzima
endogamy: *n.* endogamia
endogenote: *n.* endogenote
endometriosis: *n.* endometriosis
endomorph: *adj.* endomorfo
endomorphic: *adj.* endomórfico
endoparasite: *n.* endoparásito
endoplasmic reticulum: retículo
endoplasmatico
endorphin: *n.* endorfina
endorsable: *adj.* endosable
endorse: *v.* endosar; avalar; respaldar
endorsed bond: bono garantizado
endorsee: *n.* endosatario
endorsement: *n.* endoso
endoscope: *n.* endoscopio
endoscopic: *adj.* endoscopico
endoscopic ultrasound: ultrasonido
endoscopico
endoscopy: *n.* endoscopia
endoskeleton: *n.* endoesqueleto
endospore: *n.* endospora
endotherm: *n.* endotermo
endothermic change: cambio
endotermico
endothermic reaction: reacción
endotérmica
endow: *v.* dotar
endowment: *n.* donación
endowment fund: fondo de

beneficencia
endowment insurance: seguro de vida
endowment trust: fundación
endpoint: *n.* extremo
endurance: *n.* aguante
endure: *v.* aguantar; durar
enduring: *adj.* duradero
enema: *n.* enema
enemy: *n.* enemigo
energetic: *adj.* enérgico
energetics: *n.* energética
energize: *v.* dar energía
energy: *n.* energía
energy conservation: conservación de la energía
energy level: nivel de energía
energy pyramid: pirámide de la energía
energy transformation: transformación de la energía
enfold: *v.* envolver; incluir
engage: *v.* comprometer
engender: *v.* engendrar
engine: *n.* interna
engineer: *n.* ingeniero
engineer: *n.* ingeniero
engineer: *v.* dirigir con acierto
engineering: 1. *n.* ingeniería; 2. *adj.* relativo a la ingeniería
England: Inglaterra
English: *n.* Inglés
engraftment: *n.* injerto
engraver: *n.* grabador
engraving: *adj.* grabado
engross: *v.* absorber
enhancer: *n.* intensificador
enharmonic: *adj.* enharmónico
enharmonic: *n.* enharmónico
enigma: *n.* enigma
enjoy: *v.* gozar de; disfrutar
enlarge: *v.* ampliar; ensanchar
enlargement: *n.* ampliación
enlighten: *v.* ilustrar

enmity: *n.* enemistad
enologist: *n.* enólogo
enology: *n.* enología
enormous: *adj.* enorme
enough: *adv.* bastante
enoxacin: *n.* enoxacina
enrapture: *v.* embelesar; arrebatar
enrich: *v.* enriquecer
enrichment culture: cultura enriquecida
enrichment medium: medio de enriquecimiento
enroll: *v.* inscribir; registrar
enrollee: *n.* inscrito
enrollment: *n.* matriculación; inscripción
enrollment fee: derecho de inscripción
enrollment period: período de inscripción
enrollment register: registro de inscripción
enry: *n.* envidia
enry: *v.* envidiar
enshroud: *v.* envolver
enslavement: *n.* esclavización
ensue: *v.* seguir
ensure: *v.* asegurar
entablature: *n.* entablamento
entangle: *v.* enredar
enter: *v.* registrar; asentar; ingresar
enter: *v.* entrar
enter into force: entrar en vigor
enteral nutrition: nutrición enteral
entered value: valor declarado
enteritis: *n.* enteritis
enteroinvasive: *n.* enteroinvasor
enterostomy: *n.* enterostomía
enterprise: *n.* empresa
entertain: *v.* entretener; recibir
entertaining allowance: gastos de representación
entertaining expense: gasto de representación

entertainment: *n.* entretenimiento
enthalpy: *n.* entalpía
enthusiasm: *n.* entusiasmo
enthusiast: *n.* entusiasta
entice: *v.* inducir
entirety: *n.* entereza
entitic: *adj.* entítico; entésico
entitled: *adj.* tener derecho a
entitlement: *n.* derecho; autorización
entity: *n.* entidad; ente
entomology: *n.* entomología
entrance: *n.* entrada
entrance: *v.* encantar
entrant: *n.* entrante
entreat: *v.* rogar
entrecote: *n.* entrecot
entrepreneurship: *n.* calidad del empresario
entropy: *n.* entropía
entrust: *v.* confiar; encargar
entry: *n.* entrada
entry exclusion: bloqueo de entrada
entry site: centro aceptor
enumerate: *v.* detallar
enumeration: *n.* enumeración
enuresis: *n.* enuresis
envelop: *v.* envolver; forrar
envelope: *n.* envolvente
envious: *adj.* envidioso
environment: *n.* ambiente; medio ambiente
environmental: *adj.* ambiental; medio ambiental
environmental science: ciencias del medio ambiente
environmental scientist: científico ambientalista
environmental store: tienda de productos ecológicos
envoy: *adj.* enviado
envy: *n.* envidia
enzyme: *n.* enzima
enzyme activity: actividad enzimática

enzyme electrode: electrodo enzimático
enzyme immunoassay: enzimoinmunoanálisis
eon; aeon: *n.* eón
ephedrine: *n.* efedrina
epic: *n.* épica
epicene: *adj.* epiceno
epicene: *n.* epiceno
epicenter: *n.* epicentro
epicure: *n.* epicúreo
epicurean: *n.* epicúreo
Epicureanism: *n.* epicureismo
epicycle: *n.* epiciclo
epicycloids: *n.* epicicloide
epidemic: *adj.* epidémico; epidemial
epidemic: *adj.* epidémico
epidemiologist: *n.* epidemiólogo
epidemiology: *n.* epidemiología
epidermis: *n.* epidermis
epidural: *adj.* epidural
epigenetic: *adj.* epigenético
epiglottis: *n.* epiglotis
epigram: *n.* epigrama
epigraph: *n.* epígrafe
epigraphy: *n.* epigrafía
epilepsy: *n.* epilepsia
epileptic: *adj.* epiléptico
epilog: *n.* epílogo
epinephrine: *n.* epinefrina
epinephrine: *n.* epinefrina
Epiphany: *n.* Epifanía
epiphyte: *n.* epifita
Episcopalian: *n.* episcopalista
episcopate: *n.* episcopado
episiotomy: *n.* episiotomía
episode: *n.* episodio
episodic: *adj.* episódico
epistaxis: *n.* epistaxis
epistemology: *n.* epistemología
epistolary: *n.* epistolario
epitaph: *n.* epitafio
epithelial tissue: tejido epitelial
epithelioma: *n.* epitelioma

epithelium: *n.* epitelio
epithet: *n.* epíteto
epitome: *n.* epitome
epoch: *n.* época
epode: *n.* epodo; epoda
eponym: *n.* epónimo
epsilon: *n.* epsilón
equal: *adj.* igual
equal: *v.* igualar
equal employment: empleo sin discriminación
equal opportunity: igualdad de oportunidades
equalitarian: *n.* igualitario
equality: *n.* igualdad
equalization: *n.* compensación; nivelación
equalization: *n.* igualación
equalization fund: fondo de compensación
equalizer: *n.* igualador
equation: *n.* ecuación
equator: *n.* ecuador
equatorial: *adj.* ecuatorial
equatorial Guinea: Guinea Ecuatorial
equatorial plate: placa ecuatorial
equestrian: 1. *n.* jinete; 2. *adj.* ecuestre
equidistant: *adj.* equidistante
equilateral: *adj.* equilateral
equilateral triangle: triángulo equilátero
equilibrium: *n.* equilibrio
equilibrium constant: constante de equilibrio
equimolecular: *adj.* equimolecular
equinox: *n.* equinoccio
equip: *v.* equipar
equipment: *n.* equipo; equipamiento
equipment expense: gasto de los equipos
equitable: *adj.* equitativo
equitable estate: interés equitativo

equitable value: valor equitativo
equitation: *n.* equitación
equity: *n.* capital; fondos propios; equidad
equity account: cuenta patrimonial
equity capital: capital propio
equity dilution: dilución del capital
equity security: acción
equity shares: acciones
equity stake: participación en el capital
equity tax: impuesto al patrimonio neto
equity value: valor líquido
equivalent: *adj.* equivalente
equivalent equation: ecuación equivalente
equivalent expression: expresión equivalente
equivalent fractions: fracciones equivalentes
equivalent inequalities: desigualdades equivalentes
equivalent ratios: razones equivalentes
equivalent variable expressions: expresiones variables equivalentes
equivocal: *adj.* equívoco
era: *n.* era
erase: *v.* borrar
eraser: *n.* goma de borrar; borrador
erect: *adj.* erecto
erect: *adj.* erguido
erect: *v.* levantar; instalar; erigir
erectile: *adj.* eréctil
erection: *n.* erección
erector: *n.* erector
erg: *n.* ergio
ergonomics: *n.* ergonomía
ermine: *n.* armiño
erode: *v.* erosionar
erogenous: *adj.* erógeno
erosion: *n.* erosión
erotica: *n.* arte erótico

erotica: *n.* literatura erótica
err: *v.* errar
errand: *n.* recado; mensaje
errands boy: mandadero; cadete
errata: *n.* fe de erratas
erroneous: *adj.* erróneo
error: *n.* error
eructation: *n.* eructación; eructo
erudition: *n.* erudición
erupt: *v.* arrojar
eruption: *n.* erupción
erysipelas: *n.* erisipela
erythema: *n.* eritema
erythrasma: *n.* eritrasma
erythrocyte: *n.* eritrocito
erythromycin: *n.* eritromicina
erythropoietin: *n.* eritropoyetina
erythrosedimentation: *n.* eritrosedimentación
escalade: *n.* escalada
escalade: *v.* escalar
escalator: *n.* escalera
escalator clause: cláusula de ajuste
escape: *n.* escape
escape: *v.* escapar
escape velocity: velocidad de escape
escapism: *n.* escapismo
escarole: *n.* escarola
eschatology: *n.* escatología
escort: *n.* escolta
escudo: *n.* escudo
esculin agar: agar-esculina
Eskimo: *adj.* esquimal
esophagus: *n.* esófago
esoteric: *adj.* esotérico
Esperanto: *n.* esperanto
espionage: *n.* espionaje
essay: *n.* ensayo
essay: *v.* ensayar
essayist: *n.* ensayista
essence: *n.* esencia
essential: *adj.* esencial
essential person: persona indispensable

essential trace element: oligoelemento
establish: *v.* establecer
establishment: *n.* establecimiento; institución
estate: *n.* propiedad; inmueble; propiedades
estate duty: impuesto sucesorio
estate in common: propiedad mancomunada
estate income: ingresos testamentarios
estate tax: impuesto sucesorio; impuesto a la propiedad
esteem: *n.* estima
esteem: *v.* estimar
ester: *n.* ester
esterase: *n.* esterasa
esthete; aesthete: *n.* esteta
estimate: *n.* estimación; valoración
estimate: *v.* estimar; valorar
estimated value: valor estimado
estimation: *n.* estimación
estimator: *n.* tasador
Estonia: Estonia
estrangement: *n.* separación; alejamiento
estrogen: *n.* estrógeno
estuary: *n.* estuario
eta: *n.* eta
etcetera: *adv.* etcétera
eternal: *adj.* eterno
eternity: *n.* eternidad
ethanol: *n.* etanol
ether: *n.* éter
ethics: *n.* ética
Ethiopia: Etiopía
ethmoid: *adj.* etmoides
ethmoid: *n.* etmoides
ethnic: *adj.* étnico
ethnicity: *n.* identidad
ethnocentrism: *n.* etnocentrismo
ethnography: *n.* etnografía
ethnology: *n.* etnología

ethosuximide: *n.* etosuximida
etiology: *n.* etiología
etiquette: *n.* etiqueta
etude: *n.* estudio
etymological: *adj.* etimológico
etymologist: *n.* etimólogo
etymology: *n.* etimología
eucalyptus: *n.* eucalipto
Eucharist: *n.* eucaristía
Euclidean: *adj.* euclidiano
Euclidean geometry: geometría euclidea
eugenics: *n.* eugenesia
eugonic: *adj.* eugónico
eukaryote: *n.* eucariote
eulogize: *v.* elogiar
eulogy: *n.* elogio
euphemism: *n.* eufemismo
euphonious: *adj.* eufónico
euphorbia: *n.* euforbio
euphoria: *n.* euforia
euphoric: *adj.* eufórico
Euphrates: Eufrates
Eurasia: Eurasia
Eurasian: *adj.* eurasiático
euro: *n.* euro
Europe: Europa
European: *adj.* europeo; -a
Europeanization: *n.* europenización
Eustachian tube: tubo de Eustaquio
euthanasia: *n.* eutanasia
evacuate: *v.* evacuar
evacuation: *n.* evacuación
evacuee: *n.* evacuado
evade: *v.* evadir
evade taxes: evadir impuestos
evader: *n.* evasor
evaluate: *v.* evaluar
evaluation: *n.* evaluación
evanescent: *adj.* evanescente
evangelism: *n.* evangelismo
evangelist: *n.* evangelista; evangelizador
evaporate: *v.* evaporar

evaporated milk: leche evaporada
evaporation: *n.* evaporación
evasion: *n.* evasión
evasive statement: evasiva
eve: *n.* víspera
even: *adj.* igual; plano
even number: número par
evening: *n.* tarde; velada
evening dress: vestido de noche
evenness: *n.* igualdad
event: *n.* evento
ever: *adv.* siempre
everlasting: *adj.* eterno
every: *adj.* cada; todo
evict: *v.* lanzar; desahuciar; desalojar
eviction: *n.* lanzamiento; desahucio; desalojo; desalojamiento
eviction proceedings: procedimiento de desahucio
evidence: *n.* evidencia; prueba
evil: *adj.* malo
eviscerate: *v.* eviscerar
eviscerate: *vt.* eviscerar
evocation: *n.* evocación
evoke: *v.* evocar
evolutionary: *adj.* evolutivo
evolution: *n.* evolución
evolutionist: *n.* evolucionista
evolve: *v.* desarrollar
ewe: *n.* oveja
ex cathedra: *adv.* ex cátedra
ex libris: *n.* ex libris
ex officio: *adj.* ex oficio
exacerbation: *n.* exacerbación
exact: *adj.* exacto
exaggerated: *adj.* exagerado
exaltation: *n.* exaltación
exam: *n.* examen
examination: *n.* examen; revisión; auditoria
examination of books: revisión de libros
examine: *v.* examinar; revisar
examinee: *n.* examinando

examiner: *n.* examinador
example: *n.* ejemplo
example in context: ejemplo en contexto
exasperate: *v.* irritar; agravar; enconar
exasperated: *adj.* exasperado
exasperating: *adj.* exasperante
exasperation: *n.* exasperación
excavate: *v.* excavar; zanjar
excavation: *n.* excavación
excavator: *n.* excavadora
exceed: *v.* exceder; superar
excellency: *n.* excelencia
excellent: *adj.* excelente
except: *prep.* excepto
except: *v.* exceptuar
exception: *n.* excepción
exceptional: *adj.* excepcional
excerpt: *n.* selección; cita
excerpt: *v.* citar; escoger
excess: 1. *n.* exceso; 2. *adj.* excesivo; sobrante
excess capacity: capacidad excedente
excess load: sobrecarga
excess reserve: reserva excesiva; encaje excesivo
excess valuation: sobrevaloración; sobrevaluación
excessive: *adj.* excesivo
exchange: *n.* cambio; intercambio; bolsa
exchange: *v.* cambiar; intercambiar
exchange broker: agente de cambios
exchange certificate: certificado de cambio
exchange commission: comisión de cambios
exchange control: control de cambios
exchange gap: brecha cambiaria
exchange house: casa de cambio
exchange license: licencia de cambios
exchange market: mercado de cambios
exchange parity: paridad de cambio
exchange policy: política de cambio
exchange rate: tipo de cambio
exchangeable: *adj.* canjeable; intercambiable
excisable: *adj.* imponible
excise duty: derechos arancelarios
excise tax: impuesto al consumo
excision: *n.* excisión
excitability: *n.* excitabilidad; excitación
excitation: *n.* excitación
excitation energy: energía de excitación
excite: *v.* excitar
excited: *adj.* excitado
excitement: *n.* excitación
exciter: *n.* excitador
exclamatory: *adj.* exclamatorio
exclude: *v.* excluir
exclusion: *n.* exclusión
exclusion chromatography: cromatografía de exclusión
exclusive: *adj.* exclusivo
exclusive agent: agente exclusivo
exclusive representative: representante exclusivo
exclusive right: derecho exclusivo
exclusivism: *n.* exclusivismo
exclusivist: *adj.* exclusivista
excommunication: *n.* excomunión
excoriation: *n.* excoriación
excrement: *n.* excremento
excreta: *n.* excrementos
excretion: *n.* excreción
excretory: *n.* excretoria
exculpation: *n.* exculpación
excursion: *n.* excursión
excuse: *n.* excusa
execute: *v.* ejecutar
executed sale: venta consumada

execution: *n.* ejecución
execution creditor: acreedor ejecutante
execution sale: venta judicial
executive: 1. *n.* ejercicio; práctica; 2. *adj.* ejecutivo; jefe del estado
executive board: junta directiva; junta ejecutiva
executive body: órgano ejecutivo
executive committee: comisión ejecutiva; comité ejecutivo
executive director: director ejecutivo
executive secretary: secretario ejecutivo; secretaria ejecutiva
executive staff: personal ejecutivo
executive summary: sumario ejecutivo
executor: *n.* ejecutor
executor albacea: ejecutor
executory: *n.* ejecutorio
executory sale: venta acordada
exempt: *adj.* exento; franco; libre
exempt: *v.* eximir
exemption: *n.* exención; franquicia
exercise: *n.* ejercicio
exercise tolerance: tolerancia al ejercicio
exert: *v.* ejercer
exhalation: *n.* exhalación
exhaust: *n.* escape
exhaust: *v.* agotar; escapar
exhaust pipe: tubo de escape
exhausted: *adj.* agotado
exhausting: *adj.* agotador
exhibit: *n.* exposición; exhibición
exhibit: *v.* manifestar; mostrar; exhibir
exhibition: *n.* exhibición
exhibition hall: salón de exposiciones
exhibitionism: *n.* exhibicionismo
exhibitionist: *n.* exhibicionista
exhibitor: *n.* expositor; exhibidor

exhilarate: *v.* alegrar
exhumation: *n.* exhumación
exile: *n.* destierro
exile: *v.* desterrar; expatriar
exile: *n.* exilio
ex-interest: sin interés
exist: *v.* existir; vivir
existence: *n.* existencia
existentialism: *n.* existencialismo
existentialist: *n.* existencialista
exit: *n.* salida
exodus: *n.* éxodo
exoenzyme: *n.* exoenzima
exogamy: *n.* exogamia
exogenote: *n.* exogenote
exon: *n.* exón
exoneration: *n.* exoneración
exorbitant: *adj.* exorbitante
exorcism: *n.* exorcismo
exorcist: *n.* exorcista
exoskeleton: *n.* exoesqueleto
exosphere: *n.* exosfera
exothermic: *adj.* exotérmico
exothermic change: cambio exotérmico
exothermic reaction: reacción exotérmica
exotic: *adj.* exótico
exotic species: especies exóticas
exotoxin: *n.* exotoxina
expand: *v.* ampliar; expandir; extender
expand: *v.* expandir
expansion: *n.* expansión
expansion bolt: el perno de expansión
expansion slot: ranura de expansión
expansionism: *n.* expansionismo
expansive: *adj.* expansivo
expatriation: *n.* expatriación
expect: *v.* esperar; suponer
expectancy: *n.* expectativa
expectation: *n.* expectativas
expectorant: *n.* expectorante

expectoration: *n.* expectoración
expectoration: *n.* esputo
expedient: *adj.* conveniente
expedite: *v.* apresurar; acelerar
expedition: *n.* expedición
expeditionary: *n.* expedicionario
expenditure: *n.* gasto; erogación; cargo; expensa
expense: *n.* gasto; cargo; erogación; expensa
expense account: cuenta de gastos
expense allowance: dietas; fondo para dietas; viáticos
expense report: rendición de gastos; informe de gastos
expense voucher: comprobante de gastos
expenses: *n.* expensas; gastos
expensive: *adj.* caro
experience: *n.* experiencia
experienced: *adj.* experimentado; con experiencia
experiment: *n.* experimento
experimental: *adj.* experimental
experimental probability: probabilidad experimental
expert: 1. *n.* experto; perito; 2. *adj.* experto
expert accountant: contable experto; contador perito
expert appraisal: tasación pericial
expert appraiser: perito tasador
expert opinion: dictamen pericial
expert system: sistema experto
expiation: *n.* expiación
expiration: *n.* espiración
expiration date: fecha de vencimiento
expire: *v.* caducar; vencer; prescribir
expired: *adj.* caducado; vencido; prescrito
expiry: *n.* caducidad; vencimiento
explain: *v.* explicar
explanation: *n.* explicación

expletive: *n.* palabra expletiva
explication: *n.* explicación
explode: *v.* volar; refutar
exploit: *n.* hazaña
exploit: *v.* explotar
exploitation: *n.* explotación
exploration: *n.* exploración
explorative: *adj.* exploratorio
explore: *v.* explorar; sondear
explorer: *n.* explorador
explosion: *n.* explosión
explosive: *n.* explosivo
exponent: *n.* exponente
exponential: *n.* exponencial
exponential curve: curva exponencial
export: *n.* exportación
export: *v.* exportar
export certificate: permiso de exportación
export company: empresa exportadora
export duty: derechos de exportación
export house: empresa exportadora
export license: licencia de exportación
export permit: permiso de exportación
export quota: cuota de exportación
exporter: *n.* exportador
exporting: *n.* exportación
expose: *v.* exponer
exposed: expuesto
exposition: *n.* exposición
expostulate: *v.* protestar
exposure: *n.* exposición; riesgo
exposure meter: exposímetro
expound: *v.* exponer; explicar
express: *adj.* expreso
express warranty: garantía escrita
expression: *n.* expresión
expressionism: *n.* expresionismo
expressive: *adj.* expresivo

expressivity: *n.* expresividad
expropriate: *v.* expropiar
expropriation: *n.* expropiación
expropriator: *n.* expropiador
ex-quay libre: franco sobre el muelle
ex-ship franco: sobre el barco
extempore: *adj.* improvisado
extend: *v.* extender; ampliar; conceder
extended: *adj.* extendido
extension: *n.* extensión
extension clamp: la abrazadera de extensión
extension cord: la extensión eléctrica el cordón eléctrico
extension ladder: la escalera de extensión
extensive: *adj.* extensivo; extenso
extensor: *n.* extensor
extent: *n.* extensión
exterior: *adj.* exterior
exterior paint: la pintura para exteriores
exterminator: *n.* exterminador
external: *adj.* externo
external audit: auditoria externa
external auditor: auditor externo
external combustion engine: motor de combustión externa
external debt: deuda externa
external funds: recursos externos
external loan: préstamo externo
external party: tercero
external sector: sector externo
external trade: comercio exterior
extinct: *adj.* extinto; extinguido
extinction: *n.* extinción
extol: *v.* exaltar
extort: *v.* arrancar
extortion: *n.* extorsión
extortionist: *n.* autor de extorsiones
extra: *adj.* extra
extra charge: cargo extra; recargo
extra load: sobrecarga

extracellular fluid: líquido extracelular
extract: *n.* extracto
extract: *v.* extraer
extraction: *n.* extracción
extractive industry: industria extractiva
extractor: *n.* extractor
extracurricular: *adj.* extracurricular
extradition: *n.* extradición
extramural: *adj.* extramural
extraordinary: *adj.* extraordinario
extraordinary dividend: dividendo extraordinario
extraordinary expense: gasto extraordinario
extrapolate: *v.* extrapolar
extrapolation: *n.* extrapolación
extrasensory: *adj.* extrasensorial
extraterrestrial: *adj.* extraterrestre
extraterrestrial life: vida extraterrestre
extravagant: *adj.* extravagante
extreme: 1. *n.* extremado; extremo; 2. *adj.* extremo
extreme unction: extremaunción
extreme value: valor extremo
extremism: *n.* extremismo
extremist: *n. adj.* extremista
extremity: *n.* extremidad
extrusion: *n.* extrusión
extrusive rock: roca extrusiva
exuberance: *n.* exuberancia
exuberant: *adj.* exuberante
exudate: *adj.* exudado
exudation: *n.* exudación
exude: *v.* sudar
exultation: *n.* exultación
eye: *n.* ojo
eyebrow: *n.* ceja
eyeglasses: *n.* gafas; lentes; anteojos
eyelash: *n.* pestaña
eyelid: *n.* párpado
eyepiece: *n.* ocular

eyes: *n.* ojos
eyesight: *n.* vista
eyetooth: *n.* colmillo
eyewitness: *n.* testigo presencial

F

fa: *n.* fa
fable: *n.* fábula
fable collection: fabulario
fabric: *n.* fábrica; tela o género
fabricate: *n.* fabricar
fabricated: *adj.* fabricado
fabrication: *n.* fabricación
fabricator: *n.* fabricante
fabulist: *n.* fabulista
facade: *n.* fachada
face: 1. *n.* cara; faz; 2. *adj.* nominal
face amount: importe nominal
face lift: levantamiento facial quirúrgico
face of a solid: cara de un cuerpo geométrico
face value: valor nominal
facet: *n.* faceta
facetious: *adj.* chistoso
face-to-face interview: entrevista en persona
facial: *adj.* facial
facial: *n.* tratamiento facial
facial features: cara
facies: *n.* rasgos
facilitate: *v.* facilitar
facility: *n.* facilidad; instalación; servicio
facsimile: *n.* facsímile
fact: *n.* hecho

faction: *n.* facción
factious: *adj.* faccioso
factor: *n.* factor
factor of production: factor de producción
factor tree: árbol de factores
factorial: *adj.* factorial
factorization: *n.* división en factores
factory: *n.* fábrica; factoría
factory certificate: certificado de fábrica
factory cost: coste de fábrica
factory expense: gasto de fábrica
factory manager: director de fábrica
factory number: número de fabricación
factory overhead: gasto de fábrica
factory ship: buque factoría
factory trademark: marca de fábrica
factory worker: obrero de fábrica
factotum: *n.* factótum
factsheet: *n.* hoja informativa; hoja de datos
facultative anaerobe: anaerobio facultativo
faculty: *n.* facultad
fade: *v.* marchitar; decolorar; desteñir
fæcal culture: coprocultivo
fæces: *n.* heces
Faeros: Feroes
Fahrenheit: Fahrenheit
Fahrenheit scale: escala Fahrenheit
fail: *v.* fracasar; fallar; quebrar
failure: *n.* fracaso; fallo; quiebra
failure to prosecute: abandono del proceso
failure to report: dejar de informar
fainting: *n.* desmayo
fair: 1. *n.* feria; 2. *adj.* justo
fair competition: competencia justa
fair market value: valor equitativo en el mercado
fair pay: remuneración justa

fair value: valor equitativo; valor justo
fairground: *n.* ferial
fair-market value: valor equitativo de mercado
faith: *n.* fe
faithful: *n.* fiel
fake: *n.* falsificación; impostor
fake: *v.* falsificar
fake money: moneda falsa; dinero falso
fakir: *v.* faquir
falangism: *n.* falangismo
falaropo: *n.* faisán
falcon: *n.* halcón
falconry: *n.* halconería
fall: *n.* baja; caída
fall: *v.* bajar; caer
fall behind: atrasar
fall due: vencer
fall equipment: la protección contra caídas
fallacious: *adj.* falaz
fallacy: *n.* falacia
fallibility: *n.* falibilidad
fallopian: *adj.* de Falopio
fallopian tube: trompa de Falopio
false: *adj.* falso
false money: moneda falsa
false negative: negativo falso
false positive: positivo falso
false statement: declaración falsa
false teeth: dentadura postiza
falsehood: *n.* falsedad
falsetto: *n.* falsete
falsification: *n.* falsificación
falsifier: *n.* falsificador
falsify: *v.* falsificar
falsity: *n.* falsedad
falter: *n.* vacilación
fame: *n.* fama
familiar: *adj.* íntimo; familiar
family: *n.* familia
family allowance: subsidio familiar

family concern: negocio familiar
family employment: empleo de familia
family enterprise: empresa familiar
family maximum benefits: beneficios máximos de familia
family medical history: antecedentes médicos familiares
family members: parientes
family name: nombre de familia
family partnership: sociedad familiar
famine: *n.* hambre
famished: *adj.* famélico
famous: *adj.* famoso
fan: 1. *n.* ventilador; 2. *v.* aventar
fan: *v.* aventar
fanatic: *n.* fanático; -a
fanaticism: *n.* fanatismo
fancied: *adj.* imaginario
fancy: *n.* fantasía
fandango: *n.* fandango
fang: *n.* colmillo
fantasia: *n.* fantasía
fantasy: *n.* literatura fantástica; fantasía
far: 1. *adj.* lejano; largo; 2. *adv.* lejos
farad: *n.* farad; faradio
farce: *n.* farsa
farcical: *adj.* absurdo
fare: *n.* tarifa; precio del billete
fare: *v.* acontecer
farewell: *n.* despedida; adiós
farina: *n.* harina
farm: *n.* granja
farm: *v.* labrar; cultivar
farm bank: banco agrario
farm shop: tienda de granja; tienda rural
farm work: labores agrícolas
farm worker: peón; trabajador agrícola
farmer: *n.* granjero; agricultor
farming: 1. *n.* agricultura; agro; 2.

adj. concerniente a la agricultura
farmyard: *n.* corral de granja
farsightedness: *n.* hipermetropía
farther: *adv.* más lejos
farthing: *n.* cuarto de penique
fascia: *n.* fachada
fascia board: la moldura de la fachada
fascicle: *n.* fascículo
fascinating: *n.* fascinador; fascinante
fascination: *n.* fascinación
fascism: *n.* fascismo
fase: *n.* fase
fashion: *n.* forma; uso; estilo
fast: *adj.* rápido
fasten: *v.* ajar
fastener: *n.* sujetador
fastidious anaerobe: anaerobio exigente
fat: *adj.* grasas
fatal: *adj.* fatal
fatalist: *n.* fatalista
fate: *n.* fatalidad
father-in-law: suegro
fatigue: *n.* fatiga; cansancio
fatiguing: *adj.* fatigoso
fatty acid: ácido graso
fatty food: comida grasosa
fatty stool: heces con grasa
faucet: *n.* grifo
fault: *n.* falta
faust: *n.* fausto
Faustian: *adj.* faustiano; faústico
fauvism: *n.* fauvismo
favor: *n.* favor
favorable outcomes: resultados favorables
favorite: *adj.* favorito
favoritism: *n.* favoritismo
fax: *n.* fax
fax: *v.* faxear
feasibility: *n.* factibilidad
feasibility study: estudio de factibilidad

feasible: *adj.* viable; factible
feast: *n.* fiesta; banquete; festín
February: febrero
fecal culture: coprocultivo
feces: *n.* heces
federal: *adj.* federal
federal grants: subvenciones federales
federal tax: impuesto federal; impuesto nacional
federalism: *n.* federalismo
federation: *n.* federación
fee: *n.* honorario; emolumento; tarifa; comisión
fee splitting: división de honorarios
feedback: *n.* retroacción
feet: *n.* pies
felicitation: *n.* felicitación
felicity: *n.* felicidad
fellow: *n.* compañero; camarada
felon: *n.* felón
felonious homicide: homicidio con felonía
felony: *n.* delito grave; felonía
felt: *n.* fieltro
female: *n.* hembra
feminine: *adj.* femenino
feminine: *adj.* femenino
feminism: *n.* feminismo
femur: *n.* fémur
fence: *n.* cerca
fennel: *n.* hinojo
ferment: *n.* fermento
ferment: *adj.* fermento
fermentation: *n.* fermentación
fermentation test: prueba de la fermentación
fermented: *adj.* fermentado
fermi: *n.* fermi
ferocious: *adj.* feroz
ferocity: *n.* ferocidad
ferritin: *n.* ferritina
ferrochelatase: *n.* ferroquelatasa
ferromagnetic material: material

ferromagnético
ferrous: *adj.* ferroso
ferroxidase: *n.* ferroxidasa
fertile: *adj.* fértil
fertility: *n.* fertilidad
fertilization: *n.* fecundación
fertilizer: *n.* fertilizante
fervor: *n.* fervor
festival: *n.* festival
festivity: *n.* festividad
festoon: *n.* festón
fetal: *n.* fetal
fetal hæmoglobin: hemoglobina fetal
fetid; foetid: *adj.* fétido
fetidness: *n.* fetidez
fetish: *n.* fetiche
fetishism: *n.* fetichismo
fetus: *n.* feto
feud: *n.* contienda
feudalism: *n.* feudalismo
fever: *n.* fiebre
few: pocos; algunos
fez: *n.* fez
fhilopatry: *n.* filopatria
fiancé: *n.* novio
fiasco: *n.* fiasco
fib: *v.* embuste; mentir
fiber; fibre: *n.* fibra
fiberglass: *n.* vidrio fibroso
fibre optics: fibra óptica
fibrillation: *n.* fibrilación
fibrin: *n.* fibrina
fibrinase: *n.* plasmina
fibrinogen: *adj.* fibrinógeno
fibrinogen: *n.* fibrinógeno
fibrinogenase: *n.* trombina
fibrinolysin: *n.* plasmina
fibroblast: *n.* fibroblasto
fibroid: *n.* fibroide
fibrosis: *n.* fibrosis
fibula: *n.* fíbula
ficain: *n.* ficaína
ficin: *n.* ficaína

fickle: *adj.* inconstante
fiction: *n.* ficción
fictitious asset: activo ficticio
fictitious name: nombre ficticio
fiddle: *n.* violín
fidelity: *n.* fidelidad
fidget: *n.* persona agitada
fidget: *v.* agitar
fidgety: *n.* inquieto
fiduciary: *adj.* fiduciario
fiduciary money: moneda fiduciaria
field: *n.* terreno; campo
field auditor: auditor viajante
field manager: gerente regional
field of activity: campo de actividad
field of operations: campo de operaciones
field office: oficina regional
field representative: representante de área
field salesman: vendedor viajero
field survey: encuesta de mercado
fiend: *n.* diablo
fierce: *adj.* fiero; cruel
fiesta: *n.* fiesta
fifteen: quince
fifty: cincuenta
fig: *n.* higo; higuera
fight: *n.* lucha
figuration: *n.* figuración
figurative: *adj.* figurado
figure: *n.* cifra; número; figura
figure of speech: figura retórica
figured: *adj.* calculado
figurehead: *adj.* testaferro
figurine: *n.* figura
fiharhnarri: la tabla de fibra
filament: *n.* filamento
filch: *v.* birlar; hurtar
file: *n.* fichero; archivo
file: *v.* archivar
file an application: hacer una solicitud
file clerk: archivista; archivador

file conversion: conversión de archivos
file copy: copia de archivo
file deletion: borrado de archivos
file for civil action: entablar una acción civil
file name: nombre de fichero; nombre de archivo
file room: archivo; habitación de archivo
file server: servidor de archivos
file transfer protocol (FTP): protocolo de transferencia de ficheros
filet; fillet: *n.* filete
filial: *adj.* filial
filigree: *n.* filigrana
filing cabinet: archivo; fichero
filing card: ficha; ficha de archivo
filing date: fecha de solicitud
fill: *n.* abundancia
fill: *v.* llenar
fillet: *n.* cortar en filetes
fill-in reaction: reacción de relleno
filling (teeth): *n.* empaste
film: *n.* película; filme
film: *v.* filmar
film advertising: publicidad cinematográfica
film industry: industria cinematográfica
film library: filmoteca
filming: *n.* filmación
filter: *v.* filtrar
filter: *n.* filtro
filter: *v.* filtrar
filter flask: frasco de filtración
filter hybridization: hibidación sobre filtro
filtration: *n.* filtración
fimbriae: *n.* fimbria
final: *adj.* final
final dividend: dividendo final
final settlement: liquidación final
finale: *n.* final

finalist: *n.* finalista
finality of decision: finalidad de la decisión
finance: *n.* finanza
finance: *v.* financiar; solventar
finance bill: ley de presupuestos
finance company: compañía financiera
finance department: departamento de finanzas
finance director: director financiero
finance manager: gerente financiero
financial: *adj.* financiero
financial account: cuenta financiera
financial accounting: contabilidad financiera
financial asset: activo financiero
financial backing: respaldo financiero
financial burden: carga financiera
financial charge: cargo financiero
financial company: compañía financiera
financial condition: situación financiera
financial cost: coste financiero; costo financiero
financial department: departamento financiero
financial director: director financiero
financial engineering: ingeniería financiera
financial expense: gasto financiero
financial flow: flujo financiero
financial hardship: privación económica
financial income: ingresos financieros
financial institution: institución financiera
financial investment: inmovilizado financiero
financial liability: responsabilidad

financiera
financial management: gestión financiera
financial manager: gerente financiero
financial position: situación financiera
financial profit: beneficio financiero
financial rate: índice financiero
financial ratio: índice financiero
financial report: informe financiero
financial resources: recursos financieros
financial security: título financiero
financial services: servicios financieros
financial standing: situación financiera
financial statement: estado financiero
financial support: apoyo financiero
financial year: año financiero
financier: *n.* financista
financing: 1. *n.* financiación; financiamiento; 2. *adj.* financiero
find: *n.* hallazgo
find: *v.* hallar; descubrir; encontrar
finding: *n.* fallo; decisión
fine: 1. *n.* multa; 2. *adj.* fino
fine: *v.* multar
finely: *adv.* en trozos menudos
finery: *n.* vestido de gala
finger: *n.* dedo
fingernail: *n.* uña
fingerprint: *n.* huella
fingerprinting: *n.* obtención de la huella genética
finish: *v.* acabar; terminar
finish: *n.* fin; termino
finish: *v.* acabar; rematar
finished product: producto terminado
finite: *adj.* finito
finite group: el grupo finito

Finland: Finlandia
Finn: *n.* finlandés; -esa
Finnish: *n.* finlandés
fiord: *n.* fiordo
fiord: *adj.* fiordo
fir: *n.* abeto
fire: *n.* fuego
fire: *v.* despedir
fire drill: simulacro de incendios
fire insurance: seguro de incendio
fireworks: *n.* fuegos artificiales
firm: 1. *n.* firma; casa; 2. *adj.* firme
firm contract: contrato en firme
firm letter of credit: carta de crédito irrevocable
firm name: firma social
firm offer: oferta firme
firm order: pedido en firme
firm signature: firma social
first: 1. *n. adj.* primero; 2. *adv.* primeramente
first class: primera clase
first degree: de primer grado
first draft: anteproyecto; borrador
first hand: primera mano
first lien: primer gravamen
first mortgage: primera hipoteca
first name: nombre de pila
first payment: pago inicial
first person: *n.* primera persona
first price: precio inicial
first world: primer mundo
first-class: de primera clase
first-in; first-out: primero que llega primero sale
first-preferred share: acción de primera preferencia
firth: *n.* estuario
fiscal: *adj.* tributario; impositivo; fiscal
fiscal year: año fiscal
fish: pescado
fish: *v.* pescar
fish hook: anzuelo

fishery: *n.* pesquería
fishing industry: industria pesquera
fission: *n.* fisión
fissure: *n.* fisura
fist: *n.* puño
fist: *v.* empuñar; dar puñetazos
fistula: *n.* fístula
fit: *n.* ajuste; encaje
fit: *v.* ajustar; encajar
fitfulness: *n.* capricho
fitting: 1. *adj.* apropiado; 2. prueba
five: cinco
fix: *n.* apuro; aprieto
fix: *v.* fijar; reparar
fixative: *adj.* fijador
fixed: fijo; no corriente
fixed asset: activo fijo; activo inmovilizado; inmovilizado material
fixed chargef: cargo fijo
fixed cost: coste fijo
fixed debt: deuda fija
fixed exchange: rata; tipo de cambio fijo
fixed expense: gasto fijo
fixed income: ingresos fijos
fixed interest: interés fijo
fixed liability: pasivo no exigible a corto plazo
fixed price: precio fijo
fixed rate: tipo de interés fijo; tasa fija; tarifa fija
fixed rent: alquiler fijo
fixed term: plazo fijo
fixed-rate depreciation: depreciación lineal
fixed-rate security: título de interés fijo; valor de interés fijo
fixed-term bond: bono a plazo fijo
fixed-term deposit: depósito a plazo fijo
fixer: *n.* fijador
fixing bath: baño fijador
fixture: *n.* accesorio; instalación
flaccidity: *n.* flaccidez

flag: *n.* bandera; insignia
flagellar stain: tinción flagelar
flagellation: *n.* flagelación
flagellator: *n.* flagelador
flagellum: *n.* flagelo
flagrant: *adj.* escandaloso; flagrante
flake: *n.* escama; copo
flame: *n.* llama
flame: *v.* llamear
flamenco: *n.* flamenco
flan: *n.* flan
flange: *n.* pestaña
flange: *v.* rebordear
flank: *n.* costado
flank: *v.* flanquear; orillar
flanking sequence: secuencia flanqueadora
flannel: *n.* franela
flannelette: *n.* franela
flap: *n.* falda
flash: *n.* flash
flashback: *n.* flashback
flask: *n.* frasco
flat: *adj.* uniforme; lineal
flat charge: cargo global
flat cost: coste global
flat market: mercado poco activo
flat price: precio global
flat rate: tarifa fija; precio alzado
flat sales: ventas poco activas
flat yield: renta neta
flatness: *n.* planicie
flatten: *v.* aplastar; aplanar
flatulence: *n.* flatulencia
flavor: *n.* aroma; sabor
flavor: *v.* saborear; condimentar
flaw: *n.* defecto; ráfaga
flaw: *v.* agrietar
flea: *n.* pulga
flection: *n.* flexión
flee: *v.* huir
fleece: *n.* lana
fleet: 1. *n.* flota; 2. *adj.* veloz
flemish: *adj.* flamenco

flesh: *n.* carne
fleshpot: *n.* olla
flexible: *adj.* flexible
flexible copper: el cobre flexible
flexible duct: conducto flexible
flexible timetable: horario flexible
flexitime: *n.* horario flexible
flexor: *n.* flexor
flight: *n.* vuelo; fuga
flight attendant: *n.* auxiliar de vuelo
flight crew: tripulación de vuelo
flimsy: *adj.* débil
fling: *n.* tiro
fling: *v.* tirar; arrojar
flip: *v.* voltear
flirt: *n.* coqueta
flirt: *v.* flirtear
float: *n.* flotador
float: *v.* flotar; emitir
floating: *adj.* flotante; variable
floating asset: activo variable; activo flotante
floating capital: capital circulante
floating debt: deuda variable; deuda flotante
floating liability: pasivo variable; pasivo flotante
floating policy: póliza flotante
floating rate: tipo de interés flotante
floccose: *adj.* flocoso; -a
flock: *n.* manada; rebaño; tr. reunirse
flood: *n.* inundación
flood plain: llanura de aluvión
floor: *n.* enlosar; piso
floor drain: el desague del piso
floor joist: la vigueta del piso
floor leveler: el nivelador de piso
floor tile: la baldosa; la loseta
flooring: *n.* solado; instalación del piso
flop: *n.* negocio o producto que no ha tenido éxito
flop: *v.* fallar; fracasar
floppy disk: disquete flexible

floppy disk: disketa floppy
flora: *n.* flora
florescence: *n.* florescencia
floriculture: *n.* floricultura
florin: *n.* florín
florist: *n.* florista
florist shop: floristería
flotation: *n.* emisión; flotación
flotation cost: coste de emisión
flotilla: *n.* flotilla
flour: *n.* harina
flourish: *n.* floreo
flourish: *n.* floreo
flout: *n.* mofa
flout: *v.* mofar
flow: *n.* flujo
flow: *v.* fluir
flow cytometry: citometría de flujo
flow injection: inyección en flujo
flow production: producción continua
flow rate: caudal
flow switch: el interruptor de flujo
flowchart diagram: de flujo; flujograma
flower: *n.* flor
flower: *n.* flor
flower arrangement: arreglo floral
flowered: *adj.* floreado
flowering: *n.* florecimiento
flowing: 1. *n.* manantial; 2. *adj.* fluido
flu: *n.* gripe
fluconazole: *n.* fluconazol
fluctuate: *v.* fluctuar; variar
fluctuation: *n.* fluctuación; variación
fluency: *n.* fluidez
fluent: *adj.* afluente; liquido; con fluidez
fluently: *adv.* con fluidez
fluff: *n.* plumón
fluid: *n.* fluido
fluid friction: fricción de fluido
fluorescein: *n.* fluresceína

fluorescent: *adj.* fluorescente
fluorescent lamp: tubo fluorescente
fluorescent light: luz fluorescente
fluorescent stain: tinción fluorescente
fluorescent-antibody test: prueba del anticuerpo fluorescente
fluoridation: *n.* fluorización
fluorometry: *n.* fluorimetría
fluoroscope: *n.* fluoroscopio
fluoroscopy: *n.* fluoroscopia
flurry: *n.* agitación
flurry: *v.* agitar; confundir
flush: *n.* tope
flush end: extremo romo
flu-shot: vacuna de influenza; de gripe
fluster: *n.* aturdimiento
fluster: *v.* confundir
flute: *n.* flauta
flutist: *n.* flautista
flutter: *n.* tumulto
flutter: *v.* agitar
fluvial: *adj.* fluvial
flux: *n.* flujo
fly: *n.* mosca; bragueta
flying: *adj.* volador
FM: FM
foal: *n.* potro; buche
foam: *n.* espuma
foamy stools: heces espumosas
focal: *adj.* focal
focal point: punto de enfoque
focus: *n.* foco
focus group: grupo de muestra
foe: *n.* enemigo
foehn: *n.* fohn
fog: *n.* niebla; confusión
foil: *n.* chapa metálica; rastro; pasta
folate: *n.* folato
fold: *v.* plegar; doblar
folder: *n.* carpeta
folding: *adj.* plegable
foliate: *n.* foliado

foliage: *n.* follaje; hojas
folic acid: ácido fólico
folio: *n.* folio
folk: 1. *n.* gente; pueblo; 2. *adj.* popular
folk music: música folclórica
folk singer: cantante de música folk
folklore: *n.* folklore
folkloric: *adj.* folklórico; folclórico
folklorist: *n.* folklorista; folclorista
follicle: *n.* folículo
follitropin: *n.* folitropina
follow: *v.* seguir; suceder; copiar
follow-up: *n.* continuación
folly: *n.* locura; disparate
fomentation: *n.* fomento
fomite: *n.* fómite
fond: *adj.* aficionado
fondle: *v.* acariciar
fondue: *n.* fondue
font: *n.* fuente; tipo de letra
font: *n.* fuente
fontanel: *n.* fontanela
food: *n.* comida
food: *v.* engañar; embaucar
food chain: cadena alimentaría
food coloring: colorante alimenticio
food industry: industria alimentaría
food processor: procesador de alimentos
food stuff: productos alimenticios; comestibles
food web: red alimentaría
food-borne illness: enfermedad transmitida por alimentos
foolhardy: *adj.* temerario
foot: *n.* pie
football: *n.* fútbol; balón de fútbol
football fanatic: aficionado al fútbol; futbolero
footing: *n.* zapata; el cimiento
footmark: *n.* huella
footpath: *n.* camino para peatones
footprint: *n.* huella; pisada

footprinting: *n.* obtención de la pisada
footwall: *n.* labio inferior
for: *prep.* para; por
forage: *n.* forraje
forbear: *n.* antepasado
forbid: *v.* impedir; prohibir
force: *n.* fuerza
force: *v.* forzar
force majeure: fuerza mayor
forced: *adj.* forzado
forced heir: heredero forzoso
forced sale: venta forzosa
forceps: *n.* fórceps
forceps delivery: parto con forceps
fore: 1. *adj.* anterior; 2. *adv.* anteriormente
fore: *n.* delantera; proa
forearm: *n.* antebrazo
forecast: *v.* pronosticar; calcular
foreclose: *v.* ejecutar
foreclosure: *n.* ejecución
foreclosure of a mortgage: ejecución de hipoteca
foreclosure sale: venta judicial
forefather: *n.* antepasado
forego: *v.* renunciar
foreground: *n.* primer piso
forehead: *n.* frente
foreign: *adj.* externo; exterior; extranjero
foreign affairs: asuntos exteriores
foreign aid: ayuda externa
foreign bank: banco extranjero
foreign bill: letra externa; letra sobre el exterior
foreign commerce: comercio exterior
foreign competition: competencia externa
foreign corporation: empresa extranjera
foreign creditor: acreedor extranjero; acreedor externo

foreign currency: moneda extranjera
foreign currency account: cuenta en moneda extranjera
foreign currency deposit: depósito en moneda extrajera
foreign currency reserve: reserva de moneda extranjera
foreign debt: deuda externa
foreign debtor: deudor externo
foreign exchange: cambio exterior; moneda extranjera
foreign exchange law: ley cambiaria
foreign exchange market: mercado de divisas
foreign exchange rate: tipo de cambio de divisas
foreign legal adoption: adopción legal extranjera
foreign loan: préstamo externo
foreign market: mercado externo
foreign object: objeto extraño
foreign sector: sector externo
foreign trade: comercio exterior
foreign trade department: departamento de comercio exterior
foreign trade director: director de comercio exterior
foreign trade manager: director de comercio exterior
foreign trade zone: zona franca
foreign work test: límite de trabajo en el extranjero
foreigner: *n.* extranjero
foreman: *n.* capataz; mayordomo
foremost: 1. *adj.* delantero; 2. *adv.* primero
forenoon: *n.* mañana
forensic: *adj.* forense
forensic medicine: medicina forense
foresay: *v.* pronosticar
foresee: *v.* prever
forest: *n.* bosque
forestall: *v.* impedir
forestation: *n.* forestación

forester: *n.* guarda forestal
forestry: *n.* ingeniería forestal
forewarn: *v.* prevenir
foreword: *n.* advertencia; prólogo
forfeit: *n.* multa
forfeit: *v.* perder el derecho a
forfeiture: *n.* confiscación
forge: *n.* fragua
forge: *v.* falsificar; fraguar
forged: *adj.* fundido
forgery: *n.* falsificación
forget: *v.* olvidar
forgive: *v.* perdonar
forint: *n.* forint
fork: *n.* tenedor
forklift: la carretilla elevadora; el montacargas
form: el formulario
form: *n.* forma
form: *v.* formar
form letter: circular
formal: *adj.* formal; ceremonioso
formal dehyde: formaldehído
formalism: *n.* formalismo
formalist: *n.* formalista
format: *n.* formato
format: *v.* formatear
formation: *n.* constitución; formación
formation deed: escritura de constitución
formation expense: gasto de constitución
formative: *adj.* formativo
formatting: *n.* formateado
forment: *v.* fomentar
formula: *n.* fórmula
formulary: *n.* formulario
formulate: *v.* formular
fornication: *n.* fornicación
forsake: *v.* abandonar
forsooth: *adv.* ciertamente
forsythia: *n.* forsitia
fort: *adj.* fuerte

fortification: *n.* fortificación
fortified: *adj.* fortificado
fortify: *v.* fortificar; reforzar
fortissimo: *adv.* fortísimo
fortitude: *n.* fortaleza
fortnight: *n.* quincena
fortran: *n.* fortrán
fortress: *n.* fortaleza
fortune: *n.* fortuna
forum: *n.* foro
forward: 1. *adj.* anticipado; futuro; 2. *adv.* adelante
forward: *v.* enviar; remitir
forward exchange rate: tipo de cambio futuro
forward integration: integración vertical
forward market: mercado a término; mercado futuro
forward mutation: mutación directa
forward purchase: compra a término; compra futura
forward quotation: cotización futura
forward sale: venta a término; venta futura
forwarder: *n.* expedidor; despachante; transitario
forwarding: 1. *n.* expedición; envío; despacho; 2. *adj.* concerniente al envío
forwarding address: dirección para el envío
forwarding agent: agente de aduanas; transitario
fossil: *n.* fósil
fossil fuel: combustible fósil
fossil record: registro fósil
foster: *adj.* adoptivo
foster: *v.* adoptar; mimar; criar
foster care: cuidado tutelar
foster home: hogar de cuidado tutelar
foul: *n.* sucio; fraude

foul dealing: mala fe; trato con mala fe
foul-smelling: heces con muy mal olor
foul-smelling stools: heces con muy mal olor
found: *v.* fundar; fundir
foundation: *n.* fundación; fundamento
founder: *n.* fundador
founder's share: acción de fundador
founding member: miembro fundador
founding shareholder: accionista fundador
foundry: *n.* fundición
fount: *n.* fuente
fountain: *n.* fuente
four: cuatro
fourteen: catorce
fourth: cuarto
fourth degree: cuarto grado
fowl: *n.* ave; carne de ave
fox: *n.* zorro
foxtrot: *n.* foxtrot
foxy: *adj.* astuto
foyer: *n.* vestíbulo
fractal: *n.* fractal
fractile: *n.* fractil
fraction: *n.* fracción
fractional currency: moneda fraccionaria
fracture: *n.* fractura
fragment: *n.* fragmento
fragment: *v.* fragmentar
fragmentation: *n.* fragmentación
fragrance: *n.* fragancia
frame: *n.* estructura; armadura
frame: *v.* formar; ajustar
framed: *adj.* enmarcado
frameless: *adj.* sin marco
framework: *n.* entramado
framing: *n.* armazón
franc: *n.* franco

France: Francia
franchise: *n.* franquicia; concesión
franchise: *v.* dar en concesión; franquiciar
Franciscan: *n.* franciscano
Franco: *adj.* franco; exento; libre
frangipani: *n.* franchipaniero
frank: *adj.* franco; sincero
franking: *n.* franqueo
frankness: *adj.* franqueza
fraternal: *adj.* fraternal
fraternization: *n.* fraternización
fratricide: *adj.* fratricidio
fraud: *n.* fraude; engaño
fraudulent: *adj.* fraudulento
fraudulent bankruptcy: quiebra fraudulenta
freak: *n.* capricho
freckle: *n.* peca
free: *adj.* gratuito; gratis
free: *v.* liberar
free access: libre acceso
free competition: libre competencia
free dollar: dólar libre
free economy: economía libre
free energy: energía libre
free enterprise: libre empresa
free exchange: cambio libre
free exchange market: mercado libre de cambios
free exchange rate: tipo de cambio libre
free fall: caída libre
free fatty acids: ácidos grasos no esterificados
free market: de libre mercado
free market economy: economía de libre mercado
free market mercado: mercado abierto
free of charge: libre de gastos
free of duty: libre de derechos
free of encumbrance: libre de gravamen

free of general average: sin avería general
free on board: libre a bordo
free on dock: libre en el muelle
free on quay: libre en el muelle
free on rail: libre sobre el vagón
free on truck: libre sobre camión
free pamphlet: folleto gratis
free port: puerto libre
free rate: tasa no regulada
free sample: muestra gratis
free time: *n.* tiempo libre
free trade: comercio libre
free verse: verso libre
free zone: zona franca; zona libre
freebie: *n.* producto o servicio gratis
freedom: *n.* libertad
freehold: *n.* dominio absoluto
freehold estate: propiedad de dominio absoluto
freehold in deed: posesión real
freehold in law: título sin posesión real
freehold property: propiedad de dominio absoluto
freeholder: *n.* propietario absoluto
freelance: *n.* trabajo por su cuenta
freelance: *adj.* free-lance
free-living organism: organismo autónomo
freesia: *n.* fresia
freeware: *n.* producto o servicio gratis
freeze: *n.* bloqueo
freeze: *v.* bloquear; congelar
freezer: *n.* congelador; freezer
freezing: *n.* congelación
freight: *n.* carga; cargamento
freight: *v.* fletar
freight bill: carta de porte
freight elevator: montacargas
freight free: porte franco
freight note: albarán de carga
freight notice: aviso de recepción

freight prepaid: porte pagado
freight rate: tarifa de fletamento
freight receipt: guía de carga
freight station: estación de carga
freight train: tren de carga
freight yard: patio de carga
freightage (cost): *n.* flete; carga
freighter: *n.* fletador; transportista; fletero
French: *n.* francés
french fries: patatas fritas
French Guyana: Guayana Francesa
French Polynesia: Polinesia Francesa
french toast: torrija; tostada francesa
French-Canadian: *adj.* francocanadiense
Frenchman: *n.* francés
Frenchwoman: *n.* francesa
frenum: *n.* frenillo
frenzy: *n.* frenesí
frequency: *n.* de frecuencias; frecuencia
frequency distribution: la distribución de frecuencia
frequency modulation: frecuencia modulada
frequency table: tabla de frecuencias
frequent: *adj.* frecuente
frequent: *v.* frecuentar
frequentative: *adj.* frecuentativo
fresh: *adj.* fresco; reciente
freshen: *v.* refrescar
friar: *n.* fraile
fricassee: *n.* fricasé
friction: *n.* fricción
friction factor: factor de fricción
frictional coefficient: coeficiente de fricción
fridge: *n.* frigorífico
fried: *adj.* frito; -a
friend: *n.* amistad; amigo
frigate: *n.* fragata
fright: *n.* susto; miedo

frighten: *v.* asustar; espantar
frigid: *adj.* frígido
fringe: *adj.* adicional; extra
fringe: *n.* franja
fringe benefit: beneficio adicional
frisbee: *n.* frisbee
fritillary: *n.* fritilaria
fritter: 1. *n.* fritada; fritura; 2. *adv.* atrás
fritter: *v.* desmenuzar; esparcir
frivolity: *n.* frivolidad
frivolous: *adj.* frívolo
frock: *n.* vestido; blusa; bata
frog: *n.* rana
frolic: *n.* travesura
from: *prep.* de; desde
frond: *n.* fronda
front: 1. *n.* frente; 2. *adj.* delantero
front desk manager: encargado de recepción
frontal: *adj.* frontal
front-end cost: coste inicial; coste de entrada
front-end estimation: estimación por la izquierda
front-end fee: comisión inicial
frontier: *n.* frontera
frontispiece: *n.* frontispicio
frozen: *adj.* congelado; inmovilizado
frozen account: cuenta inmovilizada
frozen asset: activo inmovilizado
frozen price: precio invariable; precio congelado
fructokinase: *n.* fructocinasa
fructosamine: *n.* fructosamina
fructose: *n.* fructosa
frugal: *adj.* frugal
frugality: *n.* frugalidad
fruit: *n.* fruta
fruit bowl: frutero
fruit farmer: fruticultor
fruit growing: *n.* fruticultura
fruit merchant: frutero
fruit store: frutería

fruit tree: frutal
fruiting body: órgano fructífero
fruity: *adj.* afrutado; frutoso
frusemide: *n.* furosemida
frustrated: *adj.* frustrado
frustration: *n.* frustración
fry: *n.* fritada; fritura
fry: *v.* freír
frying pan: sartén
fuchsia: *n.* fucsia
fuel: *n.* combustible
fuel rod: varilla de combustible
fugitive: *adj.* fugitivo
fugue: *n.* fuga
fulcrum: *n.* fulcro
fulfill: *v.* cumplir
full: *adj.* lleno; completo
full authority: autoridad absoluta
full blood count: hemograma completo
full endorsement: garantía absoluta
full liability: responsabilidad total
full load: carga máxima
full loss: pérdida total
full meeting: sesión plenaria
full member: miembro de tiempo completo
full payment: pago total
full retirement age: edad de jubilación completa
full time: jornada completa; horario completo
fuller: *adj.* fullereno
fullerene: fullereno
full-time: a tiempo completo
full-time student: estudiante de tiempo completo
fully insured: totalmente asegurado
fully-paid: completamente pagado
fully-paid share: acción pagada
fulmination: *n.* fulminación
fulminator: *n.* fulminador
fulsome: *adj.* de mal gusto
fumble: *v.* manosear; balbucear

fumigant: *n.* sustancia fumigatoria
fumigation: *n.* fumigación
fumigator: *n.* fumigador
fun: *n.* broma
function: *v.* funcionar
function: *n.* función
function: *v.* funcionar
function notation: notación de función
functional: *adj.* funcional
functional administration: administración funcional
functional assessment: evaluación funcional
functional authority: autoridad funcional
functional test: prueba funcional
functionalism: *n.* funcionalismo
functionary: *n.* funcionario
fund: *n.* fondo; capital
fund: *v.* financiar
fund flow: flujo de fondos; movimiento de fondos
fund raising: obtención de fondos
fundamental: *adj.* fundamental
fundamental tone: tono fundamental
fundamentalism: *n.* fundamentalismo
funded: *adj.* costeada
funded debt: deuda consolidada
funded liability: pasivo consolidado
funded security: valor de interés
fundholder: *n.* rentista de fondos
funding bond: bono de consolidación
funeral: *n.* funeral
funeral home: funeraria
fungal: *adj.* fungal
fungemia: *n.* fungemia
fungible: *adj.* fungible
fungicide: *n.* fungicida
fungus: *n.* hongo
funicular: *n.* funicular
funny: *adj.* cómico; divertido

fur: *n.* piel
fur: *v.* cubrir o forrar con pieles
furious: *adj.* furioso
furnace: *n.* hornilla
furnish: *v.* amueblar; proveer
furniture: *n.* mobiliario; muebles
furniture and fixtures: muebles e instalaciones
furosemide: *n.* furosemida
furtive: *adj.* furtivo
furuncle (boil): *n.* furúnculo
fury: *n.* furia
fuse: *n.* fusible
fuse: *v.* fusionar
fuselage: *n.* fuselaje
fuss: *n.* alboroto; ajetreo
fustian: *n.* fustán
futility: *n.* futilidad
future: *adj.* futuro
future contract: contrato futuro
future currency: divisa futura
future delivery: entrega futura
future exchange: cambio futuro
future exchange rate: tipo de cambio futuro
future income: ingresos futuros
future market: mercado futuro; mercado a término
future operation: operación de futuro
future profit: ganancia futura
future purchase: compra futura
future value: valor futuro
futures market: mercado de títulos futuros
futurism: *n.* futurismo

G

gabardine: *n.* gabardina
gaelic: *n.* gálico
gag: *n.* mordaza
gag: *v.* amordazar
gage: *n.* prenda; fianza
gage: *v.* medir; calcular
gaiety: *n.* alegría; diversión
gain: *n.* ganancia
gain: *n.* ganancia; beneficio
gain: *v.* ganar; beneficiarse
gainful: *adj.* lucrativo
gainful employment: empleo remunerado
gainful occupation: actividad remunerada
gait: *n.* paso; andar
gala: *n.* gala
galactose: *n.* galactosa
galaxy: *n.* galaxia
gale: *n.* viento fuerte; explosión; temporal
gall: *n.* rencor; rozadura
gall: *v.* rozar
gall bladder: vesícula biliar
gallantry: *n.* galantería; gallardía; nobleza
gallbladder: *n.* vesícula biliar
gallery: *n.* galería
galley: *n.* galera; galerada
galley proof: galerada
galliard: *n.* gallarda
gallon: *n.* galón
gallows: *n.* horca
gallstone: *n.* piedras de la vesícula
galop: *n.* galopa
galvanism: *n.* galvanismo

galvanometer: *n.* galvanómetro
Gambia: Gambia
Gambian: *adj.* gambiano
gambit: *n.* gambito
gamble: *v.* jugar
game: *n.* juego; caza
game theory: ley de probabilidades
gamelan: *n.* gamelán
gametophyte: *n.* gametofito
gamma: *n.* gamma
gamma radiation: radiación gamma
gamma ray: rayo gamma
gamut: *n.* gama
gang: *n.* pandilla
ganglion: *n.* ganglio
gangrene: *n.* gangrena
gangster: *n.* gángster
gangsterism: *n.* gangsterismo
gap: *n.* boquete
gap: *v.* hacer brecha en; desgarrar
gape: *n.* abertura
gape: *v.* bostezar
garage: *n.* garaje
garage attendant: garajista
garb: *n.* vestidura; aspecto
garb: *v.* vestir
garbage: *n.* basura
garden: *n.* jardín; huerto
gardener: *n.* jardinero; -a
gardenia: *n.* gardenia
gardening: *n.* jardinería
gargle: *n.* gargarismo
gargling: *n.* gárgaras; gargarismos
garlic: *n.* ajo
garment: *n.* prenda de vestir
garment: *v.* vestir
garnet: *n.* granate
garnish: *n.* adorno; guarnición
garnish: *v.* adornar; guarnecer; guarnecer
garnishment embargo: retención del salario
garrison: *n.* guarnición
garrote: *n.* garrote

garrulous: *adj.* gárrulo
gas: *n.* gas
gas: *v.* gasear
gas giant: gigante gaseoso
gas station: gasolinera
gas sterilizer: esterilizador para gas
gascon: *n.* gascón
gasohol: *n.* gasohol
gasoline: *n.* gasolina
gasometer: *n.* gasómetro
gastrectomy: *n.* gastrectomía
gastric contents: contenido gástrico
gastric juice: jugo gástrico
gastricsine: *n.* gastricsina
gastrin: *n.* gastrina
gastritis: *n.* gastritis
gastroenteritis: *n.* gastroenteritis
gastroenterologist: *n.* gastroenterologista
gastroenterology: *n.* gastroenterología
gastrointestinal: *adj.* gastrointestinal
gastrointestinal system: sistema gastrointestinal
gastronome: *n.* gastrónomo
gastronomy: *n.* gastronomía
gastropod: *n.* gasterópodo
gastroscope: *n.* gastroscopio
gastroscopy: *n.* gastroscopia
gate: *n.* puerta; verja
gather: *n.* frunce
gather: *v.* fruncir; reunir; amontonar
gatt: *n.* gatt
gaucho: *n.* gaucho
gauge: *n.* calibre; medida
gauge: *v.* medir; calcular.
gauntlet: *n.* guantelete
gaur: *n.* gaur
gauss: *n.* gauss
gauze: *n.* gasa
gavotte: *n.* gaviota
gaze: *n.* mirada fija
gaze: *v.* mirar
gazelle: *n.* gacela

gazpacho: *n.* gazpacho
gear: *n.* utensilios; marcha
gear: *v.* engranar; conectar
gearing ratio: ajuste general
gecko: *n.* geco
geisha: *n.* geisha
gel: *n.* gel
gelatin: *n.* gelatina
gem: *n.* gema
gemini: *n.* géminis
gemstone: *n.* gema
gendarme: *n.* gendarme
gender: *n.* género
gene: *n.* gen
gene bank: genoteca
gene coupling: apareamiento genético
gene deletion: deleción genética
gene disruption: interrupción genética
gene dosage: dosis genética
gene library: Genoteca
gene manipulation: manipulación genética
gene tagging: marcado genético
gene targeting: reconocimiento genético
gene therapy: terapia genética
gene therapy: terapia genética
gene tracking: seguimiento genético
gene tree: árbol genético
genealogy: *n.* genealogía
general: *adj.* general
general agent: agente general
general anesthesia: anestesia general
general average: avería gruesa
general balance: balance general
general cost: costo general
general covenant: garantía general
general creditor: acreedor ordinario
general expense: gasto general
general guarantee: garantía general
general lien: gravamen general

general management: dirección general
general manager: director general; administrador general
general meeting: reunión general
general mortgage: hipoteca colectiva
general office: oficina de administración
general partner: socio colectivo
general partnership: empresa colectiva
general reserve: reserva general
general share: acción ordinaria
general store: tienda de artículos varios
general strike: huelga general
generalization: *n.* generalización
generalized: *adj.* generalizado
generalship: *n.* generalato
generate: *v.* generar
generation: *n.* generación
generator: *n.* generador
generatrix: *n.* generatriz
generic: *adj.* genérico
generosity: *n.* generosidad
generous: *adj.* generoso
genetic: *adj.* genético
genetic background: contexto genético
genetic code: código genético
genetic disorder: trastorno genético
genetic drift: deriva genética
genetic engineering: ingeniería genética
genetic load: carga genética
genetic marker: marcador genético
genetic transfer: transferencia genética
genetics: *n.* genética
genie: *n.* genio
genitals: *n.* genitales
genitive: 1. *n.* genitivo; 2. *adj.* genitivo

genitourinary: *adj.* genitourinario
genius: *n.* genio
genocide: *n.* genocidio
genome: *n.* genoma
genomic library: genoteca genómica
genotype: *n.* genotipo
genre: *n.* género
gentamicin: *n.* gentamicina
gentian: *n.* genciana
gentle: *adj.* suave; honrado
gentleman: *n.* caballero; señor
genuflection: *n.* genuflexión
genuine: *adj.* genuino
genus: *n.* género
geocentric: *adj.* geocéntrico
geochemistry: *n.* geoquímica
geode: *n.* geoda
geodesic dome: domo geodésico
geodesy: *n.* geodesia
geographer: *n.* geógrafo
geographical: *adj.* geográfico
geography: *n.* geografía
geological: *adj.* geológico
geologist: *n.* geólogo
geology: *n.* geología
geomancy: *n.* geomancia
geometric: *adj.* geométrico
geometric mean: media geométrica
geometric progression: progresión geométrica
geometric ratio: razón geométrica
geometric series: la serie geométrica
geometrical: *adj.* geométrico
geometry: *n.* geometría
geomorphology: *n.* geomorfología
geophysics: *n.* geofísica
geopolitics: *n.* geopolítica
georgette: *n.* georgette
geostrophic: *adj.* geostrófico
geothermal activity: actividad geotérmica
geranium: *n.* geranio
gerbil: *n.* gerbo
geriatric: *adj.* geriátrico

geriatrician: *n.* geriatra
geriatrics: *n.* geriatría
germ: *n.* germen
german measles: rubéola
germicide: *n.* germicida
germination: *n.* germinación
gerontocracy: *n.* gerontocracia
gerontologist: *n.* gerontólogo
gerontology: *n.* gerontología
gerund: *n.* gerundio
gesso: *n.* yeso
gestapo: *n.* gestapo
gestation: *n.* gestación
gestation period: periodo de gestación
gestational protein: proteína gravídica
gesticulation: *n.* gesticulación
gesture: *n.* gesto
get: *v.* obtener; adquirir
get rid of: Quitar
geyser: *n.* geiser
Ghana: Ghana
Ghanaian: *adj.* ghanés; -esa
ghastly: *adj.* horrible
Ghent: Gante
gherkins: *n.* pepinillo
ghetto: *n.* gueto; ghetto
giant: *adj.* gigante
gibbet: *n.* horca
gibbet: *v.* ahorcar
gibbon: *n.* gibón
gibe: *n.* burla
gibe: *v.* mofarse
Gibraltar: Gibraltar
giddiness: *n.* vértigo
gift: *n.* regalo; presente
gift: *v.* obsequiar
gift tax: impuesto a las donaciones
gigabyte: *n.* gigabyte
gigantic: *adj.* gigante; *n.* gigante
gigantism: *n.* gigantismo
gigue: *n.* giga
gild: *v.* dorar; dar lustre

gill: *n.* agalla; branquia
gilt-edged: con buenas referencias o calidad
gilt-edged security: título de primera línea
gin: *n.* ginebra; trampa; grúa
gin rummy: gin rummy
ginger: *n.* jengibre
ginger ale: refresco de jengibre
ginger beer: cerveza de jengibre
gingham: *n.* guinga
gingival: *adj.* gingival
ginkgo: *n.* gingco
ginseng: *n.* ginson; ginseng
giraffe: *n.* jirafa
girdle: *n.* corsé; faja
girl: *n.* muchacha; niña
give: *v.* dar; entregar; conceder
given: *adj.* dado; aficionado
gizzard: *n.* molleja
glacial: *adj.* glacial
glacier: *n.* glaciar
glad: *adj.* alegre
gladiator: *n.* gladiador
gladiolus: *n.* gladiolo
glamour: *n.* glamour
glance: *n.* vistazo
glance: *v.* lanzar una mirada
gland: *n.* glándula; bellota
glands: *n.* glande
glandular kallikrein: calicreína hística
glare: *n.* resplandor; mirada
glare: *v.* deslumbrar
glasnost: *n.* glasnost
glass: *n.* vidrio; vaso
glasses: *n.* lentes; anteojos
glaucoma: *n.* glaucoma
glaze: *n.* glaseado
glaze: *v.* glasear
glazed: *adj.* glaseado
gleam: *n.* brillo
gleam: *v.* destellar; resplandecer
glioma: *n.* glioma

glitter: *n.* brillo; resplandor
glitter: *v.* brillar; resplandecer
global: *adj.* global
global entry: asiento global
global warming: calentamiento global
global winds: vientos globales
globe: *n.* globo
globe trotter: trotamundos
globular cluster: cúmulo globular
globulin: *n.* globulina
glomerular filtrate: filtrado glomerular
glomerular filtration: filtración glomerular
glomeruli: *n.* glomérulos
gloom: *n.* oscuridad; tinieblas
glorification: *n.* glorificación
glory: *n.* gloria
gloss: *n.* glosa
gloss: *v.* abrillantar; glosar
glossary: *n.* glosario
glottis: *n.* glotis
glottochronology: *n.* glotocronología
glove: *n.* guante
glove compartment: guantera
gloxinia: *n.* gloxinea
glucagon: *n.* glucagón
glucose: *n.* glucosa
glucose tolerance test: examen de tolerancia a la glucosa
glue: *n.* cola
glue: *v.* encolar
glutamate: *n.* glutamato
glutamic acid: ácido glutámico
glutaminase: *n.* glutaminasa
glutamine: *n.* glutamina
gluten: *n.* gluten
glutethimide: *n.* glutetimida
gluteus: *n.* glúteo
glutton: *n.* glotón
gluttonous: *adj.* glotón
gluttony: *n.* glotonería
glycated hemoglobin:

glicohemoglobina
glycerine: *n.* glicerina
glycerol: *n.* glicerol
glycine: *n.* glicina
glycogen: *n.* glicógeno
glycogen synthase: glucógeno-sintasa
glycohemoglobin: *n.* glicohemoglobina
glycosuria: *n.* glicosuria; glucosuria
glyptographer: *n.* gliptografo
glyptography: *n.* gliptografia
gnocchi: *n.* ñoquis
gnome: *n.* gnomo; nomo
gnomon: *n.* gnomon
gnosticism: *n.* gnosticismo
gnu: *n.* flu
go: *v.* ir; andar; dirigirse
goal: *n.* meta; objeto; fin; gol
goat: *n.* cabra; macho cabrio
goatee: *n.* perilla
goblet: *n.* copa
goby: *n.* gobio
god: *n.* dios
godchild: *n.* ahijado; ahijada
godfather: *n.* padrino
godmother: *n.* madrina; comadre
godson: *n.* abrigado
go-go: *n.* gogó
going concern: empresa en marcha
going inventory: inventario permanente
going price: precio de venta
gold: *n.* oro; dinero
gold certificate: certificado de oro
gold coin: moneda de oro
gold dust: oro en polvo; oro fino
gold mine: mina de oro
gold reserve: reserva de oro
gold standard: patrón oro
golden: *adj.* dorado
golf club: palo de golf
golf course: cancha de golf
golf; golfing: *n.* golf

golfer: *n.* golfista
gonadorelin: *n.* gonadorelina
gonadotropin: *n.* gonadotropina
gondola: *n.* góndola
gondolier: *n.* gondolero
gone: *adj.* agotado; débil; arruinado
gong: *n.* gong
gonococcus: *n.* gonococo
gonorrhea: *n.* gonorrea
good: 1. *adj.* bueno; sano; 2. *n.* bien; mercancía
good cause: razón justificada
good evening: buenas tardes; buenas noches
good faith: buena fe
good money: salario elevado
good title: título válido
good will: fondo de comercio; crédito comercial
goodbye: *n.* adiós
goods and services: bienes y servicios
goods in transit: mercancía en tránsito
goods on consignment: mercancía en consignación
goose: *n.* ganso
goose berry: grosella espinosa; uva espina
goose fish: rape
Gothic: 1. *adj.* gótico; 2. *n.* gótico
gouache: *n.* guache
goulash: *n.* gulash
gourmet: *n.* gourmet; gastrónomo
gout: *n.* gota
govern: *v.* gobernar
governing board: consejo de administración
governing body: organismo rector
government: *n.* gobierno
government accountancy: contabilidad pública
government accounts: cuentas públicas

government agency: agencia gubernamental
government association: sociedad pública
government authorities: autoridades gubernamentales
government bank: banco estatal; banco público
government body: organismo gubernamental
government bond: bono estatal; título público
government budget: presupuesto gubernamental
government company: sociedad pública; empresa estatal
government debt: deuda pública; renta pública
government department: departamento gubernamental
government enterprise: empresa del estado
government inspector: inspector estatal
government loan: préstamo estatal
government monopoly: monopolio estatal
government office: oficina pública; oficina de gobierno
government property: bien fiscal
government security: bono estatal; valor fiscal
government stock: bono estatal; valor fiscal
government subsidy: subvención oficial
government tax: impuesto estatal; impuesto gubernamental
governor: *n.* gobernador
governorship: *n.* gobierno
gown: *n.* bota; vestido
gown: *v.* vestir con toga
grace: *n.* gracia
grace period: período de gracia

gradation: *n.* gradación
grade: *n.* grado; calidad; grado
grade: *v.* nivelar; graduar; clasificar
gradient: *n.* gradiente
gradual: *adj.* gradual
gradual metamorphosis: metamorfosis gradual
gradualism: *n.* gradualismo
gradually: *adv.* lentamente
graduate: *n.* graduado
graduate: *v.* graduar
graduate association: colegio de graduados
graduated tail: cola graduada
graduation: *n.* graduación
graffiti: *n.* graffiti
graft: *n.* soborno; coima
grain: *n.* grano; cereal
grain board: junta de cereales
grain cereal: grano
grain exchange: bolsa de granos
grainy; granular: *adj.* granulado
gram: *n.* gramo
gramicidin: *n.* gramicidina
gramineous: *adj.* gramíneo
grammar: *n.* gramática
grammatical: *adj.* gramatical
grammatical rule: regla gramatical
gramophone: *n.* gramófono
granary: 1. *n.* granero; 2. *adj.* granero
grand: *adj.* grande
grand opera: gran ópera
grandad: *n.* abuelo
grandchild: *n.* nieto; nieta
granddaughter: *n.* nieta
grandfather: *n.* abuelo
grandiloquent: *adj.* grandilocuente
grandiloquent: *n.* grandilocuente
grandma: *n.* abuela
grandmother: *n.* abuela
granite: *n.* granito
grant: *n.* concesión; subvención
grant: *v.* otorgar; conceder

grant-in-aid: subvención; subsidio
granulated: *adj.* granulado
granulocyte: *n.* granulosito
grape: *n.* uva
grapefruit: *n.* pomelo
graph: *n.* gráfica; diagrama
graph: *v.* representar gráficamente
graph of an inequality: gráfica de una desigualdad
graph paper: papel milimetrado
grapheme: *n.* grafema
graphic: *adj.* gráfico
graphic accent: acento ortográfico
graphic aid: ayuda visual
graphic design: diseño gráfico
graphite: *n.* grafito
graphologist: *n.* grafólogo; -a
graphology: *n.* grafología
grassland: *n.* pradera
grated: *adj.* rallado
grateful: *adj.* agradecido
gratification: *n.* gratificación
gratified: *adj.* gratificado
gratis: *adv.* gratis
gratitude: *n.* gratitud
gratuitous: *adj.* gratuito
gratuitous inducer: inductor gratuito
grave: 1. *n.* grave; 2. *adj.* grave
gravel: *n.* grava
gravida: *n.* mujer grávida
gravimetry: *n.* gravimetría
gravitational potential energy: energía potencial gravitatoria
gravity: *n.* gravedad
gravy: *n.* salsa (hecha con el jugo de la carne)
gravy boat: salsera
gray: *adj.* gris
gray mullet: lisa; mújol
grease: *n.* grasa
grease: *v.* aceitar; enmantequillar
greased: *adj.* engrasado
greaseproof paper: papel encerado o

parafinado
greasy: *adj.* grasiento
Great Britain: Gran Bretaña
greatest common factor (GCF):
máximo común divisor (MCD)
Greco-Roman: *adj.* grecorromano
Greece: Grecia
greedy: *adj.* glotón; codicioso
Greek: *adj.* griego
green beans: habichuelas
green pepper: pimiento verde
green vegetables: vegetales verdes
greengage: *n.* ciruela claudia
greengrocer: *n.* verdulero
greenhouse effect: efecto
invernadero
Greenland: Groenlandia
gregarious: *adj.* gregario
gregorian chant: canto gregoriano
Grenada: Granada
Grenadian: *adj.* granadino; -a
grenadier: *n.* granadero
grenadine: *n.* granadina
griddle: *n.* plancha
gridiron: *n.* parrilla
griffon: *n.* grifón
grill: *n.* grill
grill: *v.* gratinar
grind: *v.* moler; machacar
grinding machine: rectificadora
gringo: *n.* gringo; -a
grippe: *n.* gripe
gristle: *n.* cartílago
grocery: *n.* tienda de comestibles;
almacén
groin: *n.* escollera; ingle
gross: 1. *adj.* bruto; 2. *n.* gruesa
gross: *v.* ganar en bruto
gross amount: importe bruto; monto
bruto
gross average: monto promedio
gross domestic product: producto
bruto interior
gross earning: ganancia bruta;

beneficio bruto
gross income: renta bruta; ingresos
brutos
gross income tax: impuesto a los
ingresos brutos
gross internal product: producto
bruto interno
gross margin: beneficio bruto;
margen bruto
gross mutation: mutación
voluminosa
gross national product: producto
bruto nacional
gross pay: remuneración bruta;
salario bruto
gross profit: ganancia bruta;
beneficio bruto
gross rate: tasa bruta; tipo bruto
gross sale: venta bruta
gross ton: tonelada larga
gross tonnage: porte bruto
gross trading: venta bruta
gross value: valor bruto
gross weight: peso bruto
grotesque: *adj.* grotesco
grotto: *n.* gruta
ground: *adj.* de color café negro
ground water: aguas subterránea
grounded: conectado a tierra
groundnut: *n.* cacahuete
groundwater: aguas freáticas
group: *n.* grupo
group: *v.* agrupar
group depreciation: depreciación
conjunta
group dynamics: dinámica de grupo
grouping: *n.* modo de agrupar
grouping symbols: símbolos de
agrupación
grow: *v.* crecer
growing: creciente
growth: *n.* crecimiento
growth factor: factor de crecimiento
growth hormone: somatotropina

growth rate: tasa de crecimiento
gruel: *n.* gachas
gruyere: *n.* gruyere
Guadeloupe: Guadalupe
Guam: Guam
guanaco: *n.* guanaco
guanase: *n.* guanina-desaminasa
guanine: *n.* guanina
guano: *n.* guano
guanosine: *n.* guanosina
Guarani: *n.* guarani
guarantee: *n.* garantía; aval
guarantee: *v.* garantizar; avalar
guarantee deposit: depósito en garantía
guarantee fund: fondo de garantía
guaranteed: *adj.* garantizado
guaranteed bond: bono garantizado
guaranteed debt: deuda garantizada
guaranteed wage: salario garantizado
guarantor: *n.* avalista; garante
guaranty: *n.* garantía
guard: *n.* vigilante; guarda; guardián
guard: *v.* custodiar; cuidar
guardhouse: *n.* cuartel de la guardia
guardian: *n.* guardián
Guatemala: Guatemala
Guatemalan: *adj.* guatemalteco
guava: *n.* guayaba
guayabera: *n.* guayabera
guayule: *n.* guayule
guerrilla: *n.* guerrillero
guess: *v.* adivinar
guide: *n.* guía
guidebook: *n.* guía
guideline: *n.* guía; normas; pautas
guild: *n.* corporación; gremio
guilder: *n.* gulden
guillotine: *n.* guillotina
guilty: *adj.* culpable
Guinea: Guinea
Guinean: *adj.* guineo; -a
guitar: *n.* guitarra

guitarist: *n.* guitarrista
gulag: *n.* gulag
gulf: *n.* golfo
gully: *adj.* barranco
gum: *n.* goma
gum arabic: goma arábiga
gumbo: *n.* gumbo
gumbo: *n.* quingombó
gummy: *adj.* gomoso
guru: *n.* gurú; guru
gustatory: *adj.* gustativo
gutta-percha: gutapercha
gutteral: *adj.* guteral
Guyana: Guyana
Guyanese: *adj.* guyanés; -esa
gymnasium: *n.* gimnasio
gymnast: *n.* gimnasta
gymnastics: *n.* gimnasia; gimnástica
gymnosperm: *n.* gimnosperma
gynecocracy: *n.* ginecocracia
gynecological examination: examen ginecológico; examen de la pelvis
gynecologist: *n.* ginecólogo
gynecology: *n.* ginecología
gyrocompass: *n.* girocompás
gyropilot: *n.* giropiloto
gyroscope: *n.* giroscopio
gyrostabilizer: *n.* giroestabilizador
habanera: *n.* habanera
habeas corpus: habeas corpus
habit: *n.* hábito; costumbre
habitat: *n.* hábitat
habitat destruction: destrucción del hábitat
habitat fragmentation: fragmentación del hábitat
hacienda: *n.* hacienda
hacker: *n.* violador de información; pirata de informático

H

haddock: *n.* abadejo
haem: *n.* hemo
haem synthase: ferroquelatasa
haematology: *n.* hematología
haemeprotein: *n.* hemoproteína
haemolysis: *n.* hemólisis
haemolyzed blood: sangre
hemolizada
haggle: *n.* regateo
haggle: *v.* regatear
hagiographer: *n.* hagiógrafo
hagiography: *n.* hagiografía
ha-ha!: *intj.* ¡ja-ja!
haiku: *n.* hai kai
hail: *n.* llamada; granizo
hail: *v.* granizar; aclamar
hair: *n.* cabello; pelo
hair penetration test: prueba de la
penetración capilar
hair stylist: estilista
hairbrush: *n.* cepillo de cabeza
haircut: *n.* corte de pelo
hairdresser: *n.* peluquero
hairless: *adj.* calvo
hairline: *n.* raya
hairlock: *n.* rizo
hairpin: *n.* horquilla
hairpin loop: horquilla
Haiti: Haití
Haitian: *adj.* haitiano; -a
hake: *n.* merluza
halcyon: *adj.* sereno; tranquilo
half: 1. *n.* mitad; 2. *adj.* medio; -a
half-life: semivida; vida media
half-plane: semiplano
halibut: *n.* halibut
halitosis: *n.* halitosis

hall: *n.* vestíbulo
hallelujah!: *intj.* ¡aleluya!
hallucinations: *n.* alucinaciones
halo: *n.* halo
halogen: *n.* halógeno
halt: 1. *adj.* cojo; 2. *n.* alto; parado
halt: *v.* parar; detener
halt!: *intj.* ¡alto!
halva; halvah: *n.* halva
halve: *v.* dividir en dos; partir por la
mitad
ham: *n.* jamón
hamburger: *n.* hamburguesa
Hamitic: *n.* camita
hamlet: *n.* caserío
hammer: *n.* martillo
hammock: *n.* hamaca
hamster: *n.* hámster
hand: 1. *n.* mano; 2. *adj.* de mano;
manual
hand: *v.* entregar; dar
handball: *n.* balonmano
handful: *n.* puñado
handicap: *n.* impedimento;
desventaja
handicapped individual: individuo
con impedimento
handicraft: *n.* destreza; mano de
obra
handiwork: *n.* trabajo manual
handkerchief: *n.* pañuelo
handle: *v.* atender; manejar
handsome: *adj.* hermoso; elegante;
liberal
handy: *adj.* manual; manejable.
hang: *v.* colgar
hangar: *n.* hangar
hanging wall: labio superior
hangover: *n.* resaca
haphazard: 1. *adj.* casual; 2. *n.*
casualidad; accidente
haploid: *n.* aploide
haplotype: *n.* aplotipo
happen: *v.* acontecer

happy: *adj.* feliz; dichoso; contento
hapsburg: *n.* hapsburgo; habsburgo
hapten: *adj.* hapteno
haptoglobin: *n.* haptoglobina
harakiri; hara-kiri: *n.* haraquiri
harangue: *n.* arenga
harass: *v.* acosar; fatigar; cansar
harassment: *n.* hostigamiento
harbor: 1. *n.* puerto; 2. *adj.* portuario
hard: 1. *adj.* duro; difícil; 2. *adv.* duramente; fuertemente
hard disk: disco duro
hard-boiled egg: huevo duro
harden: *v.* endurecer
hardiness: *n.* ánimo; valor; dureza
hardship: *n.* apuro; penalidad
hardship case: caso de privación
hardware: *n.* quincalla; ferretería; hardware
hare: *n.* liebre
harem: *n.* harén
harlequin: *n.* arlequín
harm: *n.* daño; perjuicio
harm: *v.* dañar; perjudicar
harmattan: *n.* harmatán
harmless: *adj.* inofensivo
harmonic: *adj.* armónico
harmonica: *n.* armónica
harmonics: *n.* armonía
harmonious: *adj.* armonioso
harmonium: *n.* armonio
harmonization: *n.* armonización
harmony: *n.* armonía
harp: *n.* arpa
harpist: *n.* arpista
harquebus: *n.* arcabuz
harry: *v.* acosar; atormentar
harsh: *adj.* áspero
hart: *n.* ciervo
harvest: *n.* cosecha
harvest: *v.* cosechar
hasidic: *adj.* hasidico
hasidism: *n.* hasidismo
haste: *n.* prisa

hasten: *v.* apresurar
hat: *n.* sombrero
hate: *n.* odio; aversión
hate: *v.* odiar
haul: *v.* jalar
haul: *n.* tirón; ganancia
haul: *v.* acarrear; transpolar
haunch: *n.* cadera
Havana: La Habana
Havanan: *n.* habanero; -a
have: *v.* haber; tener; tomar
havoc: *n.* destrucción
havoc: *v.* destruir
Hawaii: Hawai
Hawaiian: *adj.* hawaiano; -a
Hawaiian: *n.* hawaiano
hazard: *n.* peligro
hazard: *v.* arriesgar
haze: *n.* confusión
he: 1. *pron.* pers. (3.a pers. sing. masc.) el; 2. *pron.* indef. aquel que; el que
head: 1. *n.* cabeza; 2. *adj.* delantero; mas alto;
head: *v.* acaudillar; dirigir
head and neck: cabeza y cuello
headache: *n.* dolor de la cabeza
heading: encabezamiento; título
headland: *n.* promontorio
headstone: *n.* lápida
heal: *v.* curar; cicatrizar
health: *n.* salud; sanidad
health information: información medico
health information privacy: información medico privacidad del paciente
health insurance: seguro de salud
healthy: *adj.* sano; -a
heap: *n.* montón
heap: *v.* amontonar
hear: *v.* oír; decir
hearing: *n.* audiencia; vista
hearing aid: audífono; prótesis

auditiva
hearing difficult in: dificultad para oír
hearing officer: funcionario de audiencias
hearing proceedings: actuación de audiencia
hearing process: proceso de audiencia
hearing test: examen de los oídos
hearsay: *n.* rumor
heart: *n.* corazón
heart attack: ataque cardíaco
heart disease: enfermedad del corazón
heart murmur: murmullos
hearten: *v.* animar
heartfelt: *adj.* cordial
hearth: *n.* chimenea; brasero
hearts of artichoke: corazones de alcachofas
hearty: *adj.* cordial; robusto
heat: *n.* calor
heat: *v.* calentar
heat capacity: capacidad térmica
heat engine: motor térmico
heat intolerance: intolerancia al calor
heat shock: choque térmico
heat sterilization: esterilización por calor
heater: *n.* estufa; radiador
heave: *n.* esfuerzo
heave: *v.* levantar
heaven: *n.* cielo; paraíso
heaviness: *n.* densidad
Hebraism: *n.* hebraísmo
Hebraist: *n.* hebraísta
Hebrew: *adj.* hebreo
Hebrides: Hébrides
hecatomb: *n.* hecatombe
hectare: *n.* hectárea
hectogram: *n.* hectogramo
hectoliter: *n.* hectolitro

hectometer: *n.* hectómetro
hedge: *n.* cercado
hedonism: *n.* hedonismo
hedonist: *n.* hedonista
heed: *n.* atención
heedful: *adj.* atento; cuidadoso
heel: *n.* talón; calcañal
Hegelian: *adj.* hegeliano
hegemony: *n.* hegemonía
heifer: *n.* novilla
height: *n.* altura
height of a parallelogram: altura de un paralelogramo
height of a trapezoid: altura de un trapecio
height of a triangle: altura de un triangulo
heighten: *v.* elevar
heir: *adj.* heredero
heir: *n.* heredero; -a
helical: *adj.* helicoidal
helicopter: *n.* helicóptero
heliocentric: *adj.* heliocéntrico
heliotrope: *n.* heliotropo
heliport: *n.* helipuerto
helix: *n.* hélice
hell: *n.* infierno
hellebore: *n.* heleboro; eloboro
hello!: *intj.* ¡hola!; ¡aló!
helmet: *n.* yelmo
helminth: *n.* helminto
helminthology: *n.* helmintología
help: *n.* ayuda; socorro
help: *v.* ayudar
helper: *n.* auxiliar
helpmate: *n.* compañero
hem: *n.* borde; hemo
hem: *v.* poner bastilla
hem synthase: ferroquelatasa
hemagglutination: *n.* hemoaglutinación
hematologic system: sistema hematológico
hematologist: *n.* hematólogo;

especialista en la sangre
hematology: *n.* hematología
hematoma: *n.* hematoma
hematopoietic agent: medicina para producir mas sangre
hematuria: *n.* hematuria
hemeprotein: *n.* hemoproteina
hemiplegia: *n.* hemiplejía
hemisphere: *n.* hemisferio
hemistich: *adj.* hemistiquio
hemoglobin: *n.* hemoglobina
hemoglobin: hemoglobina
hemolysis: *n.* hemólisis
hemolyzed blood: sangre hemolizada
hemophilia: *n.* hemofilia
hemophiliac: *n.* hemofílico; -a
hemophiliac: *adj.* hemofílico
hemoptysis: *n.* hemoptisis
hemorrhage: *n.* hemorragia
hemorrhoids: *n.* hemorroides
hemostasis: *n.* hemóstasis
hemostat: *n.* hemóstato
hemp: *n.* cáñamo
hen: *n.* gallina
hence: *adv.* desde; de aquí que
henceforward: *adv.* de aquí en adelante.
henequen: *n.* henequén
henna: *n.* henna; alheña
heparin: *n.* heparina
heparinized blood: sangre heparinizada
heparinized syringe: jeringuilla heparinizada
hepathlon: *n.* hepatlón
hepatic clearance: depuración hepática
hepatica: *n.* hepática
hepatitis: *n.* hepatitis
hepatologist: *n.* especialista en el hígado
heptagon: *n.* heptágono
heptameter: *n.* heptámetro

herald: *n.* heraldo; precursor
herald: *v.* anunciar
heraldry: *n.* heráldica
herb: *n.* hierba
herb garden: herbario
herbage: *n.* herbaje
herbal remedy: remedio hierbal
herbalist: *n.* herbalario
herbicide: *n.* herbicida
herbivore: *n.* herbívoro
Herculean: *adj.* hercúleo
herd: *n.* manada
herd: *v.* reunir en manada
here: *adv.* aquí; acá
hereditary: *adj.* hereditario
hereditary: *n.* enfermedades hereditarias
hereditary diseases: enfermedades hereditarias
heredity: *n.* herencia
herein: *adv.* dentro
heresy: *n.* herejía
heretofore: *adv.* hasta ahora
herewith: *adv.* esto; de este modo
hermaphrodite: *n.* hermafrodita
hermit: *n.* ermitaño; -a
hermit crab: ermitaño
hermitage: *n.* ermita
hernia: *n.* hernia
hero: *n.* héroe
heroic: *adj.* heroico
heroine: *n.* heroína
heroism: *n.* heroísmo
herpes: *n.* herpes
herpetology: *n.* herpetología
herring: *n.* arenque
hers: *pron. poss.* el suyo
herself: *pron.* ella misma
hertz: *n.* hertzio; hercio
hesitate: *v.* vacilar
heterodoxy: *n.* heterodoxia
heteroduplex analysis: análisis heterodúplex
heteroduplex mapping: cartografía

heterodúplex
heterodyne: *n.* heterodino
heterogeneous mixture: mezcla heterogénea
heterogenote: *adj.* heterogenote
heteropycnosis: *n.* heteropicnosis
heteroscedaticity: *n.* heterocedasticidad
heterosexual: *adj.* heterosexual
heterothroph: *adj.* heterótrofo
heterotroph: *adj.* heterotrofo
heterozygote: *adj.* heterocigoto
heterozygous: *adj.* heterocigoto
heuristics: *n.* heurística
hex: *n.* hechizo; hexadecimal
hexaclorophene: *adj.* hexaclorofeno
hexadecimal: *adj.* hexadecimal
hexagon: *n.* hexágono
hexagonal: *adj.* hexagonal
hexameter: *n.* hexámetro
hey!: *intj.* ¡eh!
Hezbollah: *n.* Hezbolá
hiatus: *n.* hiato
hiatus: *n.* interrupción
hibernal: *adj.* hibernal
hibernate: *v.* invernar
hibernation: *n.* hibernación
hibiscus: *n.* hibisco
hiccup: *n.* hipo
hiccup: *v.* decir con hipo
hidden: escondido; oculto
hide: 1. *n.* cuero; 2. *adj.* alto
hide: *v.* esconder
hierarchy: *n.* jerarquía
hieroglyph: *n.* jeroglífico
hieroglyphic: *adj.* jeroglífico
high: *adj.* alto
high blood pressure: alta presión sanguínea
high cholesterol: colesterol elevado
high density disk: disco de alta densidad
high heat: fuego fuerte
high resolution: alta definición; alta resolución
high tech: de alta tecnología
high triglycerides: triglicéridos elevados
highly: *adv.* sumamente; en sumo grado
highness: *n.* altura
high-rise: el edificio de muchos pisos
hiker: *n.* caminante
hilarity: *n.* hilaridad
hill: *n.* colina; cerro
hill: *v.* amontonar
hilt: *n.* empuñadura
him: *pron.* pers. m. el; le; lo; a el
Himalayas: Himalaya
hinder: *v.* impedir
Hindi: *n.* hindi
hindrance: *n.* estorbo
Hindu: *n.* hindú
Hinduism: *n.* hinduismo
Hindustan: Indostán
Hindustani: *n.* indostanes
hinge: *n.* bisagra
hinge templates: las plantillas para bisagras
hint: *n.* insinuación
hint: *v.* apuntar
hip: *n.* cadera
hip post: el poste de la lima
hipped: *adj.* de varias aguas
Hippocratic: *adj.* hipocrático
hippodrome: *n.* hipódromo
hippopotamus: *n.* hipopótamo
hippurate test: prueba del hipurato
hippy: *n.* hippie
hire: *n.* alquiler; jornal
hire: *v.* alquilar; asalariar
hirsutism: *n.* hirsutismo
Hispanist: *n.* hispanista
Hispano-America: *n.* Hispanoamérica
hiss: *n.* silbido
hiss: *v.* silbar

histamine: *n.* histamina
histidine: *n.* histidina
histochemistry: *n.* histoquímica
histocompatibility test: prueba de histocompatibilidad
histogram: *n.* histograma
histologist: *n.* histólogo; -a
histology: *n.* histología
histone: *n.* histona
histopathology: *n.* histopatología
historical: *adj.* histórico
historical: *adj.* histórico
history: *n.* historia
histrionics: *n.* histrionismo
hit: *n.* golpe; éxito
hit: *v.* golpear; acertar; censurar
hither: *adv.* acá
hitherto: *adv.* hasta aquí
Hittite: *n.* hitita
HIV: virus VIH; virus del sida
ho ho ho!: *intj.* ¡jo; jo!
hoard: *n.* cúmulo; depósito
hoard: *v.* atesorar
hoarse: *adj.* ronco
hoax: *n.* engaño
hoax: *v.* engañar
hobble: *n.* cojera
hobble: *v.* cojear
hobby: *n.* afición;; hobby
hobgoblin: *n.* duende
hockey: *n.* hockey
hoe: el azadón
hog: *n.* cerdo
hoist: el montacargas
hoist: *n.* grúa
hoist: *v.* alzar; colgar
hold: *n.* asa; mango; sujeción; autoridad
hold: *v.* sostener
hold a hearing: celebrar una audiencia
hold-down: el soporte
holding: *n.* posesión
hole: *n.* agujero

holiday: *n.* día festivo; día feriado
holiness: *n.* santidad
holistic: *adj.* holístico
Holland: Holanda
hollandaise: *n.* holandesa
hollow: 1. *adj.* hueco; ahuecado; 2. *n.* cavidad; hoyo
Holocaust: *n.* Holocausto
hologram: *n.* holograma
holograph: *n.* hológrafo
holter: *n.* cardíaco ambulatorio
holter monitor: cardíaco ambulatorio
holy: *adj.* santo; sagrado
holy grail: santo grial
Holy Grail: *n.* Santo Grial
home: 1. *n.* casa; hogar; domicilio; 2. *adj.* casero; nativo
home: *adv.* en casa
home office: la oficina en casa
home theater: el cine doméstico
homeless: *n.* sin hogar
homeless person: persona sin hogar
homeopath: *n.* homeópata
homeopathy: *n.* homeopatía
homeostasis: *n.* homeóstasis
homestead: *n.* heredad; casa solariega
homicide (killer): *n.* homicida
homily: *n.* homilía
hominid: *n.* homínido
homo sapiens: homo sapiens
homoduplex: *n.* homodúplex
homogeneous mixture: mezcla homogénea
homogenized milk: leche homogeneizada
homogenote: *adj.* homogenote
homogenuity: *n.* homogeneidad
homograph: *adj.* homógrafo
homologous structures: estructuras homologas
homology: *n.* homología
homolosine: *adj.* homolosenoidal

homomorphism: *n.* homomorfismo
homonym: *n.* homónimo
homophone: *n.* homófono
homophonic: *adj.* homofónico
homoplasy: *n.* homoplasía
homoscedasticity: *n.* homocedasticidad
homosexual: *adj.* homosexual
homozygote: *adj.* homocigote
homozygous: *adj.* homocigoto
Honduran: *adj.* hondureño; -a
Honduras: Honduras
honest: *adj.* honesto; honrado
honesty: *n.* honestidad; honradez
honey: *n.* miel; dulzura
honey: *v.* endulzar con miel
honey moon: a luna de miel
honeydew melon: melón
Hong Kong: Hong-Kong
Honolulu: Honolulú
honor: *n.* honor
honorable: *adj.* honorable; honrado
honorarium: *n.* honorarios
honorary: *adj.* honorario
honorary member: miembro honorario
honorific: *adj.* honorífico
honors: *n.* honores
hood: *n.* capucha
hook: *n.* gaucho
hook: *v.* enganchar; pescar
hoop: *n.* argolla
hoot: *n.* grito
hoot: *v.* silbar
hop: *n.* brinco
hop: *v.* brincar
hope: *n.* esperanza; confianza
hope: *v.* esperar
hopeful: *adj.* esperanzado
hopeless: sin esperanza
horah: *n.* hora
horde: *n.* multitud
horizon: *n.* horizonte
horizontal: *adj.* horizontal

hormonal: *adj.* hormonal
hormone: *n.* hormona
hormone patch: parche de hormona
horn: *n.* cuerno
hornet: *n.* avispón; moscardón
horrendous: *adj.* horrendo
horrible: *adj.* horrible
horror: *n.* horror
horror-stricken: *adj.* horrorizado
horse: *n.* caballo
horseman: *n.* jinete
horsepower: *n.* caballo de vapor; fuerza motriz
hortative; hortatory: *adj.* hortatorio
horticulture: *n.* horticultura
horticulturist: *n.* horticultor
hose: *n.* media; calcetín; forma.
hospice: *n.* hospicio
hospice care: cuidado de hospicio
hospitable: *adj.* hospitalario
hospital: *n.* hospital
hospital room: cuarto de hospital
hospital stay: hospitalización; estadía en el hospital
hospitality: *n.* hospitalidad
hospitalization: *n.* hospitalizaciones
hospitalized: *adj.* hospitalizado
host: *n.* hostia
host cell: célula hospedadora
host computer: ordenador central
hostel: *n.* hostería
hostel: *n.* hostería; albergue
hostess: *n.* ama; dueña; patrona
hostile: *adj.* hostil
hostility: *n.* hostilidad
hot: 1. *adj.* caliente; violento; 2. *n.* calor
hot dog: perro caliente
hot flashes: sensación de calor en la cara
hot spot: punto caliente
hot tub: el jacuzzi
hotel: *n.* hotel
hotelkeeper: *n.* hotelero; -a

hotline: *n.* línea de emergencia
hot-mop: *v.* poner brea
hot-water heater: calentador para el agua
hot-water pipe: tubo para agua caliente
hound: *n.* podenco
hound: *v.* cazar con perros
hour: *n.* hora; momento
hour hand: *n.* horario
houri: *n.* hurí
hourly: *adv.* por horas; horario
house: 1. *n.* casa; residencia; edificio; 2. *adj.* casero
house: *v.* alojar
house of representatives: cámara de representantes
household: *n.* hogar
household chores: trabajos; quehaceres domésticos
household expenses: gastos de la casa
household goods: enseres de la casa; domésticos
household of another: hogar de otro
household worker: empleado; trabajador doméstico
householder: *n.* jefe de familia
housekeeper: *n.* ama de llaves
housekeeping gene: gen de mantenimiento
housing: *n.* albergue
housing assistance: ayuda para la vivienda
hover: *v.* cubrir con las alas; revolotear
how: *conj.* de que modo; a cómo; cuánto
however: 1. conj sin embargo; 2. *adv.* como sea
howl: *n.* chillido
howl: *v.* decir a gritos; chillar
hubcap: *n.* tapacubos
hue: *n.* tinte; matiz

huff: *n.* enfado
huff: *v.* encolerizar; hincharse
hug: 1. *adj.* enorme; 2. *n.* abrazo
huguenot: *n.* hugonote
hula: *n.* hula
hull: *n.* casco; cáscara
human: *adj.* humano
humanism: *n.* humanismo
humanitarian: *adj.* humanitario
humanitarian aid: ayuda humanitaria
humanitarianism: *n.* humanitarismo
humanities: *n.* humanidades
humankind: *n.* humanidad
humanoid: *n.* humanoide
humble: *adj.* humilde
humble: *v.* humillar
humectant: *adj.* humectante
humerus: *n.* húmero
humid: *adj.* húmedo
humid subtropical: subtropical húmedo
humidifier: *n.* humedecedor; humectador
humidity: *n.* humedad
humidophilic: *adj.* humidofílico
humiliation: *n.* humillación
humility: *n.* humildad
humor: *n.* humor; carácter
humor: *v.* mimar
humorist: *n.* humorista
humorless: sin sentido del humor
humorous: *adj.* humorístico
humus: *n.* humus
hundred: cien; ciento
hung window: la ventana de guillotina
Hungarian: *n.* húngaro
Hungarian: *adj.* húngaro; -a
Hungary: Hungría
Hunger: hambre
hunger: *n.* hambre
hungry: *adj.* hambriento; deseoso
hunt: *n.* caza

hunt: *v.* cazar; buscar; perseguir
hurdle: *n.* valla; barrera
hurdle: *v.* saltar vallas
hurl: *n.* lanzamiento
hurl: *v.* tirar; lanzar; arrojar
hurricane: *n.* huracán
hurried: *adj.* hecho de prisa;
precipitado
hurry: *n.* prisa; premura
hurry: *v.* activar; correr
hurt: *n.* daño; herida
hurt: *v.* dañar
husband: *n.* marido
husband: *v.* gestionar; administrar
bien
husk: *n.* cáscara; pellejo
hustle: *n.* prisa
hustle: *v.* apresurar; mezclar
hut: *n.* choza
hyacinth: *n.* jacinto
hyaluronate lyase: hialuronato liasa
hybrid: *adj.* híbrido
hybridization: *n.* hibridación
hybridoma: *n.* hibridoma
hydra: *n.* hidra
hydrant: *n.* boca de agua
hydration: *n.* hidratación
hydraulic: *adj.* hidráulico
hydraulic system: sistema hidráulico
hydrocarbon: *n.* hidrocarburo
hydrocephalus: *n.* hidrocefalia
hydrocephalus: *n.* hidrocefalia
hydrodynamics: *n.* hidrodinámica
hydroelectric: *adj.* hidroeléctrico
hydroelectric power: energía
hidroeléctrica
hydroelectricity: *n.* hidroelectricidad
hydrogen carbonate:
hidrogenocarbonato
hydrogen ion: Ion hidrógeno
hydrogenation: *n.* hidrogenación
hydrography: *n.* hidrografía
hydroid: *adj.* hidroideo
hydrology: *n.* hidrología

hydrolysis: *n.* hidrólisis
hydrometer: *n.* hidrómetro
hydrophobia: *n.* hidrofobia
hydrophone: *n.* hidrófono
hydrophyte: *n.* hidrofita
hydroponics: *n.* hidroponía;
hidroponía
hydrops: *n.* hidropesía
hydropsy: *n.* hidropesía
hydrosphere: *n.* hidrosfera
hydrostatics: *n.* hidrostática
hydrotherapy: *n.* hidroterapia
hydrothermal vent: chimenea
hidrotermal
hydroxide ion: Ion hidróxido
hydroxyl group: grupo hidróxilo
hyena: *n.* hiena
hygiene: *n.* higiene
hygienics: *n.* higiene
hygienist: *n.* higienista
hygrometer: *n.* higrómetro
hymen: *n.* himen
hymn: *n.* himno
hymnal: *adj.* himnario
hymnal: *n.* himnario
hyperacidity: *n.* hiperacidez
hyperactivity: *n.* hiperactividad
hyperbaric: *adj.* hiperbárico
hyperbola: *n.* hipérbola
hyperbole: *n.* hipérbole
hyperbolic: *adj.* hiperbólico
hyperbolic geometry: geometría
hiperbólica
hyperboloid: *adj.* hiperboloide
hypercholesterolemia: *n.*
hipercolesterolemia
hypercorrection: *n.* ultracorrección
hypercritical: *adj.* hipercrítico
hyperglycemia: *n.* hiperglicemia
hyperglycemic factor: glucagón
hyperlipidemia: *n.* hiperlipidemia
hyperopia: *n.* hipermetropía
hyperplasia: *n.* hiperplasia
hypersensitive: *adj.* hipersensible

hypersensitivity: *n.* hipersensibilidad
hypertension: *n.* hipertensión
hyperthermia: *n.* hipertermia
hyperthyroidism: *n.* hipertiroidismo
hypertonic: *adj.* hipertónico -ica
hypertrophy: *n.* hipertrofia
hyperventilation: *n.* hiperventilación
hypha: *n.* hifa
hyphen: *n.* guión
hypnosis: *n.* hipnosis
hypnotherapy: *n.* hipnoterapia
hypnotism: *n.* hipnotismo
hypnotist: *n.* hipnotizador (a); hipnotista
hypoallergenic: *adj.* hipoalergénico
hypochondriac: *adj.* hipocondríaco
hypocrisy: *n.* hipocresía
hypocrite: *adj.* hipócrita
hypocritical: *adj.* hipócrita
hypocycloid: *n.* hipocicloide
hypocycloid: *adj.* hipocicloide
hypodermic: *n.* inyección hipodérmica
hypodermic needle: aguja hipodérmica
hypoglycemia: *n.* hipoglicemia
hypophysis: *n.* hipófisis
hypostasis: *n.* hipóstasis
hypotension: *n.* hipotensión
hypotenuse: *n.* hipotenusa
hypothalamus: *n.* hipotálamo
hypothermia: *n.* hipotermia
hypothesis: *n.* hipótesis
hypothyroid: *n.* hipotiroide; hipotiroideo
hypothyroid: *adj.* hipotiroide; hipotiroideo
hypothyroidism: *n.* hipotiroidismo
hypoxia: *n.* hipoxia
hypthalamus: *n.* hipotálamo
hyssop: *n.* hisopo
hysterectomy: *n.* histerectomía
hysteria: *n.* histeria; histerismo

I

iamb: *n.* yambo
ibex: *n.* íbice
ibuprofen: *n.* ibuprofen
ice: 1. *n.* hielo; 2. *adj.* de hielo; glacial
ice: *v.* cubrir con capa de azúcar
ice age: glaciación
ice cream: helado
ice cube: cubito de hielo
ice wedging: geliración
iceberg: *n.* iceberg
ice-cream: *n.* mantecado
Iceland: Irlanda
Icelander: *n.* islandés; -esa
Icelandic: *n.* islandés
ichthyology: *n.* ictiología
icing sugar: azúcar glasé
icon: *n.* icono
iconoclast: *n.* iconoclasta
iconoscope: *n.* iconoscopio
icosahedron: *n.* icosaedro
icterus: *n.* ictericia
icy: *adj.* helado; glacial
idea: *n.* idea
ideal: *adj.* ideal
idealism: *n.* idealismo
idealistic: *adj.* idealista
identical: *adj.* idéntico
identification: *n.* identificación
identification process: proceso de identificación
identification system: sistema de identificación
identity: *n.* identidad
identity property of addition: propiedad de identidad de la suma
identity property of multiplication: propiedad de identidad de la

multiplicación
ideogram; ideograph: *n.* ideograma
ideography: *n.* ideografía
ideologue: *n.* ideólogo
ideology: *n.* ideología
idiocy: *n.* idiotez
idiomatic expression: expresión idiomática
idiosyncrasy: *n.* idiosincrasia
idiot: *adj.* idiota
idle: *adj.* ocioso
idle: *v.* gastar ociosamente; holgar
idol: *adj.* ídolo
idolatry: *n.* idolatría
idyl: *n.* idilio
if: *conj.* si; en caso que
igloo: *n.* iglú
igneous rock: roca ígnea
ignite: *v.* encender
ignition: *n.* ignición
ignoble: *adj.* innoble
ignominious: *adj.* ignominioso
ignoramus: *n.* ignorante
ignorance: *n.* ignorancia
ignorant: *adj.* ignorante
iguana: *n.* iguana
ileum: *n.* íleon
iliad: *n.* iliada
ilium: *n.* ilion
ill: 1. *adj.* enfermo; doliente; 2. *adv.* mal
illegal: *adj.* ilegal
illegible: *adj.* ilegible
illicit drugs: drogas ilícitas
illiterate: *adj.* ignorante
illness: *n.* enfermedad
illogical: *adj.* ilógico
illuminance: *n.* iluminancia
illuminate: *v.* iluminar
illuminated: *adj.* iluminado
illumination: *n.* iluminación
illuminator: *n.* iluminador
illumine: *v.* iluminar; alumbrar
illusion: *n.* ilusión

illusionist: *n.* ilusionista
illustrate: *v.* ilustrar
illustration: *n.* ilustración
illustrator: *n.* ilustrador
illustrious: *adj.* ilustre; célebre
image: *n.* imagen; símbolo
imagery: *n.* imaginería
imaginary: *adj.* imaginario
imagination: *n.* imaginativa
imaginative: *adj.* imaginativo
imagine: *v.* imaginar; discurrir; suponer
imagist: *n.* imaginista
imam: *n.* imán
imbibe: *v.* beber; chupar
imitate: *v.* imitar; copiar
imitation: *n.* imitación
imitator: *n.* imitador
immanence: *n.* inmanencia
immature: *adj.* inmaduro
immaturity: *n.* inmadurez
immeasurable: *adj.* inmensurable
immediate: *adj.* inmediato
immediately: *adv.* inmediatamente
immemorial: *adj.* inmemorial
immense: *adj.* inmenso
immerse: *v.* inmergir; sumergir
immersion: *n.* inmersión
immersion lens: objetivo de inmersión
immersion objective: objetivo de inmersión
immersion oil: aceite de inmersión
immigration: *n.* inmigración
immigration records: expedientes de inmigración
imminent: *adj.* inminente
immoderate: *adj.* inmoderado
immodest: *adj.* inmodesto
immodesty: *n.* inmodestia
immoral: *adj.* inmoral
immorality: *n.* inmoralidad
immortality: *n.* inmortalidad
immovable: *adj.* inmóvil; inmovible

immune: *adj.* inmunitario; -ia
immune adherence: inmunoadherencia
immune complex: inmunocomplejo
immune response: reacción inmunológica
immune system: sistema inmunitario
immunity: *n.* inmunidad
immunization: *n.* inmunización
immunoassay: *n.* inmunoanálisis
immunochemistry: *n.* inmunoquímica
immunodeficiency: *n.* inmunodeficiencia
immunodiffusion: *n.* inmunodifusión
immunodiffusion radial: inmunodifusión radial
immunofixation: *n.* inmunofijación
immunofluorescence: *n.* inmunofluorescencia
immunogenetics: *n.* inmunogenética
immunogenic: *adj.* inmunógeno; inmunizador
immunoglobulin: *n.* inmunoglobulina
immunological: *adj.* inmunológico
immunologist: *n.* inmunólogo; -a
immunology: *n.* inmunología
immunoprecipitation: *n.* inmunoprecipitación
immunoradiometry: *n.* inmunorradiometría
immunosuppressive: *n.* inmunosupresivos
immunotherapy: *n.* inmunoterapia
imp: *n.* diablillo; duende
impact: *n.* impacto
impairment: *n.* impedimento
impala: *n.* impala
impar: *v.* deteriorar; dañar; acusar
impartial: *adj.* imparcial
impartiality: *n.* imparcialidad
impassivity: *n.* impasibilidad

impatience: *n.* impaciencia
impatient: *adj.* impaciente
impedance: *n.* impedancia
impede: *v.* impedir; dificultar
impediment: *n.* impedimento
impedimenta: *n.* impedimenta
impel: *v.* impulsar; empujar
impenitence: *n.* impenitencia
imperative: *adj.* imperativo
imperfect: *adj.* imperfecto; defectuoso
imperfective: *adj.* imperfectivo
imperialism: *n.* imperialismo
imperil: *v.* exponer; arriesgar
imperious: *adj.* imperioso
impermeable: *adj.* impermeable
impersonal: *adj.* impersonal
impersonality: *n.* impersonalidad
impersonate: *v.* personificar
impertinence: *n.* impertinencia
impertinent: *adj.* impertinente
imperturbability: *n.* imperturbabilidad
impetigo: *n.* impétigo
impetuosity: *n.* impetuosidad
impetuous: *adj.* impetuoso
impiety: *n.* impiedad
impish: *adj.* endiablado; travieso
implacability: *n.* implacabilidad
implant: *n.* implante
implant: *v.* implante
implantation: *n.* implantación
implement: *n.* instrumento; herramienta
implicate: *v.* implicar
implication: *n.* implicación
implicit: *adj.* implícito
implicit differentiation: derivación implícita
implicit function: la función implícita
implore: *v.* implorar; rogar
import: *n.* importación
import: *v.* importar

importance: *n.* importancia
important: *adj.* importante
importer: *n.* importador
importing: *n.* importación
importune: *v.* importunar; porfiar
impose: *v.* imponer
impostor: *n.* impostor
imposture: *n.* impostura; engaño
impotence: *n.* impotencia
impoverish: *v.* empobrecer
impracticability: *n.* impracticabilidad
impractical: *adj.* impráctico
imprecise: *adj.* impreciso
imprecision: *n.* imprecisión
imprecision profile: perfil de imprecisión
impregnable: *adj.* impregnable
impregnate: *v.* impregnar; imbuir
impresario: *adj.* empresario
impresario: *n.* empresario
impress: *n.* impresión
impressionism: *n.* impresionismo
impressionist: 1. *adj.* impresionisto; -a; 2. *n.* impresionista
imprinting: impronta
imprison: *v.* aprisionar
impromptu: 1. *n.* improvisación; 2. *adv.* de improviso
impromptu: *n.* impromptu
improper: *adj.* impropio
improper fraction: fracción impropia
improper integral: la integral impropia
improve: *adj.* descarado
improve: *v.* perfeccionar; reformar
improvisation: *n.* improvisación
imprudence: *n.* imprudencia
imprudent: *adj.* imprudente
impudence: *n.* impudencia
impugn: *v.* impugnar; rechazar
impulse: *n.* impulso
impulsive: *adj.* impulsivo

impunity: *n.* impunidad
impute: *v.* imputar; atribuir
in: 1. *adv.* dentro; 2. *prep.* en; dentro de; sobre; entre
in absentia: in absentia
in advance: por adelantado
in as much: por cuánto; en cuánto; puesto que; ya que
gin rummy: gin rummy
in situ: in situ
in vitro: en vitro
in vivo: in vivo
inaccessibility: *n.* inaccesibilidad
inaccuracy: *n.* inexactitud
inaccurate: *adj.* inexacto
inactive: *adj.* inactivo
inactivity: *n.* inactividad
inadaptability: *n.* inadaptabilidad
inadequacy: *n.* insuficiencia
inalienable: *adj.* inalienable
inanimate: *adj.* inanimado
inanition: *n.* inanición
inarticulate: *adj.* inarticulado
inaudible: *adj.* inaudible
inaugurate: *v.* inaugurar
inauguration: *n.* inauguración
inauspicious: *adj.* impropicio
inborn: *adj.* innato; nativo
inbreeding: endogamia
incandescence: *n.* incandescencia
incandescent light: luz incandescente
incandescent light: luz incandescente
incapable: *adj.* incapaz
incapacitation: *n.* privación de la capacidad
incapacity: *n.* incapacidad
incarceration: *n.* encarcelación
incarnate: *v.* encarnar
incarnation: *n.* encarnación
incautious: *adj.* incauto
incendiary: *adj.* incendiario
incense: *n.* incienso

incentive: *n.* incentivo
incest: *n.* incesto
inch: *n.* pulgada
inchoative: *adj.* incoativo
incidence: *n.* incidencia
incident: *n.* incidente
incision: *n.* incisión
incisor: *n.* incisivo
incite: *v.* incitar; animar
incitement: *n.* incitación
inclement: *adj.* inclemente
inclement: *n.* inclemente
inclination: *n.* inclinación
incline: *n.* pendiente
incline: *v.* inclinar
inclined plane: plano inclinado
inclinometer: *n.* inclinómetro
include: *v.* incluir; comprender; englobar
inclusion body: cuerpo de inclusión
incognito: *adv.* incógnito
incoherent: *adj.* incoherente
income: *n.* ingreso
income tax return: declaración de impuestos
incompatibility: *n.* incompatibilidad
incompatible: *adj.* incompatible
incompetence: *n.* incompetencia
incompetent: *adj.* incompetente
inconsiderate: *adj.* desconsiderado
inconsistent: *adj.* inconsistente
inconsolable: *adj.* inconsolable
inconstancy: *n.* inconstancia
incontinence: *n.* incontinencia
inconvenience: *n.* inconveniente
incorrect: *adj.* incorrecto
incorrigibility: *n.* incorregibilidad
incorrigible: *adj.* incorregible
incorruptible: *adj.* incorruptible
increase: *n.* aumento; cremento
increase: *v.* aumentar; incrementar
increasing: 1. *adj.* creciente; 2. *n.* acrecimiento
incredibility: *n.* incredibilidad

incredulity: *n.* incredulidad
increment: *n.* incremento
incrimination: *n.* incriminación
incubate: *v.* incubar
incubation: *n.* incubación
incubator: *n.* incubadora
incubus: *n.* incubo
inculpate: *v.* inculpar
incur: *v.* incurrir
incurable: *adj.* incurable
incursion: *n.* incursión
indebted: *adj.* adeudado
indecency: *n.* indecencia
indecent: *adj.* indecente
indecision: *n.* indecisión
indecorum: *n.* indecoro
indeed: *adv.* verdaderamente; en realidad
indefatigable: *adj.* infatigable
indefensible: *adj.* indefendible
indefinite: *adj.* indefinido
indelicacy: *n.* falta de delicadeza
indelicate: *adj.* indelicado
indemnify: *v.* indemnizar
indemnity: *n.* indemnidad; indemnización
independence: *n.* independencia
independent: *adj.* independiente
independent events: sucesos independientes
indescribable: *adj.* indescriptible
index: *n.* índice
index contours: curva de nivel índice
index finger: *n.* dedo índice
index fossil: fósil indicador
index of refraction: índice de refracción
index of therapeutic groups: índice de grupos terapéuticos
India: India
Indian: *adj.* indio; -a
indicate: *v.* indicar; señalar
indicative: *adj.* indicativo

indicator: *n.* indicador
indicator electrode: electrodo indicador
indict: *v.* procesar
indifference: *n.* indiferencia
indigenous: *adj.* indígena; innato
indigenous flora: flora indígena
indigent: *adj.* indigente
indigestion: *n.* indigestión
indignant: *adj.* indignado
indignation: *n.* indignación
indignity: *n.* indignidad
indigo: *n.* azul índigo
indirect: *adj.* indirecto
indirect discourse: *n.* estilo indirecto
indirect object: complemento indirecto
indirect object: complemento indirecto
indiscreet: *adj.* indiscreto
indiscretion: *n.* indiscreción
indispose: *n.* indisponer
indisposition: *n.* indisposición
individual: 1. *adj.* invididual; solo; único; 2. *n.* individuo
individual: *adj.* individual
individualism: *n.* individualismo
individualist: *n.* individualista
individuality: *n.* individualidad
indivisible: *adj.* indivisible
indoctrination: *n.* adoctrinamiento
indole: *adj.* índole
indolence: *n.* indolencia
indolent: *adj.* indolente
indomitable: *adj.* indomable; indómito
Indonesia: Indonesia
Indonesian: *adj.* indonesio; -a
indoor: *adj.* interior
indoors: *adv.* dentro
indorse: *v.* endosar
induce: *v.* inducir; mover
inducement: *n.* incentivo; estímulo
inducer: *n.* inductor

induct: *n.* dispensa
induct: *v.* introducir
inductance: *n.* inductancia
induction: *n.* inducción
inductor: *n.* inductor
indulgence: *n.* indulgencia
indulgent: *adj.* indulgente
industrial: *adj.* industrial
industrialism: *n.* industrialismo
industrialist: *adj.* industrial
industrialized: *adj.* industrializado
industrious: *adj.* industrioso
industry: *n.* industria
ineffable: *adj.* inefable
inefficiency: *n.* ineficacia
inefficient: *adj.* ineficaz
inelegance: *n.* inelegancia
inept: *adj.* inepto
ineptitude: *n.* ineptitud
ineptness: *n.* ineptitud
inequality: *n.* desigualdad
inequity: *n.* injusticia
inequity: *n.* inequidad
inert: *adj.* inerte; flojo
inertia: *n.* inercia
inevitable: *adj.* inevitable
inexcusable: *adj.* inexcusable
inexhaustible: *adj.* inagotable
inexpensive: *adj.* barato
inexperience: *n.* inexperiencia
inexpressive: *adj.* inexpresivo
infallibility: *n.* infalibilidad
infamy: *n.* infamia
infancy: *n.* infancia
infant: 1. *n.* infante; criatura; 2. *adj.* infantil
infanticide: *n.* infanticida
infanticide: *adj.* infanticidio; -a
infantile: *adj.* infantil
infantilism: *n.* infantilismo
infantry: *n.* infantería
infarct; infarction: *n.* infarto
infatuate: *v.* apasionar; cegar
infatuate: *adj.* apasionado

infect: *v.* infectar
infected: *adj.* infecto
infection: *n.* infección
infectious: *adj.* infeccioso
infectious disease: enfermedad infecciosa
infectious waste: desechos infecciosos
infer: *v.* inferir; deducir
inference: *n.* inferencia
inferior: *adj.* inferior
inferior: *n.* inferior
inferiority: *n.* inferioridad
infernal: *adj.* infernal
inferno: *n.* infierno
inferred: *adj.* inferido
infertility: *n.* infertilidad
infest: *v.* infestar
infidelity: *n.* infidelidad
infiltrate: *v.* infiltrar
infiltration: *n.* infiltración
infiltrator: *n.* infiltrado
infinite: *adj.* infinito
infinite limit: el límite infinito
infinitesimal: *adj.* infinitesimal
infinitesimal: *n.* infinitésimo
infinitesimal: *n.* infinitesimal
infinitive: *n.* infinitivo
infinity: *n.* infinidad
infirm: *adj.* enfermizo; inválido
infirmary: *n.* enfermería
inflame: *v.* inflamar
inflammation: *n.* inflamación
inflammatory: *adj.* inflamatorio
inflammatory response: reacción inflamatoria
inflate: *v.* inflar
inflation: *n.* inflación
inflect: *v.* torcer; modular
inflection: *n.* inflexión
inflexibility: *n.* inflexibilidad
inflict: *v.* infligir
influence: *n.* influencia
influence quantity: magnitud influyente

influential: *adj.* influyente
influenza; flu: *n.* influenza
inform: *adj.* informe
inform: *v.* informa; avisar
informal: *adj.* informal
informant: *adj.* informante
information: *n.* información
information technology: informática; tecnología de la información
informative: *adj.* informativo
informed: *adj.* informado
infraction: *n.* infracción
infrared (radiation): *adj.* infrarrojo
infrared radiation: radiación infrarroja
infrared rays: rayos infrarrojos
infrasound: *n.* infrasonido
infrastructure: *n.* infraestructura
infrequent: *adj.* infrecuente
infringe: *v.* infringir
infuriate: *v.* enfurecer
infuriated: *adj.* enfurecido
infusion: *n.* infusión
ingénue: *n.* ingenua
ingenuity: *n.* ingenio
ingenuous: *adj.* ingenuo
ingenuousness: *n.* ingenuidad
ingestion: *n.* ingestión
ingot: *n.* lingote
ingrain: *v.* fijar; empreñar
ingratiate: *v.* hacer aceptable
ingratiating: congraciador
ingratiating: *adj.* congraciador
ingratitude: *n.* ingratitud
ingredient: *n.* ingrediente
inguinal swelling: hinchazón de la ingle
inguinal tenderness: dolor de la ingle
inhabit: *v.* habitar
inhabitant: *n.* habitante
inhabited: *adj.* habitado

inhalant: *n.* inhalante
inhalation: *n.* inhalación
inhaler: *n.* inhalador
inherit: *v.* heredar
inheritance: *n.* herencia
inhibin: *n.* inhibina
inhibited: *adj.* inhibido
inhibition: *n.* inhibición
inhibitor: *n.* inhibidor
inhibitory concentration: concentración inhibidora
inhibitory quotient: cociente inhibidor
inhospitable: *adj.* inhóspito; inhospitalario
inhumane: *adj.* inhumano
inhumanity: *n.* inhumanidad
inimical: *adj.* enemigo
iniquitous: *adj.* inicuo
iniquity: *n.* iniquidad
initial: *adj.* inicial
initialize: *v.* inicializar
initials: *n.* iniciales
initiate: *adj.* iniciado
initiate: *v.* iniciar; comenzar
initiative: *adj.* iniciativa
initiator: *n.* iniciador
initiator site: centro iniciador
inject: *v.* inyectar
injection: *n.* inyección
injection in joint: inyección intraarticular
injunction: *n.* mandato; precepto
injure: *v.* injuriar
injustice: *n.* injusticia
ink: *n.* tinta
ink pot: tintero
inkling: *n.* sospecha
inkstand: *n.* tintero
inland: *adj.* interior; regional
inlay: *v.* embutir
inlet: *n.* estuario
inmate: *n.* inquilino; preso
inmost: *adj.* interior

inn: *n.* posado; mesón
inner: *adj.* interno
inner core: núcleo interno
inning: *n.* entrada; oportunidad
innkeeper: *n.* posadero
innocence: *n.* inocencia
innocent: *adj.* inocentón
innovate: *v.* innovar
innovation: *n.* innovación
innovative: *adj.* innovador
innovator: *n.* innovador
innumerable: *adj.* innumerable
inoculation: *n.* inoculación
inoffensive: *adj.* inofensivo
inoperable: *adj.* inoperable
inoperative: *adj.* inoperante
inopportune: *adj.* inoportuno
inorganic: *adj.* inorgánico
inpatient: *n.* paciente hospitalizado
input: *n.* entrada
input device: dispositivo de entrada
input force: fuerza aplicada
input rate: velocidad de procesamiento
input work: trabajo aportado
input-output table: tabla de entrada-salida
inquest: *n.* encuesta
inquire: *v.* inquirir
inquiry: *n.* petición
inquisition: *n.* inquisición
inquisitive: *adj.* inquisitivo
inquisitor: *n.* inquisidor
insanity: *n.* locura
insatiable: *adj.* insaciable
inscription: *n.* inscripción
insect: *n.* insecto
insecticide: *n.* insecticida
insectivore: *n.* insectívoro
insecure: *adj.* inseguro
insecurity: *n.* inseguridad
insemination: *n.* inseminación
inseparable: *adj.* inseparable
insert: *v.* meter; insertar; introducir

insert: *n.* inserto
insertion mutation: mutación por inserción
inshore: *adj.* cercano a la orilla
inside: 1. *n.* interior; de dentro; forro; 2. *adj.* interno
inside: *adv.* dentro
insidious: *adj.* insidioso
insight: *n.* penetración
insight learning: aprendizaje por discernimiento
insignificant: *adj.* insignificante
insincerity: *n.* insinceridad
insinuate: *v.* insinuar; indicar
insinuating: *adj.* insinuador
insinuation: *n.* insinuación
insipid: *adj.* insípido
insist: *v.* insistir; exigir
insistence: *n.* insistencia
insolence: *n.* insolencia
insolent: *adj.* insolente
insolvency: *n.* insolvencia
insomnia: *n.* insomnia
insomniac: *n.* insomne
inspect: *v.* inspeccionar; reconocer
inspector: *n.* inspector
inspiration: *n.* inspiración
inspire: *v.* inspirar; sugerir
install: *v.* instalar; colocar
installation: *n.* instalación
instance: *n.* instancia
instant: 1. *adj.* inmediato; 2. *n.* instante
instantaneous: *adj.* instantáneo
instantaneous speed: velocidad instantánea
instead: *adv.* en cambio
instead of: en vez de
instigation: *n.* instigación
instigator: *n.* instigador
instinct: *n.* instinto
institute: *n.* instituto
institute: *v.* instituir
institution: *n.* institución

instruct: *v.* instruir; educar
instruction: *n.* instrucción
instructions about medicines: instrucciones sobre las medicinas
instructor: *n.* instructor
instrument: *n.* instrumento
instrumental: *adj.* instrumental
instrumental dependability: seguridad instrumental
instrumentalism: *n.* instrumentalismo
instrumentalist: *n.* instrumentista
instrumentation: *n.* instrumentación
insubordinate: *adj.* insubordinado
insubordination: *n.* insubordinación
insufferable: *adj.* insufrible
insufficiency: *n.* insuficiencia
insufficient: *adj.* insuficiente
insular: 1. *n.* insular; 2. *adj.* insular
insularity: *n.* insularidad
insulate: *v.* aislar
insulation: *n.* aislamiento
insulator: *n.* aislador; aislante
insulin: *n.* insulina
insult: *n.* insulto
insult: *v.* insultar; ofender
insulting: *adj.* insultante
insulting: *adj.* insultante
insurance: *n.* seguros
insure: *v.* asegurar; garantizar
insured status: cómo estar asegurado
insurgent: *n.* insurgente
insurrection: *n.* insurrección
insurrectionist: *n.* insurrecto
intact: *adj.* intacto
intake: *n.* adquisición; consumo; ingestión
intangible: *adj.* intangible
integer: *n.* número entero
integrability: *n.* integrabilidad
integral: 1. *adj.* integral; 2. *n.* integral
integral calculus: el cálculo integral

integrate: *v.* integrar
integrated: *adj.* integrado
integrated circuit: circuito integrado
integration: *n.* integración
integration by parts: la integración por partes
integrity: *n.* integridad
intellect: *n.* intelecto
intellectual: *adj.* intelectual
intellectualism: *n.* intelectualismo
intelligence: *n.* inteligencia
intelligent: *adj.* inteligente
intelligentsia: *n.* inteligencia
intelligible: *adj.* inteligible
intemperance: *n.* intemperancia
intend: *v.* pensar; intentar
intense: *adj.* intenso
intensifier: *n.* intensificador
intensify: *v.* intensificar
intensity: *n.* intensidad
intensive: *adj.* intensivo
intent: *n.* intención
intention: *n.* intencionalidad
inter: *v.* enterrar
interactive: *adj.* interactivo
intercalate: *v.* intercalar
intercalating agent: agente intercalable
intercede: *v.* interceder
intercept: *v.* interceptar
interception: *n.* interceptación
interceptor: *n.* interceptor
interchangeability: *n.* intercambiabilidad
intercom: *n.* interfono
interconnect: *v.* interconectar
intercostal: *adj.* intercostal
intercourse: *n.* acto sexual
interdict: *v.* prohibir; vedar
interdiction: *n.* interdicto
interdisciplinary: *adj.* interdisciplinario
interest: *n.* interés
interest: *v.* interesar

interested: *adj.* interesado
interesting: *adj.* interesante
interface: *n.* interface; interfaz
interference: *n.* interferencia
interference filter: filtro interferencial
interferon: *n.* interferona
interim: *n.* ínterin; ínterin
interior: 1. *adj.* interior; 2. *n.* interior
interior decorator: decorador de interiores; interiorista
interjection: *n.* interjección
interlace: *v.* entrelazar
interleukin: *n.* interleukin
interlocution: *n.* interlocución
interlocutor: *n.* interlocutor; -a
interlocutory: *adj.* interlocutorio
interlude: *n.* intervalo; intermedio
intermediary: *adj.* intermediario
intermediate: *adj.* intermedio
intermediate host: huésped intermediario
interment: *n.* entierro; funeral
intermezzo: *n.* intermezzo
interminable: *adj.* interminable
intermission: *n.* intermedio; pausa
intermittent: *adj.* intermitente
intern: *n.* interno; -a
internal: *adj.* interno
internal combustion engine: motor de combustión interna
internal energy: energía interna
internal quality control: control interno de la calidad
internal revenue service (IRS): servicios de impuestos internos
internal-combustion: motor de combustión
international: *adj.* internacional
international standard: norma internacional
International System of Units: Sistema Internacional de Unidades
international unit: unidad

internacional
internationalism: *n.* internacionalismo
Internet: *n.* Internet
internist: *n.* internista
internment: *n.* internamiento
internship: *n.* internado
interphase: *n.* interfase
interphone: *n.* interfono
Interpol: *n.* INTERPOL
interpolation: *n.* interpolación
interpret: *v.* interpretar
interpretation: *n.* interpretación
interpreter: *n.* intérprete
interracial: *adj.* interracial
interregnum: *n.* interregno
interrogation: *n.* interrogación
interrogative: *adj.* interrogativo
interrogator: *n.* interrogador
interrogatory: *n.* interrogatorio
interrupt: *v.* interrumpir; estorbar
interrupter: *n.* interruptor
interruption: *n.* interrupción
intersect: *v.* entrecortar; cruzarse
intersecting lines: rectas secantes
intersection: *n.* intersección
interstitial collagenase: colagenasa intersticial
intertidal zone: zona intermareal
interurban: *adj.* interurbano
interval: *n.* intervalo
interval scale: escala de intervalo
intervening sequence: secuencia interpuesta
intervention: *n.* intervención
interview: *n.* entrevista
interviewer: *n.* entrevistador
intestate: *adj.* intestado
intestinal: *adj.* intestino
intestinal cramps: calambres intestinales
intestine: *n.* intestino
intimacy: *n.* intimidad
intimidation: *n.* intimidación

into: *prep.* en; dentro
intolerable: *adj.* intolerable
intolerance: *n.* intolerancia
intolerant: *adj.* intolerante
intonation: *n.* entonación
intone: *n.* entonar
intoxicant: *n.* intoxicante
intoxicate: *v.* intoxicar
intoxication: *n.* intoxicación
intracellular fluid: líquido intracelular
intractable: *adj.* intratable
intramural: *adj.* intramuros
intramuscular: *adj.* intramuscular
intransigence: *n.* intransigencia
intransigent: *adj.* intransigente
intransitive: *adj.* intransitivo
intrauterine: *adj.* intrauterino
intrauterine device: aparato intrauterino
intravenous: *adj.* intravenoso
intravenous pyelogram: pielograma intravenoso
intrepid: *adj.* intrépido
intricate: *adj.* intrincado
intrigue: *n.* intriga
introduce: *v.* introducir; insertar
introduction: *n.* introducción
introductory: *adj.* introductorio
introit: *n.* introito
intron: *n.* intrón
intron splicing: eliminación de intrones
introspection: *n.* introspección
intrude: *v.* entremeterse
intruder: *n.* intruso
intrusion: *n.* intrusión
intrusive rock: roca intrusiva
intuitive: *adj.* intuitivo
inuline: *n.* inulina
inundate: *v.* inundar; abrumar
inundation: *n.* inundación
invade: *v.* invadir
invader: *n.* invasor

invalid: *adj.* inválido
invalidate: *v.* invalidar; anular
invariant: *adj.* invariante
invasive: *adj.* invasor
invasive procedure: procedimiento cruento
invective: 1. *n.* invectiva; 2. *adj.* ofensivo; injurioso
inveigle: *v.* engatusar; seducir
invent: *v.* inventar; descubrir
invention: *n.* invención; invento
inventive: *adj.* inventivo
inventiveness: *n.* inventiva
inventor: *n.* inventor; autor
inventory: *n.* inventario
inverse: *adj.* inverso
inverse function: la función inversa
inverse operations: operaciones inversas
inverse property of addition: propiedad inversa de la suma
inverse property of **multiplication:** propiedad inversa de la multiplicación
inversion: *n.* inversión
inversion loop: lazo de inversión
invertebrate: *n.* invertebrado
inverter: *n.* inversor
invest: *v.* investir
investigate: *v.* investigar; explorar
investigation: *n.* investigación
investigator: *n.* investigador
investment: *n.* inversión
invidious: *adj.* injusto; abominable
invigorate: *v.* vigorizar
invigorating: *adj.* vigorizador
invincible: *adj.* invencible
invitation: *n.* invitación
invite: *v.* invitar; brindar
invocation: *n.* invocación
invoke: *v.* invocar
involuntary: *adj.* involuntario
involuntary muscle: músculos involuntarios

involute: *n.* involuta
involution: *n.* involución
involve: *v.* envolver; comprometer
invulnerability: *n.* invulnerabilidad
invulnerable: *adj.* invulnerable
inward: *adj.* interno
iodinase: *n.* ioduro-peroxidasa
iodine: *n.* yodo
ion: *n.* Ion
ionic: *adj.* iónico
ionic activity: actividad iónica
ionic activity coefficient: coeficiente de actividad iónica
ionic bond: enlace iónico
ionic compound: compuesto iónico
ionic strength: fuerza iónica
ionized calcium: Ion calcio
ionosphere: *n.* ionosfera
iontophoresis: *n.* iontoforesis
iota: *n.* iota
ipso facto: ipso facto
Iran: Irán
Iranian: *adj.* iraní; iranio; -a
Iraq: Iraq
Iraqi: *adj.* iraquí
irate: *n.* iracundo
ire: *n.* ira
Ireland: Irlanda
iridescence: *n.* iridiscencia
iris: *n.* iris
Irish: *n.* irlandés
Irishman: *n.* irlandés
Irishwoman: *n.* irlandesa
iritis: *n.* iritis
iron: *n.* hierro
iron deficiency anemia: deficiencia de hierro
ironic: *adj.* irónico
ironical: *adj.* irónico
ironist: *n.* ironista
irony: *n.* ironía
irradiance: *n.* irradiancia
irradiation: *n.* irradiación
irradicate: *v.* arraigar

irrational: *adj.* irracional
irrational number: numero irracional
irrationality: *n.* irracionalidad
irregular: *adj.* irregular
irregular galaxy: galaxia irregular
irrelevant: *adj.* impertinente
irreproachable: *adj.* irreprochable
irresolution: *n.* irresolución
irresponsibility: *n.* irresponsabilidad
irresponsible: *adj.* irresponsable
irreverence: *n.* irreverencia
irreversible: *adj.* irreversible
irrigate: *v.* irrigar; regar
irrigation: *n.* irrigación
irritable: *adj.* irritable
irritant: *n.* agente irritante
irritate: *v.* irritar
irritated: *adj.* irritado
irritating: *adj.* irritante
irritation: *n.* irritación
ischemia: *n.* isquemia
ischium: *n.* isquión
Islam: Islam
Islamic: *adj.* islámico
islamite: *n.* islamita
island: *n.* isleta; isla
island arc: arco de islas
islander: *n.* islefio; -a
isle: *n.* isla
islet: *n.* isleta
ism: *n.* ismo
isobar: *n.* isóbara
isoelectrical point: punto isoeléctrico
isoelectrofocusing: isoelectroenfoque
isoenzyme: *n.* isoenzima
isoform: *n.* isoforma
isogonic: *adj.* isogónico; isógono
isogram: *n.* isograma
isolate: *v.* aislar; incomunicar
isolation: *n.* aislamiento
isolation medium: medio de aislamiento
isolationism: *n.* aislacionismo
isoleucine: *n.* isoleucina
isomer: *n.* isómero
isomerism: *n.* isomería
isometric: *adj.* isométrico
isometrics: *n.* isometría
isomorphism: *n.* isomorfismo
isoniazid: *n.* isoniazida
isoproterenol: *n.* isoprenalina
isopycnose: *n.* isopicnosis
isosceles: *adj.* isósceles
isosceles triangle: triangulo isósceles
isoschizomer: *n.* isoesquizómero
isotherm: *n.* isoterma
isotonic: *adj.* isotónico
isotonics: *n.* isotonia
isotope: *n.* isótopo
isozyme: *n.* isoenzima
Israel: Israel
Israeli: *adj.* israelí
issue a decision: emitir una decisión
isthmus: *n.* istmo
Italian: *adj.* italiano; -a
Italianism: *n.* italianismo
italics: *n.* itálica
Italy: Italia
itch: *n.* picor; prurito; sarna
itch: *v.* picar
itching: *n.* picazón
item: *n.* ítem; artículo
itemize: *v.* detallar
iteration: *n.* iteración
iterative: *adj.* iterativo
iterative function: la función iterada
iteron: *n.* iterón
itinerant worker: obrero; -a itinerante
itinerary: *n.* itinerario
its: su; suyo
itself: mismo; sí mismo
IUD: dispositivo intrauterino
ivory: *n.* marfil
IVP: pielograma intravenosa

J

jacaranda: *n.* jacaranda
jack: el cabrio corto
jackass: *n.* asno
jacket: *n.* chaqueta; cazadora
jackhammer: *n.* martillo neumático
jackknife: *n.* navaja de bolsillo
jacobean: *n.* jacobino
jacobian: *adj.* jacobiano
Jacobin: *n.* jacobino
jade: 1. *n.* mujeruela; picarona;
2. *adj.* verde
jade: *v.* cansar; embotar
jag: *n.* diente; púa
jaguar: *n.* jaguar
jai alai: jai alai
jail: *n.* cárcel
jail: *v.* encarcelar
jainism: *n.* jainismo; yainismo
Jakarta: Yakarta
jalousie: *n.* celosía
jam: *n.* mermelada
Jamaica: Jamaica
Jamaican: *adj.* jamaicano; -a;
jamaiquino; -a
jamb: *n.* jamba
janitor: *n.* casero
jansenism: *n.* jansenismo
January: enero
Japan: Japón
Japanese: *n.* japonés
Japanese: *adj.* japonés; -esa
jar: *n.* jarra
jar: *n.* jarro
jar: *v.* chocar
jargon: *n.* jerga; jerigonza
jasmine: *n.* jazmín
jasper: *n.* jaspe

jaundice: *n.* ictericia
Java: Java
Javanese: *adj.* javanés; -esa
Javanese: *n.* javanés
javelin: *n.* jabalina
jaw: *n.* quijada; mandíbula
jazz: *n.* jazz
jealous: *adj.* celoso-a
jealousy: *n.* celos
jeans: *n.* jeans
Jeep: Jeep
jeer: *n.* mofa; burla
Jehovah: *n.* Jehová
jejunum: *n.* yeyuno
jellabah: *n.* chilaba
jelly: *n.* gelatina; jalea
jeopardize: *v.* arriesgar; exponer
jerboa: *n.* jerbo
jerk: *n.* sacudida
jerk: *v.* mover
jersey: *n.* jersey
Jerusalem: Jerusalén
jest: *n.* broma
jest: *v.* bromear
Jesuit: *n.* Jesuita
Jesus Christ: Jesucristo
jet: *n.* chorro; surtidor
jet: *v.* echar; arrojar
jet streams: corriente de chorro
Jew: *n.* judío; -a
jeweller: *n.* joyero
jewelry: *n.* joyas; prendas; joyería
Jewish: *adj.* judío
jicama: *n.* jícama
jig: *n.* giga
jigsaw: rompecabezas
jigsaw puzzle: puzzle
jingoist: *n.* jingoísta
jinn; jinni: *n.* genio
jinni: *n.* genio
job: *n.* trabajo; tarea
job training: entrenamiento
jockey: *n.* jockey; yoquey
jog: *n.* empujoncito

jog: *v.* empujar
join: *v.* juntar; unir
joint: *n.* unión; junta; articulación
joint compound: Conjunto compuesto
joint fluid: líquido sinovial
joint ownership: propiedad en conjunto
joint venture: empresa en conjunto
jointer: *n.* marcador de juntas
joist: *n.* vigueta
joke: *n.* broma
joke: *v.* burlarse de
joker: *n.* bromista; comodín
joking: *adj.* jocoso
jolt: *n.* traqueteo; golpe
jolt: *v.* sacudir
jonquil: *n.* junquillo
Jordan: Jordania
Jordan: Jordán
Jordanian: *adj.* jordano; -a
joule: *n.* julio
journey: *n.* viaje
journey: *v.* viajar
journeyman: *n.* rutinero; alquiladizo
jousting: *n.* justas
jovial: *adj.* jovial
joviality: *n.* jovialidad
joy: *n.* alegría
jubilant: *adj.* jubiloso
jubilation: *n.* júbilo
jubilee: *n.* jubileo
judaic: *adj.* judaico
judaica: *n.* cosas judaicas
Judaism: *n.* judaísmo
Judeo-Christian: judeocristiano
judge: *n.* juez; magistrado
judge: *v.* juzgar; censurar
judgment: *n.* juicio; orden judicial
judicature: *n.* judicatura
judicial: *adj.* judicial
judo: *n.* judo
jug: *n.* jarra
jug: *v.* encarcelar

jugged hare: estofado de liebre
juggle: *n.* juego de manos
juggle: *v.* hacer juegos de manos; hacer trampas
juice: *n.* jugo
juiciest: *n.* jugoso; zumoso
juicy: *adj.* jugoso
jujitsu: *n.* jiu-jitsu
julep: *n.* julepe
July: julio
jump: *n.* salto
jump: *v.* saltar; brincar
jumping gene: gen saltador
June: junio
jungle: *n.* jungla
junior: 1. *adj.* juvenil; 2. *n.* joven
juniper: *n.* junípero
junk food: comida basura; porquerías
junket: *n.* leche cuajada
junkie: *n.* yonqui
junta: *n.* junta
jurisdiction: *n.* jurisdicción
jurist: *n.* jurista
juror: *n.* jurado
jury duty: servicio de jurado
just: *adj.* justo
justice: *n.* justicia
justice of the peace: juez de paz
justifiable: *adj.* justificable
justification: *n.* justificación
justify: *v.* justificar; probar
Justinian: *n.* justiniano
jute: *n.* yute
juvenile: *adj.* juvenil

K

Kafkaesque: *adj.* kafkaiano; kafkiano
kaleidoscope: *n.* caleidoscopio
kalmia: *n.* kalmia
kamala: *n.* kamala
kanamycin: *n.* kanamicina
kangaroo: *n.* canguro
kantian: *adj.* kantiano
kapok: *n.* kapoc
kappa: *n.* kappa
karakul: *n.* karakul
karate: *n.* karate
karma: *n.* karma
karst topography: topografía karstica
karyokinesis: *n.* cariocinesis
karyotype: *n.* cariotipo
katacalcin: *n.* catacalcina
kayak: *n.* kayak
kebab: *n.* kebab
keel: *n.* quilla
keel: *v.* volcar
keen: *adj.* agudo; afilado
keep: *n.* manutención; subsistencia
keep: *v.* guardar; tener; retener
keep records: llevar cuentas; llevar registros
keeper: *n.* encargado; guarda
keeping: custodia; cuidado
keloid: *n.* queloide
kelp: *n.* quelpo
Kelvin: *n.* kelvin
Kelvin scale: escala Kelvin
kennel: *n.* perrera
keno: *n.* keno
Kenya: Kenia
kepi: *n.* quepis; kepis

keratin: *n.* queratina
keratitis: *n.* queratitis
kerchief: *n.* pañuelo
kernel: *n.* grano; almendra
ketchup: *n.* catsup
ketone body: compuesto cetónico
kettle: *n.* marmita
key: *n.* clave
keyboard: *n.* teclado
keyhole saw: el serrucho de calar
Keynesian: *adj.* keynesiano
keystone species: especies clave
khaki: *n.* caqui; kaki
khamsin: *n.* kamsín
khan: *n.* kan
khanate: *n.* kanato
kibbutz: *n.* kibbutz
kick: *n.* puntapié; coz
kid: *n.* chicos; niños; cabrito; chivo
kid: *v.* bromear
kidnap: *v.* secuestrar; raptar
kidnapper: *n.* secuestrador
kidnapping: *n.* secuestro
kidney: *n.* riñón
kidney beans: frijoles rojos
kidney kallikrein: calicreína hística
kidney stone: cálculo renal; piedras
kidney transplant: transplante del riñón
kill: *v.* matar; destruir
killing: 1. *n.* matanza; 2. *adj.* destructivo; irresistible
kiln: *n.* horno
kilo: *n.* kilo
kilobaud: *n.* kilobaudio
kilobit: *n.* kilobitio
kilobyte: *n.* kilobyte
kilocalorie: *n.* kilocaloría
kilocycle: *n.* kilociclo
kilogram: *n.* kilogramo
kilogram-meter: *n.* kilográmetro
kilohertz: *n.* kilohercio
kilojoule: *n.* kilojulio
kiloliter: *n.* kilolitro

kilometer: *n.* kilómetro
kilometer distance: kilometraje
kiloton: *n.* kilotón
kilovolt: *n.* kilovoltio
kilowatt: *n.* kilovatio
kilowatt-hour: kilovatio-hora
kilt: *n.* falda escocesa
kimono: *n.* kimono
kin: *adj.* pariente
kind: 1. *adj.* bueno; amable; 2. *n.* genero; especie; clase
kindergarten: *n.* jardín infantil; kindergarten
kindle: *v.* encender
kind-of-property: tipo de propiedad
kinematics: *n.* cinemática
kinescope: *n.* cinescopio
kinesologist: *n.* cinesiólogo; -a; trines-; quine-
kinesthesia: *n.* cinestesia
kinesthetic: *adj.* cinestético
kinetic energy: energía cinética
kinetics: *n.* cinética
king: *n.* rey
king medium: medio de rey
kingdom: *n.* reino; monarquía
kinin: *n.* cinina
kiosk: *n.* kiosco; quiosco
kipper: *n.* arenque
kirsch: *n.* kirsch
kiss: *n.* beso; dulce; merengue
kiss: *v.* besar
kit: *n.* conjunto; equipo de reactivos
kitchen: *n.* cocina
kitchen cabinets: los gabinetes para la cocina
kitchen foil: papel de aluminio
kitchen sink: fregadero
kitchen tissue: papel de cocina
kitchen ware: artículos de cocina
kitsch: *n.* kitsch
kitty: *n.* gatito
kiwi: *n.* kiwi
kleptomania: *n.* cleptomanía

kleptomaniac: *n.* cleptómano
knack: *n.* costumbre
knapsack: *n.* mochila
knavish: *adj.* bribón
knead: *v.* amasar
knee: *n.* rodilla
kneel: *v.* arrodillar
kneepads: *n.* rodilleras
knees: *n.* rodillas
knife: *n.* cuchillo; navaja
knife: *v.* acuchillar
knife grinder: afilador
knight: *n.* caballero; caballo
knitting: *n.* trabajo de punto
knitting machine: máquina de tejer
knob: *n.* perilla; tirador de puerta
knob of butter: nuez de mantequilla
knock: *n.* golpe; censura; criticar; censurar
knockout: *n.* nocaut; noqueo
knoll: *n.* toque de campanas
knot: *adj.* nudo
knot: *v.* anudar
know: *v.* saber; conocer; entender
knuckle bone: hueso de coyuntura
koala: *n.* koala
kohlrabi: *n.* colirrábano
kopeck: *n.* copec
Koran: *n.* Corán; Alcorán
Korea: Corea
Korean: *n.* coreano
Korean: *adj.* coreano
kosher: *adj.* kosher
koto: *n.* koto
Krakow: Cracovia
krishna: *n.* krisna
Krishna: *n.* Krisna
krona: *n.* corona
krugerrand: *n.* krugerrand
kudu: *n.* kudu
kummel: *n.* kummel; camelo
kumquat: *n.* kuncuat
kung fu: kung fu
Kuwait: Kuwait

Kuwaiti: *adj.* kuwaití
kvass: *n.* kwas; kvas
kymograph: *n.* quimógrafo
kyphosis: *n.* cifosis
kyrie: *n.* kirie

L

la: *n.* la
lab: *n.* laboratorio
label: *n.* rótulo; etiqueta
label: *v.* rotular
labeling: *n.* marcado
labia: *n.* labios
labium: *n.* labio
labor: *n.* labor; trabajo
labor and delivery: parto
laboratory: *n.* laboratorio
laboratory: *n.* laboratorio; taller
laboratory examinations: exámenes de laboratorio
laboratory medicine: ciencias de laboratorio clínico
laboratory tests: exámenes de laboratorio
laborer: *n.* trabajador; obrero
laburnum: *n.* laburno
labyrinth: *n.* laberinto
lac; lacquer: *n.* laca
lace: *n.* encaje; puntilla
lace: *v.* atar; enlazar; apretarse
laceration: *n.* laceración
laces: *n.* lazos
lack: *n.* carencia; falta
lack: *v.* necesitar
lack of severity: falta o insuficiencia de gravedad

lacked blood: sangre hemolisada
laconic: *adj.* lacónico
lacquer: la laca
lacrimal fluid: secreción lacrimal
lacrosse: *n.* lacrosse
lactase: *n.* lactasa
lactate: *n.* lactato
lactation: *n.* lactancia
lactic: *adj.* láctico
lactic acid: ácido láctico
lactose: *n.* lactosa
lactotropic hormone: prolactina
lactotropin: *n.* prolactina
lacuna: *n.* laguna
lad: *n.* muchacho; chico
ladder: *n.* escalera de mano
ladle: *n.* cucharón
lady: *n.* señora; señorita; dama
ladylike: *adj.* afeminado
ladyship: *n.* señoría
lag: 1. *adj.* rezagado; 2. *n.* retraso
lag: *v.* revestir
lag phase: fase de latencia
lager: *n.* cerveza reposada
lagging strand: cadena discontinua
lagoon: *n.* laguna
laity: *adj.* laicado
lake: *n.* lago; laguna
lama: *n.* lama
lamb: *n.* cordero
lambda: *n.* microlitro; lambda
lame: 1. *adj.* cojo; pobre; 2. *n.* lame
lame: *v.* cojear
lamé: *n.* lamé
lament: *n.* lamento
lamentation: *n.* lamentación
laminar flow: flujo laminar
lamination: *n.* laminación
lamp: *n.* lámpara
lampholder: *n.* portalámparas
lamprey: *n.* lamprea
lancer: *n.* lancero
lancet: *n.* lanceta
land: *n.* terreno; tierra

land: *v.* desembarcar
land breeze: brisa terrestre
landform: *n.* accidente geográfico
landform region: región con accidentes geográficos
landholder: *n.* terrateniente
landing: *n.* aterrizaje; desembarcos
landlady: *n.* propietaria; ama
landlord: *n.* propietario; dueño
landscape: *n.* paisaje
language: *n.* lenguaje; lengua
languid: *adj.* lánguido
languor: *n.* languidez
lank: *adj.* largo; flaco
lanolin: *n.* lanolina
lantern: *n.* linterna
Laos: Laos
lap: *n.* falda; seno
laparoscope: *n.* laparoscopio
laparoscopy: *n.* laparoscopia
laparotomy: *n.* laparotomía
lapel: *n.* solapa
lapidary: *n.* lapidario
lapis lazuli: lapislazuli
lapp: *n.* lapon
lapse: *n.* lapso
laptop: *n.* laptop
larceny: *n.* robo
lard: *n.* lardo; manteca; grasa de cerdo
larder: *n.* despensa
large: *adj.* grande; abultado
large intestine: intestino grueso; intestino grande
largess: *n.* largueza
largo: *n.* largo
largo: *adv.* largo
lariat: *n.* lazo
lark: *n.* alondra; (fam.) parranda
larva: *n.* larva
laryngitis: *n.* laringitis
laryngology: *n.* laringología
laryngoscope: *n.* laringoscopio
laryngoscopy: *n.* laringoscopia

larynx: *n.* laringe
lasagna: *n.* lasaña
lascivious: *adj.* lascivo
laser: *n.* láser
lash: *n.* látigo
lash: *v.* fustigar
lass: *n.* muchacha
lassitude: *n.* lasitud
lasso: *n.* lazo
last: 1. *adj.* último; postrero; 2. *n.* intima
latch: *n.* picaporte; pestillo
late: 1. *adj.* tardío; lejano; 2. *adv.* tarde
lateen: *n.* latina
latency: *n.* latencia
latent: *adj.* latente
later: *adj.* más tarde
latest: *Super.* el ultimo; el mas reciente
latex: *n.* látex
lather: *n.* espuma de jabón
lather: *v.* enjabonar
latifundium: *n.* latifundio
Latin: *n.* latín
latinize: *v.* latinizar
Latino: *adj.* Latino; -a
latitude: *n.* latitud
latrine: *n.* letrina
lattice: *n.* enrejado
lattice: *v.* enrejar
laud: *n.* alabanza
laud: *v.* alabar
laudable: *adj.* laudable
laudanum: *n.* láudano
laudatory: *adj.* laudatorio
laugh: *n.* risa
launch: *n.* botadura; lancha
launch: *v.* botar
launcher: *n.* lanzador
launching: lanzamiento
laundromat: *n.* lavadoras automáticas
laundry: *n.* lavandería

laurel: *n.* laurel; lauro
lava: *n.* lava
lava flow: colada de lava
lavage: *n.* lavado
lavatory: *n.* lavatorio
lavender: *n.* lavanda
lavish: *adj.* pródigo; gastador
lavish: *v.* prodigar; malgastar
law: *n.* ley; derecho
law of conservation of energy: ley de la conservación de la energía
law of conservation of mass: ley de conservación de la masa
law of conservation of **momentum**: ley de la conservación del momento
law of cosines: la ley de los cosenos
law of reflection: ley de reflexión
law of sines: la ley de los senos
law of superposition: ley de la superposición
law of universal gravitation: ley de la gravitación universal
lawful: *adj.* legítimo
lawful admission: admisión legal; entrada legal
lawful permanent resident: residente legal permanente
lawless: *adj.* ilegal
lawn: *n.* césped
lawyer: *n.* abogado; licenciado
laxative: *adj.* laxante
layer: *n.* capa; poner en capas; lecho; gallina ponedora
laying: *n.* capa; tendido (de un cable)
layman: *n.* lego; seglar
layoff (worker): *v.* despedir; suspender
laziness: *n.* pereza
lazy: *adj.* perezoso
lead: *n.* plomo
leader: *n.* líder
leader sequence: secuencia guía
leadership: *n.* liderazgo; liderato; dirección

leading: *adj.* director
leading digit: digito dominante
leading strand: cadena adelantada
leaf: *n.* hoja
league: *n.* legua; liga
league: *v.* asociar
league of nations: sociedad de naciones
leak: *n.* gotera; fuga
leak: *v.* dejar escapar
leaky mutation: mutación parcial
lean: *n.* carne magra; inclinación
lean: *v.* inclinar
leanness: *n.* flaqueza; pobreza
leap: *n.* salto
leap: *v.* saltar; brincar
learn: *v.* aprender
learned: *adj.* docto; culto
learner: *n.* aprendiz
learning: *n.* aprendizaje
lease: *n.* arrendamiento
lease: *v.* arrendar
leash: *adj.* pequeño; poco
least: 1. *adj.* más pequeño; 2. *adv.* menos
leather: *n.* cuero
leave: *n.* licencia; despedida
leave: *v.* dejar
leaven; leavening: *n.* levadura
lecherous: *adj.* lujurioso
lecithin: *n.* lecitina
lector: *n.* lector
lecture: *n.* conferencia; discurso
lecture: *v.* dar lecciones
leeks: *n.* puerros
leer: *n.* mirada de reojo
lees: *n.* pl. heces; sedimento
leeward: *n.* sotavento
left: 1. *adj.* izquierdo; 2. *n.* izquierda
leg: *n.* pierna
legacy: *n.* legado
legal dependency: dependencia legal
legal guardian: tutor legal; guardián legal

legalese: *n.* jerga legal
legalization: *n.* legalización
legate: 1. *n.* legado; 2. *adj.* legado
legation: *n.* legación
legato: 1. *adj.* ligado; 2. *adv.* ligado
legend: *n.* leyenda; letrero
legible: *adj.* legible
legion: *n.* legión
legionnaire: *n.* legionario
legionnaires disease: enfermedad del legionario
legislate: *adj.* legislativo
legislature: *n.* legislatura
legitimate: legítimo
legitimate: *v.* legitimar
legs of a right triangle: catetos de un triángulo rectángulo
legume: *n.* legumbre
leisure: 1. *n.* ocio; 2. a desocupado
lemma: *n.* lema
lemming: lemming
lemon: *n.* limón; amarillo limón
lemonade: *n.* limonada
lemony: *n.* sabor a limón
lempira: *n.* lempira
lemur: *n.* lemur
lend: *v.* prestar
lender: *n.* prestamista
lending: *n.* prestación; prestamo
length: *n.* longitud
lengthen: *v.* alargar
lenience: *n.* lenidad; clemencia
Leninism: *n.* leninismo
lens: *n.* cristalino; lente
lentil: *n.* lenteja
lento: *adj.* lento
leo: *n.* leo
leopard: *n.* leopardo
leotard: *n.* leotardo
leper: *n.* leproso
leprosarium: *n.* leprosería
leprosy: *n.* lepra
leptotene: *n.* leptotena
lesion: *n.* lesión

less: 1. *adj.* menor; 2. *adv.* menos
lessen: *v.* reducir; disminuir; aliviar
lesser: *adj.* menor; más pequeño
lesson: *n.* lección; enseñanza
lesson: *v.* instruir
lest: *conj.* no sea que
let: *v.* conceder; arrendar
lethal: *adj.* letal
lethal concentration: concentración letal
lethality assessment: evaluación del intento mortal
lethargy: *n.* letargo; aletargamiento
letter: *n.* letra; carta
letter of denial: carta de negación
lettuce: *n.* lechuga
leucine: *n.* leucina
leukemia: *n.* leucemia
leukemia: *n.* leucoma
leukocyte: *n.* leucocito
levant: *n.* levante
level: *n.* contenido; nivel
level: *v.* igualar; apuntar
level of care: nivel de cuidado
level of severity: nivel de gravedad
lever: *n.* plomada
levitation: *n.* levitación
levy: *v.* imponer impuestos; recaudar
lewd: *adj.* lascivo
lexical: *adj.* léxico
lexicographer: *n.* lexicógrafo
lexicography: *n.* lexicografía
lexicon: *n.* léxico
liability: *n.* riesgo; deuda; responsabilidad
liability: obligación; responsabilidad
liable: *adj.* sujeto; responsable
liaison: *n.* enlace
liana: *n.* bejuco
liar: *v.* mentir
libation: *n.* libación
libation: *n.* libación
libel: *n.* libelo
libeler; libelist: *n.* libelista

liberal: *adj.* liberal
liberalism: *n.* liberalismo
liberality: *n.* liberalidad
liberator: *n.* liberador; libertador
libertine: *n.* libertino; -a
liberty: *n.* libertad
libido: *n.* deseos sexuales
libra: *n.* libra
librarian: *n.* bibliotecario
library: *n.* biblioteca
library of Congress: Biblioteca del Congreso
librettist: *n.* libretista
libretto: *n.* libreto
license: *n.* licencia; permiso
lichen: *n.* liquen
lichenology: *n.* liquenología
lid: *n.* tapa; tapadera
lidocaine: *n.* lidocaína
lien: *n.* derecho de retención
lieutenant: *n.* teniente
life: *n.* vida
life expectancy: expectativas de vida
life history: historia de vida
life insurance policy: póliza de seguro de vida
life science: ciencias de la vida
lifelike: *adj.* natural; vivo
lifelong: 1. *adj.* de toda la vida; 2. *adv.* durante toda la vida
lifestyle: *n.* estilo de vida
lifetime: *n.* vitalicias
lifetime member: miembro vitalicio
lifetime reserve: reserva vitalicia
lift: *n.* fuerza de elevación
ligament: *n.* ligamento
ligand: *n.* ligando
ligase chain reaction: reacción en cadena por la ligasa
ligation: *n.* ligación
ligature: *n.* ligadura
light: 1. *adj.* luminoso; 2. *n.* luz
light: *v.* encender; alumbrar
light microscope: microscopio

óptico
light switch: interruptor
light work: trabajo ligero
lighten: *v.* aligerar; iluminar
lighter: *n.* encendedor; lancha
lighting: *n.* iluminación
lightning: *n.* rayo
light-year: año luz
lignocaine: *n.* lidocaína
like terms: términos semejantes
likelihood: *n.* probabilidad
likelihood ratio: razón de verosimilitud
likely: *adj.* probable
likeness: *n.* semejanza
liking: *n.* gusto
lilac: *n.* lila
Lilliputian: *adj.* liliputiense
lily: *adj.* lirio
lima bean: fríjol
limb: *n.* miembro
limbic: *adj.* límbico
limbo: *n.* limbo
lime: *n.* lima; limero; cal
limestone: *n.* piedra caliza
limit: *n.* límite
limit of detection: límite de detección
limitation: *n.* limitación
limitation of movement: limitación de movimiento
limiting factor: factor limitante
limnology: *n.* limnología
limousine: *n.* limusina
limp: *n.* cojera
lincomycin: *n.* lincomicina
line: *n.* línea; recta
line graph: grafica lineal
line of reflection: línea de reflexión
line of symmetry: línea de simetría
line plot: diagrama lineal
line symmetry: simetría lineal
lineage: *n.* linaje; raza
lineality range: intervalo analítico

lineament: *n.* lineamiento
linear: *adj.* linear; lineal
linear absorption coefficient: coeficiente de absorción lineal
linear algebra: el álgebra lineal
linear attenuation coefficient: coeficiente de atenuación lineal
linear equation: la ecuación lineal
linear feet: los pies lineales
linear function: función lineal
linear inequality: desigualdad lineal
linear transformation: la transformación lineal
linearity: *n.* rectilinealidad; linealidad
lined up: arreglados; en fila
lineic: *adj.* lineico -ica
lineic absorbance: absorbancia linéica
linen: *n.* lino
linen: *adj.* lino
liner: *n.* revestimiento; el encofrado
linesman: *n.* juez de línea
lineup: *n.* alineación
ling: *n.* bacallao
linger: *v.* demorar
lingerie: *n.* lencería
lingua franca: lengua franca
linguistic: *adj.* lingüístico
linguistics: *n.* lingüística
liniment: *n.* linimento
lining: *n.* forro
link: *n.* conexión; eslabón
link: *v.* enlazar
linkage: *n.* ligamiento
linkage group: grupo de ligamiento
linked gene: gen ligado
linker: *n.* ligador
linking number: número total de vueltas
linnet: *n.* jilguero
linoleum: *n.* linóleo
linotype: *n.* linotipia; linotipo
linseed: *adj.* linaza

linseed: *n.* linaza
lintel: *n.* dintel
lion: *n.* león
lioness: *n.* leona
lip: *n.* labio
lip: *v.* besar; susurrar
lip: *n.* labio
lipase: *n.* lipasa
lipid: *adj.* lípido
lipoma: *n.* lipoma
liposuction: *n.* liposucción
liquefaction: *n.* liquefacción
liquefier: *n.* licuadora
liqueur: *n.* licor
liquid: 1. líquido; 2. *adj.* líquido
liquidate: *v.* liquidar
liquidize: *v.* triturar
liquor: *n.* licor
list: *n.* lista
list: *v.* anotar; listar; registrar
listen: *v.* escuchar
listing: *n.* listado
litany: *n.* letanía
litchi: *n.* lichi
liter: *n.* litro
literal: *adj.* literal
literary: *adj.* literario
literati: *n.* literatos
literature: *n.* literatura
lithe: *adj.* flexible
lithium: *n.* litio
lithium ion: ion litio
lithograph: *n.* litografía
lithographer: *n.* litógrafo
lithography: *n.* litografía
lithosphere: *n.* litosfera
litigation: *n.* litigación; litigio
litocholic acid: ácido litocólico
litter: *n.* mantillo; litera
littoral: *adj.* litoral
liturgist: *n.* liturgista
liturgy: *n.* liturgia
live: *adj.* vivo; de actualidad
live: *v.* vivir; existir; habitar

liver: *n.* hígado
livestock: *n.* ganado; rebaño
livid: *n.* lívido
living: 1. *adj.* vivo; animado; 2. *n.* modo de vivir
living expenses: gastos de subsistencia
living room: la sala
living will: testamento en vida
living with: viviendo con
lizard: *n.* lagarto
llama: *n.* llama
load: *n.* carga
loader: *n.* cargadora
loaf: *n.* barra; hogaza de pan
loam: *n.* limo arcilloso arenoso
loam: *v.* prestar
loathe: *v.* aborrecer
lobby: *n.* lobby; salón de entrada; vestíbulo
lobe: *n.* lóbulo
lobectomy: *n.* lobectomía
lobelia: *n.* lobelia
lobotomy: *n.* lobotomía
lobster: *n.* langosta
lobule: *n.* lobulillo
local: *adj.* local
local winds: vientos locales
locale: *n.* local
localism: *n.* localismo
locality: *n.* localidad
localization: *n.* localización
locate: *v.* poner; establecer
located: *adj.* localizado; situado
location: *n.* localización
locative: *adj.* locativo
lochia: *n.* loquios
lock: *n.* cerradura; rizo
lock: *v.* cerrar
lock casing: la caja del pestillo
lock mortiser: la embutidora de cerraduras
lock nut: la tuerca de seguridad
locksmith: *n.* cerrajero

locomotive: *n.* locomotora
locoweed: *adj.* loco
locus: *n.* locus
locution: *n.* locución
lod score: lod
lodge: *n.* logia; casa de campo
lodge: *v.* alojar
lodging: *n.* alojamiento; hospedaje
loess: *n.* loes
loft: *n.* desván galería
log: *n.* leño; tronco
log: *v.* cortar troncos
logarithm: *n.* logaritmo
loggia: *n.* logia
logic: *n.* lógica
logical: *adj.* lógico
logician: *adj.* lógico
logistics: *n.* logística
logit: *n.* logit
logo: *n.* logo; logotipo
logography: *n.* logografía
logos: *n.* logos
loin: *n.* lomo; solomillo
loll: *v.* colgar
lomentum: *n.* momento
loneliness: *n.* soledad
lonely: *adj.* solo
long: 1. *adj.* largo; extenso; 2. *adv.* mucho
long beam: el larguero
long-day plant: planta de día largo
long-distance: de larga distancia
longitude: *n.* longitud
longitudinal comparison: comparación longitudinal
longitudinal wave: onda longitudinal
long-lived: *adj.* longevo
longshore drift: deriva litoral
look: *n.* mirada
look: *v.* mirar; expresar o indicar
looking after your interests: velando por sus intereses
lookout: *n.* vigilancia

loony: *adj.* loco
loop: *n.* lazo; asa
loop: *v.* enlazar
loose: 1. *adj.* flojo; suelto; 2. *n.* relajamiento
loose: *v.* soltar
loosen: *v.* desatar
lop: *v.* podar
loquacious: *adj.* locuaz
loran: *n.* lorán
Lord: *n.* Lord
lordosis: *n.* lordosis
lose: *v.* perder
loss: *n.* pérdida
loss of balance: pérdida del equilibrio
loss of bladder control: pérdida del control para orinar
loss of consciousness: pérdida del conocimiento
loss of coordination: pérdida de coordinación
loss of hearing: pérdida del oído
loss of judgment: pérdida de juicio
loss of major functions: pérdida de funciones básicas
loss of memory: pérdida de la memoria
loss of rectal control: pérdida del control para defecar
loss of sensation: pérdida de la sensibilidad
loss of speech: pérdida del habla
loss of voice: pérdida de la voz
lost: *adj.* perdido
lost check: cheque perdido
lot: *n.* lote
lotion: *n.* loción
lottery: *n.* lotería
lottery ticket seller: lotero
lotto: *n.* lotería
lotus: *n.* loto
loud: 1. *adj.* alto; fuerte; llamativo; 2. *adv.* en alta voz

louder: *adv.* más fuerte
loudness: *n.* volumen
lounge: *n.* salón de tertulia
lounge: *v.* gastar ociosamente
louvers: *n.* persianas
lovable: *adj.* amable
love: *n.* amor
love: *v.* amar; querer
lover: *n.* amante; novio
low: 1. *adj.* bajo; común; 2. *n.* mugido; 3. *adv.* bajo;
low: *v.* mugir; berrear
low back pain: dolor de espalda; dolor de riñones
lower: *v.* bajar; abatir
lower extreme: extremo inferior
lower quartile: cuartil inferior
low-income: de pocos ingresos
loyal: *adj.* fiel
loyalty: *n.* lealtad
lozenge: *n.* pastilla; tableta
lubricant: *n.* lubricante
lubrication: *n.* lubricación
lucid: *adj.* lúcido
luck: *n.* suerte; azar
lucky: *adj.* afortunado; feliz
lucrative: *adj.* lucrativo
ludicrous: *adj.* absurdo
luggage: *n.* equipaje
lugubrious: *adj.* lúgubre
luliberin: *n.* luliberina
lullaby: *n.* nana
lumbago: *n.* lumbago
lumbar: *adj.* lumbar
lumbar puncture: punción lumbar
lumber: *n.* madera de construcción
lumber: *v.* amontonar
lumen: *n.* lumen; luz
luminescent: *adj.* luminiscente
luminiscence: *n.* luminiscencia
luminometer: *n.* luminómetro
luminous: *adj.* luminoso
luminous flux: flujo luminoso
luminous intensity: intensidad

luminosa
lump: *n.* masa
lunar: *adj.* lunar
lunar eclipse: eclipse lunar
lunch: *n.* almuerzo
lung: *n.* pulmón
lupine: *n.* lupino
lupus: *n.* lupus
lure: *n.* cebo
lush: *adj.* jugoso
lust: *n.* codicia; lujuria
lust: *v.* codiciar
luster: *adj.* brillo; lustre
lusty: *adj.* robusto
lute: *n.* laúd
luther: *n.* lutero
lutheran: *adj.* luterano
lutheranism: *n.* luteranismo
lutropin: *n.* lutropina
luxury: *adj.* de lujo
luxury items: artículos de lujo
lycopod: *n.* licopodio
lymph: *n.* linfa
lymph node: ganglio linfático
lymphatic: *adj.* linfático
lymphatic system: sistema linfático
lymphoblast: *n.* linfoblasto
lymphocyte: *n.* linfocito
lymphoma: *n.* linfoma
lynching: *n.* linchamiento
lynx: *n.* lince
lyre: *n.* lira
lyric: *adj.* lírico
lyricism: *n.* lirismo
lysine: *n.* lisina
lysis: *n.* lisis
lysogenic: *adj.* lisogénico -ica
lysosome: *n.* lisosoma
lysozyme: *n.* lisozima

M

macabre: *adj.* macabro
macadam: *n.* macadán
macadamia: *n.* macadamia
macaque: *n.* macaco
macaroni: *n.* macarrones; pastas
macaroon: *n.* macarrón
mace: *n.* maza; macis
macerate: *v.* macerar
macerate: *v.* macerar
machiavelli: *n.* maquiavelo
machination: *n.* maquinación
machine: *n.* máquina
machine tool: máquina herramienta
machinery: *n.* maquinaria
machinist: *n.* maquinista
machismo: *n.* machismo
mackintosh: *n.* impermeable
macrame: *n.* macramé
macro: *n.* macro; macroinstrucción
macrobiotic: *adj.* macrobiótico
macrobiotics: *n.* macrobiótica
macrocephaly: *n.* macrocefalia
macrocode: *n.* macrocodificación
macroconidia: *n.* macroconidia
macroglobulin: *n.* macroglobulina
macromolecule: *n.* macromolécula
macroscopic: *adj.* macroscópico
mad: *adj.* loco
mad: *v.* enloquecer
mad scientist: científico loco
madam: *n.* señora
madden: *v.* enloquecer
made: *adj.* hecho; fabricado
madeira: *n.* madeira
madhouse: *n.* manicomio

madras: *n.* madras
madrigal: *adj.* madrigal
maestro: *n.* maestro
mafia: *n.* mafia
mag media: cinta magnética
magazine: *n.* revista; almacén
magenta: *n.* magenta
magic: 1. *adj.* mágico; 2. *n.* magia
magic: *adj.* mágico
magician: *n.* mágico
magistrate: *n.* magistrado
magma: *n.* magma
magma chamber: cámara magmática
magnanimity: *n.* magnanimidad
magnanimous: *adj.* magnánimo
magnesium: *n.* magnesio
magnesium ion: Ion magnesio
magnet: *n.* imán
magnetic: *adj.* magnético
magnetic declination: declinación magnética
magnetic domain: dominio magnético
magnetic field: campo magnético
magnetic field lines: líneas del campo magnético
magnetic force: fuerza magnética
magnetic pole: polo magnético
magnetic tape: cinta magnética
magnetism: *n.* magnetismo
magneto: *n.* magneto
magnetometer: *n.* magnetómetro
magnetosphere: *n.* magnetosfera
magnetron: *n.* magnetrón
magnificent: *adj.* magnífico
magnify: *v.* amplificar
magnitude: *n.* cuantía; magnitud
magnolia: *n.* magnolia
magnum: *n.* magnum
magus: *n.* mago
mahatma: *n.* mahatma
mahogany: *n.* caoba
maid: *n.* virgen

mail: *n.* correo; correspondencia; malla
mail: *v.* enviar por correo
mailbox: *n.* buzón
mailing address: dirección postal
mailing list: lista de distribución
maim: *v.* mutilar
main: *adj.* principal
main sequence: secuencia principal
mainland: *n.* tierra firme
mainly: *adv.* mayormente
maintain: *v.* mantener
maintain records: mantener los registros
maintenance: *n.* mantenimiento
maintenance dialysis: diálisis regular
maize: *n.* maíz
majestic: *adj.* majestuoso
majesty: *n.* majestad
major: *adj.* mayor
major joints: coyunturas principales
majordomo: *n.* mayordomo
majority: *n.* mayoría
make payment: pagar; hacer un pago
make sure: verificar; cerciorarse
maker: *n.* fabricante
makeshift: *adj.* provisional
make-up: *n.* composición; maquillaje
making models: hacer modelos
maladroit: *adj.* torpe
malady: *n.* mal; enfermedad
malaga: *n.* málaga
malaise: *n.* malestar
malamute: *n.* malamut
malaria: *n.* malaria
malcontent: *adj.* malcontento
male: 1. *adj.* masculino; 2. *n.* varón; macho
malediction: *n.* maldición
malefactor: *n.* malhechor
malevolence: *n.* malevolencia

malevolent: *adj.* malévolo
malice: *n.* malicia
malicious: *adj.* malicioso
malign: *adj.* maligno
malign: *v.* calumniar
malignancy: *n.* malignidad
malignant: *adj.* maligno; grave
mall: *n.* alameda
malleable: *adj.* maleable
malleolus: *adj.* maleolo
malnutrition: *n.* desnutrición
malpractice: *n.* inmoralidad
malt: *n.* Malta
maltase: *n.* maltasa
malted: *adj.* malteado
maltose: *n.* maltosa
maltreat: *v.* maltratar
maltreatment: *n.* maltrato;
maltratamiento
mambo: *n.* mambo
mammal: *n.* mamífero
mammary gland: glándula mamaria
mammatropic hormone: prolactina
mammogram: *n.* mamograma
mammography: *n.* mamografía
mammoplasty: *n.* mamoplastia
man: *n.* hombre
man: *v.* tripular
manacle: *n.* manilla
manacle: *v.* esposar
manage: *v.* manejar
manageable: *adj.* manejable
management: *n.* administración;
manejo
manager: *n.* manager
manager of farm: administrador;
gerente
mandarin: *n.* mandarina
mandate: *n.* mandato
mandible: *n.* mandíbula
mandolin: *n.* mandolina
mandrake: *n.* mandrágora
mandrill: *n.* mandril
maneuver: *n.* maniobra

maneuver: *v.* maniobrar
manful: *adj.* varonil
manger: *n.* pesebre
mango: *n.* mango
mangy: *adj.* sarnoso
manhood: *n.* masculinidad
mania: *n.* manía
manic-depressive: *adj.*
maniacodepresivo; -a
manicure: *n.* manicura
manicurist: *n.* manicurista
manifest: *adj.* manifiesto
manifest: *v.* manifestar
manifestation: *n.* manifestación
manila: *n.* manila
manipulated variable: variable
manipulada
manipulation: *n.* manipulación;
manipuleo
manipulator: *adj.* manipulador
manipulator: *n.* manipulador
mankind: *n.* humanidad
manliness: *n.* valentía
manly: *adj.* varonil
manna: *n.* maná
mannequin: *n.* maniquí
manner: *n.* manera
mannered: *adj.* amanerado
mannerism: *n.* manierismo
mannerly: *adv.* ademán
mannose: *n.* manosa
manometer: *n.* manómetro
manometry: *n.* manometría
manor: *n.* feudo
mansard: *n.* mansarda
mansion: *n.* mansión
manslaughter: *n.* homicidio
impremeditado
mantilla: *n.* mantilla
mantissa: *n.* mantisa
mantle: *n.* manto
mantle: *v.* tapar; envolver
mantra: *n.* mantra
manual: *adj.* manual

manufacturer: *n.* fabricante
manufacturing: *n.* manufactura
manure: *n.* estiércol; abono
manure: *v.* abonar
manuscript: *n.* manuscrito
many: *adj.* muchos
manzanita: *n.* manzanita
Maoism: *n.* maoísmo
map: *n.* mapa
map projection: proyección cartográfica
mapping: *n.* cartografía
mar: *v.* estropear
maracas: *n.* maracas
maraschino: *n.* marrasquino
marathon: *n.* maratón
marble: *n.* mármol
March: marzo
march: *n.* marcha
march: *v.* poner en marcha
mare: *n.* yegua
margarine: *n.* margarina
margin: *n.* margen; margarina
margin of error: margen de error
marginalia: *n.* notas marginales
Maria: *n.* Maria
marijuana: *n.* marihuana
marimba: *n.* marimba
marine: *adj.* marino
marine biology: biología marina
marine climate: clima marino
mariner: *n.* marinero; marino
marionette: *n.* marioneta
marital: *adj.* marital
marital status: estado civil
maritime: *adj.* marítimo
maritime: masa de aire marítima
marjoram: *n.* mejorana
mark: *n.* marca; huella
mark: *v.* marcar
marker: *n.* marcador
market: *n.* mercado; bolsa
market value: valor en el mercado
marketing: *n.* mercadeo;

mercadotecnia
marketplace: *n.* plaza del mercado
markup: *n.* margen
marmalade: *n.* mermelada
marmot: *n.* marmota
marquis: *n.* marqués
marquise: *n.* marquesa
marriage: *n.* matrimonio; boda
married: *adj.* casado
marrow: *n.* médula; esencia
marry: *v.* casar
marsh: *n.* pantano
marshal: *n.* maestro de ceremonias
marsupial: *n.* marsupial
mart: *n.* emporio
marten: *n.* marta
martial: *adj.* marcial
Martian: *n.* marciano
martini: *n.* martini
martyrdom: *n.* martirio
martyrology: *n.* martirologio
marvelous: *adj.* maravillosa
Marxism: *n.* marxismo
Marxist: *n.* marxista
marzipan: *n.* mazapán
masculine: *adj.* masculino
maser: *n.* maser
mash: *n.* masa
mash: *v.* amasar
mashie: *n.* mashie
mask: *n.* mascarilla; máscara; antifaz
mask: *v.* enmascarar
masochism: *n.* masoquismo
masochist: *n.* masoquista
masochistic: *n.* masoquista
mason: *n.* masón; albañil
masonry: *n.* masonería
masquerade: *n.* mascarada
mass: *n.* masa; misa
mass concentration: concentración de masa
mass extinction: extinción en masa
mass fraction: fracción de masa
mass movement: movimiento de

masas
mass number: número de masa
mass production: producción en serie
mass rate: caudal de masa
mass spectrometer: espectrómetro de masas
massacre: *n.* masacre
massage: *n.* masaje
massage: *v.* dar masaje
masseter: *n.* masetero
masseur: *n.* masajista
massic: *adj.* másico
massif: *n.* macizo
massive: *adj.* masivo
mast: *n.* mástil
mastaba: *n.* mastaba
mastectomy: *n.* mastectonía
master: *n.* patrón; maestro
master: *v.* dominar
master of ceremonies: maestro de ceremonias
masterly: 1. *adj.* magistral; 2. *adv.* magistralmente
masterpiece: *n.* obra maestra
master's degree: maestría
masterwork: *n.* obra maestra
mastery: *n.* maestría
mastic: *n.* mástique
masticate: *v.* masticar
mastication: *n.* masticación
mastiff: *n.* mastiff
mastitis: *n.* mastitis
mastoid: *n.* mastoides
mastoiditis: *n.* mastoiditis
masturbate: *v.* masturbarse
mat: 1. *adj.* mate; 2. *n.* estera
mat: *v.* enmarañar
matador: *n.* matador
match: *n.* cerilla; compañero
match: *v.* hermanar
matchless: *adj.* sin igual
mate: *n.* pareja; compañero; socio; consorte; mate

mate: *v.* aparejarse
material: *adj.* material
material fact: hecho pertinente
material participation: participación material
materialism: *n.* materialismo
materialistic: *adj.* materialista
maternal: *adj.* materno
maternity: *n.* maternidad
math: *n.* mates
mathematical: *adj.* matemático
mathematician: *n.* matemático
mathematics: *n.* matemáticas
matinee: *n.* función de tarde; matinée
mating: *n.* apareamiento
mating system: sistema de apareamiento
matins: *n.* oración matinal
matriarchal: *adj.* matriarcal
matriarchy: *n.* matriarcado
matricide: *adj.* matricidio
matriculant: *adj.* matriculador
matriculation: *n.* matrícula
matrilineal: *adj.* por línea materna
matrimony: *n.* matrimonio
matrix: 1. *n.* matriz; 2. *adj.* matricial
matrix algebra: álgebra matricial
matron: *n.* matrona
matte: *adj.* mate
matter: *n.* materia; cuestión; asunto; materia
matter: *v.* importar
mattress: *n.* colchón
maturation: *n.* maduración
mature: *adj.* maduro
mature: *v.* madurar
maturity: *n.* madurez
maudlin: *adj.* sentimental
mausoleum: *n.* mausoleo
mauve: 1. *n.* malva; 2. *adj.* de color malva
maxilla: *n.* hueso maxilar
maxim: *n.* máxima
maximal: *adj.* máximo

maximum: 1. *n.* maximum; 2. *adj.* máximo
maximum amount: cantidad máxima
maximum reduction: reducción máxima
maxixe: *n.* machicha
May: mayo
may: *v.* poder
maybe: quizá
mayonnaise: *n.* mayonesa
mayor: *n.* alcalde
maze: *n.* laberinto; confusión
mazurka: *n.* mazurca
me: *n.* mi; me
mead: *n.* pradera
meal: *n.* comida; harina
mean: *n.* promedio; media
mean life: vida media
mean time: tiempo medio
meander: *n.* meandro
meaning: *adj.* significado
meantime: *adv.* mientras tanto
measles: *n.* rubella; sarampión
measles virus: virus del sarampión
measure: *n.* mensura; medida; dimensión
measure: *v.* medir
measure of variance: la medida de variación
measurement: *n.* medida; medición
measuring curve: curva de medida
measuring function: función de medida
measuring instrument: instrumento de medida
measuring interval: intervalo de medida
measuring system: sistema de medida
meat: *n.* carne
mecanotherapy: *n.* mecanoterapia
mecca: *n.* meca
mechanic: *n.* mecánico

mechanical: *adj.* mecánico
mechanical advantage: ventaja mecánica
mechanical digestion: digestión mecánica
mechanical energy: energía mecánica
mechanical wave: onda mecánica
mechanical weathering: desgaste mecánico
mechanics: *n.* mecánica
mechanism: *n.* mecanismo
mechanization: *n.* mecanización
meconium: *n.* meconio
medal: *n.* medalla
medalist: *n.* medallista
medallion: *n.* medallón
meddle: *v.* entremeterse
media: *n.* medios
medial: *adj.* medial
median: 1. *n.* mediana; 2. *adj.* mediano
mediation: *n.* mediación
mediator: *n.* mediador
medical: *adj.* medico; medicinal
medical appliances: aparatos; utensilios médicos
medical background: datos médicos
medical coverage: protección médica
medical device: producto sanitario
medical equipment: equipo médico
medical improvement: mejoramiento médico
medical opinion: opinión médica
medical reasons: razones médicas
medical sources: fuentes médicas
medical tests: exámenes médicos
medically determinable: médicamente determinable
medicated: *adj.* medicinal
medication: *n.* medicamento; medicación
medicinal: *adj.* medicinal

medicine: *n.* medicina
medieval: *adj.* medieval
mediocre: *adj.* mediocre
mediocrity: *n.* mediocridad
meditate: *v.* meditar; considerar
meditation: *n.* meditación
Mediterranean: *adj.* mediterráneo
medium: 1. *adj.* mediano; 2. *n.* medio
medley: *n.* mezcolanza
medulla: *n.* médula
meek: *adj.* manso
meet: *v.* encontrar
meet a test: llenar; cubrir; reunir
meet requirements: reunir las condiciones
meeting: *n.* reunión; mitin
megabyte: *n.* megabyte
megahertz (mhz): *n.* megahercio
megakaryoblast: *n.* megacarioblasto
megakaryocyte: *n.* megacariocito
megalomaniac: *n.* megalómano
megalopolis: *n.* megalópolis
megaphone: *n.* megáfono
megaton: *n.* megatón
megawatt: *n.* megavatio
meiosis: *n.* meiosis
melancholic: *adj.* melancólico
melancholy: *n.* melancolía
melanin: *n.* melanina
melanism: *n.* melanismo; melanosis
melanoma: *n.* melanoma
mellifluous: *adj.* melifluo
mellow: *adj.* maduro
mellow: *v.* madurar
melodeon: *n.* melodión; melodina
melodious: *adj.* melodioso
melodrama: *n.* melodrama
melody: *n.* melodía; canción
melon: *n.* melón
melt: *v.* derretir; disolver
melt down: fusión (del núcleo de un reactor)
meltdown: fusión

melting: *n.* fusión
melting point: punto de fusión
member: *n.* miembro
membership: *n.* membresía; asociación
membrane: *n.* membrana
membranous: *adj.* membranoso
memo: *n.* memo
memorandum: *n.* memorando
memorial: *n.* memorial
memorize: *v.* memorizar
memory: *n.* memoria
menace: *n.* amenaza
menace: *v.* amenazar
menacing: *adj.* amenazador
mend: *v.* remendar
meningitis: *n.* meningitis
meniscus: *n.* menisco
mennonite: *n.* menonita
menopause: *n.* menopausia
menorah: *n.* menorá
menorrhagia: *n.* menorragia
menstrual: cólicos con la regla
menstrual cramps: cólicos con la regla
menstrual cycle: ciclo menstrual
menstrual history: historia menstrual
menstrual period: regla periódico
menstruation: *n.* menstruación
mental: *adj.* mental
mental impairment: impedimento mental
mental incompetence: incompetencia mental
mental retardation: retraso mental
mental status: estado mental
mentalism: *n.* mentalismo
mentalist: *n.* mentalista
menthol: *n.* mentol
mentholated: *adj.* mentolado
mention: *n.* mención
mention: *v.* mencionar
mentor: *n.* mentor

menu: *n.* menú; lista de platos
meperidine: *n.* petidina
Mercalli scale: escala de Mercalli
mercantilism: *n.* mercantilismo
mercenary: *n.* mercenario
merchandise: *n.* mercancías
merchant: *n.* mercante; mercader
merchant marine: marina mercante
merciful: *adj.* misericordioso
merciless: *adj.* despiadado
mercurochrome: *n.* mercurocromo
mercury barometer: barómetro de mercurio
mercy: *n.* gracia; perdón
mere: *adj.* solo; lago; mero
merge: *v.* fusionar
meridian: *n.* meridiano
meringue: *n.* merengue
merino: *n.* merino
merit: *n.* mérito
merit: *v.* merecer
meritocracy: *n.* meritocracia
meritorious: *adj.* meritorio
mermaid: *n.*. sirena
merrily: *adv.* alegremente
mescal: *adj.* mezcal
mescaline: *n.* mescalina
mesh: *n.* malla
mesh: *v.* enredar; engranar
mesmerism: *n.* mesmerismo
mesmerize: *v.* hipnotizar
mesomorph: *n.* mesomorfo
mesosphere: *n.* mesosfera
mesquite: *n.* mezquita
mess: *n.* revoltijo
mess: *v.* dar rancho
message: *n.* mensaje
messenger: *n.* mensajero
Messiah: *n.* Mesías
messianism: *n.* mesianismo
mesurand: *adj.* mesurando
meta-analysis: *n.* metanálisis
metabolic: *adj.* metabólico
metabolism: *n.* metabolismo

metacarpal: *n.* metacarpo
metal: *n.* metal
metalanguage: *n.* metalenguaje
metalinguistics: *n.* metalingüística
metallic: *adj.* metálico
metallic bond: enlace metálico
metalloid: *n.* metaloide
metallurgical: *adj.* metalúrgico
metallurgy: *n.* metalurgia
metamorphic rock: roca metamórfica
metamorphosis: *n.* metamorfosis
metamyelocyte: *n.* metamielocito
metanephrine: *n.* metanefrina
metaphase plate: placa metafásica
metaphor: *n.* metáfora
metaphrase: *n.* metáfrasis
metaphysics: *n.* metafísica
metastasis: *n.* metástasis
metatarsus: *n.* metatarso
metempsychosis: *n.* metempsicosis
meteor: *n.* meteoro
meteorite: *n.* meteorito
meteoroid: *n.* meteoroide
meteorologist: *n.* meteorólogo
meteorology: *n.* meteorología
meter: *n.* metro
methanol: *n.* metanol
method: *n.* método
method of measurement: método de medición
methodical: *adj.* metódico
methodism: *n.* metodismo
methodist: *n.* metodista
methodology: *n.* metodología
meticulous: *adj.* meticuloso
metonymy: *n.* metonimia
metric: *adj.* métrico
metrics: *n.* métrica
metro: *n.* metro
metronome: *n.* metrónomo
metropolis: *n.* metrópoli
metropolitan: *adj.* metropolitano
mettle: *n.* ánimo

mew: *n.* maullido
mewl: *v.* lloriquear
mezzotint: *n.* mezzotinto
mi: *n.* mi
miasma: *n.* miasma
microbicide: *n.* microbicida
microbiology: *n.* microbiología
microcephaly: *n.* microcefalia
microchemistry: *n.* microquímica
microchip: *n.* microchip
microcircuit: *n.* microcircuito
microclimate: *n.* microclima
microcomputer: *n.* microcomputadora
microelectronics: *n.* microelectrónica
microfiche: *n.* microficha
microfilm: *n.* microfilme
microgram: *n.* microgramo
micrography: *n.* micrografía
micrometer: *n.* micrómetro
micrometry: *n.* micrometría
micromillimeter: *n.* micromilímetro
micron: *n.* micrón
microorganism: *n.* microorganismo
microphone: *n.* micrófono
micropipette: *n.* micropipeta
microprocessor: *n.* microprocesador
microscope: *n.* microscopio
microscopic: *adj.* microscópico
microscopy: *n.* microscopia; microscopía
microsecond: *n.* microsegundo
microsequencing: *n.* microsecuenciación
microsurgery: *n.* microcirugía
microtiter plate: placa de microvaloración
microtiter well: pocillo de microvaloración
microtome: *n.* micrótomo
microwave: *n.* microonda
mid: 1. *adj.* medio; 2. *pre.* entre
midcontinent: *n.* medio del continente
midday: *n.* mediodía
middle: *n.* centro; medio
middleman: *n.* intermediario
midnight: *n.* media noche
midnight: 1. *n.* medianoche; 2. *adj.* media noche
mid-ocean ridge: cordillera oceánica central
midrash: *n.* midrash
midstream urine: orina del chorro medio
midway: *n.* medio camino
midwife: *n.* comadrona; partera
mien: *n.* porte
might: *n.* fuerza
mighty: *adj.* fuerte
migraine: *n.* migraña
migrate: *v.* emigrar
migration: *n.* migración
mike: *n.* micrófono
mil: *n.* mil
mild: *adj.* leve
mile: *n.* milla
mileage: *n.* distancia en millas
militancy: *n.* militancia
militant: *n.* militante
militarism: *n.* militarismo
militarist: *n.* militarista
military: *adj.* militar
military police: policía militar
military service: servicio militar
militia: *n.* milicia
militiaman: *n.* miliciano
milk: *n.* leche
milk: *v.* ordeñar
milking machine: máquina de ordenar
milky: *adj.* lechoso
mill: *n.* molino; taller
mill: *v.* triturar
millennium: *n.* milenio; milenario
millibar: *n.* milibar
milligram: *n.* miligramo

milliliter: *n.* mililitro
millimeter: *n.* milímetro
million: millón
millionth: *adj.* millonésimo
millisecond: *n.* milisegundo
mime: *n.* mimo
mimesis: *n.* mimética
mimicry: *n.* mímica
mimosa: *n.* mimosa
minaret: *n.* minarete
mince: *v.* desmenuzar; picar
mind: *n.* mente; espíritu
mind: *v.* notar; observar
minded: *adj.* inclinado; dispuesto
mindful: *adj.* atento
mine: 1. *adj.* mío; 2. *n.* mina
mine: *v.* extraer
minelayer: *n.* minador
miner: *n.* minero
mineral: 1. *adj.* mineral; 2. *n.* mineral
mineral oil: aceite mineral
mineral spirit: solvente
mineral water: agua mineral
minesweeper: *n.* tragaminas
mingle: *v.* mezclar
mini pill: píldora mini
miniature: 1. *adj.* miniatura; 2. *n.* miniatura
miniature golf: minigolf
miniaturist: *n.* miniaturista
miniaturization: *n.* miniaturización
minicomputer: *n.* minicomputadora
minim: 1. *n.* mínima; 2. *adj.* mínima
minimal: *adj.* mínimo
minimalism: *n.* minimalismo
minimize: *v.* reducir al mínimo
minimum: 1. *n.* mínimo; 2. *adj.* mínimo
minimum wage: sueldo mínimo
mining: *n.* minería
minion: 1. *adj.* lindo; 2. *n.* válido
miniseries: *n.* miniserie
miniskirt: *n.* minifalda

minister: *n.* ministro
ministry: *n.* ministerio; sacerdocio
mink: *n.* visión
minocycline: *n.* minociclina
minor: 1. *n.* menor; 2. *n.* menor
minority: *n.* minoría
mint: *n.* menta
mint: *v.* acunar
minuend: *n.* minuendo
minuet: *n.* minuet; minueto
minus: *adj.* menos
minuscule: 1. *n.* minúsculo; 2. *adj.* minúsculo
minute: *n.* minuto
minute chromosome: minicromosoma
minute hand: minutero
miracle: *n.* milagro
mirage: *n.* espejismo
mire: *n.* lodo; cieno
mirror: *n.* espejo
mirror: *v.* reflejar
misadventure: *n.* desventura
misanthrope: *n.* misántropo; -a
miscalculate: *v.* calcular
miscarriage: *n.* aborto espontáneo; aborto
miscarry: *v.* malograrse
miscellany: *n.* miscelánea
mischance: *n.* desgracia
mischief: *n.* daño; malicia
miscible: *adj.* miscible
misconduct: *n.* mala conducta
misdeed: *n.* fechoría
misdemeanor: *n.* mala conducta
misdivision: *n.* maldivisión
misdoer: *n.* criminal
misdoing: *n.* maldad
miser: *n.* avaro; tacaño
miserable: *adj.* miserable
miserly: *adj.* mísero
misery: *n.* miseria
misfortune: *n.* infortunio; desventura
misgiving: *n.* duda

misgovern: *v.* gobernar mal
misguide: *v.* dirigir mal
mishandle: *v.* manejar mal
mishap: *n.* accidente
mislay: *v.* traspapelar; perder
mismatch: *n.* malapareamiento
misogynist: *n.* misógino
misplace: *v.* colocar mal
misprint: *n.* errata de imprenta
misprint: *v.* imprimir con erratas
misshape: *v.* deformar
missile: *n.* misil
missing: *adj.* perdido; desaparecido
missing person: persona
desaparecida
mission: *n.* misión
missionary: *n.* misionero
missive: *n.* misiva
misspend: *v.* malgastar
mist: *n.* niebla
mistake: *n.* error
mistake: *v.* interpretar mal
mister: *n.* señor
mistral: *n.* mistral
mistreatment: *n.* maltrato
mistress: *n.* señora; ama de casa
mistrust: *n.* desconfianza
mistrust: *v.* sospechar
misunderstand: *v.* entender mal
misunderstanding: *n.* mal
entendido; equivocación
misusage: *n.* abuso
misuse: *n.* abuso
misuse: 2. *v.* usar mal
misuse of benefits: mal uso de
beneficios
mite: *n.* óbolo
miter: *n.* mitra
miter box: la caja de ángulos
miter saw: la sierra de cortar en
ángulos
mitigate: *v.* mitigar
mitochondria: *n.* mitocondria
mitosis: *n.* mitosis

mitten: *n.* mitón
mix: *n.* mezcla
mix: 2. *v.* mezclar
mixed: *adj.* mixto
mixed number: número mixto
mixer: *n.* mezcladora
mixture: *n.* mixtura; mezcla
moan: *n.* gemido; lamento
moan: *v.* lamentar
moat: *n.* foso
mob: *n.* gentío
mob: *v.* promover alborotos
mobile: *adj.* móvil; movible
mobile home: casa móvil; casa
movible
mobile phase: fase móvil
mobility: *n.* movilidad
mobilize: *v.* movilizar
moccasin: *n.* mocasín
mocha: *n.* moca
modal: *adj.* modal
modality: *n.* modalidad
mode: *n.* moda
model: 1. *adj.* modelo; ejemplar; 2.
n. modelo
model: *v.* moderar
modeler: *n.* modelador
modeling: *n.* modelización;
modelado
modem: *n.* modem
moderate: *adj.* moderado
moderate: *v.* moderar
moderation: *n.* moderación
moderato: *adv.* moderato
moderator: *n.* moderador
modern: 1. *adj.* moderno; 2. *n.*
moderno
modernism: *n.* modernismo
modest: *adj.* modesto
modesty: *n.* modestia
modified formula: fórmula
modificada
modifier: *n.* modificador
modify: *v.* modificar; cambiar

modiste: *n.* modista
modular: *adj.* modular
modulation: *n.* modulación
modulator: *n.* modulador
module: *n.* módulo
modulus: *n.* módulo
modus operandi: modus operandi
modus vivendi: modus vivendi
mohair: *n.* moer
moire: *n.* moare
moire; moiré: *n.* moaré
moist: *adj.* húmedo; jugoso
moisten: *v.* humedecer
moisture: *n.* humedad
moisture barrier: la barrera contra humedad
molal: *adj.* molal
molality: *n.* molalidad
molar: *n.* molar
molar absorption coefficient: coeficiente de absorción molar
molar absorptivity: absortividad molar
molar concentration: concentración molar
molar conductivity: conductividad molar
molar decadic absortivity: absortividad decimal molar
molar heat capacity: capacidad térmica molar
molasses: *n.* melaza
mold: *n.* molde
molding: *n.* moldura
mole: *n.* mol
mole fraction: fracción de sustancia
molecular (physics): *adj.* molecular
molecular biology: biología molecular
molecular compound: compuesto molecular
molecular genetics: genética molecular
molecular hybridization: hibridación molecular
molecular mass: masa molecular
molecular pathology: patología molecular
molecular weight: peso molecular
molecule: *n.* molécula
molest: *v.* molestar
mollify: *v.* ablandar
mollusk: *n.* molusco
molten: *adj.* derretido
molting: *n.* muda
moment: *n.* momento; ocasión
moment magnitude scale: escala de magnitud del momento
moment of inertia: momento de inercia
momentary: *adj.* momentáneo
momentary: *n.* momentáneo
momentum: *n.* momento
monad: *n.* mónada
monarchy: *n.* monarquía
monastery: *n.* monasterio
monasticism: *n.* ascetismo; monaquismo; monacato
monetarism: *n.* monetarismo
monetary: *adj.* monetario
money: *n.* dinero; plata capital; riqueza
money order: giro postal
mongolism: *n.* mongolismo
mongoloid: *n.* mongoloide
mongoose: *n.* mangosta
mongrel: 1. *adj.* mestizo; cruzado; 2. *n.* mestizo; cruzado
monism: *n.* monismo
monitor: *n.* monitor
monitor: *v.* seguir; observar; controlar
monitoring: *n.* monitorización
monk: *n.* monje
monoblast: *n.* monoblasto
monochromatic: *adj.* monocromático
monochrome: *n.* monocromo

monocle: *n.* monóculo
monoclonal antibody: anticuerpo monoclónico
monocot: *n.* monocotiledeinea
monocromator: *n.* monocromador
monocyte: *n.* monocito
monogamy: *n.* monogamia
monogram: *n.* monograma
monograph: *n.* monografía
monolingual: *adj.* monolingüe
monolith: *n.* monolito
monologue: *n.* monólogo
monomer: *n.* monómero
monometer: *n.* monómetro
monomial: *n.* monomio
mononucleosis: *n.* mononucleosis
monophonic: *adj.* monofónico
monophyly: *n.* monofilia
monoplane: *n.* monoplano
monopolize: *v.* monopolizar
monopolizer: *n.* monopolizador
monopoly: *n.* monopolio
monorail: *n.* monoriel
monoski: *n.* monoesquí
monotheism: *n.* monoteísmo
monotone: *adj.* monótono
monotony: *n.* monotonía
monotreme: *n.* monotrema
monsoon: *n.* monzón
monster: *n.* monstruo
monstrosity: *n.* monstruosidad
monstrous: *adj.* monstruoso
montage: *n.* montaje
month: *n.* mes
monthly: 1. a mensual; 2. *n.* revista mensual; 3. *adv.* mensualmente
monthly benefit: beneficio mensual
monthly premium: prima mensual
monument: *n.* monumento
monumental: *adj.* monumental
mood: *n.* modo; humor
moodily: *adv.* caprichosamente
moon: *n.* luna
moorish: *n.* moro

mop: *n.* trapeador; estropajo
mop: *v.* fregar
mope: *n.* apático; abatido
moraine: *n.* morena
moral: 1. *adj.* moral; 2. *n.* moraleja; honestidad
morale: *n.* moral
moralism: *n.* moralismo
moralist: *n.* moralista
morality: *n.* moralidad
moralize: *v.* moralizar
moralizer: *n.* moralizador
moralizing: *adj.* moralizador
morass: *n.* pantano; cenagal
moratorium: *n.* moratoria
moray: *n.* morena
morbid: *adj.* mórbido
morbid entity: entidad morbosa
morbidity: *n.* morbosidad
mordant: *adj.* mordaz
mordent: *n.* mordente
morel: *n.* morilla
moreover: *adv.* además; también
morganatic: *adj.* morganático
moribund: *adj.* moribundo
moribund: *n.* moribundo
Mormon: *n.* mormón
Mormonism: *n.* mormonismo
morning: *n.* mañana
morning-after pill: píldora del dia siguiente
morose: *adj.* moroso
morpheme: *n.* morfema
morphine: *n.* morfina
morphology: *n.* morfología
morsel: *n.* pedazo
mortal: *adj.* mortal
mortality: *n.* mortalidad
mortar: *n.* mortero; hormigón
mortgage: *n.* hipoteca
mortgage: *v.* hipotecar
mortification: *n.* mortificación
mortify: *v.* mortificar
mortise: *n.* cerradura

mortise and tenon: cerradura y espaldon
mortise gauge: trocha para cerradura
mortise lock: mecha para cerradura
mortising chisel: cerradura para formón
mortuary: 1. *adj.* mortuorio; funerario; 2. *n.* depósito de cadáveres
mosaic: 1. *n.* mosaico; 2. *n.* mosaico
mosaic law: ley mosaica
moselle: *n.* vino del mosela
Moslem; Muslim: *n.* musulmán
mosque: *n.* mezquita
mosquito: *n.* mosquito
moss: *n.* musgo
most: la mayor parte
motel: *n.* motel
motet: *n.* motete
moth: *n.* polilla
mother: *n.* madre
motherhood: *n.* maternidad
mother-in-law: suegra
motif: *n.* motivo; asunto
motility: *n.* motilidad
motility medium: medio para motilidad
motion: *n.* moción; movimiento
motionless: *adj.* inmóvil
motivated: *adj.* motivado
motivation: *n.* motivación
motoneuron: *n.* motoneurona
motor: 1. *n.* motor; 2. *adj.* motor
motor neuron: neurona motora
motor vehicle: vehículo de motor
motorboat: *n.* motora
motorcycle: *n.* moto; motocicleta
motorist: *n.* motorista
mottle: *n.* mancha
mottle: *v.* motear; jaspear
motto: *n.* lema; divisa
mould: *n.* molde; moldura
mould: *v.* moldear
mound: *n.* montón de tierra
mound: *v.* amontonar

mount: *n.* monte
mount: vt. montar
mountain: *n.* monte; montaña
mountain range: cordillera
mountaineer: *n.* montañero
mountaineering: *n.* montañismo
mountainous: *adj.* montañoso
mounting: *n.* montaje; montura
mounting screw: el tornillo de fijación
mourn: *v.* lamentar
mournful: *adj.* dolorido; triste
mourning: *n.* lamento; luto
mouse: *n.* ratón
mousetrap: *n.* ratonera; trampa
moussaka: *n.* mousaka; moussaka
mousse: *n.* mousse; espuma
mousseline: *n.* muselina
mouth: *n.* boca
mouthful: *n.* bocado
mouthpiece: *adj.* boquilla
movable: 1. *adj.* movible; 2. *n.* mueble
move: *n.* movimiento; movida
move: *v.* mover
movement: *n.* movimiento
movie: *n.* cine
mow: *v.* segar; cortar la hierba
moxalactam: *n.* latamoxef
mozetta; muzetta: *n.* muceta
mozzarella: *n.* mozzarella
MRI scan: imagen por resonancia magnética
much: 1. *adj.* mucho; 2. *adv.* mucho; casi; 3. *pron.* mucho
mucid: *n.* mohoso
mucilage: *n.* mucílago
mucous: *adj.* mocoso
mucus: *n.* moco; mucosidad
mucus in stools: heces con moco
mud: *n.* barro
mud: *v.* embarrar
muddle: *n.* confusión
muddle: *v.* confundir

mudguard: *n.* guardabarros
muezzin: *n.* muecín
muffle: *n.* mufla; amortiguador de sonido
muffle: *v.* amortiguar
muffle: *n.* mufla
mujaheddin: *n.* mujahedín; muyahidin
mulatto: *n.* mulato
mule: *n.* mulo
muleta: *n.* muleta
multiband: *n.* multibanda
multicellular: *adj.* multicelular
multicolor: *adj.* multicolor
multicolored: *adj.* multicolor
multicopy plasmid: plásmido multicopia
multiculturalism: *n.* multiculturalismo
multidimensional: *adj.* multidimensional
multilateral: *adj.* multilateral
multilingual: *adj.* multilingüe
multimedia: *n.* multimedia
multinational: *adj.* multinacional
multipara: *n.* multípara
multiparametric analyzer: multianalizador
multiple: 1. *n.* múltiplo; 2. *adj.* múltiple
multiple alleles: alelo múltiple
multiple births: nacimientos múltiples
multiple crossing: cruzamiento múltiple
multiple drug abuse: politoxicomanía
multiple variable: de varias variables
multiple-choice: de opción múltiple
multiple-well plate: placa de pocillos múltiples
multiplex: *n.* múltiplex
multiplicand: *n.* multiplicando

multiplication: *n.* multiplicación
multiplicative: *adj.* multiplicativo
multiplicative identity: identidad de la multiplicación
multiplicative inverse: inverso multiplicativo
multiplier: *n.* multiplicador
multisite mutation: mutación multicéntrica
multitasking: *n.* multitarea
multitude: *n.* multitud
mummy: *n.* momia
mumps: *n.* paperas
mumps virus: virus de la parotiditis; virus de las paperas
munch: *v.* mascar
municipal: *adj.* municipal
municipality: *n.* municipio
munificence: *n.* munificencia
munificent: *adj.* munificente; munífico
munitions: *n.* municiones
mupirocin: *n.* mupirocina
mural: 1. *adj.* mural; 2. *n.* pintura mural
murder: 1. *n.* asesinato; *v.* asesinar
murky: *adj.* lóbrego
murmur: *n.* murmullo
murmur: *v.* susurrar; murmurar
murmurings: *n.* murmullos
muscatel: *n.* moscatel
muscle: *n.* músculo
muscle biopsy: biopsia de los músculos
muscle spasm: calambre muscular
muscle tissue: tejido muscular
muscle weakness: debilidad muscular
musculature: *n.* musculatura
musculo-skeletal system: sistema músculo-esquelético
museum: *n.* museo
music: *n.* música
music cabinet: musiquero

musical: *adj.* musical
musical music: comedia musical
musician: *n.* músico
musicologist: *n.* musicologista
musicology: *n.* musicología
musing: *n.* (zool) mejillón
musketeer: *n.* mosquetero
musketry: *n.* mosqueteria
muslin: *n.* muselina
mussy: *adj.* desaliñado; desordenado
must: *n.* mosto
must: *v.* deber; tener que
mustache; moustache: *n.* mostacho
mustard: *n.* mostaza
muster: *n.* asamblea; reunión
muster: *v.* juntar; reunir
mutagenic repair: reparación mutágena
mutagenicity test: prueba de mutagenicidad
mutation: *n.* mutación
mutation rate: frecuencia de mutación
mutation site: centro de mutación
mute: *n.* mudo
mute: *adj.* mudo
muteness: *n.* mudez
mutilate: *v.* mutilar
mutilation: *n.* mutilación
mutilator: *n.* mutilador
mutineer: *n.* amotinado
mutineer: *v.* amotinado
mutiny: *n.* motín
mutualism: *n.* mutualismo
myasthenia: *n.* myastenia
mycetoma: *n.* micetoma
mycology: *n.* micología
mycolysin: *n.* micolisina
myelitis: *n.* mielitis
myeloblast: *n.* mieloblasto
myelocyte: *n.* mielocito
myelogram: n mielograma
myocarditis: *n.* miocarditis
myocardium: *n.* miocardio

myoglobin: *n.* mioglobina
myopia: *n.* miopía
myriad: *n.* miríada
myrrh: *n.* mirra
myrtle: *n.* mirto
myself: *pron.* pers. yo mismo; mi; mismo; a mi; me
mystery: *n.* misterio
mystic: *adj.* místico
mysticism: *n.* misticismo
myth: *n.* mito; fábula
myxedema; myxoedema: *n.* mixedema

N

nacre: *n.* nácar
nafcillin: *n.* nafcilina
nag: *n.* jaca
nag: *v.* regañar
nah-jongg: ma-jong
nail: *n.* una; clavo
nail: *v.* clavar
naive: *adj.* cándido; ingenuo
naked: *adj.* desnudo
nalidixic acid: ácido nalidíxico
name: *n.* nombre
nanometer: *n.* nanómetro
nanosecond: *n.* nanosegundo
nanotechnology: *n.* nanotecnología
nanotube: *n.* nanotubo
nap: *n.* lanilla; borrar
nap: *v.* dormitar; tomar la siesta
nape: *n.* nuca
napkin: *n.* servilleta; papal
napoleonic: *adj.* napoleónico
narcoanalysis: *n.* narcoanálisis
narcolepsy: *n.* narcolepsia
narcosis: *n.* narcosis
narcosynthesis: *n.* narcosíntesis

narcotic: *adj.* narcótico
narcotism: *n.* narcotismo
narration: *n.* narración
narrative: 1. narrativa; 2. *adj.* narrativo
narrativo: *v.* estrechar; disminuir; escoger
narrator: *n.* narrador
narrow: *adj.* estrecho; minucioso
narthex: *n.* nartex
nasal: *adj.* nasal
nasal mucus: muco nasal
nasal secretion: secreción nasal
nascent: *adj.* naciente
nastiness: *n.* suciedad
nasty: *adj.* sucio; asqueroso
nation: *n.* nación
national: *adj.* nacional
national anthem: himno nacional
national archives: archivos nacionales
national guard: guardia nacional
national press conference: conferencia nacional de prensa
nationalism: *n.* nacionalismo
nationality: *n.* nacionalidad
nationalization: *n.* nacionalización
native language: lengua materna
nativism: *n.* nativismo
natural: *adj.* natural
natural number: el número natural
natural resource: recurso natural
natural selection: selección natural
naturalism: *n.* naturalismo
naturalist: *n.* naturalista
naturalization: *n.* naturalización
naturalization certificate: acta de naturalización
naturalize: *v.* naturalizar
naturalness: *n.* naturalidad
nature: *n.* naturaleza
naturist: *n.* naturista
naught: *n.* nada; cero
naughty: *adj.* desobediente; ave so

nausea: *n.* náusea
nauseating: *adj.* nauseabundo
nautical: *adj.* náutico
nautilus: *n.* nautilo
nave: *n.* nave
navigate: *v.* navegar
navigation: *n.* navegación
navigator: *n.* navegante
navy: *n.* marina de guerra; armada
nay: 1. *n.* no; voto en contra; 2. *adv.* no; de ningún modo
Nazism: *n.* nazismo
neap: *adj.* ínfimo
neap tide: marea muerta
near: 1. *adj.* próximo; 2. *adv.* cerca; 3. *prep.* cerca de;
near: *v.* acercarse
near future: próximamente
nearly: *adv.* casi; cercanamente
nearsightedness: *n.* miopía
neat: 1. *adj.* pulcro; limpio; 2. *n.* vacuna
nebula: *n.* nebulosa
necessary: *adj.* necesario
necessitate: *n.* cuello; mástil
necessitate: *v.* necesitar
necessity: *n.* necesidad
neck: *n.* cuello
necklace: *n.* collar
necktie: *n.* corbata
necrology: *n.* necrología
necromancy: *n.* necromancía
necrophilia: *n.* necrofilia
necrophobia: *n.* necrofobia
necropolis: *n.* necrópolis
necrosis (gangrene): *n.* necrosis
nectar: *n.* néctar
nectarine: *n.* nectarina
need: *n.* necesidad
need: *v.* necesitar
needle: *n.* aguja
needlewoman: *n.* costurera
needy: *adj.* necesitado; pobre
nees: *n.* rodillas

nefarious: *adj.* nefario
negation: *n.* negación
negative: *adj.* negativo
negative integers: números enteros negativos
neglect: *n.* negligencia
neglect: *v.* descuidar
negligee: *n.* negligé
negligence: *n.* negligencia
negligible: *adj.* insignificante; despreciable
negotiable: *adj.* negociable
negotiate: *v.* negociar
negotiation: *n.* negociación
negotiator: *n.* negociador
negro: 1. *adj.* negro; 2. *n.* negro
negroid: *adj.* negroide
neigh: *n.* relincho
neigh: *v.* relinchar
neighbor: *n.* vecino
neighboring: *adj.* cercano
neither: 1. *pron.* ningún; 2. *adj.* ninguno; 3. *conj.* ni
nekton: *n.* nekton
neoclassicism: *n.* neoclasicismo
neocolonialism: *n.* neocolonialismo
neologism: *n.* neologismo
neomycin: *n.* neomicina
neon: *n.* neón
neon light: luz de neón
neon sign: *n.* letrero de neón
neonatal: *adj.* neonatal
neonatology: *n.* neonatología
neoplasm: *n.* neoplasma; neoplasia
neoplatonism: *n.* neoplatonismo
nephelometry: *n.* nefelometría
nephew: *n.* sobrino
nephoscope: *n.* nefoscopio
nephralgia: *n.* nefralgia
nephrectomy: *n.* nefrectomía
nephritis: *n.* nefritis
nephrolith: *n.* nefrólito
nephrologist: *n.* especialista en los riñones

nephrology: *n.* nefrología
nephron: *n.* nefrón
nephrotomy: *n.* nefrotomía
nepotism: *n.* nepotismo
neritic zone: zona neritica
nerve: *n.* nervio
nerve impulse: impulso nervioso
nervous: *adj.* nervioso
nervous system: sistema nervioso
nervous tissue: tejido nervioso
nervousness: *n.* nerviosidad
nest: *n.* nido
nest: *v.* anidar
nesting: *n.* anidación; nidificación
nestle: *v.* recostarse
net: 1. *adj.* neto; 2. *n.* red
net earnings: ganancias netas
net force: fuerza neta
net income: ingreso neto
net loss: pérdida neta
net profit: ganancia neta; utilidad neta
netilmicin: *n.* netilmicina
network: *n.* red
networking: *n.* conexión de redes
neuralgia: *n.* neuralgia
neurasthenia: *n.* neurastenia
neuritis: *n.* neuritis
neurobiology: *n.* neurobiología
neurolinguistics: *n.* neurolingüística
neurolinguistics: *n.* neurolinguistica
neurologist: *n.* neurólogo; especialista en los nervios
neurology: *n.* neurología
neuroma: *n.* neuroma
neuropathology: *n.* neuropatalogía
neuropathy: *n.* neuropatía
neurosurgeon: *n.* neurocirujano
neurosurgery: *n.* neurocirujía
neurotic: *adj.* neurótico
neurotransmiter: *n.* neurotransmisor
neuter: *adj.* neutro
neutral: *adj.* neutro
neutrality: *n.* neutralidad

neutralization: *n.* neutralización
neutralization test: prueba de la neutralización
neutralizer: *n.* neutralizador
neutron: *n.* neutrón
neutron star: estrella de neutrones
neutrophil: *n.* neutrofilocito; neutrófilo
neutrophilocyte: *n.* neutrofilocito; neutrófilo
never: *adv.* nunca
nevertheless: *adv.* no obstante; sin embargo
new: *adj.* nuevo
newborn: *adj.* recién nacido
newcomer: *n.* recién llegado
newly: *adv.* nuevamente
newness: *n.* novedad
news: *n.* noticias; novedades
news flash: flash informativo
news tug: Noticias
newsletter: *n.* noticiero electrónico
newspaper: *n.* periódico
newspaper record: récord de periódico
newsprint: *n.* papel de prensa
Newton: *n.* newton
next: *adj.* próximo; inmediato
nexus: *n.* nexo
niacin: *n.* niacina
niacinamide: *n.* nicotinamida
nib: *n.* pico; pluma
nice: *adj.* bonito; guapo
niche: *n.* nicho
nick: *n.* mella
nick translation: traslación de mellas
nickel: *n.* moneda de cinco centavos
nicotiana: *n.* nicotiana
nicotinamide: *n.* nicotinamida
nicotine: *n.* nicotina
nicoumalone: *n.* acenocumarol
niece: *n.* sobrina
night: *n.* noche

night sweats: sudores por la noche
nightclub: *n.* club nocturno
nightingale: *n.* ruiseñor
nightly: 1. *adj.* nocturno; 2. *adv.* por la noche
nightmare: *n.* pesadilla
nihilism: *n.* nihilismo
nihilist: *n.* nihilista
nil: *n.* nada
nimble: *adj.* ágil; ligero
nimbostratus: *n.* nimboestrato
nimbus: *n.* nimbo
nine: nueve
ninth: *adj.* noveno
nip: 1. *n.* pellizco; mordisco
nip: *v.* pellizcar; mordisquear
nipple: *n.* pezón; tetilla
nirvana: *n.* nirvana
nitrocellulose filter: filtro de nitrocelulosa
nitrofurantoin: *n.* nitrofurantoína
nitrogen fixation: fijación del nitrógeno
nitrous oxide: óxido nitroso
no: *adv.* no
no!: *intj.* ¡no!
nobility: *n.* nobleza
noble: *adj.* noble
noble gas: gas noble
nobody: 1. *n.* nadie; 2. *pron.* ninguno
nocturnal: *adj.* nocturno
nod: *n.* nodo; reverencia; cabezada
node: *n.* nodo
nodule: *n.* nódulo
noise: *n.* ruido
noise: *v.* divulgar
noiseless: *adj.* silencioso
nom de plume: nombre de pluma
nomad: 1. *adj.* nómada; 2. *n.* nómada
nomenclature: *n.* nomenclatura
nominal: *adj.* nominal
nominal scale: escala nominal
nominal value: valor nominal
nominate: *v.* nominar

nomination: *n.* nominación
nominative: *adj.* nominativo
nonagenarian: *adj.* nonagenario
nonalcoholic: *adj.* no alcohólico
non-aligned: no alineado
nonbelligerant: no beligerante
non-citizens: no ciudadanos; extranjeros
non-coding strand: cadena intranscrita
noncompliance: incumplimiento
nonconductor: *n.* no conductor
nonconformist: anticonformista
nonconformity: disconformidad
none: *pron.* ninguno; nadie
non-fattening: no engordante
nonfermenter: no fermentador
nonfiction: *n.* no ficción
noninfectious disease: enfermedad no infecciosa
nonintervention: no intervención
non-linear: no lineal
nonmaterial: no material
nonmetal: no metal
non-negative: no negativo
nonobservance: *n.* inobservancia
nonpoint source: fuente dispersa
nonpolar bond: enlace no polar
nonproliferation: no proliferación
non-receipt: no recibido
non-renewable: no renovable
nonrenewable resource: recurso no renovable
nonsense: *n.* tontería; bobada
nonstandard: *adj.* no estándar
nonstandard: no estándar
nonstandard analysis: análisis no estándar
nonstop: 1. *adj.* directo; sin parada; 2. *adv.* sin parar
nontechnical: *adj.* no técnico
nontechnical: no técnico
nonvascular plant: planta no vascular

nonviolence: *n.* no violencia
nonviolent: *adj.* no violento
nonwork day: día no laborable
noodles: *n.* tallarines
nook: *n.* rincón
noon: *n.* mediodía
nor: *conj.* ni; tampoco
norm: *n.* norma
normal: *adj.* normal
normal distribution: la distribución normal
normal fault: falla normal
normal values: valores de referencia
normality: *n.* normalidad
normalize: *v.* normalizar
Norman: *adj.* normando
Normandy: Normandía
north: *n.* norte
North America: Norteamérica
North American: *adj.* norteamericano; -a
North Korea: Corea del Norte
North Korean: *adj.* norcoreano
North Sea: Mar del Norte
northeast: *n.* nordeste
northeasterly: *adv.* del nordeste
northeastern: *adv.* del nordeste
norther: *n.* nortada
northerly: *adv.* desde; hacia el norte
northern: *adj.* del norte
northern blot: transferencia norte
Northern Hemisphere: hemisferio boreal
Northerner: *n.* norteño
northland: *n.* tierra del norte
northward: *adv.* hacia el norte
northwest: 1. *adj.* noroeste; 2. *n.* noroeste
northwestern: *adj.* hacia el noroeste
nortriptyline: *n.* nortriptilina
Norway: Noruega
Norwegian: 1. *n.* Noruego; 2. *adj.* noruego
nose: *n.* nariz

nose: *v.* oler; olfatear
nosebleed: sangre de la nariz
nosocomial: *adj.* nosocomial;
hospitalario
nosographic sensitivity: sensibilidad
nosográfica
nosologic specificity: especificidad
nosológica
nosology: *n.* nosología
nostalgia: *n.* nostalgia
nostril: *n.* nariz
nosy: *adj.* averiguador
not: *adv.* no
notable: *adj.* notable
notation: *n.* notación
notch: *n.* muesca; paso
notch: *v.* hacer muescas en; entallar
note: *n.* nota; apunte; signo
note: *v.* notar; marcar
notebook: *n.* libro de notas; agenda
nothing: 1. *n.* nada; 2. *pron.* nada; 3.
adv. de ninguna manera
notice: *n.* so; noticia; carta
notification: *n.* notificación
notify: *v.* notificar; avisar; comunicar
notional: *adj.* nocional
notochord: *n.* notocordio
notwithstanding: 1. *adv.* no
obstante; 2. *prep.* a pesar de; 3. *conj.*
a pesar de que
nought: *n.* nada; cero
noun: *n.* nombre; sustantivo
nourish: *v.* nutrir; abrigar
nourishing: *adj.* nutritivo
novation: *n.* novación
novel: 1. a novelo; 2. *n.* novela
novelette: *n.* novela corta
novelist: *n.* novelista; novelador
novelty: *n.* novedad; innovación
November: *n.* noviembre
novice: 1. *n.* novicio; principiante; 2.
adj. novato
novitiate: *adj.* noviciado
novobiocin: *n.* novobiocina

now: *adv.* ahora; actualmente
nowadays: *adv.* hoy en día
nowhere: *adv.* en ninguna parte
nubile: *n.* casamentero
nuclear: *adj.* nuclear
nuclear energy: energía nuclear
nuclear fission: fisión nuclear
nuclear reactor: reactor nuclear
nucleic: *adj.* nucleico
nucleic acid: ácido nucleico
nucleoside: *n.* nucleósido
nucleus: *n.* núcleo
nuclide: *adj.* nucleido
nude: *adj.* desnudo
nudge: *n.* codazo ligero
nudge: *v.* empujar ligeramente con el
codo
nuisance: *n.* molestia; estorbo
null: *adj.* nulo
null: *v.* anular
null mutation: mutación completa
nullification: *n.* anulación
nullify: *v.* anular; invalidar
numb: *adj.* entorpecido
numb: *v.* adormecer
number: *n.* número
number: *v.* numerar
number concentration:
concentración de número
number content: contenido de
número
number fact family: familia de
operaciones numéricas
number flow rate: caudal de número
number fraction: fracción de
número
number holder: nombre del
asegurado
number line: recta numérica
number of entities: número de
entidades
number sentence: enunciado
numérico
number system: sistema numérico

number theory: teoría de números
numbering machine: numeradora
numbness: *n.* adormecimiento
numeral: *n.* número
numerator: *n.* numerador
numerical: *adj.* numérico
numerical expression: expresión numérica
numerical taxonomy: taxonomía numérica
numerical value: valor numérico
numerology: *n.* numerología
numerous: *adj.* numeroso
numismatics: *n.* numismática
numismatist: *n.* numismátista
nun: *n.* monja; religiosa
nuncio: *n.* nuncio
nuncupative (will): *adj.* nuncupativo
nuptials: *n.* nupcias
nurse: *n.* ama; nodriza
nurse: *v.* amamantar; cuidar
nursery: *n.* crianza; cuarto de los niños
nursing care: cuidado de enfermería
nursing home: asilo de ancianos
nurture: *n.* crianza; educación
nurture: *v.* nutrir; alimentar
nutcracker: *n.* cascanueces
nutmeg: *n.* nuez moscada
nutria: *n.* nutria
nutrient: *n.* nutriente
nutrient agar: agar nutritivo
nutrient broth: caldo nutritivo
nutriment: *n.* nutrimento
nutrition: *n.* nutrición
nutritional: *adj.* nutritivo
nutritional history: historia nutricional
nutritionist: *n.* especialista en dietas y nutrición; nutricionista
nux vomica: nuez vómica
nyctalopia: *n.* nictalopía
nylon: *n.* nilón
nymph: *n.* ninfa

nystagmus: *n.* nistagmo

O

oafish: *adj.* idiota
oar: *n.* remo
oar: *v.* remar
oasis: *n.* oasis
oath: *n.* juramento
oatmeal: *n.* harina de avena
obdurate: *adj.* obstinado; duro
obedience: *n.* obediencia
obedient: *adj.* obediente
obeisance: *n.* obediencia
obelisk: 1. *n.* obelisco; 2. *adj.* obelisco
obesity: *n.* obesidad
obey: *v.* obedecer
obfuscate: *v.* ofuscar
obituary: *n.* obituario
obituary: *adj.* obituario
object: *n.* objeto
object: *v.* objetar
objection: *n.* objeción
objectionable: *adj.* objetable
objective: 1. *n.* objetivo; 2. *adj.* objetivo
objectivism: *n.* objetivismo
objectivity: *n.* objetividad
objector: *n.* objetor
oblation: *n.* oblación
obligation: *n.* obligación
oblige: *v.* obligar; complacer
obliging: *adj.* complaciente
oblique: *adj.* oblicuo
obliterate: *v.* obliterar
obliteration: *n.* obliteración
oblivion: *n.* olvido
oblong: *adj.* oblongo
obnoxious: *adj.* detestable

oboe: *n.* oboe
oboist: *n.* oboísta
obscene: *adj.* obsceno
obscenity: *n.* obscenidad
obscurantism: *n.* oscurantismo
obscure: *adj.* oscuro
obscurity: *n.* oscuridad
obsequious: *adj.* obsequioso; servicial; zalamero
observance: *n.* observancia
observant: *adj.* observador
observation: *n.* observación
observatory: 1. *n.* observatorio; 2. *adj.* observatorio
observe: *v.* observar; guardar
observer: *n.* observador
obsession: *n.* obsesión
obsessive: *adj.* obsesivo
obsolete: *adj.* obsoleto
obstacle race: carrera de obstáculos
obstetrician: *n.* obstetra
obstetrics: *n.* obstetricia
obstinacy: *n.* obstinación
obstinate: *adj.* obstinado
obstruct: *v.* obstruir; atascar
obstruction: *n.* obstrucción
obstructionism: *n.* obstruccionismo
obstructionist: *n.* obstruccionista
obtain: *v.* lograr; obtener; conseguir
obtuse: *adj.* obtuso; romo
obtuse angle: ángulo obtuso
obtuse triangle: triángulo obtusángulo
obviate: *v.* obviar; impedir
obvious: *adj.* obvio
ocarina: *n.* ocarina
occasion: *n.* ocasión
occasion: *v.* ocasionar
occident: *n.* occidente; oeste
occidental: *adj.* occidental
occipital: *adj.* occipital
occiput: *n.* occipucio
occluded: *adj.* ocluido
occluded front: oclusión

occlusion: *n.* oclusión
occult: *adj.* oculto; secreto
occultism: *n.* ocultismo
occultist: *n.* ocultista
occupancy: *n.* ocupación
occupant: *n.* ocupante
occupation: *n.* ocupación
occupational: *adj.* ocupacional
occupational history: datos ocupacionales
occupy: *v.* ocupar
occurrence: *n.* ocurrencia
ocean: *n.* océano
oceanic: *adj.* oceánico
oceanographer: *n.* oceanógrafo
oceanography: *n.* oceanografía
oceanology: *n.* oceanología
ocelot: *n.* ocelote
ocher: *n.* ocre
ochlocracy: *n.* oclocracia
ocotillo: *n.* ocotillo
octagon: *n.* octágono
octagonal: *adj.* octagonal
octahedron: *n.* octaedro
octant: *n.* octante
octave: *n.* octava
octet: *n.* octeto
octillion: *n.* octillón
October: octubre
octogenarian: 1. *n.* octogenario; 2. *adj.* octogenario
octometer: *n.* octómetro
octopus: *n.* pulpo
octuple: *adj.* óctuplo
ocular: *adj.* ocular
ocular micrometer: micrómetro ocular
oculist: *n.* oculista
ode: *n.* oda
odious: *adj.* odioso
odium: *n.* odio
odometer: *n.* odómetro
odontologist: *n.* odontólogo
odontology: *n.* odontología

odor: *n.* olor; fragancia
odorous: *adj.* oloroso
odyssey: *n.* odisea
off: 1. *adj.* apartado; alejado; 2. *adv.* lejos; a distancia; fuera
offal: *n.* despojos; asaduras; achuras
offend: *v.* ofender
offended: *adj.* ofendido
offender: *n.* ofensor
offense: *n.* ofensa; ofensiva
offensive: *adj.* ofensivo
offer: *n.* oferta
offer: *v.* ofrecer
offering: *n.* ofrenda
offertory: *n.* ofertorio
office: *n.* oficina
office worker: oficinista
officer: *n.* oficial; funcionario
official: 1. *adj.* oficial; 2. *n.* oficial
officiant: *n.* oficiante
officiate: *v.* oficiar
officious: *adj.* oficioso
offing: *n.* alta mar
offset: *adj.* ajuste; descuento; reducción
offshoot: *n.* vástago; ramal
offspring: *n.* hijo; descendencia; prole
ofloxacin: *n.* ofloxacina
often: *adv.* a menudo
ogre: *n.* ogro
oh no!: *intj.* ¡ay no!
ohm: *n.* ohm
oil: *n.* aceite; óleo
oil: *v.* engrasar
oil-based paint: la pintura al aceite
oilskin: *adj.* impermeable
ointment: *n.* ungüento
OK!; okay!: *intj.* ¡Okay!
okapi: *n.* okapi
old: *adj.* viejo; añejo; de edad; usado
old age: edad avanzada
olefin: *n.* olefina
oleomargarine: *n.* oleomargarina

olfactory: *adj.* olfatorio
oligarchy: *n.* oligarquía
oligoprobe: *n.* oligosonda
olive: *n.* oliva; verde olivo; aceituna
olive grove: olivar
olive grower: olivarero
olive growing: olivicultura
olive oil: aceite de oliva
olive-colored: oliváceo
Olympics: *n.* Olimpiada
omega: *n.* omega
omelet: *n.* omelet
omen: *n.* agüero
omicron: *n.* ómicron
omit: *v.* omitir
omnibus: *n.* ómnibus
omnidirectional: *adj.* omnidireccional
omnipotence: *n.* omnipotencia
omniscient: *adj.* omnisciente
omnivore: *n.* omnívoro
omphalic: *adj.* umbilical
on: *prep.* en
on grade: a nivel
onager: *n.* onagro
oncofetal antigen: antígeno oncofetal
oncogene: *n.* oncogén
oncologist: *n.* oncologista; especialista en cáncer
oncology: *n.* oncología
oncovirus: *n.* oncovirus
one: *art.* uno; a
one stop: completo
one-half support: la mitad del mantenimiento
onerous: *adj.* oneroso; molesto
oneself: *pron.* uno mismo
one-step: *n.* en un paso
one-way: de una sola-dirección
ongoing benefits: beneficios regulares
onion: *n.* cebolla
online: en línea

on-line; on line: en línea
onlooker: *n.* mirón; espectador
only: *adv.* solo; solamente
onomastics: *n.* onomástica
onomatopoeia: *n.* onomatopeya
onomatopoeic: *adj.* onomatopéyico
onset: *n.* arremetido; embestida
onshore: 1. *adj.* de tierra; 2. *adv.*
hacia la tierra
ontogeny: *n.* ontogenia; ontogénesis
ontological: *adj.* oncológico
ontology: *n.* ontología
onward: 1. *adj.* hacia adelante; 2.
adv. hacia adelante
onyx: *n.* ónice; ónix; ónique
oology: *n.* oología
oophorectomy: *n.* ooforectomia
op art: op-art
opal: *adj.* ópalo
opale mutation: mutación ópalo
opalescence: *n.* opalescencia
opalescent: *adj.* opalescente
opaque: *adj.* opaco
opaque material: material opaco
open: *adj.* abierto
open circulatory system: sistema
circulatorio abierto
open cluster: cúmulo abierto
open sesame!: ¡ábrete sísame!
open system: sistema abierto
open-air theater: teatro al aire libre
opener: *n.* abridor
opening: *n.* abertura; apertura
open-ocean zone: zona de mar
abierto
opera: *n.* ópera
opera buffa: ópera bufa
opera house: ópera
opera singer: operista
operate: *v.* actuar; efectuar
operating system: código
operacional; sistema operativo
operation: *n.* operación
operational definition: definición

operativa
operative: *n.* operario
operator: *n.* operador
operetta: *n.* opereta
operon: *n.* operón
ophiology: *n.* ofiología
ophthalmia: *n.* oftalmia
ophthalmic: *adj.* oftálmico
ophthalmologist: *n.* oftalmólogo;
especialista en los ojos
ophthalmology: *n.* oftalmología
ophthalmoscope: *n.* oftalmoscopio
opiate: *n.* opiata
opossum: *n.* oposum
opponent: 1. *adj.* oponente; 2. *n.*
opositor
opportune: *adj.* oportuno
opportunism: *n.* oportunismo
opportunist: *n.* oportunista
opportunity: *n.* oportunidad
oppose: *v.* oponer; objetar
opposing: *adj.* opuesto
opposite: 1. *adj.* opuesto; 2. *n.* lo
contrario; 3. *prep.* en frente de
opposition: *n.* oposición
oppress: *v.* oprimir
oppression: *n.* opresión
oppressive: *adj.* opresivo
oppressor: *n.* opresor
oppressor: *n.* opresor
opprobious: *adj.* oprobioso
opprobrium: *n.* oprobio
oppugn: *v.* opugnar; combatir
opsonization: *n.* opsonización
optic: *adj.* óptico
optic nerve: nervio óptico
optical: *adj.* óptico
optical axis: eje óptico
optical density: densidad óptica
optical fiber: fibra óptica
optical telescope: telescopio óptico
optician: *n.* óptico
optics: *n.* óptica
optimal: *adj.* óptimo

optimism: *n.* optimismo
optimist: *n.* optimista
optimum: *n.* óptimo
option: *n.* opción
optional: *adj.* optativo; facultativo
optional method: método opcional; método alternativo
optometrist: *n.* optometrista
optometry: *n.* optometría
opulent: *adj.* opulento
opuntia: *n.* opuncia
or: *prep.* o
oracle: *n.* oráculo
oral: *adj.* oral
oral contraceptive: anticonceptivo oral
oral sex: sexo oral
orange: 1. *adj.* (color) naranja; 2. *n.* (fruta) naranja
orangeade: *n.* naranjada
orangutan: *n.* orangután
oration: *n.* oración; discurso
orator: *n.* orador
oratorio: *adj.* oratorio
oratory: *n.* oratoria; capilla; oratoria
orb: *n.* orbe; círculo
orbit: *n.* órbita
orbital velocity: velocidad orbital
orchard: *n.* huerto
orchestra: *n.* orquesta
orchestration: *n.* orquestación
orchid: *n.* orquídea
ordain: *v.* ordenar
order: *n.* orden
order of magnitud: orden de magnitud
order of operations: orden de las operaciones
ordered pair: par ordenado
ordinal: *adj.* ordinal
ordinal scale: escala ordinal
ordinance: *n.* ordenanza
ordinary: *adj.* ordinario; usual
ordinate: *n.* ordenada

ordination: *n.* ordenación
ore: *n.* mina; mineral
oregano: *n.* orégano
organ: *n.* órgano
organ donation card: tarjeta para donar órganos
organ donor: donante de órgano
organ system: sistema de órganos
organdie: *n.* organdí
organdy: *n.* organdí
organelle: *n.* organelo
organic: *adj.* orgánico
organic acid: ácido orgánico
organic compounds: compuesto orgánico
organic rock: rota orgánica
organism: *n.* organismo
organist: *n.* organista
organization: *n.* organización
organize: *v.* organizar
organizer: *n.* organizador
orgasm: *n.* orgasmo
orient: *n.* oriente
orient: *v.* orientar
oriental: *adj.* oriental
orientate: *v.* orientar
orientation: *n.* orientación
orifice: *n.* orificio
origami: *n.* origami
origin: *n.* origen
original: 1. *adj.* original; 2. *n.* original
originality: *n.* originalidad
originator: *n.* causante
orlon: *n.* orlón
ornament: *n.* ornamento
ornamental: *adj.* ornamental
ornamentation: *n.* ornamentación; ornato
ornate: *adj.* ornado; florido
ornithology: *n.* ornitología
ornithopter: *n.* ornitóptero
orography: *n.* orografía
orphan: 1. *adj.* huérfano; 2. *n.*

huérfana
orphanage: *n.* orfanato; orfelinato
orphon: *n.* orfón
orthodox: *adj.* ortodoxo
Orthodox Church: Iglesia ortodoxa
orthodoxy: *n.* ortodoxia
orthogenesis: *n.* ontogénesis
orthogonal: *adj.* ortogonal
orthographic: *adj.* ortográfico
orthography: *n.* ortografía
orthopedic: *adj.* ortopédico
orthopedics: *n.* ortopedia
orthopedist: *n.* ortopedista
orthorhombic: 1. *n.* otorrómbico; 2.
adj. orthorhombic
oscar: *n.* oscar
oscillator: *n.* oscilador
oscillograph: *n.* oscilógrafo
osmolality: *n.* osmolalidad
osmometry: *n.* osmometría
osmosis: *n.* ósmosis
osmotic coefficient: coeficiente
osmótico
osmotic concentration:
concentración osmótica
osmotic pressure: presión osmótica
ossicle: *n.* osículo
ossuary: *n.* osario
ostentatious: *adj.* ostentoso
osteoarthritis: *n.* osteoartritis
osteocalcin: *n.* osteocalcina
osteology: *n.* osteología
osteomyelitis: *n.* osteomielitis
osteopath: *n.* osteópata
osteopathy: *n.* osteopatía
osteoporosis: *n.* osteoporosis
ostracism: *n.* ostracismo
ostrich: *n.* avestruz
otalgia: *n.* otalgia
other: *adj.* otro
otherwise: *adv.* de otro modo
otic exudate: exudado ótico
otiose: *adj.* ocioso
otolaringologist: *n.* otolaringólogo

otolaryngologist: *n.* especialista en
los oídos
otolaryngology: *n.* otolaringología
otorhinolaryngology: *n.*
otorrinolaringología
otoscope: *n.* otoscopio
ottoman: *n.* otomana
ounce: *n.* onza
our: *adj.* poss. nuestro; -a; -os; -as
ours: *pron.* (poss). nuestro
ourselves: *pron.* (reflex). nosotros
mismos; nos
oust: *v.* desahuciar
outbid: *v.* pujar; ofrecer más que
outbreak: *n.* explosión; erupción;
tumulto
outcast: *adj.* desterrado; paria
outclass: *v.* ser superior a
outcome: *n.* resultado
outcry: *n.* griterío
outdoor: *adj.* al aire libre
outdoor lighting: la iluminación al
aire libre
outer: *adj.* exterior
outer core: núcleo externo
outfit: *n.* equipo; menesteres
outfit: *v.* equipar; habilitar
outing: *n.* excursión; paseo
outlander: *n.* extranjero
outlast: *v.* durar mas que
outlaw: *n.* bandido
outlaw: *v.* proscribir
outlay: *n.* desembolso
outlay: *v.* bolsar
outlet: *n.* salida
outlier value: valor aberrante
outline: *n.* contorno; perfil
outline: *v.* delinear
outlive: *v.* sobrevivir
outlook: *n.* perspectiva; aspecto
outlying: *adj.* remoto
outmatch: *v.* aventajar
outnumber: *v.* excederse en número
outpatient: *n.* paciente externo

outpatient treatment: tratamiento ambulatorio
output: *n.* producción; rendimiento; salida
output device: dispositivo de salida
output force: fuerza desarrollada
output rate: rendimiento
output work: trabajo producido
outrage: *n.* ultraje
outrage: *v.* violentar; violar
outright: *adv.* enteramente
outrun: *v.* aventajar; dejar atrás
outset: *n.* principio; inauguración
outside: 1. *adj.* exterior; ajeno; 2. *adv.* fuera; 3. *prep.* fuera de
outside: *n.* exterior;
outsider: *n.* forastero; intruso
outskirts: *n.* cercanías; suburbios
outstand: *v.* sobresalir
outstanding: *adj.* saliente; notable
outward: 1. *adj.* exterior; externo; 2. *adv.* exteriormente
outwear: *v.* gastar; consumir
outweigh: *v.* pesar más que
ouzo: *n.* ouzo
oval: 1. *n.* óvalo; 2. *adj.* oval; ovalado; óvalo
ovariectomy: *n.* ovariectomía
ovary: *n.* ovario
ovation: *n.* ovación
oven: *n.* horno; hornillo
over: *adv.* encima; por encima
over there: allá
overall: *n.* mono; guardapolvo
overawe: *v.* intimidar
overbalance: *n.* exceso de
overbalance: *v.* preponderar
overbear: *v.* dominar; derribar
overbearing: *adj.* dominador
overburden: *n.* carga excesiva
overcast: *adj.* nublado
overcast: *v.* nublar; oscurecer
overcharge: *n.* cargo excesivo
overcharge: *v.* recargar

overcoat: *n.* abrigo
overcome: *v.* vencer; superar
overcritical: *adj.* criticón
overdo: *v.* exagerar; agobiar
overdose: *n.* sobredosis
overestimated: *adj.* sobreestimado
overexposure: *n.* sobreexposición
overfeed: *v.* sobrealimentar
overflow: *n.* rebosadero; desbordamiento; inundación
overflow: *v.* inundar
overgrown: *adj.* demasiado; desarrollado
overhand: *n.* proyección
overhand: *v.* sobre; salir por
overhang: *n.* voladizo
overhanging end: extremo saliente
overhaul: *n.* revisión
overhaul: *v.* examinar
overhead: *adv.* por encima
overhear: *v.* oír por casualidad
overheat: *v.* recalentar
overjoy: *n.* alboroto
overjoy: *v.* alborozar
overlapping: *adj.* sobrepuesto
overlapping sequence: secuencia superpuesta
overlay: *n.* cubierta
overlay: *v.* cubrir; abrumar
overleaf: *adv.* al dorso
overlook: *v.* vigilar; pasar por alto; cuidar de
overlord: *n.* jefe supremo
overnight: 1. *adj.* de noche; 2. *adv.* toda la noche
overpass: *n.* viaducto; paso superior
overpass: *v.* atravesar; exceder
overpayment: *n.* sobrepago; pago en exceso
overpayment recovery: recuperación de sobrepago
overpayment refund: reembolso de sobrepago
overpopulated: *adj.* superpoblado

overpower: *v.* dominar
override: *v.* recorrer; fatigar
overrule: *v.* anular; revocar
overrun: *v.* cubrir enteramente; infectar
oversea: 1. *adj.* de ultramar; 2. *adv.* ultramar
oversee: *v.* dirigir; revisar
overseer: *n.* director; inspector
overshadow: *v.* sombrear
oversight: *n.* inadvertencia; omisión
oversleep: *v.* dormir demasiado
overstate: *v.* exagerar
overstep: *v.* exceder; pasar
overt: *adj.* abierto
overtake: *v.* alcanzar; sobrepasar
overthrow: *n.* derrocamiento
overthrow: *v.* derrocar; trastornar
overtop: *v.* descollar sobre; exceder en
overture: *n.* obertura
overturn: *n.* vuelco
overturn: *v.* volcar; derrocar
overvalued: *adj.* sobrevalorado
overwhelm: *v.* abrumar
overwork: *n.* exceso de trabajo
overwrought: *adj.* abrumado de trabajo
oviduct: *n.* oviducto
ovulation: *n.* ovulación
ovum: *n.* óvulo
owe: *v.* deber; adeudar
owl: *n.* lechuza
own: *adj.* propio; particular
own: *v.* confesar
owner: *n.* dueño; propietario
ownership: *n.* posesión
oxacillin: *n.* noxacilina
oxbow lake: meandro abandonado
oxidant: *adj.* oxidante
oxidation: *n.* oxidación
oxtail: *n.* rabo de buey
oxyacetylene: 1. *n.* oxiacetileno; 2. *adj.* oxiacetilénico

oxygen: *n.* oxígeno
oxygen saturation: saturación de oxígeno
oxygenation: *n.* oxigenación
oxymoron: *n.* oxímoron
oxytocin: *n.* oxitocina
oyster: *n.* ostra; ostión
oyster bar: ostrería
oyster bed: ostrero
oyster culture: ostricultura
oyster vender: ostrero
ozone: *n.* ozono
ozonosphere: *n.* ozonosfera

P

pa: *n.* papá
pabulum: *n.* pébulo
pace: *n.* paso
pace: *v.* medir a pasos; marcar el paso
pacemaker: *n.* marcapasos
pachytene: *n.* paquitena
Pacific: Pacífico
Pacific time: hora del Pacífico
pacification: *n.* pacificación
pacifier: *n.* pacificador
pacifism: *n.* pacifismo
pacifist: *n.* pacifista
pacify: *v.* pacificar; calmar
pack: *n.* paquete; manada
pack: *v.* empaquetar; apretar; empacar
package: *n.* paquete
package: *v.* empaquetar
packaging: *n.* empaque; empaquetamiento
packed column: columna preparada
packet: *n.* paquete; bolsita

packet: *v.* empaquetar
pack-mule: mula de carga
pact: *n.* pacto
pad: *n.* losa; plataforma; cojinete; postizo
pad: *v.* rellenar; forrar
padding: *n.* relleno
paddle: *v.* remar
paddock: *n.* dehesa; candado
padlock: *v.* cerrar con candado
paean: *n.* peán
paganism: *n.* paganismo
page: *n.* página; paje
page: *v.* paginar
pageant: *n.* espectáculo público
pagination: *n.* paginación
pagoda: *n.* pagoda
pahoehoe: *n.* pahoehoe
paid: *adj.* pagado; asalariado
pail: *n.* cubo; balde
pain: *n.* dolor; sufrimiento
pain: *v.* doler
painless: *adj.* sin dolor; sin penas
paint: *n.* pintura
paint: *v.* pintar
paint brush: la brocha de pintar
paint sprayer: la pistola pintadora/la pintadora neumática
painter: *n.* pintor
painting: *n.* pintura; cuadro
pair: *n.* par; pareja
pair: *v.* emparejar
pajamas: *n.* pijama
Pakistan: Pakistán
Pakistani: *adj.* pakistaní; paquistaní
palace: *n.* palacio
palate: *n.* paladar
palatial: *adj.* palaciego
palatinate: *v.* palatinado
pale: *adj.* pálido
pale: *v.* palidecer
paleographer: *n.* paleógrafo; -a
paleography: *n.* paleografía
paleontologist: *n.* paleontólogo

paleontology: *n.* paleontología
Palestine: Palestina
Palestinian: *adj.* palestino
palette: *n.* paleta
palimsest: *n.* palimpsesto
palindrome: *n.* palíndromo
paling: *n.* estaca
palisade: *n.* palizada
pallet: *n.* paleta
palliate: *v.* paliar; encubrir
palliative: 1. *adj.* paliativo; -a; 2. *n.* paliativo
pallium: *n.* palio
pallor: *n.* palidez
palm: *n.* palma; palmo
palm: *v.* manipular
palm farmer: palmero
palm of hand: palma de la mano
palmetto: *n.* palmito
palpation: *n.* palpación
palpitate: *v.* palpitar
palpitation: *n.* palpitación
palsy: *n.* perlesía; parálisis
palsy: *v.* paralizar
paltry: *adj.* vil; ruin
pampa: *n.* pampa
pamper: *v.* mimar; atracar
pamphlet: *n.* folleto; panfleto
pamphleteer: *n.* panfletista
pan: *n.* cazuela; cazo
panacea: *n.* panacea
Panama: Panamá
Panamanian: *adj.* panameño; -a
pancake: *n.* crepe; panqueque
panchromatic: *adj.* pancromático
pancreas: *n.* páncreas
pancreatic: *adj.* pancreático
panda: *n.* panda
pandemic: *adj.* pandémico
pandemonium: *n.* pandemonio; pandemonium
pane: *n.* cristal
panegyric: 1. *n.* panegírico; 2. *adj.* panegírico

panel: *n.* panel
paneling: *n.* paneles
panelist: *n.* miembro del panel
pang: *n.* dolor agudo
Pangaea: Pangea
pangolin: *n.* pangolín
panic: *adj.* pánico
panicky: *adj.* pánico
pannier: *n.* cesta grande
panoply: *n.* panoplia
panorama: *n.* panorama
pant: *n.* palpitación; pantalones
pant: *v.* palpitar; anhelar
pantaloon: *n.* bufón; pantalón
pantheism: *n.* panteísmo
pantheon: *n.* panteón
panther: *n.* pantera
pantograph: *n.* pantógrafo
pantomime: *n.* pantomima
pantothenic: *adj.* pantoténico
pantry: *n.* despensa; repostería
pants: *n.* pantalones
pantyhose: *n.* medias pantis
panzer: *adj.* blindado
pap: *n.* papilla; papas
pap smear: examen de Papanicolau
papacy; popedom: *n.* papado
papain: *n.* papaína
paparazzi: *n.* paparazzi
papaya: *n.* papaya
paper: *n.* papel; artículo
paper: *v.* empapelar
paperwork: *n.* papeleo
papilla: *n.* papila
papilloma: *n.* papiloma
paprika: *n.* pimentón; paprika
Papuan: *adj.* Papú
papyrus: *n.* papiro
par: 1. *adj.* a la par; 2. *n.* paridad; par
parable: *n.* parábola
parabola: *n.* parábola
parabolic: *adj.* parabólico
paracentesis: *n.* paracentesis
parachute: *n.* paracaídas

parade: 1. *n.* desfile; cabalgata; parada
parade: *v.* desfilar; pasearse
paradigm: *n.* paradigma
paradise: *n.* paraíso
paradox: *n.* paradoja
paragraph: *n.* párrafo; artículo corto
Paraguay: Paraguay
Paraguayan: *adj.* paraguayo; -a
parallax: *n.* paralaje
parallel: 1. *adj.* paralelo; 2. *n.* paralelo-a
parallel: *v.* paralelizar
parallel bars: barras paralelas
parallel circuit: circuito paralelo
parallel lines: rectas paralelas
parallelism: *n.* paralelismo
parallelogram: *n.* paralelogramo
parallepiped: 1. *n.* paralelepípedo; 2. *adj.* paralepípedo
paralysis: *n.* parálisis
paralyze: *v.* paralizar
paramecium: *n.* paramecio
paramedic: *n.* auxiliar médico
parameter: *n.* parámetro
parametric: *adj.* paramétrico
parametric curve: la curva paramétrica
paramilitary: *adj.* paramilitar
paramount: *adj.* superior
paramour: *n.* amante
paranoia: *n.* paranoia
paranormal: *adj.* paranormal
parapet: *n.* parapeto
paraphernalia: *n.* parafernalia
paraphrase: *n.* paráfrasis
paraphyletic: *adj.* parafilético
paraplegic: 1.*n.* parapléjico 2. *adj.* parapléjico
parapsychologist: *n.* parasicólogo
parapsychology: *n.* parasicología
parasite: *n.* parásito
parasite: 1. *n.* parásito; 2. *adj.* parásito

parasitic: *adj.* parasitario; parásito
parasitism: *n.* parasitismo
parasitology: *n.* parasitología
parasol: *n.* quitasol; sombrilla
parasympathetic: *adj.* parasimpático
parathion: *n.* paratión
parathormone: *n.* paratírina
parathyroid: *n.* paratiroides
parathyroid hormone: paratíroides
paratyphoid fever: fiebre paratifoidea
parcel: 1. *n.* parcela; 2. *adj.* paquete
parcel: *v.* empaquetar; parcelar
parch: *v.* tostar; abrasar
Parcheesi: *n.* parchís
parchment: *n.* pergamino
pardon: 1. *n.* perdón; indulto;
pardon: *v.* perdonar; dispensar
paregoric: *n.* elixir paregórico
parenchyma: *n.* parénquima
parent: *n.* padre o madre
parentage: *n.* parentela; paternidad; maternidad
parenteral nutrition: nutrición parenteral
parenthesis: *n.* paréntesis
paresis: *n.* paresis; paresia
parhelion: *n.* parhelia; parhelio
pariah: *n.* paria
parietal: *adj.* parietal
Paris: París
parish: *n.* parroquia
parishioner: *n.* parroquiano
Parisian: *n.* parisiense
parity: *n.* paridad
park: *n.* parque
park: vt. parquear
parka: *n.* parka
parking lot: parking; estacionamiento
parking meter: parquímetro
parley: 1.*n.* parlamento; 2. *v.* parlamentar
parliament: *n.* parlamento

parliamentarian: *n.* parlamentario
parliamentary law: reglamento parlamentario
parlor: *n.* sala; locutorio
Parnassus: Parnaso
parodist: *n.* parodista
parody: *n.* parodia
parody: *v.* parodiar
parole: *n.* palabra de honor régimen de libertad provisional
paronychia: *n.* paroniquia
paroxysm: *n.* paroxismo
parquet: *n.* parqué
parricide: 1. *n.* parricida; 2. *adj.* parricidio
parricide (act): *n.* parricidio
parry: *n.* parada
parry: *v.* parar; rechazar
parsimonious: *adj.* parsimonioso
parsley: *n.* perejil
parson: *n.* cura; sacerdote; pastor
part: *n.* parte
part of speech: *n.* parte de la oración
part time: tiempo parcial
partake: *v.* compartir; comer; beber
partial: 1. *n.* tono parcial; 2. *adj.* parcial
partial derivative: la derivada parcial
partial pressure: presión parcial
partial udication: udicación parcial
partiality: *n.* parcialidad
participant: *n.* participante; partícipe
participate: *v.* participar
participating: *adj.* participando
participating hospital: hospital participante
participation: *n.* participación
participle: *n.* participio
particle: *n.* partícula
particle accelerator: acelerador de partículas
particle counter: contador de partículas

particular: 1. *n.* particular; 2. *adj.*
particular
particular property: propiedad
particular
particular quantity: magnitud
particular
parting: 1. *adj.* de partida; 2. *n.*
punto de partida
partisan: 1. *adj.* partidario; 2. *n.*
partidario;-a
partita: *n.* partita
partition: *n.* partición
partition: *v.* repartir
partition coefficient: coeficiente de
reparto
partitive: *adj.* partitivo
partly: *adv.* en parte
partner: *n.* compañero; cónyuge
partnership: *n.* sociedad; propiedad
común
partridge: *n.* perdiz
part-time: a tiempo parcial
parturition: *n.* parto
party: *n.* partido; -a
pas: *n.* paso
pascal: *adj.* pascal
Pascal's principle: principio de
Pascal
paschal: *adj.* pascual
pass: *n.* pase
pass: vt. pasar
passable: *adj.* pasable
passacaglia: *n.* pasacalle
passage: *n.* pasaje; transición
passenger: *n.* pasajero; -a
passepied: *n.* paspié
passer-by: *n.* transeúnte
passim: *adv.* passim
passion: *n.* pasión
passion flower: pasionaria
passionate: *adj.* apasionado
passionless: *adj.* poco apasionado
passive: *adj.* pasivo
passive immunity: inmunidad pasiva

passive transport: transporte pasivo
passivity: *n.* pasividad
passport: *n.* pasaporte
password: *n.* contraseña
past: 1. *n.* pasado; 2. *adj.* pasado
past participle: participio pasado
past tense: tiempo pasado
pasta: *n.* pasta
paste: *n.* pasta; engrudo
paste: *v.* pegar; empastar
pastel: 1. *n.* pastel; 2. *adj.* pastel
pasteurization: *n.* pasteurización
pasteurized milk: leche pasteurizada
pastiche: *n.* pastiche
pastille: *n.* pastilla
pastime: *n.* pasatiempo
pastor: *n.* pastor
pastoral: *adj.* pastoral; pastoril
pastrami: *n.* pastrami
pastry: *n.* pastelería
pasture: *n.* pasto; dehesa
pasture: *v.* pastorear; pastar
pasty: *n.* empanada; empanadilla
pat: 1. *adj.* bueno; apto; exactor; 2.
adv. oportunamente
pat: *v.* dar golpecitos
patch: *v.* remendar
patch: *n.* parche; remiendo
patch: *v.* remendar
patch repair: reparación por escisión
pate: *n.* paté
paten: *n.* patena
patent: 1. *adj.* patentado; 2. *n.*
patente
patent: *v.* patentar
patent medicine: medicamento
patentado
paternalism: *n.* paternalismo
paternity: *n.* paternidad
paternoster: *n.* paternóster
path: *n.* senda; sendero; vereda
pathlenght: paso de luz
pathless: *adj.* intransitable
pathobiochemistry: *n.* bioquímica

clínica
pathogen: *n.* microbio patógeno
pathogen: *n.* patógeno
pathogenesis: *n.* patogénesis
pathologic entity: entidad patológica
pathologist: *n.* patólogo; -a
pathology: *n.* patología
pathophysiology: *n.* fisiopatología
patience: *n.* paciencia
patient: 1. *adj.* paciente; 2. *n.* paciente
patient privacy: privacidad del paciente
patina: *n.* pátina
patio: *n.* patio
patriarchal: *adj.* patriarcal
patriarchy: *n.* patriarcado
patrilineal: *adj.* patrilineal
patrimony: *n.* patrimonio
patriotism: *n.* patriotismo
patrol: *n.* patrulla; ronda
patrol: *v.* rondar; patrullar
patron: 1. *adj.* patrocinador; 2. *n.* patrono; patrocinador
patron saint: patrono
patronage: *n.* patrocinio; protecci*ó*n
patronymic: 1. *n.* patronímico; 2. *adj.* patronímico
pattern: patrón; modelo
pattern: *v.* modelar
pauper: *n.* pobre
pause: *n.* pausa
pavan (e): *n.* pavana
pave: *v.* empedrar; pavimentar
pavement: *n.* pavimento
pavilion: *n.* pabellón
pavilion: *v.* patear; sobar
pawn: *n.* peón
pawn: *v.* dar en prenda; empeñar
pay: *n.* salario; sueldo; paga
pay: *v.* pagar
pay back: reembolsar; restituir
pay stub: talón de pago; talonario
payable: *adj.* pagadero; pagable

payday: *n.* día de paga
payee: *n.* representante; tutor del beneficiario
payment: *n.* pago; paga
payments in kind: pagos en especie
pay-per-view: pagar-para-ver
payroll: *n.* planilla de sueldos
PC: PC
pea: *n.* guisante; chícharo
peace: *n.* la paz
peace time: época de paz
peaceful: *adj.* pacífico; tranquilo
peacekeeping: *n.* mantenimiento de la paz
peach: *n.* melocotón; durazno
peak: *n.* cumbre; pico; cima.
peak level: concentración máxima
peal: *n.* estruendo fragor
peal: *v.* repicar; resonar; vocear
peanut: *n.* cacahuete; maní
peanut butter: mantequilla de cacahuete
pearl: *n.* perla; margarita.
pearl barley: cebada perlada
peasant: 1. *n.* campesino; labrador; 2. *adj.* campesino; labrador
peat: *n.* turba
pebble: *n.* guijarro; china
pecan: *n.* pacana
peccadillo: *n.* pecadillo
peccary: *n.* pecari
peck: *n.* picotazo
peck: *v.* picotear; picar
pectin: *n.* pectina
pectoral: 1. *n.* pectoral; 2. *adj.* pectoral
pecuniary: *adj.* pecuniario
pedagogue: *n.* pedagogo
pedagogy: *n.* pedagogía
pedal: *n.* pedal
pedantic: *adj.* pedante; pedantesco
pedantry: *n.* pedantería
pederast: *n.* pederasta
pedestal: *n.* pedestal

pedestrian: 1.*n.* peatón
pediatric: *adj.* pediátrico
pediatrician: *n.* pediatra; especialista en los niños
pediatrics: *n.* pediatría
pedicure: *n.* pedicura
pedigree: *n.* genealogía; árbol genealógico
pedlar: *n.* revendedor
pedodontics: *n.* pedodoncia
pedology: *n.* pedología
pedometer: *n.* podómetro
pedophile: *n.* pedófilo
pedophilia: *n.* pedofilia
peduncle: *n.* pedúnculo
pee; peepee: *n.* pipì
peel: *n.* peladura; piel
peel: vt. pelar; mondar
peeled: *adj.* pelado
peeling: *de*scamación
peer: *n.* par
peer group: grupo de comparación; grupo comparable
peer review: revisión por expertos
peerage: *n.* dignidad de par; paría
peeress: *n.* paresa
peevishness: *n.* mal humor; desagrado
pefloxacine: *n.* pefloxacina
peg: *n.* clavija; pinza
pejorative: 1. *n.* peyorativo; 2. *adj.* peyorativo
pekinese; pekingese: *n.* pequinés
pelagic: *adj.* pelágico
pelargonium: *n.* pelargonio
pellagra: *n.* pelagra
pellet: *n.* sedimento
pellicle: *n.* película
pellmell: *adv.* confusamente
pelt: *n.* cuero; piel
pelvic: 1. *n.* pélvico; 2. *adj.* pélvico
pelvic examination: examen pélvico
pelvis: *n.* pelvis
pemmican: *n.* pemicán

pemphigus: *n.* pénfigo
penal: *adj.* penal
penalise: *v.* penar; castigar
penalty: *n.* pena; penalti; penalidad
penalty deductions: deducciones por penalidad
penance: *n.* penitencia
pence: *n.* peniques
pencil: *n.* lápiz; pincel
pencil-sharpener: sacapuntas
pend: *v.* estar pendiente de
pendant: 1. *n.* pendiente; 2. *adj.* pendiente
pending: *adj.* indeciso
pendulum: *n.* péndulo
penetrancy: *n.* penetrancia
penetrate: *v.* penetrar; con-mover
penetrating: *adj.* penetrante
penetration: *n.* penetración
penguin: *n.* pingüino
penicillin: *n.* penicilina
penicillium: *n.* penicilium
peninsula: *n.* península
penis: *n.* pene
penitence: *n.* penitencia
penitentiary: *n.* penitenciaría
penknife: *n.* cortaplumas
pennant: *n.* banderin; insignia
penniless: *adj.* pobre
Pennsylvania: Pensilvania
penny: 1. *adj.* de penique; de poco valor; 2. *n.* penique; centavo
penologist: *n.* penalista
pension: *n.* pensión; retiro
pension: *v.* jubilar
pension plan: plan de pensión
pensioner: *n.* pensionado; -a; pensionista
pensive: *adj.* pensativo; triste
pent: *adj.* acorralado; encerrado
pentacle: *n.* pentáculo
pentagon: *n.* pentágono
pentahedron: *n.* pentaedro
pentameter: *n.* pentámetro

pentathlon: *n.* pentatlón
pentatonic: *adj.* pentatónico
pentecost: *n.* Pentecostés
pentecostal: *adj.* pentecostal
penthouse: *n.* penthouse
pentode: *n.* pentodo; péntodo
pentose: *n.* pentosa
penuche: *n.* panocha
penumbra: penumbra
penury: *n.* penuria; escasez
peonage: *n.* condición de peón
peony: *n.* peonía
people: *n.* pueblo; gente
people: *v.* poblar
peplum: *n.* peplo
pepper: *n.* pimienta
peppercorns: *n.* granos de pimienta
peppermint: *n.* menta
pepsin: *n.* pepsina
peptic: *adj.* péptico
peptide: *n.* péptido
peptone broth: caldo peptonado
per: *prep.* por
per capita: per cápita
per cent: por ciento
perambulate: *v.* recorrer; transitar por
percale: 1. *n.* percal; 2. *adj.* percal
perceive: *v.* percibir; conocer
percent: *n.* por ciento; porcentaje
percent of change: porcentaje de cambio
percent of decrease: porcentaje de disminución
percent of increase: porcentaje de aumento
percentile: *n.* percentil
perception: *n.* percepción
perceptual: *adj.* perceptivo
perch: 1. *n.* percha
perch: *v.* posar; perchar
perchance: *adv.* por ventura
percolation: *n.* percolación
percussion: *n.* percusión

percussionist: *n.* músico de percusión
percutaneous: *adj.* percutaneo
perdition: *n.* perdición
peregrination: *n.* peregrinación
peremptory: *adj.* perentorio; autoritario
perennial: *adj.* perenne
perfect: *adj.* perfecto
perfect: *v.* perfeccionar
perfect square: cuadrado perfecto
perfection: *n.* perfección
perfectionist: *n.* perfeccionista
perfective: *adj.* perfectivo
perfidious: *adj.* pérfido
perfidy: *n.* perfidia
perforate: *v.* perforar; taladrar
perforation: *n.* perforación
perform: *v.* desempeñar; efectuar; ejecutar
performance: *n.* prestación; funcionamiento
performance characteristic: característica de funcionamiento
performance standard: norma de funcionamiento
performance status: estado general
performer: *n.* ejecutante; actor; músico
perfume: *n.* perfume
perfume: *v.* perfumar; embalsamar
perfumery: *n.* perfumería
perfusion: *n.* perfusión
perhaps: *adv.* quizá; acaso; tal vez
periapt: 1. *n.* periapto; 2. *adj.* periapto
pericardial effusion: derrame pericárdico
pericardial fluid: líquido pericárdico
pericarditis: *n.* pericarditis
pericardium: *n.* pericardio; pericráneo
peridural: *adj.* peridural
perilous: *adj.* peligroso

perimeter: *n.* perímetro
period: *n.* período; regla; época
periodic: *adj.* periódico
periodic function: función periódica
periodic table: *n.* tabla periódica
periodical: 1. *adj.* periódico;
2. *n.* periódico
periodontal: *adj.* periodontal
periosteum: *n.* periostio
peripatetic: *adj.* peripatético
peripheral: *n.* equipo periférico
peripheral nervous system: sistema nervioso periférico
periphery: *n.* periferia
periphrasis: *n.* perífrasis
periphrastic: *adj.* perifrástico
periscope: *n.* periscopio
perish: *v.* perecer; sucumbir
peristalsis: *n.* peristalsis; peristaltismo
peristyle: *n.* peristilo
peritoneal fluid: líquido peritoneal
peritoneum: *n.* peritoneo
peritonitis: *n.* peritonitis
perjure: *v.* perjurar
perjurer: *n.* perjuro
perjury: *n.* perjurio
permafrost: permagelido
permafrost: *n.* permagélido
permanent: *adj.* permanente
permanent magnet: imán permanente
permeable: *adj.* permeable
permeate: *v.* atravesar
permission: *n.* permiso
permission sheet: hoja de autorización
permissive: *adj.* permisivo
permissiveness: *n.* permisividad
permit: *v.* permitir
permit: *n.* permiso
permit: *v.* permitir; consentir
permutation: *n.* permutación
pernicious: *adj.* pernicioso

peroration: *n.* peroración
peroxidase: *n.* peroxidasa
peroxidase test: prueba de la peroxidasa
peroxide: *n.* peróxido
perpendicular: *adj.* perpendicular
perpendicular lines: rectas perpendiculares
perpetrate: *v.* perpetrar; cometer
perpetration: *n.* perpetración
perpetrator: *n.* perpetrador
perpetual: *adj.* perpetuo
perpetuity: *n.* perpetuidad
perplex: *v.* dejar perplejo; confundir
perplexed: *adj.* perplejo
persecute: *v.* perseguir; acosar
persecution: *n.* persecución
persecutor: *n.* perseguidor
perservering: *adj.* perseverante
perseverance: *n.* perseverancia
persevere: *v.* perseverar; persistir
Persian: *n.* persa
persist: *v.* persistir; porfiar
persistence: 1. *n.* persistencia; 2. *adj.* persistente
person: *n.* persona
personage: *n.* personaje
personal: *adj.* personal
personal computer (PC): ordenador personal
personal effects: efectos personales
personal expenses: gastos personales
personal grooming: aseo personal
personal interview: entrevista personal
personalize: *v.* personalizar
personals: *n.* anuncios personales
personification: *n.* personificación
personify: *v.* personificar
personnel: *n.* personal
person-to-person: de persona a persona
perspective: *n.* perspectiva

perspicacious: *adj.* perspicaz; sutil
perspicacity: *n.* perspicacia
perspiration: *n.* sudor
perspire: *v.* transpirar; sudar
persuade: *v.* persuadir
persuasion: *n.* persuasión
persuasive: *adj.* persuasivo
persuasiveness: *n.* persuasiva
pert: *adj.* atrevido; insolente
pertness: *n.* frescura; impertinencia
perturb: *v.* perturbar
Peru: Perú
peruse: *v.* leer
Peruvian: *adj.* peruano; -a
pervade: *v.* penetrar; esparcirse por
perverse: 1. *n.* perverso; 2. *adj.* perverso
perversity: *n.* perversidad
pervert: *adj.* pervertido
pervert: *v.* pervertir
peseta: *n.* peseta
peso: *n.* peso
pessary: 1. *n.* pesario; 2. *adj.* pesario
pessimism: *n.* pesimismo
pessimist: *n.* pesimista
pessimistic: *adj.* pesimista
pest: *n.* peste; plaga
pester: *v.* molestar; importunar
pesticide: *n.* pesticida
pestilence: *n.* pestilencia
petal: *n.* pétalo
petard: *n.* petardo
petition: *n.* petición; solicitud
petition: *v.* suplicar; solicitar
petrified fossil: fósil petrificado
petrify: *v.* petrificar
petrochemical: *adj.* petroquímico
petrodollar: *n.* petrodólar
petrol: *n.* gasolina
petrolatum: *n.* petrolato
petroleum: *n.* petróleo
petrous: *adj.* petrosal; petroso
petticoat: 1. *adj.* de mujer; 2. *n.* enaguas; falda; mujer

petty: *adj.* pequeño; menor
petunia: *n.* petunia
pew: *n.* banco de iglesia
pH: pH
pH scale: escala pH
phaeton: *n.* faetón
phage: *n.* fago
phage typing: tipificación con fagos
phagocyte: *n.* fagocito
phalange: *n.* falange
phalanx: *n.* falange
phallus: *n.* falo
phantasm: *n.* fantasma
phantasmagoria: *n.* fantasmagoria
phantom: *n.* fantasma
pharmaceutical: 1. *adj.* farmacéutico;
2. *n.* producto fármaco
pharmaceutical form: forma farmacéutica
pharmacist: *n.* farmacéutico
pharmacokinetics: *n.* farmacocinética
pharmacologist: *n.* farmacólogo
pharmacology: *n.* farmacología
pharmacopeia: *n.* farmacopea
pharmacy: *n.* farmacia
pharyngitis: *n.* faringitis
pharynx: *n.* faringe
phase: *n.* fase
phasmid: *n.* fásmido
phenology: *n.* fenología
phenomenology: *n.* fenomenología
phenotype: *n.* fenotipo
phenylpyruvic acid: ácido fenilpirúvico
phenytoin: *n.* fenitoína
pheromone: *n.* feromona
phi: *n.* phi; fi
Philadelphia: Filadelfia
philanthropic: *adj.* filantrópico
philanthropist: *n.* filántropo
philanthropy: *n.* filantropía
philately: *n.* filatelia

philharmonic: *n.* orquesta filarmónica
Philippines: Filipinas
philodendron: *n.* filodendro
philologist: *n.* filólogo
philology: *n.* filología
philosopher: *n.* filósofo
philosophical: *adj.* filosófico
philosophy: *n.* filosofía
philter: *n.* filtro
phlebitis: *n.* flebitis
phlebotomy: *n.* flebotomía
phlegm: *n.* flema
phlegmatic: *adj.* flemático
phloem: *n.* floema
phlox: *n.* flox
Phoenician: 1. *adj.* fenicio; 2. *n.* fenicio
phone: *n.* teléfono
phone: *v.* telefonear
phonemics: *n.* fonética; fonémica
phonetic: *adj.* fonético
phonetics: *n.* fonética
phonics: *n.* fónica
phonogram: *n.* fonograma
phonograph: *n.* fonógrafo
phonography: *n.* fonografía
phonology: *n.* fonología
phosgene: *n.* fosgeno
phosphate: *n.* fosfato
phosphorescence: *n.* fosforescencia
phosphorescent: *adj.* fosforescente
phosphoric acid: ácido fosfórico
phosphorism: *n.* fosforismo
phosphorus: *n.* fósforo
photo: *n.* foto
photo finish: fototerminado
photocell: *n.* fotocélula
photochemical smog: neblina toxica fotoquímica
photochemistry: *n.* fotoquímica
photocomposition: *n.* fotocomposición
photoconductivity: *n.*

fotoconductibilidad
photocopier: *n.* fotocopiadora
photoelectric effect: efecto fotoeléctrico
photoelectron: *n.* fotoelectrón
photoemission: *n.* fotoemisión
photogenic: *adj.* fotogénico
photogrammetry: *n.* fotogrametría
photograph: *n.* fotografía
photographer: *n.* fotógrafo; -a
photography: *n.* fotografía
photokinesis: *n.* fotocinesis
photokinetic: *adj.* fotocinético
photomap: *n.* fotomapa
photometer: *n.* fotómetro; espectrómetro
photometry: *n.* espectrometría
photomontage: *n.* fotomontaje
photomultiplier: *n.* fotomultiplicador
photon: *n.* fotón
photoperiodism: *n.* fotoperiodicidad
photophobia: *n.* fotofobia
photopia: *n.* fotopía
photorealism: *n.* fotorealismo
photosphere: *n.* fotosfera
photosynthesis: *n.* fotosíntesis
phototelegraphy: *n.* foto telegrafía
phototherapy: *n.* fototerapia
phototonus: *n.* fototonía
phrasal verb: verbo con partícula
phrase: *n.* frase
phraseological: *adj.* fraseológico
phrasing: *n.* fraseo
phrenologist: *n.* frenólogo
phrenology: *n.* frenología
Phrygian: *n.* frigio
phylactery: *n.* filacteria
phylogenetic: *adj.* filogenético
phylogeny: *n.* filogenia
phylum: *n.* filum
physiatrics: *n.* fisiatría
physical: *adj.* físico
physical abuse: abuso físico

physical change: cambio físico
physical examination: examen
físico
physical property: propiedad física
physical therapy: fisioterapia
physician: *n.* médico
physics: *n.* física
physiognomy: *n.* fisonomía
physiography: *n.* fisiografía
physiological: *adj.* fisiológico
physiological variation: variación
fisiológica
physiologist: *n.* fisiólogo; -a
physiology: *n.* fisiología
physiopathology: *n.* fisiopatología
physiotherapist: *n.* fisioterapeuta
physiotherapy: *n.* fisioterapia
physique: 1. *adj.* físico; 2. *n.* físico;
presencia
phytogeography: *n.* fitogeografía
phytoplankton: *n.* fitoplancton
pi: *n.* pi
pianissimo: *adv.* pianísimo
pianist: *n.* pianista
piano: *n.* piano
pica: *n.* pica
picaresque: 1. *n.* picaresca; 2. *adj.*
picaresca
piccolo: *n.* piccolo
pichon: *n.* tanagra de tucán
pickax: *n.* piqueta
picket line: piquete
picnic: *n.* jira campestre; día de
campo; picnic
picnic: *v.* ir de merienda
picnicker: *n.* participante del picnic
pictogram: *n.* pictografía;
pictograma
pictograph: *n.* pictografía;
pictograma
pictography: *n.* pictografía
picture: *n.* pintura; cuadro
picture: *v.* dibujar; pintar
pie: *n.* empanada; pastel

piece: *n.* pieza
piece goods: géneros en piezas
pier: *n.* estribo; muelle; rompeolas
pierce: *v.* agujerear; taladrar
piercing: *adj.* penetrante; agudo
pietism: *n.* pietismo; piedad;
religiosidad
piety: *n.* piedad
piezoelectricity: *n.* piezoelectricidad
pig: *n.* cerdo; cochino
pigeon: *n.* paloma; pichón
piggy: *adj.* glotón
pigheaded: *adj.* cabezudo; terco
pigment: *n.* pigmento
pigtail: *n.* trenza; coleta
pilaster: *n.* pilastra
pilchard: *n.* aguja
pile: *n.* pila
pile: *v.* pilar; amontonar
pile driver: el vibrador hidráulico
pilfer: *v.* ratear; sisar
pilgrim: *n.* pegregino
pill: *n.* píldora; pastilla
pillage: *n.* pillaje; robo
pillage: *v.* saquear; robar
pillager: *n.* pillador
pillar: *n.* pilar; poste
pillow: *n.* almohada; cojín
pilon: *n.* columna
pilot: *n.* piloto
pilot: *v.* pilotar
piloting: *n.* pilotaje
pimento; pimiento: *n.* pimiento
pimpernel: *n.* pimpinela
pimple: *n.* grano; pupa
pin: *n.* alfiler; clavija
pin: *v.* prender; sujetar
pincer: *n.* pinza
pinch: *n.* pizca
pine: *n.* pino
pine kernels: piñones
pine nut: piñón
pineapple: *n.* piña
ping: *n.* silbido de bala; zumbido

ping-pong: ping-pong
pinion: *n.* piñón
pink: 1. *adj.* sonrosado; rosado 2. *n.* clavel
pinky: *adj.* rosado
pinochle: *n.* pinacle
pint: *n.* pinta
pinto: *n.* pinto
pioneer: *n.* explorador; promotor; pionero
pioneer: *v.* explorar
pioneer species: especies pioneras
pipe: *n.* chimenea; pipa; caña; conducto
pipe cutters: cortatubos
pipe vise: prensatubos
pipe wrench: Pipeta de tuerca
piperacillin: *n.* piperacilina
pipet: *n.* pipeta
pipette: *n.* pipeta
piping: *n.* cañería; tubería
piquant: *adj.* picante; áspero
pique: *v.* provocar; excitar
piracy: *n.* piratería
piranha: *n.* piraña
pirate: *n.* pirata
pirate: *v.* robar; plagiar
pirogue: *n.* piragua
pirouette: *n.* pirueta
pistachio: *n.* pistacho
pistil: *n.* pistilo
pistol: *n.* pistola; revólver
pistol: *v.* tirar con pistola
piston: *n.* pistón; émbolo
pit: *n.* hoyo; abismo; foso
pita: *n.* pita
pitch: *n.* pez; tono; tiro
pitch: *v.* lanzar
pitched: *adj.* inclinado
pitcher: *n.* cántaro; jarro
pitiless: *adj.* despiadado; inhumano
pituitary: *adj.* pituitaria
pituitary gland: glándula pituitaria
pity: *n.* piedad; lástima

pity: *v.* apiadarse de; compadecer
pivot: *n.* pivote; espiga
pizza: *n.* pizza
pizzeria: *n.* pizzería
pizzicato: *n.* pizzicato
pizzicato: *adv.* pizzicato
placard: *n.* cartel; edicto
place: *v.* colocar
place: *n.* sitio; local; distrito
place: *v.* poner; colocar
place: *n.* plaza
place value: valor posicional
placebo: *n.* placebo
placenta: *n.* placenta
placental mammal: mamífero placentario
placid: *adj.* plácido; sosegado
placidity: *n.* placidez
plagiarism: *n.* plagio
plagiarist: *n.* plagiario; -a
plague: *n.* plaga; peste;
plague: *v.* plagar; apestar; infectar
plain: 1. *adj.* claro; sincero; 2. *n.* llano; llanura
plaintiff: *n.* demandante
plait: *n.* trenza; pliegue
plait: *v.* trenzar; plegar
plan: *n.* plan; proyecto
plan: *v.* planear; proyectar
plan; system: plan o sistema
planar chromatography: cromatografía planar
plane: 1. *adj.* plano; 2. *n.* plano; avión
plane: *v.* allanar
plane mirror: espejo plano
planetarium: *n.* planetario
planetesimal: *adj.* planetesimal
planisphere: *n.* planisferio
plank: *n.* tablón
plankton: *n.* plankton
planned: *adj.* planificado; -a
planner: *n.* planificador (a)
planning: *n.* planificación

plant: *n.* planta; instalación;
plant: *v.* plantar; sembrar
plantain: *n.* plátano
plantation: *n.* plantación
plantation shutters: las persianas de plantación
planter: *n.* plantador (a)
plaque: *n.* placa
plasma: *n.* plasma
plasma cell: pasmosito
plasma kallikrein: calicreina plasmática
plasma level: concentración plasmática
plasmablast: *n.* plasmoblasto
plasmacyte: *n.* plasmocito
plasmid: *n.* plásmido
plasmin: *n.* fibrinolísina
plaster: *n.* emplasto; yeso
plaster: *v.* emplastar; enyesar
plasterboard: *n.* enyesado
plastic: 1. *adj.* plástico; 2. *n.* plástico
plastic surgery: cirugía plástica
plastron: *n.* plastrón
plate: *n.* plato; vajilla; cubierto
plate: *v.* poner placa
plate tectonics: tectónica de placas
plateau: *n.* meseta
platelet: *n.* plaqueta
platelet: *n.* trombocito; plaqueta
platform: *n.* plataforma
platinum: *n.* platino
platitude: *n.* trivialidad; vulgaridad
platonism: *n.* platonismo
platter: *n.* platón
play: *v.* desempeñar
player: *n.* actor; jugador
playroom: *n.* soda de juegos
plaza: *n.* plaza
plea: *n.* súplica; ruego; argumento
plead: *v.* alegar; defender en juicio
pleasant: 1. *adj.* agradable; 2. *n.* placentero
please: *v.* gustar; agradar

pleasure: *n.* placer; deleite
pleat: *n.* pliegue
pleat: *v.* plegar; arrugar
plebiscite: *n.* plebiscito
plectrum: *n.* plectro
pledge: *n.* promesa; voto
pledge: *v.* prometer; brindar por
plenary: *adj.* plenario
plenitude: *n.* plenitud
plentiful: *adj.* abundante
plenty: *n.* profusión
plenum: *n.* pleno
pleomorphic: *adj.* pleomórfico
pleonasm: *n.* pleonasmo
plethora: *n.* plétora
pleura: *n.* pleura
pleural aspiration: punción pleural
pleural effusion: derrame pleural
pleural fluid: líquido pleural
pleurisy: *n.* pleuresía
pliable: *adj.* flexible
pliers: *n.* alicates; pinzas
plot: *n.* complot
plough: *n.* arado
plough: *v.* arar; surcar
pluck: *n.* ánimo; valor; coraje
pluck: *v.* dar un tirón; pelar
plucking: *n.* arranque glaciar
plug: *n.* taco; boca de agua
plug: *v.* tapar
plug in: *v.* enchufar
plum: *n.* ciruela
plumb: 1. *adj.* vertical; 2. *n.* plomada; plomo
plumb: *v.* aplomar
plumb bob: plomada
plumb line: el lino de la plomada
plumbeous: *adj.* plomizo
plumber: *n.* plomero; fontanero
plumber's tape: la cinta aislante
plumbing: fontanería; cañería; plomería
plumed: *adj.* con plumas
plummet: *n.* plomada

plunder: *n.* robo; botín
plunder: *v.* saquear; pillar
plunge: *n.* zambullida
plunge: *v.* zambullirse
pluperfect: *adj.* pluscuamperfecto
plural: 1. *adj.* plural; 2. *n.* plural
pluralism: *n.* pluralismo
plurality: *n.* pluralidad
plus: *prep.* más
plutocracy: *n.* plutocracia
pluvial: 1. *adj.* pluvial; 2. *n.* pluvial
pneumatic: 1. *adj.* neumático; 2. *n.* neumática
pneumoconiosis: *n.* neumoconiosis
pneumonectomy: *n.* neumonectomía
pneumonia: *n.* neumonía
pneumothorax: *n.* neumotórax
poached: *adj.* escalfado
poacher: *n.* cazador o pescador furtivo
poaching: *n.* caza ilegal
pocket: *n.* bolsillo; saco
pocket: *v.* embolsar
podiatrist: *n.* podólogo; -a
podiatry: *n.* podiatría
podium: *n.* podio
poem: *n.* poema
poet: *n.* poeta
poet laureate: poeta laureado; -a
poetaster: *n.* poetastro; -a
poetess: *n.* poetisa
poetic: 1. *adj.* poético; 2. *n.* poética
poetry: *n.* poesía
pogrom: *n.* pogromo
poignant: *adj.* picante
poinciana: *n.* poinciana
point: n punto; punta
point: *v.* aguzar
point mutation: mutación puntual
point of order: cuestión de orden
point of view: punto de vista
point source: fuente localizada
pointed: *adj.* agudo; puntiagudo
pointer: *n.* puntero

pointillism: *n.* puntillismo
points: *n.* puntas de pie
poise: *n.* equilibrio; serenidad
poise: *v.* equilibrar
poison: *n.* veneno
poison: *v.* envenenar; corromper
poisoning: *n.* intoxicación
poisonous: *adj.* venenoso
poke: *n.* empuje; codazo
poke: *v.* atizar
poker: *n.* póquer
polar: *adj.* polar
polar bond: enlace polar
polar zone: zona polar
polarization: *n.* polarización
polarized light: luz polarizada
polarizing microscope: microscopio de polarización
polarography: *n.* polarografía
pole: *n.* poste; asta; polo
polemic: *n.* polémica
polemicist: *n.* polemista
police: *n.* policía
policeman: *n.* policía
policewoman: *n.* policía
policy: *n.* póliza; normativa; política
policy number: número de póliza
polio: *n.* polio
polio; poliomyelitis: *n.* poliomielitis
poliomyelitis: *n.* poliomielitis
Polish: *n.* polaco
polish: *n.* pulimento; cultura
polish: *v.* pulir
polished: *adj.* fin; refinado; galante; culto
politburo: *n.* politburó
polite: *adj.* culto; cortés
political: *adj.* político
political science: ciencias políticas
politics: *n.* política
polka: *n.* polca
poll: *n.* votación; encuesta
poll: *v.* empadronar; obtener
pollen: *n.* polen

pollination: *n.* polinización
pollinator: *n.* polinizador
pollinosis: *n.* polinosis
pollutant: *n.* contaminante
pollute: *v.* corromper
pollution: *n.* contaminación; polución
polo: *n.* polo
polonaise: *n.* polonesa
poloroid camera: *n.* cámara polaroid
poltergeist: *n.* poltergeista
polyandry: *n.* poliandria
polyatomic ion: ion poliatomico
polychromatic: *adj.* policromado
polychrome: 1. *n.* policromo; 2. *adj.* policromo
polychromy: *n.* policromía
polyclinic: *n.* policlínica
polydipsia: *n.* polidipsia
polyester: *n.* poliéster
polygamous: *adj.* polígamo
polygamy: *n.* poligamia
polygon: *n.* polígono
polygraph: *n.* polígrafo
polygyny: *n.* poliginia
polyhedron: *n.* poliedro
polylinker: *n.* poliligador
polymer: *n.* polímero
polymerism: *n.* polimerismo
polymorphism: *n.* polimorfismo
polynomial: *n.* polinomio
polyp: 1. *n.* pólipo; 2. *adj.* pólipo
polyphagia: *n.* polifagia
polyphonic: *adj.* polifónico
polyphony: *n.* polifonía
polysemy: *n.* polisemia
polytheism: *n.* politeísmo
polytonality: *n.* politonalidad
polyunsaturated: *adj.* poliinsaturado
polyuria: *n.* poliuria
polyvinyl alcohol: alcohol polivinilito
pomade: *n.* pomada
pomegranate: *n.* granada

pommel: *n.* golpear
pommel: *v.* cascar
pomology: *n.* pomología
pompano: *n.* pámpano
pomposity: *n.* pomposidad
pompous: *adj.* pomposo
poncho: *n.* poncho
pond: *n.* estanque; pantano
ponder: *v.* ponderar; meditar
poniard: *n.* pupal
poniard: *v.* apufialar
pontiff: *n.* pontífice
pontificate: *v.* pontificar
pontoon: *n.* pontón
pony: *n.* jaca; caballito
poodle: *n.* perro de lanas
pool: *n.* charco; mezcla; balsa
pool: *v.* mancomunar
pool: *n.* pool
pooled income: ingreso combinado
poop deck: castilla de popa
poor: *adj.* pobre; necesitado
pop art: arte popular
pope: *n.* papa
popedom: *n.* papado
poplar: *n.* álamo; chopo
poplin: *n.* popelina
poppy: *n.* amapola
poppyseed: *n.* semilla de amapola
popular: *adj.* popular
popularity: *n.* popularidad
populate: *v.* poblar
populated: *adj.* poblado
population: *n.* población
population density: densidad de populación
population outbreak: explosión demográfica
populism: *n.* populismo
porcelain: *n.* porcelana
porch: *n.* porche
porcupine: *n.* puercoespin
pore: *n.* poro
pore: *v.* reflexionar

pork: *n.* carne de cerdo
pork: *n.* puerco
pork fat: tocino
porn: *n.* porno
porno: *n.* porno
porous: *adj.* poroso
porphyria: *n.* porfiria
port: *n.* oporto; puerto
portable: *adj.* portátil
portal: *n.* portal
portcullis: *n.* rastrillo
portend: *v.* presagiar
portent: *n.* prestigio
portentous: *adj.* portentoso; extraordinario
porter: *n.* portero; conserje
portfolio: *n.* portafolio
porthole: *n.* portilla
portico: *n.* pórtico
portion: *n.* porción
portly: *adj.* corpulento
portrait: *n.* retrato
pose: *n.* pose; postura
pose: *v.* colocar en cierta postura
position: *v.* situar
position: *n.* posición
positional cloning: clonación posicional
positive: 1. *adj.* positivo; 2. *n.* positivo
positive integers: números enteros positivos
positivism: *n.* positivismo
positivist: *n.* positivista
possess: *v.* poseer; reunir
possession: *n.* posesión
possessive: *adj.* posesivo
possible: *adj.* posible; permitido
post: *n.* poste; puesto
postage: *n.* franqueo
postage free: libre de franqueo
postal: *n.* postal
postcard: *n.* postal
poster: *n.* cartel; letrero

poster: *n.* póster
posterior: 1. *adj.* posterior; 2. *n.* nalgas; trasero
postgraduate: 1. *adj.* post-graduado; 2. *n.* post-graduado
posthumous: *adj.* póstumo
postimpressionism: *n.* postimpresionismo
postimpressionist: *n.* postimpresionista
postmeridian: *adj.* postmeridiano
postnatal: *adj.* postnatal
postoperative: *adj.* postoperatorio
postpartum: *adv.* de posparto
postpone: *n.* posponer
postpone: *v.* posponer; aplazar
postscript: *n.* posdata
postulate: 1. *n.* postulado; 2. *adj.* postulado
posture: *n.* postura
pot: *n.* pote; puchero
potable: *adj.* potable
potage: *n.* potaje
potash: *n.* potasa
potassium: *n.* potasio
potato: *n.* patata
potato peeler: cosa para pelar patatas
potato starch: fécula
potency: *n.* potencia
potent: *adj.* potente
potentate: *adj.* potentado
potential: 1. *n.* potencial; 2. *adj.* potencial
potential difference: diferencia de potencial
potential energy: energía potencial
potentiometer: *n.* potenciómetro
potentiometry: *n.* potenciometría
pothole: *n.* bache; hoyo
potion: *n.* poción
potpourri: *n.* popurrí
pouch: *n.* bolsa; cartuchera
poultry: *n.* aves

pounce: *n.* arenilla
pounce: *v.* espolvorear con grasilla o arenilla
pound: *v.* golpear
pound: *n.* libra (peso); libra esterlina
poundage: *n.* impuesto
pour: *v.* verter; echar; derramar
poverty: *n.* pobreza
powder: *n.* polvo
powder: *v.* pulverizar empolvar
powder-blue: azul pálido
power: *n.* potencia; poder; energía
power: *v.* accionar
power failure: fallo en la alimentación de corriente
power of attorney: poder notarial
power off: apagado
power on: encendido
powerless: *adj.* impotente
practicability: *n.* practicabilidad
practical: *adj.* práctico
practice: *n.* práctica
practice: *v.* practicar
practitioner: *n.* profesional; médico o abogado
pragmatics: *n.* pragmática
pragmatism: *n.* pragmatismo
pragmatist: *n.* pragmatista
prairie: *n.* pradera
praise: *n.* alabanza
praise: *v.* alabar
praline: *n.* praline
pram: *n.* cochecito de niño
prattle: *n.* charla
prattle: *v.* charlar
pray: *v.* rogar; rezar
prayer: *n.* oración
preach: *v.* predicar; sermonear
preadolescence: *n.* preadolescencia
prealbumin: *n.* transtiretina
preamble: *n.* preámbulo
prebend: *n.* prebenda
precaution: *n.* precaución
precede: *v.* preceder

precedent: *n.* precedente; decisión judicial
precept: *n.* precepto
precinct: *n.* recinto
precious: *adj.* precioso; querido
precipice: *n.* precipicio
precipitate: *v.* precipitar
precipitation: *n.* precipitación
precipitin: *n.* precipitina
precipitin line: línea de precipitación
precise: *adj.* preciso
precision: *n.* precisión
preclude: *v.* excluir
precocious: *adj.* precoz
precociousness: *n.* precocidad
precognition: *n.* precognición
pre-columbian: pre-colombino
preconception: *n.* preconcepción
precursor: *n.* precursor (a)
predation: *n.* depredación
predator: *n.* depredador
predecessor: *n.* predecesor (a)
predestination: *n.* predestinación
predestined: *adj.* predestinado
predetermined: *adj.* predeterminado
predicate: 1. *n.* predicado; 2. *adj.* predicado
predication: *n.* predicación
predict: *v.* predecir
predicting: predecir
prediction: *n.* predicción
predilection: *n.* predilección
predisposition: *n.* predisposición
predominant: 1. *adj.* predominante; 2. *n.* predominante
predominate: *v.* predominar
predrill: *v.* pretaladrar
prefabrication: *n.* prefabricación
preface: *n.* prefacio
prefecture: *n.* prefectura
prefer: *v.* preferir; promover
preference: *n.* preferencia
preferential: *adj.* preferencial; preferente

preferment: *n.* ascenso; promoción
preferred: *adj.* preferente
prefix: *n.* prefijo
pregnancy: *n.* embarazo
pregnancy test: prueba para el embarazo
pregnant: *adj.* embarazada; encinta
prehistoric: 1. *adj.* prehistórico; 2. *n.* prehistórico
preimage: *n.* preimagen
prejudice: *n.* prejuicio; preocupación;
prejudice: *v.* prevenir
prejudicial: *adj.* prejudicial
prelacy: *n.* prelacia
prelate: *n.* prelado
preliminary: *adj.* preliminar
prelims: *n.* preliminares
prelude: *n.* preludio
prelude: *v.* preludiar
premature: *adj.* prematuro
premedication: *n.* medicación previa
premeditated: *adj.* premeditado
premier: 1. *adj.* primero; principal; 2. *n.* jefe del estado
premise: *n.* premisa
premium: *n.* primo
premolar: *n.* premolar
premonition: *n.* premonición
prentice: *n.* aprendiz
prenuptial: *adj.* prenupcial
preoccupation: *n.* preocupación
preordination: *n.* preordinación
prep: *v.* preparar
preparation: *n.* preparación; preparado
preparatory: *adj.* preparatorio
prepare: *v.* preparar; prevenir
preponderance: *n.* preponderancia
preponderant: *adj.* preponderante
preposition: *n.* preposición
prepositional: *adj.* preposicional
prepossess: *v.* predisponer
prepossessing: *adj.* simpático; agradable
preposterous: *adj.* absurdo
prepubescence: *n.* prepubescencia
prepuce: *n.* prepucio
Pre-Raphaelite: prerrafaelita
prerequisite: 1. *adj.* previamente necesario; 2. *n.* requisito previo
prerogative: 1. *adj.* privilegiado; 2. *n.* prerrogativa
presage: *n.* presagio
presage: *v.* presagiar
presbycusis: *n.* presbicusis
presbyopia: *n.* presbiopía
presbyter: *n.* presbítero; sacerdote
presbyterian: *n.* presbiteriano
preschool: *n.* preescolar
prescience: *n.* presciencia
prescind: *v.* prescindir; prescribe
prescribe: *v.* recetar
prescription: *n.* receta; prescripción
presence: *n.* presencia
present: 1. *n.* presente; regalo; 2. *adj.* presente
present: *v.* presentar
present participle: participio presente
presentable: *adj.* presentable
presentation: *n.* presentación
present-day: de hoy día
presentiment: *n.* presentimiento
preservation: *n.* preservación
preservation medium: medio conservante
preservative: *n.* conservante
preserve: *n.* conserva; confitura
preserve: *v.* conservar; preservar
preside: *v.* presidir; gobernar
presidency: *n.* presidencia
president: *n.* presidente
president-elect: presidente electo
press: *v.* oprimir; apretar
press: *n.* prensa
press conference: conferencia de prensa

pressed wood: la madera prensada
pressing: *adj.* apremiante
pressure: *n.* presión
pressure cooker: olla a presión
pressure flow: flujo por presión
pressure group: grupo de presión
pressure-wash: *v.* lavar a presión
pressurized: *adj.* presurizado
prestidigitation: *n.* prestidigitación
prestige: *n.* prestigio
prestigious: *adj.* prestigioso
presto: *adj.* presto
presume: *v.* presumir
presumption: *n.* presunción
presupposition: *n.* presuposición
pretence: *n.* pretensión
pretend: *v.* aparentar
pretender: *n.* pretendiente
pretension: *n.* pretensión
pretentious: 1. *n.* pretencioso; 2. *adj.* pretencioso
preterit: 1. *adj.* pretérito; 2. *n.* pretérito
pretext: *n.* pretexto
pretorian: *n.* pretoriano
pretty: *adj.* bonito; bello
pretzel: *n.* galleta salada
prevail: *v.* estar en boga o de moda
prevalence: *n.* prevalencia
prevaricate: *v.* engañar
prevaricator: *n.* prevaricador
prevent: *v.* impedir; evitar
prevention: *n.* prevención
preview: *n.* inspección; previa; avance
preview: *v.* ver o inspeccionar de antemano
previous: *adj.* previo
previous illnesses: enfermedades anteriores
prevision: *n.* previsión
prey: *n.* presa; botín
prey: *v.* cazar
price: *n.* precio; valor

price: *v.* apreciar; valorar
price-fixing: fijación de precios
priceless: *adj.* inapreciable
prickle: *n.* pincho
prickle: *v.* sentir una punzada; sentir picazón
pride: *n.* orgullo; soberbia
pride: *v.* enorgullecer
priest: *n.* sacerdote; cura
priggish: *adj.* pedante
prim: *adj.* estirado
primary: *adj.* primario; primordial
primary colors: colores primarios
primary sample: muestra primaria
primary standard: patrón primario
primary succession: sucesión primaria
primate: 1. *adj.* primado; 2. *n.* primado
prime: *adj.* primero; básico primario; primo
prime factorization: descomposición en factores primos
prime meridian: primer meridiano
prime minister: primer ministro
prime number: el número primo
prime plasmid: plásmido primero
primer: *n.* cebador
primer extension: prolongación del cebador
primeval: *adj.* primitivo; original
primidone: *n.* primidona
primitive: *adj.* primitivo
primitive triangle: el triángulo primitivo
primogeniture: *n.* primogenitura
primosome: *n.* primosoma
prince: *n.* príncipe
princedom: *n.* principado
princess: *n.* princesa
principal: 1. *adj.* principal; 2. *n.* capital
principal parts: partes principales
principality: *n.* principado

principle: *n*. principio; causa
print: *v*. imprimir
printed: *adj*. impreso
printed matter: impresos
printer: el impresor; la impresora
printer: *n*. impresora; impresor
printer driver: intérprete de
impresora
printing: *n*. impresión; edición;
imprenta
printing press: prensa; imprenta
prion: *n*. prión
prior: 1. *adj*. prior; 2. *n*. prior
prioress: *n*. priora
priority: *n*. prioridad
priory: 1. *adj*. priorato; 2. *n*. priorato
prism: *n*. prisma
prison: *n*. prisión
prison camp: campo de prisioneros
prisoner: *n*. preso
privacy: *n*. privacidad
privacy act: ley de confidencialidad
private: *adj*. privado; particular
private insurance: seguro privado
private insurer: asegurador privado
privatization: *n*. privatización
privilege: *n*. privilegio
privy: *n*. excusado; retrete
prize: 1. *adj*. premiado; 2. *n*. premio
prize: *v*. apreciar
pro: *n*. profesional
pro forma: pro forma
pro rata: prorrata
proangiotensin: *n*. proangiotensina
probability: *n*. probabilidad
probability of an event:
probabilidad de un suceso
probable: *adj*. probable
probation: *n*. prueba; ensayo
probative: *adj*. probatorio
probe: *n*. sonda; exploración
probe: *v*. sondar; sondear
probit: *n*. probit
problem: *n*. problema

procaine: *n*. procaína
procedure: *n*. procedimiento
proceed: *v*. proceder; avanzar
proceeding: *n*. procedimiento
process: *n*. proceso
process: *v*. tramitar
processing: *n*. procesamiento
procession: *n*. procesión
processor: *n*. procesador
proclaim: *v*. proclamar
proclamation: *n*. proclamación
proclitic: 1. *n*. proclítico; 2. *adj*.
proclítico
procrastinate: *v*. diferir
procreate: *v*. procrear
proctologist: *n*. proctólogo
proctology: *n*. proctología
proctoscopy: *n*. proctoscopia
procure: *v*. lograr; obtener
prod: *n*. empuje
prod: *v*. pinchar
prodigal: 1. *adj*. pródigo; 2. *n*.
pródigo
prodigious: *adj*. prodigioso
prodigy: *n*. prodigio
prodrug: *n*. profármaco
produce: *n*. producto
produce: *v*. producir
producer: *n*. productor
product: *n*. producto
production: *n*. producción
productivity: *n*. productividad
prof: *n*. profesor
profanation: *n*. profanación
profane: 1. *adj*. profano; 2. *n*.
profano
profane: *v*. profanar
profanity: *n*. profanidad
profess: *v*. profesar
profession: *n*. profesión
professional: 1. *adj*. profesional; 2.
n. profesional
professor: *n*. profesor
professor emeritus: *n*. profesora

emérita
professorship: *n.* profesorado
proffer: *n.* oferta; propuesta
proffer: *v.* ofrecer
proficiency: *n.* pericia; destreza
proficiency testing: ensayo de
aptitud
proficient: 1. *adj.* perito; experto 2.
n. perito
profile: *n.* perfil; contorno
profile: *v.* perfilar
profit: *n.* provecho; beneficio
profit: *v.* servir; aprovechar
profitable: *adj.* provechoso
profiteer: *n.* usurero
profound: *adj.* profundo
profuse: 1. *adj.* profuso; 2.*n.* profuso
progenitor: *n.* progenitor
progeny: *n.* progenie; prole; linaje
progesterone: *n.* progesterona
prognosis: *n.* pronóstico
prognostication: *n.* pronóstico
program: *v.* programer
program: *n.* programa
programmed: *adj.* programado
programmer: *n.* programador
programming: *n.* programación
progranulocyte: *n.* progranulocito
progress: *n.* progreso
progression: *n.* progresión
progressive: 1. *adj.* progresivo;
2. *n.* progresista
progressive illness: enfermedad
progresiva
prohibit: *v.* prohibir; privar
prohibition: *n.* prohibición
prohibitive: *adj.* prohibitivo
project: *n.* proyecto; plan
project: *v.* proyectar; arrojar
project manager: el gerente del
trabajo
projectile: *n.* proyectil
projection: *n.* proyección
projectionist: *n.* proyeccionista

projective: *adj.* proyectivo
projector: *n.* proyector
prokaryote: *n.* procariote
prolactin: *n.* prolactina
prolapse: *n.* prolapso
proletarian: *n.* proletario
proletariat: *n.* proletariado
proliferate: *v.* multiplicar; proliferar
proliferation: *n.* proliferación
prolific: *adj.* prolífico
proline: *n.* prolina
prolix: *adj.* difuso; prolijo
prologue: *n.* prólogo
prolong: *v.* prolongar
prolonged: *adj.* prolongado
promenade: *n.* paseo; vuelta
prominence: *n.* protuberancia solar
prominent: *adj.* prominente
promiscuous: *adj.* promiscuo
promise: *n.* promesa
promise: *v.* prometer
promising: *adj.* prometedor
promissory: *n.* promisorio
promissory note: pagaré; vale
promonotory: *n.* promonotorio
promote: *v.* promover
promoter: *n.* promotor (a)
promotion: *n.* promoción
prompt: *adj.* pronto; puntual
prompt: *v.* incitar; mover
pronase: *n.* micolisina
prone: *adj.* prono; inclinado
proneness: *n.* postración; disposición
prong: *n.* púa; punta; gajo
pronominal: *adj.* pronominal
pronormoblast: *n.* pronormoblasto
pronoun: *n.* pronombre
pronounce: *v.* pronunciar
pronouncing: *n.* de pronunciación
pronunciation: *n.* pronunciación
proof: *n.* demostración; prueba
proof-reading: corrección de
pruebas de imprenta
propaganda: *n.* propaganda

propagandist: *n.* propagandista
propagate: *v.* propagar
propane: *n.* propano
propel: *v.* propulsar
propellant: *adj.* propelente
propensity: *n.* propención
proper: *adj.* propio
proper fraction: fracción propia
properness: *n.* propiedad
property: *n.* propiedad
property tax: impuesto de propiedad
property valuation: tasación de la propiedad
prophage: *n.* profago
prophecy: *n.* profecía
prophecy: *v.* profetizar
prophet: *n.* profeta; profetisa
prophylaxis: *n.* profilaxis
propitiation: *n.* propiciación
proplasmacyte: *n.* proplasmocito
proportion: *n.* proporción
proportionality: *n.* proporcionalidad
proportionate: *adj.* proporcionado
proposal: *n.* propuesta; oferta
propose: *v.* proponer
proposition: *n.* proposición
propound: *v.* proponer
propranolol: *n.* propranolol
proprietary: *n.* propietario; corrección
propulsion: *n.* propulsión
prorate: *v.* prorratear; dividir
prosaic: *adj.* prosaico
proscenium: *n.* proscenio
proscribe: *v.* proscribir
proscription: *n.* proscripción
prose: *n.* prosa
prosecute: *v.* procesar
prosecutor: *n.* fiscal
prosody: *n.* prosodia
prospect: *n.* perspectiva
prospect: *v.* explotar
prospecting: *n.* sondeo
prospectus: *n.* prospecto

prosper: *v.* prosperar
prostaglandin: *n.* prostaglandina
prostate: *n.* próstata
prostate cancer: cáncer de la próstata
prostate examination: examen de la próstata
prostatic fluid: líquido prostático
prostatism: *n.* prostatismo
prostatitis: *n.* prostatitis
prosthesis: *n.* prótesis
prosthetic group: grupo prostético
prosthetics: *n.* protética
prostitute: *n.* prostituta
prostitute: *v.* vender; prostituir
prostitution: *n.* prostitución
prostrate: *v.* postrar
prostration: *n.* postración
protagonist: *n.* protagonista
protease: *n.* proteasa
protect: *v.* proteger
protection: *n.* protección
protectionism: *n.* proteccionismo
protectionist: *n.* proteccionista
protective tariff: tarifa proteccionista
protector: *n.* protector
protectorate: *n.* protectorado
protegee: *n.* protegido
protein: *n.* proteína
protein binding: unión a proteínas
protest: *n.* protesta
protest: *v.* protestar
protestant: 1. *adj.* protestante; 2. *n.* protestante
Protestantism: *n.* protestantismo
protestation: *n.* protestación
prothrombin: *n.* protrombina
protirelin: *n.* protirelina
protist: *n.* protista
protocol: *n.* protocolo
proton: *n.* protón
protoplasm: *n.* protoplasma
protoporphyrin: *n.* protoporfirina

prototroph: *n.* prototrofo
prototype: *n.* prototipo
protozoan: *n.* protozoario
proud: *adj.* orgulloso
prove: *v.* demostrar; probar
provencal: *adj.* provenzal
provence: *n.* provenza
proverb: *n.* proverbio
provide: *v.* proveer; proporcionar; suministrar
provide services: proveer servicios
provided: a condición de que
providence: *n.* providencia
provider: *n.* proveedor
provider of services: proveedor de servicios
province: *n.* provincia
provincial: *adj.* provincial
provincialism: *n.* provincialismo
provision: *n.* provisión
provision: *v.* aprovisionar; abastecer
provision of law: estipulación legal; disposición legal
provisional: *adj.* provisional
provisions: *n.* provisiones
provocateur: *n.* agente provocador
provocation: *n.* provocación
provocative: *adj.* provocador
provoke: *v.* provocar; indignar
provoked: *adj.* provocado
prow: *n.* proa
prow: *v.* rondar
proximity: *n.* proximidad
proxy: *n.* poder; apoderado; delegado
prozone effect: efecto prozona
prudence: *n.* prudencia
prudent: *adj.* sensato; prudente
prune: *n.* ciruela pasa
prune: *v.* mondar; podar
pruners: el cortador de ramas
pry: *v.* levantar con palanca
pry bar: la pata de cabra
psalm: *n.* salmo

psalmist: *n.* salmista
psalmody: *n.* salmodia
psaltery: *n.* salterio
pseudocast: *n.* seudocilindro
pseudonym: *n.* pseudónimo
pseudopod: *n.* pseudópodo
pseudoscience: *n.* pseudociencia
psi: *n.* psi
psoriasis: *n.* psoriasis
psychiatric problems: problemas psiquiátricos
psychiatrist: *n.* especialista en problemas emocionales
psychiatrist: *n.* psiquiatra
psychiatry: *n.* psiquiatría
psychobiology: *n.* psicobiología
psychogenic: *adj.* psicógeno
psychokinesis: *n.* psicocinesis.
psycholinguistics: *n.* psicolingüística
psychological: *adj.* psicológico
psychologist: *n.* especialista en problemas emocionales
psychology: *n.* psicología
psychometrics: *n.* psicometría
psychopharmacology: *n.* psicofármaco logia
psychosis: *n.* psicosis
psychosomatic: *adj.* psicosomático
psychosurgery: *n.* psicocirugía
psychotic: *adj.* psicótico
psychrometer: *n.* psicrómetro
pteridophyte: *n.* pteridofita
ptomaine: *n.* tomaína
ptosis: *n.* ptosis
ptyalin: *n.* tialina
pub: *n.* taberna
puberty: *n.* pubertad
pubescence: *n.* pubescencia
pubic: *adj.* púbico
pubic hair: pelo púbico
pubis: *n.* pubis
public: *adj.* público
public defender: defensora de oficio
public health: salud pública

public office: cargo público
public opinion: opinión publica
public record: registro civil
publication: *n.* publicación
publicist: *n.* publicista
publicity: *n.* publicidad
publisher: *n.* editor
puck: *n.* puck
pucker: *n.* arruga
pucker: *v.* plegar mal
pudding: *n.* pudín; budín
pudenda: *n.* partes pudendas
puerile: *adj.* pueril
puerilism: *n.* puerilismo
puerperal: *adj.* puerperal
puff: *n.* abultamiento
puff pastry: hojaldre
puffy: *adj.* hinchado
pugilism: *n.* pugilato
pugilist: *n.* pugilista
pugnacity: *n.* pugnacidad
pulitzer prize: premio pulitzer
pull: *n.* tirón; estirón; tirador
pull: *v.* tirar; coger; abatir
pull wire: jalar alambre
pulley: *n.* polea
pullman: *n.* coche-cama
pulmonary: *adj.* pulmonar
pulmonary tuberculosis:
tuberculosis pulmonar
pulmonologist: *n.* especialista en los
pulmones
pulp: *n.* pulpa
pulpit: *n.* púlpito
pulsar: *n.* pulsar
pulsate: *v.* pulsar
pulsation: *n.* pulsación
pulse: *n.* pulso; latido
pulverize: *v.* pulverizar
pulverizer: *n.* pulverizador
puma: *n.* puma
pump: *v.* bombear; impeler
pump: *n.* bomba
pumpernickel: *n.* pumpernickel

pumpkin: *n.* calabaza; zapallo
pun: *n.* equívoco
punch: *n.* ponche; punzón
punchbowl: *n.* ponchera
punctilious: *adj.* puntilloso
punctual: *adj.* puntual
punctuated equilibria: equilibrio
puntuado
punctuation: *n.* puntuación
puncture: *n.* punción; pinchazo
puncture: *v.* pinchar
pungent: *adj.* pungente
punish: *v.* castigar
punishable: *adj.* castigable
punitive: *adj.* punitivo
pupa: *n.* pupa
pupil: *n.* pupila; alumno
puppet: *n.* títere; muñeco
puppy: *n.* cachorro
purchase: *n.* compra; adquisición;
purchase: *v.* comprar; adquirir
pure: *adj.* puro; limpio
purgative: *adj.* purgante; purgativo
purgatory: *n.* purgatorio
purge: *n.* purga
purge: *v.* purgar
purification: *n.* purificación
purifier: *n.* purificador; depurador
purify: *v.* purificar
Purim: *n.* purim
purism: *n.* purismo
purist: *n.* purista
puritan: *n.* puritano
Puritanism: *n.* puritanismo
purity: *n.* pureza
purple: 1. *n.* purpúreo; púrpura;
2. *adj.* purpúreo
purport: *n.* significado; idea
principal
purport: *v.* significar
purpose: *n.* intención; objeto; fin
purpura: *n.* púrpura
purse: *n.* bolsa
pursue: *v.* perseguir; continuar

pursuer: *n.* seguidor
pursuit: *n.* seguimiento
purulence: *n.* purulencia
purulent: *adj.* purulento
purvey: *v.* proveer; abastecer
pus: *n.* pus
push: *n.* empujón; embestida
push: *v.* empujar
pushing: *adj.* emprendedor; activo
pusillanimity: *n.* pusilanimidad
pustulation: *n.* pustulación
pustule: *n.* pústula
put: *adj.* puesto
put: *v.* poner; proponer; imponer
put in: *v.* meter
putative: *adj.* putativo
putative marriage: matrimonio supuesto
putrid: *adj.* pútrido; putrefacto
putter: *n.* putter
putty: *v.* enmasillar
putty knife: la espátula
puzzle: *n.* enigma; acertijo;
puzzle: *v.* confundir; desconcertar
pyelogram: *n.* pielograma
pyelography: *n.* pielografía
pylon: *n.* pilón
pyocin: *n.* piocina
pyocin typing: piocinotipia
pyogenic: *adj.* piógeno
pyramid: *n.* pirámide
pyre: *n.* pira
pyrethrum: *n.* piretrina
pyroclastic flow: flujo piroclastico
pyromancy: *n.* piromancia
pyrotechnics: *n.* pirotenia
pyruvic acid: ácido pirúvico; piruvato
python: *n.* pitón
pyx: *n.* píxide

Q

quadrangle: *n.* cuadrángulo
quadrangular: *adj.* cuadrangular
quadrant: *n.* cuadrante
quadraphonic: *adj.* cuadrifónico
quadrate: *n.* cuadrado
quadratic: *adj.* cuadrático
quadratic formula: fórmula cuadrática
quadrennial: *adj.* cuadrienal
quadrennium: *n.* cuadrienio
quadriceps: *n.* cuadriceps
quadrilateral: *adj.* cuadrilátero
quadrille: *n.* cuadrilla
quadriplegia: *n.* cuadriplejía
quadriplegic: *adj.* cuadripléjico
quadruple: *n.* cuádruplo
quadruplet: *n.* cuádruplo; cuatrillizo
quadruplicate: *adj.* cuadruplicado
quaker: *n.* cuáquero
quakerism: *n.* cuaquerismo
qualification: *n.* calificación
qualified: *adj.* calificado
qualified person: persona cualificada
qualifier: *n.* calificativo
qualifying: *adj.* calificativo
qualitative: *adj.* cualitativo
qualitative analysis: análisis cualitativo
qualitative observation: observación cualitativa
qualitology: *n.* cualitología
qualitometrics: *n.* cualitometría
quality: *n.* calidad
quality assessment: evaluación de la calidad
quality assurance: garantía de la calidad

quality audit: auditoria de la calidad
quality control: control de la calidad
quality management: gestión de la calidad
quality policy: política de calidad
quantification: *n.* cuantificación
quantifier: *n.* cuantificador
quantitative: *adj.* cuantitativo
quantitative analysis: análisis cuantitativo
quantitative observation: observación cuantitativa
quantity: *n.* cantidad; magnitud
quantum (physics): 1. *adj.* cuántico; 2. *n.* cuántico
quarantine: *n.* cuarentena
quart: *n.* cuartilla
quarter: *n.* cuartel
quarter hour: cuarto de hora
quarterfinal: *n.* cuarto de final
quarterfinalist: *n.* cuartofinalista
quarters of coverage: trimestres de protección; créditos
quartet; quartette: *n.* cuarteto
quartile: *n.* cuartil
quartz: *n.* cuarzo
quartzite: *n.* cuarcita
quasar: *n.* quásar
quasi contract: cuasicontrato
Quasimodo: *n.* cuasimodo
quassia: *n.* cuasia
quaternion: *n.* cuaternión
quatrain: *n.* cuarteta
question: *n.* pregunta
question: *v.* poner en duda; cuestionar
questionable pay: pago dudoso
questionable retirement: retiro dudoso
questionnaire: *n.* cuestionario
quetzal: *n.* quetzal
queuine: *n.* queuina
quickly: *adv.* rápidamente
quill: *n.* pluma de ave

quilt: *n.* cobertor
quince: *n.* membrillo
quindecennial: 1. *n.* quindenio; 2. *adj.* quindecenal
quinidine: *n.* quinidina
quintal: *n.* quintal
quintessence: *n.* quintaesencia
quintet: *n.* quinteto
quintuple: 1. *adj.* quíntuplo; 2. *n.* quíntuplo
quintuplet: *n.* quintillizo; -a
quintuplicate: *adj.* quintuplicado
quip: *n.* sarcasmo; ocurrencia
quit: *adj.* absuelto; sin obligaciones
quit: *v.* dejar; abandonar
quite: *adv.* completamente
quiver: *n.* temblor; estremecimiento
quiver: *v.* temblar
quixotic: *adj.* quijotesco
quorum: *n.* quórum
quota: *n.* cuota
quotation: *n.* cotización
quote: *v.* cotizar
quotidian: *adj.* cotidiano
quotient: *n.* cociente

R

rabbet: *v.* rebajar
rabbi: *n.* rabí; rabino
Rabbinate: *n.* rabinato
rabble: *n.* chusma; multitud
rabid: *adj.* rabioso
rabies: *n.* rabia; hidrofobia
rabies virus: virus de la rabia
race: *n.* raza; casta
race: *v.* corner; desafiar
race relations: relaciones raciales
racing: *n.* caballo de carrera

racing car: carro de carreras
racism: *n.* racismo
racist: *n.* racista
rack: *n.* estante; percha
rack: *v.* atormentar; torturar
racket: *n.* raqueta; pala
rad: *n.* rad
radar: *n.* radar
radar operator: radarista
radial: *adj.* radial
radial symmetry: simetría radial
radian: *n.* radián
radiant energy: energía radiante
radiant excitance: excitancia radiante
radiant flux: flujo radiante
radiant intensity: intensidad radiante
radiant power: potencia radiante
radiate: *adj.* radiado
radiate: *v.* radiar; centellear
radiation: *n.* radiación
radiation sickness: *n.* radiotoxemia
radiation therapy: radioterapia; terapia de radiación
radiation zone: zona radiactiva
radiator: *n.* radiador
radical: *adj.* radical; fundamental
radical expression: expresión radical
radicalism: *n.* radicalismo
radicle: *n.* radícula
radio: *n.* radio
radio beacon: radiofaro
radio broadcasting: radiodifusión
radio frequency: radiofrecuencia
radio ham: radioaficionado
radio listener: radioescucha; radioyente
radio location: radiolocalización
radio navigation: radio navegación
radio operator: *n.* radiotelegrafista
radio station: radioemisora
radio telephone: radioteléfono

radio telescope: radiotelescopio
radio waves: ondas de radio
radioactive: *adj.* radiactivo; radioactivo
radioactive dating: datación radiactiva
radioactive decay: desintegración radiactiva
radioactive element: elemento radiactivo
radioactive tagging: radiomarcado
radioactivity: *n.* radiactividad
radiocarbon: *n.* radiocarbono
radiochemistry: *n.* radioquímica
radiocommunication: *n.* radiocomunicación
radiocompass: *n.* radiocompás
radiogram: *n.* radiograma
radiograph: *n.* radiografía
radiography: *n.* radiografía
radioisotope: *n.* radisótopo; isótopo radiactivo
radiolocation: *n.* radiolocalización
radiologist: *n.* radiólogo; -a
radiology: *n.* radiología
radionuclide: *n.* radionucleido
radiophone: *n.* radiófono
radioscopy: *n.* radioscopía
radiosonde: *n.* radiosonda
radiotelegraphy: *n.* radiotelegrafía
radiotelephone: *n.* radioteléfono
radiotelephony: *n.* radiotelefonía
radiotherapy: *n.* radioterapia
radius: *n.* radio
radius of a circle: radio de un círculo
radula: *n.* radula
raffia: *n.* rafia
raffle: *n.* rifa; lotería
raffle: *v.* rifar; sortear
raft: *n.* balsa
rag: *n.* trapo; harapo
rag: *v.* romper; hacer jirones
rage: *n.* rabia; ardor

rage: *v.* rabiar; encolerizarse
ragged: *adj.* andrajoso; harapiento
raglan: *n.* raglán
ragout: *n.* ragú
ragtime: *n.* ragtime
raid: *n.* invasión
raid: *v.* atacar por sorpresa
rail: *n.* carril; rail
rail: *v.* poner barrera o barandilla
railing: *n.* barandilla; pasamano
railroad: *n.* ferrocarril
railroad employment: empleo ferroviario
railroad industry: industria ferroviaria
railroad retirement: retiro ferroviario
railroad retirement board: junta de retiro ferroviario
railway: 1. *adj.* ferroviario; 2. *n.* ferrocarril
rain: *n.* lluvia
rain: *v.* llover
rain forest: selva lluviosa
rain gauge: pluviómetro
rainbows: *n.* arco iris
raincoat: *n.* impermeable
rainfall: *n.* aguacero
rainstorm: *n.* tempestad de lluvia
raise: *n.* aumento; alza
raise: *v.* criar; cultivar; levantar
raisin: *n.* pasa
rajah: *n.* rajá
rake: *n.* rastro; rastrillo
rake: *v.* rastrillar; raspar
rally: *n.* rally; reunión popular
rally: *v.* reunir
ram: *n.* carnero
ram: *v.* atacar; clavar
ramble: *n.* paseo; excursión
ramble: *v.* pasear; divagar
ramie: *n.* ramina; ramio
ramification: *n.* ramificación
ramp: *n.* rampa

rampant: *adj.* exuberante; excesivo
rampart: *n.* terraplén; muralla
ranch: *n.* hacienda; rancho
rancher: *n.* ranchero; -a
rancid: *adj.* rancio
rancor: *n.* rencor
rand: *n.* rand
random: 1. *adj.* azaroso; al azar; 2. *n.* azar; acaso
random access: acceso aleatorio
random error: error aleatorio
random priming: cebado aleatorio
random sample: muestra aleatoria
randomization: *n.* aleatorización; distribución al azar
range: *n.* rango; fila; viaje
range: *v.* alinearse; variar
range of a data set: rango de un conjunto de datos
range of a function: rango de una función
rani: *n.* rani
rank: 1. *adj.* exuberante; denso; 2. *n.* fila; grado; rango
rank: *v.* alinear; ordenar
ranking: *n.* clasificación
ransack: *v.* registrar; explotar
ransom: *n.* rescate
ransom: *v.* rescatar
rap: *n.* manotón; censura
rap: *v.* golpear; criticar duramente
rap: *n.* rap
rapacity: *n.* rapacidad
rape: *n.* rapto; violación sexual
rape: *v.* raptar; violar
rapid: *adj.* rápido
rapier: *n.* estoque; espadín
rapine: *n.* rapiña
rapport: *n.* relación; informe
rapture: *n.* rapto; arrebato
rare: *adj.* raro
rarefaction: *n.* rarefacción
rarefy: *v.* enrarecer; enrarecerse
rarely: *adv.* raramente

rascal: *n.* bribón; canalla
rash: 1. *adj.* aventurero; 2. *n.* brote; erupción
rasp: *n.* ronquido; ronquera
rasp: *v.* raspar
rasping: *n.* raspadura
rastafarian: 1. *adj.* rastafariano; 2. *n.* rastafariano; -a
rat: *n.* rata
rate: *n.* cantidad; tasa; grado
rate: *v.* valuar; estimar
rate of conversion: velocidad de transformación
rate of reaction: velocidad de reacción
ratepayer: *n.* contribuyente
rather: *adv.* bastante; mejor; mas
ratification: *n.* ratificación
ratify: *v.* ratificar
ratio: 1. *n.* razón; cociente; proporción
ratio scale: escala racional
ration: *v.* racionar
rational: 1. *adj.* racional; 2. *n.* racional
rational function: función racional
rational number: número racional
rationalism: *n.* racionalismo
rationalist: *n.* racionalista
rationality: *n.* racionalidad
rationalization: *n.* racionalización
rattan: *n.* rota
rattle: *n.* sonajero; estertor
rattle: *v.* hacer sonar; traquetear
ravage: *n.* estrago; daño
ravage: *v.* destruir; arruinar
rave: *v.* desvariar; delirar
raven: *n.* cuervo
ravenous: *adj.* voraz; hambriento
ravine: *n.* hondonada; barranco
ravioli: *n.* ravioles
ravish: *v.* encantar
raw: *adj.* crudo; -a
ray: *n.* rayo

ray: *v.* irradiar; radiar
rayon: *n.* rayón
raze: *v.* arrasar; asolar
razor: *n.* navaja de afeitar
Re: *n.* re
reach: *n.* alcance; extensión
reach: *v.* alargar; extender; alcanzar
react: *v.* reaccionar
reactance: *n.* reactancia
reactant: *n.* agente reactor
reaction: *n.* reacción
reaction norm: norma de reacción
reactionary: *adj.* reaccionario
reactivity: *n.* reactividad
reactor vessel: reactor de embarcación
read: *v.* leer; interpretar
readability: *n.* lectura mínima
readable: *adj.* legible; ameno
reader: *n.* lector; corrector (de pruebas)
reading: *n.* lectura
reading frame: marco de lectura
reading frameshift: desplazamiento del marco de lectura
readjust: *v.* reajustar
readthrough: *n.* translectura
ready: *adj.* listo; preparado
ready-to-use medium: medio preparado
reaffirm: *v.* reafirmar
reagent: *adj.* reactivo
reagent strip: tira reactiva
reagents kit: equipo de reactivos
reagin: *n.* reagina
real: *adj.* real
real estate: bienes raíces
real estate salesman: agente de bienes raíces
real image: imagen real
real number: número real
real time: *n.* tiempo real
realism: *n.* realismo
realist: *n.* realista

reality: *n.* realidad
realization: *n.* realización
realize: *v.* comprender; ver
really: *adv.* realmente
realm: *n.* reino; campo; dominio
reap: *v.* segar; cosechar
rear: *adj.* posterior; trasero
rear: *v.* levantar; elevar; criar
rearguard: *n.* retaguardia
rearmost: *adj.* último
reason: *n.* razón; entendimiento
reason: *v.* razonar
reasonable: *adj.* razonable
reasoning: *n.* razonamiento
rebate: *n.* descuento
rebate: *v.* descontar
rebel: *n.* rebelde
rebel: *v.* rebelarse; sublevarse
rebellion: *n.* rebelión
rebelliousness: *n.* rebeldía
reboot: *n.* reiniciar
rebuff: *n.* desaire; rechazo
rebuff: *v.* rechazar
rebuild: *v.* reconstruir
rebuke: *n.* censura; reproche
recall: *n.* aviso
recall: *v.* hacer volver; revocar
recapitulation: *n.* recapitulación
recede: *v.* retroceder; retirarse; alejarse
receipt: *n.* abono; recibo
receive: *v.* recibir; tomar
receiver: *n.* receptor; recibidor
recent: *adj.* reciente
reception: *n.* recepción
receptionist: *n.* recepcionista
receptive: *adj.* receptivo
receptor: *n.* receptor
recess: *n.* intermisión; tregua; hora de recreo
recess: *n.* receso
recession: *n.* recesión
recessional: 1. *adj.* recesional; 2. *n.* himno recesional

recessive allele: alelo recesivo
recipe: *n.* fórmula; receta
recipient: *n.* receptor; reclamante; destinatario
recipient cell: célula receptora
reciprocal: 1. *adj.* recíproco; 2. *n.* número recíproco
reciprocity: *n.* reciprocidad
recital: 1. *adj.* recital; 2. *n.* recital
recitation: *n.* recitado; recitación
recitative: 1. *adj.* recitativo; 2. *n.* recitativo
recite: *v.* recitar
reckless: *adj.* descuidado
reckon: *v.* considerar; calcular
reckoning: *n.* cómputo; cuenta
reclaim: *v.* reclamar; ganar terreno al mar
recline: *v.* reclinar
recluse: 1. *adj.* retirado; solitario; 2. *n.* ermitaño
recognition: *v.* reconocer
recognize: *n.* reconocimiento
recognize: *vt.* reconocer
recoil: *n.* retroceso; reculada
recoil: *v.* recular; retroceder
recollect: *v.* recordar
recombination repair: reparación por recombinación
recombinator: *n.* recombinador
recombinogenic element: recombinador
recommend: *v.* recomendar
recommendation: *n.* recomendación
recompense: *n.* recompensa
recomputation: *n.* volver a calcular
reconcile: *v.* reconciliar
reconciliation: *n.* reconciliación
reconnaissance: *n.* reconocimiento
reconnection: *n.* reconexión
reconnoiter: *v.* reconocer
reconsideration: *n.* reconsideración
reconstitution: *n.* reconstitución
reconstruct: *v.* reconstruir

reconstruction: *n.* reconstrucción
reconstructionist: 1. *adj.* reconstruccionista; 2. *n.* reconstruccionista
reconstructive: *adj.* reconstructivo
recontact: *n.* contacto adicional
record: *n.* record; registro; archivo; récord
recorded: *adj.* anotado; registrado; grabado
recount: *v.* contar de nuevo; referir
recoup: *v.* recobrar; recuperar
recover: *v.* recobrar; recuperar
recovery: *n.* recobro; recuperación
recreate: *v.* recrear; divertir
recreation: *n.* recreación; recreo
recreational: *adj.* recreativo
recrimination: *n.* recriminación
recrudescence: *n.* recrudecimiento
recruit: *n.* recluta
recruit: *v.* reclutar; abastecer
recruitment: *n.* reclutamiento
rectal: *adj.* rectal
rectal examination: tacto rectal
rectangle: *n.* rectángulo
rectangular: *adj.* rectangular
rectangular prism: prisma rectangular
rectification: *n.* rectificación
rectifier: *n.* rectificador
rectify: *v.* rectificar
rectilinear: *adj.* rectilinear
rectilinearity: *n.* rectilinealidad
rectitude: *n.* rectitud
recto: 1. *adj.* recto; 2 *n.* rector.
rectum: *n.* recto
recuperation: *n.* recuperación
recur: *v.* recurrir; repetirse
recurrent: *adj.* recurrente
recycle: *v.* reciclar
recycling: *n.* reciclaje
red: *adj.* rojo; enrojecido
red blood cell: glóbulo rojo
red cell: eritrocito

redden: *v.* enrojecer; ruborizarse
redeem: *v.* redimir
redeemer: *n.* redentor
redefine: *v.* redefinir
redemption: *n.* redención
redness: *n.* enrojecimiento
redo: *v.* volver a hacer
redouble: *n.* redoble; redoblo
redoubtable: *adj.* formidable; temible
redress: *v.* enderezar; reparar
redskin: *n.* piel roja; indio
reduce: *v.* reducir; disminuir
reduced: *adj.* reducido
reduced benefits: beneficios reducidos
reducer: *n.* reductor
reduction: *n.* reducción
redundant: *adj.* redundante
re-echo: *v.* resonar
reef: *n.* arrecife
reel: *n.* carrete
reel: *v.* devanar; enrollar
re-elect: *v.* reelegir
re-enforce: *v.* reforzar
reenlist: *v.* reengrancharse
reentry permit: permiso de reingreso
re-establish: *v.* restablecer
refectory: *n.* refectorio
refer: *v.* referir; dirigir
referee: *n.* árbitro
reference: *n.* referencia
reference distribution: distribución de referencia
reference electrode: electrodo de referencia
reference individual: individuo de referencia
reference laboratory: laboratorio de referencia
reference limit: límite de referencia
reference material: material de referencia

reference method: método de referencia
reference point: punto de referencia
reference population: población de referencia
reference procedure: procedimiento de referencia
reference range: intervalo de referencia
reference sample: muestra de referencia
reference value: valor de referencia
referendum: *n.* referendum
referential: *adj.* de referencia
referral: *n.* referencia; referido
refill: *v.* rellenar
refinancing: *n.* refinanciamiento
refine: *v.* refinar; purificar
refined: *adj.* refinado
refinement: *n.* refinamiento
reflect: *v.* reflejar; repercutir
reflectance spectrometry: espectrometría de reflectancia
reflecting telescope: telescopio reflector
reflection: 1. *n.* reflexión; reflejo; 2. *adj.* reflexivo
reflection factor: factor de reflexión
reflex: *n.* reflejo
reflexive: *adj.* reflexivo
reflux: *n.* reflujo
reforestation: *n.* reforestación
reform: *n.* reforma
reformatory: *adj.* reformatorio
reformer: *n.* reformador
refractive index: índice de refracción
refractometry: *n.* refractometría
refrain: *n.* estribillo
refresh: *v.* refrescar; reanimar
refresher course: *n.* curso de repaso
refreshing: 1. *adj.* refrescante; 2. *n.* refrescante
refrigerant: *adj.* refrigerante

refrigerate: *v.* refrigerar
refrigeration: *n.* refrigeración
refrigerator: *n.* refrigerador
refugee: *n.* refugiado
refund: *n.* reembolso
refund: *v.* reembolsar; devolver
refund form: formulario de reembolso
refuse: *n.* basura; desecho
refuse: *v.* rehusar; rechazar
refutation: *n.* refutación
refute: *v.* refutar
regain: *v.* recuperar; recobrar
regal: 1. *adj.* regio; 2. *n.* regio
regale: *v.* regalar; recrear
regard: *n.* mirada; consideración
regard: *v.* mirar; contemplar
regardless: *adv.* a pesar de; sin considerar
regatta: *n.* regata
regency: *n.* regencia
regenerated: *adj.* regenerado
regenerator: *n.* regenerador
regent: 1. *adj.* regente; 2. *n.* reggae
reggae: *n.* reggae
regicide: *n.* regicido
regimen: *n.* régimen
regiment: *n.* regimiento
region: *n.* región
regional: *adj.* regional
regionalism: *n.* regionalismo
register: *n.* registro; archivo
register: *v.* registrar; inscribir
registered: *adj.* registrado
registrar: *n.* registrador(a)
regression: *n.* regresión
regret: *n.* pena
regret: *v.* sentir; lamentar
regretful: *adj.* pesaroso
regrettable: *adj.* lamentable
regular: *adj.* regular
regular polygon: polígono regular
regular reflection: reflexión regular
regular services: servicios regulares

regular tessellation: teselado regular
regulate: *v.* regular; ajustar
regulation: *n.* reglamento
regulator: *n.* regulador
regulator gene: gene regulador
regulon: *n.* regulón
regurgitation: *n.* regurgitación
rehabilitation: *n.* rehabilitación
rehearse: *v.* ensayar
reign: *n.* reino; reinado
reign: *v.* reinar
reimburse: *v.* reembolsar; indemnizar
reimbursement: *n.* reembolso
rein: *n.* rienda
reincarnation: *n.* reencarnación
reindeer: *n.* reno
reinforce: *v.* reforzar
reinforcement: *n.* refuerzo
reinstate: *v.* reanudar; restablecer; reinstalar
reiterate: *v.* reiterar; repetir
reiteration: *n.* reiteración
reject: *v.* rechazar
rejoice: *v.* alegrar; regocijar
rejoin: *v.* reunirse con
rejoinder: *n.* respuesta
rejuvenation: *n.* rejuvenecimiento
relapse: *n.* recaída
relate: *v.* relatar; referir
related to: relacionado con
relation: *n.* relación
relational: *adj.* relacional
relationship: *n.* parentesco; relación
relative: 1. *adj.* relativo; 2. *n.* pariente
relative age: edad relativa
relative atomic mass: masa atómica relativa
relative dating: datación relativa
relative density: densidad relativa
relative error: error relativo
relative humidity: humedad relativa
relative inaccuracy: inexactitud

relativa
relative molecular mass: masa molecular relativa
relative quantity: magnitud relativa
relatively prime numbers: números relativamente primos
relativism: *n.* relativismo
relativity: *n.* relatividad
relax: *v.* relajar; soltar
relaxant: *n.* relajante
relaxation: *n.* relajación; aflojamiento
relaxing: *n.* relaxina
relay: *n.* relevo; parada
relay: *v.* relevar; mudar
release: *n.* liberación
release factor: factor de terminación
release splicing: eliminación de intrones
relent: *v.* ablandarse; aplacarse
relevant: *adj.* pertinente
reliability: *n.* fiabilidad
reliable: *adj.* fidedigno; veraz
reliance: *n.* confianza
relic: *n.* reliquia; vestigio
relief: *n.* relevo; relieve; ayuda; auxilio
relieve: *v.* relevar; auxiliar
religion: *n.* religión
religious: *adj.* religioso
relinquish: *v.* abandonar; dejar
reliquary: 1. *adj.* relicario; 2. *n.* relicario
relish: *n.* buen sabor; gusto
relish: *v.* saborear; paladear
reload: *v.* recargar
relocate: *v.* mudarse; cambiarse
reluctance: *n.* aversión; repugnancia; reluctancia
rem: *n.* rem
remain: *v.* quedar; sobrar
remainder: *n.* resto
remand: *n.* devolución
remark: *n.* observación; nota

remark: *v.* notar; observar
remarriage: *n.* volver a casarse
remedy: *n.* remedio; medicamento
remedy: *v.* remediar; curar
remember: *v.* recordar; acordarse de
remind: *v.* acordar; recordar
remission: *n.* remisión
remit: *v.* remitir; restituir
remittance: *n.* remesa; envío; giro
remodeling: *n.* remodelación
remonstrance: *n.* protesta; amonestación
remonstrate: *v.* protestar; censurar
remora: *n.* rémora
remorseless: *adj.* implacable
remote: 1. *adj.* remoto; 2. *n.* remoto
remote control: control remoto
removal: *n.* remoción; traslado; mudanza
remove: *v.* eliminar; extraer
remuneration: *n.* remuneración
remunerative: *adj.* remunerador
renaissance: *n.* renacimiento
renal: *adj.* renal
renal analysis: análisis de función de los riñones
renal calculus: cálculo renal
renal clearance: depuración renal
renal failure: insuficiencia renal
renal transplant: transplante del riñón
renal tubule: túbulo renal
renaturation: *n.* renaturalización
rend: *v.* desgarrar
render: *v.* rendir
rendezvous: *n.* cita
renegade: 1. *adj.* renegado; 2. *n.* renegado
renew: *v.* renovar
renewable resource: recurso renovable
renewal commission: comisión por renovación

renin; rennin: *n.* renina
renounce: *v.* renunciar; abdicar
renovate: *v.* renovar
renovation: *n.* renovación
renown: *n.* renombre; fama
rent: *n.* renta; arrendamiento
rent: *v.* alquilar
rental income: ingreso de rentas
renter: *n.* arrendatario; inquilino
renunciation: *n.* renuncia
reopen: *v.* reabrir; reanudar
repair: *n.* reparación; reparo
repair: *v.* reparar; restaurar
repairman: *n.* reparador(a)
reparation: *n.* reparación
repast: *n.* comida; comilona
repatriate: *adj.* repatriado
repatriation: *n.* repatriación
repay: *v.* reembolsar; compensar
repayment: *n.* reembolso
repeat: *n.* repetición
repeat: *v.* repetir
repeatability: *n.* repetibilidad
repeatedly: *adv.* repetidamente
repeating decimal: decimal periódico
repel: *v.* repeler; repulsar
repent: *v.* arrepentirse de
repentance: *n.* arrepentimiento
repercussion: *n.* repercusión
repertory: *n.* repertorio
repetition: *n.* repetición
repetitious: *adj.* repetidor
repetitive: *adj.* repetitivo
replace: *v.* reemplazar; sustituir
replacement: *n.* reemplazo
replacement rate: porcentaje de reemplazo
replacement vector: vector por sustitución
replenish: *v.* llenar; henchir; llenar de nuevo
replica: *n.* réplica
replication: *n.* replicación

replication fork: horquilla de replicación
replicon: *n.* replicón
replicon fusion: fusión de replicones
reply: *n.* respuesta
reply: *v.* responder; contestar
report: *n.* informe
report: *v.* informar; notificar
reporter: *n.* reportero
reporter gene: gen indicador
reporting: *n.* reportaje
reporting events: acontecimientos
represent: *v.* representar; simbolizar
representation: *n.* representación
representative: *n.* representante
representative payee: representante del beneficiario
repress: *v.* reprimir; contener
repression: *n.* represión
repressive: *adj.* represivo
reprimand: *n.* reprimenda
reprint: *n.* reimpresión
reprint: *v.* reimprimir
reprisal: *n.* represalia
reprive: *n.* suspensión; indulto
reprive: *v.* suspender la ejecución de
reproach: *n.* reproche
reprobate: *n.* réprobo
reproduce: *v.* reproducir
reproducibility: *n.* reproducibilidad
reproduction: *n.* reproducción
reproductive: *adj.* reproductivo
reproductive system: sistema reproductivo
reprove: *v.* reprobar; censurar
reptile: *n.* reptil
republic: *n.* república
republican: *adj.* republicano
repudiate: *v.* repudiar; rechazar
repudiation: *n.* repudiación; repudio
repugnance: *n.* repugnancia
repulse: *n.* rechazo; repulsa
repulse: *v.* repulsar; rechazar
repulsion: *n.* repulsión

reputable: *adj.* de buena reputación
reputation: *n.* reputación; fama
repute: *v.* reputar; juzgar
request: *n.* petición; ruego
request for hearing: petición de audiencia; vista
requiem: *n.* réquiem
require: *v.* estipular; requerir
requirement: *n.* requisito
requisition: *n.* requisitoria
requiste: *adj.* necesario; preciso
requiste: *n.* requisito
requite: *v.* corresponder; pagar
rescind: *v.* rescindir
rescission: *n.* rescisión
rescue: *n.* rescate; liberación
rescue: *v.* rescatar; libertar
resection: *n.* resección
resell: *v.* revender
resemble: *v.* asemejarse a
resent: *v.* resentirse de
resentful: *adj.* resentido
resentment: *n.* resentimiento
reserpine: *n.* reserpina
reservation: *n.* reserva; reservación
reserve: *n.* reserva; silencio
reserve: *v.* reservar; retirar
reserve fund: fondo de reserva
reservist: *n.* reservista
reservoir: *n.* depósito; embalse
reshuffle: *n.* recomposición
reshuffle: *v.* revolver otra vez
reside: *v.* residir
residence: *n.* residencia; domicilio
residence time: periodo de permanencia
residency: *n.* residencia
resident: *n.* residente
resident status: estado legal de residente
residential: *adj.* residencial
residual: *n.* variancia residual
residue: *n.* residuo; resto
resign: *v.* renunciar; dimitir

resignation: *n.* dimisión; renuncia
resilience; resiliency: *n.* resiliencia
resin: *n.* resina
resist: *v.* resistir; oponerse
resistance: *n.* resistencia
resistivity: *n.* resistividad
resistor: *n.* resistencia; resistor
resolute: *adj.* resuelto
resolution: *n.* resolución
resolve: *n.* resolución
resolve: *v.* resolver
resolved: *adj.* resuelto
resonance: *n.* resonancia
resonant: *adj.* resonante
resonator: *n.* resonador
resort: *n.* concurrencia
resort: *v.* acudir; frecuentar
resound: *v.* hacer resonar
resounding: *adj.* sonoro
resources: *n.* recursos; bienes
respect: *n.* respecto; atención
respect: *v.* respetar; estimar
respectability: *n.* respetabilidad
respectful: *adj.* respetuoso
respecting: *prep.* con respecto a
respiration: *n.* respiración
respirator: *n.* respirador
respiratory: *adj.* respiratorio
respiratory difficulty: dificultad respiratoria
respite: *n.* respiro; tregua
respite: *v.* dar tregua a
respite care: relevo de descanso
resplendent: *adj.* resplandeciente
respond: *v.* responder; contestar
responding variable: respuesta variable
response: *n.* respuesta
responsibility: *n.* responsabilidad
responsible: *adj.* responsable; solvente
rest: *n.* descanso; reposo; resto
rest: *v.* descansar; parar
rest home: casa de reposo

restaurant: *n.* restaurante
restitute: *v.* restituir
restitution: *n.* restitución
restive: *adj.* intranquilo; alborotado
restless: *adj.* inquieto
restlessness: *n.* intranquilidad; desasosiego
restock: *v.* reaprovisionar; repoblar
restoration: *n.* restauración
restore: *v.* restaurar; instaurar
restrain: *v.* refrenar; aprisionar
restraint: *n.* limitación; restricción
restraint: *v.* restringir; limitar
restricted function: *n.* restricción
restriction: función restringida
restriction: *n.* restricción
restriction enzyme: enzima de restricción
restriction mapping: cartografía de restricción
restriction site: centro de restricción
result: *n.* resultado
result: *v.* resultar
resume: *v.* reasumir
résumé: *n.* el curriculum
resumption of payments: reanudación de pagos
resurge: *v.* resurgir
resurrect: *v.* resucitar
resurrection: *n.* resurrección
resuscitator: *n.* resucitador
retail: *n.* venta al por menor
retain: *v.* retener; guardar
retainer: *n.* dependiente; partidario
retaining wall: el muro de apoyo
retaliate: *v.* vengarse
retaliation: *n.* venganza
retard: *v.* retardar; retrasar
retarded: *adj.* retardado
retention: *n.* retención
reticence: *n.* reticencia
reticulocyte: *n.* reticulocito
reticulum: *n.* retículo
retina: *n.* retina

retinene: *adj.* retinal
retinitis: *n.* retinitis
retinol: *n.* retinol
retinol (vitamin a): *n.* retinol
retinopathy: *n.* retinopatía
retinoscope: *n.* retinoscopio
retinoscopy: *n.* retinoscopia
retinue: *n.* séquito
retire: *v.* retirar; jubilar
retired: *adj.* jubilado
retirement: *n.* retiro
retirement: *n.* retiro; jubilación
retirement plan: plan de retiro
retirement planner: planificador de beneficios
retiring: *adj.* retraído
retort: *n.* retorta
retort: *v.* rebatir
retouch: *v.* retocar
retouching: 1. *adj.* retoque; 2. *n.* retoque
retrace: *v.* repasar
retract: *v.* retractar; retraer
retractable: *adj.* retractable
retraction (statement): *n.* retractación
retractor: *n.* retractor
retreat: *n.* retirada; retiro
retrieve: *n.* recuperación; cobra
retrieve: *v.* reparar; desquitarse de
retriever vector: vector recuperador
retroactive: *adj.* retroactivo
retroactivity: *n.* retroactividad
retrocede: *v.* hacer retrocesión de
retrograde: 1. *adj.* retrógrado; 2. *n.* retrógrada
retrograde: *n.* retrógrada
retrograde pyelogram: pielograma retrógrado
retroposon: *n.* retrotransposón
retrospective: *n.* retrospectiva
retrotransposon: *n.* retrotransposón
retrovirus: *n.* retrovirus
return: *n.* retorno; devolución

return: *v.* volver; devolver
return pipe: el tubo de retorno
reunion: *n.* reunión
reunite: *v.* reunir; juntar
revaluation of assets: reevaluación de bienes
revalue: *v.* revalorizar
revanchism: *n.* revanchismo
revanchist: *n.* revanchista
reveal: *v.* revelar
reveal: *n.* regocijo
revelation: *n.* revelación
revenge: *n.* venganza
revenge: *v.* vengar
revenue: *n.* renta; rédito
reverberate: *v.* reflejar
reverberation: *n.* reverberación; reverbero
revere: *v.* reverenciar
reverence: *n.* reverencia
reverend: 1. *adj.* reverendo; venerable; 2. *n.* clérigo
reverent: *adj.* reverente
reverie: *n.* ensueño
reversal: *n.* revocación; echarse atrás
reverse: 1. *adj.* invertido; inverso; 2. *n.* revés; contrario
reverse: *v.* invertir; trastrocar
reverse fault: falla inversa
reverse mutation: reversión
reversible: *adj.* reversible
reversion: *n.* reversión
revert: *v.* volver atrás
review: *n.* revista; revisión
review: *v.* revisar
revile: *v.* ultrajar
revise: *v.* revisar; corregir
revisionism: *n.* revisionismo
revive: *v.* reanimar; resucitar; restablecer
revivify: *v.* hacer revivir
revocation: *n.* revocación
revoke: *v.* revocar; retirar
revolt: *n.* rebelión

revolt: *v.* rebelarse
revolution: *n.* revolución
revolutionary: *adj.* revolucionario
revolutionize: *v.* revolucionar
revolve: *v.* revolver; dar
revolver: *n.* revólver
revolving: *adj.* giratorio
revolving door: la puerta giratoria
revue: *n.* revista
revulsion: *n.* revulsión
reward: *n.* premio; recompense
reward: *v.* premiar
rhapsody: *n.* rapsodia
rheostat:
rhetoric: *n.* retórica
rhetorical: *adj.* retórico
rheum: *n.* reuma
rheumatic: *adj.* fiebre reumática
rheumatic fever: *n.* fiebre reumática
rheumatism: *n.* reumatismo
rheumatoid factor: factor reumatoide
rheumatology: *n.* reumatología
rhinitis: *n.* rinitis
rhinoplasty: *n.* rinoplastia
rhizoid: *adj.* rizoide
rho: *n.* rho
rhombic: *adj.* rombal; rómbico
rhombus: *n.* rombo
rhubarb: *n.* ruibarbo
rhyme: *n.* rima
rhyme: *v.* rimar
rhymester: *n.* rimador
rhyming: *n.* de rimas
rhythm: *n.* ritmo
rhythm method: método de ritmo
rib: *n.* costilla
ribald: *adj.* obsceno; blasfemo
ribbon: *n.* cinta
riboflavin: *n.* riboflavina
ribonucleic: *adj.* ribonucleico
riboprobe: *n.* ribosonda
ribose: *n.* ribosa
ribosome: *n.* ribosoma

rice: *n.* arroz
rice field/paddy: *n.* arrozal
rich: *adj.* rico; acomodado riqueza
richness: *n.* riqueza; opulencia
Richter scale: escala de Richter
rickets: *n.* raquitismo
rickettsia: *n.* riketsia
riddle: *n.* enigma; misterio
riddle: *v.* adivinar; descifrar
ride: *n.* paseo- a caballo o en coche
ride: *v.* montar
rider: *n.* jinete; caballero
ridge: *n.* espinazo
ridge board: la tabla del caballete
ridicule: 1. *adj.* ridículo; 2. *n.* ridículo
riesling: riesling
rifampicin: *n.* rifampicina
rife: 1. *adj.* frecuente; abundante; 2. *n.* rifle; fusil; carabina
rife: *v.* hurtar; despojar
rifle: *n.* rifle
rift: 1. *n.* raja; abertura; 2. *v.* rajar; dividir
rift valley: valle de fisura
rigging: *n.* aparejo
right: *adj.* derecho; -a
right: *adj.* recto
right angle: ángulo recto
right now: ahora mismo
right to a hearing: derecho a una audiencia
right triangle: triángulo rectángulo
righteous: *adj.* recto; justo
rightful: *adj.* justo; legítimo
rightly: *adv.* rectamente; derechamente
rigid: *adj.* rígido; tieso
rigor: *n.* rigor; dureza
rill: *n.* arroyuelo; riachuelo
rill: *v.* correr formando un arroyuelo
rim: *n.* canto; borde
rind: *n.* corteza; cáscara
ring: *n.* anillo; sortija

ring: *v.* sonar; repicar
ring of fire: cinturón de fuego
ringing: 1. *adj.* resonante; 2. *n.* toque
ringing: *n.* zumbido
ringing in the ears: zumbido en los oídos
rinse: *v.* enjuagar; aclarar
riot: *n.* tumulto; desenfreno
riot: *v.* armar alboroto
rip: *n.* rasgadura
rip: *v.* rasgar; romper
rip current: corriente de resaca
riparian: *adj.* ribereño
ripe: *adj.* maduro; sazonado
ripen: *v.* madurar; sazonar
riposte: *n.* respuesta; réplica
riposte: *v.* responder
ripple: *n.* rizo; ondulación
ripple: *v.* ondular; rizare
rise: *n.* distancia vertical
riser pipe: el tubo vertical
rising: 1. *adj.* ascendiente; naciente; 2. *n.* subida; ascensión
risk factor: *n.* factor de riesgo
risky: *adj.* arriesgado; peligroso
risotto: *n.* risotto
rite: *n.* rito
ritual: 1. *adj.* ritual; 2. *n.* ritual
ritualism: *n.* ritualismo
rival: *n.* rival; competidor
rival: *v.* competir; emular
rivalry: *n.* rivalidad; competencia
rive: *v.* rajar; hender
river: *n.* río
riverside: *n.* ribera
rivet: el remache
rivulet: *n.* riachuelo; arroyo
Riyadh: Riad; Riyad
RNA: ARN
roach: *n.* cucaracha
roadhouse: *n.* posada en el camino; parador
roadside: *n.* borde del camino
roadway: *n.* calzada

roam: *v.* rodar; vagar
roar: *n.* rugido; bramido
roar: *v.* rugir; bramar
roast: *n.* asado; carne para asar
roast: v asar; tostar
roaster: *n.* tostador
rob: *v.* robar; saquear
robbery: *n.* robo
robe: *n.* traje; túnica
robot: *n.* robot
robotics: *n.* robótica
robotry: *n.* automática
robust: *adj.* robusto
robustness: *n.* robustez
roc: 1. *adj.* rocho; 2. *n.* rocho
rock: *n.* roca; rock; peña
rock: *v.* mecer; acunar
rock chips: rocalla
rock cycle: ciclo de la roca
rocker: *n.* mecedora; cohete
rocket: *n.* cohete
rock-forming minerals: minerales formadores de rocas
rock'n'roll: *n.* rócanról
rococo: *n.* rococó
rod: *n.* vara; varilla; bastón
rodent: 1. *adj.* roedor; 2. *n.* roedor
rodeo: *n.* rodeo
rods: bastones
roentgenology: *n.* roentgenología
rogue: *n.* pícaro; bribón
roguish: *adj.* bellaco; pícaro
roisterer: *n.* fanfarrón
role: *n.* rol
roll: *n.* rollo
roller: *n.* rulo; rulero
roller skate: patín de ruedas

rolling: 1. *adj.* rodante; girante; 2. *n.* rodadura; balanceo
rolling circle: círculo rodador
rolling friction: fricción de rodamiento
rolling shutters: las persianas

enrollables
roman: 1. *adj.* romano; 2. *n.* romano; -a
romance: *n.* romance; novela; historia
romanesque: *adj.* románico
romanization: *n.* romanización
romantic: 1. *adj.* romántico; encantado; 2. *n.* romántico; -a
romanticism: *n.* romanticismo
romanticist: 1. *adj.* romántico; 2. *n.* romántico; -a
Rome: *n.* Roma
rondel; rondelle: *n.* rondel
rondo: 1. *adj.* rondo; 2. *n.* rondó
rood: *n.* cruz; crucifijo
roof: *n.* techo; tejado; bóveda
roofing: la techumbre/la instalación del tejado
roofless: *adj.* sin techo; desamparado
rooftop: la azotea
rook: *n.* roque; grajo
room: *n.* habitación; cuarto; ocasión
room and board: alojamiento y comida
room temperature: temperatura ambiente
roomy: *adj.* amplio; espacioso
roost: *n.* dormidero
roost: *v.* retirarse al dormidero
rooster: *n.* gallo
root: *v.* plantar firmemente
root: *n.* raíz
root canal: tratamiento de canal dental
root cap: cofia
rope: *n.* cuerda; soga
rope: *v.* atar
rosace: *n.* rosetón
rosary: *n.* rosario
rose: *n.* rosa
rosé: *n.* rosado
rosebud: *n.* capullo
rosebush: *n.* rosal

rosetta stone: *n.* piedra de Roseta
rosette: *n.* roseta
Rosicrucian: *n.* rosacruz
rostrum: *n.* tribuna
rosy: *adj.* sonrosado; florido; risueño
rot: *n.* podredumbre
rot: *v.* pudrirse; corromperse
Rotarian: *adj.* rotario
rotary: *n.* máquina rotativa
rotary switch: el interruptor Oratorio
rotate: *v.* girar; rodar
rotation: *n.* rotación
rotational: *adj.* rotacional
rotational frequency: frecuencia rotacional
rotational symmetry: simetría de rotación
rote: *n.* rutina
rotenone: *n.* rotenona
rotor: *n.* rotor
rototiller: la aflojadora de tierra
rotten: *adj.* podrido
rotund: *adj.* redondo de cuerpo
rotunda: *n.* rotonda
rouge: *n.* arrebol
rouge: *v.* pintar; dar color
rough: áspero
rough-in: de mano gruesa
roughly: *adv.* ásperamente; aproximadamente
roughness: *n.* aspereza; tosquedad
roulette: *n.* ruleta
round: *n.* ronda
round: *v.* redondear
round numbers: números redondos
rouse: *v.* despertar; provocar
rout: *n.* rota; derrota
rout: *v.* derrotar; poner en fuga
route: *n.* ruta; itinerario
routine: *adj.* rutinario
routine: *n.* rutina
routine examination: examen sistemático
roux: *n.* roux

rover: *n.* vagabundo; veleta
row: *n.* riña; pelotera
row: *v.* remar; bogar
royal: *adj.* real; regio; magnífico
royalist: *n.* realista
royalties: *n.* royalties
royalty: *n.* realeza; derechos de autor
rubber: *n.* goma; caucho
rubbish: *n.* basura; desperdicios; disparate
rubdown: *n.* masaje
rubella; rubeola: *n.* rubéola
ruble: *n.* rublo
rubric: *n.* rúbrica
ruby: *n.* rojo; rubí
ruck: *v.* arrugar
rudder: *n.* timón
rude: *adj.* rudo; tosco
rudiment: *n.* rudimento
ruffian: *n.* rufián
rug: *n.* alfombra; felpudo
rugby: *n.* rugby
ruin: *n.* ruina; destrucción
ruin: *v.* arruinar; estropear
rule: *n.* regla; regulación
rule: *v.* gobernar; dirigir; contener
ruling: *n.* resolución
rum: *n.* ron; aguardiente
rumba; rhumba: *n.* rumba
rumble: *n.* rumor; retumbo
rumble: *v.* retumbar
ruminant: 1. *adj.* rumiante; 2. *n.* rumiante
ruminate: *v.* rumiar; masticar
rummage: *n.* búsqueda
rummy: 1. *adj.* raro; extraño; 2. n borracho
rumor: *n.* rumor; fábula
rumor: *v.* rumorear
rump: *n.* anca
rumpus: *n.* alboroto
run: *n.* distancia horizontal; serie
run off: prueba de trascripción (no iniciada)

run on: prueba de trascripción (iniciada)
runaway: 1. *adj.* desbocado; 2. *n.* fugitivo
runaway plasmid: plásmido autorreplicable
rune: *n.* runa
rung: *n.* peldaño; travesaño
runner: *n.* corredor; mensajero
runner-up: *n.* subcampeón
running: *n.* carrera; corrida
runoff: *n.* escorrentía
rupee: *n.* rupia (moneda)
rupture: *n.* ruptura
rupture: *v.* romper; quebrar; fracturar
rural: *adj.* rural
ruse: *n.* ardid; astucia; estafa
rust: *n.* orín; herrumbre; moho
rust: *v.* enmohecer
rustic: *adj.* rústico; rural; agreste
rustle: *n.* susurro; crujido
rustle: *v.* hacer susurrar o crujir
rusty: *adj.* oxidado; mohoso
ruthless: *adj.* despiadado

S

Sabbath: *n.* DIA de descanso
Sabbath: *n.* sábado
sabbatical: *adj.* sabático
saber: *v.* acuchillar
saber: *n.* saboteador
saboteur: *n.* sable
sac: *n.* saco
saccharin: *n.* sacarina
saccharine: *adj.* sacarino
sacking: *n.* saqueo
sacrament: *n.* sacramento
sacred: *adj.* sagrado; sacro

sacrifice: *n.* sacrificio; inmolación
sacrifice: *v.* sacrificar; inmolar
sacrilege: *n.* sacrilegio
sacristy: *n.* sacristía
sacroiliac: 1. *adj.* región sacroilíaca;
2. *n.* región sacroilíaca
sacrum: *n.* sacro
sad: *adj.* triste; mustio
sadden: *v.* entristecer
saddle: *n.* silla
sadist: *n.* sádico; -a
sadistic: *adj.* sádico
sadness: *n.* tristeza
safari: *n.* safari
safe: *adj.* seguro
safeguard: *n.* salvaguardia; carta de
seguridad
safeguard: *v.* proteger
safety: *n.* seguridad; inocuidad
safety plan: plan de seguridad
saffron: *n.* azafrán
safranin: *n.* safranina
saga: *n.* saga
sagacious: *adj.* sagaz
sagacity: *n.* sagacidad
sage: 1. *adj.* sabio; cuerdo; 2. *n.*
salvia
Sagittarius: *n.* sagitario
sail: *n.* vela; paseo o excursión en
barco
sailboat: *n.* bote de vela
sailing: *n.* navegación; barco de vela
sailor: *n.* marinero
saint: 1. *adj.* santo; 2. *n.* santo; -a
sake: *n.* causa; motivo; sake; saki
salaam: *n.* zalema
salad: *n.* ensalada
salad bowl: ensaladera
salamander: *n.* salamandra
salami: *n.* salami
salaried: *adj.* asalariado
salaried employment: empleo
asalariado
salary: *n.* salario; sueldo; paga

sale: *n.* venta; salida
salicylate: *adj.* salicilato
salicylic acid: ácido salicílico;
salicilato
salient: *n.* saliente
salinity: *n.* salinidad
saliva: *n.* saliva
salivary: *adj.* salival
salivation: *n.* salivación
sallow: *adj.* pálido
sally: *n.* salida; excursión
sally: *v.* hacer una salida
salmon: *n.* salmón
salmonella: *n.* salmonela
salon: *n.* salón
salsa: *n.* salsa
salsify: *n.* salsifí
salsify: *v.* salsifí
salt: *n.* sal
salt: *v.* salar; sazonar
salt cod: bacalao salado
saltcellar; saltshaker: *n.* salero
salts: *n.* sales
salty; salted: *adj.* salado
salutation: *n.* saludo; salutación
salute: *n.* saludo
salute: *v.* saludar
salvage: *n.* salvamento
salvage: *v.* salvar
salvation: *n.* salvación
salve: *n.* ungüento; pomada
salve: *v.* curar con ungüentos
salvia: *n.* salvia
samba: *n.* samba
same: 1. *adj.* mismo; igual; 2. *adv.*
mismo
sameness: *n.* igualdad; identidad
samisen: *n.* samisén
samovar: *n.* samovar
sampan: *n.* sampán
sample: *n.* muestra
sampler: *n.* muestreador
sampling: *n.* muestreo
sanatorium: *n.* sanatorio

sanctification: *n.* santificación
sanctify: *v.* santificar
sanction: *n.* sanción; ratificación
sanction: *v.* sancionar; ratificar
sanctity: *n.* santidad
sanctuary: *n.* santuario; templo; asilo
sand: *n.* arena
sandal: *n.* sandalia
sandalwood: *n.* sándalo
sandbank: *n.* banco de arena
sandbar: *n.* barra de arena
sandpaper: *n.* papel de lija
sandwich: *n.* sándwich; emparedado; bocadillo
sandwich toaster: sandwichera; sandwichero
sandy: *adj.* arenoso
sane: *adj.* sano
sangfroid: *n.* sangre fría
sangria: *n.* sangría
sanguine: *adj.* colorado; rubicundo
sanitary: *adj.* sanitario; higiénico
sanitary pads: toallas sanitarias
sanitation: *n.* saneamiento
Sanskrit: *n.* sánscrito
sap: *n.* savia; vigor
sap: *v.* extraer la savia de; minar
sapper: *n.* zapador
sapphire: *n.* azul zafiro
saraband (e): *n.* zarabanda
sarcasm: *n.* sarcasmo
sarcastic: *adj.* sarcástico
sarcoma: *n.* sarcoma
sarcophagus: *n.* sarcófago
sarcosine: *n.* sarcosina
sardine: *n.* sardina
sardonyx: *n.* sardónica; sardónice
Sargasso: *n.* sargazo
sari: *n.* sari
sarong: *n.* sarong
sarsaparilla: *n.* zarzaparrilla
sash: *n.* faja; ceñidor
sassafras: *n.* sasafrás

Satanism: *n.* satanismo
satchel: *n.* saco de mano; maletín
sate: *v.* saciar
sateen; satin: *n.* satín
satellite: *n.* satélite
satellitism test: prueba del satelitismo
satiate: *adj.* saciado
satiate: *v.* saciar; hartar
satiation: *n.* saciedad
satin: *n.* satén; satín; raso
satire: *n.* sátira
satirist: *n.* satírico; a
satirize: *v.* satirizar
satisfaction: *n.* satisfacción
satisfactory: *adj.* satisfactorio
satisfied: *adj.* satisfecho
satisfy: *v.* satisfacer; contentar
saturant: *v.* saturar
saturate: *n.* sustancia saturativa
saturated hydrocarbon: hidrocarburo saturado
saturated solution: solución saturada
saturated zone: zona saturada
saturation: *n.* saturación
saturation fraction: fracción saturante
Saturday: sábado
sauce: *n.* salsa; condimento
sauce: *v.* aderezar; sazonar
saucepan: *n.* cazuela; cacerola
saucer: *n.* platillo
sauciness: *n.* descaro; gracia
Saudi Arabia: Arabia Saudita
Saudi; Saudi-Arabian: *adj.* saudita; saudí
sauna: *n.* sauna
saunter: *n.* paseo
saunter: *v.* pasear
sausage: *n.* embutido; salchicha
sausage meat: carne de salchicha
sausage roll: salchicha envuelta en hojaldre

sauté: *n.* saltear
savage: 1. *adj.* salvaje; inculto; 2. *n.* sabana; pampa; salvaje
savannah: *n.* sabana
save: *prep.* salvo; excepto
save: *v.* salvar; librar
saving: 1. *adj.* ahorrativo; económico; 2. *n.* ahorro; economía
savings account: cuenta de ahorros
savior: *n.* salvador (a)
savor: *n.* sabor; gusto
savor: *v.* sabotear
savory: *adj.* sabroso
Savoy: Saboya
Savoyard: 1. *adj.* saboyano; -a; 2. *n.* saboyano
saw: *n.* sierra
saw: *v.* serrar
sawdust: *n.* serrín; aserrín
sax: *n.* saxo
saxifrage: *n.* saxifraga; saxifragia
Saxon: 1. *adj.* sajón; 2. *n.* sajón
Saxony: Sajonia
saxophone: *n.* saxofón
saxophonist: *n.* saxofonista
say: *n.* dicho; afirmación
say: *v.* decir; recitar
saying: *n.* dicho; aserto; relato
scab: *n.* costra; postilla
scabbard: *n.* vaina
scabies: *n.* escabies; sarna
scabrous: *adj.* escabroso
scaffold: *n.* andamio; tablado
scaffold: *v.* construir andamios
scaffolding: *n.* andamiaje
scalar: *adj.* escalar
scalar: *v.* escalar
scald: *v.* escaldar; abrasar; quemar
scald; scalding: *n.* escaldadura
scalding: *n.* escaldadura
scale: *n.* escala
scale drawing: dibujo a escala
scale factor: factor de escala
scale model: modelo a escala

scaled: *adj.* escamado
scalene: *adj.* escaleno
scalene triangle: triangulo escaleno
scallion: *n.* cebolleta; cebollín
scallop: *n.* escalope
scalp: *v.* escalpar
scalpel: *n.* bisturí; escalpelo
scamp: *n.* golfo; bribón
scamp: *v.* chapucear
scamper: *n.* fuga precipitada
scamper: *v.* huir
scan: *v.* buscar; repasar; escudriñar
scan MRI: imágenes por resonancia magnética
scandal: *n.* escándalo
scandalize: *v.* escandalizar
Scandinavia: Escandinavia
Scandinavian: *adj.* escandinavo
scanner: *n.* escáner; escanógrafo
scansion: *n.* escansión
scant: *adj.* escaso; corto
scant: *v.* escatimar; reducir
scanty: *adj.* escaso; limitado
scapegrace: 1. *adj.* incorregible; 2. *n.* pícaro
scapula: *n.* escápula
scapular: *adj.* escapulario
scar: *n.* cicatriz
scarce: 1. *adj.* escaso; 2. *n.* escaso
scarcely: *adv.* apenas
scarceness: *n.* escasez; penuria
scarcity: *n.* escasez
scare: *n.* susto; pánico
scare: *v.* asustar; alarmar
scarecrow: *n.* espantapájaros
scarf: *n.* pañuelo; bufanda
scarify: *v.* escarificar
scarlet: *n.* escarlatina; rojo escarlata
scarlet fever: *n.* escarlatina
scatology: *n.* escatología
scatter: *v.* dispersar; poner en fuga
scatter plot: diagrama de dispersión
scattering: *n.* dispersión
scavenger: *n.* carroñero

scene: *n.* escena; escenario
scenery: *n.* escenario; paisaje
scent: *n.* olfato; olor
scent: *v.* oler; olfatear
schedule: *n.* lista; catálogo
schedule: *v.* catalogar; planear
scheme: *n.* esquema
scheme: *v.* proyectar; urdir
scherzo: *n.* scherzo
schism: *n.* cisma
schistosomiasis: *n.* esquistosomiasis
schizo: *n.* esquizo; -a
schizophrenia: *n.* esquizofrenia
schizophrenic: *adj.* esquizofrénico; -a
schizophrenic: *n.* esquizofrenia
scholar: *n.* escolar; alumno
scholarship: *n.* beca
scholasticism: *n.* escolasticismo
school: *adj.* escolar
school: *n.* escuela
schooling: *n.* instrucción; enseñanza
sciatic: *adj.* ciático
sciatic nerve: nervio ciático
sciatica: *n.* ciática
science: *n.* ciencia; sabiduría
science fiction: ciencia ficción
scientific: *adj.* científico
scientific inquiry: investigación científica
scientific law: ley científica
scientific notation: notación científica
scientific theory: teoría científica
scientist: *n.* científico; -a
scientologist: *n.* cientólogo
scientology: *n.* cientología
scintillate: *v.* centellear; chispear
scintillation: *n.* centelleo
scintillation counter: contador de centelleo
scintillation detector: detector de centelleo
scintillator: *n.* contador de centelleo

scion: *n.* vástago; renuevo
scission: *n.* corte; división
scissors: *n.* tijeras
sclera: *n.* esclerótica
scleritis: *n.* escleritis
scleroma: *n.* escleroma
sclerosis: *n.* esclerosis
scoff: *n.* burla
scoff: *v.* mofarse de
scold: *n.* regañón
scold: *v.* regañar
scoliosis: *n.* escoliosis
scone: *n.* especie de bizcocho
scooter: *n.* escúter; patineta; embarcación de motor
scope: *n.* alcance; propósito
scorbutus: *n.* escorbuto
scorbutus: *v.* chamuscar; abrasar
scorching: *adj.* ardiente; abrasador
scorn: *n.* desdén; desprecio
scorn: *v.* desdeñar; despreciar
scorpio: *n.* escorpio
scorpion: *n.* escorpión; alacrán
scot: *n.* escocés
scotch: *n.* whisky escocés
scotoma: *n.* escotoma
scotswoman: *n.* escocesa
Scottish: *n.* escocés
scoundrel: *n.* granuja; bribón
scour: *v.* fregar; restregar; limpiar
scourge: *n.* látigo; azote
scourge: *v.* azotar; castigar
scowl: *n.* ceño; sobrecejo
scowl: *v.* mirar con ceño
scrabble: *n.* garabatos; borrón
scrabble: *v.* garabatear; emborronar
scraggy: *adj.* desigual
scramble: *n.* lucha; contienda
scramble: *v.* gatear
scrambled egg: huevos revueltos
scrap: los desperdicios/el desecho
scrape: *n.* raspadura; aprieto
scrape: *v.* raspar; rascar
scratch: *n.* arañazo; rasguño

scratch: *v.* arañar; rasguñar
scream: *n.* chillido; grito
scream: *v.* chillar
screen: *n.* pantalla; biombo
screen: *v.* ocultar; encubrir
screening: *n.* cribado; detección
precoz
screw: *n.* tornillo
scribble: *n.* garabatos
scribble: *v.* escribir de prisa
scribe: *n.* escriba
script: *n.* escritura
scripture: *n.* escritura
scripture: *n.* Sagrada Escritura;
Biblia
scrofula: *n.* escrófula
scroll: *n.* rollo; escrito
scrotum: *n.* escroto
scrub: *n.* fregado
scrub: *v.* fregar
scrubby: *adj.* desmirriado; bajo
scruff: *n.* pescuezo; nuca
scruple: *n.* escrúpulo
scruple: *v.* tener escrúpulo
scrupulous: *adj.* escrupuloso
scrutinise: *v.* escrutar; escudriñar
scuffle: *n.* lucha
scuffle: *v.* luchar
sculptor: *n.* escultor
sculpture: *n.* escultura
sculpture: *v.* esculpir
scum: *n.* espuma; escoria
scum: *v.* espumar
scurf: *n.* caspa
scurrilous: *adj.* chabacano
scutcheon: *n.* escudo de armas
scuttle: *n.* escotillón; trampa; cubo
del carbón
scythe: *n.* guadaña
sea: *n.* mar; océano
sea-floor spreading: expansión del
suelo oceánico
seafood: *n.* mariscos
seal: *n.* sello; sigilo

seal: *v.* sellar; precintar; lacrar
sealskin: *n.* piel de foca
seam: *n.* costura; grieta
seam: *v.* coser
seamless: sin costura
seaplane: *n.* hidroplano
search: *n.* busca; búsqueda;
investigación
search: *v.* examinar; registrar
searching: *adj.* escrutador
seashore: *n.* playa; costa
seasickness: *n.* mareo
seaside: *n.* playa; costa
season: *v.* sazonar
seasoned: *adj.* sazonado
seasoning: *n.* condimento; sazón
seaward: *adv.* hacia el mar
sebum: *n.* sebo
sec: *adj.* seco
secant: *n.* secante
secede: *v.* separarse
secluded: *adj.* retirado; -a
seclusion: *n.* retraimiento;
apartamiento
second: 1. *adj.* segundo; 2. *n.*
segundo
second hand: *n.* segundero
second person: *n.* segunda persona
second son: segundón
secondary: *adj.* secundario
second-born: *adj.* segundogénito
secrecy: *n.* secreto
secret: *n.* secreto
secretariat: *n.* secretaría
secretary: *n.* secretario
secrete: *v.* esconder; ocultar
secretin: *n.* secretina
secretion: *n.* secreción
secretive: *adj.* callado
sect: *n.* secta; grupo
sectarianism: *n.* sectarismo
section: *n.* sección; trozo
section: *v.* seccionar
sectional: *adj.* por secciones

sector: *n.* sector
secularism: *n.* secularismo
secularize: *v.* secularizar
secure: *adj.* seguro; tranquilo
secure: *v.* asegurar
security: *n.* seguridad
sedan: *n.* sedán
sedate: *v.* sedar; calmar
sedation: *n.* medicina tranquilizante
sedation: *n.* sedación
sedative: 1. *adj.* sedante; sedativo;
2. *n.* sedante; sedativo
sedentary: *adj.* sedentario
seder: *n.* seder
sediment: *n.* sedimento
sedimentation: *n.* sedimentación
sedition: *n.* sedición
seduce: *v.* seducir; inducir
seducer: *n.* seductor
seduction: *n.* seducción
see: *v.* ver
seed: *n.* semilla
seeing: *n.* vista; acción de ver
seek: *v.* buscar; inquirir; pedir;
ambicionar
seem: *v.* parecer
seeming: *adj.* aparente; fingido
seep: *v.* colar; pasar
seer: *n.* profeta; vidente
seesaw: *n.* columpio de tabla;
balanceo
seethe: *v.* hervir
seether: *n.* olla; caldera
segment: *n.* segmento
segregation: *n.* segregación
Seine: Sena
seismic wave: onda sísmica
seismogram: sismograma
seismograph: sismógrafo
seismometer: *n.* sismómetro
seize: *v.* coger; tomar
seizer: *n.* agarrador
seizure: *n.* captura; detención;
convulsión

seldom: *adv.* raramente
select: *adj.* selecto; escogido
select: *v.* escoger; elegir
selection: *n.* selección
selective: *adj.* selectivo
selector: *n.* selector
selenium: *n.* selenio
self: *adj.* mismo; idéntico
self-criticism: *n.* autocrítica
self-destruction: *n.* autodestrucción
self-determination: *n.*
autodeterminación
self-dialysis: *n.* autodiálisis
self-directed: *adj.* autodirigido
self-discipline: *n.* autodisciplina
self-expression: *n.* autoexpresión
self-image: *n.* autoimagen
selfish: *adj.* interesado; egoísta
selfishness: *n.* egoísmo; amor propio
self-sufficiency: *n.* autosuficiencia
sell: *n.* engaño; estafa
sell: *v.* vender; enajenar
seltzer: *n.* agua efervescente
semantic: *adj.* semántico
semantics: *n.* semántica
semblance: *n.* semejanza; aspecto;
forma
semeiologic value: valor
semiológico
semeiology: *n.* semiología
semen: *n.* semen; esperma
semester: *n.* semestre
semicircle: *n.* semicírculo
semicircular: *adj.* semicircular
semicircular canals: canales
semicirculares
semicolon: *n.* punto y coma
semiconductor: *n.* semiconductor
semifinal: *n.* semifinal
semifinalist: *n.* semifinalista
seminal: *adj.* seminal
seminar: *n.* seminario
seminarian: *n.* seminarista
seminary: *n.* semillero; plantel;

seminario
semiology: *n.* semiología
semiotics: *n.* semiótica
semiprecious: *adj.* semiprecioso
Semitic: *adj.* semítico
semitone: *n.* semitono
semitransparent: *adj.*
semitransparente
semolina: *n.* sémola
senator: *n.* senador
senatorship: *n.* senaduría
sender: *n.* remitente
senescence: *n.* senescencia; senilidad
senility: *n.* senilidad; senilísimo
senior: *adj.* mayor
senior citizen: persona mayor
sensation: *n.* sensación
sensational: *adj.* sensacional;
efectista
sensationalism: *n.* sensacionalismo
sense: *n.* sentido; juicio
senseless: *adj.* insensible; inerte
sensibility: *n.* sensibilidad
sensitive: *adj.* sensitivo
sensitivity: *n.* sensibilidad
sensor: *n.* sensor
sensory: 1. *adj.* sensorial; sensorio;
2. *n.* sensorial; sensorio
sensual: *adj.* sensual
sensualist: *n.* sensualista
sensuous: *adj.* voluptuoso; sensible
sensuousness: *n.* sensualidad
sentence: *n.* sentencia
sententious: *adj.* sentencioso
sentient: *adj.* sensible; sensitivo
sentiment: *n.* sentimiento
sentimentalism: *n.* sentimentalismo
sentry: *n.* centinela
sepal: *n.* sépalo
separable: *adj.* separable
separate: *adj.* separado
separate: *v.* separar; despegar
separation: *n.* separación
separatism: *n.* separatismo

separatist: *n.* disidente; separatista
separator: *n.* separador
sephardi: *n.* sefardita
sephardic: *adj.* sefárdico
sephardim: *n.* sefardles
sepia: *n.* sepia
September: *n.* septiembre
septet: *n.* septeto
septicemia: *n.* septicemia
septuagenarian: 1. *adj.*
septuagenario; -a; 2. *n.* septuagenario
septum: *n.* septo; septimo
septuplet: *n.* septillizo; -a
sepulcher: *n.* sepulcro; tumba
sepulture: *n.* sepultura
sequel: *n.* secuela; conclusión
sequence: *n.* secuencia
sequence: *n.* serie; sucesión;
secuencia
sequencing: *n.* secuenciación
sequential: *adj.* en secuencia
sequestrate: *v.* secuestrar
sequestration: *n.* secuestración
seraglio: *n.* serrallo
serape: *n.* sarape
seraph: *n.* serafín
serenade: *n.* serenata
serenader: *n.* él que da serenatas
serene: 1. *adj.* sereno; calmado; 2. *n.*
sereno
serenity: *n.* serenidad
serf: *n.* ciervo; esclavo
serfdom: *n.* servidumbre
serge: *n.* sarga
sergeancy: *n.* sargentía
sergeant: *n.* sargento; escudero
serial: *adj.* de serie; en serie
serial: *n.* serial
sericulture: *n.* sericultura
series: *n.* serie; sucesión; progresión
serine: *n.* serina
serious: *adj.* serio; formal
sermon: *n.* sermón
sermorelin: *n.* sermorelina

serology: *n.* serología
serotonin: *n.* serotonina
serpent: *n.* serpiente
serrated: *adj.* dentellado; serrado
serried: *adj.* apretado; apiñado
serum: *n.* suero
servant: *n.* sirviente; criado
server: *n.* servidor
service: *n.* servicio
serviceable: *adj.* servible; útil
servile: 1. *adj.* servil; bajo; 2. *n.* esclavo
servility: *n.* servilismo
servitude: *n.* servidumbre; trabajo forzado
servomechanism: *n.* servomecanismo
servomotor: *n.* servomotor
sesame: *n.* sésamo
session: *n.* junta; sesión
sestet: *n.* sextilla
set: *n.* set; equipo; colección
setback: *n.* revés; contrariedad
settee: *n.* banco; sofá
setting: 1. *adj.* poniente; 2. *n.* puesta; ocaso
settle: *n.* escaño; banco
settle: *v.* colocar; asentar
settled: *adj.* fijado; establecido
settlement: *n.* acuerdo
settler: *n.* poblador; colono
sever: *v.* separar; dividir
several: 1. *adj.* vanos; 2. *pron.* algunos
severe: *adj.* severo; grave
severe: *v.* coser
sewage: *n.* aguas de alcantarilla
sewer: *n.* colector; alcantarilla
sewer: *v.* alcantarillar; desaguar
sewing: *n.* costura
sewing machine: máquina de coser
sex: *n.* sexo; naturaleza
sex chromosomes: cromosomas sexuales

sex ratio: proporción de sexos
sex symbol: Símbolo de sexo
sexagenarian: 1. *adj.* sexagenario; -a; 2. *n.* sexagenario
sexagesimal: 1. *adj.* sexagesimal; 2. *n.* sexagesimal
sexism: *n.* sexismo
sexist: *n.* sexista
sexless: *adj.* asexual; neutro
sex-linked gene: gen ligado al sexo
sextant: *n.* sextante
sextet; sextette: *n.* sexteto
sexton: *n.* sacristán; enterrador
sextuple: 1. *adj.* séxtuplo; 2. *n.* séxtuplo
sextuplet: *n.* sextillo; séxtuplo
sexual abuse: abuso sexual
sexual counselor: consejero sobre el sexo
sexual desires: deseos sexuales
sexual relations: relaciones sexuales
sexual reproduction: reproducción sexual
sexual selection: selección sexual
sexually transmitted diseases STD: enfermedades transmitidas sexualmente
sexy: *adj.* sexy
sh!: intj. ¡sh!
shabby: *adj.* raído; gastado; andrajoso
shack: *n.* cabana; choza
shadow: *n.* sombra; oscuridad
shadow: *v.* sombrear; oscurecer
shaft: *n.* astil; asta
Shakespearean; Shakespearian: *adj.* shakesperiano
shako: *n.* chaco
shaky: *adj.* trémulo; tembloroso
shallot: *n.* chalote; cebolleta
shallow: *adj.* bajo; poco; profundo
sham: 1. *adj.* fingido; 2. *n.* simulación; farsa
sham: *v.* fingir

shaman: *n.* shamán; chamán
shame: *n.* vergüenza; bochorno
shame: *v.* avergonzar; abochornar
shamefaced: *adj.* tímido; vergonzoso
shampoo: *n.* champú
shamrock: *n.* trébol
shape: *n.* forma
shapeless: *adj.* deforme
share: *n.* parte; acción; porción; interés
share: *v.* dividir; distribuir
shareholder: *n.* accionista
shareware: *n.* software gratuito
shark: *n.* tiburón
shark: *v.* estafar
sharp: *adj.* agudo; cortante
sharpen: *v.* afilar; aguzar
shawl: *n.* chal; rebozo; toquilla
she: *pron. pers.* ella
shear: *v.* cortar; esquilar
sheath: *n.* vaina; funda
shed: *n.* cobertizo; refugio
shed: *v.* verter; derramar
sheen: *n.* lustre; brillo
sheep: *n.* oveja; rebaño
sheet: *n.* hoja; lámina
sheikdom: *n.* jeque
sheikh: *n.* principado de jeque
shekel: *n.* shekel; ciclo
shelf: *n.* estante; anaquel
shell: *n.* concha; caparazón
shell: *v.* descascarar; desvainar
shellfish: *n.* marisco
shelter: *n.* resguardo; protección
shelter: *v.* resguardar; proteger
shepherd: *v.* pastorear
sherry: *n.* jerez
shiatsu: *n.* shiatsu
shield: *n.* escudo
shield: *v.* escudar; resguardar
shilling: *n.* chelín
shimmy: *n.* vibraciones
shin: *n.* espinilla
shine: *n.* brillo; resplandor

shine: *v.* brillar; resplandecer
Shinto: *n.* shintoismo
ship: *n.* buque; barco
ship: *v.* embarcar; enviar
shipwreck: *n.* naufragio; desastre
shipwreck: *v.* hacer naufragar
shirk: *v.* eludir; evitar
shirt: *n.* camisa
shiva: *n.* siva
shiver: *n.* temblor; escalofrío
shiver: *v.* temblar
shoal: 1. *adj.* poco profundo; 2. *n.* bajo; muchedumbre
shock: *n.* choque
shoe: *n.* zapato; bota
shoe: *v.* calzar; herrar
shoemaker: *n.* zapatero
shoot: *n.* vástago; pimpollo
shoot: *v.* herir o matar; disparar
shooting: *n.* tiro; fusilamiento; filmación
shop: *n.* tienda; comercio
shopwindow: *n.* escaparate; vidriera
shoran: *n.* shoran
shore: *n.* orilla; costa; playa
short: 1. *adj.* corto; pequeño; 2. *adv.* brevemente; secamente
short circuit: *n.* cortocircuito
short course: *n.* cursillo
shortage: *n.* escasez
shorten: *v.* acortar; reducir
shorthand: *n.* taquigrafía
shortly: *adv.* en breve
shoulder: *n.* hombro; codo; paletilla; paleta
shoulder: *v.* echarse sobre las espaldas
shout: *n.* grito; exclamación
shout: *v.* gritar; vocear
shove: *n.* empujón
shove: *v.* empujar
shovel: *n.* pala
shovel: *v.* mover con palas
show: *n.* presentación; exhibición

show: *v.* mostrar; enseñar
shower: *n.* chubasco; chaparrón
shower: *v.* regar; mojar
showy: *adj.* vistoso; ostentoso
shred: *n.* tira; trozo largo
shred: *v.* hacer tiras
shrewish: *adj.* regañón
shrill: *adj.* agudo; penetrante
shrill: *v.* chillar
shrimp: *n.* langostino; camarón; gamba; quisquilla
shrine: *n.* urna; relicario
shrivel: *v.* arrugar; fruncir
shroud: *n.* mortaja; sudario
shroud: *v.* amortajar
shrub: *n.* arbusto
shrug: *v.* encoger los hombros
shuck: *n.* cáscara; exterior
shuck: *v.* descascarar
shun: *v.* huir; rehuir
shut: *adj.* cerrado
shut: *v.* cerrar
sick: *adj.* enfermo (a)
sicken: *v.* enfermar; cansar
sickliness: *n.* indisposición
sickness: *n.* enfermedad
side: *n.* lado
sideboard: *n.* aparador; bufete
sidelong: *adj.* oblicuo; inclinado
sidereal: *adj.* sidéreo; sideral
sidewalk: *n.* acera; andén
sideward: *adv.* de lado
siege: *n.* sitio; asedio
sienna: *n.* siena
siesta: *n.* siesta
sieve: *n.* tamiz
sieve: *v.* cernir; tamizar
sievert: *n.* siévert
sift: *v.* cernir; cribar
sigh: *n.* suspiro
sigh: *v.* suspirar
sight: *n.* vista; vislumbre
sight: *v.* avistar; vislumbrar
sightless: *adj.* ciego

sigma: *n.* sigma
sigmoidal: *adj.* sigmoide; sigmoideo
sigmoidoscope: *n.* sigmoidoscopio
sigmoidoscopy: *n.* sigmoidoscopia
sign: *n.* signo; señal
sign: *v.* firmar; suscribir
signal: *n.* señal
signalize: *v.* señalar; distinguir
signature: *n.* firma; rúbrica
significance: *n.* significado; significación
significant: *adj.* significativo
signify: *v.* significar; indicar
silage: *n.* ensilaje
silence: *n.* silencio
silence: *v.* imponer silencio a; hacer callar
silencer: *n.* silenciador
silent: *adj.* silencioso
silhouette: *n.* silueta
silica: m. sílice
silicosis: *n.* silicosis
silk: *n.* seda
sill: *n.* umbral de ventana
silliness: *n.* tontería
silo: *n.* silo
silver: 1. *adj.* de plata; 2. *n.* plata
silviculture: *n.* silvicultura
similar: *adj.* similar
similarity: *n.* similitud
simile: *n.* sonrisa
simile: *v.* sonreír (se)
simmer: 1. *n.* hervir a fuego lento; 2. *n.* hacer cocer a fuego lento
simoom: *n.* monzón; simún
simp: *n.* bobo; mentecato
simple: 1. *adj.* simple; sencillo; 2. *n.* simple; simplón
simplex: 1. *adj.* simplex; 2. *n.* simplex
simplified: *adj.* simplificado
simplify: *v.* simplificar
simulation: *n.* simulación
simultaneous: *adj.* simultáneo

sin: *n.* pecado; culpa
sin: *v.* pecar; cometer
since: 1. *prep.* desde; después de; 2. *adv.* desde entonces; 3. *conj.* desde que
sincerity: *n.* sinceridad
sine: *n.* seno
sine qua non: sine qua non
sinecure: *n.* sinecura
sinew: *n.* tendón; energía
sinew: *v.* fortalecer
sing: *v.* cantar
singe: *n.* chamusco
singe: *v.* chamuscar
singer: *n.* cantante
single: *adj.* solo; único
single: *v.* singularizar; escoger
singsong: 1. *adj.* monótono; 2. *n.* cadencia uniforme
singular: *adj.* singular
singularity: *n.* singularidad
sinigrase: *n.* tioglucosidasa
sinister: *adj.* izquierdo; siniestro
sinless: *adj.* puro; libre de pecado
sinner: *n.* pecador
sinous: *adj.* sinuoso; tortuoso
sinus: *n.* seno
sinusitis: *n.* sinusitis
sire: *n.* señor; padre; abuelo
siren: *n.* sirena
sirloin: *n.* solomillo
sirroco: *n.* siroco
sisal: *n.* sisal
sisomicin: *n.* sisomicina
sister: *n.* hermana
sisterhood: *n.* hermandad
sit: *v.* sentar
sitar: *n.* sitar
sitcom: *n.* diaria
site: *n.* sitio; lugar
sitting: *n.* la acción de sentarse; estar sentado
situate: *v.* situar
situation: *n.* situación

six: seis
sixpence: *n.* moneda de medio chelín
sixteen: dieciséis
sixth: *adj.* sexto
size: *n.* medida; talla
size: *v.* clasificar según tamaño
skald: *n.* escaldo
skate: *n.* patín; raya
skate: *v.* patinar
skeletal: *adj.* esquelético
skeleton: *n.* esqueleto; osamenta
skeptic: *n.* escéptico
skepticism: *n.* escepticismo
skew: 1. *adj.* oblicuo; inclinado; 2. *n.* oblicuidad
skew: *v.* sesgar; torcer
ski: *n.* esquí
skier: *n.* esquiador
skiff: *n.* esquife
skiing: *n.* esquí
skilift: *n.* telesquí
skill: *n.* conocimiento práctico
skilled: *adj.* práctico
skillful: *adj.* hábil; mafioso
skim: *n.* desnatar
skimpy: *adj.* escaso; tacaño
skin: *n.* piel
skin: *v.* pelar
skink: *n.* esquinco; estinco
skinned: *adj.* pelado
skip: *n.* salto; brinco
skip: *v.* saltar; brincar
skipper: *n.* saltador; patrón; capitán
skirt: *n.* falda; saya
skirt: *v.* bordear; rodear
skit: *n.* parodia
skit: *v.* asustarse
skulk: *v.* esconderse
skull: *n.* cráneo; calavera; cerebro
sky: *n.* cielo; firmamento
skylark: *n.* alondra
slab: *n.* labia; plancha
slack: *adj.* flojo; débil; poco firme
slacken: *v.* aflojar; relajar

slag: *n.* escoria
slake: *v.* apagar; extinguir
slalom: *n.* esquiar en zig zag
slam: *n.* portazo
slam: *v.* cerrar de golpe
slander: *n.* calumnia
slander: *v.* calumniar
slang: *n.* lenguaje vulgar
slant: *n.* sesgo; inclinación
slap: *n.* palmada; manotazo
slap: *v.* pegar; abofetear
slash: *n.* cuchillada
slash: *v.* acuchillar
slate: *n.* pizarra
slaughter: *n.* muerte; matanza
slaughter: *v.* matar; esclavizar
slavery: *n.* esclavitud
slavic: *adj.* eslavo; -a
slavic: *n.* eslavo
sledge: *n.* trineo
sleek: *adj.* liso
sleek: *v.* pulir
sleep: *n.* sueño
sleep: *v.* dormir
sleeper: *n.* durmiente
sleet: *n.* agua de nieve
sleeve: *n.* manga
sleight: *n.* destreza; habilidad
slender: *adj.* delgado; tenue
slice: *n.* rebanada; tajada
slice: *v.* rebanar
sliced: *adj.* en rebanadas
slide: *n.* deslizamiento
slide: *v.* resbalar; deslizarse
slight: *adj.* ligero
slight: *v.* despreciar; menospreciar
slim: *adj.* delgado; esbelto
slim: *v.* ponerse a régimen para adelgazar.
slimy: *adj.* viscoso; limoso
sling: *n.* eslinga
slipper: *n.* zapatilla
slit: *n.* abertura; estrecha
slogan: *n.* eslogan; lema

sloop: *n.* balandro
slop: *n.* cuesta; ladera
slop: *v.* inclinar
slope: *n.* pendiente
slot: *n.* hendidura; abertura
sloth: *n.* pereza; galbana
sloven: *adj.* desaseado
slovenen: *adj.* esloveno
slovenly: *adj.* desaliñado
slowly: *adv.* lentamente
sluggish: *adj.* flojo; perezoso
sluggish: *adv.* perezosamente
slum: *n.* barrio o calle miserable
slumber: *n.* sueño
slump: *n.* hundimiento
slump: *v.* hundirse
slut: *n.* mujerzuela
sly: *adj.* astuto; travieso
smack: *n.* sabor; golpe
smack: *v.* chasquear el látigo
small: *adj.* pequeño; menudo
smallpox: *n.* viruela
smashing: *adj.* extraordinario
smatter: *n.* barniz; conocimiento superficial
smear: *n.* untar
smeary: *adj.* graso
smell: *n.* olfato; olor
smell: *v.* oler
smelt: *v.* fundir
smelting: *n.* fundición
smile: *n.* sonrisa
smile: *v.* sonreírse
smite: *v.* golpear; herir
smith: *n.* forjador; herrero
smock: *n.* camisa; bata
smog: *n.* esmog
smog: *n.* niebla mezclada con humo
smoke: *n.* humo
smoked: *adj.* ahumado
smoking: 1. *adj.* humeante; 2. *n.* acción de fumar
smooth: *adj.* liso
smooth: *v.* alisar; allanar

smother: *n.* humareda
smother: *v.* sofocar; ahogar
smug: *adj.* pulido; satisfecho
smuggle: *v.* pasar de contrabando
smut: *n.* suciedad; mancha
smut: *v.* ensuciar; manchar
snack: *n.* bocado; comida ligera; sorbo
snag: *n.* nudo; tronco flotante
snail: *n.* caracol
snake: *n.* culebra; serpiente
snapdragon: *n.* boca de dragón
snappy: *adj.* chispeante; vivo
snapshot: *n.* instantánea
snapshot: *v.* hacer una instantánea
snare: *n.* lazo; trampa
snare: *v.* atrapar; coger en un lazo
snarl: *n.* gruñido
snarl: *v.* regañar; gruñir
sneeze: *n.* estornudo
snip: *n.* incisión; recorte
snip: *v.* cortar; recortar
sniper: *n.* buen tirador
snivel: *n.* moquear; gimotear
snob: *n.* snob; esnob
snobbery: *n.* snobismo; esnobismo
snobbish: *n.* pretencioso
snorkel: *n.* esnorquel
snort: *n.* resoplido; bufido
snout: *n.* trompa
snow: *n.* nieve
snub: *n.* repulsa; desaire
snub: *v.* reprender
snuffle: *n.* inspiración ruidosa por la nariz
snuffle: *v.* respirar con la nariz obstruida
snug: *adj.* cómodo; abrigado
snuggle: *v.* arrimar
soak: *n.* remojo
soak: *v.* empapar; remojar
soap: *n.* jabón
soap: *v.* enjabonar; dar jabón; adular
soar: *n.* vuelo; remonte

soar: *v.* elevarse
sob: *n.* sollozo
sob: *v.* sollozar
sober: *adj.* sobrio; moderado
sobriety: *n.* sobriedad
sociability: *n.* sociabilidad
sociable: *adj.* sociable
social: *adj.* social
socialism: *n.* socialismo
socialist: *n.* socialista
socialite: *n.* persona de alta sociedad
socialization: *n.* socialización
socialized medicine: *n.* medicina estatal
society: *n.* sociedad
sociobiology: *n.* sociobióloga
socioeconomic: *n.* socioeconómico
sociolinguistics: *n.* sociolingüística
sociologist: *n.* sociólogo
sociology: *n.* sociología
sociopath: *n.* sociópata
sock: *n.* calcetín
socket: *n.* hueco
socratic: *adj.* socrático
soda: *n.* soda
sodden: *adj.* mojado; empapado
sodden: *v.* mojar; empapar
sodium: *n.* sodio; ion sodio
sodomy: *n.* sodomía
soever: *adv.* por mucho; por mas que sea
sofa: *n.* sofá
soft: *adj.* blando; dúctil
soften: *v.* ablandar; reblandecer
softness: *n.* blandura; ductilidad
software: *n.* software
soggy: *adj.* mojado; hecho una sopa
soil: *n.* tierra; terreno; suelo
soil: *v.* ensuciar; manchar
soiree: *n.* reunión nocturna
sojourn: *n.* estancia
sojourn: *v.* estar; permanecer
sol: *n.* sol
solace: *n.* solaz; consuelo; alivio

solace: *v.* consolar; confortar
solanum: *n.* solanácea
solar: 1. *adj.* solar; 2. *n.* solar
solar plexus: *n.* plexo solar
solarium: *n.* solana; solario
solder: *n.* soldadura
solder: *v.* soldar; estañar
solder; soldering: *n.* soldadura
soldering: *n.* soldadura
soldier: *n.* soldado
soldiery: *n.* profesión o ejercicio militar
sole: *adj.* solo
solecism: *n.* solecismo
solemnity: *n.* solemnidad
solemnize: *v.* solemnizar
solenoid: *n.* solenoide
sol-fa; solfeggio: *n.* solfeo
solicit: *v.* pedir
solicitor: *n.* abogado; agente; corredor
solicitous: *adj.* solícito
solicitude: *n.* solicitud
solid: *adj.* sólido
solidi: *n.* solidez; consistencia
solidify: *v.* solidificar; consolidar
solid-state: *n.* estado sólido
soliloquy: *n.* soliloquio
solipsism: *n.* solipsismo

solitaire: 1. *adj.* solitario; 2. *n.* solitario
solitude: *n.* soledad
solo: 1. *adj.* solo; 2. *n.* solo
soloist: *n.* solista
solstice: *n.* solsticio
solubility: *n.* solubilidad
solute: *n.* soluto
solution: *n.* solución
solvatation: *n.* solvatación
solve: *v.* resolver; aclarar
solvency: *n.* solvencia
solvent: 1. *adj.* disolvente; solvente; 2. *n.* solvente

soma: *n.* cuerpo
somatoliberin: *n.* somatoliberina
somatology: *n.* somatalogía
somatomedin: *n.* somatomedina
somatorelin: *n.* somatorelina
somatropin: *n.* somatotropina
somber: 1. *adj.* sombrío; 2. *n.* sombrío
someone: *n.* alguien
somersault: *n.* salto mortal
somersault: *v.* dar un salto mortal
sometimes: *adv.* algunas veces; a veces
somewhat: 1. *n.* algo; alguna cosa; una parte; 2. *adv.* algo
somewhere: *adv.* en alguna parte
somnambulism: *n.* somnambulismo
somnambulist: *n.* somnambulista
somnolence: *n.* somnolencia
son: *n.* hijo
sonar: *n.* sónar
sonata: *n.* sonata
sonatina: *n.* sonatina
song: *n.* canto; copla; poesía
sonic: *adj.* sónico
sonnet: *n.* soneto
sonogram: *n.* sonograma
sonorous: *adj.* sonoro
soon: *adv.* pronto; presto
soot: *n.* hollín; tizne
soot: *v.* cubrir de hollín
soothe: *v.* aliviar; suavizar; tranquilizar
soothsayer: *n.* adivino
sophism: *n.* sofisma
sophist: *n.* sofista
sophistication: *n.* sofisticación
soporific: *n.* soporífero
soprano: *n.* soprano
sorbonne: *n.* sorbona
sorcerer: *n.* hechicero
sordid: *adj.* interesado; bajo; vil
sordidness: *n.* sordidez
sore: 1. *adj.* penoso; doloroso; 2. *n.*

úlcera; disgusto
sores: *n.* úlceras
sorghum: *n.* sorgo
sorrow: *n.* dolor; pesar
sorrow: *v.* disgusto
sorrowful: *adj.* afligido; pesaroso
sorry: *adj.* afligido
sort: *n.* clase; especie
sort: *v.* ordenar; arreglar
souffle: *n.* suflé
soul: *n.* alma; espíritu
sound: *n.* son; sonido
sound: *v.* sonar
sounding: *n.* sondeo
soup: *n.* sopa
sour: *adj.* ácido; agrio
sour: *v.* agriar; avinagrar
source: *n.* origen; causa
south: *n.* sur
southeast: *n.* sudeste
southerly: *adv.* del sur
Southern Hemisphere: hemisferio austral
southerner: *n.* sureño; -a
souvenir: *n.* recuerdo
sovereign: *adj.* soberano
sow: *v.* sembrar; esparcir
soy: *n.* soya
soybean: *n.* soja
spa: *n.* balneario
space: *n.* espacio
space-time: *n.* espacio-tiempo
spacing: *n.* espaciamiento
spacious: *adj.* espacioso
spade: *n.* espada
spaghetti: *n.* espaguetis
span: *n.* palmo; extensión
spare: *adj.* de reserva; de recambio
sparing: *adj.* escaso; piadoso.
spark: *n.* parque; jardín; chispa
spark: *v.* chispear; echar chispas
sparrow: *n.* gorrión; pardal
sparse: *adj.* esparcido; esparramado
spasm: *n.* espasmo

spasmodic: *adj.* espasmódico
spastic: *adj.* espástico; -a
spate: *n.* aguacero; chaparrón
spate: *v.* inundar
spathe: *n.* espata
spatter: *n.* salpicadura; chapoteo
spatter: *v.* salpicar; rociar
spatula: *n.* espátula
spawn: *n.* huevos de peces
spawn: *v.* desovar
speak: *v.* hablar; pronunciar; proferir
speaker: *n.* orador; locutor
spear: *n.* lanza; arpón
spear: *v.* atravesar con arpón
special: *adj.* especial
special case: caso especial
specialist: *n.* especialista
specialization: *adj.* especializado
specialize: *n.* especialidad
specialized: *n.* especialidad
specialty: *n.* especialidad
speciation: *n.* especiación
specie: *n.* efectivo; metálico
species: *n.* especie
specific: 1. *adj.* específico; 2. *n.* específico
specification: *n.* especificación
specificity: *n.* especificidad
specify: *v.* especificar
specimen: *n.* espécimen; ejemplo
speck: *n.* manchita
speck: *v.* manchar
speckled: *n.* salpicado
specs: *n.* gafas
spectacle: *n.* espectáculo
spectacular: 1. *adj.* espectacular; 2. *n.* espectacular
spectator: *n.* espectador
specter: *n.* espectro
spectinomycin: *n.* espectinomicina
spectrograph: *n.* espectrógrafo
spectrometer: *n.* espectrómetro
spectrometry: *n.* espectrometría
spectrophotometer: *n.*

espectrómetro
spectrophotometry: *n.*
espectrometría
spectroscope: *n.* espectroscopio
spectroscopy: *n.* espectroscopía
spectrum: *n.* espectro
speculate: *v.* especular
speculation: *n.* especulación
speculum: *n.* especulo
speech: *n.* palabra; habla; dialecto
speechless: *adj.* sin habla; mudo
speed: *n.* velocidad; rapidez;
prontitud
spell: *n.* hechizo; encanto
spell: *v.* deletrear; hechizar; encantar
spellbind: *v.* hechizar; encantar
spelling reform: *n.* reforma
ortográfica
spend: *v.* gastar; consumir
spendthrift: *adj.* derrochador
sperm: *n.* esperma; semen;
espermatozoide
sperm count: *n.* cuenta espermática
spermatophyte: *n.* espermatofita
spermatozoid: *n.* espermatozoide
spermicide: *n.* espermicida;
espermaticida
spew: *v.* vomitar
sphenoid: *n.* esfenoides
sphere: *n.* esfera
spherical: *adj.* esférico
spheroid: *n.* esferoide
sphincter: *n.* esfínter
sphinx: *n.* esfinge
sphygmomanometer: *n.*
esfigmomanómetro
spice: *n.* especia
spick-and-span: *adj.* nuevo; reciente
spicy: *adj.* picante; sazonado con
especias
spider: *n.* araña
spike: *n.* pincho
spike: *v.* clavar
spiky: *adj.* puntiagudo

spill: *n.* vuelco
spill: *v.* verter; derramar
spin: *v.* hilar; rodar
spina bifida: espina bífida
spinach: *n.* espinaca
spinal: *adj.* espinal
spindle: *n.* huso
spine: *n.* espina; espinazo
spineless: *adj.* invertebrado
spinet: *n.* espineta
spinster: *n.* solterona
spiral: *n.* espiral
spiramycin: *n.* espiramicina
spire: *n.* cima; cúspide
spirit: *n.* espíritu; aparición
spirited: *adj.* vivo; brioso
spiritism: *n.* espiritismo
spiritual: 1. *adj.* espiritual; 2. *n.*
espiritual
spiritualism: *n.* espiritualismo
spiritualist: *n.* espiritista
spirochete: *n.* espiroqueta
spirograph: *n.* espirógrafo
spirometer: *n.* espirómetro
spirometry: *n.* espirometría
spirt: *n.* chorro; surtidor
spirt: *v.* arrojar a chorro
spit: banco de arena
spit: *n.* saliva
spit: *v.* escupir; echar
spiteful: *adj.* rencoroso; maligno
splattered: *adj.* estrellado
splay: *n.* extensión
splay: *v.* extender
spleen: *n.* bazo; bilis
splendid: *adj.* espléndido
splendor: *n.* esplendidez; esplendor
spliceosome: *n.* espliceosoma
splicing: *n.* eliminación de intrones
splinker: *n.* esplínquer
splint: *n.* astilla; tablilla
splint: *v.* entablillar
splinter: *n.* astilla; raja; cacho
splinter: *v.* hacer astillas

split: 1. *adj.* hendido; 2. *n.*
hendidura; división;
split: *v.* hender; partir
splotch: *n.* mancha
splotch: *v.* hender; partir; manchar
spokesman: *n.* portavoz
spondee: *n.* espondeo
sponge: *n.* esponja
sponsor: *n.* fiador; esponsor;
patrocinador
sponsored: *adj.* patrocinado
sponsorship: *n.* esponsorización
spontaneity: *n.* espontaneidad
spontaneous: *adj.* espontáneo
spool: *n.* carrete; bobina
spoon: *v.* sacar con cuchara
sporadic: *adj.* esporádico
spore: *n.* espora
sporicide: *n.* esporicida
sporophyte: *n.* esporofito
sport: *n.* deporte
sportcaster: *n.* comentarista
deportivo; -a
sporting: *adj.* deportivo
sports: *adj.* deportivo
sports: *n.* deportes; deportismo
sports medicine: *n.* medicina
deportiva
sportsman: *n.* deportista
sportsmanship: *n.* deportividad
spotless: *adj.* limpio; sin mancha
spotlight: *n.* reflector
spots: *n.* manchas
spotted: *adj.* manchado
spouse: *n.* cónyuge; esposo; -a
spout: *n.* pico; chorro
spout: *v.* echar; arrojar
sprain: *n.* torcedura
sprain: *v.* torcer; distender
sprawl: *v.* abrir; extender
spray: *v.* rociar
spray: *n.* espray; spray
spread: *v.* esparcir
spreadsheet: *n.* hoja de cálculo

sprig: *n.* ramita
spring: *n.* manantial
sprinkle: *v.* rociar; salpicar
sprint: *n.* sprint; esprint
sprinter: *n.* esprinter
sprite: *n.* duende; hada
spud: *n.* patatas
spumy: 1. *adj.* espumoso; 2. *n.*
espumoso
spur: *n.* espuela; aguijón
spur: *v.* picar; aguijar
spurious: *adj.* espurio
spurn: *v.* despreciar
spurt: *n.* chorro; borbotón
sputum: *n.* esputo
spy: *n.* espía
spy: *v.* espiar; acechar
squadron: *n.* escuadra
squall: *n.* racha; chubasco
squall: *v.* chillar
squalor: *n.* escualidez; suciedad;
miseria
squander: *v.* malgastar; despilfarran
square: *n.* cuadrado
squared: *adj.* elevado al cuadrado
squash: *n.* calabaza; pulpa
squash: *v.* aplastar; machacar
squat: *adj.* sentado en cuclillas
squat: *v.* agacharse
squatty: *adj.* regordete
squeal: *n.* chillido
squeal: *v.* chillar
squeamish: *adj.* delicado;
escrupuloso
squeeze: *n.* apretón; abrazo estrecho
squeeze: *v.* apretar; exprimir
squid: *v.* calamar
squirm: *v.* retorcerse
squirrel: *n.* ardilla
squirt: *v.* chorrear
stab: *n.* puñalada
stab: *v.* dar puñaladas
stability: *n.* estabilidad
stabilize: *v.* estabilizar

stabilizer: *n.* estabilizador; estabilizante
stable: *adj.* estable
stable: *n.* establo
staccato: *adj.* staccato
stack: *n.* pila; montón
stack: *v.* apilar
stadium: *n.* estadio
staff: *v.* proveer de personal
staff: *n.* planilla; personal
stag: *n.* ciervo
stage: *n.* escenario; tablas
stage: *v.* exhibir al público
stagflation: *n.* estagflacion
stagger: *v.* alternar; vacilar
stagnate: *v.* estancarse; detenerse
staid: *adj.* grave; serio
stain: *n.* mancha; tinte
stain: *v.* manchar
stainless: *adj.* limpio
stair: *n.* escalón; peldaño; escalera
stake: *n.* estaca; hoguera
stake: *v.* estacar; apostar; aventurar
stalactite: *n.* estalactita
stalagmite: *n.* estalagmita
stale: *adj.* pasado; viejo
stalinism: *n.* stalinismo ; estalinismo
stalk: *n.* tallo; caña
stalk: *v.* cazar al acecho
stallion: *n.* semental
stalwart: *adj.* fornido; robusto
stamen: *n.* estambre
stamina: *n.* vitalidad
stamp: *n.* estampa; huella
stamp: *v.* estampar; sellar; triturar
stampede: *n.* huída en desorden
stampede: *v.* ahuyentar
stamper: *n.* estampador
stanch: *v.* estancar
stand: *n.* puesto; situación; posición
stand: *v.* ponerse en pie; levantarse
standard: 1. *adj.* estándar; 2. *n.* estándar
standardized: *adj.* estandarizado

standpoint: *n.* punto de vista
standstill: *n.* alto; descanso
staphylococcus: *n.* grapa
staple: *v.* engrapar
staple: *n.* estrella; lucero
star: *v.* sembrar; marcar con asterisco
star: *n.* estribor
starboard: *n.* almidón
starch: *v.* almidonar
starch: *n.* mirada fija
stare: *adj.* tieso; rígido
stark: *v.* arrancar
start up: *v.* asustar
startle: *n.* hambre
starvation: *v.* morir de hambre; matar de hambre
starve: *n.* éxtasis
stasis: *n.* determinación urgente
stat: *n.* estado; situación
state: *v.* exponer; declarar
state: *adj.* establecido
stated: *n.* declaración; manifestación
statement: *n.* estadista
statesman: 1. *adj.* estático; 2. *n.* estático
static: *n.* estación
station: *v.* estacionar; situar
station: *n.* papelería; artículos de escritorio
stationery: *n.* estadística
statistic: *n.* estadista
statistician: *n.* estadística
statistics: *n.* estator
stator: *n.* estatuaria
statuary: *n.* estatua
statue: *n.* estatuilla
statuette: *n.* estatura
stature: *n.* estado; estatus
status: *n.* ley decreto
statute: *adj.* firme; constante
staunch: *n.* sitio; servicio
stead: *adj.* firme
steadfast: *n.* estabilidad; seguridad
steadiness: *n.* bistec; filete

steak: *n.* hurto
steal: *v.* hurtar; robar
steal: *n.* disimulo
stealth: *n.* vapor
steam: *v.* evaporar
steam: *n.* vapor
steamer: *n.* esteatorea
steatorrhea: *n.* acero
steel: *v.* acerar; endurecer
steel: *n.* aguja; campanario
steeple: *n.* novillo
steer: *v.* gobernar; dirigir
steer: *n.* gobierno; dirección
steerage: *n.* piloto; timonero
steersman: *n.* estela
stela; stele: *adj.* estelar
stellar: *n.* tallo; tronco
stem: *n.* esténcil
stencil: *n.* estenógrafo; -a
stenographer: *n.* estenografía
stenography: *n.* estenotipo
stenotype: *n.* estenotipista
stenotypist: *n.* estenotipia
stenotypy: *n.* estentóreo
stentorian: *n.* paso; escalón
step: *v.* poner; sentar; plantar
step: *n.* hijastra; entenada
stepdaughter: *n.* padrastro
stepfather: *n.* estepa
steppe: *n.* hijastro
stepson: *n.* estéreo
stereo: *n.* estereoquímica
stereochemistry: *adj.* estereofónico
stereophonic: *n.* estereoscopio
stereoscope: *adj.* estéril; infecundo
sterile: *n.* esterilidad
sterility: *n.* esterilización
sterilization: *v.* esterilizar
sterilize: *n.* esterilizador
sterilizer: *n.* esterlina
sterling: 1. *adj.* duro; vigoroso; 2. *n.*
popa
stern: *n.* esternón
sternum: *n.* esteroide

steroid: *adj.* estertoroso
stertorous: *n.* estetoscopio
stethoscope: *n.* estibador
stevedore: *n.* cocido; estofado
stew: *v.* estofar; guisar
stew: *n.* mayordomo; administrador
steward: *v.* pegarse; pegar
stick: *n.* esparadrapo
sticking-plaster: *adj.* espeso; duro
stiff: *v.* atiesar; dar rigidez
stiffen: *n.* rigidez; tirantez
stiffness: *v.* ahogar; sofocar
stifle: *n.* estigma; mancha
stigma: *n.* estilete
stiletto: *n.* quietud; inmovilidad
stillness: *n.* estimulante
stimulant: *adj.* avaro; tacaño
stimulate: *v.* estimular; incitar
stimulate: *adj.* estimulante
stimulating: *n.* estimulación
stimulation: *n.* estimulan
stimulon: *n.* estímulo
stimulus: *n.* corrupción
stink: *v.* oler mal
stink: *n.* estipendio
stipend: *v.* estipular; especificar
stipulate: *n.* estipulación
stipulation: 1. *adj.* estribo; 2. *n.*
estribo; peldaño
stirrup: *n.* puntada
stitch: *v.* coser; bordar
stitch: *n.* acción; existencias; reserva
stock: *n.* estacada
stockade: *n.* accionista
stockholder: *n.* media; calcetín
stocking: 1. *adj.* estoico; 2. *n.*
estoico; -a
stoic: *n.* estoicismo
stoicism: *n.* fogonero
stoker: *n.* estola
stole: *n.* estómago
stomach: *n.* estomas
stomata: *n.* estomatitis
stomatitis: *n.* obra de sillería;

mampostería
stonework: *adj.* pedregoso; duro
stony: *n.* heces
stool: *n.* alto; parada
stoop: *v.* agacharse; inclinarse
stoop: *n.* stop
stop: *v.* parar; terminar; acabar
stop: *n.* detención
stoppage: *n.* tapón; estorbo
stopper: *n.* almacenamiento
storage: *n.* copia; abundancia
store: *v.* abastecer; proveer
store: *n.* almacén
storehouse: *n.* almacenero
storekeeper: *n.* piso; planta
storey: *n.* tormenta
storm: *n.* historia; leyenda
story: *n.* frasco; jarro
stoup: *adj.* fuerte; recio; resistente
stout: *n.* fuerza; vigor
stoutness: *n.* estufa; cocina
económica
stove: *n.* estrabismo
strabismus: *v.* rodar; andar perdido
straggle: *adj.* recto; derecho
straight: *v.* enderezar
straighten: *adj.* recto; honrado
straightforward: *adv.*
inmediatamente
straightway: *n.* colar; cepa; tensión
strain: *v.* extender
strain: *adj.* colador
strainer: *v.* colador; filtro
strainer: 1. *adj.* estrecho; angosto;
2. *n.* estrecho; pasaje
strait: *v.* estrechar
straiten: *n.* cadena
strand: *adj.* extraño; raro
strange: *n.* extrañeza
strangeness: *n.* extraño; extranjero
stranger: *v.* estrangular; asfixiar
strangle: *n.* estafilococo
strangler: *n.* estrangulador
strangulation: *n.* estrangulación

strap: *n.* correa
stratagem: *n.* estratagema
strategic: *adj.* estratégico
strategist: *n.* estratega
strategy: *n.* estrategia
stratification: *n.* estratificación
stratocumulus: *n.* estratocúmulo
stratosphere: *n.* estratosfera;
estratosfera
stratospheric: *adj.* estratosférico
stratum: *n.* estrato
stratus: *n.* estrato
straw: *n.* paja
strawberry: *n.* fresa
stray: *adj.* descarriado
stray: *v.* desviarse
streak: *n.* raya; línea
streak: *v.* rayar; listar
streaked: *adj.* listado
stream: *n.* corriente; río
stream: *v.* correr; fluir
street: *n.* calle; vía pública
strength: *n.* fuerza; energía
streptococcus: *n.* estreptococo
streptomycin: *n.* estreptomicina
stress: *n.* estrés; fuerza
stress: *v.* cargar; dar importancia
stretch: *v.* estirar
stricken: *adj.* golpeado; herido;
absoluto
stricture: *n.* estrechez
stride: *n.* paso largo
stride: *v.* andar a paso largo
strident: *adj.* estridente
strife: *n.* disputa; contienda
strife: *v.* golpear
striking: *adj.* notable; impresionante
string: *n.* cordón; cinta
stringency: *n.* rigor
stringent: *adj.* rígido; severo
strip: *n.* tira; faja
strip: *v.* despojar
stripe: *n.* raya; lista
striped: *adj.* rayado

striptease: *n.* desnudarse
strive: *v.* esforzarse; hacer todo lo posible
strobila: *n.* estróbilo
stroboscope: *n.* estroboscopio
stroke: *n.* derrame cerebral
stroll: *n.* paseo; vuelta
stroll: *v.* callejear
strong: *adj.* fuerte; robusto
strophe: *n.* estrofa
struck: *adj.* herido; afectado
structural: *adj.* estructural
structure: *n.* estructura
struggle: *n.* esfuerzo; lucha
struggle: *v.* luchar; bregar
strumpet: *n.* ramera; prostituta
strumpet: *v.* andar con aire orgulloso
strychnine: *n.* estricnina
stub: *n.* cepa; persona rechoncha
stubborn: *adj.* obstinado; terco
stucco: *n.* estuco
stuck-up: *adj.* tieso; estirado
stud: *n.* poste; montante
stud: *v.* tachonar; clavetear
student: *n.* estudiante
studio: *n.* estudio; taller
study: *n.* estudio; despacho
study: *v.* estudiar; meditar
stuff: *v.* rellenar
stuffing: *n.* relleno
stuffy: *adj.* mal ventilado; resfriado
stumble: *n.* tropiezo; tropezón
stun: *n.* aturdimiento
stun: *v.* aturdir
stupefaction: *n.* estupefacción
stupefy: *v.* causar estupor; atontarse
stupendous: *adj.* estupendo
stupidity: *n.* estupidez
stupor: *n.* estupor
sturdiness: *n.* robustez; fuerza
sturdy: *adj.* robusto; fornido
sturgeon: *n.* esturión
stutter: *n.* tartamudeo
stutter: *v.* tartamudear

sty: *n.* pocilga; orzuelo
style: *n.* estilo; título
style: *v.* llamar; nombrar
styling: *n.* estilización
stylish: *adj.* elegante
stylist: *n.* estilista
stylistics: *n.* estilística
stylograph: *n.* estilógrafo
stylus: *n.* estilo
suave: *adj.* suave; afable
subarctic: *n.* subartino
subcommittee: *n.* subcomité
subcontinent: *n.* subcontinente
subcontractor: *n.* subcontratista
subculture: *n.* subcultura
subcutaneous: *adj.* subcutáneo
subdivision: *n.* subdivisión
subdominant: *n.* subdominante
subduction: *n.* subducción
subdue: *v.* sojuzgar; someter
subgroup: *n.* subgrupo
subject: 1. *adj.* sometido; dominado; *n.* sujeto; súbdito; tema
subject: *v.* sujetar; someter
subjection: *n.* sometimiento
subjective: *adj.* subjuntivo
subjectivism: *n.* subjetivismo
subjectivity: *n.* subjetividad
subjugate: *v.* subyugar; sojuzgar; dominar
subjugation: *n.* subyugación
subjunctive: 1. *adj.* subjuntivo; 2. *n.* subjuntivo
sublimation: *n.* sublimación
submarine: *n.* submarino
submaxillary: 1. *adj.* submaxilar; 2. *n.* submaxilar
submerge: *v.* sumergir; hundir
submersible: *adj.* sumergible
submersion: *n.* sumersión
submissiveness: *n.* sumisión
submit: *v.* someter; remitir
subordinate: 1. *adj.* subordinado; 2. *n.* subordinado

subordinate: *v.* subordinar
subordinating: 1. *adj.* subordinante;
2. *n.* subordinante
suborn: *v.* sobornar; cohechar
subornation: *n.* soborno
suborner: *n.* sobornador
subpoena: *n.* citación legal
subrogation: *n.* subrogación
subscribe: *v.* subsistir; firmar
subscriber: *n.* suscriptor; subscriptor
subscript: *n.* subíndice
subscription: *n.* firma; suscripción
subsequent: 1. *adj.* subsiguiente
subside: *v.* menguar; disminuir
subsidence: *n.* hundimiento;
descenso
subsidiary: 1. *adj.* subsidiario; 2.*n.*
subsidiario
subsidize: *v.* subvencionar
subsidy: *n.* subsidio
subsist: *v.* subsistir; existir
subsistence: *n.* subsistencia
subsoil: *n.* subsuelo
subsonic: *adj.* subsónico
subspace: *n.* subespacio
subspecies: *n.* subespecie
substance: *n.* sustancia
substandard: *adj.* no estándar
substantial: *adj.* substancial;
substancioso
substantiate: *v.* probar; establecer
substantive: *n.* sustantivo
substitute: *n.* sustituto; -a
substrate: *n.* substrato
substratum: *n.* sustrato
subterfuge: *n.* subterfugio
subterranean: *adj.* subterráneo
subtilisin: *n.* subtilisina
subtility: *n.* sutileza
subtitle: *n.* subtítulo
subtle: *adj.* sutil; raro; fino
subtlety: *n.* sutileza
subtotal: *n.* subtotal
subtract: *v.* sustraer; restar

subtraction: *n.* substracción
subtrahend: *n.* substraendo;
sustraendo
subtropical: *adj.* subtropical
suburb: *n.* suburbio
suburbanite: *n.* suburbano
suburbia: *n.* suburbios
subvention: *n.* subvención
subversive: 1. *adj.* subversivo; 2. *n.*
subversivo; -a
subway: *n.* paso o conducto
subterráneo
succeed: *v.* suceder; tener éxito
success: *n.* éxito; fortuna
successful: *adj.* prospero; dichoso
succession: *n.* sucesión
successive: *adj.* sucesivo
successor: *n.* sucesor
succinct: *adj.* sucinto
succor: *n.* socorro; auxilio
succor: *v.* socorrer; asistir
succulent: *adj.* suculento
such: *adj.* tal; semejante
suchlike: *adj.* tal; semejante
suck: *n.* chupada; mamada
suck: *v.* chupar
suckle: *v.* amamantar
sucrose: *n.* sucrosa; glucosidasa
sucrose: *n.* sucrosa
suction: *adj.* succión
suction: *n.* succión
suddenly: *adv.* de repente
suddenness: *n.* precipitación
suds: *n.* jabonaduras; espuma
sue: *v.* demandar; poner pleito
suffer: *v.* sufrir; padecer
suffering: *n.* sufrimiento
suffice: *v.* bastar; ser suficiente
sufficiency: *n.* suficiencia
sufficient: *adj.* suficiente
suffix: *n.* sufijo
suffocation: *n.* sofocación; sofoco
suffrage: *n.* sufragio; voto
suffuse: *v.* banal; cubrir

sugar: *n.* azúcar
sugar: *v.* azucarar; confitar
sugary: *adj.* azucarado
suggest: *v.* sugerir; insinuar
suggestibility: *n.* sugestibilidad
suggestion: *n.* sugerencia
suicide: *n.* suicidio
suit: *n.* solicitación; súplica
suit: *v.* convenir; acomodar
suitable: *adj.* propio; conveniente
suitcase: *n.* maleta
suite: *n.* serie; séquito
suiting: *n.* tela para trajes
sulbactam: *n.* sulbactam
sulfa: *n.* sulfa
sulfadiazine: *n.* sulfadiazina
sulfonamide: *n.* sulfonamida
sullen: *adj.* hosco; arisco
sully: *n.* mancha; mancilla
sully: *v.* manchar; ensuciar
sulphur: *n.* azufre; trueno; rayo
sultana: *n.* pasa sultana
sultanate: *n.* sultanato
sultry: *adj.* bochornoso
sum: *n.* suma; adición
sum: *v.* sumar
sumerian: *n.* sumerio
summarize: *v.* resumir
summary: *n.* sumario
summation: *n.* suma
summer: *n.* verano; estío
summer: *v.* veranear
summit: *n.* cúspide; cima
summon: *v.* llamar; requerir; convocar
sumptuous: *adj.* suntuoso
sun: *n.* sol
sunbeam: *n.* rayo de sol
sunburning: *n.* quemadura del sol
Sunday: domingo
sunflower: *n.* girasol
sunni: *n.* sunita
sunny: *adj.* soleado
sunrise: *n.* amanecer

sunset: *n.* ocaso; puesta del sol; atardecer
sunshade: *n.* parasol; sombrilla
sunshine: *n.* sol
sunspot: *n.* mancha solar
sup: *n.* sorbo
sup: *v.* dar de cenar; beber
superb: *adj.* soberbio
supercoil: *n.* superhélice
superficial: *adj.* superficial
superficiality: *n.* superficialidad
superfine: *adj.* superfino; extrafino
superfluous: *adj.* superfluo
superhelix: *n.* superhélice
superhero: *n.* superhéroe
superintend: *v.* vigilar; dirigir
superintendent: *n.* superintendente
superior: 1. *adj.* superior; rector;
2. *n.* superior; rector
superiority: *n.* supremacía
superlative: 1. *adj.* superlativo;
2. *n.* superlativo
supermarket: *n.* supermercado
supernatural: *adj.* sobrenatural
supernova: *n.* supernova
superpower: *n.* superpotencia
supersede: *v.* reemplazar
supersensitive: *adj.* supersensible
supersonic: *adj.* supersónico
superstition: *n.* superstición
superstructure: *n.* superestructura
supertonic: *n.* supertónica
supervise: *v.* inspeccionar; intervenir
supervision: *n.* inspección; revisión; supervisión
supervisor: *n.* inspector; interventor
supine: 1. *adj.* supino; 2. *n.* supino
supper: *n.* cena
supper: *v.* cenar; dar de cenar
supplant: *v.* suplantar
supple: *adj.* suave; flexible
supplement: *n.* suplemento
supplementary: *adj.* suplementario
supplicate: *v.* suplicar; pedir

supplication: *n.* súplica; suplicación
supplier: *n.* suministrador; proveedor
supply: *n.* suministro
supply: *v.* surtir; proveer; abastecer
support: *n.* suporte; apoyo; respaldo
support: *v.* apoyar; respaldar
suppose: *v.* suponer; dar por sentado
supposition: *n.* suposición
suppository: *n.* supositorio
suppress: *v.* suprimir; omitir
suppression: *n.* supresión; omisión
suppressor: *n.* supresor
suprarenal: *adj.* suprarrenal
supremacist: *n.* supremacista
supremacy: *n.* supremacía
supreme: *adj.* supremo
surcharge: *n.* sobrecarga
sure: 1. *adj.* seguro; cierto;
2. *adv.* ciertamente
surf: *n.* marejada; resaca
surface: *n.* superficie
surfactant: *adj.* surfactivo
surfeit: *n.* exceso; empacho
surfeit: *v.* hartar; saciar
surfer: *n.* surfista
surge: *n.* ola; oleada
surgeon: *n.* cirujano
surgery: *n.* cirugía
surgy: *adj.* agitado
surmount: *v.* vencer; coronar
surname: *n.* apellido
surname: *v.* apellidar
surpass: *v.* sobrepujar; aventajar
surpassing: *adj.* superior; excelente
surplus: *n.* sobrante; exceso;
superávit
surprise: *n.* sorpresa
surprise: *v.* sorprender
surreal: 1. *adj.* surrealista; 2. *n.*
surrealista
surrealism: *n.* surrealismo
surrealist: *n.* surrealista
surrender: *n.* rendición
surreptitious: *adj.* subrepticio

surround: *v.* rodear; cercar
survey: *n.* encuesta; peritaje
survey: *v.* encuestar; sondear
surveying: *n.* agrimensura
survival: *n.* supervivencia
survive: *v.* sobrevivir
surviving: *n.* sobreviviente
survivor: *n.* sobreviviente
survivorship: *n.* supervivencia
suspect: *v.* sospechar; recelar
suspend: *v.* suspender; colgar
suspense: *n.* suspensión;
interrupción; suspenso
suspension: *n.* suspensión
suspensory: *adj.* suspensorio
suspicion: *n.* sospecha; recelo
sustain: *v.* sostener; aguantar
sustenance: *n.* sustento
suture: *n.* sutura
suzerain: *n.* soberano
swab: *n.* hisopo; torunda
swallow: *n.* bocado; trago
swallow: *v.* tragar
swan: *n.* cisne
sward: *adj.* césped
swarm: *n.* enjambre
swarm: *v.* enjambrar
swastika: *n.* esvástica
swath: *n.* faja; ringlera
sway: *n.* oscilación; vaivén
sway: *v.* oscilar; mecerse
swear: *v.* jurar
sweat: *n.* sudor
sweat: *v.* sudar
sweater: *n.* suéter
sweating: *n.* sudoración
Swede: 1. *adj.* sueco; -a; 2. *n.* sueco
sweep: *n.* barredura; barrendero
sweep: *v.* barrer
sweet: 1. *adj.* dulce; azucarado;
2. *n.* dulzura
sweetbread: *n.* molleja; lechecilla
sweetcorn: *n.* maíz tierno; elote
sweeten: *v.* endulzar; azucarar

sweetener: *n.* endulzante
sweetener artificial: azúcar artificial
sweetheart: *n.* novia; prometida
swell: *v.* hincharse
swelling: *n.* hinchazón; inflamación
swift: *adj.* veloz; rápido
swim: *n.* nadar; nado
swim: *v.* nadar; flotar
swimmer: *n.* nadador
swindle: *v.* estafar; timar
swine: *n.* cerdo; marrano
swing: *n.* balanceo; oscilación
swing: *v.* balancear; mecer
swirl: *n.* remolino
swirl: *v.* hacer girar
switch: *n.* vara flexible
switch: *v.* azotar
switchboard: *n.* cuadro de mandos
swollen: *adj.* hinchado; crecido
sword: *n.* espada
sybarite: *n.* sibarita
sycophant: *adj.* sicofante
syllabary: *n.* silabario
syllabi: *n.* silabeo
syllable: *n.* sílaba
syllabus: *n.* sumario; compendio
syllogism: *n.* silogismo
symbiosis: *n.* simbiosis
symbol: *n.* símbolo; signo
symbolic: *adj.* simbólico
symbolically: *adv.* simbólicamente
symbolism: *n.* simbolista
symbolist: *v.* simbolizar
symbolize: *n.* simbolismo
symmetrical: *adj.* simétrico
symmetry: *n.* simetría
symmetry: *n.* simetría
sympathetic: *adj.* simpático
sympathize: *v.* simpatizar; compadecerse
sympathizer: *n.* simpatizante
sympatric: *adj.* simpático
symphony: *n.* sinfonía
symposium: *n.* simposio

symptom: *n.* síntoma
symptom: *n.* sintomatología
symptomatology: *n.* síntoma
synagogue: *n.* sinagoga
synapomorphy: *n.* sinapomorfía
synapse: *n.* sinapsis
synchronic: *adj.* sincrónico
synchronizer: *n.* sincronizador
synchronous: *adj.* sincrónico
syncline: *n.* sinclinal
syncope: *n.* síncope
syncretism: *n.* sincretismo
syndicalism: *n.* sindicalismo
syndrome: *n.* síndrome
synecdoche: *n.* sinécdoque
synergetic: *adj.* sinérgico (a)
synergismy: *n.* sinergia
synergy: *n.* sinergia
synod: *n.* sínodo
synonym: *n.* sinonimia
synonymy: *n.* sinónimo
synopsis: *n.* sinopsis
syntax: *n.* sintaxis
synthesis: *n.* síntesis
synthesizer: *n.* sintetizador
synthetic: *adj.* sintético
syntopic: *adj.* sintópico
syphilis: *n.* sífilis
syringe: *n.* jeringa
syrup: *n.* almíbar; jarabe
systaltic: *adj.* sistáltico
system: *n.* sistema
systematics: *n.* sistemática
systemic: *adj.* sistémico
systole: *n.* sístole
systolic: *adj.* sistólico

T

T.B. test: prueba de tuberculina
tabard: *n.* tabardo
tabernacle: *n.* tabernáculo
table: *n.* mesa; tabla; índice
table: *v.* poner sobre la mesa; dejar un asunto
table tennis: tenis de mesa
tablespoon: *n.* cuchara
tablet: *n.* tableta; pastilla; comprimido
tabloid: *n.* tabloide
taboo: *n.* tabú
tabor; tabour: *n.* tamboril
tabulate: *v.* tabular
tabulation: *n.* tabulación
tachometer: *n.* tacómetro
tachycardia: *n.* taquicardia
taciturn: *adj.* taciturno
tack: *v.* Ajar con tachuelas
tackle: *n.* equipo; avios
tackle: *v.* asir; agarrar
tact: *n.* tacto; discreción
tactful: *adj.* discreto; diplomático
tactical: *adj.* táctico
tactician: *n.* táctico
tactics: *n.* táctica
tactile: *adj.* táctil
tadpole: *n.* renacuajo
taffeta: *n.* tafetán
tag: *n.* etiqueta
tag: *v.* poner membrete o etiqueta
taiga: *n.* taiga
tail: *n.* cola; fila
tailing: *n.* prolongación
tailor: *n.* sastre
taint: *n.* mancha
taint: *v.* manchar

take: *v.* tomar/llevar
take down: *v.* retirar
take out: *v.* sacar/quitar
taking: *n.* tomar; entrada en posesión
talc: *n.* talco
talcum powder: talco
tale: *n.* cuento; fábula
talent: *n.* talento
talisman: *n.* talismán
talk: *n.* habla; charla
talk: *v.* hablar; decir
tall: *adj.* alto; exagerado
tallow: *n.* sebo
tallow: *v.* ensebar
tally: *n.* cuenta; etiqueta
tally: *v.* llevar la cuenta; marcar
talmud: *n.* talmud
talmudist: *n.* talmudista
talon: *n.* garra
tamale: *n.* tamale
tamarind: *n.* tamarindo
tambourine: *n.* pandereta
tame: *adj.* sumiso; dócil
tame: *v.* domar; domesticar
tamer: *n.* domador
tamil: *n.* tamil
tamper: *n.* apisonador
tamper: *v.* entremeterse; sobornar
tampon: *n.* tampón
tan: *n.* tostar
tan: *v.* curtir; adobar
tang: *n.* sabor fuerte y picante
tangent: 1. *adj.* tangente; 2. *n.* tangente
tangential: *adj.* tangencial
tangerine: 1. *adj.* tangerino; -a; 2.*n.* mandarina; tangerina
tangible: *adj.* tangible
tangle: *n.* enredo; embrollo
tangle: *v.* enredar
tango: *n.* tango
tank: *n.* tanque; depósito
tankard: *n.* jarro con tapas y asa
tanker: *n.* tanquista

tantalize: *v.* atormentar
tantamount: *adj.* equivalente
Taoism: *n.* taoísmo
tap: *n.* toquecito; grifo
tap: *v.* dar golpecitos
tape: *n.* cinta
tape: *v.* atar con cinta; medir con cinta
taper: *n.* cerilla; velilla
taper: *v.* disminuir; afilar
tapestry: *n.* tapicería; tapiz
tapestry: *v.* tapizar
tapeworm: *n.* tenia; solitaria
tapioca: *n.* tapioca
tar: *n.* brea; alquitrán
tar: *v.* alquitranar
tarantella: *n.* tarantela
tardy: *adj.* tardío
target: *n.* blanco; objetivo
tariff: *n.* tarifa
taro: *n.* taro
tarot: *n.* tarot
tarpon: *n.* tarpón
tarragon: *n.* estragón
tarry: *adj.* alquitranado; embreado
tarry: *v.* esperar; tardar
tarsier: *n.* tarsero
tarsus: *n.* tarso
tart: 1. *adj.* agrio; 2. *n.* tarta
task: *n.* tarea; labor
task: *v.* atarear; abrumar
tassel: *n.* bona
taste: *n.* gusto; sabor
taste: *v.* gustar; saborear
tasteful: *adj.* de buen gusto
tattoo: *n.* tatuaje
tau: *n.* tau
taunt: *n.* mofa; pulla
taut: *adj.* tirante; tieso.
tautology: *n.* tautología
tavern: *n.* taberna
tawdry: *adj.* charro; llamativo
tax: *n.* contribución; tributo; *vtr.* poner impuestos; *pl.* gastos de

aduana.
taxable: *adj.* tributable
taxation: *n.* tributación
taxi: *n.* taxi
taxidermy: *n.* taxidermia
taxonomy: *n.* taxonomía
tea: *n.* té
teach: *v.* enseñar
teacher: *n.* maestro; profesor
teaching: 1. *adj.* docente; 2. *n.* enseñanza
team: *n.* yunta; equipo
team: *v.* enganchar; unir
teapot: *n.* tetera
tear: *n.* lágrima
tearful: *adj.* lagrimoso
tearing: *n.* lagrimeo
tease: *n.* aburrimiento
tease: *v.* molestar; importunar
teaspoon: *n.* cucharita; cucharilla
teat: *n.* pezón; teta
technical: *adj.* técnico
technician: *n.* técnico
technicolor: *n.* technicolor
technique: *n.* técnica
technocracy: *n.* tecnocracia
technocrat: *n.* tecnócrata
technological: *adj.* tecnológico
technology: *n.* tecnología
teddy bear: oso de juguete
teddy boy: gamberro
tedium: *n.* tedio
tee: *n.* tee; punto de salida
teem: *v.* abundar
teepee: *n.* tipi
teeth: *n.* dientes; dentadura
teicoplanin: *n.* teicoplanina
telecommunication: *n.* telecomunicación
teleconferencing: *n.* teleconferencia
telegram: *n.* telegrama
telegraph: *n.* telégrafo
telegraph operator: telegrafista
telegraphy: *n.* telegrafía

telekinesis: *n.* telequinesia
telemarketing: *n.* telemárketing
telemeter: *n.* telémetro
telemetry: *n.* telemetría
teleology: *n.* teleología
telepathy: *n.* telepatía
telephone: *n.* teléfono
telephone directory: guía telefónica
telephone interview: entrevista telefónica
telephone number: número de teléfono
telephone operator: telefonista
telephony: *n.* telefonía
telephoto: *n.* telefoto
teleprompter: *n.* teleprompter
telescope: *n.* telescopio
teletext: *n.* teletex; teletexto
teletype: *n.* teletipo
television: *n.* televisión
television set: televisor
television viewer: televidente
telex: *n.* telex
tell: *v.* decir; contar; hablar
temerity: *n.* temeridad
temper: *n.* temple; genio
tempera: *n.* témpera
temperament: *n.* temperamento
temperate: *adj.* templado
temperate phage: fago atenuado
temperate zones: zonas templadas
temperature: *n.* temperatura
tempest: *n.* tempestad
tempestuous: *adj.* tempestuoso
template: *n.* molde
temple: *n.* templo
tempo: *n.* tempo
temporal: *adj.* temporal; de tiempo
temporary: *adj.* temporal; provisional; interino; temporario
temporary benefits: beneficios temporeros
temporary magnet: imán temporal
tempt: *v.* tentar; inducir

temptation: *n.* tentación
tempter: *n.* tentador
tempting: *adj.* tentador
tenable: *adj.* defendible
tenacity: *adj.* tenacidad; tesón
tenant: *n.* inquilino; arrendatario
tend: *v.* cuidar; vigilar
tendentious: *adj.* tendencioso
tender: 1. *adj.* tierno; afable; doloroso;
2. *n.* oferta
tender: *v.* ofrecer; proponer
tenderloin steak: solomillo
tenderness: *n.* ternura; sensibilidad
tendon: *n.* tendón
tendonitis: *n.* tendonitis
tenement: *n.* habitación
tenet: *n.* credo; dogma
tennis: *n.* tenis
tennis court: cancha de tenis
tennis player: tenista
tenor: *n.* tenor
tense: 1. *adj.* tirante; 2. *n.* tiempo; tensión
tension: *n.* tensión; esfuerzo mental
tent: *n.* tienda
tent: *v.* acampar bajo tiendas
tentative: 1. *adj.* tentativo; 2. *n.* tentativo
tenuous: *adj.* tenue; raro
tepid: *adj.* tibio; templado
tequila: *n.* tequila
tercet: *n.* terceto; tercerilla
term: *n.* término
terminal: 1. *adj.* terminal; 2. *n.* terminal
terminal velocity: velocidad terminal
terminally ill: enfermo mortal
terminate: *v.* terminar
terminating decimal: decimal exacto
termination: *n.* terminación
termination notice: aviso de

terminación
terminator: *n.* terminador
terminology: *n.* terminología
terminus: *n.* terminal
termite: *n.* termita; hormiga
terms of an expression: términos de una expresión
ternary: *adj.* ternario
terrace: *n.* terraplén; terraza
terra-cotta: terracota
terrain: *n.* terreno
terramycin: *n.* terramicina
terrazzo: *n.* terrazo
terrestrial: *adj.* terrestre
terrestrial planets: planetas telúricos
terrier: *n.* terrier
terrific: *adj.* terrífico
terrified: *adj.* aterrorizado
terrify: *v.* aterrorizar; espantar
territorial: *adj.* territorial
territory: *n.* territorio
terror: *n.* terror
terrorism: *n.* terrorismo
terrorist: *n.* terrorista
terse: *adj.* breve
tertiary: *adj.* terciario
tessellation: *n.* teselado
tessitura: *n.* tesitura
test: *n.* prueba; examen; test
test: *v.* probar; poner a prueba
test instructions: instrucciones sobre las pruebas
test tube: tubo de ensayo
testate: *adj.* testado
testator: *n.* testador(a)
testicle: *n.* testículo
testify: *v.* testificar
testimonial: *adj.* testimonial
testimony: *n.* testimonio
testing laboratory: laboratorio de ensayo
testis: *n.* testículos
testosterone: *n.* testosterona

tetanus: *n.* tétanos
tether: *n.* traba; maniobra
tetracosactide: *n.* tetracosáctida
tetracycline: *n.* tetraciclina
tetrad: *n.* tétrade
tetrahedral: *adj.* tetraédrico
tetrahedron: *n.* tetraedro
tetralogy: *n.* tetralogía
tetrameter: *n.* tetrámero
tetrode: *n.* tétrodo
teutonic: *adj.* teutónico
text: *n.* texto
textbook: *n.* libro de texto
textile: *n.* textil
texture: *n.* textura
thalamus: *n.* tálamo
thalophyte: *n.* talofita
than: *cnj.* que
thank: *n.* gracias
thank: *v.* agradecer
thankful: *adj.* agradecido
thankless: *adj.* ingrato
thatch: *n.* paja; techo de paja
thatch: *v.* cubrir de paja
thaw: *n.* deshielo
thaw: *v.* deshelar
thaw: *v.* descongelar
theater: *n.* teatro
theater of the absurd: teatro del absurdo
theater-in-the-round: teatro circular
theatrical: *adj.* teatral
theft: *n.* robo; hurto
theism: *n.* teísmo
thematic: *adj.* temático
theme: *n.* tema; transposición
then: *adv.* entonces; después; luego
thence: *adv.* desde allí; desde entonces
thenceforth: *adv.* de allí en adelante
theocracy: *n.* teocracia
theodolite: *n.* teodolito
theofibrate: *n.* clofibrato de etofilina
theologian: *n.* teólogo

theology: *n.* teología
theophylline: *n.* teofilina
theorem: *n.* teorema
theoretical: *adj.* teorético; teórico
theoretical probability:
probabilidad teórica
theoretician: *n.* teórico
theory: *n.* teoría
theosophy: *n.* teosofía
theramin: *n.* teramín
therapeutic index: índice
terapéutico
therapeutic level: concentración
terapéutica
therapeutic range: intervalo
terapéutico
therapeutics: *n.* terapéutica
therapist: *n.* terapeuta
therapy: *n.* terapia
therapy: *n.* terapia
there: *adv.* ahí; allí; allá
thereabout: *adv.* por ahí; por allí
thereafter: *adv.* después de eso; de
allí en adelante
thereby: *adv.* con eso; con lo cual;
así; por allí cerca
therefor; therefore: *adv.* por lo
tanto; por consiguiente
thereupon: *adv.* sobre eso; encima
de eso
therewith: *adv.* con esto
thermal energy: energía térmica
thermal expansion: expansión
térmica
thermionics: *n.* termiónica
thermochemistry: *n.* termoquímica
thermodynamics: *n.* termodinámica
thermogram: *n.* termografía
thermograph: *n.* termógrafo
thermography: *n.* termografía
thermolysin: *n.* termolisina
thermometer: *n.* termómetro
thermos: *n.* termo
thermosphere: *n.* termosfera

thermostat: *n.* termostato
thesaurus: *n.* tesauro
thesis: *n.* tesis
theta: *n.* theta
theurgy: *n.* teurgia
thews: *n.* músculos
thiamine; thiamin: *n.* tiamina
thick: 1. *adj.* espeso; grueso; 2. *n.*
espesor; grueso
thicken: *v.* espesar
thickness: *n.* espesura; grueso
thief: *n.* ladrón
thigh: *n.* muslo
thighbone: *n.* fémur
thimble: *n.* dedal
thin: *adj.* delgado
thin: *v.* adelgazar
thing: *n.* cosa
think: *v.* pensar; creer; estimar
thinness: *n.* delgadez
thioglucosidase: *n.* tioglucosidasa
thioglycolate broth: caldo con
tioglicolato
third: 1. *adj.* tercero; 2. *n.* tercero
third class: en tercera clase
third degree: de grado tres
third person: *n.* tercera persona
third prong: tercero terminal
third-class: en tercera clase
thirst: *n.* sed
thirst: *v.* tener sed
thirsty : *adj.* sediento
thither: *adv.* allá; hacia allá
thong: *n.* correa
thoracentesis: *n.* toracocentesis
thoracic: *adj.* torácico
thorax: *n.* tórax
thorn: *n.* espina; púa
thoroughfare: *n.* carretera
thoroughly: *adv.* completamente
though: 1. *adv.* sin embargo;
2. *conj.* aunque
thought: *n.* pensamiento
thoughtless: *adj.* irreflexivo

thrash: *v.* trillar; azotar
thrashing: *n.* trilla
thread: *n.* hilo; fibra
thread: *v.* enhebrar; roscar
threaded: *adj.* roscado
threat: *n.* amenaza
threaten: *v.* amenazar
threatened species: especie amenazada
three-dimensional: *adj.* tridimensional
threepence: *n.* moneda de tres peniques
three-way plug: el enchufe de tres puntas
threonine: *n.* treonina
threshold: *n.* umbral; entrada
thrice: *adv.* tres veces
thrift: *n.* economía
thrill: *n.* emoción; exaltación
thrill: *v.* emocionar; estremecerse
thriller: *n.* persona o cosa emocionante
thrive: *v.* prosperar; adelantar
throat: *n.* garganta
throb: *n.* latido; palpitación
throb: *v.* latir; palpitar
throe: *n.* dolor; congoja
thrombin: *n.* trombina; tombasa
thrombocyte: *n.* trombocito; plaqueta
thrombosis: *n.* trombosis
thrombus: *n.* trombo
throne: *n.* trono
throng: *n.* gentío; tropel
throng: *v.* apretar; atestar
throttle: *n.* garganta; acelerador
throttle: *v.* ahogar; sofocar
through: prep. por; a través
throughout: 1. *adv.* por todas partes; 2. prep. en todo; durante todo
throw: *n.* tirada; lance
throw: *v.* lanzar; disparar
throw away: tirar; botar

throw rug: el tapete
thrust: *n.* empuje; acometida
thrust: *v.* empujar; hincar
thug: *n.* malhechor; ladrón
thumb: *n.* pulgar; dedo gordo
thunder: *n.* trueno; estruendo
thunder: *v.* fulminar; tronar
thunderstorm: *n.* tronada
Thursday: jueves
thus: *adv.* de este modo
thwart: 1. *adj.* trasversal; 2. *n.* riestra
thwart: *v.* desbaratar; frustrar
thyme: *n.* tomillo
thymidine: *n.* timidina
thymin: *n.* timopoyetina
thymine: *n.* timina
thyroid: *n.* glándula tiroidea
thyroxin: *n.* tiroxina
ti: *n.* si
tiara: *n.* tiara
tibia: *n.* tibia
tic: *n.* tic
ticarcillin: *n.* ticarcilina
tick: *n.* garrapata
ticket: *n.* billete; boleto
ticket: *v.* rotular; marcar
tickle: *n.* ticket
tickle: *v.* hacer cosquillas
ticktack: *n.* tictac
tidbit: *n.* buen bocado
tide: *n.* marea; temporada
tide: *v.* llevar
tie: *v.* amarrar; atar
tier: *n.* fila
tier: *v.* apilar
tierce: *adj.* tercera
tierce: *n.* tercera
tiger: *n.* tigre
tight: *adj.* apretado; estrecho
tighten: *v.* apretar; estirar
tightness: *n.* tensión; tirantez
tigress: *n.* tigresa
tilde: *n.* tilde
tile: *n.* azulejo; baldosa

tile: *v.* azulejar
tile cutter: la cortabaldosas
till: 1. *n.* cajón o gaveta del dinero; 2.
prep. hasta; 3. cnj. hasta que
till: *v.* labrar
tiller: *n.* agricultor
tilt: *n.* inclinación
tilt: *v.* inclinar; volcar
tilth: *n.* labranza
timbale: *n.* timbal
timber: *n.* madera
time: *n.* tiempo
time capsule: cápsula del tiempo
time out: tiempo muerto
time sharing: tiempo compartido
time warp: salto en el tiempo
timeless: *adj.* eterno; infinito
timer: *n.* contador
time-saving: que ahorra tiempo
timid: *adj.* tímido; temeroso
timidity: *n.* timidez
timorous: *adj.* timorato
timpani: *n.* tímpanos
timpanist: *n.* timbalero; -a
tin: *n.* estaño; hojalata
tin: *v.* estañar; enlatar
tin snips: *n.* tinte; baño
tincture: *v.* teñir
tincture: *n.* yesca; mecha
tinder: *n.* tiña
tinea: *n.* matiz; tinte
tinge: *v.* colorear; teñir
tinge: *n.* comezón
tingle: *n.* hormigueo
tingling: hormigueo
tingling sensation: hormigueo
tingling taste: *n.* tinidazol
tinidazole: *n.* retiñir
tinkle: *v.* sonar
tinkle: *adj.* en lata
tinned: *n.* tinnitus
tinnitus: *n.* tinte
tint: sombreado
tinted: *n.* ferrotipo

tintype: *n.* hojalatería
tinwork: *adj.* diminuto; menudo
tiny: *n.* punta
tip: *adj.* cavilante; achispado
tipsy: *n.* punta del pie
tiptoe: *v.* andar de puntillas
tiptoe: *adj.* superior; excelente
tiptop: *n.* cumbre; cima
tiptop: *n.* llanta
tire: *v.* cansar (se)
tire: *adj.* cansado
tired: *adj.* incansable
tireless: *adj.* cansado; aburrido
tiresome: *n.* incansable; infatigable
tirol: *n.* tejido
tissue: *n.* tisú
titanic: *n.* titánico
tithe: *n.* décimo; diezmo
title: *n.* titulo; inscripción
title: *v.* titular; roturar
titration: *n.* valoración
titter: *n.* risita ahogada o disimulada
titter: *v.* reír con disimulo
toast: *n.* tostada
toast: *vt.* tostar; brindar
toasted: *adj.* tostado
toaster: *n.* tostadora
tobacco: *adj.* atabacado
tobacco: *n.* tabaco
tobacco plantation: tabacal
toboggan: *n.* tobogán
tobramycin: *n.* tobramicina
toccata: *n.* tocata
today: *adv.* hoy
toe: *n.* dedo del pie; pezuña
toe kick: la tabla contragolpes
toenail: *v.* clavar en ángulo
tofu: *n.* tofú; queso de soya
toga: *n.* toga
together: *adv.* juntos; juntamente; a
un tiempo
toil: *n.* afán; fatiga
toil: *v.* sudar; afanarse
toilet: *n.* tocador; utensilio de tocador

token: *n.* trabajo; símbolo
tolerable: *adj.* tolerable
tolerance: *n.* tolerancia
tolerance rule: regla de tolerancia
tolerance test: prueba de tolerancia
tolerant: *n.* tolerante
tolerate: *v.* tolerar; aguantar
toll: *n.* tañido; doble de campanas
toll: *v.* cobrar o pagar peaje
toll free: llamada gratis; libre de cargo
tomato: *n.* tomate
tomato patch: tomatal
tomato plant: tomatera
tomb: *n.* tumba
tombstone: *n.* lápida o piedra sepulcral
tomcat: *n.* gato
tome: *n.* tomo
tomogram: *n.* tomograma
tomography: *n.* tomografía
tomorrow: *adv.* mañana
tom-tom: tam-tam
ton: *n.* tonelada
tonality: *n.* tonalidad
tone: *n.* tono
tone: *v.* entonar; armonizar
tongue: *n.* tono
tonic: *n.* lengua; *adj.* tónico
tonicity: *n.* tonicidad
tonight: *adv.* esta noche
tonnage: *n.* tonelaje
tonsil: *n.* amígdala
tonsillectomy: *n.* tonsilectomía
tonsure: *n.* tonsura
too: *adv.* también; además; demasiado
too much: demasiado
tool: *n.* utensilio; herramienta
tooth: *n.* diente; muela
toothless: *n.* palillo
top plate: la placa superior
topaz: *n.* topacio
topic: *n.* asunto; tema

topographer: *n.* topógrafo
topographic map: mapa topografico
topography: *n.* topografía
topology: *n.* topología
toponymy: *n.* toponimia
topple: *v.* derribar; volcar
topsoil: *n.* suelo superior
Toque: *n.* toca
Torah: *n.* tora
Torch: *n.* antorcha
Torii: *n.* torii
torment: *n.* tormento
torment: *v.* atormentar
tormented: *adj.* atormentado
tormenter; tormentor: *n.* atormentador(a)
tornado: *n.* tornado
torpedo: *n.* torpedo
torpedo boat: torpedero
torrent: *n.* torrente
torsion: *n.* torsión
torso: *n.* cuerpo; torso
torte: *n.* torta
torticolis: *n.* tortícolis
tortilla: *n.* tortilla
tortoise: *n.* tortuga
torture: *n.* tortuga
tory: *v.* torturar
toss: *n.* conservador; mezclar
toss-up: *n.* cara y cruz
total: 1. *adj.* total; entero; 2. *n.* total; entero
totalitarianism: *n.* totalitarismo
totality: *n.* totalidad
totem: *n.* tótem
touch: *n.* toque; tacto
touch: *v.* tocar
touching: *adj.* conmovedor; enternecedor
touch-sensitive: sensible al tacto
touchy: *adj.* quisquilloso
tough: *adj.* duro; recio
toughen: *v.* endurecer; dificultar
toupee: *n.* tupé

tour: *n.* paseo; viaje largo; excursión
touring: *n.* turismo
tourism: *n.* turismo
tourist: 1. *adj.* de turista; 2. *n.* turista
tourmaline: *n.* turmalina
tournament: *n.* torneo; campeonato
tournedo: *n.* turnedo
tourniquet: *n.* torniquete
tow: *n.* remolque; estopa
tow: *v.* remolcar
toward; towards: prep. hacia; cerca de
towel: *n.* toalla
towel rack: toallero
toweling: *n.* tela de toalla
tower: *n.* torre
tower: *v.* encumbrarse; elevarse
town: *n.* pueblo; ciudad; villa
toxemia: *n.* toxemia
toxic level: concentración tóxica
toxicity: *n.* toxicidad
toxicologist: *n.* toxicólogo
toxicology: *n.* toxicología
toxin: *n.* toxina
toy: *n.* juguete
toy: *v.* jugar; divertirse
trace: *n.* traza; rastro; pisada
trace: *v.* rastrear; seguir la pista de; trazar
trace element: oligoelemento; elemento traza
trace fossil: vestigios fósiles
traceability: *n.* trazabilidad
tracer: *n.* trazador
trachea: *n.* tráquea
tracheotomy: *n.* traqueotomía
trachoma: *n.* tracoma
tract: *n.* tracto
traction: *n.* tracción
tractor: *n.* tractor
trade: *n.* comercio; oficio
trade: *v.* trocar; cambiar
trade union: sindicato; unión obrera
trade winds: vientos alisios

trade-off: compensar
trader: *n.* comerciante; traficante
tradition: *n.* tradición
traditional: *adj.* tradicional
traduce: *v.* calumniar; difamar
traffic: *n.* tráfico
traffic: *v.* traficar
traffic island: isleta
trafficker: *n.* traficante
tragedian: *adj.* trágico
tragedy: *n.* tragedia
tragicomedy: *n.* tragicomedia
tragopon: *n.* trogon; vireo
Trail: *n.* huella; pista
trail: *v.* arrastrar
trailer sequence: secuencia remolque
train: *n.* tren
trainer: *v.* adiestrar
training: *n.* instrucción; preparación
trait: *n.* rasgo; característica
traitor: *n.* traidor
tram: *n.* trama; tranvía
trample: *n.* pisoteo
trample: *v.* atropellar; pisotear
trampoline: *n.* trampolín
tramway: *n.* tranvía
trance: *n.* rapto; arrobamiento; trance
tranquil: *adj.* tranquilo
tranquility: *n.* tranquilidad
tranquilizer: *n.* tranquilizante
transact: *v.* tramitar
transaction: *n.* transacción
transatlantic ocean: trasatlántico
transcend: *v.* exceder
transcendence: *n.* trascendencia
transcendental: *adj.* trascendental
transcendentalism: *n.* trascendentalismo
transcript: *n.* trascrito; trascripto
transcript mapping: cartografía del trascrito
transcription: *n.* transcripción

transducer: *n.* transductor
transducing phage: fago transductor
transept: *n.* transepto
transfer: *n.* traspaso; transferencia
transfer: *v.* transferir; traspasar
transfer factor: factor de transferencia
transfer of business: *n.* transferibilidad
transferability:
transference: *n.* transferencia
transferring: *n.* transferrina
transfiguration: *n.* transfiguración
transfix: *v.* traspasar
transform: *v.* transformar; transfigurar.
transformant: *n.* transformado
transformation: transformación
transformational: *adj.* transformacional
transformer: *n.* transformador
transfusion: *n.* transfusión
transfusion blood: transfusión de sangre
transgenic: *adj.* transgénico; -a
transgress: *v.* violar; quebrantar
transgression: *n.* transgresión
transgressor: *n.* transgresor
transient: 1. *adj.* pasajero; 2. *n.* transeúnte
transistor: *n.* transistor
transit: *n.* tránsito
transition: *n.* transición
transition metal: metal de transición
transitive: *adj.* transitivo
transitory: *adj.* transitorio
transketolase: *n.* transcetolasa
translate: *v.* traducir; cambiar
translation: *n.* traducción; traslación
translator: *n.* traductor
transliteration: *n.* trasliteración
translucent: *adj.* traslúcido
translucent material: material traslúcido

transmigration: *n.* trasmigración
transmission: *n.* transmisión
transmission factor: factor de transmisión
transmit: *v.* transmitir; traspasar
transmittance: *n.* transmitancia
transmitter: *n.* transmisor
transparency: *n.* transparencia; dispositiva
transparent: *adj.* transparente
transparent material: material transparente
transpiration: *n.* transpiración
transplant: *n.* trasplante
transponder: *v.* trasplantar
transponible: *n.* transponedor
transport: *n.* transporte
transport: *v.* transportar; deportar
transport medium: medio de transporte
transport number: número de transporte
transportation: *n.* transportación
transposition: *n.* transposición
transposon: *n.* transposón
transtyretin: *n.* transtiretina
transubstantiation: *n.* transubstanciación
transudate: *adj.* trasudado
transversal: *n.* transversal
transverse: *n.* transverso
transverse wave: onda transversal
transvestite: *n.* transvestido
trap: *n.* trampa; equipaje
trap: *v.* atrapar
trapeze: *n.* trapecio
trapeze artist: trapecista
trapezium: *n.* trapecio
trapezoid: *n.* trapecio; trapezoide
trappist: *n.* trapense
trash: *n.* broza; basura
trash: *v.* podar
trauma: *n.* trauma
travel: *n.* viaje

travel: *v.* viajar; caminar
travel expenses: gastos de viaje
traveler: *n.* viajero
traveler's check: cheque de viajero
traverse: *v.* atravesar
traverse: 1. *adj.* transversal; 2. *n.* paso; pasaje
tray: *n.* bandeja
tread: *n.* pisada
tread: *v.* pisar; pisotear
treason: *n.* traición
treasure: *n.* tesoro; caudal
treasure: v atesorar
treasurer: *n.* tesorero
treatable: *adj.* tratable
treating physician: médico de tratamiento
treatise: *n.* tratado
treatment: *n.* tratamiento
treatment: *n.* trato
treaty: *n.* tratado
treble: *n.* triple
treble: *v.* triplicar
tree: *n.* árbol
tree diagram: diagrama de árbol
trekking: *n.* trekking
tremble: *v.* temblar
trembling: *n.* temblor
tremendous: *adj.* tremendo
tremolo: *n.* trémolo
trench: *n.* trinchera; foso; zanja
trench: *v.* excavar
trenchant: *adj.* agudo
trend: *n.* dirección; tendencia
trend: *v.* dirigirse; tender
trepanation: *n.* trepanación
trephine: *n.* trefina
tress: *n.* trenza; rizo
trey: *n.* tres
triad: *n.* triada
trial: *n.* ensayo; prueba
trial and error: ensayo y error
triangle: *n.* triángulo
triangular: *adj.* triangular

triangular prism: prisma triangular
tribal: *adj.* tribal
tribe: *n.* tribu
tribulation: *n.* tribulación
tribune: *n.* tribuna
tributary: *adj.* afluente; tributario
trice: *n.* instante
tricentennial: *adj.* tricentenario
trichinosis: *n.* triquinosis
trichoptera: *n.* tricóptero
trichotomy: *n.* tricotomía
trick: 1. *adj.* ingenioso; 2. *n.* truco
trick: *v.* burlar; engañar
trick photography: trucaje
trickle: *n.* chorrear un poco
trickle: *v.* gotear
tricky: *adj.* tramposo
tricorne: *n.* tricornio
tricot: *n.* tricot
tricuspid: *adj.* tricúspide
triennial: *adj.* trienal
trifocal: *adj.* trifocal
trigger: *n.* disparador
triglyceride: *n.* triglicérido
trigonometric: *adj.* trigonométrico
trigonometric ratio: razón trigonométrica
trigonometry: *n.* trigonometría
trihedral: *n.* triedro
trilateral: *adj.* trilateral
trill: *n.* trino
trilogy: *n.* trilogía
trim: 1. *adj.* acicalado; compuesto; 2. *n.* adorno; aseo
trim: *v.* ajustar; adaptar; adornar
trimester: *n.* trimestre
trimethoprim: *n.* trimetoprima
trimming: *n.* guarnición; adorno
trinket: *n.* dije; joya
trinomial: *n.* trinomio
trio: *n.* trío
triode: *n.* tríodo
triple: *adj.* triple
triple bond: enlace triple

triplet: *n.* terceto; tersillo; trillizo
triplicate: *adj.* triplicado
tripod: *n.* trípode
triptych: *n.* tríptico
trisection: *n.* trisección
trismus: *n.* trismo
triton: *n.* tritón
triumph: *n.* triunfo
triumph: *v.* triunfar
triumphant: *adj.* triunfante
triumvirate: *n.* triunvirato
trivial: *adj.* trivial
trochaic: *adj.* trocaico
trochee: *n.* troqueo
troika: *n.* troica
trolley: *n.* tranvía; volquete
trolley: *n.* trole
trolleybus: *n.* trolebús
trombone: *n.* trombón
trombonist: *n.* trombonista
troop: *n.* tropa; escuadrón
troop: *v.* agruparse
troop carrier: transporte de tropas
troop tren: tren militar
trooper: *n.* soldado de caballería
trope: *n.* tropo
trophozoite: *n.* trofozoito
trophy: *n.* trofeo
tropic: *adj.* trópico
tropical: *adj.* tropical
tropical zone: zona tropical
tropics: *n.* zona tropical
tropism: *n.* tropismo
troposphere: *n.* troposfera
trot: *n.* trote; paso vivo
trot: *v.* hacer trotar
troubadour: *n.* trovador
troubleshooting: solución de problemas
troublous: *adj.* agitado; confuso
trough: *n.* artesa; pita; valle
trough level: concentración mínima
troupe: *n.* trouppe; compañía
trousseau: *n.* ajuar; equipo de novia

trout: *n.* trucha
troy: *n.* trío; troya
truce: *n.* tregua
truck: *n.* carro; camión
truck: *v.* trasportar
trucker: *n.* camionero; conductor
truckload: *n.* camionada
trudge: *n.* marcha
trudge: *v.* viajar a pie
true: *adj.* verdadero; exacto
true negative: negativo verdadero
true positive: *adj.* positivo verdadero
true value: valor verdadero
trueness: *n.* veracidad
truffle: *n.* trufa
trumpet: *n.* trompeta
trunk: *n.* tronco; baúl
truss: *n.* armadura
trust: *n.* fideicomiso
trust account: cuenta de fideicomiso
trust fund: fondo de fideicomisos
trustee: *n.* administrador
truth: *n.* verdad; fidelidad
try: *n.* prueba; intento
try: *v.* intentar; ensayar
trying: *adj.* penoso
trypanosome: *n.* tripanosoma
trypsin: *n.* tripsina
tuatara: *n.* tuatara; tuatera
tuba: *n.* tuba
tubal: *adj.* tubárico
tubal ligation: ligadura de trompas
tube: *n.* tubo
tube bender: la dobladora de tubos
tube feet: pies ambulantes
tubercle: *n.* tubérculo
tuberculin test: prueba de tuberculina
tuberculosis: *n.* tuberculosis
tuberose: *n.* tuberosa
tubing: *n.* tubería
tubule: *n.* túbulo
tuck: *n.* pliegue; alforza
tudor: *n.* tudor

Tuesday: martes
tuft: *n.* copete; mono
tuition: *n.* matrícula
tularemia: *n.* tularemia
tulip: *n.* tulipán
tulle: *n.* tul
tumble: *n.* tumbo
tumbler: *n.* vaso; cubilete
tumefaction: *n.* tumefacción
tumescence: *n.* tumescencia
tumor: *n.* tumor
tumor marker: marcador tumoral
tumor suppressor gene: gen
oncosupresor
tumult: *n.* tumulto
tumultuous: *adj.* tumultuoso
tun: *n.* tono; barril
tun: *v.* acordar; afinar
tuna: *n.* atún
tundra: *n.* tundra
tune: *n.* tonada
tunic: *n.* túnica
tunnel: *n.* túnel
tunny: *n.* atún
turban: *adj.* turbante
turbid: *adj.* turbio; borroso
turbidimetry: *n.* turbidimetría
turbine: *n.* turbina
turbocompressor: *n.*
turbocompresor
turbojet: *n.* turborreactor
turboprop: *n.* turbopropulsor
turbot: *n.* turbo
turbulence: *n.* turbulencia
turbulent: *adj.* turbulento
turgescence: *n.* turgencia
turgid: *adj.* turgente
turkey: *n.* pavo
turmoil: *n.* alboroto; tumulto
turn: *n.* vuelta; turno
turn: *v.* volver; dar vuelta a
turning: 1. *adj.* giratorio; rotatorio;
2. *n.* vuelta; rodeo
turnover: *n.* recambio metabólico;

ciclo metabólico
turpentine: *n.* trementina
turpitude: *n.* torpeza
turquoise: *n.* turquesa
turret: *n.* torrecilla; torreón
turret: *n.* torreón
turtle: *n.* tortuga
tusk: *n.* colmillo (de elefante)
tusk: *v.* herir con los colmillos
tutor: *n.* tutor
twang: *n.* timbre nasal
twang: *v.* producir un sonido agudo
tweed: *n.* mezcla de lana
twelve: doce
twenty: veinte
twice: *adv.* dos veces; doble
twin: *n.* gemelo mellizo
twine: *n.* bramante
twine: *v.* enroscar
twirl: *n.* vuelta; giro
twirl: *v.* torcer; retorcer
twisted: *adj.* torcido
two: dos
two-dimensional: *adj.* bidimensional
twofold: *n.* doble; duplicado
tympani: *n.* tímpanos
tympanist: *n.* timbalero
tympanum: *n.* tímpano
type: *n.* tipo; letras impresas
type: *v.* escribir a máquina
typewriter: *n.* máquina de escribir
typhoid: *n.* fiebre tifoidea
typhoid fever: *n.* fiebre tifoidea
typhoon: *n.* tifón
typhus: *n.* tifus; tifo
typical: *adj.* típico
typing: *n.* tipificación
tyrannical: *adj.* tiránico
tyrannize: *v.* tiranizar
tyrant: *n.* tirano
tyrol: *n.* tirol
tyrolean: *n.* tiroles
tyrosine: *n.* tirosina

U

ugaritic: *adj.* ugarítico
ugh!: *intj.* ¡uf!
ugliness: *n.* fealdad; afeamiento
ugly: *adj.* feo; disforme
ukulele: *n.* ukelele; *adj.* ukele
ulcer: *n.* úlcera
ulceration: *n.* ulceración
ulna: *n.* ulna
ulnar: *n.* ulnar
ultimatum: *n.* ultimatum
ultracentrifugation: *n.* ultracentrifugación
ultrafiltration: *n.* ultrafiltración
ultramarine: *adj.* ultramarino
ultramodern: *adj.* ultramoderno
ultrasound: *adj.* ultrasonido
ultraviolet radiation: radiación ultravioleta
ultraviolet ray: rayos ultravioletas
ululate: *v.* ulular
umbilical: *adj.* umbilical
umbilical cord: cordón umbilical
umbilicus: *n.* ombligo
umbra: *n.* umbra
umbrage: *n.* sombra; umbría
umbrella: *n.* paraguas
umpire: *n.* árbitro; juez
umpire: *v.* arbitrar
unabashed: *adj.* desvergonzado
unable: *adj.* incapaz
unacceptable: *adj.* inaceptable
unaccomplished: *adj.* incompleto
unaccountable: *adj.* inexplicable
unaccustomed: *adj.* insólito
unacquainted: *adj.* ignorado
unaffected: *adj.* inafectado
unanswerable: *adj.* incontestable

unarmed: *adj.* desarmado
unattached: *adj.* suelto
unauthorized: *adj.* desautorizado; sin autorización
unaware: 1. *adj.* inconsciente; 2. *adv.* de improviso
unbalanced force: fuerza desequilibrada
unbelievable: *adj.* increíble
unbending: *adj.* inflexible
unbind: *v.* desatar; desligar
unbosom: *v.* confesar
unbound: *adj.* no unido
unbreakable: *adj.* irrompible
unbroken: *adj.* intacto
unburden: *v.* descargar
unbutton: *v.* desabotonar
uncanny: *adj.* misterioso
uncertain: *adj.* incierto; dudoso
uncertainty: *n.* certidumbre
uncle: *n.* tío
uncle by marriage: tío político
unclean: *adj.* sucio; poco claro
unclear: *adj.* poco claro
unclouded: *adj.* esperado
uncollectible: *adj.* incobrable
uncomfortable: *adj.* incómodo
uncommon: *adj.* poco común
uncommunicative: *adj.* poco comunicativo
uncompromising: *adj.* inflexible
unconcern: *n.* indiferencia
unconscious: *adj.* inconsciente
unconventional: *adj.* poco convencional
uncork: *v.* descorchar; destapar
uncountable: *adj.* no contable
uncouple: *v.* desatraillar; desconectar
uncouth: *adj.* tosco; rústico
uncover: *v.* destapar; descubrir
unction: *n.* extremaunción
unctuous: *adj.* untuoso
uncultivated: *adj.* baldío; silvestre
uncultured: *adj.* indeciso

undeceive: *adj.* inculto
undecided: *v.* desengañar
undeliverable: *adj.* imposible de entregar
undeniable: *adj.* innegable
under: 1. *adv.* debajo; 2. *prep.* bajo; debajo de
under age: menor de edad
under oath: bajo juramento
underclass: *n.* clase marginada
underclothes: *n.* ropa interior
undercurrent: *adj.* corriente submarina
underestimate: *v.* menospreciar
underexposure: *n.* subexposición
underground: 1. *adj.* subterráneo; secreto; 2. *adv.* bajo tierra
underlie: *v.* estar debajo de
underline: *v.* subrayar
underling: *n.* inferior; subordinado
undermine: *v.* socavar
undermost: 1. *adj.* ínfimo; 2. *adv.* debajo de todo
underneath: 1. *adv.* debajo; 2. *prep.* debajo de
underpass: *n.* paso inferior
underpay: *n.* pago insuficiente
underpay: *v.* pagar insuficientemente
underpayment: *n.* pago insuficiente; pago de menos
underrate: *v.* menospreciar
undersecretary: *n.* subsecretario
undersigned: *adj.* suscrito; abajo firmante
undersoil: *n.* subsuelo
understand: *v.* comprender; entender
understory: *n.* sotobosque
undertake: *v.* emprender; comprometerse
undertaking: *n.* empresa; empeño
undertone: *n.* voz baja
undervalue: *v.* estimar demasiado bajo

underwater: *adj.* submarino
underwear: *n.* ropa interior
underwood: *n.* maleza
undeserved: *adj.* inmerecido
undesirable: *adj.* indeseable
undigested: *adj.* indigesto
undisciplined: *adj.* indisciplinado
undo: *v.* deshacer; anular
undocumented: *adj.* indocumentado
undoubted: *adj.* indudable
undress: *v.* desnudar
undulant fever: fiebre ondulante
unearned income: ingreso no derivado del trabajo
uneasiness: *n.* intranquilidad
uneasy: *adj.* intranquilo
uneducated: *adj.* ineducado; ignorante
unemployment: *n.* desempleo
unending: *adj.* inacabable
unequal: *adj.* desigual
uneven: *adj.* desnivelado
unevennes: *n.* desnivel
unexpected: *adj.* inesperado; fortuito
unexposed: *adj.* no expuesto
unfair: *adj.* inicuo; injusto
unfaithful: *adj.* infiel
unfavorable outcome: resultado desfavorable
unfeigned: *adj.* sincero; real
unfit: *adj.* incapaz; inhábil
unfit: *v.* inhabilitar
unfold: *v.* desplegar
unforeseen: *adj.* imprevisto
unfortunate: *adj.* infeliz; desgraciado
unfrequented: *adj.* solitario
unfriendly: *adj.* enemigo
unfurl: *v.* enrollar
ungovernable: *adj.* ingobernable
ungrammatical: *adj.* antigramatical
ungrateful: *adj.* ingrato
unguent: *n.* ungüento
unhappily: *adv.* infelizmente

unhealthy: *adj.* malsano; enfermizo
unheard: *adj.* que no se ha oído
unholy: *adj.* impío; malo
unhurt: *adj.* sin daño; ileso
unicameral: *adj.* unicameral
unicellular: *adj.* unicelular
unidirectional: *adj.* unidireccional
unification: *n.* unificación
uniform: *n.* uniforme
unify: *v.* unificar; unir
unilateral: *adj.* unilateral
unimaginative: *adj.* imaginativo; poco imaginativo
unimportant: *adj.* sin importancia
uninhabited: *adj.* inhabitado
uninsured: *adj.* no asegurado
unintelligent: *adj.* ininteligente
union: *n.* unión
union dues: cuota de sindicato
unique: *adj.* único
unison: *n.* concordancia; armonía; unísono
unit: *n.* unidad
unit rate: *n.* tasa unitaria
unitarian: *adj.* unitario
unitarianism: *n.* unitarismo
unite: *v.* unir; juntar
united: *adj.* unido
unity: *n.* unidad
universal: *adj.* universal
universalist: *n.* universalista
universe: 1. *adj.* universo; 2. *n.* universo
university: *n.* universidad
unjust: *adj.* injusto
unkempt: *adj.* despeinado
unkind: *adj.* duro; intratable
unlace: *v.* desenlazar
unlatch: *v.* abrir; quitar el cerrojo
unlawful: *adj.* ilegal
unless: *conj.* a menos que
unlettered: *adj.* iletrado
unlike: *adj.* desigual; distinto
unload: *v.* descargar

unlock: *v.* abrir; revelar secretos
unloose: *v.* desatar; desencadenar
unlucky: *adj.* de mala suerte
unmake: *v.* deshacer; destruir
unmask: *v.* descubrir; desenmascarar
unmixed: *adj.* sin mezcla
unnatural: *adj.* antinatural
unnavigable: *adj.* innavegable
unnecessary: *adj.* innecesario
unnerve: *v.* acobardar
unpack: *v.* desembalar; desempacar
unpardonable: *adj.* imperdonable
unpleasant: *adj.* antipático; desagradable
unpopularity: *n.* impopularidad
unpretentious: *adj.* sin pretensiones
unqualified: *adj.* no calificado
unravel: *v.* desenredar; deshilar
unreal: *adj.* irreal; falso
unreality: *n.* irrealidad
unreasonable: *adj.* desrazonable
unrest: *n.* intranquilidad
unrighteous: *adj.* injusto
unripe: *adj.* verde; crudo
unroll: *v.* desenrollar
unruffled: *adj.* tranquilo; sereno
unsatisfactory: *adj.* insatisfactorio
unsaturated solution: solución no saturada
unsaturated zone: zona insaturada
unscrupulous: *adj.* inescrupuloso
unsociable: *adj.* insociable
unsocial: *adj.* insocial
unsportsmanlike: *adj.* antideportivo
until: *adv.* hasta
untreatable: *adj.* no tratable
unusual: *adj.* inusual
up: arriba
update: *v.* actualizar
upgrade: *v.* mejorar
uphill: cuesta arriba
upper extreme: extremo superior
upper quartile: cuartil superior
upset: 1. *adj.* volcado; 2. *n.* vuelco

upset: *v.* volcar; trastornar
upside: *n.* de arriba; parte superior
upside down: boca abajo
upside-down: al revés; patas arriba
upsilon: *n.* ípsilon
upstairs: *adv.* arriba
upstream: *adv.* en dirección de arriba
up-to-date: al día
upwelling: *adj.* afloramiento
uracile: *adj.* uracilo
urban: *adj.* urbano
urban renewal: renovación urbana
urbanity: *n.* urbanidad
urchin: *n.* chiquillo
urea: *n.* urea
urease: *n.* ureasa
ureter: *n.* uréter
urethra: *n.* uretra
urethral exudate: exudado uretral
urge: *n.* impulso; instinto
urge: *v.* urgir; impulsar
urgency: *n.* urgencia
urgent: *adj.* urgente
uric acid: ácido úrico; urato
uricase: *n.* urato-oxidasa
uridine: *n.* uridina
urinal: *adj.* orinal; urinario
urinalysis: *n.* análisis de orina; urinálisis
urinary bladder: vejiga urinaria
urinary cast: cilindro urinario
urinary kallikrein: calicreína cística
urinary sediment: sedimento urinario
urinary stone: cálculo urinario
urinary tract: sistema urinario
urinate: *v.* orinar
urine: *n.* orina
urine culture: cultivo de orina; urocultivo
urine sample: muestra de orina
urine sediment: sedimento urinario
urine stream: chorro urinario

urn: *n.* urna
urobilinogen: *adj.* urobilinógeno
urogenital: *adj.* urogenital
urography: *n.* urografía
urolith: *n.* cálculo urinario
urologist: *n.* urólogo
urology: *n.* urología
us: *pron.* personal (caso objetivo) nos
usage: *n.* uso
use: *n.* uso
use: *v.* usar; emplear
used: *adj.* usado
useful: *adj.* útil
user: *n.* usuario
usher: *n.* acomodador; ujier
usher: *v.* conserje
usual: *adj.* usual
usufruct: *adj.* usufructo
usurp: *v.* usurpar
usury: *n.* usura
utensil: *n.* utensilio
uterus: *n.* útero; matriz
uticaria: *n.* uticaria
utilitarian: *adj.* utilitarista
utilitarian: *n.* utilitarista
utilitarianism: *n.* utilitarismo
utilities: *n.* servicios públicos (gas; electricidad; etc.)
utility cabinet: el gabinete de servicios
utility knife: la cuchilla/la navaja
utility room: despensa
utilize: *v.* utilizar; aprovechar
utopian: *adj.* utópico
utter: *adj.* total; completo
utter: *v.* proferir; pronunciar
utterly: *adv.* totalmente; completamente
uveitis: *n.* uveítis
uvula: *n.* úvula

V

vacancy: *n.* vacío; hueco; vacante
vacant: *adj.* vacante; vacío; hueco
vacate: *v.* dejar vacante
vacation: *n.* vacaciones
vacation pay: pago de vacaciones
vaccinate: *v.* vacunar
vaccination: *n.* vacunación
vaccine: *n.* vacuna
vacillation: *n.* vacilación
vacuole: *n.* vacuola
vacuous: *adj.* vacuo; desocupado
vacuum: *n.* vacío
vacuum cleaner: la aspiradora
vagabond: *adj.* vagabundo
vagabond: *n.* vagabundo; -a
vagina: *n.* vagina
vaginal: *adj.* vaginal
vaginal sex: sexo vaginal
vaginal suppository: supositorio vaginal
vaginitis: *n.* vaginitis
vagrancy: *n.* vagancia
vagrant: *adj.* vago
vague: *adj.* vago; incierto
vain: *adj.* vano; vanidoso
vainglorious: *adj.* vanaglorioso
vainglory: *n.* vanagloria
vale: *n.* valle
valediction: *n.* despedida
valence: *n.* valencia
valet: *n.* paje; camarero
valiant: *adj.* valiente; bravo
valid: *adj.* válido
validate: *v.* validar
validation: *n.* validación
validity: *n.* validez
valise: *n.* maleta; valija

valley: *n.* valle
valley glacier: glaciar de valle
valor: *n.* valentía; valor
valorous: *adj.* valeroso
valour: *n.* valor; valentía
valuable: *adj.* valioso
valuables: *n.* objetos de valor
value: *n.* valor; importe
value: *v.* valorar; tasar
valve: *n.* válvula
vampire: *n.* vampiro; vampiresa
vampirism: *n.* vampirismo
van: *n.* carro de carga; camión de mudanzas
vandal: *n.* vándalo
vandalism: *n.* vandalismo
vanguard: *n.* vanguardia
vanilla: *n.* vainilla
vanillin: *n.* vainillina
vanish: *v.* desvanecerse; desaparecer
vanity: *n.* vanidad
vanquish: *v.* vencer; sujetar
vapid: *adj.* insípido; soso
vapor light: luz de vapor
vaporization: vaporización
vara: *n.* vara
variable: 1. *adj.* variable; 2. *n.* variable
variable expression: expresión variable
variance: *n.* variación; variancia
variant: *adj.* variante
variation: *n.* variación
varicose veins: *n.* varices; várices
variety: *n.* variedad
variety show: variedades
various: *adj.* vario
varnish: *n.* barniz; charol
varnish: *v.* barnizar; encubrir
varnished: *adj.* barnizado
vary: *v.* variar; cambiar
vary inversely: variar inversamente
varying: *adj.* variante
vascular: *adj.* vascular

vascular plant: planta vascular
vascular tissue: tejido vascular
vase: *n.* florero; jarrón
vasectomy: *n.* vasectomía
vasoconstriction: *n.* vasoconstricción
vasoconstrictor: *n.* vasoconstrictor
vasodilatation: *n.* vasodilatación
vasodilator: *n.* vasodilatador
vasomotor: *n.* vasomotor
vasopressin: *n.* vasopresina
vassal: 1. *adj.* vasallo; súbdito; 2. *n.* vasallo
vassalage: *n.* vasallaje
vast: *adj.* vasto; extenso
vaticinate: *v.* vaticinar; adivinar
vaticination: *n.* vaticinio
vaudeville: *n.* vodevil
vault: *n.* bóveda; cúpula; cueva
vault: *v.* abovedar
veal: *n.* carne de ternera
vector: *n.* vector
vector space: espacio vectorial
veda: *n.* veda
veer: *v.* virar
vegetable: 1. *adj.* vegetal; de hortaliza; 2. *n.* vegetal; planta
vegetarian: *n.* vegetariano
vegetarianism: *n.* vegetarianismo
vegetate: *v.* vegetar
vegetation: *n.* vegetación
vehemence: *n.* vehemencia
vehement: *adj.* vehemente
vehicle: *n.* vehículo; carruaje
veil: *n.* veto
veil: *v.* velar; cubrir
veiling: *n.* tela para velos
vein: *n.* vena; veta; filón
vein: *v.* vetear
velcro: *n.* velcro
vellum: *n.* vitela; pergamino
velocity: *n.* velocidad
velodrome: *n.* velódromo

velour: *n.* velveton
velum: *n.* velo
velvet: *n.* terciopelo; vello
velveteen: *n.* velvetón
vendor: *n.* vendedor
veneer: *n.* chapa; enchapado
veneer: *v.* cubrir; ocultar
venerate: *v.* venerar; reverenciar
veneration: *n.* veneración
venereal: *adj.* venéreo
venereal: *n.* venéreo
venetian: *adj.* veneciano
vengeful: *adj.* vengativo
venom: *n.* veneno; malicia
venous blood: sangre venosa
vent: *n.* orificio; agujero
vent: *v.* desahogar; descargar
ventilate: *v.* ventilar; airear
ventilation: *n.* ventilación
ventral: *adj.* ventral
ventricle: *n.* ventrículo
ventriloquism: *n.* ventriloquia
ventriloquist: *n.* ventrílocuo
venture: *n.* aventura; riesgo
venture: *v.* aventurar; arriesgar
veracious: *adj.* verídico
veracity: *n.* veracidad
veranda: *n.* terraza; galería
verb: *n.* verbo
verbal model: modelo verbal
verbalization: *n.* expresión verbalmente
verbatim: *adj.* al pie de la letra
verbena: *n.* verbena
verbiage: *n.* verboragia; verborrea
verbose: *adj.* verboso
verdant: *adj.* verde; verdoso
verdict: *n.* veredicto; dictamen
verdure: *n.* verdor; verdura
verge: *n.* borde; margen
verge: *v.* acercarse
verger: *n.* sacristán alguacil de vara
verification: *n.* verificación
verify: *v.* verificar; comprobar;

justificar
vermicelli: *n.* fideos
vermicide: *n.* vermicida
vermiform: *adj.* vermiforme
vermilion: *n.* bermellón; rojo
vermin: *n.* sabandijas; alimaña
verminous: *adj.* verminoso
vermouth: *n.* vermut; verma
vernacular: *adj.* vernáculo; indígena
vernal: *adj.* vernal
versatile: *adj.* flexible; hábil
verse: *n.* verso; versículo
versed: *adj.* versado; práctico
versifier: *n.* versificador
versify: *v.* versificar
version: *n.* versión; traducción
verso: *n.* verso
versus: *prep.* contra; comparado con
vertebra: *n.* vértebra
vertebrate: *adj.* vertebrado
vertex: *n.* vértice
vertex of a polygon: vértice de un polígono
vertex of a solid: vértice de un cuerpo geométrico
vertex of an angle: vértice de un ángulo
vertical: *adj.* vertical
vertical angles: ángulos opuestos por el vértice
vertical line test: prueba de línea vertical
vertigo: *n.* vértigo
vertone: *n.* armónico
very: *adv.* muy bien
vesicle: *n.* vesícula
vesper: 1. *adj.* vespertino; 2. *n.* anochecer; tarde
vespers: *n.* vísperas
vessel: *n.* vasija; recipiente
vest: *n.* chaleco; chaquetilla
vestibule: *v.* vestir
vestment: *n.* vestíbulo
vet: *n.* veterano; veterinario

vet: *v.* reconocer
veteran: *n.* veterano
veterinarian: *n.* veterinario
veto: *n.* veto; prohibición
vex: *v.* vejar; molestar
via: *prep.* vía; por
viable: *adj.* viable
viaduct: *n.* viaducto
vial: *n.* vial
vibrant: *adj.* vibrante
vibraphone: *n.* vibráfono
vibrate: *v.* vibrar; retemblar
vibration: *n.* vibración
vibrato: *n.* vibrato
vibrator: *n.* vibrador
vicar: *n.* vicario
vicarage: *n.* vicaría
vice: *n.* vicio; falta; cercanía
vice-presidency: vicepresidencia
vice-president: vice-presidente
vicious: *adj.* vicioso
vicissitude: *n.* vicisitud
victim: *n.* víctima
victor: *n.* vencedor; triunfador
victorious: *adj.* victorioso
victory: *n.* victoria
victualler: *n.* abastecedor; proveedor
vicuna: *n.* vicuña
video: *n.* video
video camera: video cámara
video cassette: video casete
video cassette: videocasete
video conference: video conferencia
video game: video juego
video library: videoteca
videoconference: *n.* videoconferencia
videodisc; videodisk: *n.* videodisco
videophone: *n.* videófono
videotape: *n.* videocinta
vie: *v.* competir; rivalizar
view: *n.* vista; panorama
view: *v.* ver; mirar; contemplar
viewer: *n.* espectador; inspector

vigil: *n.* vigilia
vigilance: *n.* vigilancia
vigilant: *adj.* vigilante
vigor: *n.* vigor
vigor: *n.* vigor; fuerza
vile: *adj.* vil; repugnante
vilification: *n.* vilipendio
vilify: *v.* difamar; envilecer
vilifying: *adj.* vilipendiador
vilifying: *n.* vilipendiador
villa: *n.* quinta; casa de campo; villa
village: *n.* aldea; pueblo caserío
villain: *n.* malvado; bellaco; pícaro
villainous: *adj.* villano
villainy: *n.* villanía
vinaigrette: *n.* vinagreta
vindicate: *v.* vindicar
vindication: *n.* vindicación
vindictive: *adj.* vindicativo
vine: *n.* vid
vinegar: *n.* vinagre
vinegary: *adj.* avinagrado; vinagroso
vineyard: *n.* viña; viñedo
viniculture: *n.* vinicultura
vintage: *n.* vendimia; cosecha
vintner: *n.* vinatero
vinyl: *adj.* vinilo
viola: *n.* viola
violate: *v.* violar; violentar
violation: *n.* violación
violence: *n.* violencia; fuerza
violent: *adj.* violento
violet: *adj.* violeta
violin: *n.* violín
violinist: *n.* violinista
violist: *n.* viola
violoncellist: *n.* violonchelista
violoncello: *n.* violonchelo
viper: *n.* víbora
virago: *n.* marimacho
viral: *adj.* virulento
viral oncogene: oncogén vírico
viremia: *n.* viremia
virgin: 1. *adj.* virgen; inmaculado;

2. *n.* virgen
virgin forest: bosque virgen
virginal: *adj.* virginal
virgo: *adj.* virgo
virility: *n.* virilidad
virion: *n.* virión
viroid: *adj.* viroide
virologist: *n.* virólogo
virology: *n.* virología
virtual: *adj.* virtual
virtual image: imagen virtual
virtual memory: memoria virtual
virtue: *n.* virtud
virtuosity: *n.* virtuosismo
virtuoso: *n.* virtuoso
virtuous: *adj.* virtuoso
virulence: *n.* virulencia
virus: *n.* virus
visa: *n.* visa
visage: *n.* cara; semblante
viscera: *n.* víscera
viscosity: *n.* viscosidad
visible: *adj.* visible
visible light: luz visible
vision: *n.* visión; vista
vision test: examen de la vista
visionary: *adj.* visionario
visit: *n.* visita
visit: *v.* visitar; inspeccionar
visit: *n.* visita
visitation: *n.* visitación
visitor: *n.* visitante
visor: *n.* visera
vista: *n.* vista
visual: *adj.* visual
vitalism: *n.* vitalismo
vitality: *n.* vitalidad
vitamin: *n.* vitamina
vitamin deficiency: *n.* déficit
vitamínico
vitiate: *v.* viciar
vitreous: *adj.* vítreo
vitriolic: *adj.* vitriólico
vital: *adj.* vital

vituperate: *v.* vituperar; censurar
vituperation: *n.* vituperio
vituperative: *adj.* vituperioso
vivacity: *n.* vivacidad; viveza
vivify: *v.* vivificador; avivar
viviparous: *adj.* vivíparo
vocable: *n.* voz; vocablo; palabra
vocabulary: *n.* vocabulario
vocal: *adj.* vocal
vocal cords: cuerdas vocales
vocalist: *n.* vocalista
vocalization: *n.* vocalización
vocation: *n.* vocación
vocational: *adj.* vocacional
vocational evaluation: evaluación vocacional
vocational rehabilitation: rehabilitación vocacional
vocative: *adj.* vocativo
vocciferate: *v.* vocear; vociferar
vociferating: *adj.* vociferante
vociferous: *adj.* vociferador
vodka: *n.* vodka
vogue: *n.* boga; moda
voice: *n.* voz
voice: *v.* expresar; divulgar
voice-over: voz superpuesta
void: 1. *adj.* vacío; nulo; inválido; 2. *n.* vacío
void: *v.* anular; vaciar
volatility: *n.* volatilidad
volcanic neck: cuello volcánico
volcano: *n.* volcán
volition: *n.* volición
volley: *n.* descarga
volley: *v.* volear; dirigir
volley: *n.* volea
volleyball: *n.* voleibol; voleibol
volt: *n.* volt; voltio
voltage: *n.* voltaje
voltage source: fuente de voltaje
voltaic: *adj.* voltaico
voltammeter: *n.* voltamperímetro
voltmeter: *n.* voltímetro

volume: *n.* volumen
volume flow rate: caudal de volumen
volume fraction: fracción de volumen
volume of a solid: volumen de un cuerpo geométrico
volume rate: caudal de volumen
volumetric flask: matraz aforado
volumetric pipet: pipeta aforada
volumetry: *n.* volumetría
volumic: *adj.* volúmico; -a
volumic mass: masa volúmica
voluminous: *adj.* voluminoso
voluntary: *adj.* voluntario
voluntary muscle: músculos voluntarios
volunteer: *n.* voluntario
voluptuary: *n.* voluptuoso
vomit: *n.* vómito
vomit: *v.* vomitar; provocar
vomiting: *n.* vómito
voodoo: *n.* vudú
voracious: *adj.* voraz
voracity: *n.* voracidad
vortex: *n.* vórtice
vorticella: *n.* vorticela
votary: *n.* partidario; monde
vote: *n.* voto
vote: *v.* votar
voter: *n.* votante
voting: *n.* votación
vouch: *v.* garantizar; atestiguar; certificar
voucher: *n.* fiador; garante
vouchsafe: *v.* conceder; otorgar
vow: *n.* promesa solemne; voto
vow: *v.* prometer solemnemente; votar
vow of poverty: voto de pobreza
vowel: *n.* vocal
vowel point: punto vocálico
voyage: *n.* viaje
voyage: *v.* atravesar

voyager: *n.* viajero
vulgar: *adj.* vulgar
vulgarism: *n.* vulgarismo
vulgarity: *n.* vulgaridad
vulnerability: *n.* vulnerabilidad
vulnerable: *adj.* vulnerable
vulture: *n.* buitre
vulva: *n.* vulva

W

wad: *n.* taco; guata
wad: *v.* colocar algodón en; acolchar
wadding: *n.* algodón
wading: *adj.* zancuda
wafer: *n.* oblea; hostia
waft: *n.* ráfaga de aire; viento; olor
waft: *v.* mecer
wag: *v.* sacudir; menear
wage earner: trabajador asalariado
wage statement: informe de sueldo
wager: *n.* apuesta
wager: *v.* apostar
wages: *n.* salarios; sueldos
waggery: *n.* broma; chanza
waggish: *adj.* bromista
wagon: *n.* carreta; carromato; vagón
wagonload: *n.* vagón
waif: *n.* cosa o animal sin dueño;
niño abandonado
wail: *n.* gemido; lamento
wail: *v.* llorar
waiscoat: *n.* chaleco
waist: *n.* cintura; talle
wait: *n.* espera
wait: *v.* esperar; aguardar
waiter: *n.* camarero; mozo
waiting: 1. *adj.* que espera; 2. *n.* espera
waiting period: período de espera

waitress: *n.* camarera; criada
waive: *v.* renunciar a
waiver: *n.* dispensa; dispensación
wake: *n.* vigilia
wake: *v.* velar un cadáver
waken: *v.* despertar
wales: *n.* Gales
walk: *n.* caminata; paseo
walk: *v.* andar; caminar
walkie-talkie: transmisor-receptor
portátil.
walkout: *n.* huelga de obreros.
wall: *n.* pared; muro
wall: *v.* emparedar; amurallar
wallaby: *n.* wallabi
wallet: *n.* cartera; mochila
wallow: *n.* revuelco
wallow: *v.* revolcarse
walnut: *n.* nuez; nogal
waltz: *n.* vals
wan: *adj.* pálido
wand: *n.* vara; varilla mágica
wander: *v.* atravesar; recorrer a la
ventura
wane: *n.* mengua; disminución
wane: *v.* menguar
want: *n.* deseo; necesidad
want: *v.* querer; desear
wanting: *adj.* falto; defectuoso;
necesitado
wanton: 1. *adj.* insensible; perverso;
2. *n.* libertino; prostituta
war: *n.* guerra
war: *v.* guerrear
ward: *n.* pupilo; tutela
ward: *v.* guardar; defender
warden: *n.* guardián; carcelero
wardrobe: *n.* guardarropa
warehouse: *n.* almacén
warehouse: *v.* almacenar
warfare: *n.* guerra; arte militar
warines: *n.* cautela
warm: *adj.* caliente; cálido
warm: *v.* calentar; acalorar

warmth: *n.* calor moderado; entusiasmo; simpatía
warn: *v.* avisar; advertir
warning: *n.* aviso; amonestación
warrant: *n.* autorización; decreto
warrant: *v.* autorizar; justificar
warren: *n.* conejera. vivero
wary: *adj.* cauteloso; prudente
wash: *n.* lavado; jabonado
wash: *v.* lavar
washed-out: descolorido
washing: *n.* lavado
washing machine: máquina de lavar
washstand: *n.* palangana
washy: *adj.* aguado; diluido
wasp: *n.* avispa
wastage: *n.* pérdida; derroche
wasteful: *n.* gastador; derrochador
wasteless: *adj.* sin desperdicio
watch: *n.* vigilancia; velación
watch: *v.* mirar; velar
watchful: *adj.* vigilante; cuidadoso
watchman: *n.* sereno
watchword: *n.* santo y seña; lema
water: *n.* agua
water: *v.* regar; rociar
water cycle: ciclo del agua
water filter: filtro de agua
water heater: calentador del agua
water leak: fuga de agua
water main: agua matriz
water meter: medidor de agua
water pipe: tubo de agua
water pollution: contaminación del agua
water quality: calidad del agua
water table: nivel freático
water tank truck: camión cisterna
water valve: válvula de agua
water vapor: vapor de agua
water vascular system: sistema vascular de agua
water-based paint: la pintura al agua

waterfall: *n.* catarata
waterline: *n.* línea de flotación
watermelon: *n.* sandía
waterproof: *adj.* impermeable
waterspout: *n.* canalón; manga
watertight: *adj.* hermético; estanco
watery: *adj.* acuoso; mojado
watt: *n.* watt; vatio
wattage: *n.* vataje
watt-hour: *n.* vatio-hora
watt-hour meter: el medidor de vatios por hora
wattmeter: *n.* vatímetro
wave: *n.* onda; ola
wave: *v.* agitar; blandir
wave height: altura de una ola
wavelength: *n.* longitud de onda
wavenumber: *n.* número de onda
waver: *v.* oscilar; ondear
wax: *n.* cera
wax: *v.* encerar
waxy cast: cilindro céreo
way: *n.* vía; camino; manera; modo
wayfarer: *n.* caminante
waylay: *v.* acechar
we: *pron.* pers. nosotros
weak: *adj.* débil; flojo
weaken: *v.* debilitar; enflaquecer
weakness: *n.* debilidad
weakness muscle: debilidad muscular
wealth: *n.* riqueza
wean: *v.* destetar
weapon: *n.* arma
wear: *n.* use; desgaste; deterioro
wear: *v.* llevar o traer puesto; usar
wearer: *n.* portador
weariness: *n.* cansancio
wearisome: *adj.* aburrido
weary: *adj.* cansado; aburrido
weary: *v.* cansar
weather: *n.* tiempo
weather: *v.* airear; solear
weather stria: el burlete

weathering: *n.* desgaste
weave: *n.* tejido
weave: *v.* tejer
web: *n.* tela; tejido
weber: *n.* weber
wedding: *n.* boda; matrimonio
wedge: *n.* cuña
wedge: *v.* acuñar
wedlock: *n.* matrimonio
Wednesday: miércoles
weed: *n.* mala hierba
weedwacker: *n.* desyerbador
week: *n.* semana
weekend: *n.* fin de semana
weep: *v.* llorar; derramar
weep hole: hueco para drenaje
weer: *v.* creer; pensar
weigh: *v.* pesar; medir
weighing: *n.* pesada; peso
weight: *n.* peso
weighted benefits: beneficios ajustados
weighting scheme: esquema de pesaje
weird: *adj.* misterioso; sobrenatural
welcome: *n.* bienvenida
welcome: *v.* dar la bienvenida
weld: *n.* soldadura autógena
weld: *v.* soldar con autógena
welder: *n.* soldador
welding: la soldadura
welfare: *n.* bienestar
welfare department: departamento de bienestar público
welfare reform: reformas al sistema de bienestar público
well: 1. *n.* pozo; fuente; manantial; 2. *adv.* bien; muy bien; mucho
wench: *n.* muchacha
wend: *v.* seguir su camino
west: *n.* oeste; occidente
westbound: *adv.* con rumbo al oeste
westbound: *n.* con rumbo al oeste
westerly: 1. *adj.* occidental;

2. *n.* viento del oeste; 3. *adv.* del oeste
western: 1. *adj.* occidental; 2. *n.* película del oeste
western: *adv.* del oeste
western blot: test western blot
westerner: *n.* habitante del oeste
westward: *adv.* hacia el oeste
wet: 1. *adj.* mojado; húmedo; 2. *n.* humedad
wet: *v.* mojar
wet cell: celda húmeda
wet-dry vac: la aspiradora de agua
wetland: *n.* humedal; pantano
whale: *n.* ballena
wharf: *n.* muelle; andén
wheat: *n.* trigo
wheedle: *v.* engatusar; halagar
wheel: *n.* rueda; disco
wheel: *v.* proveer de ruedas
wheel and axle: rueda y eje
wheelbarrow: la carretilla
wheelchair: *n.* silla; silla de ruedas
when: 1. *adv.* cuando; 2. *conj.* cuando
whence: *adv.* de donde; por eso; por tanto
whenever: *conj.* cuando; cuando quiera que
whensoever: 1. *adv.* cuando quiera; 2. *conj.* cuando quiera que
where: *adv.* donde; adonde; en donde
whereabouts: *n.* paradero
whereabouts unknown: paradero desconocido
whereas: *conj.* mientras que
whereby: *adj.* por donde; por medio del cual
wherein: *adv.* donde; en que; como
whereto: *adj.* adonde
whereupon: *adv.* entonces; con lo cual
wherever: *adv.* dondequiera que
whet: *n.* afiladura; aperitivo

whet: *v.* afilar; aguzar; estimular
whether: *conj.* si
whey: *n.* suero de leche
which: pro*n.* cual; que; el (la; etc.) que
whichever: pro*n.* rel. cualquiera
while: 1. *n.* rato; 2. *v.* pasar el rato
while: 1. *conj.* mientras que; al mismo tiempo que; 2. *n.* mientras
whim: *n.* capricho; antojo
whip: *n.* látigo; azote
whip: *v.* azotar; fustigar
whirl: *n.* vuelta; giro
whirl: *v.* hacer girar
whirlpool: *n.* remolino
whisk: *n.* escobilla; cepillo
whisk: *v.* cepillar; barren
whisker: *n.* patilla; pelo de la barba
whiskey: *n.* whisky
whisper: *n.* cuchicheo
whistle: *v.* decir al oído
whistle: *n.* silbido
whit: *v.* silbar
white: *adj.* blanco; pálido
white blood cell: glóbulos blancos
white cell: leucocito
white cell count: recuento de glóbulos blancos
white dwarf: enana blanca
whiten: *v.* blanquear
whiter: *adv.* adonde; hacia donde
whiz: *v.* silbar; zumbar
whizz:
who: pro*n.* quien; quienes
whoever: quienquiera que
whole: *adj.* entero; todo
whole blood: sangre total; sangre íntegra
whole numbers: números enteros
wholesale: *n.* venta al por mayor
wholesome: *adj.* saludable
whom: pro*n.* que; a quien
whoop: *n.* alarido; grito
whoop: *v.* decir a gritos

whoopee!; yippee!: *intj.* ¡yupi!
whooping cough: tos ferina
whop: *n.* carcoma
whopping: *v.* dar una paliza a
whore: *n.* prostituta
whose: pro*n.* de quien?
wicket: *n.* portillo
wide: *adj.* ancho; extenso
wide-angle lens: gran angular
widen: *v.* ensanchar
widow: *n.* viuda
widower: *n.* viudo
width: *n.* anchura
wield: *v.* empuñar; esgrimir
wife: *n.* esposa
wig: *n.* peluca
wights and measures: pesos y medidas
wild: 1. *adj.* salvaje; silvestre; 2. *adv.* violentamente
wild: *n.* yermo; desierto
wildcat: *n.* gato montés
wildlife: *n.* vida silvestre
wildness: 1. *n.* ferocidad; fiereza; testamento
will: *n.* testamento
willow: *n.* sauce
wilt: *v.* marchitarse
win: *v.* ganar; triunfar
wince: *n.* sobresalto
winch: *n.* torso
wind: *n.* viento; aire; aliento
wind: *v.* husmear
windfall: *n.* rama o fruta caída del árbol
windfall benefits: beneficios inesperados
winding: 1. *adj.* sinuoso; 2. *n.* vuelta; bobinado
windmill: *n.* molino de viento
window: *n.* ventana; escaparate
window sash: el bastidor de vidriera
windpipe: *n.* tráquea
windward: *n.* barlovento

windy: *adj.* ventoso
wine: *n.* vino
wine glass: copa para vino
wine grower: vinicultor; -a
wine merchant: viñatero
wine shop: vinatería
wineglass: *n.* copa para vino
winegrower: *n.* vinicultor; -a
winery: *n.* vinería
wing: *n.* ala; paleta de hélice
wing: *v.* volar
wink: *n.* guiño; parpadeo
wink: *v.* guiñar
winner: *n.* ganador
winning: *adj.* ganancioso; triunfador
winnow: *v.* aventar; entresacar
winsome: *adj.* atrayente; simpático
winter: *n.* invierno
winter: *v.* invernar
winterless: *adj.* sin invierno
wipe: *n.* frotadura
wipe: *v.* enjugar; secar
wiper: *n.* limpiador; paño
wire: *n.* alambre; telégrafo
wire: *v.* proveer de alambres; atar con alambre
wisdom: *n.* sabiduría
wise: *adj.* sabio; doctor; erudito
wish: *n.* deseo; anhelo
wish: *v.* desear; querer
wishful: *adj.* deseoso
wisp: *n.* puñado; rastro
wit: *n.* puñado; rastro
witch: *n.* bruja; hechicera
wite cell count: recuento de glóbulos blancos
with: *prep.* con; de; en compañía
withal: *adj.* además; también
withdraw: *v.* retirar; quitar; separar
withdrawal: *n.* síndrome de abstinencia
wither: *v.* marchitar
withhold: *v.* negar; suspender
within: 1. *adv.* dentro; adentro; 2.

prep. dentro de
without: 1. *adv.* fuera; 2. *prep.* fuera de; sin; 2. cnj
withstand: *v.* aguantar; soportar
witness: *n.* testigo; testimonio
witness: *v.* dar testimonio.
witty: *adj.* agudo; ingenioso
wizard: *n.* brujo; hechicero
woe: *n.* dolor; pena
woeful: *adj.* miserable
wolf: *n.* lobo
woman: *n.* mujer
wombat: *n.* wombat
wonder: *n.* maravilla; portento
wonder: *v.* preguntarse
wonderful: *adj.* maravilloso; prodigioso
wont: 1. *adj.* habituado; 2. *n.* hábito; costumbre; uso
wonted: *adj.* habitual
wood: *n.* madera; bosque
woodcreeper: *n.* trepatronco; trepador
wooded: *adj.* plantado de árboles
woodland: 1. *adj.* silvestre; 2. *n.* bosque; arbolado
woodpecker: *n.* pájaro carpintero
woodwork: *n.* ebanistería
word: *n.* palabra
word: *v.* redactar; enunciar
word processing: procesamiento de palabras
word processor: procesador de palabras
wordless: *adj.* mudo
work: *n.* trabajo; tarea
work: *v.* trabajar; funcionar
work activity: actividad de trabajo
work test: límite de trabajo
worker: *n.* trabajador; obrero
workforce: *n.* fuerza laboral
workhouse: *n.* hospicio; asilo
working: *n.* obra; trabajo
working class: clase obrera

working conditions: condiciones de trabajo
workmanlike: *adj.* esmerado
workmanship: *n.* destreza o habilidad en el trabajo
worksheet: *n.* hoja de cálculos
workshop: *n.* taller; fábrica
world bank: banco mundial
world map: mapamundi
worm: *n.* gusano; lombriz
worm: *v.* limpiar de lombrices; conseguir por medio de artimañas
worn: *adj.* gastado; roto
worry: *n.* inquietud; preocupación
worry: *v.* inquietar; preocupar
worse: *adj.* peor
worsen: *v.* empeorar
worship: *n.* adoración; culto
worship: *v.* adorar
worth: *n.* valor; valía
worthless: *adj.* sin valor
wound: *n.* herida
wound: *v.* herir
wrangle: *n.* disputa; riña
wrangle: *v.* disputar
wrap: *n.* abrigo
wrap: *v.* envolver
wrapper: *n.* envoltura; funda
wrath: *n.* ira; cólera
wreak: *v.* descargar
wreath: *n.* corona
wreck: *n.* destrucción; ruina
wreck: *v.* destruir; arruinar
wrench: *n.* llave; torcedura violenta; dolor
wrench: *v.* retorcer
wrest: *n.* torsión violenta
wrest: *v.* torcer; arrancar
wrestle: *v.* luchar
wriggle: *v.* menearse rápidamente
wring: *v.* torcer; retorcer
wrinkle: *n.* arruga
wrinkle: *v.* arrugar
wrist: *n.* muñeca

write: *v.* escribir
writing: *n.* escritura
written evidence: constancia por escrito
wrong: *adj.* injusto; equivocado
wrong: *v.* agraviar; ofender
wrongly: *adv.* mal; erróneamente
wry: *adj.* torcido; ladeado

X

xanthine: *n.* xantina
xanthoma: *n.* xantoma
x-axis: eje x
x-coordinate: coordenada x
xenobiotic: *n.* xenobiótico -ica
xenophilia: *n.* afición a lo extranjero
xenophobe: *n.* xenófobo; -a
xenophobia: *n.* aversión a lo extranjero
xerophyte: *n.* xerofita
xi: *n.* xi
x-intercept: interseccion en x
Xmas (abrev. de Christmas): Navidad
X-ray: *n.* rayo X; radiografía
X-ray: *v.* radiografiar
X-ray machine: aparato de rayos X
x-ray of the chest: radiografía del tórax
X-rays: rayos X; radiografía
xylem: *n.* xilema
xylograph: *n.* xilografía
xylography: *n.* xilografía
xylophone: *n.* xilófono
xylophonist: *n.* xilofonista
xylose: *n.* xilosa

Y

yacht: *n.* yate
yacht: *v.* pasear en yate
yacht: *n.* yate
yachting: *n.* navegación en yate
yah!: *intj.* ¡ja; ja!
yak: *n.* yac
yang: *n.* yang
yard: *n.* yarda (medida = 0;91 metros)
yardage: *n.* medida en yardas; tela
yarn: *n.* hilado
yarn: *v.* inventar y contar historietas
y-axis: eje y
y-coordinate: coordenada y
year: *n.* año
yearn: *v.* suspirar por
yeast: *n.* levadura
yeast extract: extracto de levadura
yell: *n.* grito; voz
yell: *v.* decir a gritos
yellow: *adj.* amarillo
yellow fever: fiebre amarilla
yes: *adv.* sí; ciertamente
yeshiva: *n.* yeshiva
yesterday: *adv.* ayer
yet: 1. *adv.* todavía; 2. *conj.* con todo
yield: *n.* producción; rendimiento
yield: *v.* producir; rentar
yin: *n.* yin
y-intercept: intersección en y
yoga: *n.* yoga
yogi: *n.* yogui
yogurt maker: yogurtera
yoke: *n.* yugo
yolk: *n.* yema de huevo
yom kippur: yom kippur
yonder: *adj.* aquel; aquellos; *adv.* Allá; mas allá

yoo-hoo!: *intj.* ¡juju!
you: pro*n.* tu; ti; te; vosotros; usted; ustedes; le; la les
young: *adj.* joven; temprano
younger: menor de; más joven que
your: *adj.* poss. tu; vuestro; su; el de usted o de ustedes
yours: pro*n.* poss. tuyo; vuestro; suyo; de usted; de ustedes
yourself: pro*n.* usted mismo
youth: *n.* juventud
yo-yo: yoyo; yoyó
Yuan: *n.* yuan
yum yum!: *intj.* ¡ñam ñam!
yuppie; yuppy: *n.* yupi
yurt: *n.* yurt

Z

zarzuela: *n.* zarzuela
zeal: *n.* celo; fervor
zealot: *n.* fanático
zebra: *n.* cebra
zein: *n.* ceína; zeína
zen: *n.* zen
zenith: *n.* cenit; apogeo
zephyr: *n.* céfiro
zeppelin: *n.* zeppelín
zero: cero
zero gravity: gravedad nula
zest: *n.* entusiasmo; gusto; sabor
zeta: *n.* zeta
zigzag: *n.* zigzag
zinc: *n.* cinc
zinc: *v.* cubrir con cinc; galvanizar
zinc-finger: dedo de zinc
zinnia: *n.* cinnia
zion: *n.* sion
zionism: *n.* sionismo
zionist: sionista

zip: *v.* comprimir
zip code: código postal
zipper: *n.* ziper; cierre de cremallera
zircon: *n.* circón; zircón
zombie: *n.* zombi
zone: *n.* zona
zone: *v.* dividir en zonas
zoning: *n.* zonificación
zoo: *n.* zoo; parque zoológico
zoogeography: *n.* zoogeografía
zoography: *n.* zoografía
zooid: *n.* zooide
zoology: *n.* zoología
zoom lens: zoom
zoophyte: *n.* zoófito
zygoma: *n.* cigoma; zigoma
zygotene: *n.* cigotena
zymase: *n.* cimaza; zimasa
zymogen: *n.* zimógeno; proenzima
zymology: *n.* cimología
zymurgy: *n.* cimurgia; zimurgia

SECTION TWO

Spanish English

Dictionary

A

abad: *nm.* abbot
abadejo: *nm.* codfish
abadesa: *nf.* abbess
abadía: *nf.* abbey
abajarse: *vr.* to go down
abajo: *av.* down; under; below
abalanzar: *vt.* to balance; *vi.*to rush on
abanderado: *nm.* standard-bearer
abanderar: *vt.* to conscript
abandonado: *aj.* abandoned
abandonar: *vt.* to abandon
abandono: *nm.* abandonment
abanicar: *vt.* to fan
abanico: *nm.* fan
abaratamiento: *nm.* action of lowering the price
abaratar: *vt.* to cheapen; to lower the price of
abarcar: *vt.* to embrace
abarrotar: *vt.* to stow
abastecedor: 1. *nm.* caterer; 2. *aj.* caterer
abastecer: *vt.* to supply
abate: *nm.* priest
abatido: *aj.* dejected; suffering; discouraged; demolished
abatimiento: *nm.* suffering; discouragement
abatir: *vt.* to cause suffering; to discourage
abdicar: *vt.* to abdicate; renounce
abdomen: *nm.* abdomen; stomach
abeja: *nf.* bee
abejón: *nm.* large bee
abejorreo: *nm.* buzzing sound made by a bee
abejorro: *nm.* bumble-bee
abertura: *nf.* aperture; opening
abeto: *nm.* silver-tree; fir-tree
abierto: *aj.* open; clear
abismado: *aj.* defected

abismal: *aj.* abysmal
abismar: *vt.* to put something in the abyss; to disparage
abismo: *nm.* abyss
abjuración: *nf.* forswearing
abjurar: *vt.* to forswear; to abjure; to publicly renounce something or someone
ablandamiento: *nm.* the act of softening (thing)
ablandar: *vt.* to soften; mollify; to soften
ablución: *nm.* ablutions
abnegación: *nf.* to put oneself at the service of others; self-denial
abnegado: *aj.* self-denying
abobado: *aj.* stupid; silly
abocar: *vt.* to take or catch with the mouth
abofetear: *vt.* to slap; to box
abogacía: *nf.* advocacy; profession of a lawyer
abogado: *nm.* lawyer; advocate
abogar: *vi.* to defend; to be an advocate for; to advocate
abolengo: *nm.* ancestry
abollado: *aj.* curled
abombar: *vt.* to give a convex
abominar: *vt.* to abominate; to detest
abonable: *aj.* which can be subscribed to
abonado: *aj.* paid
abonador: *nmf.* person who makes a payment
abono: *nm.* security; guarantee; subscription
abordable: *aj.* accessible
abordaje: *nm.* boarding passengers
abordar: *vt.* to board a ship; *vi.* to put into a port
aborrecer: *vt.* to hate; abhor; *r.* to hate each other
aborrecer: *vt.* to hate; to abhor
aborrecible: *aj.* hateful

aborrecible: *aj.* detestable
aborrecimiento: *nm.* hatred
abortar: *vt.* to miscarry; to abort
aborto: *nm.* miscarriage
abotonar: *vt.* to button; *r.* to button up
abotonarse: *vr.* to button oneself up
abovedar: *vt.* to cover a space with a curved structure; to make a curved structure
abrazadera: *nf.* clamp; brace
abrazar: *vt.* to hug
abrazo: *nm.* hug
abrecartas: *nm.* letter opener
abrelatas: *nm.* tin-opener
abreviado: *aj.* abbreviated
abreviar: *vt.* to abridge; shorten
abreviatura: *nf.* abbreviation
abridor : *aj.* open;
abrigado: *aj.* covered or protected with a coat or blanket
abrigar: *vt.* to shelter; protect; cover
abrigo: *nm.* overcoat; shelter; protection
abril: *nm.* April
abrillantado: *nm.* the process of shining something
abrillantar: *vt.* to make shiny
abrir: *vt.* to open; unlock; uncover; to gain; split; inaugurate; to; *vi.* to open; unfold
abrir: *vt.* to open
abrochar: *vt.* to button on; fasten
abrumado: *aj.* overwhelmed
abrumador: *aj.* overwhelming
abrumar: *vt.* to crush; overwhelm
ábside: *nm.* apse
absolución: *aj.* absolution
absolutamente: *av.* absolutely
absolutismo: *nm.* absolutism
absolutista: *nmf.* absolutist
absoluto: *aj.* absolute
absorber: *vt.* to absorb
abstemio: *aj.* abstaining

abstención: *nf.* abstention
abstencionismo: *nm.* abstention from voting
abstencionista: *nmf.* one who abstains from voting
abstenerse: *vr.* to abstain; refrain
abstinencia: *nf.* abstinence
abstracción: *nf.* abstraction
abstracto: *aj.* abstract
abstraer: *vt.* to abstract
abstraído -da: *aj.* abstracted; absent
absurdidad: *nf.* absurdity
absurdo: *aj.* absurd; nonsense
abuchear: *vt.* to scoff; boo
abuela: *nf.* grandmother
abuelo: *nm.* grandfather
abultado -da: *aj.* big; bulky
abultar: *vt.* to enlarge
abundancia: *nf.* abundance
abundante: *aj.* abundant
abundar: *vi.* to abound
aburguesarse: *vr.* to become part of the bourgeoisie
aburrido: *aj.* bored
aburrimiento: *nm.* boredom
aburrir: *vt.* to annoy; tire; bore; weary
aburrir: *vt.* to bore
abusar: *vt.* to abuse
abusivo: *aj.* abusive
abuso: *nm.* abuse
abusón: *aj.* abusing
abusón;-a: *nmf.* abuser
acá: *av.* here
acabado: *aj.* finished; exhausted
acabado -da: *aj.* perfect; complete
acabar: *vt.* to finish; to exhaust
academia: *nf.* academy; school
academia: *nf.* academy
académico: *aj.* academic
acallar: *vt.* to quiet; to silence
acalorado: *aj.* hot
acalorado -da: *aj.* excited
acaloramiento: *nm.* heated

discussion; heated words; anger
acalorar: *vt.* to warm; to produce heat
acalorarse: *vr.* to be overheating; to become angry
acampada: *nf.* camping
acampanado: *aj.* bell-shaped
acampar: *vi.* to camp
acanalado: *aj.* grooved; channeled
acantilado -da: 1. *aj.* bold; steep; 2. *nm.* cliff
acaparar: *vt.* to monopolize; buy up
acariciador: *aj.* caressing
acariciar: *vt.* to fondle; to caress
acarrear: *vt.* to transport a load; to carry consequences
acarreo: *nm.* transporting of a load
acaso: *nm.* chance
acatar: *vt.* to respect; revere; conform
acaudalado: *aj.* rich; wealthy
acaudalar: *vt.* to learn much; to make a fortune
acaudillar: *vt.* to lead a military group
acceder: *vt.* to accede
accesorio: *aj.* accessory; additional
accidentado: *aj.* involved in an accident
accidental: *aj.* accidental
accidentar: *vt.* to cause an accident
accidente: *nm.* accident
acción: *nf.* action; share of company stock
accionar: *vt.* to take action
accionista: *nmf.* shareholder; participant in an enterprise
acechar: *vt.* to waylay; lie in ambush
aceitar: *vt.* to oil
aceite: *nm.* oil
aceitera: *nf.* oil container
aceitero: *aj.* pertaining to oil
aceitoso: *aj.* oily
aceituna: *nf.* olive

aceitunado: *aj.* olive-colored
aceitunero;-a: *nmf.* olive merchant, olive grower
aceituno: *nm.* olive tree
aceleración: *nf.* acceleration
acelerada: *nf.* acceleration
acelerado: *aj.* accelerated
acelerador: *nm.* accelerator pedal
acelerar: *vt.* to accelerate; haste; hurry; to make haste
acelerar: *vt.* to accelerate
acelerón: *nm.* quick; sudden acceleration
acento: *nm.* accent; tone
acento: *nm.* accent
acentuación: *nf.* accentuation
acentuado: *aj.* accentuated; accented
acentuar: *vt.* to accentuate; to accent
acentuarse: *vr.* to be accentuated; to be accented
acepción: *nf.* acceptation; meaning
aceptabilidad: *nf.* acceptability
aceptable: *aj.* acceptable
aceptación: *nf.* acceptance
aceptar: *vt.* to accept; agree
acequia: *nf.* canal; gutter
acera: *nf.* pavement
acerado: *aj.* covered with steel
acerar: *vt.* to put steel on something
acerca de: *av.* about
acercar: *vt.* to move close; to draw nearer
acercarse: *vr.* to move closer; to draw nearer
acerería: *nf.* steelwork
acero: *nm.* steel; sword
acero: *nm.* steel
acertado -da: *aj.* right; correct
acertar: *vt.* to hit the mark; to be right
acertijo: *nm.* riddle; puzzle
achacar: *vt.* to impute
achaque: *nm.* thane
achatar: *vt.* to flatten

achicado: *aj.* made smaller
achicar: *vt.* to reduce; to make smaller
achicarse: *vr.* to become smaller
achicharrar: *vt.* to cook crisp; roast
acicate: *nm.* stimulant
ácido -da: *aj.* acid; sour
acierto: *nm.* success; good hit
aclamación: *nf.* acclamation
aclamar: *vt.* to shout; acclaim
aclaración: *nf.* clarification; explanation
aclarado: *aj.* explained
aclarar: *vt.* to clarify, to explain; to clear up; to make lighter
aclararse: *vr.* to become clear; to clear up
aclaratorio: *aj.* clarifying; explanatory
aclimatable: *aj.* able to be climate-controlled
aclimatación: *nf.* acclimation
aclimatar: *vt.* to acclimate
aclimatarse: *vr.* to become acclimated
acobardar: *vt.* to daunt; to frighten
acobardarse: *vr.* to cower; to be cowardly
acogedor: *aj.* comfortable; enjoyable for the manner in which one is treated
acoger: *vt.* to welcome; receive; to protect; to shelter
acogerse: *vr.* to protect oneself; to take refuge
acogida: *nf.* refuge
acogido;-a: *nmf.* person cared for in a special place (hospice; nursing home; etc.)
acolchar: *vt.* to quilt
acometedor: *aj.* audacious
acometer: *vt.* to attack; assault
acometida: *nf.* attacking or working vigorously to solve a problem

acometividad: *nf.* audacity
acomodación: *nf.* arranging; arrangement
acomodado: *aj.* arranged; comfortably well-off; convenient; fit; rich
acomodador;-a: *nmf.* usher, attendant; restaurant host or hostess
acomodar (se): *vt.* to arrange
acomodo: *nm.* arranging; arrangement
acompañado: *aj.* accompanied; escorted
acompañamiento: *nm.* accompaniment
acompañante: *nmf.* escort; companion
acompañar: *vt.* to accompany; to lead along
acompañarse: *vr.* to accompany each other
acompasado: *aj.* rhythmic; calm
acomplejado: *aj.* having a complex
acomplejar: *vt.* to give a complex
acomplejarse: *vr.* to have a complex
acondicionado: *aj.* made ready for use
acondicionador: *nm.* conditioner
acondicionamiento: *nm.* making ready for use
acondicionar: *vt.* to dispose; to make ready for use
acongojar: *vt.* to vex; *r.* to become vexed
aconsejable: *aj.* advisable
aconsejar: *vt.* to counsel; to advise
aconsejarse: *vr.* to seek counsel, to seek advice
acontecer: *vi.* to happen; to occur
acontecimiento: *nm.* event
acopiar: *vt.* to store
acopio: *nm.* storing
acorazado: *aj.* ironclad
acordado: *aj.* agreed-upon

acordar: *vt.* to agree; become uniform; *r.* to remember
acordar: *vt.* to make a deal; to come to an accord
acordarse: *vr.* to remember
acorde: 1. *aj.* agreed; 2. *nm.* chord
acordonado: *aj.* cordoned off
acordonar: *vt.* to cordon off
acorralado: *aj.* corralled; surrounded; pinned down; cornered
acorralar: *vt.* to corral; to surround; to pin down; to corner
acortar: *vt.* to shorten
acortarse: *vr.* to be abbreviated; to be made smaller or shorter
acosar: *vt.* to pursue closely
acostar: *vt.* to lay down; *vi.* to
acostumbrado: *aj.* accustomed
acostumbrar: *vt.* to accustom
Acotación: *nf.* bounds
Acre: *nm.* air; wind; briskness
acrecentamiento: *nm.* growth
Acrecentar: *vt.* to make larger, to make bigger; to increase
Acreditación: *nf.* accreditation
Acreditado: *aj.* accredited
Acreditar: *vt.* to accredit; to vouch for; to guarantee; to extend credit
Acreedor: *nmf.* creditor; deserving or worthy person
acreedor: *aj.* deserving
activación: *nf.* activation
activar: *vt.* to activate
actividad: *nf.* activity
activismo: *nm.* activism
activista: *nmf.* activist
activo: *aj.* active
acto: *nm.* act; event; ceremony
actor: *nm.* actor; player
actriz: *nf.* actress
actuación: *nf.* performance
actual: *aj.* current; present; up-to-date
actualidad: *nf.* actuality; present

time
actualización: *nf.* modernization
actualizar: *vt.* to make current; to bring up-to-date
actualmente: *av.* currently; nowadays
actuar: *vt.* to act; to put a thing in action; *vi.* to digest
acuarela: *nf.* water-color
acuarelista: *nmf.* watercolor painter
acuario: *nm.* aquarium
acuartelamiento: *nm.* quartering (of soldiers)
acuartelar: *vt.* to quarter (soldiers)
acuático: *aj.* aquatic
acuchillar: *vt.* to cut or stab with a knife
acuciar: *vt.* to stimulate
acueducto: *nm.* aqueduct
acuerdo: *nm.* resolution; determination; agreement
acumulable: *aj.* able to be accumulated
acumulación: *nf.* accumulation
acumulador: *nm.* car battery
acumular: *vt.* to accumulate; heap together
acunar: *vt.* to rock in a cradle
acuosidad: *nf.* wateriness
acuoso: *aj.* watery
acurrucarse: *vt.* to huddle
acusación: *nf.* accusation
acusado: 1. *aj.* accused; 2 *nm.* accused
acusador;-a: *nmf.* accuser
acusar: *vt.* to accuse
acusativo: *nm.* accusative; in grammar
acusatorio: *aj.* accusatory
acústica: *nf.* acoustics
adagio: *nm.* proverb
adaptable: *aj.* adaptable
adaptación: *nf.* adaptation
adaptado: *aj.* adapted

adaptador: *nm.* adapter
adaptar: *vt.* to adapt
adaptarse: *vr.* to become adapted to
adecuación: *nf.* adaptation
adecuado: *aj.* adequate
adecuar: *vt.* to fit; accommodate; adequate
adecuarse: *vr.* to adapt oneself
adelantado: *aj.* fast (clock); advanced; ahead of
adelantamiento: *nm.* progress; advancement; growth
adelantar: *vt.* to move forward; to go in
adelantarse: *vr.* to move oneself forward; to go ahead
adelante: *av.* ahead; forward
adelante: *vi.* come in!
adelanto: *nm.* progress; advancement
adelgazado -da: *aj.* made slender or thin
adelgazador: *aj.* slimming
adelgazamiento: *nm.* slimming down
adelgazar: *vi.* to get thin
ademán: *nm.* gesture
además: *av.* moreover
adentrarse: *vr.* to go inside
adentro: *av.* within; inside
aderezar: *vt.* to adorn; embellish; dress; to season
adeudar: *vt.* to owe; to be dutiable
adeudarse: *vr.* to go into debt
adeudo: *nm.* debt
adherencia: *nf.* adherence
adherente: *aj.* adhesive
adherir: *vi.* to adhere
adherirse: *vr.* to be adhering to; to be stuck to
adhesión: *nf.* adhesion
adhesivo: *nm.* adhesive
adición: *nf.* addition
adicionar: *vt.* to make additions
adiestrar: *vt.* to teach; to coach

adinerado: *aj.* wealthy
adinerado;-a: *nmf.* wealthy or rich person
adinerarse: *vr.* to enrich oneself
adiós: *inf.* good-bye; (tam.) bye-bye
adivinación: *nf.* guess; fortune telling
adivinado: *aj.* guessed; solved
adivinador;-a: *nmf.* fortune teller
adivinanza: *nf.* con. prediction
adivinanza: *nf.* riddle
adivinar: *vt.* to predict; to guess
adivino;-a: *nmf.* fortune teller
adjetivar: *vt.* to give adjectival value
adjudicación: *nf.* adjudication
adjudicar: *vt.* to adjudge; *r.* to appropriate
adjuntar: *vt.* to attach
adjunto -a: *aj.* joined; annexed; attached
administración: *nf.* administration
administrador: *nmf.* administrator
administrar: *vt.* to administrate
administrarse: *vr.* to be administrated
administrativo: *aj.* administrative
admirable: *aj.* admirable
admiración: *nf.* admiration
admirado -da: *aj.* astonished
admirador: *nmf.* admirer; fan
admirar: *vt.* to admire; marvel; *r.* to wonder
admirarse: *vr.* to be amazed
admirativo: *nm.* exclamation point
admisibilidad: *nf.* admissibility
admisión: *nf.* admission
admitido: *aj.* admitted
admitir: *vt.* to admit; to concede
admonición: *nf.* warning
adobar: *vt.* to dress; prepare
adoctrinamiento: *nm.* indoctrination
adoctrinar: *vt.* to instruct; to indoctrinate
adolecer: *vi.* to suffer

adolescencia: *nf.* adolescence
adolescente: *nmf.* adolescent
adolorido: *aj.* painful; hurting
adónde: *av.* where
adondequiera: *av.* to wherever
adopción: *nf.* adoption
adoptar: *vt.* to adopt
adoptivo: *aj.* adoptive
adoquinar: *vt.* to pave
adorable: *aj.* adorable
adoración: *nf.* adoration
adorado: *aj.* adored
adorador;-a: *nmf.* worshiper
adorar: *vt.* to worship; to adore
adormecedor: *aj.* causing
drowsiness
adormecerse: *vr.* to fall asleep (part
of the body); to become drowsy
adormecido: *aj.* drowsy
adormecimiento: *nm.* drowsiness
adormilarse: *vr.* to be drowsy
adornado: *aj.* adorned; decorated;
made beautiful
adornamiento: *inn.* adornment;
decoration
adornar: *vt.* to decorate; to adorn; to
beautify
adorno: *nm.* ornament; decoration
adquirido: *aj.* acquired
adquirir: *vt.* to acquire; obtain
adquisición: *nf.* acquisition
adrede: *av.* purposely; intention-ally
adscribir: *vt.* to ascribe; to assign
adscribirse: *vr.* to be ascribed; to be
assigned
adscripción: *nf.* ascription
aduana: *nf.* custom-house
aducir: *vt.* to adduce
adueñarse: *vr.* to become an owner
adulación: *nf.* flattery
adular: *vt.* to flatter; soothe; coax
adultero: *nmf.* adulterer
adulto: *aj.* adult; grown-up
advenedizo: *aj. & nm.* foreign;

strange
advenimiento: *nm.* arrive; advent
adverbio: *nm.* adverb
adversidad: *nf.* calamity; adversity
advertencia: *nf.* warning; advice
advertido: *aj.* warned
advertir: *vt.* to warn; to notice
adviento: *nm.* advent
adyacente: *aj.* adjacent
aéreo: *aj.* aero
aeróbicos: *nmpl.* aerobics; aerobic
exercise
aerobio: *aj.* aerobic
aeroclub: *nm.* airplane flying club
aerodeslizador: *nm.* hovercraft
aerodinámica: *nf.* aerodynamics
aerodinámico: *aj.* aerodynamic
aeródromo: *nm.* aerodrome
aerofaro: *nm.* airplane signal or
warning tower
aerógrafo: *nm.* airbrush
aerograma: *nf.* aerogram
aerolínea: *nf.* airline
aeromodelismo: *nm.* airplane model
building
aeromodelista: *aj.* pertaining to
airplane model building
aeromodelo: *nm.* airplane model
aeromoza: *nf.* flight attendant
aeronáutica: *nf.* aeronautics
aeronáutico: *aj.* aeronautic
aeronaval: *aj.* air-naval
aeronave: *nf.* airship
aeroplano: *nm.* airplane
aeropuerto: *nm.* airport
aerosol: *nm.* aerosol
aerostática: *nf.* balloon or blimp
flying
aerostático: *aj.* blimp; dirigible
aerostato: *nm.* blimp; dirigible
afabilidad: *nf.* affability
afamado: *aj.* famous; famed
afamar: *vt.* to make famous
afamarse: *vr.* to become famous

afán: *nm.* effort
afanador;-a: *nmf.* hard-worker; cleaning person
afanar: *vt.* to try hard; *vi.* to toil; labor; *r.* to toil too much
afanarse: *vr.* to work hard; to work with effort
afanoso: *aj.* hardworking
afear: *vt.* to deform; disfigure; deface
afección: *nf.* affection
afectar: *vt.* to feign; *r.* to be moved
afecto: *aj.* inclined; with a fondness for
afectuoso: *aj.* affectionate
afeitado: *aj.* shaved
afeitadora: *nf.* electric shaver
afeitar: *vt.* to shave
afeitarse: *vr.* to shave oneself
afeminación: *nf.* effeminacy
afeminado: *nm.* effeminate man; homosexual
afeminamiento: *nm.* effeminacy
afeminar: *vt.* to effeminate; *r.* to become weak
afeminarse: *vr.* to become effeminate
aferrar: *vt.* to grasp; grapple; seize
afianzado: *aj.* guaranteed
afición: *nf.* fondness
aficionado: *aj.* fond of; interested in
aficionado;-a: *nmf.* fan
aficionar: *vt.* to inspire affection
aficionarse: *vr.* to become fond of
afijo: *aj.* affix
afilador: *aj.* sharpening
afilar: *vt.* to whet; grind; *r.* to grow thin
afiliarse: *vr.* to become affiliated with
afinar: *vt.* to polish; to tune; *r.* to become polished
afinidad: *nf.* relationship; resem-blance
afirmación: *nf.* affirmation

afirmar: *vt.* to affirm; assert; *r.* to maintain firmly
afirmativa: *nf.* affirmative
afligir: *vt.* to afflict; *r.* to grieve
afluencia: *nf.* affluence; crowd
afluente: *aj.* copious; affluent
afluir: *vt.* to flow into
afonía: *nf.* loss of voice
afónico: *aj.* without sound
aforo: *nm.* gauging
afortunado -da: *aj.* fortunate; happy
afrenta: *nf.* affront
afrentar: *vt.* to face; to affront; insult; *r.* to be affronted
afrentarse: *vr.* to come face to face with a
afrentoso: *aj.* outrageous
afrontar: *vt.* to confront
afuera: *av.* away; outside
afuera: *av.* outside
agachar: *vt.* to lower; bow down
agarradera: *nf.* handle
agarrado: *aj.* mean; close fisted
agarrador: *nm.* potholder
agarrar: *vt.* to grasp; com. to obtain; *r.* to clinch
agarrarse: *vr.* to grab hold of; to take hold of
agarrón: *nm.* fight
agasajar: *vt.* to receive and treat kindly
agatas: *av.* on all fours
agencia: *nf.* agency
agenciar: *vt.* to procure for someone else
agenda: *nf.* notebook
agente: *nm.* agent; actor
agigantado: *aj.* excessively enlarged
agigantar: *vt.* to enlarge greatly
agigantarse: *vr.* to become giant
ágil: *aj.* nimble
agitación: *nf.* agitation
agitado: *aj.* agitated
agitanado -da: *aj.* gipsy-like

agitar: *vt.* to agitate; ruffle; fret; *r.* to flutter; palpitate
agitarse: *vr.* to be shaken up; to be
agitador: *nmf.* agitator
aglomeración: *nf.* accumulation
aglomerado: *nm.* pressed material; particle board
aglomerante: *nm.* material that hardens (cement; resin; plaster; etc.)
aglomerarse: *vr.* to come together; to accumulate
aglutinar: *vt.* to glue together
agobiar: *vt.* to bend the body down
agolpar: *vt.* to heap; *r.* to crowd together
agonía: *nf.* agony
agonizar: *vt. vi.* to be dying
agosto: *nm.* August
agotación: nm
agotado: *aj.* tired; exhausted; unavailable
agotador: *aj.* tiring; exhausting
agotamiento: *nm.* tiring; exhaustion
agotar: *vt.* to tire; to exhaust; to run out
agotarse: *vr.* to become tired; to be exhausted; to be out of
agraciado: *aj.* graced; shown favor
agraciar: *vt.* to favor; to favor with a gift; to grace
agradable: *aj.* pleasing; pleasant
agradar : *vi.* to please; *r.* to be pleased
agradecer: *vi.* to thank; to give thanks
agradecido: *aj.* thankful
agradecimiento: *nm.* acknowledgement
agrado: *nm.* pleasure
agrandar: *vt.* to enlarge; to make something big
agrandarse: *vr.* to become enlarged
agrario: *aj.* agrarian
agraviar: *vt.* to wrong; offend; *vt.* to

be aggrieved
agravio: *nm.* offence; insult
agredir: *vt.* to assault; attack
agregación: *nf.* aggregation; aggregate
agregado -da: *aj.* aggregate
agregar: *vt.* to aggregate; to add; to collect; *r.* to become united
agregarse: *vr.* to join; to be added to
agresor: *nmf.* aggressor; *aj.* aggressive; assaulting
agriar: *vt.* to make sour; *r.* to turn sour or acid
agrícola: *aj.* agricultural
agricultor;-a: *nmf.* farmer
agricultura: *nf.* agriculture
agrietar: *vt.* to crack
lagrimón: *nm.* a big tear
agrio -a: *aj.* sour; acid
agrisar: *vt.* to color grey
agro: *nm.* fertile field
agronomía: *nf.* agronomy
agrónomo: *aj.* agronomic; farming
agropecuario: *aj.* having to do with agriculture and animal farming
agrupación: *nf.* grouping; group
agrupamiento: *nm.* grouping process
agrupar: *vt.* to group; cluster; *r.* to gather in groups
agruparse: *vr.* to become grouped
agua: *nm.* water
aguacero: *nm.* downpour
aguado: *aj.* flexible; easily bent; overly stretched; watery
aguador;-a: *nmf.* water boy; water girl
aguafiestas: *nmf.* party pooper; wet blanket
aguafiestas: *nmf.* someone who takes the fun out of a party; party pooper; wet blanket
aguamarina: *nf.* aquamarine
aguamiel: *nm.* mixture of honey and water

aguanieve: *nf.* sleet
aguanieves: *nf.* sleet; snow-water
aguantable: *aj.* tolerable
aguantar: *vt.* to tolerate; to put up with
aguantarse: *vr.* to be able to stand (tolerate)
aguante: *nm.* tolerance
aguar: *vt.* to dilute with water; *r.* to become inundated
aguardar: *vt.* to wait for; expect; *vi.* to wait
aguardiente: *nm.* spirituous liquor
aguarrás: *nm.* oil of turpentine
aguarse: *vr.* (figurative) to become inundated with water
aguazal: *nm.* flooded land
agudeza: *nf.* acuteness; subtlety
agudizar: *vt.* to intensify
agudizarse: *vr.* to become sharpened (senses)
agudo: *aj.* pointed; sharp
agüero: *nm.* augury
aguerrido: *aj.* experienced in warfare; spirited
aguijar: *vt.* spur; to incite
aguijón: *nm.* stinger; thorn
aguijonear: *vt.* to sting; to prick with a thorn
águila: *nf.* eagle
aguileño: *aj.* with an eagle-like nose
aguilucho: *nm.* eaglet
aguja: *nf.* needle; knitting-needle
agujerar; agujerear: *vt.* to perforate
agujereado: *aj.* perforated
agujero: *nm.* hole; pincushion
agujeta: *nf.* shoestring
agujetero: *nm.* pincushion
agusanado: *aj.* wormy; filled with worms
agusanarse: *vr.* to become filled with worms
aguzar: *vt.* to sharpen; to stimulate
aherrojar: *vt.* to put a ball and chain on someone
aherrumbrarse: *vr.* to become rusted
ahí: *av.* there; in that place
ahijado: *nm.* godson; godchild
ahijar: *vt.* to adopt as a godchild
ahogado: *aj.* drowned
ahogado: *nmf.* drowning victim
ahogar: *vt.* to choke; throttle; *r.* to become suffocated
ahogar: *vt.* to drown
ahogo: *nm.* drowning
ahondar: *vi.* to go deeper; to go deeper into (water; earth; subject; situation; etc.)
ahora: *av.* now; at present; just now; *conj.* whether; or
ahorcar: *vt.* to hang; *rvt.* to hang oneself
ahorrador;-a: *nmf.* saver; person who likes to save; thrifty person
ahorrar: *vt.* to economize; save; spare
ahorrarse: *vr.* to save for oneself (money; time; effort; etc.)
ahorrativo: *aj.* saving; thrifty
ahorro: *nm.* savings
ahuecamiento: *nm.* hollowed-out part of something
ahuecar: *vt.* to make hollow
ahuecarse: *vr.* to become hollow
ahumado: *aj.* smoked
ahumar: *vt.* to smoke; to give a smoke flavor to something
ahumarse: *vr.* to become smoked
ahuyentar: *vt.* to drive away
airado: *aj.* angry
airar: *vt.* to anger
airarse: *vr.* to become very angry
aire: *nm.* air; wind
aireado: *aj.* ventilated; aired out
airear: *vt.* to give air; ventilate
airearse: *vr.* to air out
aires: *nmpl.* airs (of pretension)

airoso: *aj.* windy; putting on airs
aislacionismo: *nm.* isolationism
aislacionista: *aj.* isolationist
aislacionista: *nmf.* isolationist
aislado: *aj.* isolated
aislador: *nm.* insulator
aislamiento: *nm.* isolation
aislar: *vt.* to insulate; to become isolated
aislarse: *vr.* to become isolated
ajedrez: *nm.* chess
ajeno: *aj.* another's; foreign; strange
ajetreo: *nm.* fatigue
ajo: *nm.* garlic
ajuar: *nf.* bridal apparel
ajustado: *aj.* tight-fitting; exact-fitting; adjusted
ajustado -da: *aj.* exact; right
ajustador: *aj.* adjusting
ajustar: *vt.* to adjust; regulate; fit; *r.* to settle matters
ajustarse: *vr.* to become adjusted to
ajuste: *nm.* adjustment
ajusticiado;-a: *nmf.* person who receives the death penalty
ajusticiar: *vt.* to execute; put to death
ala: *nf.* wing
alabanza: *nf.* praise
alabar: *vt.* to praise
alacena: *nf.* cupboard; closet
alacrán: *nm.* scorpion
alado -da: *aj.* winged
alambicado: *aj.* distilled
alambique: *nm.* still
alambre: *nm.* wire
alameda: *nf.* poplar grove
álamo: *nm.* poplar tree
alarde: *nm.* ostentation
alargado: *aj.* elongated; lengthened
alargamiento: *nm.* lengthening
alargar: *vt.* to elongate; to lengthen
alargarse: *vr.* to become longer; to last a long time

alarido: *nm.* outcry; shout
alarma: *nf.* alarm
alarmado: *aj.* alarmed
alarmante: *aj.* alarming
alarmar: *vt.* to alarm
alarmarse: *vr.* to be alarmed
alarmista: *nmf.* alarmist
alba: *nf.* dawn
albañil: *nm.* mason; bricklayer
albar: *aj.* white
albarda: *nf.* pack-saddle
albaricoque: *nm.* apricot
albedrío: *nm.* free-will
albergar: *vt.* to lodge; shelter; harbor;
vi. to lodge
albergue: *nm.* lodging; shelter
albero: *aj.* white albino
albinismo: *nm.* albinism
albino;-a: *nmf.* albino
albor: *nm.* brightness of the dawn
alborada: *nf.* dawn
alborear: *vi.* to dawn
albornoz: *nm.* burnoose
alborotador : *aj.* riotous
alborotar: *vt.* to disturb; in & *r.* to get excited
alcachofa: *nf.* artichoque
alcalde: *nm.* mayor
alcaldesa: *nf.* mayor (woman)
alcaldía: *nf.* city hall; office of mayor
alcance: *nm.* pursuit; arm's length
alcantarilla: *nf.* underground sewer
alcantarillado: *nf.* sewerage
alcanzable: *aj.* reachable
alcanzar: *vt.* overtake; reach; *vi.* to attain
alcázar: *nm.* castle; fortress
alcoba: *nf.* alcove; bedroom
alcohol: *nm.* alcohol
alcohólico: *aj.* alcoholic
alcohólico: *nmf.* alcoholic
alcoholímetro: *nm.* alcohol-level

measuring device
alcoholismo: *nm.* alcoholism
alcoholizado: *aj.* drunk; inebriated
alcoholizar: *vt.* to add alcohol to
alcoholizarse: *vr.* to become drunk
alcohómetro: *nm.* alcohol-level
measuring device
alcornoque: *nm.* cork tree
aldaba: *nf.* knocker; clapper
aldea: *nf.* small village
aldeano;-a: *nmf.* person who lives in
a small town
aleación: *nf.* alloy
aleccionador: *aj.* lesson-giving; said
of something that teaches someone a
lesson
aleccionamiento: *nm.* the giving of
lessons; training
aleccionar: *vt.* to teach
alegar: *vt.* to allegate
alegrar: *vt.* to make happy
alegrarse: *vr.* to be happy; to
become happy
alegre: *aj.* happy
alegría: *nf.* happiness

alegrón: *nm.* great unexpected joy or
happiness
alejamiento: *nm.* distance
alejar: *vt.* to remove; separate; *vi.* to
go away
alejarse: *vr.* to distance oneself
alentado: *aj.* encouraged
alentador: *aj.* encouraging
alentar: *vt.* to encourage
alentarse: *vr.* to be encouraged
alero: *nm.* eaves
alerta: *nf.* watchword; *av.* vigilantly;
carefully
aleta: *nf.* small sing
aletargar: *vt.* to lethargize; *r.* to fall
into lethargy
aletear: *vi.* to flap wings
aleteo: *nm.* flapping

alfabeto: *nm.* alphabet
alfarería: *nf.* pottery
alfil: *nm.* bishop (chess)
alfiler: *nm.* pin; scarf-pin
alfiletero: *nm.* box of pins;
pincushion
alfombra: *nf.* carpet
alga: *nf.* seaweed
algo: *pron.* some
algodón: *nm.* cotton
alguacil: *nm.* constable
algún: *aj.* some
alguno;-a : *pron.* something
alhaja: *nf.* jewel; gem
aliado: *aj.* allied
alianza: *nf.* alliance; confederacy
aliarse: *vr.* to ally oneself
alicaído: *aj.* depressed; weakened
alicates: *nm.* pl. pincers
aliento: *nm.* breath
aligeramiento: *nm.* lightening
aligerar: *vt.* to lighten
alimentación: *nf.* feeding;
nourishment
alimentador: *nm.* apparatus used for
feeding material into a machine;
feeder
alimentar: *vt.* to feed; nourish; *r.* to
feed oneself
alimentario: *aj.* alimentary;
pertaining to feeding
alimentarse: *vr.* to eat; to nourish
oneself (also figurative)
alimenticio: *aj.* nutritive
alimento: *nm.* food; nourishment
aliñar: *vt.* to arrange; adorn
alineación: *nf.* alignment (e. g. ; of a
cars wheels)
alineado: *aj.* aligned
alineamiento: *nm.* the act of putting
in a straight line; lining up
alinear: *vt.* to line up; to put in a
straight line
alinearse: *vr.* to form a straight line

alisador: *nm.* something used to smooth (e. g. ; hair)
alisar: *vt.* to make smooth; to make straight (e. g; hair)
alisarse: *vr.* to become smooth; to become straight (e. g. ; hair)
alisios: *nm.* pl. east winds
alistado: *aj.* listed
alistamiento: *nm.* listing
alistar: *vt.* to enlist
alistarse: *vr.* to enlist
aliviador: *aj.* relieving
aliviar: *vt.* to relieve
aliviarse: *vr.* to be relieved; to be cured
alivio: *nm.* relief
allí: *av.* there; in that place; then
allá: *av.* there; in that place; thither
allanamiento: *nm.* flattening of land
allanar: *vt.* to flatten land
allanarse: *vr.* to become flat (land)
allegado -da: *nmf.* relation; inti-mate friend; *aj.* near
alma: *nf.* soul; mind; spirit; strength; vigor
almacén: *nm.* warehouse; shop
almacenaje: *nm.* warehousing
almacenamiento: *nm.* warehousing
almacenar: *vt.* to store; deposit
almacenista: *nmf.* warehouse worker
almeja: *nf.* mussel
almendra: *nf.* almond; kernel
almendro: *nm.* almond-tree
almíbar: *nm.* syrup
almidonar: *vt.* to starch
almirantazgo: *nm.* admiralty
almirante: *nm.* admiral
almohada: *nf.* pillow; bolster
almohadilla: *nf.* small pillow; cushion
almohadillado: *aj.* padded; stuffed with cotton or other material
almohadillar: *vt.* to pad; to stuff with cotton or other material

almohadón: *nm.* large pillow
almorzar: *vi.* to eat brunch
almuerzo: *nm.* brunch
alocado: *aj.* crazy-acting; without sense
alocución: *nf.* allocution; speech
alojamiento: *nm.* lodging
alojar: *vt.* to host; to accommodate
alojarse: *vr.* to accommodate oneself; to stay overnight
alondra: *nf.* lark
alpiste: *nm.* canary-seed
alquilar: *vt.* to rent
alquiler: *nm.* wages; hire; renter
alquitrán: *nm.* tar
alrededor: *av.* around
alrededores: *nmpl.* surroundings
altamente: *av.* highly
altanería: *nf.* arrogance
altanero: *aj.* arrogant
altar: *nm.* stone for sacrifices; altar
altavoz: *nm.* megaphone; loudspeaker
alterabilidad: *nf.* alterability
alterable: *aj.* alterable
alteración: *nf.* alteration
alterado: *aj.* changed; altered; upset
alterar: *vt.* to alter; change
alterarse: *vr.* to be altered
alternador: *nm.* alternator
alternante: *aj.* alternating
alternar: *vt.* to alternate
alternativa: *nf.* alternative
alternativo: *aj.* alternative
alterno: *aj.* alternate
alteza: *nf.* highness; excellence; nobility
altibajo: *nm.* pl. the sinuosities of uneven ground
altibajos: *nmpl.* ups and downs or highs and lows; especially of life
altímetro: *nm.* altimeter
altiplanicie: *nm.* plateau; high plain
altiplano: *nm.* high plain; plateau

altísimo: *nm.* the Most High; God
altisonancia: *nf.* high-pitched sound
altisonancia: *nf.* pompousness; especially in one's use of language
altisonante: *aj.* high-pitched; disagreeable to the ears
altitud: *nf.* altitude; height
altivez: *nf.* arrogance
altiveza: *nf.* arrogance
altivo: *aj.* arrogant
alto: *aj.* tall; high
altoparlante: *nm.* loudspeaker
altura: *nf.* height; loftiness
alubia: *nf.* bean; French bean
alud: *nm.* avalanche; snow-slip
aludido: *aj.* alluded
aludir: *vi.* to allude
alumbrado: *aj.* lit-up; well lighted
alumbramiento: *nm.* childbirth
alumbrar: *vt.* to light; lighten
alumbrarse: *vr.* to become well-lit
alumnado: *nm.* student body
alumno: *nm.* disciple; pupil; student
alunizaje: *nm.* moon-landing
alunizar: *vt.* to land on the moon
alusión: *nf.* allusion
alusivo: *aj.* allusive
alza: *nf.* rise in price
alzacuello: *nm.* ecclesiastical collar
alzada: *nf.* height of a horse
alzado: *aj.* conceited; proud
alzamiento: *nm.* uprising; revolt
alzar: *vt.* to raise; to heave; lift up
ama: *nf.* mistress; landlady
amabilidad: *nf.* kindliness; kindness
amable: *aj.* amiable; kind
amado: *aj.* loved; beloved
amadrinar: *vt.* to act as godmother
amaestrado: *aj.* trained; coached; taught; tamed
amaestrador;-a: *nmf.* trainer; coach; teacher
amaestramiento: *nm.* mastering
amaestrar: *vt.* to instruct; *r.* to train;

teach oneself
amaestrar: *vt.* to train; to coach; to teach; to tame
amagar: *vt.* to threaten; *vi.* to show a threatening attitude
amainar: *vt.* to lower the sails
amamantamiento: *nm.* nursing
amamantar: *vt.* to breast-feed; to nurse (a baby)
amanecer: *nm.* dawn
amansar: *vt.* to tame; subdue; *r.* to become tamed
amante: *aj.* loving
amapola: *nf.* poppy
amar: *vt.* to love; like
amaraje: *nm.* sea landing
amarar: *vi.* to land at sea (seaplane)
amargado: *aj.* embittered
amargar: *vt.* to make bitter
amargarse: *vr.* to become bitter
amargo: *aj.* bitter
amargura: *nf.* bitterness
amarillear: *vi.* to yellow
amarillento: *aj.* yellowish
amarillees: *nf.* yellowness
amarillismo: *nm.* yellow journalism
amarillista: *nmf.* journalist who sensationalizes the news;
amarillo: *aj.* yellow
amarilloso: *aj.* yellowish
amarra: *nf.* cable; hawser
amarrar: *vt.* to tie; fasten
amarse: *vr.* to love each other
amartelar: *vt.* to enamor; *r.* to fall in love
amartillar: *vt.* to hammer
amatista: *nf.* (Mvi.) amethyst
ámbar: *nm.* amber
ambición: *nf.* ambition
ambicionar: *vt.* to aspire to
ambicioso: *aj.* ambitious
ambidextro: *aj.* ambidextrous
ambientación: *nf.* ambience of a scene

ambientador: *aj.* creating an atmosphere; applying air fresheners
ambiental: *aj.* environmental
ambientar: *vt.* to create an atmosphere
ambiente: *nm.* surrounding; atmosphere
ambigüedad: *nf.* ambiguity
ámbito: *nm.* situations affecting someone
ambivalencia: *nf.* ambivalence
ambivalente: *aj.* ambivalent
ambos: *pron.* both
ambulancia: *nf.* ambulance
ambulante: *aj.* roving
ambulatorio: *nm.* dispensary
amedrentar: *vt.* to put fear into someone; to provoke fear
amenaza: *nf.* threat
amenazador: *aj.* threatening a
amenazar: *vt.* to threaten; menace
amenizar: *vt.* to make pleasant or agreeable
americana: *nf.* coat; jacket
ameritado: *aj.* merited; deserved
ameritar: *vt.* to deserve
ametralladora: *nf.* machine-gun
amigable: *aj.* friendly; amicable
amigacho;-a: *nmf.* good friend; informally used
amígdalas: *nf.* pl. amygdalate; tonsils
amigo: 1. *aj.* friendly; 2. *nmf.* friend
amigote: *nm.* great friend
amiguero: *aj.* easily able to make friends
amistad: *nf.* friendship; amity
amistoso: *aj.* friendly
amo: *nm.* master; proprietor
amolar: *vt.* to grind
amonestar: *vt.* to advise
amontonado: *aj.* piled
amontonamiento: *nm.* piling up
amontonar: *vt.* to pile

amontonarse: *vr.* to become piled up
amor: *nm.* love; tenderness
amoralidad: *nf.* amorality
amoratado: *aj.* livid; ghastly
amorcillo: *nm.* cupid
amordazar: *vt.* to gag
amorío: *nm.* love affair
amoroso: *aj.* loving; full of love; tenderhearted
amortajamiento: *nm.* act of covering with a shroud
amortajar: *vt.* to cover with a shroud
amortiguar: *vt.* to temper; mitigate
amotinar: *vt.* to excite to rebellion
amparar: *vt.* to shelter
ampararse: *vr.* to protect oneself
amparo: *nm.* favor; aid; protection
ampliación: *nf.* enlargement
ampliado: *aj.* enlarged; widened
ampliadora: *nf.* photographic enlarger
ampliar: *vt.* to amplify; enlarge
amplificación: *nf.* amplification
amplificador: *nm.* amplifier
amplificar: *vt.* to amplify
amplio: *aj.* ample
amplitud: *nf.* amplitude; wideness
ampolla: *nf.* blister on the skin
amueblar: *vt.* to furnish
amurallado: *aj.* with or surrounded by large walls
amurallar: *vt.* to build a large wall
anacrónico: *aj.* anachronistic
anacronismo: *nm.* anachronism
añadido: *aj.* added
añadidura: *nf.* addition
añadir: *vt.* to add; join to augment
añado: *av.* by swimming or floating
anaerobio: *aj.* anaerobic
anaerobio: *nm.* anaerobic organism
analfabeto: *aj.* m. & *nf.* illiterate; ignorant
análisis: *nm.* analysis
analista: *nmf.* analyst

analítico: *aj.* analytical; analytic
analizable: *aj.* analyzable
analizador: *aj.* analyzing
analizar: *vt.* to analyze
analogía: *nf.* analogy
análogo: *aj.* analogous
anarquía: *nf.* anarchy
anatomía: *nf.* anatomy
anatómico: *aj.* anatomical
antecedente: *nm.* antecedent; past; background
ancho: *aj.* wide
ancho -cha: *aj.* broad; wide
anchoa: *nf.* anchovy
anchura: *nf.* breadth; width; wideness
ancianidad: *nf.* old age
anciano: *aj.* old
anclar: *vt.* to anchor
andada: *nf.* track; trail
andadas: nfpl. habits
andaderas: nfpl. baby's walker
andador: *aj.* walking; fond of walking
andadura: *nf.* walking
andamio: *nm.* scaffold
andar: *vt.* to walk; to associate with; to go out (dating)
andariego: *aj.* restless
andén: *nm.* sidewalk; platform
andrajoso: *aj.* ragged
anécdota: *nf.* anecdote
anecdotario: *nm.* collection of anecdotes
anecdótico: *aj.* anecdotal
añejamiento: *nm.* aging (wine)
añejar: *vt.* to age (wine)
añejarse: *vr.* to be aged
añejo: *aj.* aged (wine)
anexo: *aj.* joined
anfiteatro: *nm.* amphitheater
ángel: *nm.* angel; spiritual being
angélico: *aj.* angelical; angelic
angelito: *nm.* little angel

angelote: *nm.* big angel
angina: *nf.* angina; pl. tonsils
anglosajón : *aj.* Anglo-Saxon
angosto: *aj.* narrow
angostura: *nf.* narrowness
anguila: *nf.* eel
angular: *aj.* angular
ángulo: *nm.* angle; corner; nook
angustia: *nf.* anguish; affliction; distress
angustiado: *aj.* anguished; in anguish
angustiar: *vt.* to cause anguish; afflict
angustiarse: *vr.* to be in anguish; to be distressed
angustioso: *aj.* provoking anguish
anhelante: *aj.* greatly desirable
anhelar: *vt.* to desire passionately; to yearn
anhelo: *nm.* great desire; yearning
anidar: *vi.* to nest; to protect
anidar: *vi.* to nestle
anillo: *nm.* ring; finger ring
ánima: *nf.* soul; spirit
animación: *nf.* animation
animadamente: *av.* with desire; with will; purposefully
animado: *aj.* encouraged
animador: *aj.* encouraging
animador;-a: *nmf.* encouraging person; director of a party; audience prompter for a television program
animar: *vt.* to encourage
animarse: *vr.* to be encouraged
anímico: *aj.* pertaining to the soul
ánimo: *nm.* courage; thought; desire; will
animoso: *aj.* filled with desire or will; energetic
aniñado -da: *aj.* childish
aniñarse: *vr.* to become childlike; to act like a child
aniquilar: *vt.* to annihilate; destroy

anís: *nm.* anise
anisar: *vt.* to desire anxiously
aniversario: *nm.* anniversary
año: *nm.* year
anoche: *av.* last night
anochecer: *nm.* nightfall
anochecer: *vi.* to begin the night
anochecida: *nf.* nightfall
anomalía: *nf.* anomaly
anonadar: *vt.* to annihilate; to humble oneself greatly
anonimato: *nm.* anonymity
anónimo: *aj.* anonymous
añorar: *vt.* to pine for; to feel homesickness
anormal: *aj.* abnormal
anotar: *vt.* to annotate; to note; mark down
ansia: *nf.* feeling of anxiety
ansiado: *aj.* desired
ansiar: *vt.* to be anxious
ansiedad: *nf.* anxiety
ansioso: *aj.* anxious
antagónico: *aj.* antagonistic
antagonismo: *nm.* antagonism
antagonista: *nmf.* antagonist
antagonista: *nmf.* antagonist
antagonista: *aj.* antagonistic
antaño: *av.* formerly; yesteryear
ante: *nm.* elk; buckskin
anteanoche: *av.* the night before last
anteayer: *av.* the day before yesterday
antebrazo: *nm.* forearm
antecedente: *aj.* record
anteceder: *vt.* to precede; go before
antecesor;-a: *nmf.* predecessor
antedicho: *aj.* aforesaid
antefirma: *nf.* complimentary closing of a letter
antelación: *nf.* preference
antemano: *av.* beforehand
antena: *nf.* aerial
anteojera: *nf.* blinders for horses

anteojo: *nm.* eye-glass
antepasado: *aj.* previous
antepecho: *nm.* breastwork
antepenúltimo: *aj.* before the next-to-last
anteponer: *vt.* to prefer; place before
anteproyecto: *nm.* preliminary study
antepuesto: *aj.* placed in front of or with a higher priority
anterior: *aj.* previous
anterioridad: *nf.* anticipation
anteriormente: *av.* previously
antes: *av.* before; sooner; earlier; beforehand; rather
antesala: *nf.* antechamber
antevíspera: *nf.* two days before an event
antiadherente: *aj.* not adhesive
antiaéreo: *aj.* anti-aircraft
antialcohólico: *aj.* favoring prohibition of alcohol
antibiótico: *nm.* antibiotic
anticipado -da: *aj.* premature
anticipar: *vt.* to anticipate; forestall
anticomunista: *aj.* anticommunist
anticoncepción: *nf.* contraception
anticonceptivo: *aj.* contraceptive
anticonstitucional: *aj.* unconstitutional
anticristo: *nm.* Antichrist
anticuado: *aj.* antiquated
anticuario: *nmf.* antiquarian
antifaz: *nm.* veil; mask
anticuario: *nm.* antique dealer; antique store
anticuerpo: *nm.* antibody
antidemocrático: *aj.* undemocratic
antideportivo: *aj.* referring to a poor sport
antideslizante: *aj.* anti-skidding; anti-slipping
antiestético: *aj.* ugly
antifascismo: *nm.* antifascism
antifascista: *nmf.* antifascist

antifaz: *nf.* mask
antigualla: *nf.* antique
antigüedad: *nf.* antiquity; oldness; *pl.* antiques
antigüedad: *nf.* antiquity
antiguo: *aj.* ancient
antihéroe: *nm.* anti-hero
antimateria: *nf.* anti-matter
antinatural: *aj.* against nature; contrary to nature; not natural
antipatía: *nf.* antipathy; aversion
antipatía: *nf.* antipathy
antipático: *aj.* unsympathetic
antipatriótico: *aj.* unpatriotic
antiquísimo: *aj.* very ancient
antirrábico: *aj.* anti-rabies medicine
antirreglamentario: *aj.* contrary to regulations
antirrobo: *aj.* anti-theft
antisocial: *aj.* antisocial
antitesis: *nf.* antithesis; contrary
antojadizo: *aj.* with cravings
antojarse: *vr.* to make one crave
antojo: *nm.* craving
antorcha: *nf.* torch
antropófago: *nmf.* cannibal
anual: *aj.* annual
anualidad: *nf.* annuity
anuario: *nm.* annual; yearbook
anudar: *vt.* to know; to become knotted
anulación: *nf.* annulment
anular: *vt.* to annul
anularse: *vr.* to be annulled
anunciador;-a: *nmf.* announcer
anunciar: *vt.* to announce; *vt.* to make oneself known
anunciarse: *vr.* to be announced
anuncio: *nm.* announcement; advertisement
anzuelo: *nm.* fishhook; bait
aojar: *vt.* to give the evil eye
aovar: *vt.* to make something egg-shaped

apacentar: *vt.* to pasture; graze
apacible: *aj.* gentle; peaceful
apaciguador: *aj.* calming; pacifying
apaciguador;-a: *nmf.* person who calms or pacifies other
apaciguamiento: *nm.* appeasement; calming; pacifying
apaciguar: *vt.* to pacify; *r.* to be appeased
apaciguarse: *vr.* to be pacified; to be calm
apadrinamiento: *nm.* act of being a godfather
apadrinar: *vt.* to sponsor; to act as godfather for a child
apagadizo: *aj.* with a propensity to lose power
apagado: *aj.* turned off
apagar: *vt.* to extinguish; to put out; to turn off
apagarse: *vr.* to be turned off
apagavelas: *nm.* candle snuffer
apagón: *nm.* power outage
apaisado -da: *aj.* oblong; broader
apalabrar: *vt.* to agree to something
apalancamiento: *nm.* leverage
apalancar: *vt.* to lever; to move with leverage
apalanque: *inn.* leveraging
apalear: *vt.* to beat; to beat down (fruit)
aparatoso: *aj.* pompous; showy
aparcar: *vt.* to park
apareamiento: *nm.* forming of a pair; mating
aparear: *vt.* to form a pair; to mate
aparearse: *vr.* to be paired with; to be mated with
aparecer: *vi.* to appear
aparecerse: *vr.* to appear
aparecido: *nm.* ghost; specter
aparejado: *aj.* paired; mated
aparejador: *nm.* architect's assistant; works manager

aparejar: *vt.* to prepare; get ready; *r.* to get

aparejo: *nm.* apparel; harness

aparentar: *vt.* to feign

aparente: *aj.* apparent

aparentemente: *av.* apparently

aparición: *nf.* apparition

apariencia: *nf.* appearance

apartado: *aj.* separated; saved; reserved

apartado -da: *aj.* retired; aloof;

apartamento: *nm.* apartment

apartamento: *nm.* separation; withdrawal

apartar: *vt.* to separate; to save

apartarse: *vr.* to separate oneself

aparte: *nm.* separate paragraph; an aside in theater or a speech

aparto: *nm.* apparatus; appliance; device

apasionado: *aj.* passionate

apasionamiento: *nm.* passion

apasionante: *aj.* causing or creating passion; fascinating

apasionar: *vt.* to impassion; excite strongly

apasionarse: *vr.* to be passionate

apátrida: *aj.* without a country

expatriado: *aj.* expatriated

apátrida: *nmf.* man or woman without a country

apeadero: *nm.* horse block

apear: *vt.* to dismount; bring down

apedrear: *vt.* to throw stones at

apegado: *aj.* attached; accustomed

apegarse: *vr.* to become accustomed; to become attached

apego: *nm.* affection

apelable: *aj.* appealable

apelación: *nf.* appeal

apelar: *vi.* to appeal

apelativo: *aj.* appellate

apellidar: *vt.* to call; name; to proclaim; *r.* to be called

apellidarse: *vr.* to have as a last name

apellido: *nm.* surname; family name; last name

apenado: *aj.* filled with shame

apenar: *vt.* to pain; to embarrass

apenas: *av.* scarcely; hardly

apendicitis: *nf.* appendicitis

aperitivo: *nm.* appetizer

apertura: *nf.* opening; aperture

apesadumbrado: *aj.* afflicted

apesadumbrar: *vt.* to pain; grieve

apestar: *vt.* to infect with the plague

apetecer: *vt.* to desire; to feel an appetite for

apetecible: *aj.* tempting; desirable; appetizing

apetencia: *nf.* appetite

apetito: *nm.* appetite

apetitoso: *aj.* appetizing

apiadar: *vt.* to inspire pity; *r.* to have mercy on

apilado: *aj.* piled

apilamiento: *nm.* piling

apilar: *vt.* to pile

apilarse: *vr.* to be piled

apiñar: *vt.* to pack; press together; *r.* to crowd

apisonadora: *nf.* steamroller; road roller

apisonar: *vt.* to compact; to flatten

aplanador: *aj.* flattening

aplanadora: *nf.* steamroller; road roller

aplanamiento: *nm.* flattening

aplanar: *vt.* to smooth; lever; *r.* to tumble down

aplastar: *vt.* to flatten; to crush; to quash; *r.* to flatten

aplaudir: *vt.* to applaud

aplauso: *nm.* applause

aplazar: *vt.* to adjourn; put off

aplicable: *aj.* applicable

aplicación: *nf.* application;

aplicado: *aj.* hard-working; studious
aplicar: *vt.* to apply; to put
aplicarse: *vr.* to apply on self (cream; medicine; etc.)
apócrifo: *aj.* apocryphal
apodar: *vt.* to nickname
apoderado: *aj.* authorized
apoderar: *vr.* to empower; to authorize
apoderarse: *vr.* to take possession of
apodo: *nm.* nickname
apogeo: *nm.* height
apolillar: *vt.* to eat
apolítico: *aj.* apolitical
aporrear: *vt.* to cudgel; club
aportación: *nf.* donation; contribution
aportar: *vt.* to bring; furnish
aporte: *nm.* donation
aposentamiento: *nm.* lodging
aposentar: *vt.* to put up; lodge; *vt.* to take lodging
aposentarse: *vr.* to room or lodge somewhere
aposento: *nm.* room; lodging
apoyado: *aj.* supported
apoyar: *vt.* to support
apoyo: *nm.* support
acostar: *r.* to lie down
aprovechado: *aj.* well spent
apreciable: *aj.* appreciable
apreciación: *nf.* appreciation
apreciado: *aj.* appreciated
apreciar: *vt.* to evaluate; appraise; to appreciate
apreciativo: *aj.* appreciative
aprecio: *nm.* appreciation
apremiante: *aj.* urgent
apremiar: *vt.* to urge; press
aprender: *vt.* to learn
aprendiz;-a: *nmf.* learner
aprendizaje: *nm.* learning
apresar: *vt.* to seize
apresurado: *aj.* hurried

apresurar: *vt.* to hasten; quicken; hurry; *vt.* to hasten
apresurar: *vt.* to hurry
apresurarse: *vr.* to be in a hurry
apretado: *aj.* tight
apretar: *vt.* to squeeze; to hug; *r.* to crowd
apretón: *nm.* squeeze
apretujar: *vt.* to squeeze
apretujarse: *vr.* to be squeezed into
apretujón: *nm.* tight squeeze
apretura: *nf.* narrow place
aprieto: *nm.* strait; difficulty
aprisa: *av.* fast; quickly
aprisionar: *vt.* to imprison
aprobación: *nf.* approbation; approval
aprobado: *aj.* approved; passed
aprobado: *nm.* certificate of a passing score; approval
aprobar: *vt.* to approve; to pass
aprobatorio: *aj.* passing
aprovechable: *aj.* serviceable
aprovechado: *aj.* taken advantage of; well-used
aprovechamiento: *nm.* improvement
aprovechar: *vt.* to utilize; make use of; *vi.* to be useful
aprovecharse: *vr.* to take advantage of a situation for one's own benefit; to take advantage of someone
aprovisionar: *vt.* to supply; to stock provisions
aproximación: *nf.* nearing; approximation
aproximadamente: *av.* approximately
aproximado: *aj.* approximate
aproximar: *vt.* to approximate; to move toward
aproximarse: *vr.* to move closer to
aptitud: *nf.* aptitude
apto: *aj.* apt; capable
apuesto: *aj.* handsome

apuñalar: *vt.* to stab with dagger
apuntado: *aj.* noted; written down
apuntador;-a: *nmf.* prompter in theater
apuntalar: *vt.* to prop
apuntar: *vt.* to aim; level; point; *vi.* to break dawn
apuntarse: *vr.* to sign up for
apunte: *nm.* note
apurado: *aj.* in a hurry; hurry
apurar: *vt.* to hurry
apurarse: *vr.* to be in a hurry
apuro: *nm.* need; want
aquejar: *vt.* to ail; afflict
aquél; aquélla : *pron.* dem. that one
aquello : *pron. dem.* neuter. that; it. aqui; *av.* here
aquéllos; aquéllas : *pron.* dem. pl. those ones
aquietar: *vt.* to calm; to quiet
aquietarse: *vr.* to become calm; to become quiet
aquilatar: *vt.* to estimate the carats of
ara: *nf.* altar
arado: *nm.* plough
araña: *nf.* spider
arañar: *vt.* to scratch
arancel: *nm.* tariff
arbitraje: *nm.* officiating; arbitration
arbitral: *aj.* pertaining to officiating or arbitration
arbitrar: *vt.* to arbitrate
arbitrariedad: *nf.* arbitrariness
arbitrario: *aj.* arbitrary
árbitro;-a: *nmf.* referee; umpire; arbiter
árbol: *nm.* tree
arbolado: *aj.* filled with trees
arboladura: *nf.* masts and related equipment of a ship
arbolar: *vt.* to raise (flag)
arboleda: *nf.* grove; park filled with trees

arbóreo: *aj.* pertaining to trees
arbusto: *nm.* shrub; bush
arca: *nf.* coffer; chest
arcaico -ca: *aj.* archaic
arcángel: *nm.* archangel
archiduque: *nm.* archduke
archiduquesa: *nf.* archduchess
archivador: *nm.* file cabinet or box
archivar: *vt.* to file
archivero: *nm.* file cabinet
archivo: *nm.* file
arcilla: *nf.* clay
arco: *nm.* arc; bow arch
arder: *vt.* to sting or burn something
ardido: *aj.* angry; irritated
ardiente: *aj.* stinging
ardilla: *nf.* squirrel
ardor: *nm.* burning; intense fire (also figurative)
ardoroso: *aj.* burning; stinging
área: *nf.* area; space
arena: *nf.* sand; grit
arenal: *nm.* large area covered with sand
arenoso: *aj.* sandy
argüir: *vt.* to argue
agujas: *nf.* pl. pins and needles
argumentación: *nf.* argumentation
argumentar: *vi.* to argue; to give arguments
argumento: *nm.* argument
aridecer: *vt.* to make arid or dry
aridecerse: *vr.* to become arid or dry
aridez: *nf.* drought; barrenness; aridity
árido: *aj.* arid; dry
arista: *nf.* arista; edge
aristocracia: *nf.* aristocracy
aristocrático: *aj.* aristocratic
aritmética: *nf.* arithmetic
arma: *nf.* arm; weapon
armada: *nf.* navy; battle fleet
armado: *aj.* armed
armador: *nm.* outfitter

armadura: *nf.* armor
armamento: *nm.* armament
armar: *vt.* to arm; mount
armario: *nm.* cupboard; wardrobe
armazón: *nf.* frame
armería: *nf.* arms factory or shop; gun store
armero: *nm.* gun cabinet or locker
armónica: *nf.* harmonica
armónicamente: *av.* in harmony
armónico: *aj.* harmonic
armonio: *nm.* harmonium
armonioso: *aj.* harmonious
armonización: *nf.* harmonization
armonizar: *vt.* to harmonize
aro: *nm.* hoop
aroma: *nf.* scent; fragrance; aroma
aromático: *aj.* aromatic
aromatización: *nf.* air freshening; the filling of air with an aroma
aromatizador: *nm.* air freshener
aromatizar: *vt.* to aromatize
arpillera: *nf.* sackcloth
arquear: *vt.* to arch
arqueología: *nf.* archeology
arqueológico: *aj.* archeological
arquetípico: *aj.* archetypal
arquetipo: *nm.* archetype
arquitecto: *nm.* architect
arquitectónico: *aj.* architectural
arquitectura: *nf.* architecture
arrabal: *nm.* suburb; pl. environs
arraigado: *aj.* having roots; rooted
arraigar: *vi.* to sprout roots
arraigo: *nm.* order to remain in a jurisdiction; settlement of land
arrancada: *nf.* forward impulse of a horse or a car; etc
arrancado: *aj.* pulled up by the roots
arrancar: *vt.* to extirpate; root out; *vi.* to start off; con. to leave
arrancar: *vt.* to pull from the root; to start a race; to start forward
arranque: *nm.* pulling from the root;

violent impulse
arrasar: *vt.* to level; to raze; demolish
arrastradizo: *aj.* dragging; crawling
arrastrado: *aj.* ruined
arrastrar: *vt.* to drag
arrastrarse: *vr.* drag oneself; to crawl
arrastre: *nm.* dragging
arrear: *vt.* to drive
arrebatado: *aj.* grabbed; infuriated; furious extremely angry
arrebatador: *aj.* gripping
arrebatamiento: *nm.* grabbing; act of becoming extremely angry
arrebatar: *vt.* to grab forcefully; to burn too quickly (flame of a stove)
arrebatarse: *vr.* to become extremely angry
arrebato: *nm.* grabbing; act of becoming
arrecife: *nm.* causeway
arreglado: *aj.* fixed; arranged
arreglar: *vt.* to guide; regulate; *r.* to conform oneself
arreglarse: *vr.* to be fixed; to get oneself ready
arreglista: *nmf.* musical arranger
arreglo: *nm.* arrangement
arremangar: *vt.* to roll up sleeves
arremangarse: *vr.* to roll up one's sleeves
arremeter: *vt.* to assail; attack
arremetida: *nf.* attack
arrendado -da: *aj.* rented
arrendador: *nmf.* landlord; lessor
arrendamiento: *nm.* renting; leasing
arrendar: *vt.* to rent; let
arrendatario;-a: *nmf.* tenant
arrepentido: *aj.* repentant
arrepentimiento: *nm.* repentance
arrepentirse: *vr.* to repent
arresto: *nm.* detention
arriar: *vt.* to lower; to strike

arriba: *av.* above; over; on high
arribada: *nf.* arrival of a ship
arribar: *vi.* to arrive
arribo: *nm.* arrival of a ship
arriendo: *nm.* letting; renting
arriero: *nm.* muleteer
arriesgado: *aj.* at risk; risky
arriesgar: *vt.* to risk; hazard
arriesgarse: *vr.* to take a risk
arrinconado: *aj.* isolated or set apart from the rest
arrinconar: *vt.* to put in a corner; to corner
arrinconarse: *vr.* to be cornered
arrocero: *aj.* pertaining to rice
arrodillado: *aj.* bowing on knees
arrodillar: *vt.* to bow on a knee
arrodillarse: *vr.* to bow on one's knees
arrogar: *vt.* to arrogate; *r.* to appropriate to oneself
arrojado: *aj.* thrown; hurled; fearless; intrepid; brave
arrojar: *vt.* fling; hurl; to throw; to throw away; *r.* to launch
arrojarse: *vr.* to hurl oneself
arrojo: *nm.* throw; hurling of oneself
arrollar: *vt.* to roll up; wind
arropamiento: *nm.* action of putting on heavy clothes
arropar: *vt.* to put on heavier clothes
arroparse: *vr.* to put heavier clothing on oneself
arrostrar: *vt.* to face danger
arroyar: *vt.* to form channels of water
arroyo: *nm.* small river; creek
arroyuelo: *nm.* small creek
arroz: *nm.* rice
arrozal: *nm.* rice paddy or field
arruga: *nf.* wrinkle
arrugar: *vt.* to wrinkle; crumple
arruinado: *aj.* ruined
arruinar: *vt.* to throw; to demolish; to ruin
arruinarse: *vt.* to be ruined
arrullar: *vt.* to bill
arte: *nmf.* art
artesa: *nf.* trough
artesanal: *aj.* pertaining to arts and crafts
artesanía: *nf.* arts and crafts; crafted object
artesano; -a: *nmf.* artisan
artesonado -da: *aj.* paneled
articular: *vt.* to articulate
articulista: *nmf.* article writer; newspaper or magazine reporter
artículo: *nm.* article; knuckle; joint
artificial: *aj.* artificial
artificialmente: *av.* artificially
artificio: *nm.* workmanship; craft
artificio: *nm.* skill; ability
artificioso: *aj.* made with skill or ability
artillería: *nf.* artillery
artillero: *nm.* artillery soldier
artimaña: *nf.* trap; snare
artista: *nmf.* artist
artístico: *aj.* artistic
arzobispal: *aj.* pertaining to the archbishop
arzobispo: *nm.* archbishop
arzobispo: *nm.* archbishop
asa: *nf.* handle; ear of a vase
asador: *nm.* spit
asalariado: *aj.* salaried
asalariar: *vt.* to pay a salary
asaltante: *aj.* assaulting
asaltar: *vt.* to assault
asalto: *nm.* assault
asamblea: *nf.* assembly
asambleísta: *nmf.* one who is part of an assembly
asar: *vt.* to roast; *r.* to excessively hot
ascendente: *aj.* ascending
ascender: *vi.* to ascend

ascendiente: *nm.* ancestor
ascendiente: *nmf.* ancestor
ascensión: *nmf.* ascension
ascenso: *nm.* rise; promotion
ascensor: *nm.* elevator
ascensorista: *nmf.* elevator
repairman or builder
asco: *nm.* nausea; loathsomeness
asear: *vt.* to set off; adorn; *r.* to make
oneself clean
asediar: *vt.* to besiege; blockade
asegurado: *aj.* assured
asegurador;-a: *nmf.* insurer
aseguradora: *nf.* insurance company
asegurar: *vt.* to ensure; to insure
asegurarse: *vr.* to assure oneself
asemejar: *vt.* to make similar
asemejarse: *vr.* to become similar
asentaderas: *nf.* pl buttocks
asentado: *aj.* seated
asentamiento: *nm.* seating
asentarse: *vr.* to settle
asentimiento: *nm.* assent; agreement
asentir: *vi.* to assent; to agree with;
to approve
aseo: *nm.* cleanliness; neatness.
aserrar
aseo: *vt.* to saw
aserradero: *nm.* sawmill
aserrado: *aj.* having a saw-like
shape
aserradura: *nf.* incomplete cut
aserrar: *vt.* to saw
aserrín: *nm.* sawdust
aserto: *nm.* assertion
asesinar: *vt.* to assassinate
asesinato: *nm.* murder
asesino: *aj.* murdering
asesorar: *vt.* to advise; counsel; *r.* to
take advice
asexuado: *aj.* sexless
asexual: *aj.* asexual
asfalto: *nm.* asphalt
asfixiar: *vt.* to asphyxiate; suffocate

así: *av.* so; thus; in this way; like this
asiduidad: *nf.* diligence; assiduity
asiduo: *aj.* assiduous
asiento: *nm.* seat; chair; stool; bench
asignación: *nf.* assigning to a post;
assigning of money
asignar: *vt.* to assign
asignatario;-a: *nmf.* heir; person
who receives money from an
inheritance
asignatura: *nf.* subject (to study)
asilo: *nm.* asylum; sanctuary
asimetría: *nf.* asymmetry
asimétrico: *aj.* asymmetric
asistencia: *nf.* attendance; actual
presence
asistenta: *nf.* handmaid
asistente: *nm.* assistant; helper
asistido: *aj.* attended; assisted
asistir: *vt.* to attend
asno: *nm.* ass donkey
asociación: *nf.* association; fellowship
asociado: *aj.* associated
asociar: *vt.* to associate
asociarse: *vr.* to be associated
asociativo: *aj.* associating
asoleada: *nf.* over-exposure to the
sun
asolear: *vt.* to sun
asolearse: *vt.* to bask in sunlight
asomar: *vi.* to show oneself
asomarse: *vr.* to peer
asombrado: *aj.* amazed
asombrar: *vt.* to amaze
asombrarse: *vr.* to be amazed
asombro: *nm.* dread; fear
asombroso: *aj.* amazing
asordar: *vt.* to deafen
aspa: *nf.* cross; sail (windmill)
aspecto: *nm.* sight; appearance; look
aspereza: *nf.* asperity; acerbity
asperjar: *vt.* to sprinkle
áspero: *aj.* rough

aspiración: *aj.* aspiration; desire
aspirado: *aj.* vacuumed; aspirate (letter)
aspirador: *aj.* aspiring
aspiradora: *nf.* vacuum cleaner
aspirante: *aj.* aspiring; desiring
aspirar: *vt.* to inspire the air; draw breath
asquear: *vt.* to consider with disgust
asqueroso: *aj.* nasty; filthy
asta: *nf.* lance
asterisco: *nm.* asterisk
asteroide: *nm.* asteroid
astral: *aj.* pertaining to heavenly bodies
astro: *nm.* star; planet
astrofísica: *nf.* astrophysics
astrolabio: *nm.* astrolabe
astrología: *nf.* astrology
astrológico: *aj.* astrological
astrólogo;-a: *nmf.* astrologer
astronauta: *nmf.* astronaut
astronáutica: *nf.* astronautics
astronave: *nf.* space ship
astronomía: *nf.* astronomy
astronómico: *aj.* astronomical
astrónomo;-a: *nmf.* astronomer
asumir: *vt.* to assume; take upon
asunción: *nf.* assumption
asunto: *nm.* matter
asustadizo: *aj.* easily frightened
asustado: *aj.* frightened
asustar: *vt.* to frighten
asustarse: *vr.* to be frightened
asustador: *aj.* frightening
atacante: *aj.* attacking
atacar: *vt.* to attack
atadero: *nm.* hitching post
atado: *aj.* bundled; tied
atadura: *nf.* tying
atajo: *nm.* short-cut
atalaya: *nf.* watch-tower
ataque: *nm.* attack
atar: *vt.* to tie

atardecer: *nm.* sunset
atardecer: *vt.* to set (sun)
atareado: *aj.* busy with assignments
atarear: *vt.* to task; impose a task
atarearse: *vr.* to be busy with assignments
atarse: *vr.* to be tied
atascar: *vt.* to stop a leak
ataúd: *nm.* coffin
ataviar: *vt.* to deck out
atemorizar: *vt.* to frighten
atemorizarse: *vr.* to be intimidated
atemperar: *vt.* to moderate
atemperarse: *vr.* to become moderate or temperate
atención: *nf.* attention
atender: *vt.* to attend to
atenerse: *vr.* to rely on; to be dependent on
atentamente: *av.* attentively
atentar: *vt.* to attempt; to commit a crime
atenuar: *vt.* to attenuate; extenuate
aterrada: *nf.* nearness to land of a ship
aterrador: *aj.* horrible
aterraje: *nm.* touchdown point in an aircraft landing
aterramiento: *nm.* act of frightening
aterrar: *vt.* to frighten
aterrarse: *vr.* to become frightened
aterrizaje: *nm.* landing
aterrizar: *vt.* to land
aterrorizar: *vt.* to terrorize
aterrorizarse: *vr.* to become frightened
atesoramiento: *nm.* treasuring
atesorar: *vt.* to treasure up; hoard-up
atestado: *nm.* affidavit
atestar: *vt.* to cram; stuff
atestiguación: *nf.* witnessing; the act of being a witness
atestiguar: *vt.* to depose; to witness; to testify

atezado: *aj.* smooth or shiny tienda store; tent
atezar: *vt.* to make smooth or shiny
atezarse: *vr.* to become tan in appearance
atildar: *vt.* to punctuate; *r.* to dress
atinadamente: *av.* with good aim
atinado: *aj.* on the mark; just right
atinar: *vi.* to hit the target; to hit the bull's-eye
atípico: *aj.* atypical típico typical
atizar: *vt.* to stir the fire
atleta: *nmf.* athlete
atlético: *aj.* athletic
atletismo: *nm.* track and field
atmósfera: *nf.* atmosphere
atmosférico: *aj.* atmospheric
atolondrado -da: *aj.* hare-brained; giddy
atómico: *aj.* atomic
atomización: *nf.* atomization
atomizar: *vt.* to atomize
átomo: *nm.* atom; mote
atonal: *aj.* atonal
átono: *aj.* without accent
atontadamente: *av.* in a foolish manner
atontado: *aj.* dizzy or woozy
atontar: *vt.* to make someone feel dizzy or woozy
atontarse: *vr.* to feel dizzy or woozy
atormentador: *aj.* tormenting; torturing
atormentar: *vt.* to torment
atormentarse: *vr.* to torment oneself
atornillar: *vt.* to screw
atosigar: *vt.* to poison; *r.* to become worried
atracción: *nf.* attraction
atractivamente: *av.* attractively
atractivo: *nm.* attraction
atraer: *vt.* to attract
atragantarse: *vr.* to swallow wrong
atrás: *av.* backwards; behind

atrasado: *aj.* behind
atrasado -da: *aj.* late
atrasar: *vt.* to protract; postpone
atrasarse: *vr.* to get behind in
atraso: *nm.* late payment; the act of being late or behind in something
atravesar: *vt.* to traverse; to cross; to move through
atravesarse: *vr.* to move into the path of something
atrayente: *aj.* attractive
atreverse: *vr.* to dare
atrevido: *aj.* daring
atrevimiento: *nm.* daring; audacity
atribución: *nf.* attribution; conferring
atribuible: *aj.* attributable
atribuir: *vt.* to attribute; ascribe; impute
atribuirse: *vr.* to be attributed to
atributivo: *aj.* attributive
atributo: *nm.* attribute
atril: *nm.* desk; lectern; music-stand
atrincherar: *vt.* to entrench; fortify with a trench
atropar: *vt.* to form a troop or troops
atroparse: *vr.* to form part of a troop
atropellar: *vt.* to run over; to push through; to knock down; *r.* to hurry overmuch
atroz: *aj.* atrocious; cruel
atún: *nm.* tunny
aturdir: *vt.* to perturb; bewilder
audacia: *nf.* boldness; audacity
audaz: *aj.* bold; audacious
audible: *aj.* audible
audición: *nf.* audition
audiencia: *nf.* audience; hearing
audífono: *nm.* hearing aid
audiovisual: *aj.* audiovisual
auditivo: *aj.* auditory
auditor: *nm.* judge
auditorio: *nm.* auditorium
auge: *nm.* apogee
augurar: *vt.* to augur; foretell

aula: *nf.* class room
aumentado: *aj.* increased; enlarged; added
aumentar: *vt.* to augment; increase; *r.* to gather
aumentativo: *aj.* augmentative (grammatical term)
aumento: *nm.* gain; increase
aun: *av.* yet; even; aun cuando; although
auricular: *aj.* ear; *nm.* receiver
aurora: *nf.* dawn; daybreak
auscultar: *vt.* to auscultate
ausencia: *nf.* absence
ausentarse: *vr.* to absent oneself
ausente: *aj.* absent
ausente: *nmf.* person who is not present
ausentismo: *nm.* absenteeism
austeridad: *nf.* austerity
austero: *aj.* austere
auténtica: *nf.* certificate of authenticity
autenticación: *nf.* authentication
autenticar: *vt.* to authenticate
autenticidad: *nf.* authenticity
auténtico: *aj.* authentic
autentificar: *vt.* to give a certificate of authenticity
auto: *nm.* auto; car
autoadhesivo: *aj.* self-adhesive
autoanálisis: *nm.* self-analysis
autobiografía: *nf.* autobiography
autobiográfico: *aj.* autobiographical
autobús: *nm.* bus
autocamión: *nm.* bus; truck
autocrítica: *nf.* self-criticism
autodisciplina: *nf.* self-discipline
autódromo: *nm.* auto race track
autoescuela: *nf.* driving school
autogobierno: *nm.* self-government
automotor: *nm.* engine (train)
automóvil: *nm.* automobile
automovilismo: *nm.* motoring; automobile construction
automovilista: *nmf.* motorist
automovilístico: *aj.* pertaining to motoring or automobile construction
autonomía: *nf.* autonomy
autonómico: *aj.* pertaining to autonomy
autónomo: *aj.* autonomous
autopista: *nf.* highway; racetrack
autopista: *nf.* highway
autoridad: *nf.* authority; credit
autoritario: *aj.* authoritarian
autoritarismo: *nm.* authoritarianism
autoritativo: *aj.* authoritative
autorizable: *aj.* authorizable
autorización: *nf.* authorization
autorizado: *aj.* authorized
autorizar: *vt.* to authorize; legalize
autorretrato: *nm.* self-portrait
autoservicio: *nm.* self-service
autosuficiencia: *nf.* self-sufficiency
autosuficiente: *aj.* self-sufficient
autosugestión: *nf.* self-suggestion
auxiliador: *aj.* helpful
auxiliar: 1. *aj.* auxiliary; 2; *nmf.* assistant
auxiliar: *vt.* to aid; help
auxilio: *nm.* aid; help
aval: *nm.* guarantee; surety
avalar: *vt.* to confirm the veracity of something
avalorar: *vt.* to estimate the value
avaluación: *nf.* act of pricing
avaluar: *vt.* to price something; to appraise
avance: *nm.* advance
avante: *av.* ahead
avanzada: *nf.* group of military scouts
avanzado: *aj.* advanced
avanzar: *vi.* to advance
ave: *nf.* bird; fowl
avecinar: *vt.* to approach; *r.* to domicile oneself

avejentarse: *vr.* to grow old; to become old
avena: *nf.* oats
avenida: *nf.* avenue
avenir: *vt.* to reconcile; *r.* to settle differences in a friendly way
aventajado: *aj.* having an advantage; advantageous
aventajar: *vt.* to surpass; to gain an advantage
aventar: *vt.* to throw through the air
aventarse: *vr.* to dare; try; go for
aventura: *nf.* adventure
aventurado: *aj.* risky
aventurar: *vt.* to venture; to risk
aventurarse: *vr.* to take a risk; to dare
aventurero: *aj.* adventurous
avergonzado: *aj.* ashamed
avergonzar: *vt.* to shame; abash; *r.* to feel shame
avergonzarse: *vr.* to become ashamed
avería: *nf.* damage
averiguable: *aj.* able to be investigated
averiguación: *nf.* investigation
averiguar: *vt.* to inquire; investigate
avestruz: *nm.* ostrich
aviación: *nf.* aviation
aviador;-a: *nmf.* aviator
avidez: *nf.* covetousness; avidity
ávido -da: *aj.* greedy; covetous
avión: *nm.* aeroplane; airplane
avioneta: *nf.* light airplane
avioneta: *nf.* small airplane
avisar: *vt.* to inform; give notice
aviso: *nm.* information; intelligence; warning
avispa: *nf.* wasp
avivado: *aj.* stimulated; brought to life
avivar: *vt.* to quicken; enliven; encourage

avivarse: *vr.* to wake up; to become alive with energy
avizor: *aj.* watchful; *nm.* Spy
ay! : *inj.* alas!
ayer: *av.* yesterday; formerly
ayuda: *nf.* help; aid
ayudante: *nmf.* assistant
ayudar: *vt.* to help
ayudarse: *vr.* to help oneself; to help each other
ayunar: *vi.* to fast
ayuno: *nm.* fast
azada: *nf.* spade; hoe
azafata: *nf.* air hostess
azafrán: *nm.* saffron
azar: *nm.* chance; unforeseen disaster
azotar: *vt.* to whip; lash; horse-whip
azúcar: *nf.* sugar
azucarado: *aj.* sugared
azucarar: *vt.* to sugar; sweeten
azucarera: *nf.* sugar bowl
azucarero: *aj.* pertaining to sugar
azucena: *nf.* white lily; innocent or guileless person
azufre: *nm.* sulphur
azul: *aj.* blue
azulado: *aj.* bluish
azular: *vt.* to make blue; to color with blue
azulejo: *nm.* glazed tile

B

baba: *nf.* drivel; slaver
babero: *nm.* bib
babor: *nm.* port; larboard
babucha: *nf.* slipper

baca: *nf.* top (of a stagecoach)
bacalao: *nm.* codfish
bache: *nm.* hole; pot-hole
bachiller: *nmf.* high school or junior college student
bachillerato: *nm.* study at the high school or junior college level
báculo: *nm.* walking-stick; staff
badajo: *nm.* bell clapper
badén: *nm.* channel made by rainwater; rain gutter
bagaje: *nm.* baggage; luggage
bahía: *nf.* bay
bailable: *aj.* danceable
bailador: *aj.* pertaining to dance
bailante: *aj.* dancing
bailar: *vt. vi.* to dance
bailar: *vi.* to dance
bailarín;-a: *nmf.* dancer; ballet dancer; ballerina
baile: *nm.* dance
bailotear: *vi.* to dance in an arrhythmic manner
bailoteo: *nm.* arrhythmic dance
baja: *nf.* lowering
bajada: *nf.* descent; slope; ballad; song
bajamar: *nf.* water's edge
bajamente: *av.* in a low manner
bajar: to descend. to lower; let down; to reduce
bajarse: to lower oneself; to get off a vehicle
bajeza: *nf.* meanness
bajío: *nm.* lowland; sandbank
bajista: *aj.* pertaining to a bearish market; bearish
bajo: *av.* below; *prep.* under; beneath
bajo: *aj.* low; short
bajo: *prep.* under
bala: *nf.* bullet
bala: *nf.* bullet
balance: *nm.* balance
balancear: *vt.* to balance

balancearse: *vr.* to become balanced
balanceo: *nm.* balance
balancín: *nm.* rocking chair
balandro: *nm.* (Náut.) small sloop
balanza: *nf.* scale of the balance type
balaustrada: *nf.* balustrade
balazo: *nm.* bullet wound
balbucear : *vi.* to stutter; stammer
balcón: *nm.* balcony; open gallery
balconcesto: *nm.* basketball
baldar: *vt.* to cripple; to trump
balde: *nm.* bucket; gratis; free of charge
baldío: *aj.* untilled; unculti-vated
baldosa: *nf.* fine square tile
balín: *nm.* BB or pellet
balística: *nf.* ballistics
balístico: *aj.* ballistic
ballena: *nf.* whale
ballesta: *nf.* cross-bow
ballet: *nm.* ballet
balneario: *nm.* watering place; bathing place
balón: *nm.* (large) ball
balsa: *nf.* pool; pond
bañadero: *nm.* bathing area for animals
bañar: *vt.* to bathe
bañarse: *vr.* to bathe oneself
banca: *nf.* form; bench; washing-box
bancario: *aj.* bank; pertaining to the bank
bancarrota: *nf.* bankruptcy
banco: *nm.* boat; vessel; ship; bank
banda: *nf.* sash; scarf
bandada: *nf.* covery; flock (of birds)
bandeja: *nf.* tray
bandera: *nf.* flag
abanderado: *nmf.* flag bearer
abanderar: *vt.* to register a ship under a nation's flag
banderilla: *nf.* small dart with a bannerol for baiting bulls
banderín: *nf.* small flag

banderita: *nf.* small flag or pennant
bandido: *nm.* bandit; outlaw
bando: *nm.* proclamation; edict; group of animals
bañera: *nf.* bathtub
bañista: *nmf.* swimmer at a public pool
baño: *nm.* bath
banquete: *nm.* banquet
banquetear: *vt.* to feast
banquetero: *nmf.* person who prepares and serves a banquet
baraja: *nf.* complete pack of cards; game of cards
barajar: *vt.* to shuffle (cards); *vi.* to quarrel; content
baranda: *nf.* railing; banister
baratija: *nf.* something cheaply made
baratijas: *nf.* pl. trifles; toys
barato: *aj.* cheap; low-priced
barba: *nf.* beard; chin
barbado: *aj.* bearded
barbaridad: *nf.* barbarity
barbarie: *nf.* culturally ignorant person
barbarismo: *nm.* barbarianism
bárbaro: *aj.* barbaric
barbecho: *nm.* fallow
barbería: *nf.* barber shop
barbero: *nm.* barber
barbilampiño: *aj.* beardless; clean-shaven
barbilla: *nf.* chin
barbudo: *aj.* bearded
barca: *nf.* ship; boat
barniz: *nm.* varnish; glaze
barnizar: *vt.* to varnish
barón: *nm.* baron
baronesa: *nf.* baroness
barquero: *nm.* helmsman
barraca: *nf.* barrack; cabin
barranco: *nm.* precipice
barrena: *nf.* gimlet; borer

barrenar : *vt.* to bore; drill
barrendero: *nmf.* sweeper; cleaner
barreno: *nm.* large borer
barrer: *vt.* to sweep
barriada: *nf.* city ward
barriga: *nf.* abdomen; belly
barril: *nm.* barrel; earthen jug
barrizal: *nm.* place filled with clay
barro: *nm.* clay; mud; mire
barroco: *aj.* baroque
barroquismo: *inn.* the quality of being baroque
barroso: *aj.* muddy; clay-like
barruntar: *vt.* to foresee; conjecture
basamento: *nm.* base; referring to a construction project
basar: *vt.* to base; set up
basarse: *vr.* to base oneself
báscula: *nf.* weighing scale
base: *nf.* base
básico: *aj.* basic
basílica: *nf.* royal palace
bastante: *aj.* sufficient; enough; rather; quite
bastar: *vi.* to be enough
bastidor: *nm.* easel; frame
basto -ta: *aj.* coarse; homespun
bastón: *nm.* cane; stick; staff
batalla: *nf.* battle; fight; combat
batallador;-a: *nmf.* fighter; person who battles
batallar: *vi.* to battle; to struggle; to fight with
batallón: *nm.* battalion
batata: *nf.* sweet potato
bate: *nm.* bat
bateador;-a: *nmf.* batter (sport)
batear: *vt.* to bat; to swing a bat
batería: *nf.* (Mil; Elec.) battery
batidor: *nm.* beater
batiente: *aj.* beating
batir: *vt.* to beat; dash
batirse: *vr.* to become beaten (food; mixture)

batuta: *nf.* baton
baúl: *nm.* trunk; coffer
bautismo: *nm.* baptism
bautizar: *vt.* to baptize; christen
bayeta: *nf.* baise
bayoneta: *nf.* bayonet
bazar: *nm.* bazaar; emporium
bazo: *nm.* spleen
bebé: *nm.* baby
bebedero: *nm.* drinking fountain
bebedizo: *nm.* drinkable liquid; potable drink
bebedor: *nmf.* drinker
beber: *vt.* to drink; swallow
bebible: *aj.* drinkable
bebida: *nf.* drink; beverage
bebido: *aj.* under the influence of alcohol
becerro: *nm.* young bull; yearling calf
bedel: *nm.* beadle
bélico: *aj.* warlike; martial
bellaco -ca: *aj.* artful; sly
belleza: *nf.* beauty; fairness; loveliness
bello: *aj.* beautiful; pretty
bellota: *nf.* acorn
bendecir: *vt.* praise; exalt; to bless
bendición: *nf.* -ion blessing
bendito: *aj.* blessed
benedictino: *aj.* benedictine
benefactor;-a: *nmf.* benefactor
beneficencia: *nf.* beneficence
beneficiado;-a: *nf.* person who has benefited
beneficiar: *vt.* to benefit; do good to. *r.* to make profit
beneficiario;-a: *nmf.* beneficiary
beneficiarse: *vr.* to benefit from
beneficio: *nm.* benefit; favor; kind-ness
beneficioso: *aj.* beneficial
benéfico: *aj.* beneficial
benemérito: *aj.* worthy of honor

beneplácito: *nm.* good will; appro-bation
benevolencia: *nf.* benevolence
benevolente: *aj.* benevolent
benévolo: *aj.* benevolent
benjamín: *nm.* youngest son
berenjena: *nf.* eggplant
berrinche: *nm.* con. anger; sulkiness of children
berza: *nf.* cabbage
besamanos: *nm.* hand kissing of royalty
besar: *vt.* to kiss; con. to touch closely (objects)
besarse: *vr.* to kiss each other
beso: *nm.* kiss
bestia: *nf.* beast
besucón: *aj.* pertaining to over-affectionate kissing
besugo: *nm.* sea bream
bazuquear: *vt.* to kiss excessively
besuqueo: *nm.* overly affectionate kiss
beta: *nf.* scholarship or studentship; grant; part of acolle
betún: *nm.* bitumen
biberón: *nm.* feeding-bottle
Biblia: *nf.* Bible
bíblico: *aj.* biblical
bibliófilo: *nm.* book lover
bibliografía: *nf.* bibliography
bibliográfico: *aj.* bibliographic
biblioteca: *nf.* library
bibliotecario;-a: *nmf.* librarian
bicho: *nm.* small insect
bicicleta: *nf.* bicycle
bidón: *nm.* drum
biela: *nf.* crank
bien: *nm.* good; well-being; utility; benefit; pl. property; fortune; land
bienaventurado: *aj.* blessed; fortunate
bienaventuranza: *nf.* beatitude; blessedness

bienestar: *nm.* well-being; comfort
bienhechor: *aj.* referring to one who does good
bienintencionado: *aj.* well-intentioned
bienvenida: *nf.* welcome
bienvenido: *aj.* welcome
bifurcación: *nf.* fork
bigote: *nm.* moustache; whisker
bigotudo: *aj.* mustached
bilis: *nf.* bile gall
billar: *nm.* game of billiards
billetaje: *nm.* collection of tickets
billete: *nm.* bill; billete
billetero: *nm.* wallet; someone who sells lottery tickets
biofísica: *nf.* biophysics
biografía: *nf.* biography
biográfico: 1. *aj.* biographical; 2. *nm.* biographer
biología: *nf.* biology
biológico: 1. *aj.* biological; 2. *nmf.* biologist
biombo: *nm.* folding screen
biopsia: *nf.* biopsy
bioquímica: *nf.* biochemistry
bioquímico: 1. *aj.* biochemical; 2. *nmf.* biochemist
bis: *av.* twice
bisabuela: *nf.* great grandmother
bisabuelo: *nm.* great grandfather
bisagra: *nf.* hinge
bisiesto (ano): *aj.* a leap year
bistec: *nm.* steak
bisturí: *nm.* bistoury; scalpel
bisutería: *nf.* jewelry
bizco -ca: 1. *aj.* cross-eyed; 2. *nm.* squinter
bizcocho: *nm.* biscuit; hardtack
biznieta: *nf.* great granddaughter
biznieto: *nm.* great grandson
blanco: *aj.* white
blancura: *nf.* whiteness
blancuzco: *aj.* whitish

blando: *aj.* smooth; soft
blandura: *nf.* softness
blanduzco: *aj.* partly soft; rather soft
blanqueador: *aj.* whitening
blanquear: *vt.* to make something white
blanquearse: *vr.* to become white
blanquecino: *aj.* off-white
blanqueo: *nm.* whitening; whitewashing
blasón: *nm.* heraldry; blazon
blindar: *vt.* (Mil.) & (Náutica) to protect with blindage
bibliotecario -ria: *aj.* librarian
bloque: *nm.* block
bloqueador: *nm.* sun block; sunscreen
bloquear: *vt.* to block
bloqueo: *nm.* blocking
blusa: *nf.* blouse
bobada: *nf.* nonsense; stupidity
bobina: *nf.* reel or bobbin; spool
boca: *nf.* mouth
bocacalle: *nf.* entrance to a street; street that flows into a boulevard
bocadillo: *nm.* appetizer; snack
bocado: *nm.* mouthful; a bite of food
bocamanga: *nf.* cuff
bocanada: *nf.* mouthful
bocera: *nf.* food or drink that sticks to the lips
boceto: *nm.* sketch
bochorno: *nm.* hot; sultry weather
bocina: *nf.* horn; (car)
boda: *nf.* marriage; nuptials; wedding
bodega: *nf.* wine-vault
bodegón: *nm.* eating-house
bofetada: *nf.* slap; box
boga: *nf.* kind of edible fish; (Náut.) act of rowing
bogar : *vi.* to row
boicotear: *vt.* to boycott
boina: *nm.* beret; flat round cap

without peak
bola: *nm.* ball; bowl
bola: *nf.* round object; bullet
bolear: *vt.* to volley; to practice with a ball
bolera: *nf.* bowling alley
boletín: *nm.* bulletin
boleto: *nm.* ticket
boliche: *nm.* bowling
bolígrafo: *nm.* ball-point pen
bollo: *nm.* small loaf or roll; small biscuit
bolsa: *nf.* purse; bag
bolsear: *vt.* to steal; to pick someone's pocket
bolsero;-a: *nmf.* person that makes or sells bags or pursesse-snatcher
bolsillo: *nm.* pocket; purse
bolso: *nm.* handbag; purse
bomba: *nf.* pump; bomb
bombardear: *vt.* to bombard; bomb
bombardeo: *nm.* bombardment
bombardero: *nm.* bomber (airplane)
bombazo: *nm.* bombing; explosion of a bomb
bombear: *vt.* to pump
bombeo: *nm.* act of pumping
bombero: *nm.* fireman; firefighter
bombilla: *nf.* bulb
bombón: *nm.* bonbon; sweet stuff
bonachón: *aj.* of good character
bondad: *nf.* goodness; excellence; kindness
bondadoso: *aj.* kind
bonificación: *nf.* improvement; discount
bonito -ta: *aj.* pretty good; pretty
boquerón: *nm.* anchovy
boquete: *nm.* opening
boquilla: *nf.* lower opening of breeches
borda: *nf.* gunwale
bordado: *aj.* embroidered
bordado: *nm.* embroidery

bordador;-a: *nmf.* embroiderer
bordadora: *nf.* embroidery machine
bordar: *vt.* to embroider
borde: *nm.* border; outer edge
bordear: *vt.* to move along the edge
bordo: *nm.* an exterior side of a ship
borrador: *nm.* blotter
borrador: *nm.* eraser; rough draft
borrajear: *vt.* to scribble notes
borrar: *vt.* to cross out; strike out; to erase
borrasca: *nf.* storm; tempest
borrico: *nm.* ass; con. fool
borrón: *nm.* blot of ink; act of erasing
borronear: *vt.* to erase frequently
borroso: *aj.* blurred; smeared
boscaje: *nm.* small forest
boscoso: *aj.* forested
bosque: *nm.* forest
bosquejo: *nm.* sketch
bosquimano;-a; bosquimán;-a: *nmf.* bushman
bostezar: *vi.* to yawn; gape
bota: *nf.* boot; small leather winebag
bote: *nm.* thrust (spear); tin; rebound of a ball; jump
botella: *nf.* bottle; flask
botellazo: *nm.* a hit with a bottle
botica: *nf.* chemist-shop
botijo: *nm.* round earthen jar with spout and handle
botín: *nm.* buskin; half-boot
botiquín: *nm.* first aid
botón: *nm.* sprout; bud; button
botonadura: *nf.* buttons of a piece of clothing as a group
botones: *nm.* bellboy
bóveda: *nf.* arch; vault
bóveda: *nf.* curved structure
bozal: *nm.* muzzle
braga: *nf.* pl. knickers; breeches
bragueta: *nf.* fly of breeches
bramar : *vi.* to roar; to storm

brasa: *nf.* live coal; red-hot coal (or) wood
brasero: *nm.* brazier; fire-pan
braveza: *nf.* valor
bravo: *aj.* fierce; brave
bravucón: *aj.* brave only in appearance
bravuconada: *nf.* false bravery
bravura: *nf.* valor
braza: *nf.* butterfly stroke (swimming)
brazada: *nf.* stroke (swimming)
brazal: *nm.* armband
brazalete: *nm.* armlet; bracelet
brazo: *nm.* arm; branch
brea: *nf.* tar; resin; pitch
breva: *nf.* early fruit of a fig tree
breve: *aj.* brief; short; concise
brevedad: *nf.* brevity; briefness
brevedad: *nf.* brevity
breviario: *nm.* a brief; summary
bribón -na: vagrant
brigada: *nf.* brigade
brillante: *aj.* brilliant; shiny
brillantez: *nf.* brilliance
brillantina: *nf.* cosmetic used to make hair shine
brillar: *vi.* to shine
brillo: *nm.* shine
brincar : *vi.* to jump; leap
brindar: *vt.* to toast; to salute with a toast
brindis: *nm.* health; after dinner speech
brindis: *nm.* a toast
brío: *nm.* strength; force; energy
brioso: *aj.* full of energy and decision
brisca: *nf.* game of cards
británico: *aj.* British
brocha: *nf.* brush
broma: *nf.* gaiety; jollity
broma: *nf.* practical joke
bromear : *vi.* to joke; make fun

bromista: *nmf.* practical joker
bronca: *nf.* quarrel
bronce: *nm.* bronze
bronceado: *aj.* bronzed; suntanned
bronceador: *nm.* tanning lotion
broncear: *vt.* to bronze; to tan
brotar: *vi.* to bloom; to germinate; to sprout
brote: *nm.* sprout
brujo: *nm.* sorcerer; conjurer
brújula: *nf.* compass
bruma: *nf.* mist; haze
bruscamente: *av.* brusquely; without subtlety
brusco: *aj.* rough; brusque
brusquedad: *nf.* brusqueness
brutal: *aj.* brutal; brutish
bruto -ta: 1. *aj.* coarse; beastly; brutish; 2. *nm.* brute; beast
buenamente: *av.* freely; sponta-neously
buenaventura: *nf.* fortune; good luck
buenazo: *aj.* of a kind and peaceful nature
bueno -na: 1. *aj.* good; kind; upright; virtuous; 2. *av.* very well; all right
buey: *nm.* ox
bufanda: *nf.* muffler; scarf
bufete: *nm.* bureau
bufón -na: 1. *aj.* funny; comical; 2. *nm.* pedlar
buhardilla: *nf.* garret; attic
búho: *nm.* owl; con. unsocial person
buitre: *nm.* vulture
bujía: *nf.* wax candle
bullir: to boil; bubble up; to move; stir; to stir
bulto: *nm.* bulk; anything which appears bulky
buque: *nm.* (Náut.) vessel; ship
burbujear : *vi.* to bubble
burgo: *nm.* small town dependent on a larger entity

burgués: *aj.* bourgeois
burguesía: *nf.* bourgeoisie
burla: *nf.* the making fun of someone
burlarse: *vr.* to make fun of someone
burlesco: *aj.* burlesque
burlón: *aj.* referring to a person who makes fun of someone
burro: *nm.* ass; donkey
busca: *nf.* act of looking for something
buscada: *aj.* looked for; sought after
buscapiés: *nm.* a type of firecracker
buscar: *vt.* to seek; search; to look for
búsqueda: *nf.* search
busto: *nm.* bust
butaca: *nf.* arm-chair; easy-chair
buzo: *nm.* diver

C

cabal: *aj.* exact
cabalgadura: *nf.* saddle and accessories; riding horse
cabalgar: *vi.* to ride a horse
cabalgata: *nf.* procession of mounted horsemen
caballar: *aj.* pertaining to horses; horse-like
caballeresco: *aj.* pertaining to knights
caballería: *nf.* riding horse
caballeriza: *nf.* stable
caballerizo;-a: *nmf.* worker in a stable
caballero: *nm.* knight; gentleman; sir

caballerosidad: *nf.* gentlemanliness
caballeroso: *aj.* gentlemanly
caballete: *nm.* painter's easel; ridge
caballista: *nmf.* horse expert
caballitos: *nmpl.* carousel
caballo: *nm.* horse; knight
cabaña: *nf.* cabin; hut
cabecear: *vi.* to nod off
cabeceo: *nm.* nodding off
cabecera: *nf.* beginning; head; headboard
cabecilla: *nmf.* head; leader
cabellera: *nf.* long hair
cabello: *nm.* hair
cabelludo: *aj.* having a lot of hair
caber: *vi.* to fit
cabestrillo: *nm.* sling; bell-ox
cabeza: *nf.* head; chief; leader
cabezazo: *nm.* hit with the head
cabezón: *aj.* bigheaded; foolish
cabezota: *nf.* large head; person with a large head
cabezudo: *aj.* with a large head; bigheaded; foolish
cabezudo: *nm.* person with a large head
cabida: *nf.* space; capacity
cabildo: *nm.* cathedral chapter; municipal council
cabina: *nf.* cabin
cabizbajo: *aj.* sad; with head hanging low
cable: *nm.* cable; wire
cabo: *nm.* end; handle; small bun-dle; thread
cabotaje: *nm.* coasting trade
cabra: *nf.* female goat
cabrero;-a: *nmf.* goatherd
cabrío: *aj.* pertaining to goats
cabritilla: *nf.* goatskin from a young goat
cabrito: *nm.* kid; small goat
cabrón: *nm.* male goat; also used as an offensive term

cacahuete: *nm.* peanut
cacería: *nf.* hunting
cacharro: *nm.* crock; earthen pot
cachear: *vt.* to frisk
cachimba: *nf.* tobacco-pipe
cacho: *nm.* piece; slide
caco: *nm.* pickpocket
cada: *aj.* indef. each; every
cadalso: *nm.* stand; platform
cadáver : *vi.* corpse; dead body; cadaver
cadavérico: *aj.* pertaining to cadavers; cadaver-like; pale
cadena: *nf.* chain
cadera: *nf.* hip
caer: *vi.* to fall
caerse: *vr.* to fall (oneself)
café: *nm.* coffee; cafe
cafeína: *nf.* caffeine
cafetal: *nm.* coffee plantation
cafetera: *nf.* coffee-pot
cafetería: *nf.* cafeteria
cafetero: *aj.* pertaining to coffee
cafeto: *nm.* coffee plant
caída: *nf.* fall; downfall; drop; decli-nation
caído: *aj.* fallen
caja: *nf.* box; case; cashbox; cashiers office
cajero;-a: *nmf.* cashier
cajetilla: *nf.* pack of cigarettes
cajón: *nm.* drawer
cal: *nf.* lime
calabaza: *nf.* pumpkin; gourd
calabozo : *nm.* dungeon; prison cell
calamar: *nm.* squid; calamar
calambre: *nm.* cramp; muscle contraction
calar: *vt.* to pierce; to permeate
calavera: *nf.* skull
calcaño: *nm.* heel (bone)
calcar: *vt.* to trace; to copy
calceta: *nf.* stocking
calcetín: *nm.* sock

calcinar: *vt.* to calcine
calculable: *aj.* calculable
calculador: *nm.* calculator
calcular: *vt.* to calculate
cálculo: *nm.* calculation; calculus
caldeamiento: *nm.* heating
caldear: *vt.* to heat; to become heated
caldera: *nf.* boiler; kettle; cauldron
calderilla: *nf.* copper coins; copper money
caldero: *nm.* kettle
caldero: *nm.* small cauldron
caldillo: *nm.* light gravy or broth
caldo: *nm.* broth
caldoso: *aj.* with broth; similar to broth in texture; soupy
calefacción: *nf.* heating system
calendario: *nm.* calendar
calentador: *aj.* heater; heating
calentamiento: *nm.* heating
calentar: *vt.* to heat
calentura: *nf.* fever
calenturiento: *aj.* feverish
calibrar: *vt.* to calibrate
calidad: *nf.* quality
cálido: *aj.* warm; hot
cálido: *aj.* warm
calientaplatos: *nm.* hot plate
caliente: *aj.* hot; heated; fie
calificable: *aj.* able to qualify
calificación: *nf.* grade
calificado: *aj.* graded; qualified
calificador: *aj.* grading
calificar: *vt.* to qualify; to certify mark; to grade
calificativo: *aj.* qualifying
caligrafía: *nf.* calligraphy; hand wetting
callado: *aj.* quiet; silent
callar: *vt.* to quiet; to silence
callarse: *vr.* to be quiet; to be silent
calle: *nf.* street
callejear: *vi.* to walk the streets

callejero: *aj.* pertaining to streets; street-walking
callejón: *nm.* alley
callejuela: *nf.* short street
callo: *nm.* callus; corn. pl. tripe
calma: *nf.* calm
calmante: *aj.* calming; tranquilizing
calmante: *nm.* tranquilizer
calmar: *vt.* to calm; to mitigate; to quite
calmarse: *vr.* to be calm
calmoso: *aj.* slow or lazy
calor: *nm.* heat; warmth
caloría: *nf.* calorie
calórico: *aj.* fattening; with many calories
caluroso: *aj.* warm
calva: *nm.* bald head
calvo: *aj.* bald; hairless
calzado -da: *aj.* shod; calced
calzar: *vt.* to shoe; to put on
calzoncillos: *nm.* pl. drawers; pants
calzones: *nm.* pants; trousers
cama: *nf.* bed
cámara: *nf.* hall; parlor; chamber; breech
camarada: *nm.* comrade; companion
camaradería: *nf.* camaraderie
camarera: *nf.* maid; waitress
camarero: *nm.* waiter
camarote: *nm.* berth; cabin in a ship
camastro: *nm.* uncomfortable bed
cambalachear: *vt.* to exchange
cambiante: *aj.* changing
cambiar: *vt.* to change
cambiarse: *vr.* to move; to change
cambiazo: *nm.* fraud
cambio: *nm.* change
cambista: *nmf.* moneychanger
camelar: *vt.* con. to flirt with; to trick
camera video: *nm.* video
camilla: *nf.* stretcher; litter
camillero;-a: *nmf.* stretcher bearer
caminante: *nmf.* walker

caminar: *vt.* intr. to walk
caminata: *nf.* walk; stroll
camino: *nm.* roadway; path; road
camión: *nm.* truck; van; bus
camionero; -a: *nmf.* bus driver; truck driver
camioneta: *nf.* van; pickup truck
camisa: *nf.* shirt; slough
camisera: *nf.* blouse
camisería: *nf.* clothing store specializing in shirts
camisero;-a: *nmf.* shirt maker or seller
camiseta: *nf.* vest; undershirt
camisola: *nf.* camisole
camisón: *nm.* nightshirt; nightgown
campamento: *nm.* camp
campana: *nf.* bell; cloche
campanada: *nf.* one ring of a bell
campanario: *nm.* bell tower
campanear: *vi.* to ring a bell
campaneo: *nm.* ringing of a bell
campanero;-a: *nmf.* bell maker; bell ringer
campanilla: *nf.* small bell
campear: *vi.* to lead or take animals to pasture
campeón; a: *mnf.* champion
campeonato: *nm.* championship
campero: *aj.* out in the open; in the country
campesinado: *nm.* peasantry
campesino: 1. *aj.* rural; 2. *nm.* countryman
campestre: *aj.* rural; pertaining to the country
campiña: *nf.* country; countryside; agricultural field
campirano: *aj.* rural; pertaining to the country
campista: *nmf.* camper
campo: *nm.* field; country
cana: *nf.* white (or) gray hair
caña: *nf.* cane; culm; stem; reed;

glass of beer
canal: *nf.* canal
canalización: *nf.* building of a canal
canalizar: *vt.* to canalize
canalla: *nm.* rascal
canalón: *nm.* gutter
cáñamo: *nm.* hemp
cañamón: *nm.* hemp seeds
canapé: *nm.* sofa; settee
canasta: *nf.* basket
cañaveral: *nm.* canebrake; cane field
cancelar: *vt.* to annul; to cancel
cáncer: *nm.* cancer
canciller: *nm.* chancellor
canción: *nf.* song
cancionero: *nm.* music book
candado: *nm.* padlock
candela: *nf.* candle; torch
candente: *aj.* candent; red-hot
candidato -ta: *nmf.* candidate; competitor
candidez: *nf.* candidness
cándido: *aj.* candid
candil: *nm.* oil lamp
candilejas: *nf.* pl. footlights
candor: *nm.* candor
candoroso: *aj.* candid
canela: *nm.* cinnamon
cangrejo: *nm.* crab
canijo -ja: *aj.* sickly; infirm
canjear: *vt.* to exchange
caño: *nm.* tube; pipe; ditch
canoa: *nf.* canoe; launch
canon: *nm.* religious canon
cañón: *nm.* tube; pipe; cannon; gun
cañonazo: *nm.* hit with a cannonball
cañonear: *vt.* to fire a cannon; to bombard
cañonero: *aj.* armed with cannon
canónico: *aj.* canonical
canonización: *nf.* canonization
canonizar: *vt.* to canonize
cansado -da: *aj.* tired; weary
cansancio: *nm.* tiredness

cansar: *vt.* to tire
cansarse: *vr.* to become tired
cantante: *aj.* singing
cantante: *nmf.* singer
cantar: *vt.* to sing
cántaro: *nm.* jug
cantata: *nf.* cantata
cantera: *nf.* quarry
cantidad: *nf.* quantity; amount
cantina: *nf.* tavern; pub
canto: *nm.* song; chant
cantor: 1. adj singing 2. *nm.* singer; songster
canturrear: *vi.* to sing in a low voice or without paying much attention; to hum
canturreo: *nm.* singing in a low voice or without paying much attention; humming
caoba: *nf.* mahogany
caos: *nm.* chaos; confusion
caótico: *aj.* chaotic
capa: *nf.* cape; cloak; mantle; stratum
capacidad: *nf.* capacity; ability
capacitación: *nf.* training
capacitar: *vt.* to enable; to qualify; *r.* to be come enabled
capataz: *nm.* overseer; foreman
capaz: *aj.* capable
capellán: *nm.* chaplain; priest
capilla: *nf.* chapel
capirote: *nm.* pointed cap
capital: *aj.* capital; main; principal
capitalismo: *nm.* capitalism
capitalista: 1. *aj.* capitalistic; 2. *nmf.* capitalist
capitalización: *nf.* capitalization
capitalizar: *vt.* to capitalize
capitán: *nm.* leader; captain
capitana: *nf.* wife of a captain
capitanear: *vt.* to head; to lead
capitanía: *nf.* captaincy
capitol: *nm.* capitol
capitulo: *nm.* chapter

capota: *nf.* top; hood
capote: *nm.* cape with sleeves
capricho: *nm.* caprice; whim
caprichoso: *aj.* capricious
cápsula: *nf.* capsule
captar: *vt.* to catch; to attract
capturar: *vt.* to capture; arrest; seize; get
capucha: *nf.* hood attached to a cape
capullo: *nm.* bud; cocoon
cara: *nf.* face; appearance; look
carabela: *nf.* caravel
carabinero: *nm.* carabineer; frontier officer
caracol: *nm.* snail
carácter: *nm.* character; type
característica: *nf.* characteristic
característicamente: *av.* characteristically
característico: *aj.* characteristic
caracterización: *nf.* characterization
caracterizado: *aj.* characterized
caracterizar: *vt.* to characterize
caramba: inj. by jove!
caramelo: *nm.* caramel; sweet; toffee
carátula: *nf.* face of a clock
carbón: *nm.* coal; charcoal
carboncillo: *nm.* charcoal pencil
carbonera: *nf.* locker for storing coal or charcoal
carbonería: *nf.* store specializing in sale of coal or charcoal
carbonero: 1. *aj.* pertaining to coal or charcoal; 2. *nm.* charcoal maker or seller
carbónico: *aj.* containing carbon; pertaining to carbon
carbonífero: *aj.* carboniferous
carbonización: *nf.* carbonization
carbonizar: *vt.* to carbonize
carbonizarse: *vr.* to be carbonized
carbono: *nm.* carbon
carburador: *nm.* carburetor
carburante: *nm.* fuel

carcajada: *nf.* guffaw; loud laughter
carcajearse: *vr.* to guffaw; to laugh loudly
cárcel: *nf.* jail; prison
carcelero;-a: *nmf.* jailer
carcoma: *nf.* woodworm
carcomer: *vt.* to bore; to gnaw away; *r.* to become undermined
carcomerse: *vr.* to be consumed
cardo: *nm.* thistle
carear: *vt.* to bring face-to-face
carecer : *vt.* to be in want; to be in need of
careo: *nm.* judicial confrontation
carestía: *nf.* scarcity
careta: *nf.* cardboard mask
carga: *nm.* load
cargado: *aj.* charged; loaded
cargador: *nm.* charger; person who carries or loads
cargamento: *nm.* cargo
cargar: *vt.* to carry; to charge
cargarse: *vr.* to be charged; to carry
cargazón: *nf.* heaviness
cargo: *nm.* burden; weight; job; duty; charge; post; dignity
carguero: *nm.* cargo ship; freighter
caricatura: *nf.* caricature; cartoon
caricaturista: *nmf.* caricaturist; cartoon artist
caricaturizar: *vt.* to draw a caricature
caricia: *nf.* to decay; rot; caress; pat; stroke
caridad: *nf.* charity
cariño: *nm.* love; affection; care
cariñoso: *aj.* caring
cariz: *nm.* appearance
carne: *nf.* flesh; meat
carnero: *nm.* mutton; sheep
carnet: *nm.* notebook
carnicería: *nf.* meat market; butcher's shop; carnage
carnicero: *aj.* carnivorous

carnicero;-a: *nmf.* butcher
cárnico: *aj.* pertaining to meat
carnívoro: *aj.* carnivorous
carnoso: *aj.* meaty; fleshy
caro -ra: *aj.* dear; expensive
carpeta: *nf.* portfolio
carpintería: *nf.* carpentry
carraspera: *nf.* con. hoarseness
carrera: *nf.* race; running; career;
horse racing
carreta: *nf.* cart; wagon
carretada: *nf.* load
carrete: *nm.* spool; bobbin
carretera: *nf.* highway; road
carretero: *nm.* car builder
carretilla: *nf.* wheelbarrow
carretón: *nm.* two-wheeled cart or
wagon
carril: *nm.* lane
carro: *nm.* cart; truck; car
carrocería: *nf.* coachwork; body of a
car
carroza: *nf.* coach; carriage; hearse
carruaje: *nm.* carriage
carta: *nf.* letter; chart
carta: *nf.* letter
cartear: *vt.* to play low cards; *r.* to
write each other
cartearse: *vr.* to correspond by letter
cartel: *nm.* poster; place card
cartelera: *nf.* billboard;
entertainment guide; marquee
carteo: *nm.* correspondence
cartera: *nf.* wallet
carterista: *nmf.* pickpocket
cartero: *nm.* postman; mail carrier
cartilla: *nf.* primer; short treatise
cartón: *nm.* cardboard; paste-board
cartucho: *nm.* cartridge
cartulina: *nf.* thin cardboard
casa: *nf.* house; home; apartment
casadero -da: *aj.* marriageable
casado: *aj.* married
casamentero: *aj.* matchmaking

casamentero;-a: *nmf.* matchmaker
casamiento: *nm.* marriage; wedding
casar: *vt.* to marry
casarse: *vr.* to get married
cascabel: *nm.* jingle bell
cascanueces: *nm.* nut-cracker
cáscara: *nf.* rind; peel
casco: *nm.* skull; hoof; potsherd
casero: *aj.* homemade
caserón: *nm.* large house; mansion
caseta: *nf.* hut
casi: *av.* almost; nearly
casino: *nm.* casino; club
caso: *nm.* case; chance; event
casona: *nf.* large house; mansion
caspa: *nf.* dandruff; scurf
casquete: *nm.* skullcap
casta: *nf.* caste; race
castaña: *nf.* chestnut (fruit)
castellanizar: *vt.* to adapt a foreign
word to the Spanish language
castellano: *aj.* pertaining to the
Spanish language; Castilian
castellano: *nm.* Spanish language;
Castilian
castidad: *nf.* chastity
castigar: *vt.* to punish; to castigate
castigo: *nm.* punishment
castizo: *aj.* pure
casto: *aj.* chaste
casual: *aj.* accidental; chance; casual
casualidad: *nf.* coincidence
casualmente: *av.* coincidentally;
accidentally
cataclismo: *nm.* cataclysm
catacumbas: *nf.* pl. catacombs
catalejo: *nm.* telescope
catalogación: *nf.* cataloguing;
classification
catalogar: *vt.* to catalog; to classify
catálogo: *nm.* catalogue; catalog
catar: *vt.* to taste
catarata: *nf.* cataract; waterfall
catarro: *nm.* catarrh; cold (nose)

catástrofe: *nf.* catastrophe
catastrófico: *aj.* catastrophic
cátedra: *nf.* subject of study at a university
catedrático: *nm.* professor; teacher
catolicismo: *nm.* Catholicism
católico: *aj.* Catholic
catorce: *aj.* fourteen
catorceavo: *aj.* fourteenth
catorceavo: *nm.* one-fourteenth (fraction)
cauce: *nm.* river bed
caucho: *nm.* india-rubber
caudal: *nm.* abundance of water
caudaloso: *aj.* with great abundance
caudillaje: *nm.* military leadership
caudillo: *nm.* military leader
causa: *nf.* cause; motive
causal: *aj.* causal
causalidad: *nf.* causality
causante: *aj.* causing
causar: *vt.* to cause; to make
cautela: *nf.* caution
cautivar: *vt.* to take prisoner
cavar: *vt.* to dig
cavidad: *nf.* cavity
caza: *nf.* chase; hunt; game
cazabombardero: *nm.* fighter bomber (airplane)
cazador -ra: 1. *aj.* hunting; 2. *nm.* hunter
cazar: *vt.* to chase; to hunt
cazasubmarinos: *nm.* destroyer; submarine chaser
cazatalentos: *nmf.* talent searcher; headhunter
cazatorpedero: *nm.* destroyer
cazo: *nm.* ladle
cazuela: *nf.* earthen casserole
cebada: *nf.* barley
cebar: *vt.* to fatten up
cebolla: *nf.* onion
cecina: *nf.* dried beef
ceder: *vt.* to yield; give up; to cede

cegador: *aj.* blinding
cegar: *vt.* to blind; to block
cegarse: *vr.* to become blind
cegato: *aj.* suffering from myopia
cegato;-a: *nmf.* myopic person
ceguera: *nf.* blindness
ceja: *nf.* eyebrow
cejar: *vi.* to turn back
cejijunto: *aj.* with eyebrows close together
celar: *vt.* to see to; to watch over
celda: *nf.* cell
celda: *nf.* jail or prison cell
celdilla: *nf.* cell of a beehive
celebérrimo -ma: *aj.* sp. very or most celebrated
celebración: *nf.* celebration
celebrante: *aj.* celebrating
celebrar: *vt.* to celebrate; to laugh at a joke
celebrarse: *vr.* to be celebrated; to have a celebration
célebre: *aj.* well-known; famous
celebridad: *nf.* celebrity
celeste: *nm.* sky blue
celestial: *aj.* celestial; heavenly
celestina: *nf.* bawd; procurer
celo: *nm.* zeal; distrust; envy
celos: *nmpl.* jealousy
celoso: *aj.* jealous
célula: *nf.* cell
celular: *aj.* cellular
cementerio: *nm.* cemetery; church yard
cemento: *nm.* cement; concrete
cena: *nf.* supper; dinner
cenagoso -sa: *aj.* muddy; boggy
cenar: *vt.* to have supper; to sup; eat dinner; to dine
cenicero: *nm.* ashtray
ceñido: *aj.* tight; adjusted
ceñir: *vt.* to grid; to encircle; *r.* to tighten ones belt
ceñirse: *vr.* to tighten (on oneself); to

adjust
ceniza: *nf.* ash; ashes
censo: *nm.* census; tax
censurar: *vt.* to censure; to blame
centavo: *nm.* cent
centena: *nf.* hundred
centena; centenar: *nm.* one hundred
centenar: *nm.* hundred
centenario: *nm.* century; one hundred years; centenarian
centeno -na: *aj.* rye
centésimo: 1. *aj.* hundredth; 2. *nm.* one-hundredth (fraction)
centígrado: *aj.* centigrade
centigramo: *nm.* centigram
centilitro: *nm.* centiliter
centímetro: *nm.* centimeter
céntimo: *aj.* hundredth; *nm.* cent; centime
céntimo: *nm.* cent
centinela: *nmf.* sentinel; sentry; guard
centrado: *aj.* centered
central: 1. *aj.* central; 2. *nf.* central
centralismo: *nm.* centralism
centralista: *aj.* centralist
centralización: *nf.* centralization
centralizador: *aj.* centralizing
centralizar: *vt.* to centralize
centralizarse: *vr.* to be centralized
centrar: *vt.* to center
céntrico -ca: *aj.* central
centrípeto: *aj.* centripetal
centrista: *nmf.* centrist
centro: *nm.* center; purpose
centrocampista: *nmf.* halfback (soccer)
centuria: *nf.* century.
centurión: *nm.* centurion
cepillo: *nm.* brush; plane
cepo: *nm.* branch; bough
cerca: 1. *nf.* fence; wall; 2. *av.* near; close
cercado: *nm.* fence; enclosure

cercanía: *nf.* nearness; proximity
cercano: *aj.* near
cercar: *vt.* to fence
cerco: *nm.* fence; wall; hoop
cerdo: *nm.* hog; pig; pork; dirty
cerebelo: *nm.* cerebellum
cerebral: *aj.* cerebral
cerebro: *nm.* brain; cerebrum; mind
cereza: *nf.* cherry
cerezo: *nm.* wax chandler
cerrado: *aj.* closed
cerradura: *nf.* keyhole
cerrajería: *nf.* locksmith's shop
cerrajero;-a: *nmf.* locksmith
cerrar: *vt.* to close
cerrojo: *nm.* keyhole
certero: *aj.* with good aim
certeza: *nf.* certainty; truth
certidumbre: *nf.* certainty; truth
certificación: *nf.* certification
certificado: *aj.* certified
certificar: *vt.* to certify
cerumen: *nm.* earwax
cesación: *nf.* cessation
cesante: *aj.* ceasing
cesar: *vi.* to cease
cese: *nm.* cessation
chabacano: *aj.* awkward; clumsy
chacal: *nm.* jackal
chacha: *nf.* lass
chafar: *vt.* to flatten
chaleco: *nm.* vest; waistcoat
champiñón: *nm.* mushroom
champú: *nm.* shampoo
chamuscar: *vt.* to singe
chanclo: *nm.* clog
chantaje: *nm.* blackmail
chapa: *nf.* plate; metal sheet
chaparrón: *nm.* heavy shower
chapista: *nmf.* tinsmith
chapucear: *vt.* to botch; bungle
chapucero: *aj.* rough; crude
chapuzar: *vt. vi. & r.* to duck; to dive; to plunge

chaqueta: *nf.* jacket
charco: *nm.* puddle; pool
charla: *nf.* chat; chatting
charlador: *aj.* given to chatting
charlar: *vi.* to chat
charlatán;-a: *nmf.* charlatan
charlatanería: *nf.* charlatanism
charretera: *nf.* epaulet; garter
charro -rra: *aj.* coarse
chascar: *vt.* to click
chasco: *nm.* disappointment; frus-tration
chasis: *nm.* chassis; body (car)
chatarra: *nf.* scrap iron
chatarreria: *nf.* junk yard
chato -ta: *aj.* flat; *nf.* darling; pret-ty girl
chaval -la: *aj.* young; *nm.* Lad
chaveta: *nf.* cotter
chelín: *nm.* shilling
chepa: *nf.* hunch; hump
cheque: *nm.* check
chequera: *nf.* checkbook
chicle: *nm.* chewing-gum
chico: 1. *aj.* small; 2. *nmf.* boy or girl
chicote: *nm.* short piece of rope or string; etc
chifla: *nf.* hissing; whistle
chifladura: *nf.* hissing
chiflar: *vi.* to whistle
chillón -ona: *aj.* shrieking; screaming
chinche: *nmf.* bedbug
chiquillada: *nf.* group of children
chiquillo;-a: *nmf.* boy or girl
chiquitín: *aj.* very small
chiquito: 1. *aj.* tiny; 2. *nmf.* little boy or girl
chirigota: *nf.* joke
chiripa: *nf.* fluke; scratch
chirrido: *nm.* sizzle; creak
chisme: *nm.* gossip
chispa: *nf.* spark
chispazo: *nm.* spark

chiste: *nm.* witticism; joke
chistera: *nf.* basket; top hat
chistoso: 1. *aj.* funny; 2. *nmf.* funny person
chocar: *vt.* to shock; to collide; to crash
chocolate: *nm.* chocolate
chocolatera: *nf.* pot for making hot chocolate
chocolatería: *nf.* store specializing in chocolate or hot chocolate; chocolate factory
chocolatero: 1. *aj.* chocolate loving; 2. *nmf.* person who makes or sells chocolate; chocolate lover
chocolatín: *nm.* small bar of chocolate
chofer: *nm.* driver
chopo: *nm.* black poplar
choque: *nm.* shock; impact; collision
choque: *nm.* crash
chorizo: *nm.* sausage
chorro: *nm.* spurt; jet
chubasco: *nm.* squall; shower; storm
chufa: *nf.* tiger-nut
chuleta: *nf.* chop; cutlet
chulo -la: *aj.* flashy; snappy
chupar: *vt.* to suck; to absorb; *r.* to lose strength
chupete: *nm.* pacifier
chupón -na: 1. *aj.* sucking; 2. *nmf.* swindler
churruscar: *vt.* to burn (food)
chusma: *nf.* galley slaves
cíclico: *aj.* cyclic
ciclismo: *nm.* cycling
ciclista: *nmf.* cyclist
ciclo: *nm.* cycle
ciclomotor: *nm.* motorized bicycle
ciclón: *nm.* cyclone
ciego: 1. *aj.* blind; 2. *nmf.* blind person
cielo: *nm.* sky; heaven
cien: *aj.* one hundred

ciencia: *nf.* science
cienmilésimo: *aj.* hundred thousandth
cienmillonésimo: *aj.* hundred millionth
científico: 1. *aj.* scientific; 2. *nmf.* scientist
ciento: *aj.* one hundred
cierre: *nm.* closing time; zipper
ciertamente: *av.* -mente certainly
cierto: *aj.* certain; true
cifar: *vt.* cipher
cifra: *nf.* cipher; code; numerical digit
cifrado: *aj.* coded
cifrar: *vt.* to write a code
cifrarse: *vr.* to summarize or synthesize
cigarrera: *nf.* cigarette case
cigarrero;-a: *nmf.* cigarette maker or seller
cigarrillo: *nm.* cigarette
cigarro: *nm.* cigarette
cigüeña: *nf.* stork
cigüeñal: *nm.* crankshaft
cilindrada: *nf.* piston displacement
cilindro: *nm.* cylinder; roll
cima: *nf.* top; summit; peak
cimentar: *vt.* to found; to lay the foundation for
cimiento: *nm.* foundation
cinc: *nm.* zinc
cincel: *nm.* chisel; cutter
cincelar: *vt.* to chisel; carve; engrave
cinco: *aj.* five
cincuenta: *aj.* fifty
cincuentavo: *aj.* fiftieth
cincuentena: *nf.* group of fifty
cincuentenario: *nm.* fiftieth anniversary
cincuentón: *aj.* fifty-year-old
cine: *nm.* cinema; movie theater
cineasta: *nmf.* cinematographer
cineclub: *nm.* association for promoting films
cinéfilo;-a: *nmf.* movie lover
cinematografía: *nf.* cinematography
cinematográfico: *aj.* cinematographic
cinematógrafo: *nm.* movie projector
cínico: *aj.* cynical
cínico;-a: *nmf.* cynic
cinismo: *nm.* cynicism
cinta: *nf.* ribbon; tape; film
cinto: *nm.* belt
cintura: *nf.* waist
cinturón: *nm.* seatbelt
circo: *nm.* circus
circuito: *nm.* circuit
circulación: *nf.* circulation
circular: *aj.* circular
circular: *vt.* to circulate
circulatorio: *aj.* circulatory
circulo: *nm.* circle; club
circuncidar: *vt.* to circumcise
circuncisión: *nf.* circumcision
circunciso: *aj.* circumcised
circundante: *aj.* surrounding
circundar: *vt.* to surround
circunferencia: *nf.* circumference
circunflejo: *aj.* circumflex
circunlocución: *nf.* circumlocution
circunloquio: *nm.* circumlocution
circunscribir: *vt.* to circumscribe; to limit
circunscribirse: *vr.* to limit oneself
circunscripción: *nf.* circumscription
circunscrito: *aj.* circumscribed
circunspección: *nf.* circumspection; prudence
circunspecto: *aj.* circumspect; prudent
circunstancia: *nf.* circumstance
circunstancial: *aj.* circumstantial
circunvalar: *vt.* to surround
cirio: *nm.* big wax candle
ciruela: *nf.* plum
cirugía: *nf.* surgery

cirujano: *nm.* surgeon
cisma: *nm.* schism
cisne: *nm.* swan. Cita; *nf.* date; appointment
cita: *nf.* citation; reference; appointment; date
citación: *nf.* citation (ticket); summons to court
citar: *vt.* to cite a source; to make an appointment
citarse: *vr.* to make an appointment with each other
citatorio: *nm.* summons to court
ciudad: *nf.* city; town
ciudadanía: *nf.* citizenship
ciudadano;-a: *nmf.* citizen
ciudadela: *nf.* citadel
cívico: *aj.* civic
civil: *aj.* civil; civilian
civilista: *nmf.* expert in civil law
civilización: *nf.* civilization
civilizado: *aj.* civilized
civilizador: *aj.* civilizing
civilizar: *vt.* to civilize
civilizarse: *vr.* to become civilized
civismo: *nm.* civics
cizaña: *nf.* darnel
clamar: *vt.* to clamor for; cry out for
clamar: *vt.* to claim
clamor: *nm.* clamor
clamoroso: *aj.* clamorous
clan: *nm.* clan; family
clara: *nf.* white of egg
clarear: *vt.* to make clear or light
clararse: *vr.* to become transparent or light
claridad: *nf.* clarity
clarificación: *nf.* clarification
clarificador: *aj.* clarifying
clarificar: *vt.* to clarify
clarinete: *nm.* clarinet
clarividencia: *nf.* clairvoyance
clarividente: *aj.* able to see and understand clearly; having a cute

perception
claro: *aj.* clear; bright; light
clase: *nf.* class; kind; quality; rank
clasicismo: *nm.* classicism
clasicista: *nmf.* classicist; expert in classics
clásico: *aj.* classic
clasificación: *nf.* classification
clasificar: *vt.* to classify; to categorize; to arrange
clasista: *aj.* relating to socio-economic classes
claudicar: *vt.* to limp
claustro: *nm.* cloister
claustrofobia: *nf.* claustrophobia
clausurar: *vt.* to close
clavado: *aj.* nailed
clavar: *vt.* to nail; to stick
clave: *nf.* key; password
clavel: *nm.* pink; carnation
clavícula: *nf.* clavicle
clavija: *nf.* pin; peg
clavo: *nm.* nail; corn
clerecía: *nf.* clergy
clérigo: *nm.* cleric
clero: *nm.* clergy; congregation
cliente: *nmf.* client; customer
clientela: *nf.* clientele
clima: *nm.* climate; weather
climático: *aj.* climatic
climatización: *nf.* control of the climate
climatizado: *aj.* climate-controlled
climatizar: *vt.* to control the climate
climatología: *nf.* climatology; study of climates
climatológico: *aj.* pertaining to the study of climates
clínica: *nf.* clinic; surgery; dispensary
clínica: *nf.* clinic
clínico: 1. *aj.* clinical; 2. *nmf.* clinician
cloro: *nm.* chlorine

clorofila: *nf.* chlorophyll
coacción: *nf.* coerción; coaction
coaccionar: *vt.* to coerce; to force
coactivo: *aj.* coerced; forced
coágulo: *nm.* clot
coartada: *nf.* alibi
cobarde: *aj.* coward; timid
cobardemente: *av.* cowardly
cobardía: *nf.* cowardice
cobertizo: *nm.* shed; shelter
cobertor: *nm.* bedcover; bedspread; quilt
cobijar: *vt.* to cover; to lodge
cobrador: *nm.* collector; conductor; teller
cobrador: 1. *aj.* bill collecting; 2. *nm.* bill collector
cobrar: *vt.* to recover; to collect; to cash; to charge
cobre: *nm.* copper
cobrizo: *aj.* copper-colored; copper
cobro: *nm.* cashing; collection
cocer: *vt.* to boil; to cook
cocerse: *vr.* to be boiling; to be cooking
coche: *nm.* car; carriage
cochera: *nf.* garage; coach house
cochero: *nm.* coachman; driver of a carriage
cocido: *aj.* cooked
cocina: *nf.* kitchen
cocinar: *vt.* to cook; to do the cooking
cocinero;-a: *nmf.* cook
codiciar: *vt.* to covet; to long; to have
codificación: *nf.* codification
codificador: *aj.* codifying
codificar: *vt.* to codify
código: *nm.* code; codex
codo: *nm.* elbow
codorniz: *nf.* quail
coeducación: *nf.* coeducation
coexistencia: *nf.* coexistence

coexistir: *vi.* to coexist
cofradía: *nf.* confraternity; association
cofre: *nm.* coffer; trunk
cogedor: *nm.* dust pan
coger: *vt.* to take; catch
cogollo: *nm.* heart (of lettuce)
cogote: *nm.* back of the neck
cohabitación: *nf.* cohabitation
cohabitar: *vi.* to cohabit
cohete: *nm.* rocket
cohibición: *nf.* inhibition
cohibido: *aj.* inhibited; reserved
cohibir: *vt.* to restrain; to inhibit
cojin: *nm.* cushion
coincidencia: *nf.* coincidence
coincidente: *aj.* coinciding
coincidir: *vi.* to coincide
cojo -a: *aj.* crippled
col: *nf.* cabbage
cola: *nf.* tail; end seat
colaboración: *nf.* collaboration
colaboracionista: *nmf.* collaborator; one who cooperates with the enemy
colaborador: 1. *aj.* collaborating; 2. *nmf.* collaborator
colaborar: *vi.* to collaborate
colada: *nf.* wash
colador: *nm.* strainer; colander
colar: *vt.* to strain; filter; *r.* to slip through
colcha: *nf.* bedspread
colchón: *nm.* mattress
colchoneta: *nf.* quilt
coleador: *nm.* mop
colear: *vi.* to move the tail; to mop
colección: *nf.* collection
coleccionar: *vt.* to collect
coleccionista: *nmf.* collector
colecta: *nf.* collection
colectar: *vt.* to raise funds
colectividad: *nf.* collectivity
colectivización: *nf.* collectivization
colectivizar: *vt.* to form a collective

colectivo: *aj.* collective
colega: *nm.* colleague
colegial: 1. *aj.* collegiate; 2. *nm.* collegian; schoolboy
colegio: *nm.* college; school; public school
cólera: *nf.* bile
cólera: *nf.* anger
coleta: *nf.* pigtail
colgado: *aj.* hung
colgadura: *nf.* hangings; drapery
colgante: 1. *aj.* hanging; 2. *nm.* pendant; hanging ornament
colgante: *nm.* errand; pendant
colgar: *vt.* to hang; to fix
cólico: *nm.* colic
coliflor: *nf.* cauliflower
colilla: *nf.* butt; stump (of cigar)
colina: *nf.* hill; slope
colindante: *aj.* adjacent
colindar: *vi.* to be adjacent to
collar: *nm.* necklace; collar
colmado: *aj.* overflowing
colmar: *vt.* to overflow
colmillo: *nm.* eyetooth
colmo: *nm.* top; plenty; fill
colocación: *nf.* placing
colocado: *aj.* placed; placed in an employment
colocar: *vt.* to place
colonia: *nf.* colony; neighborhood
coloniaje: *nm.* colonial period
colonial: *aj.* colonial
colonialismo: *nm.* colonialism
colonialista: *aj.* colonialistic; colonialist
colonialista: *nmf.* colonialist
colonización: *nf.* colonization
colonizador: 1. *aj.* colonizing; 2. *nmf.* colonizer; colonist
colonizar: *vt.* to colonize; to settle
coloquio: *nm.* talk; conversation
color: *nm.* color
coloración: *nf.* coloration

colorado: *aj.* red
colorante: 1. *aj.* coloring; 2. *nm.* substance used for coloring; food coloring
colorear: *vt.* to color
colorete: *nm.* lipstick
colorido: *nm.* strong or bright coloring
colorista: *aj.* coloristic
colorista: *nmf.* painter; colorist
colosal: *aj.* colossal
coloso: *nm.* colossus
columna: *nf.* column
columnata: *nf.* colonnade
columnista: *nmf.* columnist
columpiar: *vt.* to swing; *r.* to swing
comadrona: *nf.* midwife
comandancia: *nf.* headquarters; office of the commander
comandante: *nmf.* commander
comandar: *vt.* to command
comando: *nm.* military commando
comarca: *nf.* region; province; shire
comarcal: *aj.* regional
comarcano: *aj.* nearby
combate: *nm.* combat
combatir: *vt.* to combat
combinación: *nf.* combination
combinado: *aj.* combined
combinado: *nm.* combination
combinar: *vt.* to combine; *r.* to combine
combustible: 1. *aj.* combustible; 2. *nm.* combustible material
combustión: *nf.* combustion
comedero: *nm.* feeding-trough
comedia: *nf.* comedy
comediante: *nmf.* comedian; comedienne
comedido -da: *aj.* courteous; polite
comedor: *nm.* dining room
comensal: *nmf.* table companion
comentar: *vt.* to comment
comentario: *nm.* comment;

commentary
comentarista: *nmf.* commentator
comenzar: *vt.* to commence; to begin
comer: *vt.* to eat
comercial: *aj.* commercial
comercialización: *nf.* commercialization
comercializar: *vt.* to commercialize
comerciante: *nmf.* businessman; merchant
comerciar: *vi.* to engage in business
comercio: *nm.* commerce; business
comerse: *vr.* to leave out; to skip something written or spoken (word; letter)
comestible: *aj.* edible
cometer: *vt.* to commit
cometido: *nm.* commitment; responsibility
comicidad: *nf.* funniness; comicalness
cómico: *aj.* comic; comical
comida: *nf.* food; meal; dinner
comienzo: *nm.* beginning; start
comillas: *nfpl.* quotation marks
comilón: *aj.* big eating; gluttonous
comisaría: *nf.* police station
comisario: *nm.* chief of police or other organization
comisión: *nf.* commission
comisionado: *aj.* commissioned
comisionar: *vt.* to commission
comité: *nm.* committee; assembly
comitiva: *nf.* retinue; suit; followers
como: *av.* as; so; like; conj. as; when; if
cómoda: *nf.* dresser
cómodamente: *av.* comfortably
comodidad: *nf.* comfort
cómodo: *aj.* comfortable
comodón: *aj.* fond of comfort
compadecer: *vt.* to feel compassion for
compadre: *nm.* close friend

compaginar: *vt.* to arrange; to put in order; *r.* to fit
compañerismo: *nm.* relationship between companions
compañero;-a: *nmf.* companion; classmate; co-worker
compañía: *nf.* company
comparable: *aj.* comparable
comparación: *nf.* comparison
comparado: *aj.* compared
comparar: *vt.* to compare
comparativo: *aj.* comparative
comparecencia: *nf.* appearance before a judge
comparecer: *vt.* to appear before a judge
compartimiento: *nm.* compartment
compartir: *vt.* to divide; to share
compás: *nm.* compass; rhythm; beat
compasión: *nf.* compassion
compasivo: *aj.* compassionate
compatriota: *nmf.* compatriot
compendiar: *vt.* to summarize; condense
compenetración: *nf.* complete identification with another person
compenetrarse: *vr.* to identify completely with each other
compensación: *nf.* compensation
compensador: *aj.* compensating
compensar: *vt.* to compensate
competencia: *nf.* competition; competence
competente: *aj.* competent
competición: *nf.* competition
competidor;-a: *nmf.* competitor
competir (se) vi(r).: to compete
competitividad: *nf.* competitiveness
competitivo: *aj.* competitive; of high quality
complacencia: *nf.* pleasing
complacer: *vt.* to please
complacido: *aj.* pleased
complaciente: *aj.* pleasing

complejidad: *nf.* complexity
complejo: *aj.* complex
complementar: *vt.* to complement
complementario: *aj.* complementary
complementarse: *vr.* to complement each other
complemento: *nm.* complement
completamente: *av.* completely
completar: *vt.* to complete
completo: *aj.* complete
complicación: *nf.* complication
complicado: *aj.* complicated
complicar: *vt.* to complicate; *r.* to become complicated
cómplice: *nmf.* accomplice
complot: *nm.* plot; conspiracy
componente: *aj.* component
componente: *nm.* component
componer: *vt.* to compose; to fix; to repair
comportar: *vt.* to bear; *r.* to behave
composición: *nf.* composition
compositor -rá: *nmf.* composer
compositor;-a: *nmf.* 1 composer
compostura: *nf.* repair
compra: *nf.* purchase; shopping
comprador: *aj.* buying
comprador;-a: *nmf.* buyer
comprar: *vt.* to buy; to purchase
comprarse: *vr.* to buy for oneself
compraventa: *nf.* buying and selling
comprender: *vt.* to comprehend; understand
comprender: *vt.* to comprehend; to understand
comprenderse: *vr.* to understand each other
comprensible: *aj.* comprehensible; understandable
comprensión: *nf.* comprehension
comprensivo: *aj.* able to understand; understanding
compresa: *nf.* compress
comprimir: *vt.* to press; squeeze

comprobable: *aj.* provable
comprobación: *nf.* verification; proof
comprobante: *nm.* proof; receipt
comprobar: *vt.* to verify; to prove
comprometedor: *aj.* compromising
comprometer: *vt.* to commit; to compromise
comprometerse: *vr.* to commit oneself; to compromise oneself
comprometido: *aj.* committed
compromiso: *nm.* commitment
compuesto: 1. *aj.* compound; composed; fixed; 2. *nm.* chemical compound
común: *aj.* common
comuna: *nf.* commune
comunal: *aj.* communal
comunicable: *aj.* communicable
comunicación: *nf.* communication
comunicado: 1. *nm.* announcement; dispatch; 2. *aj.* well-connected (hub); easily accessed
comunicante: *aj.* communicating
comunicar: *vt.* to communicate
comunicativo: *aj.* communicative; sociable
comunidad: *nf.* community; fellowship
comunión: *nf.* communion
comunismo: *nm.* communism
comunista: 1. *aj.* communist; communistic; 2. *nmf.* communist
comunitario: *aj.* community
conato: *nm.* endeavor
concebible: *aj.* conceivable
concebir: *vt.* to conceive
conceder: *vt.* to concede; admit
concejal: *nm.* councilor
concentración: *nf.* concentration
concentrado: *aj.* concentrated
concentrar: *vt.* to concentrate
concéntrico: *aj.* concentric
concepción: *nf.* conception

concepto: *nm.* concept
conceptual: *aj.* conceptual
conceptuar: *vt.* to judge; to imagine; to form an idea
concernir: *vt.* to concern; refer to
concertado: *aj.* arranged; agreed upon
concertar: *vt.* to concert; to arrange
concertista: *nmf.* perfomer; concert musician
concha: *nf.* shell; tortoise shell
conciencia: *nf.* conscience; consciousness; conscience
concienzudo: *aj.* conscientious
concierto: *nm.* concert
conciliar: *vt.* to conciliate; to win
concilio: *nm.* council
conciso: *aj.* concise; brief
concluir: *vt.* to conclude; to finish
conclusión: *nf.* conclusion; end
concluso: *aj.* conclusive
concluyente: *aj.* concluding
concordar: *vt.* to harmonize; to reconcile.
concretamente: *av.* concretely; specifically
concretar: *vt.* to concrete; to specify; to make concrete
concreto: *aj.* concrete
concupiscencia: *nf.* lust
concurrencia: *nf.* concurrence; crowd
concurrente: *aj.* attending
concurrido: *aj.* attended
concurrir: *vi.* to attend
concursante: *nmf.* competitor
concursar: *vi.* to compete in a tournament or competition
concurso: *nm.* tournament; competition
condado: *nm.* area ruled by a count; county
condal: *aj.* pertaining to a count or area ruled by a count

conde: *nm.* earl; count
condecoración: *nf.* decoration (of an award)
condecorar: *vt.* to decorate; confer
condena: *nf.* sentence; penalty
condenación: *nf.* condemnation; damnation
condenado: 1. *aj.* condemned; damned; 2. *nmf.* condemned prisoner
condenar: *vt.* to condemn; to damn
condensación: *nf.* condensation
condensado: *aj.* condensed
condensador: *nm.* condenser
condensar: *vt.* to condense
condensarse: *vr.* to become condensed
condesa: *nf.* countess
condescendencia: *nf.* congeniality; ability to adjust to others' personalities
condescender: *vi.* to adapt oneself to another person's manner of being
condescendiente: *aj.* congenial
condición: *nf.* condition
condicional: *aj.* conditional
condicionamiento: *nm.* placing of conditions
condicionar: *vt.* to place conditions
condimentar: *vt.* to season
condiscípulo: *nm.* fellow student
condiscípulo;-a: *nmf.* fellow student
condolencia: *nf.* condolence
condolerse: *vr.* to share in suffering
condominio: *nm.* condominium
conducción: *nf.* conduction
conducir: *vt.* to conduct; to drive
conducta: *nf.* conduct
conductibilidad: *nf.* conductibility
conducto: *nm.* conduit; pipe; duct; tube
conductor: *nm.* conductor; driver
conectar: *vt.* to connect
conejera: *nf.* rabbit warren
conejero: *aj.* rabbit-hunting

conejo: *nm.* rabbit
confección: *nm.* making; confection
confeccionar: *nf.* to make
confederación: *nf.* confederation
confederado: 1. *aj.* confederated; 2. *nmf.* confederate
confederar: *vt.* to confederate; to form an alliance or confederation
conferencia: *nf.* conference; conference call
conferenciante: *nmf.* conference speaker
conferenciar: *vi.* to speak at a conference
conferencista: *nmf.* conference speaker
conferir: *vt.* to confer; grant
confesar: *vt.* to confess; admit
confesional: *aj.* confessional
confesionario: *nm.* confessional
confeso: *aj.* confessed
confesor: *nm.* confessor
confiable: *aj.* trustworthy
confiado: *aj.* trusting
confianza: *nf.* confidence; trust
confiar: *vt.* to entrust; confide
confidencial: *aj.* confidential
confidente;-a: *nmf.* confidant; confidante
configuración: *nf.* configuration
configurar: *vt.* to configure
confín: *nm.* boundary; limit
confinamiento: *nm.* confinement
confinar: *vt.* to confine
confirmación: *nf.* confirmation
confirmar: *vt.* to confirm
confirmatorio: *aj.* confirming
confiscación: *nf.* confiscation
confiscar: *vt.* to confiscate
confite: *nm.* candy; bonbon
conflictivo: *aj.* conflicting
conflicto: *nm.* conflict
confluencia: *nf.* confluence
confluente: *aj.* confluent

confluir: *vi.* to flow or to run together
conformación: *nf.* conformation; structure; shape
conformar: *vt.* to conform; to adjust; *r.* to conform
conforme: *conj.* as soon as; in the same way that; according to
conformidad: *nf.* conformity
conformismo: *nm.* conformism
conformista: *nmf.* conformist
confortar: *vt.* to comfort; console
confraternar: *vt.* to create bonds of brotherhood
confraternidad: *nf.* brotherhood; meeting of friends
confraternizar: *vt.* to create bonds of brotherhood
confrontación: *nf.* confrontation frente; forehead
confundible: *aj.* easily confused
confundir: *vt.* to confuse
confusión: *nf.* confusion
confuso: *aj.* confused
congelar: *vt.* to freeze; congeal
congénito -ta: *aj.* congenital
congoja: *nf.* anguish
congregación: *nf.* congregation
congregante: *nmf.* member of a congregation
congregar: *vi.* to gather a group together
congresista: *nmf.* member of a congress
congreso: *nm.* congress
congrio: *nm.* conger
conjeturar: *vt.* to conjecture; to guess
conjugar: *vt.* to conjugate
conjunción: *nf.* conjunction
conjuntar: *vt.* to unite with harmony
conjuntivo: *aj.* conjunctive; joining
conjunto: 1. *aj.* conjoint; conjunct; 2. *nm.* whole; group

conjura; conjuración: *nf.* conspiracy against someone or something
conjurado: 1. *aj.* participating in a conspiracy; 2. *nmf.* participant in a conspiracy
conjurar: *vi.* to swear allegiance to a conspiracy or plot
juramentar: *vt.* to swear in
conjuro: *nm.* the act of swearing in
conllevar: *vt.* to help bear a burden or trouble
conmemoración: *nf.* commemoration
conmemorar: *vt.* to commemorate
conmemorativo: *aj.* commemorative
conminar: *vt.* to threaten
conmiseración: *nf.* commiseration
conmovedor: *aj.* moving
conmovedor -ra: *aj.* stirring; touching
conmover: *vt.* to move emotionally
conmutador: *nm.* switch; commuter
connatural: *aj.* innate
conocedor: 1. *aj.* expert; 2. *nmf.* knowledgeable person
conocer: *vt.* to know; to be familiar with
conocido: 1. *aj.* known; familiar; 2. *nmf.* acquaintance
conocimiento: *nm.* knowledge
conquista: *nf.* conquest
conquistador; -ra: *nmf.* conqueror
conquistar: *vt.* to conquer
consabido: *aj.* aforementioned; aforesaid
consagración: *nf.* consecration
consagrar: *vt.* to consecrate; to sanctify
consanguíneo: *aj.* blood-related
consanguinidad: *nf.* blood relationship
consciente: *aj.* conscious; aware
consecución: *nf.* acquisition

consecuencia: *nf.* consequence
consecuente: *aj.* consequent
consecuentemente: *av.* consequently
consecutivo: *aj.* consecutive
conseguir: *vt.* to get; obtain
consejero -ra: *nm.* counselor
consejo: *nm.* advice; counsel
consenso: *nm.* consensus
consensual: *aj.* consensual
consentido: *aj.* coddled; pampered
consentimiento: *nm.* consent; permission
consentir: *vt.* to consent; to coddle; to pamper
conserje: *nm.* concierge
conserjería: *nf.* janitor ship
conserva: *nf.* conserve; preserves
conservación: *nf.* conservation
conservador;-a: *nmf.* conservative; political rightist
conservadurismo: *nm.* conservatism
conservar: *vt.* to preserve; to keep; maintain
considerable: *aj.* considerable
consideración: *nf.* consideration
considerado: *aj.* considered
considerar: *vt.* to consider
consigna: *nf.* order; watch-word; assignment
consignar: *vt.* to consign
consignatario;-a: *nmf.* consignee
consiguiente: *aj.* consequent
consistencia: *nf.* consistence; consistency
consistente: *aj.* consistent
consistir: *vi.* to consist
consocio;-a: *nmf.* associate
consolación: *nf.* consolation
consolador: *aj.* consoling
consolar: *vt.* to console; comfort
consolidar: *vt.* to consolidate
consonancia: *nf.* consonance
consonante: *nf.* consonant
consonántico: *aj.* pertaining to

consonant sounds
consonar: *vt.* to harmonize; to be in consonance
consorcio: *nm.* consortium
consorte: *nmf.* consort
conspiración: *nf.* conspiracy
conspirador;-a: *nmf.* conspirator
conspirar: *vi.* to conspire
constancia: *nf.* constancy; stability
constante: *aj.* constant
constante : *nf.* mathematical constant
constantemente: *av.* constantly
constar: *vi.* to be certain or evident to someone
constatación: *nf.* confirmation; verification
constatar: *vt.* to confirm; to check; to verify
consternar: *vt.* to consternate
constitución : *nf.* constitution
constitucional: *aj.* constitutional
constituir: *vt.* to constitute
constituirse: *vr.* to be constituted
constitutivo: *aj.* constituent
constituyente: *aj.* constituent
constituyente: *nmf.* constituent
constreñir: *vt.* to constrain
construcción: *nf.* construction
constructivo: *aj.* constructive
constructor: *aj.* pertaining to construction
constructor;-a: *nmf.* builder
constructora: *nf.* building contractor; construction company
construir: *vt.* to construct
consuelo: *nm.* consolation
cónsul: *nm.* consul
consulado: *nm.* consulate
consular: *aj.* consular
consulta: *nf.* consultation
consultar: *vt.* to consult
consultivo: *aj.* consultative
consultorio: *nm.* medical or dental office

consumado: *aj.* consummate
consumar: *vt.* to consummate
consumición: *nf.* consumption
consumido: *aj.* consumed
consumidor: *aj.* consuming
consumir: *vt.* to consume
consumismo: *nm.* practice of over-consumption
consumo: *nm.* consumption
contabilidad: *nf.* accounting; accountancy; bookkeeping
contabilizar: *vt.* to track income and expenses
contable: *aj.* countable
contactar: *vt.* to contact
contacto: *nm.* contact
contado: *aj.* counted; scarce
contador;-a: *nmf.* accountant
contaduría: *nf.* accountant's office or position
contagiar: *vt.* to infect
contagio: *nm.* infection; contagious disease
contagioso: *aj.* contagious
contaminar: *vt.* to contaminate; infect
contar: *vt.* to count; to rate; to tell a story
contemplación: *nf.* contemplation
contemplador: *aj.* contemplating
contemplar: *vt.* to contemplate
contemplativamente: *av.* contemplatively
contemporaneidad: *nf.* contemporaneousness
contemporáneo: *aj.* contemporary
contemporizar : *vi.* to contempo-rize
contencioso -sa: *aj.* con-tentious; litigious
contener: *vt.* to contain
contenido: *nm.* contents
contentar: *vt.* to make content or happy
contento: *nm.* contentment

contestación: *nf.* answer; reply
contestar: *vt.* to answer; reply
contextura: *nf.* contexture; framework
contienda: *nf.* fight; dispute
contigüidad: *nf.* contiguity; nearness; proximity
contiguo -ua: *aj.* contiguous; next
continental: *aj.* continental
continente: *nm.* continent
continuación: *nf.* continuation; sequel
continuador: *aj.* continuing
continuamente: *av.* continually
continuar: *vt.* to continue
continuidad: *nf.* continuity
continuo: *aj.* continuous
contra: *prep.* against
contraatacar: *vt.* to counter-attack
contraataque: *nm.* counter-attack
contrabajo: *nm.* double bass
contrabandista: *nmf.* contrabandist; smuggler
contracción: *nf.* contraction
contracepción: *nf.* contraception
contracorriente: *nf.* headwind; crosscurrent
contracultura: *nf.* counterculture
contradecir: *vt.* to contradict
contradicción: *nf.* contradiction
contradictorio: *aj.* contradictory
contraer: *vt.* to contract
contraerse: *vr.* to be contracted
contraespionaje: *nm.* counterespionage
contragolpe: *nm.* counter coup
contraindicar: *vt.* contraindicate
contraofensiva: *nf.* counter-offense
contrapesar: *vt.* to place a counterweight; to counterbalance
contrapeso: *nm.* counterweight; counterbalance
contraponer: *vt.* to oppose
contraproducente: *aj.*

counterproductive
contrapunto: *nm.* counterpoint
contrariar: *vt.* to oppose; to block
contrariedad: *nf.* contrariety
contrario: 1. *aj.* contrary; opposing; 2. *nm.* obstacle
contrarrestar: *vt.* to; offset; counteract
contrarrevolución: *nf.* counter-revolution
contraseña: *nf.* countersign; password
contrastar: *vt.* to check; to contrast
contraste: *nm.* resistance; *nm.* contrast
contratación: *nf.* trade; deal
contratar: *vt.* to contract
contratiempo: *nm.* misfortune; mishap
contratista: *nmf.* contractor
contrato: *nm.* contract
contravención: *nm.* contravention
contravenir: *vt.* to contravene
contrayente: *nmf.* bride or groom
contribución: *nf.* contribution
contribuir: *vt.* to contribute
contribuyente: *nmf.* contributor
contristar: *vt.* to make sad
control: *nm.* check; control
controlar: *vt.* to check; control
controvertir: *vt.* to controvert; dispute
contundente: *aj.* bruising
conturbado: *aj.* perturbed
conturbar: *vt.* to disquiet; to perturb
convalidar: *vt.* to confirm
convecino -na: *aj.* neighboring
convencer: *vt.* to convince
convencimiento: *nm.* convincing
convención: *nf.* convention
conveniencia: *nf.* convenience
conveniente: *aj.* proper; convenient
convenio: *nm.* pact; agreement
convenir: *vi.* to be convenient to or

for
convento: *nm.* convent
conventual: *aj.* pertaining to a convent
conversación: *nf.* conversation
conversador: *aj.* conversing
conversar: *vi.* to converse
conversión: *nf.* conversion
converso: *aj.* converted
converso -sa: 1. *aj.* converted; 2. *nmf.* convert
convertibilidad: *nf.* convertibility
convertible: *aj.* convertible
convertir: *vt.* to convert
convicción: *nf.* conviction; certainty
convicto: 1. *aj.* convicted; 2. *nmf.* convict
convidado: 1. *aj.* invited; 2. *nmf.* invited person
convidar: *vt.* to invite; to share
convincente: *aj.* convincing
convivencia: *nf.* get-together
convivió: *nm.* get-together; sharing together of time; experience and food
convivir: *vi.* to share experiences; food; and time together
convocar: *vt.* to convoke; summon; call together
conyugal: *aj.* conjugal
cónyuge: *nmf.* spouse; consort
cooperación: *nf.* cooperation
cooperador;-a: *nmf.* one who cooperates; a cooperative person
cooperar: *vi.* to cooperate
cooperativa: *nm.* cooperative
cooperativo: *aj.* cooperative
coordenada: *nf.* coordinate
coordenado: *aj.* coordinated
coordinación: *nf.* coordination
coordinador;-a: *nmf.* coordinator
coordinar: *vt.* to coordinate
copa: *nf.* goblet; wineglass
copartícipe: *nmf.* partner
copia: *nf.* abundance; plenty

copia: *nf.* copy
copiador: *aj.* copying
copiadora: *nf.* photocopier
copiar: *vt.* to copy
copiloto: *nm.* copilot
copioso: *aj.* copious
copista: *nmf.* scribe
copla: *nf.* couplet; stanza
coproducción: *nf.* co-production
coproductor: *nmf.* co-producer
cópula: *nf.* joining; coupling
coraje: *nm.* anger; spirit; courage
corajudo: *aj.* easily angered
corazón: *nm.* heart
corazonada: *nf.* feeling or presentiment in one's heart
cordaje: *nm.* strings of a musical instrument
cordel: *nm.* cord; rope
cordero: *nm.* lamb
cordial: *aj.* cordial; hearty
cordialidad: *nf.* cordiality
cordillera: *nf.* mountain range
cordón: *nm.* lace; string
cordura: *nf.* prudence; wisdom
cornada: *nf.* thrust with horns; goring
cornamenta: *nf.* horns; antlers
cornear: *vt.* to wound with a horn
córneo: *aj.* with horns; horn-shaped
corneta: *nf.* bugle; cornet
corneta: *nm.* cornet player
cornisa: *nf.* cornice
corno: *nm.* musical horn
cornucopia: *nf.* cornucopia; horn of plenty
cornudo: *aj.* with horns
coro: *nm.* chorus; choir
corona: *nf.* crown
coronación: *nf.* coronation
coronamiento: *nm.* crowning
coronar: *vt.* to crown; to top
coronilla: *nf.* crown of the head
corpiño: *nm.* vest

corporación: *nf.* corporation
corporal: *aj.* corporal
corporativo: *aj.* corporate
corpóreo: *aj.* corporeal
corpulencia: *nf.* corpulence
corpulento: *aj.* -km corpulent
corpus: *nm.* corpus
corpúsculo: *nm.* corpuscle; particle
corral: *nm.* corral; stockyard
correa: *nf.* leather strap
correaje: *nm.* belts; belting
corrección: *nf.* correction
correccional: *aj.* correctional
correctamente: *av.* correctly
correctivo: *aj.* corrective
correctivo: *nm.* sanction
correcto: *aj.* correct
corrector: *nm.* correction fluid
corredizo: *aj.* sliding
corredor;-a: *nmf.* runner; broker
corregible: *aj.* corrigible
corregir: *vt.* to correct; amend
correlación: *nf.* correlation
correlativo: *aj.* correlative
correo: *nm.* courier; mail
correr: *vt.* to run; to race
correspondencia: *nf.* correspondence
correspondiente: *aj.* corresponding
corresponsal: *nmf.* news correspondent
corresponsalía: *nf.* post of a correspondent
corretaje: *nm.* brokerage
corretear: *vi.* to run back and forth
correteo: *nm.* running back and forth
correveidile: *nmf.* gossip; tale-bearer
corrida: *nf.* run
corrido -da: *aj.* in excess; cursive
corroboración: *nf.* corroboration
corroborar: *vt.* to corroborate
corroborativo: *aj.* corroborative
corrupción: *nf.* corruption
corsé: *nm.* corset; girdle

corta: *nf.* pruning; time for pruning
cortacésped: *nf.* awn mower
cortacircuitos: *nm.* circuit breaker
cortado: *aj.* cut
cortador;-a: *nmf.* cutter; person who cuts
cortafuego: *nm.* firebreak; fuel break
cortante: *aj.* cutting; sharp
cortaplumas: *nm.* small knife
cortar: *vt.* cut; to trim; to clip
cortauñas: *nm.* nail clippers
corte: *nm.* cut; cutting; court; yard
cortejar: *vt.* to escort; court; woo
cortés: *aj.* courteous; polite
cortesía: *nf.* courtesy; politeness
cortésmente: *av.* courteously
corteza: *nf.* bark; peel; skin; cortex
cortina: *nf.* curtain
corto: *aj.* short
cortocircuito: *nm.* short circuit
cortometraje: *nm.* short film
cosa: *nf.* thing
cosecha: *nf.* harvest; crop
cosechador: *aj.* reaping; harvesting
cosechadora: *nf.* reaper; harvesting machine
cosechar: *vt.* to reap; to harvest
cosechero;-a: *nmf.* farmer
coser: *vt.* to sew
cosido: *aj.* sewn
cósmico: *aj.* cosmic
cosmografía: *nf.* cosmography
cosmográfico: *aj.* cosmographic; cosmographical
cosmonauta: *nmf.* cosmonaut
cosmopolita: *aj.* cosmopolitan
cosmos: *nm.* cosmos
cosquilleo: *nm.* tickling
costa: *nf.* cost; price; coast
costado: *nm.* side; flank
costar: *vt.* to cost
costear: *vt.* to navigate the coast; to pay
costilla: *nf.* rib

costo: *nm.* cost
costoso -sa: *aj.* costly; expensive
costumbre: *nf.* custom
costura: *nf.* sewing; needlework; tailoring
cotejar: *vt.* to compare; confront
cotidiano: *aj.* daily; everyday
coto: *nm.* enclosed pasture
coyuntura: *nf.* conjuncture; change
craneal: *aj.* cranial
cráneo: *nm.* cranium; skull
creación: *nf.* creation
Creador: Creator; God
creador;-a: *nmf.* creator
crear: *vt.* to create
creatividad: *nf.* creativity
creativo: *aj.* creative
crecer: *vi.* to grow
crecida: *nf.* rising
crecido: *aj.* grown; large
creciente: *aj.* growing
crecimiento: *nm.* -mento growth
credencial: *nf.* credential
credibilidad: *nf.* credibility
crédito: *nm.* credit; belief
credo: *nm.* creed; credo
credulidad: *nf.* credulity
crédulo: *aj.* credulous
creencia: *nf.* belief
creer: *vt.* to believe; to think
creíble: *aj.* believable
crema: *nf.* cream
cremallera: *nf.* rack; zip fastener
crepuscular: *aj.* pertaining to the twilight
crepúsculo: *nm.* twilight
crespón: *nm.* crape
cresta: *nf.* crest; summit
creyente: *nmf.* believer
cría: *nf.* raising; breeding
criadero: *nm.* nursery
criado: *aj.* raised
crianza: *nf.* raising
criar: *vt.* to raise; rear

criatura: *nf.* creature; baby
cribar: *vt.* to sieve; sift
crimen: *nm.* crime
criminal: 1. *aj.* criminal; 2. *nmf.* criminal
criminalidad: *nf.* criminality
criminalista: *nmf.* attorney specializing in criminal law
criminología: *nf.* criminology
crío: *nmf.* young child; baby
criollo -lla: *aj.* Creole
cripta: *nf.* crypt
cristal: *nm.* crystal
cristalería: *nf.* glassware
cristalino: *aj.* crystalline
cristalino: *nm.* lens of the eye
cristalización: *nf.* crystallization
cristalizar: *vi.* to crystallize
cristiandad: *nf.* Cristendom
cristianismo: *nm.* Christianity
cristianizar: *vt.* to Christianize
cristiano: 1. *aj.* Christian; 2. *nmf.* Christian
Cristo: *nm.* Christ
criterio: *nm.* criterion
crítica: *nf.* criticism
criticar: *vt.* to criticize; censure
crítico: 1. *aj.* critical; 2. *nm.* critic
cromo: *nm.* chromium
crónica: *nf.* chronicle; news column
crónico: *aj.* chronic
cronista: *nmf.* chronicler
cronología: *nf.* chronology
cronológico: *aj.* chronological
cronometraje: *nm.* timing
cronometrar: *vt.* to time
cronómetro: *nm.* chronometer; stopwatch
croquis: *nm.* sketch
cruce: *nm.* crossing
crucero: *nm.* cruiser; intersection
crucial: *aj.* having the form of a cross; crucial
crucificado: *aj.* crucified

crucificar: *vt.* to crucify
crucifijo: *nm.* crucifix
crucifixión: *nf.* crucifixion
crucigrama: *nf.* crossword puzzle
crudeza: *nf.* rawness
crudo: 1. *aj.* raw; crude; 2. *nm.* crude oil
cruel: *aj.* cruel
crueldad: *nf.* cruelty
cruz: *nf.* cross
cruzada: *nf.* crusade
cruzado: *aj.* crossed
cruzar: *vt.* to cross; to cut across
cuadra: *nf.* stable; block
cuadrado: 1. *aj.* square; 2. *nm.* square
cuadragésimo: *aj.* fortieth
cuadragésimo: *nm.* one-fortieth
cuadrante: *nm.* quadrant
cuadrar: *vt.* to square; to make square
cuadratura: *nf.* squaring
cuadrícula: *nf.* series of boxes as on graph paper
cuadricular: *aj.* with squares
cuadrilátero: *nm.* quadrilateral; boxing ring
cuadrilla: *nf.* work group or team
cuadro: *nm.* square; picture
cuadrúpedo: *aj.* four-legged; quadruped
cuádruple: *aj.* quadruple
cuadruplicar: *vt.* to quadruple
cuajada: *nf.* setting (pudding; gelatin)
cuajar: *vt.* to set (pudding; gelatin; etc.)
cualidad: *nf.* quality; characteristic
cualitativo: *aj.* qualitative
cualquiera: 1. *pron.* indef. anyone; 2. *pron.* rel. whichever; 3. *nm.* somebody
cuando: conj. when; although
cuantificar: *vt.* to quantify

cuantioso: *aj.* many; much; a lot of
cuantitativo: *aj.* quantitative
cuanto: *aj.* as much as; as many as; all the
cuarenta: *aj.* forty
cuarenta: *nm.* forty
cuarentavo: *aj.* fortieth
cuarentavo: *nm.* one-fortieth (fraction)
cuarentena: *nf.* group of forty; Lent
cuarentón: *aj.* forty-year-old
cuaresma: *nf.* lent
cuartear: *vt.* to divide into fourths
cuartel: *nm.* section; ward; quarters; barracks
cuartelero: *aj.* pertaining to quarters
cuarteto: *nm.* quatrain; quartet
cuartilla: *nf.* quarter of large sheet of paper
cuartillo: *nm.* four-person card game
cuarto: 1. fourth; 2. n. room; quarter
cuartucho: *nm.* old; ugly; or run-down room
cuatrillizo; -a: *nmf.* quadruplet
cuatrimotor: *nm.* four-engine airplane
cuatro: *aj.* four
cuatrocientos: *aj.* four hundred
cuba: *nf.* cask; barrel
cubeta: *nf.* keg; small cask or barrel
cubierta: *nf.* cover
cubierto: 1. *nm.* knife; fork; and spoon; 2. *aj.* covered
cubierto: *nm.* table setting
cubo: *nm.* bucket
cubrecama: *nf.* bedspread
cubrecolchón: *nm.* mattress cover
cubrir: *vt.* to cover
cuchara: *nf.* spoon; ladle
cucharilla: *nf.* small spoon
cucharón: *nf.* ladle
cuchilla: *nf.* knife; cutting tool
cuchillada: *nf.* knife wound
cuchillazo: *nm.* cut or stab with a

knife
cuchillería: *nf.* cutlery
cuchillo: *nm.* knife
cuello: *nm.* neck; collar
cuenta: *nf.* count; calculation; account; bill
cuentagotas: *nm.* dropper
cuentakilómetros: *nm.* odometer
cuentarrevoluciones: *nm.* tachometer
cuentista: *aj.* story-telling; gossiping
cuentista: *nmf.* storyteller; gossip
cuento: *nm.* story; tale
cuerda: *nf.* string; rope; cord; chord
cuerdo -da: *aj.* sane
cuerno: *nm.* horn
cuero: *nm.* pelt; rawhide
cuerpo: *nm.* body; corpus
cuervo: *nm.* raven
cuesta: *nf.* hill; slope
cuestión: *nf.* question; affair; matter
cuestionable: *aj.* questionable
cuestionar: *vt.* to discuss a matter
cueva: *nf.* cave; cellar
cuidado: *nm.* care; worry
cuidado: *nm.* care
cuidadoso -sa: *aj.* careful; watchful
cuidar: *vt.* to care for
culata: *nf.* haunch; butt
culo: *nm.* seat; behind; anus
culpa: *nf.* blame; guild; fault
culpabilidad: *nf.* culpability
culpable: *aj.* culpable; guilty
culpable: *nmf.* guilty person
culpar: *vt.* to blame; censure
cultivado: *aj.* cultivated
cultivar: *vt.* to cultivate; till
cultivo: *nm.* cultivation; farming
culto: *aj.* cultured; educated
cultura: *nf.* culture; education
cultural: *aj.* cultural
cumbre: *nm.* hilltop; mountaintop; summit
cumpleaños: *nm.* birthday

cumplido: *nm.* compliment; demonstration of courtesy
cumplidor -ra: *aj.* reliable
cumplimentar: *vt.* to compliment
cumplimiento: *nm.* completion
cumplir: *vt.* to execute; to perform; to fulfill; to complete
cúmulo: *nm.* pile; group; cumulus cloud
cuna: *nf.* cradle
cuñada: *nf.* sister-in-law
cuñado: *nm.* brother-in-law
cuneta: *nf.* ditch; gutter
cuota: *nf.* quota
cupón: *nm.* coupon
cura: *nmf.* priest; cure; remedy; healing
curación: *nf.* healing; treatment
curado: *aj.* cured
curandero;-a: *nmf.* healer; quack
curar: *vt.* to heal; to cure; to heal
curativo: *aj.* incurable
curiosear: *vt.* to show curiosity; to be curious; to pry
curiosidad: *nf.* curiosity
curioso: *aj.* curious
cursar: *vt.* to haunt; to frequent; to attend; to take a course
cursillista: *nmf.* participant in a series of theme-centered courses (often religious)
cursillo: *nm.* short course
cursillo: *nm.* brief series of courses centered on a theme
curso: *nm.* course; circulation
curtir: *vt.* to tan; to harden; to become tanned
curva: *nf.* bend; curve
curvar: *vt.* to curve
curvatura: *nf.* curvature
curvilíneo: *aj.* curvilinear
curvo: *aj.* curved
cúspide: *nf.* peak; top; summit
cutis: *nmf.* skin

D

dactilógrafo -fa: *nmf.* typist; typewriter
dádiva: *nf.* gift; present
dadivoso: *aj.* giving
dado: *aj.* given
dador;-a: *nmf.* giver
dama: *nf.* lady
damnificar: *vt.* to damage; hurt
dañado: *aj.* damaged
dañar: *vt.* to hurt; to damage
dañino: *aj.* damaging
daño: *nm.* damage
dañoso: *aj.* damaging
danza: *nf.* dance; dancing
danzante: *nmf.* dancer
danzar: *vt.* to dance
danzarín;-a: *nmf.* dancer
dar: *vt.* to give
dardo: *nm.* dart
dársena: *nf.* inner harbor
datar: *vt.* to date; *vi.* to date
dato: *nm.* datum; fact
deambular: *vt.* to wander without purpose or destination
debajo: *av.* below; underneath
debate: *nm.* debate
debatir: *vt.* to debate; struggle
debe: *nm.* debit
deber: *nm.* duty; debit
deber: *vt.* to owe; to must
debidamente: *av.* correctly; suitably
debido: *aj.* correct; suitable
débil: *aj.* weak; feeble
debilidad: *nf.* weakness
debilitación: *nf.* debilitation
debilitar: *vt.* to debilitate
debilucho: *aj.* very weak
decadencia: *nf.* decadence

decadente: *aj.* decadent
decaer: *vi.* to decay
decaído: *aj.* decayed
decaimiento: *nm.* decaying
decanato: *nm.* deanship
decapitación: *nf.* decapitation
decapitar: *vt.* to decapitate
decente: *aj.* decent; dignified
decepción: *nf.* disappointment
decepcionar: *vt.* to disappoint
decididamente: *av.* decidedly
decidido: *aj.* decided
decidir: *vi.* to decide
decimal: 1. *aj.* decimal; *nm.* decimal
decímetro: *nm.* decimeter
décimo: *aj.* tenth
décimo: *nm.* one-tenth
décimo -ma: *aj.* tenth
decimoctavo: *aj.* eighteenth
decimocuarto: *aj.* fourteenth
decimonoveno: *aj.* nineteenth
decimoquinto: *aj.* fifteenth
decimoséptimo: *aj.* seventeenth
decimosexto: *aj.* sixteenth
decimotercero: *aj.* thirteenth
decir: *vt.* to say; to tell; to speak; state; utter
decisión: *nf.* decision
decisivo: *aj.* decisive
declamar: *vt.* to declaim; recite
declaración: *nf.* declaration
declarado: *aj.* declared
declarar: *vt.* to declare; state
declaratorio: *aj.* declaratory
declinar: *vt.* to decline; refuse
declive: *nm.* declivity; slope
decoloración: *nf.* discoloration
decolorante: *nm.* chemical used for removing color
decolorar: *vt.* to bleach; to remove color from clothing
decoración: *nf.* decoration
decorado: *aj.* decorated
decorado: *nm.* decorative style

decorador;-a: *nmf.* decorator
decorar: *vt.* to decorate
decorativo: *aj.* decorative
decoro: *nm.* decorum
decoroso: *aj.* with decorum; with dignity
decrecer: *vi.* to decrease
decreciente: *aj.* decreasing; diminishing
decrecimiento: *nm.* decreasing; decline
decretar: *vt.* to decree; resolve
decreto: *nm.* decree
dedal: *nm.* thimble
dedicación: *nf.* dedication
dedicado: *aj.* dedicated
dedicar: *vt.* to dedicate
dedicarse: *vr.* to dedicate oneself
dedicatoria: *nf.* dedication; of a gift; book; etc
dedo: *nm.* finger
deducción: *nf.* deduction
deducible: *aj.* deducible
deducir: *vt.* to deduce; to deduct
deductivo: *aj.* deductive
defecto: *nm.* defect; fault; weakness
defectuoso: *aj.* defective
defender: *vt.* to defend; to protect
defendible: *aj.* defendable
defendido: 1. *aj.* defended; 2. *nmf.* defendant
defensa: *nf.* bumper; defense
defensiva: *nf.* defensive
defensivo: *aj.* defensive
defensor;-a: *nmf.* defense attorney
deficiencia: *nf.* deficiency
deficiente: *aj.* deficient
déficit: *nm.* deficit
definible: *aj.* definable
definición: *nf.* definition
definido: *aj.* defined
definir: *vt.* to define; make clear
definitivamente: *av.* definitely
definitivo: *aj.* definitive

deformación: *nf.* deformation
deformar: *vt.* to deform; distort
deforme: *aj.* deformed
deformidad: *nf.* deformity
defraudar: *vt.* to defraud; to cheat
defunción: *nf.* death; demise
degeneración: *nf.* degeneration
degenerado: *aj.* degenerated
degenerar: *vi.* to degenerate
degenerativo: aj degenerative
degradación: *nf.* degradation
degradante: *aj.* degrading
degradar: *vt.* to degrade
degustación: *nf.* tasting or sampling of food or drink
degustar: *vt.* to taste
deificar: *vt.* to deify
dejadez: *nf.* laziness; negligence
dejado: *aj.* abandoned; unkempt
dejar: *vt.* to leave; to permit; to allow
delantal: *nm.* apron
delante: *av.* before; *vi.* front of
delante de: in front of
delantera: *nf.* front bumper; forward position (soccer; etc.)
delantero -ra: *aj.* front; head
delator -ra: 1. *aj.* accusing; 2. *nmf.* accuser
delegación: *nf.* delegation
delegado: 1. *aj.* delegated; 2. *nmf.* delegate
delegar: *vt.* to delegate; depute
deleitar: *vt.* to delight
deleite: *nm.* delight
deleitoso: *aj.* delightful
deletrear: *vt.* to spell
deletreo: *nm.* spelling
delgadez: *nf.* thinness; slimness
delgado: *aj.* thin; slim
delgaducho: *aj.* skinny
deliberar: *vt.* to deliberate
delicadeza: *nf.* delicacy
delicado: *aj.* delicate
delicia: *nf.* delight

delicioso: *aj.* delicious; delightful
delimitación: *nf.* boundary
delimitar: *vt.* to delimit
delincuente: 1. *aj.* guilty; delinquent;
2. *nmf.* guilty person
delineación: *nf.* delineation
delineante: 1. *aj.* delineating;
drafting;
2. *nmf.* delineator
delinear: *vt.* to delineate; to outline
delirante: *aj.* causing delirium;
delirious
delirar: *vt.* to make delirious
delirio: *nm.* delirium
denunciar: *vt.* to accuse; denounce
demanda: *nf.* demand; petition;
lawsuit
demandado;-a: *nmf.* defendant in a
lawsuit
demandante: *nmf.* plaintiff in a
lawsuit
demandar: *vt.* to demand; to sue
demarcación: *nf.* demarcation
demarcar: *vt.* to demarcate; to
delimit
demás: *av.* besides
demasía: *nf.* abundance; excess
demasiado: 1. *aj.* excessive; 2. *av.*
too much
demencia: *nf.* insanity; madness
demérito: *nm.* demerit
democracia: *nf.* democracy
demócrata: *nmf.* democrat
democrático: *aj.* democratic
democratización: *nf.*
democratization
democratizar: *vt.* to democratize
demografía: *nf.* demography
demográfico: *aj.* demographic
demoler: *vt.* to demolish; fear down
demoníaco: *aj.* demoniacal
demonio: *nm.* demon; devil
demonología: *nf.* demonology
demostrar: *vt.* to demonstrate; prove

demorar: *vt.* to delay; *vi.* to retard
demostrable: *aj.* demonstrable
demostración: *nf.* demonstration
demostrar: *vt.* to demonstrate
demostrativo: *aj.* demonstrative
denegación: *nf.* formal rejection
denegar: *vt.* to deny; to refuse; to
reject
denigrar: *vt.* to defame; revile
denominación: *nf.* denomination
denominado: *aj.* denominated
denominador: *nm.* denominator
denominar: *vt.* to name; to
denominate
denominativo: *aj.* denominative
denotar: *vt.* to denote; mean
densidad: *nf.* density
densificar: *vt.* to make dense
denso: *aj.* dense
dentado: *aj.* with teeth
dentadura: *nf.* denture; set of teeth
dental: *aj.* dental
dentar: *vi.* to teethe
dentellar: *vt.* to chatter one's teeth
dentista: *nmf.* dentist
dentrifico -ca: *aj.* tooth paste
dentro: *av.* inside; within
dentro: *prep.* inside
dentro de: within
denuncia: *nf.* denunciation
denunciador;-a: *nmf.* denouncer
denunciante: *nmf.* denouncer
denunciar: *vt.* to denounce
departamental: *aj.* departmental
departamento: *nm.* department
dependencia: *nf.* dependency
depender: *vi.* to depend in
dependiente: *aj.* dependent
dependizar: *vt.* to grant
independence
depilar: *vt.* to depilate
depistar: *vt.* to put off
deplorar: *vt.* to deplore
deponente: *aj.* deposing

deponer: *vt.* to set aside
deportar: *vt.* to banish; exile
deporte: *nm.* sport
deportista: *nmf.* sports enthusiast
deportividad: *nf.* good sportsmanship
deportivo: *aj.* sport
deposición: *nf.* deposition
depositante: *nmf.* depositor
depositar: *vt.* to deposit
depositario;-a: *nmf.* depositor; treasurer
depositarse: *vr.* to be deposited
depósito: *nm.* depot; warehouse
depósito: *nm.* deposit
depravar: *vt.* to deprave; vitiate
depreciación: *nf.* depreciation
depreciar: *vt.* to depreciate; undervalue
depresión: *nf.* depression
depresivo: *aj.* depressing
deprimente: *aj.* depressing
deprimido: *aj.* depressed
deprimir: *vt.* to depress
depuración: *nf.* purification
depurador: *aj.* purifying
depurar: *vt.* to purify
depurativo: *aj.* purifying
derecha: *nf.* right
derechazo: *nm.* hit with the right hand
derechista: *aj.* right wing
derecho: 1. *aj.* straight; 2. adv. right
de repente: *av.* suddenly
deriva: *nf.* drift
derivación: *nf.* derivation
derivada: *nf.* mathematical function
derivado: 1. *aj.* derived; 2. *nm.* derivative
derivar: *vt.* to derive
derivativo: *aj.* derivative
derogar: *vt.* to abolish; derogate
derramamiento: *nm.* spilling; overflowing

derramar: *vt.* to spill
derramarse: *vr.* to overflow
derrame: *nm.* spilling
derretir: *vt.* to melt
derribar: *vt.* to demolish; destroy; to tear down
derribo: *nm.* tearing down
derrocar: *vt.* to tear down
derrota: *nf.* course; path; defeat; rout
derrotado: *aj.* defeated
derrotar: *vt.* to rout; to defeat
derrotero: *nm.* ship's course; direction
derruir: *vt.* to tear down
derrumbamiento: *nm.* collapse; landslide
derrumbar: *vt.* to tumble down; to collapse
desabrigar: *vt.* to uncover; to expose to the elements
desabrigo: *nm.* lack of protection
desabrochar: *vt.* to unsnap; *r.* to become unfastened
desaceleración: *nf.* deceleration
desacelerar: *vi.* to decelerate; to slow down
desacertado: *aj.* off the mark; incorrect
desacertar: *vi.* to miss the mark; to be wrong
desacierto: *nm.* missing the mark
desacompañado: *aj.* unaccompanied
desaconsejado: *aj.* imprudent; unwise; ill-advised
desaconsejar: *vt.* to dissuade
desacorde: *aj.* discordant; out-of-tune
desacostumbrado: *aj.* unaccustomed
desacreditar: *vt.* to discredit
desactivar: *vt.* to deactivate
desacuerdo: *nm.* disagreement
desafecto: *aj.* lacking affection; not affectionate
desafiar: *vt.* to challenge; dare

desafinar: *vt.* to put out of tune; *vi.* to get out of tune
desafió: *nm.* challenge; duel
desafortunado: *aj.* unfortunate
desagradable: *aj.* disagreeable; unpleasant
desagradar: *vt.* to displease
desagradecer: *vi.* to show a lack of gratitude
desagradecido: *aj.* unthankful
desagradecido;-a: *nmf.* an ungrateful person
desagradecimiento: *nm.* ungratefulness; ingratitude
desagrado: *nm.* displeasure
desaguar: *vt.* to drain; empty
desagüe: *nm.* drainage; sewerage
desahogado: *aj.* relieved; less busy
desahogar: *vt.* to relieve
desahogo: *nm.* relief
desahuciar: *vt.* to deprive of hope
desairar: *vt.* to slight; snub
desaire: *nm.* ungracefulness; slight
desajustar: *vt.* to put out of adjustment
desajuste: *nm.* lack of adjustment
desalar: *vt.* to take the salt from
desalentador: *aj.* discouraging
desalentar: *vt.* to discourage
desaliento: *nm.* discouragement
desalinear: *vt.* to put out of line
desalmado: *aj.* cruel; without a soul
desalojamiento: *nm.* vacating of a house; eviction
desalojar: *vi.* to vacate
desalquilado: *aj.* vacant
desalquilar: *vt.* to stop renting; to vacate
desalquilarse: *vr.* to be vacant
desamor: *nm.* lack of love
desamparado: *aj.* defenseless; helpless
desamparar: *vt.* to forsake
desamparo: *nm.* lack of protection; help; or support
desamueblado: *aj.* unfurnished
desamueblar: *vt.* to remove furniture
desandar: *vt.* to retrace one's steps; to go back the way one came
desangramiento: *nm.* blood loss
desangrar: *vt.* to bleed copiously
desanidar: *vi.* to leave the nest
desanimado: *aj.* discouraged
desanimar: *vt.* to discourage
desánimo: *nm.* discouragement
desapacible: *aj.* unpleasant; disagreeable
desapacible: *aj.* not peaceful
desaparecer: *vi.* to disappear
desaparecido: *aj.* missing
desaparición: *nf.* disappearance
desapasionadamente: *av.* dispassionately
desapasionado: *aj.* dispassionate
desapego: *nm.* lack of affection
desapercibido: *aj.* unperceived; unnoticed
desaplicado: *aj.* lazy; lacking effort
desaplicado;-a: *nm.* f bad student
desaprobación: *nf.* disapproval
desaprobador: *aj.* disapproving; failing
desaprobar: *vt.* to disapprove
desaprovechado: *aj.* poorly used
desaprovechar: *vt.* to miss (an opportunity)
desarmable: *aj.* able to be taken apart
desarmado: *aj.* unarmed; taken apart
desarmar: *vt.* to disarm
desarme: *nm.* disarmament
desarraigado: *aj.* without roots; uprooted
desarraigar: *vt.* to uproot
desarraigarse; *vr.* to become uprooted (also figurative)
desarraigo: *nm.* uprooting
desarreglado: *aj.* moved out of place

desarreglar: *vt.* to move out of place
desarreglo: *nm.* moving out of place
desarrollado: *aj.* developed
desarrollar: *vt.* to unroll; unfurl; to develop
desarrollo: *nm.* development
desarropar: *vt.* to take off heavy clothes
desasosegar: *vt.* to disquiet; worry; *r.* to become disquieted
desasosiego: *nm.* disquiet; worry
desastrado;-a: *nmf.* unkempt person
desastre: *nm.* disaster
desastroso: *aj.* disastrous
desatado: *aj.* untied; unleashed
desatar: *vt.* to untie; to unleash
desatarse: *vr.* to be unleashed
desatención: *nf.* neglect
desatender: *vt.* to neglect; to avoid attending to
desatento: *aj.* neglectful
desatinado: *aj.* off the mark; blundering
desatinar: *vi.* to aim poorly
desatornillar: *vt.* to unscrew; to take out a screw
desautorización: *nf.* removal of authority
desautorizado: *aj.* unauthorized
desautorizar: *vt.* to take away authority
desaventajado: *aj.* disadvantageous
desayunar: *vt.* to eat breakfast
desayuno: *nm.* breakfast
desazón: *nf.* lack of seasoning
desazonado: *aj.* unseasoned
desazonar: *vt.* to remove the seasoning
desazonarse: *vt.* to feel unwell
desbancar: *vt.* to break the bank
desbloquear: *vt.* to unblock
desbloqueo: *nm.* unblocking
desbocado: *aj.* foul-mouthed
desbocado;-a: *nmf.* foul-mouthed

person
desbocar: *vt.* to break the mouth
desbordamiento: *nm.* overflow
desbordante: *aj.* overflowing
desbordar: *vt.* to pass or flow over the edge
descabalgar: *vi.* to dismount
descabezar: *vt.* to decapitate
descafeinado: *aj.* decaffeinated
descafeinar: *vt.* to decaffeinate
descalabrar: *vt.* to hit; to hurt
descalificación: *nf.* disqualification
descalificar: *vt.* to disqualify
descalzar: *vt.* to take off
descambiar: *vt.* to undo a change
descamisado: *aj.* shirtless; poor or miserable
descampado: *aj.* barren; without vegetation
descansadero: *nm.* resting place
descansado -da: *aj.* rested; tranquil
descansar: *vt.* to stop work; to rest
descanso: *nm.* rest
descaradamente: *av.* insolently
descarado: *aj.* insolent
descarado -da: *aj.* impudent; cheeky
descarado;-a: *nmf.* shameless person
descarga: *nf.* unloading
descargador;-a: *nmf.* person who unloads
descargar: *vt.* to discharge; to empty
descargo: *nm.* unloading
descarnado: *aj.* lean; thin
descarnar: *vt.* to remove the meat from a bone
descaro: *nm.* effrontery; insolence
descartar: *vt.* to reject
descasar: *vt.* to divorce; to annul
descendencia: *nf.* descendants; lineage
descendente: *aj.* descending
descender: *vt.* to descend; go down
descendiente: *nmf.* descendant
descendimiento: *nm.* descent

desceñir: *vt.* to loosen
descenso: *nm.* descent
descentrado: *aj.* not centered
descentralización: *nf.* decentralization
descentralizar: *vt.* to decentralize
descentrar: *vt.* to remove from the center
descifrable: *aj.* decipherable
descifrado: *aj.* solved; cracked; broken (code)
desciframiento: *nm.* code breaking
descifrar: *vt.* to decipher or break a code
desclavar: *vt.* to remove the nails from
desclavar: *vt.* to remove a nail
descolgar: *vt.* to take down
descolocar: *vt.* to remove
descolonización: *nf.* decolonization
descolonizar: *vt.* to decolonize
descoloramiento: *nm.* removal of color
descolorido: *aj.* discolored; pale
descomponer: *vt.* to decompose
descomposición: *nf.* breaking down; decomposition
descompostura: *nf.* breaking down; decomposition
descompuesto: *aj.* broken down; decomposed
descomunal: *aj.* extraordinary
desconcentrado: *aj.* unfocused; lacking in concentration
desconcentrar: *vt.* to distract
desconcertar: *vt.* to disconcert
desconcierto: *nm.* disorder
desconectar: *vt.* to disconnect
desconfiado -da: *aj.* distrustful
desconfianza: *nf.* lack of confidence or faith
desconfiar: *vi.* to lack faith
descongelar: *vt.* to defrost; to melt
desconocer: *vt.* not to know

desconocido: *aj.* unknown; unfamiliar
desconocimiento: *nm.* ignorance; lack of knowledge
desconsideración: *nf.* inconsideration
desconsiderado: *aj.* inconsiderate
desconsolado: *aj.* not consoled; sad
desconsolador: *aj.* not consoling
desconsolar: *vt.* to grieve
desconsuelo: *nm.* grief
descontar: *vt.* to discount
descontentar: *vt.* to make unhappy
descontento: *aj.* discontented
descontento: *nm.* discontentment
desconcentar: *vr.* to become distracted
descorazonador: *aj.* demoralizing; disheartening
descorazonar: *vt.* to break someone's heart; to disappoint; to demoralize
descorchar: *vt.* remove the bar (or) cork from
descornar: *vt.* to remove the horns from an animal
descorrer: *vt.* to run back the way one came; to draw (curtains)
descorrerse: *vr.* to draw (curtains)
descorrimiento: *nm.* drawing of the curtains
descortés: *aj.* discourteous; rude
descortezar: *vt.* to remove the core or cortex
descoser: *vt.* to remove sewn threads
descosido: *aj.* unstitched; indiscreet
descoyuntar: *vt.* to dislocate
descrédito: *nm.* discredit; loss of one's good name
descreído: *aj.* no longer believing
describir: *vt.* to describe; to define
descripción: *nf.* description
descriptible: *aj.* describable
descriptivo: *aj.* descriptive
descrito: *aj.* described

descuartizamiento: *nm.* cutting into pieces
descuartizar: *vt.* to quarter
descubierto: *aj.* discovered
descubridor;-a: *nmf.* discoverer
descubrimiento: *nm.* -miento discovery
descubrir: *vt.* to discover
descuento: *nm.* discount
descuidado: *aj.* uncared for; neglected; careless
descuidar: *vt.* to neglect; overlook
descuido: *nm.* neglect
desde: *prep.* since; from; after
desdén: *nm.* disdain
desdeñable: *aj.* despicable
desdeñar: *vt.* to disdain
desdeñoso: *aj.* disdainful
desdentado: *aj.* toothless
desdibujado: *aj.* blurred; indefinite
desdibujar: *vt.* to soften the lines of a drawing or painting
desdicha: *nf.* misfortune; unhappiness
desdichadamente: *av.* unfortunately
desdichado: *aj.* unfortunate; unhappy
desdoblamiento: *nm.* unfolding
desdoblar: *vt.* to unfold
deseable: *aj.* desirable
deseado: *aj.* desired
desear: *vt.* to desire; wish
desecar: *vt.* to dry
desechable: *aj.* disposable
desechar: *vt.* to throw out
desecho: *nm.* throw-away item
desembalar: *vt.* to unpack
desembarcadero: *nm.* wharf; pier
desembarcar: *vt.* to disembark; to unload
desembarco: *nm.* unloading of a ship
desembargar: *vt.* to remove an embargo or prohibition of commerce
desembargo: *nm.* removal of an embargo or prohibition on commerce
desembocadura: *nf.* mouth of a river
desembocar: *vi.* to flow out of a river; lake; or road
desembolsar: *vt.* to disburse; pay out
desembolso: *nm.* payment; expense
desemejante: *aj.* dissimilar
desemejanza: *nf.* dissimilarity
desempapelar: *vt.* to unwrap; to take the paper off
desempaquetar: *vt.* to unpack
desemparejado: *aj.* made uneven; mismatched
desemparejar: *vt.* to make uneven; to mismatch
desempedrar: *vt.* to remove rocks
desempeñar: *vt.* to redeem; to recover
desempleado: *aj.* unemployed
desemplear: *vt.* to dismiss from employment
desempleo: *nm.* unemployment
desempolvar: *vt.* to remove the dust from
desencadenamiento: *nm.* freeing from a chain; unleashing of a series of events
desencadenar: *vt.* to remove a chain
desencajado: *aj.* removed; dislodged
desencajar: *vt.* to dislodge; to remove something; to take out
desencajonar: *vt.* to remove from a drawer
desencantamiento: *nm.* act of reversing a spell
desencantar: *vt.* to disenchant
desencanto: *nm.* disenchantment
desencarcelar: *vt.* to free from jail
desenfadado: *aj.* appeased; content
desenfadar: *vt.* to stop irritating; to appease
desenfado: *nm.* ease; freedom
desenfocado: *aj.* unfocused; out of focus

desenfocar: *vi.* to go out of focus
desenfoque: *nm.* loss of focus
desenfreno: *nm.* unruliness;
licentiousness
desengañar: *vt.* to disillusion
desengañarse: *vr.* to be disillusioned
desengaño: *nm.* disillusionment
desengrasar: *vt.* to remove the fat
from
desenhebrar: *vt.* to take out thread
desenlace: *nm.* finale; conclusion to
a story or conference
desenlazar: *vt.* to unravel; to untie
desenmascarar: *vt.* to unmask
desenredar: *vt.* to disentangle; to
untangle
desensillar: *vt.* to remove the saddle
desentender: *vt.* to take no part in
desentenderse: *vr.* to pretend not to
understand
desenterrar: *vt.* to unearth
desentonar: *vi.* to be out of tune
desentrañar: *vt.* to remove the
entrails; to get to the bottom of the
matter
desenvainar: *vt.* to unsheathe
desenvoltura: *nf.* ease; grace
desenvolver: *vt.* to unwrap
desenvuelto: *aj.* unwrapped;
confident
deseo: *nm.* desire; wish
deseoso: *aj.* desirous; filled with
desire
desequilibrado: *aj.* unbalanced
desequilibrar: *vt.* to cause loss of
balance; to knock or throw off
balance
desequilibrio: *nm.* loss or lack of
balance
deserción: *nf.* desertion
desertar: *vt.* to desert
desértico: *aj.* desert; relating to the
desert; desert-like
desertor;-a: *nmf.* deserter

desesperación: *nf.* impatience
desesperado: *aj.* impatient
desesperante: *aj.* exasperating
desesperanza: *nf.* hopelessness
desesperanzar: *vt.* to lack hope
desesperar: *vt.* to cause impatience
desestabilización: *nf.* destabilization
desestabilizar: *vt.* to disestablish
desestimar: *vt.* to reject
desfallecer: *vt.* to weaken; to
debilitate
desfallecido: *aj.* fainting;
discouraged; weak
desfallecimiento: *nm.* fainting;
discouragement; weakness
desfasado: *aj.* out of phase
desfasar: *vt.* to go out of phase
desfase: *nm.* maladjustment
desfavorable: *aj.* unfavorable
desfavorecer: *vt.* to disfavor
desfigurado: *aj.* disfigured
desfigurar: *vt.* to disfigure
desfiladero: *nm.* defile; pass
desfilar: *vi.* to parade
desfile: *nm.* parade; march
desfloración: *nf.* deflowering
desflorar: *vt.* to deflower
desfondar: *vt.* to remove the bottom
desfonde: *nm.* removal of the bottom
desgajar: *vt.* to tear off; to break off
desgana: *nf.* lack of desire
desganado: *aj.* uninspired; without
desire
desganar: *vt.* to discourage
desgarrado: *aj.* torn
desgarrador: *aj.* tearing; clawing
desgarrar: *vt.* to tear
desgarro: *nm.* tear; rent
desgarrón: *nm.* violent tearing of
clothing
desgaste: *nm.* wearing down
desgobernar: *vt.* to misgovern
desgracia: *nf.* disgrace; misery
desgraciadamente: *av.* unfortunately

desgraciado: *aj.* disgraced; miserable
desgraciado -da: *aj.* unfortunate
desgraciado;-a: *nmf.* a disgraced person; wretch
desgraciar: *vt.* to disgrace
desgranadora: *nf.* threshing machine
desgranar: *vt.* to thresh
desgranarse: *vr.* to become threshed
desgravación: *nf.* lowering of a tax
desgravar: *vt.* to lower a tax
deshabitado: *aj.* uninhabited
deshabitar: *vt.* to move out of
deshabituar: *vt.* to break a habit
deshacer: *vt.* to undo; to untie
desharrapado -da: *aj.* ragged; shabby
deshecho: *aj.* undone; unmade
deshelar: *vt.* to defrost; to melt
desherbar: *vt.* to weed
desheredado: *aj.* disinherited
desheredar: *vt.* to disinherit
deshielo: *nm.* slush
deshilachar: *vt.* to remove extra threads from cloth
deshilvanado: *aj.* with the temporary stitches removed
deshilvanar: *vt.* to remove temporary stitches
deshinchar: *vt.* to deflate; *r.* to get down
deshojar: *vt.* to defoliate
deshonestidad: *nf.* dishonesty
deshonesto: *aj.* dishonest
deshonor: *nm.* dishonor
deshonra: *nf.* dishonor
deshonrar: *vt.* to dishonor
deshonroso: *aj.* without honor
deshora: *nf.* inopportune time
deshuesadora: *nf.* a device used for pitting fruit
deshuesar: *vt.* to bone; to remove the bone
deshumanización: *nf.*

dehumanization
deshumanizado: *aj.* dehumanized
deshumanizar: *vt.* to dehumanize
desidia: *nf.* laziness; indolence
desierto: *nm.* desert
designar: *vt.* to designate; to select
desigual: *aj.* unequal
desigualar: *vt.* to mismatch
desigualdad: *nf.* inequality
desilusión: *nf.* disillusion; disappointment
desilusionado: *aj.* disillusioned; disappointed
desilusionar: *vt.* to disillusion
desinflar: *vt.* to deflate
desintegración: *nf.* disintegration
desintegrar: *vt.* to disintegrate
desinterés: *nm.* disinterest
desinteresado: *aj.* disinterested
desinteresarse: *vr.* to become disinterested
deslavar: *vt.* to wash lightly or superficially
desleal: *aj.* disloyal leal; loyal
deslealtad: *nf.* disloyalty
deslenguado: *aj.* bad-mouthed
deslenguar: *vt.* to remove the tongue
desliar: *vt.* to untie; unpack
desligar: *vt.* to untie; to unwind; *r.* to come loose
deslinde: *nm.* the act of placing property lines
desliz: *nm.* sliding; slipping
deslizamiento: *nm.* slipping or sliding
deslizar: *vt.* to slip or slide
deslucido: *aj.* dull; discolored
deslucir: *vt.* to tarnish
deslumbrador: *aj.* blinding; amazing
deslumbramiento: *nm.* blinding with bright light; amazement
deslumbrar: *vt.* to dazzle
deslustrar: *vt.* to discolor; to take the shine off

desmandado: *aj.* disobedient to orders
desmangar: *vt.* to take off the handle of *r.* to come off
desmantelar: *vt.* to dismantle
desmayar: *vt.* to dishearten; *r.* to faint
desmayo: *nm.* depression; faltering
desmedido: *aj.* excessive; limitless
desmejorar: *vi.* to worsen
desmemoriado: *aj.* forgetful
desmentir: *vt.* to contradict; to discover a lie
desmenuzar: *vt.* to pull to pieces. to crumb
desmerecer: *vt.* to be undeserving
desmerecimiento: *nm.* undeserving
desmilitarización: *nf.* demilitarization
desmilitarizar: *vt.* to demilitarize
desmineralización: *nf.* demineralization
desmineralizar: *vt.* to demineralize
desmontar: *vt.* to dismount
desmoralización: *nf.* demoralization
desmoralizador: *aj.* demoralizing
desmoralizar: *vt.* to demoralize
desmovilización: *nf.* demobilization
desmovilizar: *vt.* to demobilize
desnacionalización: *nf.* denationalization
desnacionalizar: *vt.* to denationalize
desnatar: *vt.* to skim
desnaturalización: *nf.* the act of taking away the rights of citizenship
desnaturalizado: *aj.* not having emotional closeness with or caring for one's family
desnaturalizar: *vt.* to take away the rights of citizenship
desnivel: *nm.* incline; slope
desnivelación: *nf.* incline; slope
desnivelado: *aj.* leaning; inclined
desnivelar: *vt.* to lean or tilt

desnucar: *vt.* to break the vertebrae of the neck
desnucarse: *vr.* to break the vertebrae of one's neck
desnudar: *vt.* to strip; to undress
desnudez: *nf.* nudity
desnudismo: *nm.* nudism
desnudista: *aj.* nudist
desnudo: *aj.* naked; nude
desnutrición: *nf.* malnutrition
desnutrido: *aj.* malnourished
desobedecer: *vt.* to disobey
desobediencia: *nf.* disobedience
desobediente: *aj.* disobedient
desocupación: *nf.* unemployment; vacancy
desocupado: *aj.* not busy
desocupar: *vt.* to free up
desodorante: 1. *aj.* deodorant; 2. deodorant
desoír: *vt.* not to hear
desolar: *vt.* to desolate
desollar: *vt.* to flay; to skin
desorden: *nm.* ' disorder
desordenado: *aj.* disordered; unorganized
desordenar: *vt.* to disorder
desorganización: *nf.* disorganized place
desorganizar: *vt.* to disorganize
desorientación: *nf.* disorientation
desorientado: *aj.* disoriented
desorientar: *vt.* to disorient
desovar: *vt.* to lay eggs
despabilar: *vt.* to trim; to snuff (candle)
despachar: *vt.* to dispatch; to expedite
despacho: *nm.* attorney's office; act of dispatching
despacio: *av.* slowly
despacioso: *aj.* slow; slow-moving; slow-going
desparpajo: *nm.* con. pertness

despechado: *aj.* filled with rancor
despechar: *vt.* to wean
despecho: *nm.* spite; rancor
despectivo -a: *aj.* depreciatory
despedazar: *vt.* to break to pieces; to tear into pieces
despedazar: *vt.* to break into many pieces
despedida: *nf.* farewell; leave
despedir: *vt.* to throw; to hurl
despegado: *aj.* unstuck
despegar: *vt.* to take off (airplane); to unstick; to take off something that is stuck despegue
despeinado: *aj.* uncombed; disheveled
despeinar: *vt.* to mess up hair
despejar: *vt.* to free; to clear; *r.* to be free and easy
despellejar: *vt.* to remove the skin
despensa: *nf.* pantry
desperdiciar: *vt.* to waste
desperdicio: *nm.* waste
desperfecto: *nm.* imperfection; problem
despersonalizar: *vt.* to depersonalize
despertador: *nm.* alarm clock
despertar: *vt.* to wake up
despido: *nm.* dismissal from work
despierto: *aj.* awake
despilfarro: *nm.* squandering; lav-ishness
despintar: *vt.* to remove paint from; to remove makeup
desplazado: *aj.* displaced; moved
desplazamiento: *nm.* displacement; movement from one place to another
desplazar: *vt.* to displace; to move
desplegar: *vt.* to spread out; unfold; *r.* to spread out
despliegue: *nm.* dismissal of troops from formation
desplumar: *vt.* to remove feathers; to pluck

despoblación: *nf.* depopulation
despoblar: *vt.* to depopulate
despojar: *vt.* to strip; despoil; *r.* to undress
desposado: *aj.* recently married
desposar: *vt.* to marry; *r.* to be betrothed
desposeer: *vt.* to dispossess
desposeido;-a: *nmf.* dispossessed person
despreciable: *aj.* despicable; worthless
despreciar: *vt.* to despise; to scorn
despreciativo: *aj.* acting in a despicable manner
desprecio: *nm.* hate; despising
desprender: *vt.* to detach; to separate
desprendido: *aj.* generous
desprendimiento: *nm.* separation
despreocupación: *nf.* state of being worry-free
despreocupado: *aj.* not worried
desprestigiar: *vt.* to cause loss of prestige
desprestigio: *nm.* loss of prestige
desprevenido: *aj.* unprepared
desprovisto: *aj.* unforeseen
después: *av.* after; afterwards
despuntado: *aj.* without a point
despuntar: *vt.* to remove the point from; to break (dawn) from a point of light
desquiciar: *vt.* to unhinge; *r.* to come unhinged
destacado: *aj.* distinguished
destacar: *vt.* to emphasize; to stand out
destajo: *nm.* piecework
destapar: *vt.* to uncover; to get uncovered
destello: *nm.* sparkle; flash
desteñir: *vt.* to discolor
desterrado;-a: *nmf.* exile
desterrar: *vt.* to exile

desterrar: *vt.* to exile; banish
destierro: *nm.* exile; banishment
destinado: *aj.* destined
destinar: *vt.* to destine
destinatario;-a: *nmf.* destination
destino: *nm.* destiny
destituir: *vt.* to deprive
destornillador: *nm.* screwdriver
destornillar: *vt.* to take out a screw
destrozar: *vt.* to break to pieces
destreza: *nf.* skill; dexterity
destronamiento: *nm.* dethroning
destrozado: *aj.* broken into pieces
destrozar: *vt.* to break something into pieces
destrozo: *nm.* breaking into pieces
destrucción: *nf.* destruction
destructivo: *aj.* destructive
destructor: *aj.* destructing
destructor: *nm.* destroyer
destruir: *vt.* to destroy; lay waste
desunión: *nf.* separation
desunir: *vt.* to disunite; to separate
desusado: *aj.* out of use
desuso: *nm.* disuse
desvalido: *aj.* helpless or without resources
desvalijamiento: *nm.* robbery; theft
desvalijar: *vt.* to steal the contents of; to rob
desvalorización: *nf.* drop in value or price
desvalorizar: *vt.* to devaluate; to drop in value; to lose value
desván: *nm.* garret; loft
desvanecer: *vt.* to vanish; to blur or soften a photo or picture
desvanecerse: *vr.* to faint
desvanecimiento: *nm.* vanishing; fainting
desvariar: *vi.* to rave; rant
desvelado: *aj.* tired from lack of sleep
desvelar: *vt.* to keep awake

desvelo: *nm.* staying up late
desvenar: *vt.* to remove the veins (of vegetables)
desvencijado: *aj.* loose; partially broken
desvencijar: *vt.* to loosen; to break partially
desventurado -da: *aj.* unfortunate
desvergonzado: *aj.* shameless
desvestir: *vt.* to undress
desvestirse: *vr.* to undress oneself; to get undressed
desviación: *nf.* detour
desviar: *vt.* to detour
desvió: *nm.* deflection; deviation; detour
desvirgar: *vt.* to deflower
desvirtuar: *vt.* to cause something to lose its virtue
desvivirse: *vr.* to give of oneself completely
detalladamente: *av.* carefully; with attention to detail
detallado: *aj.* detailed
detallar: *vt.* to detail
detalle: *nm.* retail
detallista: *nmf.* person who pays attention to detail; retail seller
detectar: *vt.* to detect
detención: *nf.* detention
detener: *vt.* to stop; to check; to detain
detenerse: *vr.* to stop oneself
detenidamente: *av.* carefully; thoroughly; slowly
detenido: 1. *aj.* detained; 2. *nmf.* prisoner; arrested person
determinación: *nf.* determination
determinado: *aj.* determined
determinante: *aj.* determining
determinar: *vt.* to determine
determinativo: *aj.* determining
determinismo: *nm.* determinism
determinista: *aj.* determinist

detestable: *aj.* detestable
detestar: *vt.* to detest; to curse
detrás: *av.* behind
deuda: *nf.* debt
deudor: *aj.* indebted
deudor;-a: *nmf.* debtor
devaluación: *nf.* devaluation
devaluar: *vt.* to devaluate; to drop in value; to lose value
devastar: *vt.* to devastate
devoción: *nf.* devotion
devocionario: *nm.* devotional book
devolución: *nf.* return; restitution
devolver: *vt.* to return; to take something back
devorar: *vt.* to devour
devuelto: *aj.* returned
día: *nm.* day
diablesa: *nf.* female devil
diablillo: *nm.* little devil; referring to a mischievous child
diablo: *nm.* devil
diablura: *nf.* mischievous trick
diabólico: *aj.* diabolic
diácono: *nm.* deacon
diagnosticar: *vt.* to diagnose
dialecto: *nm.* dialect
dialogar: *vt.* to dialogue; to converse
diálogo: *nm.* dialog
diametral: *aj.* diametrical
diametralmente: *av.* diametrically
diámetro: *nm.* diameter
diapositiva: *nf.* transparency; slide
diariamente: *av.* daily
diario: 1. *aj.* daily; 2. *nm.* diary; daily newspaper
dibujante: *nmf.* sketcher; draftsman; draftswoman
dibujante: *nmf.* artist who draws
dibujar: *vt.* to draw; to design
dibujo: *nm.* drawing; sketch
dicción: *nf.* diction
diccionario: *nm.* dictionary
dicha: *nf.* joy; happiness

dicharachero: *aj.* someone who constantly speaks in sayings; funny stories or jokes
dicho: *aj.* said; expressed; aforesaid
dicho: *nm.* saying
dichoso: *aj.* joyful; happy
diciembre: *nm.* December
dictado: *nm.* dictation
dictador;-a: *nmf.* dictator
dictadura: *nf.* dictatorship
dictamen: *nm.* judicial opinion or decision
dictaminar: *vt.* to issue a judicial opinion or decision
dictar: *vt.* to dictate
dictatorial: *aj.* dictatorial
diecinueve: *aj.* nineteen
diecinueve: *aj.* nineteen
diecinueveavo: *aj.* nineteenth
diecinueveavo: *aj.* nineteenth
dieciochesco: *aj.* related to the eighteenth century
dieciocho: *aj.* eighteen
dieciséis: *aj.* sixteen
dieciseisavo: *aj.* sixteenth
diecisiete: *aj.* seventeen
diecisieteavo: *aj.* one-seventeenth
diecisieteavo: *aj.* seventeenth
diente: *nm.* tooth
diestra: *nf.* right hand
diestro: *aj.* right; skilful
dieta: *nf.* diet
dietética: *nf.* dietetics
dietético: *aj.* dietetic
dietista: *nmf.* dietician
diez: *aj.* ten
diezmar: *vt.* to tithe
difamación: *nf.* defamation
difamador;-a: *nmf.* libeler
difamar: *vt.* to defame
diferencia: *nf.* difference
diferenciación: *nf.* differentiation
diferencial: *aj.* differential
diferencial: *nm.* differential

diferenciar: *vt.* to differentiate
diferente: *aj.* different
diferir: *vt.* to defer; to differ
difícil: *aj.* difficult; hard
dificultad: *nf.* difficulty
dificultar: *vt.* to make something difficult
dificultoso: *aj.* difficult
difundido: *aj.* broadcasted
difundir: *vt.* to diffuse; to spread; to broadcast; to publish; to spread
difusión: *nf.* diffusion
difuso: *aj.* diffuse
difusor: *aj.* broadcasting; publishing
digerir: *vt.* to digest
dignamente: *av.* worthily
dignatario;-a: *nmf.* dignitary
dignidad: *nf.* dignity
dignificante: *aj.* dignifying
dignificar: *vt.* to dignify
digno: *aj.* worthy
digno -na: *aj.* worthy
dilatación: *nf.* dilation
dilatado: *aj.* dilated
dilatador: *aj.* dilating
dilatar: *vt.* to expand; to dilate
diligencia: *nf.* diligence
diligenciar: *vt.* to carry out or execute a task
diligente: *aj.* diligent
diluir: *vt.* to dilute
diluvio: *nm.* deluge
dimensión: *nf.* dimension
dimensional: *aj.* dimensional
diminutivo -va: *aj.* diminishing
dimisión: *nf.* resignation
dimitir: *vt.* to resign
dinámica: *nf.* dynamics
dinámico: *aj.* dynamic
dinamismo: *nm.* dynamism
dinamita: *nf.* dynamite
dinamitar: *vt.* to dynamite
dinamitero;-a: *nmf.* one who works with dynamite

dineral: *nm.* great deal of money
dinerillo: *nm.* small amount of money; small coin
dinero: *nm.* money
dintel: *nm.* lintel; doorhead
Dios: *nm.* God
diosa: *nf.* goddess
diploma: *nf.* diploma
diplomacia: *nf.* diplomacy
diplomado: *aj.* licensed; with diploma
diplomarse: *vr.* to earn a diploma
diplomático: *aj.* diplomatic
diplomático;-a: *nmf.* diplomat
diptongo: *nm.* diphthong
diputado -da: *nmf.* representa-tive
dique: *nm.* dike; dam
dirección: *nf.* direction; course; address
direccional: *nm.* directional signal
directa: *nf.* drive or high gear of a motor
directamente: *av.* directly
directiva: *nf.* directive
directivo: *aj.* directive; managing
directo: *aj.* direct
director;-a: *nmf.* director
directorio: *nm.* directory
dirigente: *nmf.* leader responsible for a group or activity
dirigible: *aj.* able to be guided or directed
dirigir: *vt.* to direct; to manage
discernimiento: *nm.* discernment
discernir: *vt.* to discern
disciplina: *nf.* discipline
disciplinado: *aj.* disciplined
disciplinar: *vt.* to discipline
disciplinario: *aj.* disciplinary
discípulo;-a: *nmf.* disciple
disco: *nm.* disc; record
disconforme: *aj.* not in agreement
disconformidad: *nf.* nonconformity
discontinuidad: *nf.* lack of

continuity
discontinuo: *aj.* discontinuous
discordia: *nf.* discord; disagree-ment
discreción: *nf.* discretion
discrecional: *aj.* optional; discretionary
discrepancia: *nf.* discrepancy
discreto: *aj.* discreet
discreto;-a: *nmf.* a discreet person
disculpa: *nf.* excuse
disculpable: *aj.* excusable
disculpar: *vt.* to excuse
discurrir: *vt.* to invent; contrive; *vi.* to ramble
discursivo: *aj.* pertaining to a speech
discurso: *nm.* speech
discusión: *nf.* discussion
discutible: *aj.* debatable
discutir: *vt.* to discuss; to argue
disecar: *vt.* to dissect; to stuff
disentir: *vi.* to dissent
disertación: *nf.* dissertation
disertar: *vt.* to speak at length on a subject
disfraz: *nm.* disguise; costume
disfrazar: *vt.* to disguise
disfrutar: *vt.* to enjoy
disfrute: *nm.* enjoyment
disgregación: *nf.* separation
disgregar: *vt.* to take away; to separate
disgustado: *aj.* disgusted
disgustar: *vt.* to displease; to upset
disgusto: *nm.* problem; trouble
disimulación: *nf.* pretense
disimuladamente: *av.* in a feigned or pretended manner
disimulado: *aj.* pretended; feigned
disimular: *vt.* to dissimulate; to pretend; to feign
disimulo: *nm.* dissimulation
disipado: *aj.* dissipated
disipar: *vt.* to dissipate; to disappear
dislocar: *vt.* to dislocate

disminución: *nf.* diminution; lowering; lessening
disminuir: *vt.* to diminish
disociable: *aj.* dissociable; separable
disociación: *nf.* dissociation
disociar: *vt.* to disassociate
disolubilidad: *nf.* solubility
disoluble: *aj.* soluble
disolución: *nf.* dissolution
disolvente: *aj.* dissolvent; solvent
disolvente: *nm.* dissolvent; solvent
disolver: *vt.* to dissolve; to separate
disonancia: *nf.* dissonance
disparador: *nm.* shooter
disparar: *vt.* to shoot; to dash away
disparar: *vt.* to shoot
disparejo: *aj.* uneven; unequal
disparo: *nm.* shot; discharge
dispensa: *nf.* dispensation
dispensar: *vt.* to dispense; to excuse or pardon
dispensario: *nm.* dispensary
disponer: *vt.* to dispose; arrange; to have available
disponibilidad: *nf.* availability
disponible: *aj.* available
disposición: *nf.* disposition
dispuesto: *aj.* available
disputa: *nf.* dispute; quarrel
disputar: *vt.* to dispute
distancia: *nf.* distance
distanciado: *aj.* distant
distanciamiento: *nm.* distancing
distanciar: *vt.* to separate or increase the distance between two things
distante: *aj.* distant
distar: *vi.* to be distant from
distinción: *nf.* distinction
distinguido: *aj.* distinguished
distinguir: *vt.* to distinguish
distintivo: *aj.* distinctive
distintivo: *nm.* distinguishing mark or sign
distinto: *aj.* distinct

distracción: *nf.* distraction
distraer: *vt.* to distract
distraído: *aj.* distracted
distribución: *nf.* distribution
distribuidor;-a: *nmf.* distributor
distribuir: *vt.* to distribute; divide
distributivo: *aj.* distributive
diurno: *aj.* daytime
divagación: *nf.* rambling
divergencia: *nf.* divergence
divergente: *aj.* divergent
divergir: *vi.* to diverge
diversidad: *nf.* diversity; variety
diversificación: *nf.* diversification
diversificar: *vt.* to diversify
diversificarse: *vr.* to be diversified
diversión: *nf.* diversion
diverso: *aj.* diverse
diverso -sa: *aj.* diverse; different
divertido: *aj.* fun; funny; amusing
divertir: *vt.* to amuse; to divert; to entertain
divertirse: *vr.* to have fun
dividendo: *nm.* dividend
dividir: *vt.* to divide
divinidad: *nf.* divinity
divinizar: *vt.* to make something divine
divino: *aj.* divine
divisa: *nf.* emblem
divisar: *vt.* to perceive
divisibilidad: *nf.* divisibility
divisible: *aj.* divisible
división: *nf.* division
divisor: *nm.* divisor
divisoria: *nm.* dividing line
divisorio: *aj.* dividing
divorciado: *aj.* divorced
divorciar: *vt.* to divorce
divorciarse: *vr.* to become divorced
divorcio: *nm.* divorce
divulgar: *vt.* to divulge; to spread
doblaje: *nm.* dubbing
doblar: *vt.* to double; to fold

doble: 1. *aj.* double ; 2. *nm.* double
doblegar: *vt.* to fold; to bend
doblemente: *av.* doubly
doblez: *nm.* fold; duplicity; double-dealing
doce: *aj.* twelve
doceavo: *aj.* twelfth
docena: *nf.* dozen
dócil: *aj.* docile
docilidad: *nf.* docility
doctamente: *av.* with wisdom and knowledge
docto;-a: *nmf.* expert
doctor;-a: *nmf.* doctor
doctorado: *nm.* doctorate
doctoral: *aj.* doctoral
doctorarse: *vr.* to earn a doctorate
doctrinal: 1. *aj.* doctrinal; 2. *nf.* doctrine
doctrinario;-a: *nmf.* doctrinaire person
documentación: *nf.* documentation
documentado -da: *aj.* documented; well-informed
documental: *aj.* documentary
documentar: *vt.* to document
documento: *nm.* document
dogma: *nm.* dogma
dogmático;-a: *aj.* dogmatic
dogmatismo: *nm.* dogmatism
dogmatizar: *vt.* to teach dogma
dolencia: *nf.* ailment; complaint
doler : *vi.* to ache; to hurt; r; to complain
dolerse: *vr.* to be hurting
dolor: *nm.* ache; pain
dolorido: *aj.* painful; hurting
doloroso: *aj.* physically or emotionally painful
doma: *nf.* taming
domador;-a: *nmf.* one who tames an animal
domar: *vt.* to tame; to break
domesticable: *aj.* tamable

domesticación: *nf.* domestication
domesticar: *vt.* to tame; to domesticate
doméstico: *aj.* domestic
dominación: *nf.* domination
dominante: *aj.* dominant
dominar: *vt.* to dominate
domingo: *nm.* Sunday
dominio: *nm.* dominion; domain
don: *nm.* gift; present; talent
doña: *nf.* Mrs
donar: *vt.* to give; donate
donativo: *nm.* gift; donation
doncella: *nf.* maiden; virgin
dónde: 1. *interr.* where?; 2. *conj.* where
dondequiera: *av.* anywhere; wherever
dorado: *aj.* golden
dorar (se): *vt.* to make something golden
dormido: *aj.* asleep
dormir: *vt.* to sleep
dormitar: *vi.* to nod off; to doze
dormitorio: *nm.* dormitory
dorso: *nm.* back
dos: *aj.* two
doscientos: *aj.* two hundred
dosis: *nf.* dose
dotación: *nf.* endowment; dowry
dotado: *aj.* gifted; talented
dotar: *vt.* to endow
dote: *nf.* gift; talent; dowry
dragar: *vt.* to dredge
drama: *nm.* drama
dramática: *nf.* dramatics
dramático: *aj.* dramatic
dramatismo: *nm.* drama
dramatizar: *vt.* to dramatize
dramaturgia: *nf.* dramatics
dramaturgo: *nmf.* play writer; dramatist
droga: *nf.* drug; medicine
ducha: *nf.* shower bath

ducho -cha: *aj.* skillful. ; expert
duda: *nf.* doubt
dudar: *vt.* to doubt
dudoso: *aj.* doubtful
duelo: *nm.* grief; sorrow
duende: *nm.* elf; goblin
dueño -ña: *nmf.* owner; proprietor
dulce: 1. *aj.* sweet; 2. *nm.* sweet; candy
dulcería: *nf.* candy store
dulcero: *aj.* sweet-loving
dulcificar: *vt.* to sweeten
dulzón: *aj.* over-sweet
dulzor: *nm.* sweetness
dulzura: *nf.* sweetness
dúo: *nm.* duet
duplicar: *vt.* to duplicate
duque: *nm.* duke
duquesa: *nf.* duchess
durabilidad: *nf.* durability
durable: *aj.* durable
duración: *nf.* duration; length
duración: *nf.* duration
duradero: *aj.* long-lasting
durante: *prep.* during
durar: *vi.* to last
dureza: *nf.* hardness
durmiente: *aj.* sleeping
duro: *aj.* hard

E

e: *conj.* and
ebanista: *nm.* cabinetmaker
ebrio -ebria: *aj.* drunk
ebullición: *nf.* boiling
echado: *aj.* thrown-out
echar: *vt.* to throw; to cough up
Eclesiastés: *nm.* Ecclesiastes
eclesiástico: *aj.* ecclesiastical

eclipsar: *vt.* to eclipse
eco: *nm.* echo
econometría: *nf.* econometrics
economía: *nf.* economy; economics
económicamente: *av.* economically
económico: *aj.* economical
economista: *nmf.* economist
economizar: *vt.* to economize
ecosistema: *nm.* ecosystem
edad: *nf.* age
edición: *nf.* edition
edicto: *nm.* edict; proclamation
edificación: *nf.* building; edification
edificador: *aj.* edifying
edificante: *aj.* edifying
edificar: *vt.* to edify; to build up
edificio: *nm.* building
editar: *vt.* to publish
editor; a: *nmf.* publisher
editorial: 1. *aj.* editorial; related to publishing; 2. *nm.* editorial
editorialista: *nmf.* editorial writer
educación: *nf.* education
educado: *aj.* well-mannered; educated
educador;-a: *nmf.* educator
educar: *vt.* to educate; to train
educativo: *aj.* educative
edulcorante: *nm.* synthetic sweetener
efectivamente: *av.* effectively
efectividad: *nf.* effectiveness
efectivo: 1. *aj.* effective; real; actual; 2. *nm.* cash
efecto: *nm.* effect
efectuar: *vt.* to effect; carry out
eficacia: *nf.* efficiency
eficaz: *aj.* effective; efficient
eficazmente: *av.* efficiently
eficiencia: *nf.* efficiency
eficiente: *aj.* efficient
eficientemente: *av.* efficiently
refugiar: *vt.* to seek refuge
ego: *nm.* ego

egocéntrico: *aj.* egocentric
egocentrismo: *nm.* egocentrism
egoísmo: *nm.* egoism; egotism; selfishness
egoísta: *aj.* selfish; egotistical
ególatra: *nmf.* self-worshiper
egolatría: *nf.* self-worship; excessive self-adoration
egotismo: *nm.* egotism
eje: *nm.* axis; axle
ejecución: *nf.* execution
ejecutar: *vt.* to execute
ejecutivo;-a: 1. *aj.* executive; 2. *nm.* executive
ejecutor -tora: 1. *aj.* executive; 2. *nmf.* executive
ejemplar: 1. *aj.* exemplary; 2. *nm.* exemplary person
ejemplarizar: *vt.* to give an example; to exemplify
ejemplo: *nm.* example; instance
ejercer: *vt.* to practice; exercise
ejercicio: *nm.* exercise
ejercitar: *vt.* to exercise
ejercitarse: *vr.* to get exercise
ejército: *nm.* army
el: *art. masc. sing.* the
él: *pron. pers.* he; him; it
elaboración: *nf.* elaboration
elaborar: *vt.* to elaborate
elección: *nf.* election
electivo: *aj.* elective
electo: *nmf.* person elected to office
elector;-a: *nmf.* elector
electorado: *nm.* electorate
electoral: *aj.* electoral
electricidad: *nf.* electricity
electricista: *nmf.* electrician
eléctrico: *aj.* electric
electrificación: *nf.* electrification
electrificar: *vt.* to electrify
electrizante: *aj.* electrifying
electrizar: *vt.* to electrify
electrocardiograma: *nf.*

electrocardiogram
electrochoque: *nm.* electric shock
electrocución: *nf.* electrocution
electrocutar: *vt.* to electrocute
electrocutarse: *vr.* to be electrocuted
electrodo: *nm.* electrode
electrodoméstico: *nm.* electrical appliance
electroimán: *nm.* electromagnet
electrólisis: *nf.* electrolysis
electrolito: *nm.* electrolyte
electromagnético: *aj.* electromagnetic
electrón: *nm.* electron
electrónica: *nf.* electronics
electrónico: *aj.* electronic
electrostática: *nf.* electrostatics
elegancia: *nf.* elegance
elegante: *aj.* elegant; stylish
elegantemente: *av.* elegantly
elegibilidad: *nf.* eligibility
elegible: *aj.* eligible
elegido: *aj.* elected; chosen
elegir: *vt.* to elect; to choose
elemental: *aj.* elemental
elemento: *nm.* element
elevación: *nf.* elevation; exaltation
elevado: *aj.* elevated
elevador: *nm.* elevator
elevar: *vt.* to elevate; to rise
eliminación: *nf.* elimination
eliminador;-a: *nmf.* eliminator
eliminar: *vt.* to eliminate
eliminatoria: *nf.* eliminatory round of competition
eliminatorio: *aj.* eliminatory
ella: *pron.* she
ello: *pron.* he; it; that
ellos: *pron.* they (at least one male)
elocución: *nf.* elocution
elocuencia: *nf.* eloquence
elocuente: *aj.* eloquent
elogiable: *aj.* praiseworthy
elogiar: *vt.* to eulogize; to praise

elogio: *nm.* praise; eulogy
elucidación: *nf.* elucidation; clarification
elucidar: *vt.* to elucidate
emanación: *nf.* emanation
emanar: *vi.* to emanate
emancipar: *vt.* to emancipate; *vr.* to become emancipated
embajada: *nf.* embassy; message
embajador;-a: *nmf.* ambassador
embalaje: *nm.* packing
embalar: *vt.* to pack
embarazar: *vt.* to embarrass; *vr.* to be obstructed
embarazo: *nm.* embarrassment
embarcación: *nf.* medium-sized boat
embarcadero: *nm.* wharf; loading dock
embarcar: *vt.* to load a ship
embargar: *vt.* to embargo; to prohibit commerce
embargo: *nm.* embargo
embarque: *nm.* loading of a ship
embarrar: *vt.* to splash with mud
embaucar: *vt.* to deceive
embeber: *vt.* to absorb; to soak up
embelesar: *vt.* to charm; fascinate; *vr.* to be charmed
embellecer: *vt.* to beautify
embellecimiento: *nm.* beautification; embellishment
embestir: *v.* to attack; to assail
emblema: *nm.* emblem
embocar: *vt.* to put the lips on the mouthpiece of an instrument
embolsar: *vt.* to put into a pocket; purse or bag
emboscada: *nf.* ambush
emboscar: *vt.* to ambush
embotellado: *aj.* bottled
embotellador;-a: *nmf.* bottler
embotelladora: *nf.* bottling plant
embotellamiento: *nm.* bottling
embotellar: *vt.* to bottle

embriagado: *aj.* inebriated; intoxicated; drunk
embriagador: *aj.* inebriating; intoxicating
embriagar: *vt.* to inebriate; to intoxicate
embriagarse: *vr.* to become inebriated; to become intoxicated
embriaguez: *nm.* inebriation; intoxication; drunkenness
embrollar: *vt.* to embroil; confuse
embromar: *vt.* to play a practical joke on someone; to tease
embrujar: *vt.* to bewitch
embudo: *nm.* funnel
embuste: *nm.* lie; trick
embutido -da: *aj.* recessed; *nm.* inlay; sausage
emigrar: *vi.* to emigrate
eminencia: *nf.* eminence
eminente: *aj.* eminent
eminentemente: *av.* eminently
emisión: *nf.* emission
emisor: *nm.* transmitter
emisora: *nf.* radio or television broadcasting station
emitir: *vt.* to emit; to broadcast
emoción: *nf.* emotion
emocionado: *aj.* excited; emotional
emocional: *aj.* emotional
emocionalmente: *av.* emotionally
emocionante: *aj.* exciting
emocionar: *vt.* to move; to stir
emocionarse: *vr.* to become excited
emotividad: *nf.* emotive quality
emotivo: *aj.* emotive; causing emotion
empadronar: *vt.* to register
empalmar: *vt.* to join; connect; *vi.* to connect
empanada: *nf.* turnover
empanadilla: *nf.* small turnover
empanado: *aj.* wrapped in bread
empañar: *vt.* to get misty

empanizado: *aj.* breaded
empanizar: *vt.* to bread
empapar: *vt.* to soak; saturate; *vr.* to soak
empapelado: *nm.* paper wrapping
empapelar: *vt.* to wrap up in paper
empaquetar: *vt.* to pack
emparedado: *nm.* sandwich
emparedar: *vt.* to build a wall around
emparejar: *vt.* to make even; to match
emparentado: *aj.* related by marriage
emparentar: *vi.* to become relatives by marriage
empaste: *nm.* filling
empatar: *vt.* to tie
empate: *nm.* draw
empedernido -da: *aj.* hardened
empedrado: *aj.* made of rocks
empedrar: *vt.* to place rocks
empeñar: *vt.* to make worse
empeño: *nm.* effort; pawning
empeoramiento: *nm.* worsening
empeorar: *vi.* to worsen
empeorarse: *vr.* to become worse
empequeñecer: *vt.* to make smaller; to shrink
empequeñecimiento: *nm.* shrinking
emperador: *nm.* emperor
emperatriz: *nf.* empress
empezar: *vt.* to begin
emplazar: *vt.* to summons
empleado; -a: *nmf.* employee
emplear: *vt.* to employ
emplearse: *vr.* to be employed
empleo: *nm.* employment
emplumado: *aj.* with feathers
emplumar: *vt.* to feather; to put feathers in something
empobrecer: *vt.* to make poor
empobrecerse: *vr.* to become poor
empollar: *vi.* to brood

empolvado: *aj.* dusty
empolvar: *vt.* to make dusty
empolvarse: *vr.* to become dusty
empotrar: *vt.* to plant; to interlock
emprendedor: *aj.* decisive; enterprising
emprender: *vt.* to undertake; to begin a work or business
empresa: *nf.* enterprise; business
empresarial: *aj.* business
empresario;-a: *nmf.* business owner
empujar: *vt.* to push
empuje: *nm.* push
empujón: *nm.* hard push; shove
empuñadura: *nf.* handle of a dagger or sword
empuñar: *vt.* to take hold of a dagger
en: *prep.* in; into; at; on
en seguida: *av.* immediately; right away
enaceitar: *vt.* to oil; to get oil on
enajenar: *vt.* to transport
enamoradizo: *aj.* easily enamored
enamorado -da: *aj.* in love
enamoramiento: *nm.* falling in love
enamorar: *vt.* to cause to fall in love
enamorarse: *vr.* to fall in love
enano -na: *aj.* dwarfish; *nmf.*
enarbolar: *vt.* to raise
enarcar: *vt.* to make in the shape of an arch
enardecer: *vt.* to inflame; to fire
enarenar: *vt.* to cover with sand
enarenarse: *vr.* to be covered with sand
encabezamiento: *nm.* action of leading or heading
encabezar: *vt.* to head; to lead
encadenado: *aj.* chained
encadenamiento: *nm.* chaining
encadenar: *vt.* to chain
encajado: *aj.* encased; lodged
encajar: *vt.* to put; to insert
encaje: *nm.* encasing; forcing of

something inside another object
encajonar: *vt.* to place in a drawer; to box in
encamado: *aj.* bedridden
encamar: *vt.* to put to bed
encamarse: *vr.* to be bedridden
encaminar: *vt.* to start someone down a path
encaminarse: *vr.* to follow a pursuit
encañado: *nm.* fortified with cannon
encañonar: *vt.* to aim a cannon or firearm
encantado: *aj.* charmed; enchanted
encantador: *aj.* enchanting; charming
encantamiento: *nm.* spell; charm
encantar: *vt.* to cast a spell on; to enchant
encanto: *nm.* charm; spell
encaprichamiento: *nm.* capriciousness
encapricharse: *vr.* to act capriciously; to be capricious
encarado: *aj.* referring to facial appearance
encarar: *vt.* to face; to aim
encararse: *vr.* to be facing
encarcelación: *nf.* incarceration
encarcelar: *vt.* to jail; incarcerate; *vr.* to achieve a fine reputation
encarecimiento: *nm.* increase
encargado: *aj.* in charge
encargar: *vt.* to entrust; *vr.* to take charge
encargarse: *vr.* to take charge of
encargo: *nm.* task; assignment
encariñarse: *vr.* to be fond of
encarnación: *nf.* incarnation
encarnado: *aj.* incarnate
encarnar: *vt.* to incarnate
encarnizado -da: *aj.* bloody
encasillar: *vt.* to pigeon-hole
encasquillar: *vt.* to put a tip on; *vr.* to stick

encelar: *vt.* to make jealous
encelarse: *vr.* to become jealous
encendedor: *nm.* lighter
encender: *vt.* to light; set fire to
encenderse: *vr.* to become quickly angry
encendido: *nm.* lighting; turning on; ignition
encerado -da: 1. *aj.* waxy; 2. *nm.* blackboard
encerar: *vt.* to wax
encerrado: *aj.* locked up; enclosed
encerrar: *vt.* to shut in; lock in
enchufar: *vt.* to switch on; plug in
encía: *nf.* gum
enciclopedia: *nf.* encyclopedia
enciclopédico: *aj.* encyclopedic
encierro: *nm.* locking up; enclosing
encima: *av.* on top of
encimar: *vt.* to place on top
encintar: *vt.* to tie with a belt or drawstring; to wrap with tape
enclaustrado: *aj.* hidden
enclaustrar: *vt.* to hide; to place in a secret place
enclaustrarse: *vr.* to be hidden; to be placed in a secret place
enclavar: *vt.* to nail; to pierce
encoger: *vt.* to shrink; contract
encogido: *aj.* shrunk
encogimiento: *nm.* shrinking
encolar: *vt.* to glue; to size
encolerizar: *vt.* to anger; irritate
encolerizarse: *vr.* to become very angry; to become filled with ire
encontrado: *aj.* found
encontrar: *vt.* to find; to meet
encontrarse: *vr.* to meet up with; to find (oneself)
encontronazo: *nm.* collision; dispute
encorajar: *vt.* to anger
encorajarse: *vr.* to become angry
encordonar: *vt.* to tie with rope or cord

encorvar: *vt.* to bend; to bend over
encrucijada: *nf.* crossroads
encrudecer: *vt.* to make raw; especially one's nerves; to annoy
encrudecerse: *vr.* to become annoyed
encuadernar: *vt.* to bind
encuadramiento: *nm.* framing
encuadrar: *vt.* to frame
encuadrarse: *vr.* to be framed
encuadre: *nm.* framing of a photographic scene
encubiertamente: *av.* secretly
encubierto: *aj.* covered-up or hidden
encubrimiento: *nm.* hiding or covering-up of something
encubrir: *vt.* to cover up; to hide
encubrirse: *vr.* to be covered up; to be hidden
encuentro: *nm.* encounter; chance meeting
encuesta: *nf.* poll
encuestador;-a: *nmf.* pollster
encuestar: *vt.* to poll
encumbrado: *aj.* elevated; on the mountaintop; successful; famous
encumbramiento: *nm.* act of elevating; fame; success
encumbrar: *vt.* to raise; elevate; to rise
endeble: *aj.* weak
endemoniado: *aj.* demon-possessed; extremely angry
enderezamiento: *nm.* straightening up; the act of straightening up something
enderezar: *vt.* to straighten up
enderezarse: *vr.* to straighten oneself up
endeudarse: *vr.* to go into debt
endiabladamente: *av.* devilishly
endiablado: *aj.* furious
endiosamiento: *nm.* deification
endiosar: *vt.* to make into a god; to

deify
endulzar: *vt.* to sweeten
endurecer: *vt.* to harden; to harden
endurecimiento: *nm.* hardening; hardness
enemigo: *aj.* enemy
enemistad: *nf.* enmity
enemistar: *vt.* to make an enemy
enemistarse: *vr.* to become an enemy
energético: *aj.* energy-giving
energía: *nf.* energy
enérgico: *aj.* energetic
enero: *nm.* January
enervación: *nf.* enervation
enervante: *aj.* enervating
enervar: *vt.* to enervate
enfadadizo: *aj.* easily angered
enfadado: *aj.* irritated
enfadar: *vt.* to irritate; to bother
enfadarse: *vr.* to be irritated by
enfado: *nm.* anger
enfadoso: *aj.* irritating
énfasis: *nmf.* emphasis
enfermar (se): *vt.* to become sick
enfermedad: *nf.* sickness; illness
enfermería: *nf.* hospital
enfermero; -a: *nmf.* nurse
enfermizo: *aj.* easily made sick
enfermo: *aj.* sick; ill
enfervorizar: *vt.* to fill with fervor or enthusiasm
enfilar: *vt.* to line up
enflaquecer: *vt.* to make thinner; to discourage
enflaquecido: *aj.* discouraged
enflaquecimiento: *nm.* weight loss; discouragement
enfocar: *vt.* to focus
enfoque: *nm.* focus
enfrentamiento: *nm.* confrontation
enfrentar: *vt.* to confront; to face; to meet face to face
enfrente: *av.* facing; in front

enfriador: *aj.* cooling
enfriamiento: *nm.* cooling
enfriar: *vt.* to make cold
enfurecer: *vt.* to infuriate; enrage; *vr.* to rage
enfurecimiento: *nm.* act of becoming furious; fury
engalanado: *aj.* adorned for a celebration
engalanar: *vt.* to adorn
engañadizo: *aj.* easily deceived
engañar: *vt.* to deceive; to cheat
enganchar: *vt.* to hook
engaño: *nm.* deception
engañoso: *aj.* deceptive
engendrar: *vt.* to engender; beget
engendro: *nm.* deformed creature
engomar: *vt.* gum; glue
engorda: *nf.* fattening of animals
engordar: *vt.* to make something fat
engorde: *nm.* fattening of animals
engranaje: *nm.* gearing
engrandecer: *vt.* to enlarge; amplify
engrandecimiento: *nm.* enlargement
engrasar: *vt.* to grease; lubricate
engrase: *nm.* lubrication; greasing
engrosar: *vt.* to thicken
engrudo: *nm.* paste; glue
enguantado: *aj.* gloved
enhebrar: *vt.* to thread
enhorabuena: *nf.* congratulations
enigma: *nf.* enigma
enigmático: *aj.* enigmatic
enjabonar: *vt.* to put soap on something
enjaular: *vt.* to put in a cage
enjoyar: *vt.* to put on jewels
enjuagar: *vt.* to rinse
enjuiciamiento: *nm.* the judgment of trial or judge
enjuiciar: *vt.* to examine
enlace: *nm.* the union or marriage of newlyweds
enladrillado: *aj.* bricked; of brick

enladrillar: *vt.* to lay bricks
enlazar: *vt.* to tie with rope
enloquecedor: *aj.* referring to that which drives one crazy
enloquecer: *vt.* to drive crazy
enloquecimiento: *nm.* the act of becoming or going crazy
enlutado: *aj.* mourning
enlutar: *v.* to mourn
enmaderar: *vt.* to reface with wood
enmarcar: *vt.* to frame
enmascarado -da: *aj.* mask
enmendadura: *nf.* mending; correction
enmendar: *vt.* to amend; to correct; to change
enmienda: *nf.* emendation; mending; correction
enmudecer: *vt.* to silence
enmudecerse: *vr.* to be silent
ennegrecer: *vt.* to blacken
ennoblecer: *vt.* to ennoble
enojadizo: *aj.* easily-angered
enojado: *aj.* angry
enojar: *vt.* to anger; annoy; to become angry
enojo: *nm.* anger
enojón: *aj.* frequently angry
enorgullecer: *vt.* to make proud; to be proud
enorgullecimiento: *nm.* the act of becoming prideful
enorme: *aj.* enormous; vast
enormemente: *av.* enormously
enormidad: *nf.* enormity
enrabiar: *vt.* to give rabies; to anger
enraizado: *aj.* having roots; rooted
enraizar: *vi.* to sprout roots
enramada: *nf.* ornament made of branches or twigs
enramado: *aj.* interlaced (branches)
enranciar: *vt.* to make rancid
enrarecer: *vt.* to make rare; to dissipate

enrarecido: *aj.* rare; uncommon
enredadera: *nf.* climbing vine
enredar: *vt.* to tangle
enredarse: *vr.* to become tangled
enredo: *nm.* confusion
enredoso: *aj.* difficult; confusing
enrejado: *aj.* with bars
enrejar: *vt.* to put up a protective grill
enrevesado: *aj.* frisky; compli-cated
enriquecer: *vt.* to enrich
enriquecerse: *vr.* to become rich
enriquecimiento: *nm.* enrichment
enrojecer: *vti.* to redden
enrojecerse: *vr.* to become red
enrojecimiento: *nm.* reddening
enroscar: *vt.* to twist
ensalada: *nf.* salad
ensalzar: *vt.* to extol
ensanchamiento: *nm.* widening
ensanchar: *vt.* to widen something; to make wider
ensanche: *nm.* width
ensangrentado: *aj.* bloodstained
ensangrentar: *vt.* to stain with blood
ensayar: *vt.* to try; try on; to practice
ensayista: *nmf.* essayist
ensayo: *nm.* trying; testing; essay; rehearsal
enseñado: *aj.* taught
enseñanza: *nf.* teaching; education
enseñar: *vt.* to teach; to train
enseres: *nm. pl.* household goods
ensillar: *vt.* to saddle
ensombrecer: *vt.* to cover with a shadow
ensoñación: *nf.* daydreaming
ensoñador: *aj.* daydreaming
ensoñar: *v.* to daydream
ensordecedor: *aj.* deafening
ensordecer: *vt.* to deafen
ensordecimiento: *nm.* deafness
ensuciar: *vt.* to dirty; to stain; to soil
ensueño: *nm.* daydream; fantasy

entablado: *nm.* floor or fence made of wooden planks
entablar: *vt.* to board; board up
entablillado: *nm.* the placing of a splint
entablillar: *vt.* to splint
entallar: *vt.* to carve; to engrave
ente: *nm.* being
entendedor;-a: *nmf.* understanding person
entender: *vt.* to understand
entenderse: *vr.* to understand each other
entendido: *aj.* understood
entendimiento: *nm.* understanding
entenebrecer: *vt.* to turn dark and gloomy
entenebrecerse: *vr.* to become dark and gloomy
enterado: *aj.* learned; understood
enteramente: *av.* entirely
enterar: *vr.* to inform
enterarse: *vr.* to notice; to learn that; to learn of
entereza: *nf.* integrity; wholeness
enternecedor: *aj.* causing tender-heartedness
enternecer: *vt.* to make tender
enternecidamente: *av.* tenderly; tiernamente
enternecimiento: *nm.* tenderness
entero -ra: *aj.* whole; entire; complete
enterrador: *nm.* gravedigger; person who buries
enterrar: *vt.* to inter; bury
entidad: *nf.* entity
entierro: *nm.* burial
entintar: *vt.* to fill with ink
entonación: *nf.* intonation
entonado: *aj.* tuned
entonar: *vt.* to intone; to tune
entonces: ad*v.* then; and so
entontecer: *vt.* to make someone feel dizzy or woozy
entontecerse: *vr.* to feel dizzy or woozy
entornar: *vt.* to upset
entorpecer: *v.* to lose one's physical or mental dexterity
entorpecimiento: *nm.* the act of losing one's physical or mental dexterity
entrada: *nf.* entrance; appetizer
entraña: *nf.* the center; the nucleus
entrañable: *aj.* close; intimate
entrañablemente: *av.* intimately
entrañar: *vt.* to bury deep
entrañas: *nf. pl.* entrails; bowels
entrante: *aj.* entering; next
entrar: *vi.* to enter
entreabierto: *aj.* partially open
entreabrir: *vt.* to open partially
entreacto: *nm.* intermission
entrecejo: *nm.* space between the eyebrows
entrecortado: *aj.* broken up; partly cut
entrecortar: *vt.* to cut in between
entrecubiertas: *nfpl.* space between decks
entredicho: *nm.* prohibition
entrefino: *aj.* somewhat fine
entrega: *nf.* giving or delivering
entregar: *vt.* to give or deliver
entregarse: *vr.* to give oneself to something or someone
entrelazado: *aj.* woven; knitted
entrelazar: *vt.* to braid
entrelazarse: *vr.* to be braided
entrelinear: *vt.* to write between the lines
entremedias: *av.* in between
entremés: *nm.* side dish; hors d'oeuvre
entremeter: *vt.* to insert something between things
entremezclar: *vt.* to mix in with

other things
entrenar: *vt.* to train; to coach
entrepierna: *nf.* inner thigh; crotch
entreponer: *vt.* to put between two
things
entresacar: *vt.* to take out from a
collection
entresuelo: *nm.* mezzanine
entretejer: *vt.* to interweave
entretela: *nf.* interlining
entretener: *vt.* to entertain; to amuse
entretenido: *aj.* entertained
entretenimiento: *nm.* entertainment
entrever: *vt.* to glimpse; descry
entrevista: *nf.* interview
entrevistador;-a: *nmf.* interviewer
entrevistar: *vt.* to interview
entristecedor: *aj.* saddening
entristecer: *vt.* to make sad
entristecerse: *vr.* to become sad
entrometido: *aj.* meddlesome; nosy
entronización: *nf.* enthroning
entronizar: *vt.* to enthrone
entuerto: *nm.* wrong
enturbiar: *vt.* to stir up; to muddy
enturbiarse: *vr.* to become turbid
entusiasmar: *vt.* to generate
enthusiasm
entusiasmo: *nm.* enthusiasm
entusiasta: *aj.* enthusiastic; referring
to people
entusiasta: *nmf.* enthusiast
enumeración: *nf.* enumeration
enumerar: *vt.* to enumerate
enunciar: *vt.* to enounce
envalentonamiento: *nm.* boasting;
bragging
envalentonarse: *vr.* to take courage;
to rise to the occasion
envanecer: *vt.* to cause arrogance or
vanity
envanecerse: *vr.* to become vain
envanecimiento: *nm.* the act of
becoming conceited

envasado: *aj.* bottled
envasado: *nm.* bottling
envasar: *vt.* to bottle
envase: *nm.* packing; bottling;
container
envejecer: *vt.* to age; make old
envejecido: *aj.* aging
envejecimiento: *nm.* old age
envenenamiento: *nm.* poisoning
envenenar: *vt.* to poison
enverdecer: *vi.* to turn green
envergadura: *nf.* breadth
enviado: *nm.* envoy
enviar: *vt.* to send
enviciar: *vt.* to involve someone in a
vice
envidia: *nf.* envy; grudge
envidiable: *aj.* enviable
envidiar: *vt.* to envy
envidiosamente: *av.* enviously
envidioso: *aj.* envious
envio: *nm.* sending; shipment
enviudar: *vi.* to become a widow or
a widower
envoltorio: *nm.* bundle
envoltura: *nf.* wrapping
envolver: *vt.* to wrap; wrap up
envolverse: *vr.* to become involved
enyesado: *aj.* covered with plaster
enyesado: *nm.* plastering
enyesar: *vt.* to plaster
épica: *nf.* epic poetry
episódico: *aj.* episodic
episodio: *nm.* episode; incident
época: *nf.* epoch; age; time
equidistancia: *nf.* equidistance
equidistante: *aj.* equidistant
equidistar: *vi.* to be equidistant
equilátero: *aj.* equilateral
equilibrado: *aj.* balanced
equilibrar: *vt.* to balance; to gain
equilibrium
equilibrarse: *vr.* to gain one's
equilibrium

equilibrio: *nm.* equilibrium
equilibrismo: *nm.* balancing act
equilibrista: *nmf.* tightrope walker
equipaje: *nm.* luggage; baggage
equiparar: *vt.* to compare
equivalencia: *nf.* equivalence
equivalente: *aj.* equivalent
equivaler: *vi.* to be equivalent
equivocación: *nf.* mistake
equivocadamente: *av.* mistakenly
equivocado: *aj.* wrong
equivocar: *vr.* to mistake; to make a mistake
equivocarse: *vr.* to be mistaken
eremita: *nm.* hermit; often isolated for penitence and prayer
erigir: *vt.* to erect; build
erizo: *nm.* hedgehog
ermita: *nf.* small church isolated from town
erradamente: *av.* erroneously; mistakenly
errado: *aj.* mistaken
errante: *aj.* wandering
errar: *vt.* to miss; to wander; to err
errata: *nf.* errata
errático: *aj.* erratic
erróneamente: *av.* erroneously
error: *nm.* error
eructar: *vi.* to belch
erudición: *nf.* erudition
eruditamente: *av.* eruditely
erudito: *aj.* erudite
esbeltez: *nf.* gracefulness; slenderness
esbelto: *aj.* svelte; slender
esbozo: *nm.* sketch
escabeche: *nm.* pickle
escabroso -sa: *aj.* scabrous
escala: *nf.* ladder; scale; layover
escalador;-a: *nmf.* rock climber; mountain climber
escalafón: *nm.* organizational level; by seniority or position

escalar: *vt.* to escalate; to scale; to climb
escalera: *nf.* staircase; stairs; ladder
escalerilla: *nf.* small ladder
escalofriante: *aj.* producing goose bumps; scary
escalofrío: *nm.* goose bump; shudder
escalón: *nm.* stair step
escalonadamente: *av.* in a stair-stepped fashion
escalonado: *aj.* with stair steps
escalonar: *vt.* to advance one stair step at a time
escama: *nf.* scale
escandalizar: *vt.* to scandalize
escándalo: *nm.* scandal; commotion; disturbance
escandalosamente: *av.* scandalously; noisily
escandaloso: *aj.* scandalous; with a lot of noise
escaño: *nm.* settle; bench
escapada: *nf.* escapade
escapar: *vi.* to escape; get away; to escape
escaparate: *nm.* shop window; showcase
escaparatista: *nmf.* person who decorates showcases
escaparse: *vr.* to escape
escapatoria: *nf.* means or way of escape
escape: *nm.* escape; exhaust
escarabajo: *nm.* beetle
escarcha: *nf.* frost
escarlata: *aj.* scarlet
escarola: *nf.* endive
escasamente: *av.* scarcely
escasear: *vi.* to be scarce; to run low
escasez: *nf.* scarcity
escaso -sa: *aj.* short; scarce
escatimar: *vt.* to spend the minimum necessary
escena: *nf.* scene

escenario: *nm.* stage; set

escénico: *aj.* scenic

escenografía: *nf.* scenography

escenógrafo;-a: *nm.* scene writer

esclarecer: *vt.* to enlighten; to resolve a conflict

esclarecido: *aj.* illuminated; explained

esclarecimiento: *nm.* enlightenment; resolution of a conflict

esclavitud: *nf.* slavery

esclavizar: *vt.* to enslave

esclavo;-a: *nmf.* slave

escoba: *nf.* broom

escocer: *vt.* to annoy; to displease; to choose

escogido: *aj.* chosen

escogimiento: *nm.* choosing

escolar: *nmf.* scholar

escolaridad: *nf.* level of studies

escolástico: *aj.* scholastic

escolta: *nf.* escort

escombro: *nm.* escombros; shambles

esconder: *vt.* to hide

esconderse: *vr.* to be hidden

escondidas: *av.* hidden

escondite: *nm.* hiding place

escondrijo: *nm.* hiding place

escopeta: *nf.* shotgun

escopetazo: *nm.* shot with a shotgun

escoria: *nf.* dross; refuse

escote: *nm.* low neck

escribano: *nm.* court clerk

escribano;-a: *nmf.* word from antiquity meaning writer

escribir: *nm.* writing; *vt. & vi.* to write

escribir: *vt.* to write

escribirse: *vr.* to correspond with each other

escrito: *aj.* written

escritor -ra: *nmf.* writer; author

escritorio: *nm.* desk

escritura: *nf.* scripture

escriturar: *vt.* to formalize a contract

escrúpulo: *nm.* scruple

escrupulosamente: *av.* scrupulously

escrupulosidad: *nf.* scrupulousness

escrupuloso: *aj.* scrupulous

escucha: *nf.* act of listening

escuchar: *vt.* to hear

escudar: *vt.* to shield

escudarse: *vr.* to shield oneself

escudería: *nf.* office of squire; auto or motorcycle racing team

escudero: *nm.* maker of shields; squire

escudo: *nm.* shield

escuela: *nf.* school

escuetamente: *av.* plainly; briefly; precisely

escueto: *aj.* plain; brief; precise

esculpir: *vt.* to carve; to sculpt

escultismo: *nm.* sculpting

escultor;-a: *nmf.* sculptor

escultura: *nf.* sculpture

escultural: *aj.* sculptural

escupir: *vt.* to spit

escurrir: *vt.* to drain

ese; esa: *aj.* dem. that

ése; ésa: *pron.* dem that one

esencia: *nf.* essence

esencial: *aj.* essential

esencialmente: *av.* essentially

esfera: *nf.* sphere

esférico: *aj.* spherical

esferoide: *nm.* spheroid

esforzado: *aj.* forced; with effort

esforzar: *vr.* to force; to make an effort

esforzarse: *vr.* to force oneself

esfuerzo: *nm.* force; effort

eslabón: *nm.* link

eslora: *nf.* length

esmaltar: *vt.* to enamel

esmerar: *vt.* to polish; to take pains

eso: *pron.* dem. neut. that

espaciador: *nm.* space-bar

espacial: *aj.* spatial
espaciar: *vt.* to space; to make space
espacio: *nm.* space; room
espacioso: *aj.* spacious
espada: *nf.* sword
espadachín: *nm.* sword fighter
espalda: *nf.* back
espaldilla: *nf.* disk or bone of the back
español: *aj.* Spanish
españolada: *aj.* appearing to be Spanish
españolismo: *nm.* affinity for Spanish culture
españolista: *nmf.* fan of Spanish culture
españolizar: *vt.* to introduce Spanish word into a language
españolizarse: *vr.* to become Spanish
espantadizo: *aj.* easily frightened
espantapájaros: *nm.* scarecrow
espantar: *vt.* to scare; to frighten
espantarse: *vr.* to be frightened
espanto: *nm.* fright
espantoso: *aj.* frightening
esparcir: *vt.* to scatter; to spread
especial: *aj.* special
especialista: *nmf.* specialist
especialización: *nf.* specialization
especializado: *aj.* specialized
especializar: *vt.* to specialize
especialmente: *av.* especially
especie: *nf.* species
especificación: *nf.* specification
específicamente: *av.* specifically
especificar: *vt.* to specify
específico: *aj.* specific
espécimen: *nm.* specimen
espectacular: *aj.* spectacular
espectacularmente: *av.* spectacularly
espectáculo: *nm.* show; spectacle
espectador;-a: *nmf.* spectator

especulación: *nf.* speculation
especulador;-a: *nmf.* speculator
especular: *vi.* to speculate
especulativo: *aj.* speculative
espejear: *vt.* to look in the mirror
espejismo: *nm.* mirage
espejo: *nm.* mirror
espera: *nf.* expectation
esperanza: *nf.* hope
esperanzador: *aj.* hope-inspiring
esperanzar: *vt.* to inspire hope
esperar: *vt.* to wait; to hope; to expect
espesante: *nm.* thickener
espesar: *vt.* to thicken
espesarse: *vr.* to become thick
espeso -sa: *aj.* thick; heavy
espesor: *nm.* density of a liquid; volume of a solid
espesura: *nf.* thickness
espía: *nmf.* spy
espiar: *vt.* to spy
espiga: *nf.* ear; sprig
espigado: *aj.* slender
espigar: *vt.* to pick
espigón: *nm.* sharp ear or sprig
espina: *nf.* thorn; spine
espinaca: *nf.* spinach
espinal: *aj.* spinal
espinazo: *nm.* spinal cord
espinilla: *nf.* shinbone; pimple; blackhead
espinillera: *nf.* shin guard
espino: *nm.* thorny plant about meter tall
espinoso -sa: *aj.* thorny
espionaje: *nm.* spying; espionage
espiritismo: *nm.* belief in the spirit world
espiritista: *nmf.* believer in the spirit world
espíritu: *nm.* spirit
espiritual: *aj.* spiritual
espiritualidad: *nf.* spirituality

espiritualismo: *nm.* spiritualism
espiritualista: *nmf.* spiritualist
espiritualmente: *av.* spiritually
espléndidamente: *av.* splendidly
espléndido -da: *aj.* splendid
esplendor: *nm.* splendor
esplendoroso: *aj.* brilliant; bright
espontáneamente: *av.* spontaneously
espontaneidad: *nf.* spontaneity
espontáneo: *aj.* spontaneous
esposa: *nf.* wife
esposado: *aj.* handcuffed
esposar: *vt.* to put on handcuffs
esposas: *nfpl.* handcuffs
esposo -sa: *nmf.* spouse
espuela: *nf.* Spur
espuma: *nf.* foam
espumar: *vt.* to skim; to foam
espumarajo: *nm.* foamy saliva
espumilla: *nf.* creamy pie or cake topping
espumoso: *aj.* foamy esqueleto skeleton
esputo: *nm.* sputum
esquela: *nf.* note
esquelético: *aj.* skeletal; skeleton-like
esqueleto: *nm.* skeleton
esquema: *nf.* scheme
esquemático: *aj.* schematic
esquematizar: *vt.* to make a schematic drawing
esquiar: *vi.* to ski
esquina: *nf.* corner
esquinado: *aj.* having the form of a corner; with corners
esquivar: *vt.* to avoid; to withdraw
esquivo: *aj.* withdrawn; unsociable
estabilidad: *nf.* stability
estabilización: *nf.* stabilization
estabilizador: *nm.* stabilizer
estabilizar: *vt.* to stabilize
estabilizarse: *vr.* to become stabilized

estable: *aj.* stable; firm
establecer: *vt.* to establish
establecerse: *vr.* to be established
establecimiento: *nm.* establishment
estación: *nf.* station; season of the year
estacional: *aj.* seasonal
estacionar: *vt.* to park; to station
estadio: *nm.* stadium
estadística: *nf.* statistics; statistic
estadístico: *aj.* statistical
estado: *nm.* state; condition
estafa: *nf.* trick
estafar: *vt.* to defraud; to swindle
estallar: *vi.* to burst; to explode
estallido: *nm.* noise of an explosion
estampa: *nf.* print; stamp
estampación: *nf.* imprinting
estampado: *aj.* stamped; printed
estampar: *vt.* to print; to stamp
estampilla: *nf.* postage stamp
estancar: *vt.* to staunch
estancia: *nf.* stay; room
estandarte: *nm.* standard; banner
estaño: *nm.* tin
estanque: *nm.* reservoir
estante: *nm.* shelf
estantería: *nf.* shelving
estar: *vi.* to be
estatua: *nf.* statue
estatuaria: *nf.* technique of statue-making
estatuario: *aj.* statue
estatuilla: *nf.* small statue; statuette
estatura: *nf.* stature; height
éste; ésta: *pron. dem.* this one
estepa: *nf.* step
estéril: *aj.* sterile; barren
esterilidad: *nf.* sterility
esterilización: *nf.* sterilization
esterilizador: *nm.* sterilizer
esterilizar: *vt.* to sterilize
estética: *nf.* aesthetics
esteticista: *nmf.* specialist in

cosmetics
estético: *aj.* relating to aesthetics or the study of beauty
estilarse: *vr.* to be in style
estilista: *nmf.* stylist
estilística: *nf.* stylistics
estilístico: *aj.* stylistic
estilización: *nf.* stylization
estilizar: *vt.* to stylize
estilo: *nm.* style
estima: *nf.* esteem; estimate
estimable: *aj.* estimable
estimación: *nf.* estimation
estimado: *aj.* estimated
estimar: *vt.* to esteem; to estimate
estimulante: 1. *aj.* stimulating; 2. *nm.* stimulant
estimular: *vt.* to stimulate
estímulo: *nm.* stimulus
estío: *nm.* summer
estipulación: *nf.* stipulation
estipular: *vt.* to stipulate; lay down
estirado: *aj.* presumptuous
estirar: *vt.* to stretch
estirón: *nm.* violent pull
estirpe: *nf.* stock
estival: *aj.* aestival; summer
esto: *pron; dem*
estocada: *nf.* thrust; stab
estofado -da: *aj.* stew
estofar: *vt.* to stew
estomacal: *aj.* stomach
estómago: *nm.* stomach
estorbar: *vt.* to hinder; to obstruct; to block
estorbo: *nm.* obstruction
estornudar: *vi.* to sneeze
estrafalario -ria: *aj.* con. slovenly; sloppy
estratificación: *nf.* stratification
estratificar: *vt.* to stratify
estrato: *nm.* stratus
estratosfera: *nf.* stratosphere
estrechamente: *av.* closely;

intimately
estrechamiento: *nm.* narrowing
estrechar: *vt.* to make narrow; to clasp hands
estrechez: *nf.* lack of width
estrecho: *aj.* narrow
estrechura: *nf.* lack of width; narrowness
estrella: *nf.* star
estrella fugaz: shooting star
estrellado: *aj.* star-shaped
estrellar: *vt.* to cover with stars; to crack
estrellato: *nm.* star status; referring to famous people
estrellón: *nm.* type of fireworks that forms a star in the air
estremecedor: *aj.* causing quivering; shivering; shuddering
estremecer: *vt.* to cause to quiver; shiver; or shudder
estremecerse: *vr.* to quiver; shiver; or shudder
estremecido: *aj.* quivering; shivering; shuddering
estremecimiento: *nm.* quivering; shivering; shuddering
estreñir: *vt.* to bind; restrain
estrépito: *nm.* noise
estribillo: *nm.* burden; chorus
estricto -ta: *aj.* strict; severe
estropear: *vt.* to abuse; to spoil; to ruin
estructura: *nf.* structure
estructural: *aj.* structural
estructurar: *vt.* to structure
estruendo: *nm.* crash
estrujar: *vt.* to squeeze; to crush
estudiado: *aj.* studied
estudiantado: *nm.* student body
estudiante: *nm.* student; school boy
estudiantil: *aj.* relating to students
estudiantina: *nf.* musical group made up of students

estudiar: *vt.* to study
estudio: *nm.* study
estudioso: *aj.* studious
estufa: *nf.* stove
estupendamente: *av.* -mente stupendously
estupendo: *aj.* stupendous
estupidez: *nf.* stupidity
estúpido: *aj.* extremely stupid
etapa: *nf.* stage
eternidad: *nf.* eternity
eterno: *aj.* eternal
ética: *nf.* ethics
ético: *aj.* ethical
etiqueta: *nf.* etiquette; formality
evacuar: *vt.* to evacuate; to empty
evadir: *vt.* to avoid; to evade
evaluar: *vt.* to evaluate
evangélico: *aj.* evangelical
evangelismo: *nm.* evangelism
evangelista: *nmf.* evangelist
evangelización: *nf.* evangelization
evangelizador: *aj.* evangelizing
evangelizar: *vt.* to evangelize
evaporación: *nf.* evaporation
evaporar: *vt.* to evaporate
evidencia: *nf.* evidence
evidenciar: *vt.* to show evidence; to prove with evidence
evidente: *aj.* evident
evidentemente: *av.* evidently
evitable: *aj.* avoidable
evitar: *vt.* to avoid
evocación: *nf.* evocation
evocar: *vt.* to evoke
evolución: *nf.* evolution
evolucionar: *vi.* to evolve
evolucionismo: *nm.* evolutionism
evolucionista: *aj.* evolutionist
evolutivo: *aj.* evolutional; evolutionary
exactamente: *av.* exactly
exactitud: *nf.* exactitude
exacto: *aj.* exact

exageración: *nf.* exaggeration
exageradamente: *av.* exaggeratedly
exagerado: *aj.* exaggerated
exagerar: *vt.* to exaggerate
exaltación: *nf.* exaltation
exaltado: *aj.* exalted
exaltar: *vt.* to exalt
examen: *nm.* exam
examinador;-a: *nmf.* examiner
examinar: *vt.* to examine
excedente: *nm.* surplus
exceder: *vt.* to exceed
excelencia: *nf.* excellence
excelente: *aj.* excellent
excelso: *aj.* prominent; superior
excepción: *nf.* exception
excepcional: *aj.* exceptional
excepto: *av.* except
exceptuar: *vt.* to except
excesivo: *aj.* excessive
exceso: *nm.* excess
excitabilidad: *nf.* excitability
excitable: *aj.* excitable
excitación: *nf.* excitation
excitante: *aj.* exciting
excitar: *vt.* to excite
exclamación: *nf.* exclamation
exclamar: *vi.* to exclaim
exclamatorio: *aj.* exclamatory
excluir: *vt.* to exclude; eject
exclusión: *nf.* exclusion
exclusivamente: *av.* exclusively
exclusive: *av.* exclusive
exclusividad: *nf.* exclusivity
exclusivismo: *nm.* exclusivism
exclusivista: *nmf.* person who practices exclusivism
exclusivo: *aj.* exclusive
excursión: *nf.* excursion exhalar to exhale
excursionismo: *nm.* practice of taking excursions for educational or recreational purposes
excusa: *nf.* excuse; apology

excusar: *vt.* to excuse; to avoid
exhalación: *nf.* exhalation
exhalar: *vt.* to exhale
exhibición: *nf.* exhibition
exhibicionismo: *nm.* exhibitionism
exhibicionista: *nmf.* exhibitionist
exhibir: *vt.* to exhibit
exigencia: *nf.* demand
exigente: *aj.* demanding
exigir: *vt.* to demand
eximir: *vt.* to exempt
existencia: *nf.* existence
existencial: *aj.* existential
existencialismo: *nm.* existentialism
existencialista: *nmf.* existentialist
existente: *aj.* existent
existir: *vi.* to exist; be
éxito: *nm.* outcome; success
exorable: *aj.* easily convinced
expandir: *vt.* to expand
expandirse: *vr.* to be expanded
expansión: *nf.* expansion
expansionismo: *nm.* expansionism
expansionista: *aj.* expansionist
expansivo: *aj.* expansive
expatriación: *nf.* expatriation
expatriado;-a: *nmf.* expatriate
expatriar: *vt.* to expatriate
expedición: *nf.* expedition
expedicionario: *aj.* expeditionary
expedidor;-a: *nmf.* expeditor
expedir: *vt.* to send; to ship; to expedite
expeditivo: *aj.* expeditious
expedito: *aj.* expedited
experiencia: *nf.* experience; trial
experimentación: *nf.* experimentation
experimentado: *aj.* experimented
experimental: *aj.* experimental
experimentar: *vt.* to test; to try out; to experiment
experimento: *nm.* experiment
expertamente: *av.* expertly

experto: *aj.* expert
expiración: *nf.* expiration
expirar: *vi.* to expire
explanación indicado: *aj.* indicated
explicable: *aj.* explicable
explicación: *nf.* explanation
explicar: *vt.* to explain; to expound
explicativo: *aj.* explicative
explicitar: *vt.* to be explicit
explícito: *aj.* explicit
explorador -ra: *nm.* explorer; boy scout
explosión: *nf.* explosion
explosionar: *vti.* to explode
explosivo: 1. *aj.* explosive; 2. *nm.* explosive
explotable: *aj.* exploitable
explotación: *nf.* exploitation
explotador;-a: *nmf.* exploiter
explotar: *vt.* to run; to operate; to explode; to exploit
exportable: *aj.* exportable
exportación: *nf.* exportation
exportador;-a: *nmf.* exporter
exportar: *vt.* to export
exposición: *nf.* exposition
expositivo: *aj.* expositive; explanatory
expositor;-a: *nmf.* person who explains or demonstrates something
expresado: *aj.* expressed
expresamente: *av.* expressly
expresar: *vt.* to express
expresión: *nf.* expression
expresionismo: *nm.* expressionism
expresionista: *nmf.* expressionist
expresivo: *aj.* expressive
expreso: *av.* express
exprimir: *vt.* to express
expropiar: *vt.* to expropriate
expuesto: *aj.* exposed
expulsar: *vt.* to expel
expulsión: *nf.* expulsion
expulsor: *nm.* ejector

expurgación: *nf.* expurgation
expurgar: *vt.* to expurgate
exquisitez: *nf.* exquisiteness
exquisito: *aj.* exquisite
extemporáneo: *aj.* extemporaneous
extender: *vt.* to extend; to stretch out
extendido: *aj.* extended
extensamente: *av.* extensively
extensión: *nf.* extension
extenso: *aj.* extensive
extenuación: *nf.* extenuation
extenuante: *aj.* extenuating; exhausting
extenuar: *vt.* to exhaust
exterior: 1. *aj.* exterior; 2. *nm.* exterior
exterioridad: *nf.* appearance of things
exteriorización: *nf.* manifestation of one's ideas or thoughts
exteriorizar: *vt.* to reveal; to make manifest
exteriormente: *av.* outwardly
externamente: *av.* externally
externo: *aj.* external
extinción: *nf.* extinction
extinguidor: *nm.* fire extinguisher
extinguir: *vt.* to extinguish; to put out
extinto: *aj.* extinct
extintor: *nm.* fire extinguisher
extraer: *vt.* to extract; pull out
extraescolar: *aj.* extracurricular
extrafino: *aj.* extra fine
extrajudicial: *aj.* extra-judicial
extralimitarse: *vr.* to go beyond the limits
extramuros: *av.* outside the city
extrañamente: *av.* strangely
extrañar: *vt.* to surprise
extrañeza: *nf.* amazement or surprise
extranjerismo: *nm.* inclination to prefer foreign products or culture
extranjero: *aj.* foreign

extraño: 1. *aj.* strange; 2. *nmf.* stranger
extraoficial: *aj.* unofficial; unsanctioned
extraordinaria: *nf.* bonus
extraordinario: *aj.* extraordinary
extraterrestre: 1. *aj.* extraterrestrial; 2. *nmf.* extraterrestrial
extraterritorial: *aj.* extra-territorial
extravagancia: *nf.* extravagance
extravagante: *aj.* extravagant
extraviado: *aj.* lost
extraviar: *vt.* to lead astray; to go astray
extravío: *nm.* act of being lost
extremadamente: *av.* extremely
extremado: *aj.* extreme
extremar: *vt.* to adopt an extreme attitude
extremaunción: *nf.* extreme unction; ritual of the Catholic church
extremidad: *nf.* extremity
extremismo: *nm.* extremism
extremista: *aj.* extremist
extremo: *aj.* last; furthest
exuberancia: *nf.* exuberance

F

fábrica: *nf.* manufacture; factory
fabricación: *nf.* fabrication
fabricante: *nmf.* factory worker
fabricar: *vt.* to fabricate; make
fábula: *nf.* fable; tale
fabulista: *nmf.* fabulist
facción: *nf.* faction
faccioso: *aj.* factious

fácil: *aj.* easy
facilidad: *nf.* facility
facilitación: *nf.* facilitation
facilitar: *vt.* to facilitate; to supply
fácilmente: *av.* easily
factor: *nm.* commission; merchant
factura: *nf.* form; invoice; bill
facturación: *nf.* invoicing
facturar: *vt.* to invoice
facultad: *nf.* faculty; power; ability
faja: *nf.* girdle; corset
fajado: *aj.* tucked in
fajar: *vt.* to put on a girdle or corset; to tuck in
fajo: *nm.* bundle
falaz: *aj.* deceitful; fallacious
falda: *nf.* skirt; slope
faldero: *aj.* skirt-chasing
fallar: *vt.* to ruff; to trump
fallecer: *vi.* to decease; die
fallecido: *aj.* dead
fallecimiento: *nm.* passing away
falsear: *vt.* to falsify
falsedad: *nf.* falsehood
falsete: *nm.* falsetto
falsificación: *nf.* falsification
falsificador;-a: *nmf.* liar; forger
falsificar: *vt.* to falsify
falso: *aj.* false
falta: *nf.* lack
faltar: *vt.* to offend; to insult; to miss
falto: *aj.* lacking
familia: *nf.* family; household
familiar: *aj.* familiar
familiaridad: *nf.* familiarity
familiarizar: *vt.* to familiarize
famoso: *aj.* famous
fanfarrón -na: *aj. con.* blustering
fango: *nm.* mud; slime
fardel: *nm.* bag; bundle
fardo: *nm.* bundle
farmacéutico: *aj.* pharmaceutical
farmacia: *nf.* pharmacy
fármaco: *nm.* drug sold in

pharmacies
farmacología: *nf.* pharmacology
farmacológico: *aj.* pharmacological
faro: *nm.* lighthouse; headlight
farol: *nm.* lantern; streetlamp
farola: *nf.* large lighthouse
farsa: *nf.* farce
farsante: *nmf.* hypocrite; teller of farce
fascismo: *nm.* fascism
fascista: 1. *aj.* fascist ; 2. *nm.* fascist
fase: *nf.* phase
fastidiar: *vt.* to cloy; to sicken
fastuosidad: *nf.* pomposity
fastuoso: *aj.* pompous
fatal: *aj.* fatal
fatalidad: *nf.* fatality
fatalismo: *nm.* fatalism
fatalista: 1. *aj.* fatalist; 2. *nm.* fatalist
fatalmente: *av.* fatally
fatiga: *nf.* fatigue
fatigado: *aj.* fatigued; tired
fatigar: *vt.* to fatigue; to tire
fatigosamente: *av.* tiredly
fatigoso: *aj.* fatiguing
favor: *nm.* favor
favorable: *aj.* favorable
favorecedor: *aj.* favoring
favorecer: *vt.* to favor
favorecido: *aj.* favored
favoritismo: *nm.* favoritism
favorito: *aj.* favorite
faz: *nm.* face; aspect
fe: *nf.* faith; certificate
fealdad: *nf.* ugliness
febrero: *nm.* February
febril: *aj.* relating to fever
fecha: *nf.* date
fechador: *nm.* date stamp
fechar: *vt.* to date
fécula: *nf.* starch; fecula
fecundación: *nf.* fecundation
fecundar: *vt.* to fecundate
fecundidad: *nf.* fertility

fecundizar: *vt.* to fertilize
fecundo: *aj.* fertile
federación: *nf.* federation
federado: *aj.* federated
federal: *aj.* federal
federalismo: *nm.* federalism
federalista: *nmf.* federalist
federar: *vt.* to federate
felicidad: *nf.* felicity; happiness
felicitación: *nf.* act of congratulations
felicitar: *vt.* to congratulate
feligrés -sa: *nmf.* parishioner
feliz: *aj.* happy
femenino: *aj.* feminine
feminidad: *nf.* femininity
feminismo: *nm.* feminism
feminista: *nmf.* feminist
Fender; guardacostas: coastguard
fenomenal: *aj.* phenomenal
fenómeno: *nm.* phenomenon
feo -a: *aj.* ugly
feraz: *aj.* feracious; fertile
féretro: *nm.* bier; coffin
feria: *nf.* fair; market
ferial: *aj.* relating to fairs
fermentación: *nf.* fermentation
fermentar: *vti.* to ferment
fermento: *nm.* fermented substance
ferocidad: *nf.* ferocity
feroz: *aj.* ferocious
ferozmente: *av.* ferociously
férreo: *aj.* of iron; strong; tenacious
ferrería: *nf.* ironworks
ferretería: *nf.* hardware shop
ferrocarril: *nm.* railroad; railway
ferroviario;-a: *nmf.* train worker
fértil: *aj.* fertile
fertilidad: *nf.* fertility
fertilización: *nf.* fertilization
fertilizante: *nm.* fertilizer
fertilizar: *vt.* to fertilize
férvido: *aj.* ardent; fervent
ferviente: *aj.* fervent

fervor: *nm.* fervor; eagerness; enthusiasm; love
fervoroso: *aj.* full of fervor
festejar: *vt.* to fete; entertain; to celebrate
festejo: *nm.* celebration
festín: *nm.* feast; party; banquet
festival: *nm.* festival
festividad: *nf.* festivity
festivo: *aj.* holiday; festival
fiabilidad: *nf.* trustworthiness
fiable: *aj.* trustworthy
fiador -ra: *nmf.* bail (person)
fiambre: *aj.* cold; *nm.* cold lunch
fianza: *nf.* bail
fiar: *vt.* to guarantee; to loan
ficción: *nf.* fiction
ficha: *nf.* chip; domino (piece)
fichero: *nm.* card index
ficticio: *aj.* fictitious
fidedigno: *aj.* trustworthy
fideicomiso: *nm.* a trust
fidelidad: *nf.* fidelity
fiebre: *nf.* fever
fiel: *aj.* faithful; honest; exact
fiera: *nf.* wild animal; fiend (person)
fiereza: *nf.* fierceness; cruelty
fiero: *aj.* fierce
fiesta: *nf.* feast; holiday; festivity; party
figura: *nf.* figure
figuración: *nf.* mental image
figurado: *aj.* figurative
figurar: *vt.* to figure; to represent
figurativo: *aj.* figurative
figurín: *nm.* figurine
fijación: *nf.* holding in place; fixing; fixation
fijador: *nm.* hairspray
fijamente: *av.* attentively
fijar: *vt.* to fix; to fasten
fijeza: *nf.* firmness of ideas
fijo: *aj.* fixed; in a fixed place; immovable

fila: *nf.* row; line; file
filete: *nm.* fillet; steak
filiación: *nf.* proof of identification
filial: 1. *aj.* filial; 2. *nf.* branch office of an organization
filón: *nm.* vein; seam
filosofar: *vi.* to philosophize
filosofía: *nf.* philosophy
filosófico: *aj.* philosophic
filósofo;-a: *nmf.* philosopher
filtrar: *vt.* to filter; to filtrate
fin: *nmf.* end; object; aim
finado: *aj.* dead
final: *aj.* final
finalidad: *nf.* finality
finalista: *nmf.* finalist
finalizar: *vt.* to finalize
finalmente: *av.* finally
finca: *nf.* land; estate
fingido: *aj.* faked
fingimiento: *nm.* act of faking
fingir: *vt.* to feign; to fake
fingirse: *vr.* to pretend to be something or someone
finito: *aj.* finite
fino: *aj.* fine
finta: *nf.* fake movement
fintar: *vt.* to feign
finura: *nf.* fineness
firma: *nf.* signature
firmante: *nmf.* signatory; person who signs a document
firmar: *vt.* to sign
firme: *aj.* firm; steady; solid
firmemente: *av.* firmly
firmeza: *nf.* firmness
fiscal: *aj.* fiscal
fiscalía: *nf.* office of the attorney general
fiscalizar: *vt.* to rigorously enforce the law
fisco: *nm.* tax money stored in the treasury
fisgar: *vt.* to pry; peep; to nose into

fisgón -na: *nmf.* con. Busybody
física: *nf.* physics
físicamente: *av.* physically
físico: 1. *aj.* physical; 2. *nm.* physique
físico;-a: *nmf.* physicist
fisiología: *nf.* physiology
fisiológico: *aj.* physiologic
fisiólogo;-a: *nmf.* physiologist
fisioterapeuta: *nmf.* physiotherapist
fisioterapia: *nf.* physiotherapy
flaco: *aj.* thin; skinny
flacucho: *aj.* comically thin
flacura: *nf.* thinness
flamante: *aj.* bright
flan: *nm.* carmel custard
flaquear: *vi.* to weaken
flaqueza: *nf.* thinness
flecha: *nf.* arrow
flechar: *vt.* to shoot an arrow
flechazo: *nm.* a hit with an arrow
fleco: *nm.* fringe; bangs
fletar: *vt.* to charter
flor: *nf.* flower
flojear: *vi.* to slacken; ease up; to weaken
flor: *nf.* flower; bouquet
flora: *nf.* flora
floración: *nf.* flowering
floral: *aj.* floral
floreado: *aj.* flowered
florear: *vt.* to flower
florecer: *vi.* to bloom; to flourish
floreciente: *aj.* flourishing
florecimiento: *aj.* um flourishing
floreo: *nm.* compliment
florería: *nf.* flower shop
florero: *nm.* vase
floresta: *nf.* grove
floricultura: *nf.* floriculture
florido: *aj.* flowered; filled with flowers
florín: *nm.* florin
florista: *nmf.* florist

floristería: *nf.* flower shop
flota: *nf.* fleet
flotación: *nf.* floating
flotador: *nm.* float
flotante: *aj.* floating
flotar: *vi.* to float
flote: *nm.* floating
fluidez: *nf.* fluidity; fluency
fluido: 1. *aj.* fluid; fluent; 2. *nm.* fluid
fluir: *vi.* to flow
flujo: *nm.* flow
foca: *nf.* seal
focal: *aj.* focal
foco: *nm.* focus; center; light bulb
fogata: *nf.* blaze; bonfire; campfire
fogón: *nm.* stove
fogonazo: *nm.* sudden burst of flame
fogonero;-a: *nmf.* person who stokes the fire on a train
fogosidad: *nf.* passion
fogoso: *aj.* ardent and passionate; fiery; spirited
follaje: *nm.* foliage
fomentar: *vt.* to foment; to promote
fonda: *nf. vi.* inn; guesthouse
fondeadero: *nm.* anchorage
fondear: *vt.* to sound
fondo: *nm.* bottom; money; bottom; depth
fonema: *nf.* phoneme
fonética: *nf.* phonetics
fonético: *aj.* phonetic
fonógrafo: *nm.* phonograph
fonología: *nf.* phonology
fonológico: *aj.* phonologic
fonoteca: *nf.* sound; tape or record library
fontanero: *nm.* Plumber
foráneo: *aj.* referring to outsiders or non-locals
forastero: 1. *aj.* alien; foreign; 2. *nmf.* outsider; stranger
forcejar; forcejear: *vi.* to struggle; struggling
forja: *nf.* forging; forge
forjado: *aj.* forged
forjar: *vt.* to forge
forma: *nf.* form; shape; format
formación: *nf.* formation
formal: *aj.* formal
formalidad: *nf.* formality
formalismo: *nm.* formalism
formalista: *nmf.* formalist
formalizar: *vt.* to formalize
formar: *vt.* to form
formativo: *aj.* formative
fórmula: *nf.* formula
formulación: *nf.* formulation
formular: *vt.* to formulate
formulario: *aj.* relating to formulas
formulismo: *nm.* formulism; paperwork
forro: *nm.* cover; lining
fortalecedor: *aj.* fortifying; strengthening
fortalecer: *vt.* to fortify; to strengthen
fortalecimiento: *nm.* strengthening
fortaleza: *nf.* strength
fortificación: *nf.* fortification
fortificante: *aj.* fortifying
fortificar: *vt.* to fortify
fortín: *nm.* small fort; outpost
fortísimo: *aj.* very strong
fortuito: *aj.* fortuitous
fortuna: *nf.* fortune
forzado: *aj.* forced; obliged
forzar: *vt.* to force
forzoso: *aj.* forced; obligatory; inescapable; strong; husky
forzudo: *aj.* very strong; muscular
foso: *nm.* pit; ditch
foto: *nm.* photograph
fotocopia: *nf.* photocopy
fotocopiadora: *nf.* photocopier
fotocopiar: *vt.* to photocopy
fotoeléctrico: *aj.* photoelectric

fotogénico: *aj.* photogenic
fotografía: *nf.* photography
fotografiar: *vt.* to photograph
fotográfico: *aj.* photographic
fotógrafo;-a: *nmf.* photographer
fotómetro: *nm.* light meter
fotomontaje: *nm.* photo montage
fotosíntesis: *nf.* photosynthesis
fracasado: *aj.* failed
fracasar: *vi.* to fail
fracaso: *nm.* failure
frágil: *aj.* fragile; breakable
fragilidad: *nf.* fragility
fragmentación: *nf.* fragmentation
fragmentar: *vt.* to fragment; to break into fragments
fragmentario: *aj.* fragmentary
fragmento: *nm.* fragment
fragor: *nm.* crash; din; uproar
fraguar: *vt.* to forge
fraile: *nm.* friar
franquear: *vt.* to exempt; to open; to clear
franqueo: *nm.* postage; franking (of a letter)
frasco: *nm.* bottle; flask
frase: *nf.* sentence
fraseología: *nf.* phraseology
fraternal: *aj.* fraternal
fraternidad: *nf.* fraternity
fraternización: *nf.* fraternization
fraternizar: *vi.* to fraternize
fraterno: *aj.* fraternal
fratricida: *aj.* fratricidal
fratricidio: *nm.* murder of a brother
frecuencia: *nf.* frequency
frecuentado: *aj.* frequented
frecuentar: *vt.* to frequent
frecuente: *aj.* frequent
frecuentemente: *av.* frequently
fregar: *vt.* to rub; to scrub
freír: *vt.* to fry
freno: *nm.* bridle; brake; check
frente: *nmf.* front; brow; forehead

fresca: *nf.* cool drink
fresco: *aj.* fresh
frescor: *nm.* coolness
frescura: *nf.* freshness
frialdad: *nf.* coldness
friccionar: *vt.* to rub; to massage
frigidez: *nf.* frigidity
frígido: *aj.* frigid
frigorífico: *nm.* large refrigerator; cold-storage room
frió -a: *aj.* cold; frigid
friolento: *aj.* cold-natured
frivolidad: *nf.* frivolity
Frívolo: *aj.* frivolous
Fronda: *nf.* palm
Frondosidad: *nf.* great amount of foliage
frondoso –sa: *aj.* leafy; woodsy
Confrontación: *nm.* confrontation
confrontar: *vt.* to face
frontera: *nf.* frontier; boundary
frontera: *nf.* border
fronterizo: *aj.* border
frotar: *vtvr.* to rub
fructífero: *aj.* fruitful
fructificar: *vt.* to yield or bear fruit
fructuoso: *aj.* fruitful
frustrar: *vt.* to frustrate
fruta: *nf.* fruit
frutal: *aj.* fruit-bearing
frutería: *nf.* fruit shop
frutero;-a: *nmf.* fruit seller
fruto: *nm.* fruit
fuego: *nm.* fire; light
fuente: *nf.* fountain
fuera: *adv.* out; outside; away
fuero: *nm.* law; code of laws
fuerte: *aj.* strong; intense; rough
fuerza: *nf.* force; strength; power
fuga: *nf.* flight
fugarse: *vr.* to flee
fugaz: *aj.* brief; fugitive
fugitivo: 1. *aj.* fugitive; 2. *nmf.* fugitive

fulano -na: *nmf.* so-and-so
fulgor: *nm.* shining; brightness
fulgurante: *aj.* brightly shining
fulgurar: *vi.* to shine exceptionally bright
fulminante: *aj.* fulminant
fulminar: *vt.* to strike with lightning; to fulminate
fumar: *vt.* to smoke
función: *nf.* function
funcional: *aj.* functional
funcionamiento: *nm.* functioning
funcionar: *vi.* to function
funcionario;-a: *nmf.* person with a position in government
funda: *nf.* case; sheath
fundación: *nf.* foundation
fundado: *aj.* founded
fundador;-a: *nmf.* founder
fundamental: *aj.* fundamental
fundamentar: *vt.* to place the foundation
fundamento: *nm.* fundamental
fundar: *vt.* to found; to base; to be founded
fundición: *nf.* founding or smelting of metals
fundido: *nm.* founding or smelting of metals
fundidor: *nm.* founder or smelter of metals
fundir: *vt.* to found metals; to smelt metals
fúnebre: *aj.* funeral
funeral: *nm.* funeral
funeraria: *nf.* funeral home
funerario: *aj.* funeral
furgón: *nm.* van; wagon
furgoneta: *nf.* light truck
furia: *nf.* fury
furibundo: *aj.* furious; angry
furioso: *aj.* furious
furor: *nm.* furor
fusible: 1. *aj.* fusible; 2. *nm.* fuse

fusil: *nm.* gun; rifle
fusilamiento: *nm.* execution by firing squad
fusilar: *vt.* to kill with a rifle
fusilería: *nf.* group of soldiers armed with rifles
fusilero: *nm.* infantry soldier who is armed with a rifle
fusionar: *vt.* to fuse
fútbol: *nm.* football
futura: *nf.* future wife; fiancée
futurismo: *nm.* futurism
futurista: *nmf.* futurist
futuro: *aj.* future

G

gabán: *nm.* overcoat
gabardina: *nf.* rain coat; gabardine
gabinete: *nm.* office; studio
gago: *nm.* branch (tree); section (orange)
gaita: *nf.* bagpipe
gala: *nf.* gala; celebration
galán: *nm.* gallant man
galante: *aj.* gallant
galanteador: *aj.* performing gallant acts of courting;
galantear: *vt.* treat someone extra-special
galantemente: *av.* gallantly; in a gallant manner
galanteo: *nm.* compliment paid in the act of courting
galantería: *nf.* gallantry
galanura: *nf.* elegance in language or style

galardonar: *vt.* to reward
galería: *nf.* gallery
galés: *aj.* welsh
gallardía: *nf.* elegance in language or style
gallardo: *aj.* gallant; excellent
galleta: *nf.* ship biscuit; biscuit
gallina: *nf.* hen
gallinero: *nm.* hen house; chicken coop
gallo: *nm.* cock; rooster
galopar: *vt.* to gallop
galvanizar: *vt.* to galvanize
gama: *nm.* buck; male fallow deer
gamuza: *nf.* chamois
gana: *nf.* desire
ganadería: *nf.* cattle ranching
ganadero;-a: *nmf.* cattle rancher
ganado: *nm.* cattle; livestock
ganador: *nmf.* winner
ganancia: *nf.* gain; profit
ganancioso: *aj.* profitable
ganar: *vt.* to earn; to gain; to win
gancho: *nm.* hook
gandul -ula: *aj.* loafer; idler
ganga: *nf.* gangue
ganzúa: *nf.* false key
garante: *nmf.* guarantor
garantía: *nf.* guarantee
garantizado: *aj.* guaranteed
garantizar: *vt.* to guarantee
garbanzo: *nm.* chickpea
gancho: *nm.* hook
garfio: *nm.* hook
gargajo: *nm.* phlegm
garganta: *nf.* throat
gargantilla: *nf.* necklace the size of the neck
gárgaras: *nmf.* gargling
gargarismo: *nm.* gargling
gargarizar: *vt.* to gargle
gargüero: *nm.* first part of the tracheal tube
garita: *nf.* watchtower; sentry box

garra: *nf.* claw; catch
garrafa: *nf.* carafe
garrote: *nm.* club; cudgel
gas: *nm.* gas
gaseosa: *nf.* carbonated drink
gaseoso: *aj.* gaseous
gasoducto: *nm.* gas pipe
gasolina: *nf.* gasoline
gasolinera: *nf.* gas station
gasómetro: *nm.* gas meter
gastado: *aj.* spent
gastador;-a: *nmf.* spender
gastar: *vt.* to spend; to waste
gasto: *nm.* expense
gata: *nf.* female cat
gatear: *vi.* to crawl
gatillo: *nm.* trigger
gato: *nm.* cat; jack
gavilán: *nm.* sparrow hawk
gaviota: *nf.* gull; seagull
gazpacho: *nm.* cold vegetable soup; gazpacho
gemelo -la: *aj. nmf.* twin
gemido: *nm.* howling; moaning; groaning
gemir: *vi.* to howl; to moan; to groan
gene: *nm.* gene
genealogía: *nf.* genealogy
genealógico: *aj.* genealogical
genealogista: *nmf.* genealogist
generación: *nf.* generation
generacional: *aj.* generational
general: 1. *aj.* general; 2. *nm.* general in the army
generalato: *nm.* generals; committee of generals
generalidad: *nf.* generality
generalísimo: *nm.* supreme general
generalización: *nf.* generalization
generalizado: *aj.* generalized
generalizar: *vt.* to generalize
generalmente: *av.* generally
genérico: *aj.* generic
género: *nm.* kind; sort

generosidad: *nf.* generosity
generoso: *aj.* generous
genética: *nf.* genetics
genial: *aj.* inspired; genius-like; cheerful; ingenious
genialidad: *nf.* ingenuity; talent
genio: *nm.* genius
genocidio: *nm.* genocide
genotipo: *nm.* genotype
gentilhombre: *nm.* gentleman
gentío: *nm.* crowd; throng
geocéntrico: *aj.* geocentric
geofísica: *nf.* geophysics
geofísico: 1. *aj.* geophysical; 2. *nmf.* geophysicist
geografía: *nf.* geography
geográfico: *aj.* geographic; geographical
geógrafo;-a: *nmf.* geographer
geología: *nf.* geology
geológico: *aj.* geologic; geological
geólogo;-a: *nmf.* geologist
geomagnético: *aj.* geomagnetic
geometría: *nf.* geometry
geométrico: *aj.* geometric; geometrical
geopolítica: *nf.* geopolitics
gerente: *nm.* manager; director
germen: *nm.* germ; source
germinar: *vi.* to germinate; to bud
gestación: *nf.* gestation
gestar: *v.* to gestate
gestión: *nf.* step; management; administration
gestionar: *vt.* to pursue; prosecute
gesto: *nm.* face; grimace
gestor;-a: *nmf.* administrator; manager
gigante: *aj.* giant; gigantic
gigantesco: *aj.* gigantic
gigantismo: *nm.* gigantism
gimnasia: *nf.* gymnastics
gira: *nf.* tour; excursion
girar: *vt.* to draw; to turn

girasol: *nm.* sunflower
giratorio: *aj.* able to gyrate or revolve
giro: *nm.* gyration; complete turn
gitanada: *nf.* an act or saying said or done by gypsies
gitanería: *nf.* band of gypsies
gitano;-a: *nmf.* gypsy
global: *aj.* total; global
globalmente: *av.* globally
globo: *nm.* globe; balloon
gloria: *nf.* glory
glorieta: *nf.* square
glorificación: *nf.* glorification
glorificar: *vt.* to glorify
glorioso: *aj.* glorious
glosar: *vt.* to gloss; to comment; to make a glossary
glosario: *nm.* glossary
glotón -na: *aj. nmf.* glutton
gobernable: *aj.* governable
gobernación: *nf.* governance
gobernador;-a: *nmf.* governor
gobernante: *aj. nmf.* ruler
gobernante: *nmf.* governor; ruler
gobernar: *vt.* to govern
gobierno: *nm.* government
goce: *nm.* enjoyment
gol: *nm.* goal
golfo -fa: *nmf.* little scoundrel; teddy boy; *nm.* Gulf
golondrina: *nf.* swallow
golosina: *nf.* sweet; delicacy
golpazo: *nf.* strong or violent hit
golpe: *nm.* blow; hit; beat; knock; stroke
golpear: *vt.* to hit
golpetear: *vt.* to tap repeatedly
golpeteo: *nm.* hitting; repeated punching
golpismo: *nm.* violent overthrow of the government; junta
golpiza: *nf.* violent beating
goma: *nf.* gum; rubber

gordo: *nm.* fat of meat
gordura: *nf.* excess of fat; fatness
gorra: *nf.* cap; busby; sponging
gota: *nf.* drop
gotear: *vt.* to sprinkle; to rain lightly
goteo: *nm.* dripping
gotera: *nf.* drip; dripping
gotero: *nm.* dropper
goterón: *nm.* large drop of rain
gozada: *nf.* great joy
gozar: *vt.* to enjoy
gozo: *nm.* joy; rejoicing
gozoso: *aj.* joyful
grabación: *nf.* recording
grabado: *aj.* engraved; stamped
grabar: *vt.* to record; to engrave
gracia: *nf.* grace; joke; witticism
gracias: *nmf.* thank-you; thanks
gracioso: *aj.* funny
grada: *nm.* grade; degree
graduable: *aj.* able to graduate
graduación: *nf.* graduation
graduado: *aj.* graduate
gradual: *aj.* gradual
graduar: *vt.* to graduate
graduarse: *vr.* to graduate
gragea: *nf.* small colored candy; pill
gramo: *nm.* gramme
gramófono: *nm.* gramophone
gran: *aj.* great
grana: *nf.* threshing
granar: *vt.* to seed
grande: *aj.* big; large; great
grandeza: *nf.* greatness
grandilocuencia: *nf.* grandiloquence
grandilocuente: *aj.* grandiloquent
grandiosidad: *nf.* magnificence
grandioso: *aj.* magnificent; awe-inspiring
grandote: *nmf.* big person
granero: *nm.* barn
granizo: *nm.* hail
granja: *nf.* farm; grange
granjero: *nm.* farmer

grano: *nm.* grain; grape
granulación: *nf.* granulation
granulado: *aj.* granulated
granular: *vt.* to granulate
gránulo: *nm.* granule
granuloso: *aj.* grainy
grapa: *nf.* staple; clip
grasa: *nf.* fat; grease
grasiento: *aj.* very greasy
graso: *aj.* greasy; oily; referring to skin
grasoso: *aj.* greasy; oily
gratificación: *nf.* reward; tip; bonus to a salary
gratificante: *aj.* rewarding; satisfying
gratificar: *vt.* to gratify; to reward
gratis: *adv.* gratis; free
gratitud: *nf.* gratitude
gratuitamente: *av.* freely
gratuito: *aj.* free
gravamen: *nm.* obligation; tax
gravar: *vt.* to burden; to encumber; to charge a tax
grave: *aj.* heavy; grave; serious
gravedad: *nf.* gravity
gravitación: *nf.* gravitation
gravitacional: *aj.* gravitational
gravitar: *vi.* to gravitate
gravoso: *aj.* heavy; costly
gremio: *nm.* guild; union; trade union
grey: *nf.* flock; congregation
grieta: *nf.* crack; fissure
grifo: *aj.nm.* faucet; tap
grillo: *nm.* cricket
gris: *aj.* gray; *nm.* gray
grisáceo: *aj.* grayish
gritar: *vi.* to shout
gritería: *nf.* shouting
griterío: *nm.* shouting
grito: *nm.* cry; shout
gritón: *aj.* always shouting
grosería: *nf.* rudeness; vulgarity

grosero: *aj.* rude; vulgar
grosor: *nm.* thickness; bulk
grosura: *nf.* thickness
grotesco -ca: *aj.* grotesque
grúa: *nf.* crane; derrick
grueso: *aj.* thick
gruñido: *nm.* grunt; growl
grupo: *nm.* group
gruta: *nf.* grotto; cavern
guantada: *nf.* slap
guantazo: *nm.* hit with a glove
guante: *nm.* glore
guantera: *nf.* glove compartment
guapo: *aj.* handsome; good-looking
guapura: *nf.* handsomeness
guarda: *nmf.* guard; keeper
guardabarros: *nm.* mud flap
guardabosque: *nmf.* forest ranger
guardacoches: *nmf.* parking lot
attendant
guardaespaldas: *nmf.* bodyguard
guardafrenos: *nmf.* brakeman
(railroad)
guardameta: *nmf.* goal keeper
guardamuebles: *nm.* storage shed or
warehouse; storage business
guardapelo: *nm.* locket to keep a
lock of hair
guardapolvo: *nm.* cover; cloth
guardar: *vt.* to guard; to keep; to
preserve
guardarropa: *nmf.* wardrobe;
cloakroom; closet
guardarse: *vr.* to put something in
its place
guardería: *nf.* guard; guardship
guardia: *nf.* care; protection; guard
guardián;-a: *nmf.* guardian
guarecer: *vt.* to protect from danger
guarecerse: *vr.* to protect oneself
from danger
guarida: *nf.* den; lair (of animals)
guarnecer: *vt.* to garnish; to adorn
guarnición: *nf.* garrison; garnishing;

garnish
guarnicionaría: *nf.* harness shop
gubernamental: *aj.* governmental
guerra: *nf.* war; conflict; struggle
guerrear: *vt.* to fight a war
guerrero;-a: *nmf.* warrior
guerrilla: *nf.* guerrilla warfare
guerrillero;-a: *nmf.* guerrilla fighter
guía: *nmf.* guidebook; guide; leader
guiar: *vt.* to guide; to lead
guiñar: *vt.* to wink (an eye); to wink
guión: *nm.* cross; royal standard
guisado: *nm.* stew; meat stew
guisante: *nm.* pea
guisar: *vt.* to stew; to cook
guitarra: *nf.* guitar
guitarreo: *nm.* sound of the guitar
guitarrillo: *nm.* stringed guitar
guitarrista: *nmf.* guitarist
guitarrón: *nm.* over-sized guitar
gusanillo: *nm.* tiny worm
gusano: *nm.* worm
gustar: *vt.* to taste; to try; test
gustativo: *aj.* gustative; pertaining to
the sense of taste
gusto: *nm.* pleasure

H

ha!: *int.* ah!
habano -na: *aj. nm.* cigar
habichuela: *nf.* kidney bean
hábil: *aj.* skillful; clever; able
habilidad: *nf.* ability
habilidoso: *aj.* able; capable
habilitación: *nf.* act and effect of
training a person or repairing a tool
habilitado;-a: *nmf.* person
authorized to do something because

of his ability
habilitar: *vt.* to habilitate; to qualify
hábilmente: *av.* ably
habitable: *aj.* inhabitable; able to be lived in
habitación: *nf.* dwelling; room; chamber
habitante: *nmf.* inhabitant; weller
habitar: *vt.* to inhabit; to live in a place
hábitat: *nm.* habitat
hábito: *nm.* habit
habituación: *nf.* habituation; something done by habit
habitual: *aj.* habitual
habitualmente: *av.* habitually
habituar: *vt.* to habituate; accustom
habla: *nf.* speech; speaking
hablado: *aj.* spoken
hablador: *nmf.* someone who talks too much; loudmouth; charlatan
habladuría: *nf.* gossip; foolishness; nonsense
hablar: *vi.* to speak; to talk
hacedero: *aj.* possible; doable
hacendado: *aj.* having a country estate
hacendado;-a: *nmf.* owner of a country estate
hacendoso: *aj.* hard-working when referring to working at home
hacer: *vt.* to do; to make
hacha: *nf.* ax; axe
hacia: *prep.* towards; toward; to; for
hacienda: *nf.* country estate
hado: *nm.* fate; destiny
halagar: *vt.* to flatter; to adulate; to please
hálito: *nm.* breath; vapor
hallar: *vt.* to find
hallarse: *vr.* to find oneself in a particular state or situation
hallazgo: *nm.* find
hambre: *nf.* hunger; starvation

hambriento: *aj.* hungry
harapo: *nm.* rag; tatter
harina: *nf.* flour
hartar: *vt.* to satiate; to fill; gorge
hartarse: *vr.* to completely fill oneself
harto: *aj.* weary
hastiar: *vt.* to cloy; sate; to weary; bore
hatajo: *nm.* herd; flock
hato: *nm.* outfit; belongings
haya: *nf.* beech tree
haz: *nm.* bundle; beam; pencil
hazaña: *nf.* deed; feat; exploit
hazmerreír: *nm.* laughing-stock
hebra: *nf.* piece of thread
hechizar: *vt.* to bewitch; charm; enchant; to fascinate
hecho: *aj.* done; finished; made
hechura: *nf.* the form of the finished product
heder: *vi.* to stink
helada: *nf.* freeze; freezing
heladera: *nf.* ice cream container; freezer
heladería: *nf.* place where they make or sell ice cream
heladero;-a: *nmf.* person who makes or sells ice cream
helado: *nm.* ice cream
helador: *aj.* freezing
heladora: *nf.* home ice cream maker
helar: *vt.* to freeze; to frostbite
hélice: *nf.* helix; propeller
hembra: *nf.* female
hendidura: *aj.* cleft; crevice
heno: *nm.* hay
herbáceo: *aj.* herb-like
herbario: *nm.* collection of plants
herbicida: *nf.* herbicide; weed killer
herbívoro: *aj.* herbivorous
herbolario;-a: *nmf.* person who buys and sells medicinal herbs
herboristería: *nf.* medicinal herb

store
herboso: *aj.* herbaceous
heredable: *aj.* inheritable
heredad: *nf.* heredity
heredado: *aj.* inherited
heredar: *vt.* to inherit
heredero -ra: *aj.* inheriting
hereditario: *aj.* hereditary
herencia: *nf.* inheritance
herida: *nf.* wound; stab
herido: *aj.* wounded
herir: *vt.* to wound; injure; hurt
hermana: *nf.* sister
hermanable: *aj.* brotherly
hermanar: *vt.* to equalize
hermanastro;-a: *nmf.* step-brother; step-sister
hermandad: *nf.* brotherhood; the brethren
hermano;-a: *nmf.* brother or sister
hermosear: *vt.* to beautify
hermoso: *aj.* beautiful; gorgeous; fair;
hermosura: *nf.* beauty
héroe: *nm.* hero
heroico: *aj.* heroic
heroína: *nf.* heroine
heroísmo: *nm.* heroism
herrado: *nm.* horseshoeing
herrador: *nm.* blacksmith
herradura: *nf.* horseshoe
herraje: *nm.* iron made into furniture
herramienta: *nf.* tool; instrument
herrar: *vt.* to shoe a horse
herrería: *nf.* art of working iron
herrero: *nm.* blacksmith
herrumbre: *nf.* rust; iron rust
herrumbroso: *aj.* rusty
hervir: *vi.* to boil; to hubble
heterogeneidad: *nf.* heterogeneity
heterogéneo: *aj.* heterogeneous
heterosexual: *aj.* heterosexual
híbrido -da: *aj.* hybrid
hidalgo: *aj.* altruistic; of noble spirit

hidrógeno: *nm.* to hydrogen
hiel: *nf.* bile gall; fig. gall; bitter-ness
hielo: *nm.* ice; frost
hierba: *nf.* herb; grass; weed
hierbabuena: *nf.* mint
hierro: *nm.* iron
hígado: *nm.* liver; courage
higiene: *nf.* hygiene; cleanliness
higo: *nm.* fig
hija: *nf.* daughter
hijastro -tra: *nmf.* stepson; stepdaughter
hijear: *vi.* to sprout
hijo: *nmf.* son; child
hijuelo: *nm.* sprout
hilado: *nm.* action of making thread
hilar: *vt.* to spin
hilera: *nf.* file; line; row
hilo: *nm.* thread
hilván: *nm.* basting; tacking
hilvanar: *vt.* to baste; tack
himno: *nm.* hymn; anthem
hincar: *vt.* to stick; introduce; drive
hinchar: *vt.* to inflate; puff up; blow up
hinojo: *nm.* fennel
hipercrítico: *aj.* hypercritical
hipermercado: *nm.* supermarket
hipersensible: *aj.* hypersensitive
hípico -ca: *aj.* equine; horse
hipo: *nm.* hiccup
hipócrita: *aj.* false; *nmf.* hyp-ocrite
hipotecar: *vt.* to mortgage; hypothecate
hipótesis: *nf.* hypothesis
hipotético: *aj.* hypothetical
hiriente: *aj.* wounding
hispanidad: *nf.* community of Spanish-speakers
hispanismo: *nm.* Spanish word used in another language
hispanista: *nmf.* fan of Spanish language and culture
hispano: *aj.* Hispanic

Hispanoamérica: *nf.* Spanish America
hispanohablante: *aj.* Spanish-speaking
historia: *nf.* history; tale; story
historiador;-a: *nmf.* historian
historial: *nm.* personal or business history; records
historiar: *vt.* to give a historical narration
histórico: *aj.* historic
historieta: *nf.* story; tale
hocico: *nm.* snout; muzzle
hogar: *nm.* heart; fireplace; fur-nace; home (family life)
hogareño: *aj.* homey; home-loving
hogaza: *nf.* large loaf
hoguera: *nf.* bonfire; fire
hoja: *nf.* leaf; page
hojalata: *nf.* sheet metal
hojalatería: *nf.* workshop for working with sheet metal
hojalatero: *nm.* one who works with sheet metal
hojaldre: *nm.* (or) *nf.* puff pastry
hojarasca: *nf.* pile of dried flowers fallen from a tree
hojear: *vt.* to scan; run through (book)
hola!: *in.* hallo!
holgar: *vt.* to do nothing
holgazán: *aj.* lazy
holgazanear: *vi.* to be lazy; to waste time
holgazanería: *nf.* the act of wasting time; laziness
hollín: *nm.* soot
hombrada: *nf.* a vile "macho" act
hombre: *nm.* man
hombrear: *vi.* to act "macho"; to act chauvinistic
hombría: *nf.* manliness
hombro: *nm.* shoulder
homenaje: *nm.* homage

homenajear: *vt.* to pay homage
homicidio: *nm.* homicide; manslaughter
homofonía: *nf.* homo
homófono: *aj.* homophonic
homogeneidad: *nf.* homogeneity
homogeneizar: *vt.* to homogenize
homogéneo: *aj.* homogeneous
homosexual: *aj.* homosexual
homosexualidad: *nf.* homosexuality
hondo -da: *aj.* deep; profound;
hondura: *nf.* depth
hondureño: *nmf.* person from Honduras
honestamente: *av.* honestly
honestidad: *nf.* honesty
honesto: *aj.* honest
honor: *nm.* honor
honorable: *aj.* honorable
honorario: *nm.* honorarium
honra: *nf.* honor
honrado: *aj.* honored
honrar: *vt.* to honor
honroso: *aj.* respectful; honest; honorable
hora: *nf.* hour; time; season; adv. now; at this time
horadar: *vt.* to perforate; bore
horario: *nm.* schedule
horca: *nf.* gallows; gibbet; pitchfork
horchata: *nf.* drink
horizontal: *aj.* horizontal
horizontalmente: *av.* horizontally
horizonte: *nm.* horizon
horma: *nf.* horm; mould
hormiga: *nf.* ant
hormigón: *nm.* concrete
horno: *nm.* oven; furnace
horrendo: *aj.* horrifying
horrible: *aj.* horrible
horripilante: *aj.* horrifying
horror: *nm.* horror; atrocity
horrorizar: *vt.* to horrify
horroroso: *aj.* horrifying

horroroso -SA: *aj.* horrible; horrid; hideous
hortaliza: *nf.* vegetables
hospedaje: *nm.* lodging; board
hospedar: *vt.* to host
hospedería: *nf.* lodging
hospicio: *nm.* shelter; orphanage
hospital: *nm.* hospital
hospitalario: *aj.* hospitable
hospitalidad: *nf.* hospitality
hospitalización: *nf.* hospitalization
hospitalizar: *vt.* to hospitalize
hostal: *nm.* hostel
hostelería: *nf.* hostel
hostelero;-a: *nmf.* manager or worker in a hostel
hostería: *nf.* inn; bed and breakfast
hostigamiento: *nm.* harassment; persecution
hostigar: *vt.* to harass; to persecute
hostil: *aj.* hostile; adverse
hostilidad: *nf.* hostility
hotel: *nm.* hotel
hotelero;-a: *nmf.* manager or worker in a hotel
hoy: *adv.* today; now; nowadays
hoyo: *nm.* hole; pit; dent; indentation
hoz: *nf.* sickle; gorge
hucha: *nf.* large chest (or) coffer; money-box
hueco -ca: 1. *aj.* hollow; empty; vain; conceited; 2. *nm.* hollow; cavity
huelga: *nf.* strike
huelguista: *nmf.* striker
huella: *nf.* track; print; footprint
huérfano -na: *aj.* fatherless; motherless; *nm.* orphan
huerta: *nf.* large vegetable garden (or) orchard
hueso: *nm.* bone
huésped: *nmf.* guest; lodger; boarder
huesudo: *aj.* bony
huevera: *nf.* recipient for eggs
hueverìa: *nf.* egg shop

huevero;-a: *nmf.* person who is in the business of buying or selling eggs
huevo: *nm.* egg
huida: *nf.* flight from something
huidizo: *aj.* fleeing
huir: *vi.* to flee
hulla: *nf.* coal
humanidad: *nf.* humanity
humanismo: *nm.* humanism
humanista: *nmf.* humanist
humanístico: *aj.* humanistic
humanitario: *aj.* humanitarian
humanitarismo: *nm.* humanitarianism
humanización: *nf.* humanization
humanizar: *vt.* to humanize
humanizarse: *vr.* to become human
humano: *aj.* human
humareda: *nf.* cloud of smoke; smoke
humareda: *nf.* billow of smoke; a great quantity of smoke
humeante: *aj.* smoking
humear: *vi.* to be smoking
humedad: *nf.* humidity; moisture
humedecer: *vt.* to moisten
humedecerse: *vr.* to become moist
húmedo: *aj.* humid
humildad: *nf.* humility
humilde: *aj.* humble; meek; plain
humillación: *nf.* humiliation
humillante: *aj.* humbling
humillar: *vt.* to humble
humillarse: *vr.* to humble oneself; to become humble
humo: *nm.* smoke
humor: *nm.* humor
humorismo: *nm.* humor; in a general sense
humorista: *nmf.* humorist; comic
humorístico: *aj.* comic; pertaining to humor or comedy
hundible: *aj.* sinkable hundido
hundimiento: *nm.* the sinking

hundir: *vt.* to sink
hundirse: *vr.* to sink

I

ibero -ra: *aj. & nm. nf.* Iberian
ida: *nf.* going (to a place) departure
idea: *nf.* idea; notion
ideal: *aj.* ideal
idealismo: *nm.* idealism
idealista: *nmf.* idealist
idealización: *nf.* idealization
idealizar: *vt.* to idealize
idealmente: *av.* ideally
idear: *vt.* to imagine; plan; to project
idénticamente: *av.* identically
idéntico: *aj.* identical
identidad: *nf.* identity
identificable: *aj.* identifiable
identificación: *nf.* identification
identificar: *vt.* to identify; to be identified
ideograma: *nf.* ideogram
ideología: *nf.* ideology
ideológico: *aj.* ideological
ideólogo;-a: *nmf.* ideologue
idioma: *nm.* idiom; language
idiomático: *aj.* idiomatic
idiota: adj. idiot; silly
idólatra: *nmf.* idolater; idolatress
idolatrar: *vt.* idolize; to practice idolatry
idolatría: *nf.* idolatry
ídolo: *nm.* idol
iglesia: *nf.* church
ignominia: *nf.* ignominy
ignominioso: *aj.* ignominious
ignorado -da: *aj.* unknown

ignorancia: *nf.* ignorance
ignorante: *aj.* ignorant
ignorar: *vt.* not to know; to be ignorant of
igual: *aj.* equal; level; even; equal; commensurate
igualación: *nf.* equalization
igualada: *nf.* tie
igualado: *aj.* equaled; matched; presumptuous
igualar: *vt.* to equal
igualdad: *nf.* equality
igualitario: *aj.* egalitarian
igualmente: *av.* equally
llavín: *nm.* latch key
Llegada: *nf.* arrival; coming
ilegal: *aj.* illegal
ilegalidad: *nf.* illegality
ilegalmente: *av.* illegally
ilegítimamente: *av.* illegitimately
ilegítimo: *aj.* illegitimate
ileso: *aj.* uninjured; unhurt; unharmed
iletrado: *aj.* illiterate
Llevar (se): vt*vr.* to carry
ilícitamente: *av.* illicitly
ilícito: *aj.* illicit
ilimitable: *aj.* unlimited
ilimitado: *aj.* unlimited
ilógicamente: *av.* illogically
ilógico -ca: *aj.* illogical; irrational
iluminación: *nf.* illumination
iluminado: *aj.* illuminated
iluminador: *aj.* illuminating
iluminar: *vt.* illuminate; illumine; light
ilusión: *nf.* illusion; dream; desire
ilusionar: *vt.* to deceive
ilusionismo: *nm.* illusionism; the use of illusion
ilusionista: *nmf.* artist specializing in the use of illusion; magician
iluso: *aj.* deceived; deluded; dreamer
ilusorio: *aj.* deceiving

ilustración: *nf.* illustration
ilustrado: *aj.* illustrious; knowledgeable; well-educated
ilustrador;-a: *nmf.* illustrator
ilustrar: *vt.* to illustrate
ilustrarse: *vr.* to enlighten; to be illustrated
ilustrativo: *aj.* illustrative
ilustre: *aj.* famous; in the lime-light
ilustrísimo: *aj.* most illustrious
imagen: *nf.* image; statue
imaginable: *aj.* imaginable
imaginación: *nf.* imagination
imaginar: *vt.* to imagine; conceive; to imagine; to assume
imaginario: *aj.* imaginary
imaginativo: *aj.* imaginative
imán: *nm.* magnet
imborrable: *aj.* unforgettable
imbuir: *vt.* to imbue; fill
imitación: *nf.* imitation
imitador;-a: *nmf.* imitator
imitar: *vt.* to imitate; to copy; to ape
impaciencia: *nf.* impatience
impacientar: *vt.* to make lose patience; to lose patience
impacientarse: *vr.* to become impatient
impaciente: *aj.* impatient
impacientemente: *av.* impatiently
impagable: *aj.* unpayable
impagado: *aj.* unpaid
impalpable: *aj.* impalpable
impar: *aj.* odd; uneven
imparable: *aj.* unstoppable
imparcial: *aj.* impartial
imparcialidad: *nm.* impartiality
imparcialmente: *av.* impartially
impartir: *vt.* to impart; bestow
impedido: *aj.* disabled
impedimento: *nm.* impediment; obstacle
impedir: *vt.* to impede; obstruct
impenetrabilidad: *nf.*

impenetrability
impenitencia: *nf.* impenitence
impenitente: *aj.* impenitent
impensable: *aj.* unthinkable
impensado: *aj.* unthought-of
imperante: *aj.* imperative
imperar: *vi.* to be an emperor; to rule; to command
imperativamente: *av.* imperatively
imperativo: *aj.* imperative
imperceptibilidad: *nf.* imperceptibility
imperceptible: *aj.* imperceptible
imperceptiblemente: *av.* imperceptibly
imperdible: *nm.* safety pin
imperdonable: *aj.* unpardonable
imperecedero: *aj.* not perishable
imperfección: *nf.* imperfection
imperfecto: *aj.* imperfect
imperial: *aj.* imperial
imperialismo: *nm.* imperialism
imperialista: *nmf.* imperialist
imperio: *nm.* empire
imperioso: *aj.* imperious
impermeabilizar: *vt.* to waterproof
ímpetu: *nm.* impetus; impulse
impetuosidad: *nf.* impetuosity
impetuoso: *aj.* impetuous
impiedad: *nf.* impiety
impío;-a: *nmf.* impious person
implantación: *nf.* implantation
implantar: *vt.* to implant; to introduce
implicación: *nf.* implication
implicar: *vt.* to imply; involve; implicate
implícitamente: *av.* implicitly
implícito: *aj.* implicit
implorar: *vt.* to implore; beg; beseech
impúdico -ca: *aj.* immodest
imponente: *aj.* imposing; impressive
imponer: *vt.* to impose

imponerse: *vr.* to impose oneself; to be accustomed
impopular: *aj.* unpopular
impopularidad: *nf.* lack of popularity
importación: *nf.* importation; import
importador;-a: *nmf.* importer
importancia: *nf.* importance
importante: *aj.* important
importar: *vi.* to import; be important
importe: *nm.* amount
importunar: *vt.* to bother
importuno: *aj.* bothersome
imposibilidad: *nf.* impossibility
imposibilitado: *aj.* unable to move; incapable of moving
imposibilitar: *vt.* to prevent the possibility of something
imposible: *aj.* impossible
imposición: *nf.* imposition; charge
impotencia: *nf.* impotence
impotente: *aj.* impotent
imprecisión: *nf.* imprecision
impreciso: *aj.* imprecise
impredecible: *aj.* unpredictable
impremeditado: *aj.* unpremeditated
imprenta: *nf.* printing; press
imprescindible: *aj.* essential; indispensable
impresentable: *aj.* not presentable
impresión: *nf.* impression
impresionabilidad: *nf.* impressionability
impresionable: *aj.* impressionable
impresionante: *aj.* impressive
impresionar: *vt.* to impress; to touch; to be impressed
impresionarse: *vr.* to be impressed
impresionismo: *nm.* impressionism
impresionista: *nmf.* impressionist
impreso: 1. *aj.* printed; 2. *nm.* printed material
impresor;-a: *nmf.* printer
imprevisible: *aj.* unforeseeable

imprevisión: *nf.* lack of foresight
imprevisto -ta: *aj.* unforeseen; unexpected
imprimir: *vt.* to impress; imprint; to print
improbabilidad: *nf.* improbability
improbable: *aj.* improbable
improbablemente: *av.* improbably
improductividad: *nf.* lack of productivity
improductivo: *aj.* not productive
impronunciable: *aj.* unpronounceable
improvisar: *vt.* to improvise; to extemporize
imprudencia: *nf.* imprudence
imprudente: *aj.* imprudent
impúdico: *aj.* shameless; immodest; lacking reserve; cynical
impudor: *nm.* shamelessness; immodesty; lack of reserve; cynicism
impuesto: *aj.* imposed
impuesto: *nm.* tax
impugnar: *vt.* to impugn; oppose; contradict
impulsar: *vt.* to impel; push; to force
impulsividad: *nf.* impulsivity
impulsivo: *aj.* impulsive
impulso: *nm.* impulse
impureza: *nf.* impurity
impuro: *aj.* impure
imputar: *vt.* to impute; ascribe; attribute
inacabable: *aj.* unending; inexhaustible
inaceptable: *aj.* unacceptable
inactividad: *nf.* inactivity
inactivo: *aj.* inactive
inadaptable: *aj.* not adaptable
inadaptado: *aj.* not adapted
inadecuado: *aj.* inadequate
inadecuado -da: *aj.* unsuitable
inadmisible: *aj.* inadmissible
inadvertencia: *nf.* inadvertence; lack

of warning
inadvertido: *aj.* inadvertent; without warning
inagotable: *aj.* inexhaustible; endless
inaguantable: adj. intolerable; unbearable
inalcanzable: *aj.* unreachable
inalterable: *aj.* unalterable; stable; firm
inalterado: *aj.* unaltered
inanimado: *aj.* inanimate
inapelable: *aj.* not appealable
inapetencia: *nf.* lack of appetite
inaplicable: *aj.* inapplicable
inapreciable: *aj.* despicable; worthless
inasistencia: *nf.* absence
inatento: *aj.* inattentive
inaudible: *aj.* inaudible
inaudito -ta: *aj.* unheard of; extraordinary
inauguración: *nf.* inauguration
inaugural: *aj.* inaugural
inaugurar: *vt.* to inaugurate; open
incalculable: *aj.* incalculable
incansable: *aj.* indefatigable; tireless
incansablemente: *av.* untiringly
incapacidad: *nf.* incapacity
incapacitado: *aj.* untrained; injured
incapacitar: *vt.* to incapacitate
incapaz: *aj.* incapable; unable
incautamente: *av.* incautiously
incauto: *aj.* incautious
incendiar: *vt.* to set on fire; to catch fire
incensario: *nm.* incensory
incertidumbre: *nf.* lack of certainty; doubt; uncertainty; doubt
incesante: *aj.* incessant
incesantemente: *av.* incessantly
incesto: *nm.* incest
incidencia: *nf.* incidence
incidente: *nm.* incident; event
incidir: *vi.* to fall into error

inciertamente: *av.* uncertainly; falsely
incierto: *aj.* uncertain; untrue; false
incitación: *nf.* incitation
incitador;-a: *nmf.* one who incites or provokes
incitante: *aj.* inciting; provoking
incitar: *vt.* to incite; instigate; goad
incivil: *aj.* uncivil
incivilizado: *aj.* uncivilized
inclinación: *nf.* inclination
inclinado: *aj.* leaning; inclined
inclinar: *vt.* to incline; slant; bow; to lean
incluido: *aj.* included
incluir: *vt.* to include
inclusión: *nf.* inclusion
inclusivamente: *av.* inclusively
inclusive: *av.* inclusive
incluso: *aj.* included; even
incógnito -ta: *aj.* unknown
incoloro: *aj.* colorless
incombustible: *aj.* incombustible
incomestible: *aj.* inedible
incomible: *aj.* inedible
incomodar: *vt.* to bother; to interrupt
incomodidad: *nf.* discomfort
incómodo: *aj.* uncomfortable
incomparable: *aj.* incomparable
incompetencia: *nf.* incompetence
incompetente: *aj.* incompetent
incompetente: *nmf.* incompetent person
incompleto: *aj.* incomplete
incomprensible: *aj.* incomprehensible
incomprensiblemente: *av.* incomprehensibly
incomprensión: *nf.* incomprehension
incomprensivo: *aj.* unable to understand
incomunicación: *nf.* isolation
incomunicado: *aj.* incommunicado
incomunicar: *vt.* to isolate; to put

into solitary confinement
inconcebible: *aj.* inconceivable
inconcluso: *aj.* inconclusive
incondicional: *aj.* unconditional
inconfesable: *aj.* so serious that it is
not confessable
inconfeso: *aj.* not confessed
inconformismo: *nm.* nonconformity
inconformista: *nmf.* nonconformist
inconfundible: *aj.* unable to be
confused; obvious
inconmovible: *aj.* imperturbable;
emotionally unmovable
inconquistable: *aj.* unconquerable
inconsciencia: *nf.* unconsciousness
inconsciente: *aj.* unconscious;
unaware
inconsecuente: *aj.* inconsequential
inconsistencia: *nf.* inconsistency
inconsistente: *aj.* inconsistent
inconsolable: *aj.* inconsolable
inconstancia: *nf.* inconstancy;
instability
inconstante: *aj.* inconstant; unstable
inconstitucional: *aj.* unconstitutional
inconstitucionalidad: *nf.*
unconstitutionality
incontable: *aj.* uncountable;
countless
inconveniencia: *nf.* inconvenience
inconveniente: 1. *aj.* inconvenient;
2. *nm.* problem; annoyance;
inconvenience
incorporación: *nf.* incorporation
incorporado: *aj.* incorporated
incorporar: *vt.* to incorporate
incorpóreo: *aj.* incorporeal
incorrección: *nf.* error
incorrecto -ta: *aj.* incorrect; faulty
incorregible: *aj.* incorrigible
incredulidad: *nf.* incredulity
incrédulo: *aj.* incredulous; atheistic
increíble: *aj.* incredible;
unbelievable

increíble: *aj.* incredible
incrementar: *vi.* to grow
incrementally
incremento: *nm.* increment; increase
incriminación: *nf.* incrimination
incriminar: *vt.* to incriminate
incrustar: *vt.* to incrust; implay
incubar: *vt.* to incubate; brood; hatch
incuestionable: *aj.* unquestionable
inculcar: *vt.* to inculcate; put into
inculpación: *nf.* accusation
inculpado: *aj.* accused
inculpar: *vt.* to accuse
inculto: *aj.* lacking culture
incultura: *nf.* lack of culture
incumplido: *aj.* uncompleted;
unfinished
incumplimiento: *nm.* lack of
completion
incumplir: *vi.* to leave incomplete; to
leave unfinished
indagar: *vt.* to investigate; inquire
indebidamente: *av.* incorrectly;
unsuitably
indebido: *aj.* incorrect; unsuitable
indecible: *aj.* unspeakable
indecisión: *nf.* indecision
indeciso: *aj.* indecisive; hesitate;
irresolute
indefendible: *aj.* indefensible
indefenso: *aj.* defenseless
indefinible: *aj.* indefinable
indefinidamente: *av.* indefinitely
indefinido: *aj.* indefinite
indeformable: *aj.* cannot be
deformed
indelicadeza: *nf.* indelicacy
indemnizar: *vt.* to indemnify
independencia: *nf.* independency
independiente: *aj.* independent
independientemente: *av.*
independently
independizar: *vt.* to free; emancipate
indescifrable: *aj.* indecipherable

indescriptible: *aj.* indescribable
indeseable: *aj.* undesirable
indestructible: *aj.* indestructible
indeterminable: *aj.* indeterminable
indeterminación: *nf.*
indetermination
indeterminado: *aj.* undetermined
indiano -na: 1. *aj.* itinerary; 2. *nm.*
route; programme
indicación: *nf.* indication; sign; hint
indicador: *nm.* indicator
indicar: *vt.* to indicate; to point out;
to hint; suggest
indicativo: 1. *aj.* indicative; 2. *nm.*
indicative
índice: *nm.* index; forefinger
indicio: *nm.* indication; sign
indiferencia: *nf.* indifference
indiferente: *aj.* indifferent
indignación: *nf.* indignation
indignado: *aj.* indignant
indignante: *aj.* outrageous; giving
rise to anger
indignar: *vt.* to irritate; make
indignant; to cause anger; to outrage
indignidad: *nf.* indignity
indigno: *aj.* unworthy
indirecto: *aj.* indirect
indisciplina: *nf.* lack of discipline
indisciplinado: *aj.* undisciplined
indiscreción: *nf.* indiscretion
indiscreto: *aj.* indiscreet
indiscutible: *aj.* indisputable
indispensable: *aj.* indispensable
indisponer: *vt.* to indispose; be
indisposed
indisponible: *aj.* unavailable
indisposición: *nf.* indisposition
indispuesto: *aj.* unavailable
indistintamente: *av.* indistinctly
indistinto: *aj.* indistinct
individual: *aj.* individual
individualidad: *nf.* individuality
individualismo: *nm.* individualism

individualista: *nmf.* individualist
individualización: *nf.*
individualization
individualizar: *vt.* to individualize
individuo: *nm.* individual
indivisible: *aj.* indivisible
indocumentado: *aj.* undocumented
indoloro: *aj.* painless
indomable: *aj.* indomitable;
untamable
indómito: *aj.* untamable; rebellious
inducido: *aj.* induced
inducir: *vt.* to induce; persuade
inductor: *aj.* inducing
indudable: *aj.* indubitable
indultar: *vt.* to pardon; to exempt
indulto: *nm.* pardon; indult
indumentaria: *nf.* clothing; dress
industria: *nf.* industry
industrial: *aj.* industrial
industrialización: *nf.*
industrialization
industrializar: *vt.* to industrialize
industrioso: *aj.* industrious
inédito: *aj.* unpublished
inefectivo: *aj.* ineffective
ineficacia: *nf.* inefficiency
ineficaz: *aj.* inefficient
inepto: *nmf.* incapable
ineptitud: *nf.* ineptitude
inepto: *aj.* inept; incompetent
inequívoco: *aj.* unmistakable
inerte: *aj.* inert
inesperadamente: *av.* unexpectedly
inesperado: *aj.* unexpected
inestabilidad: *nf.* instability
inestable: *aj.* unstable
inestimable: *aj.* inestimable
inevitable: *aj.* inevitable;
unavoidable
inevitablemente: *av.* unavoidably
inexactitud: *nf.* inexactitude
inexacto -ta: *aj.* inexact; inaccurate
inexistencia: *nf.* inexistence

inexistente: *aj.* nonexistent
inexorable: *aj.* inexorable
inexorablemente: *av.* inexorably
inexperiencia: *nf.* inexperience
inexperimentado: *aj.* untried
inexperto: *aj.* inexpert
inexplicable: *aj.* inexplicable
inexpresable: *aj.* inexpressible
inexpresivo: *aj.* inexpressive
inextinguible: *aj.* inextinguishable
infamar: *vt.* to defame; to dishonor; to libel
infame: *aj.* infamous
infamia: *nf.* infamy; public dishonor
infancia: *nf.* infancy
infanta: *nf.* infant girl
infante: *nm.* male infant
infantería: *nf.* infantry
infanticida: *nmf.* one who kills an infant
infanticidio: *nm.* infanticide
infantil: *aj.* infantile; childlike
infatigable: *aj.* indefatigable
infección: *nf.* infection; contagion
infectar: *vt.* to infect
infecundidad: *nf.* infertility
infecundo: *aj.* undo infertile
infelicidad: *nf.* unhappiness
infeliz: *aj.* unhappy; *nmf.* unhappy person
inferior: *aj.* inferior
inferioridad: *nf.* inferiority
infernal: *aj.* infernal
infestar: *vt.* to infest; to infect
infidelidad: *nf.* infidelity
infiel: *aj.* unfaithful
infiel: *nmf.* unfaithful person
infielmente: *av.* faithlessly
infierno: *nm.* hell; inferno
infiltración: *nf.* infiltration
infiltrado;-a: *nmf.* intruder; infiltrator
infiltrar: *vt.* to infiltrate
infiltrarse: *vr.* to infiltrate oneself

infinidad: *nf.* infinity
infinitamente: *av.* infinitely
infinitesimal: *aj.* infinitesimal
infinitivo: *nm.* infinitive
infinito: *nm.* infinite; endless; immense
inflamar: *vt.* to inflame; set on fire
inflar: *vt.* to inflate; to exaggerate; *vr.* to inflate
influencia: *nf.* influence (usually relating to people)
influir: *vt.* to influence
influyente: *nmf.* person with influence
información: *nf.* information
informado: *aj.* informed
informador;-a: *nmf.* informer
informal: *aj.* informal
informalidad: *nf.* informality
informalmente: *av.* informally
informar: *vt.* to inform; *vi.* to report
informarse: *vr.* to become informed
informática: *nf.* information systems
informativo: *aj.* informative
informe: *inn.* report
infortunado: *aj.* unfortunate
infortunio: *nm.* misfortune
infracción: *nf.* infraction; breach
infraestructura: *nf.* infrastructure
infrahumano: *aj.* subhuman
infrarrojo: *aj.* infrared
infravalorar: *vt.* to under-appreciate
infringir: *vt.* to infringe; break
infructuosamente: *av.* fruitlessly
infructuoso: *aj.* unfruitful
infundado: *aj.* unfounded
infundió: *nm.* unfounded rumor
infundir: *vt.* to infuse
infusión: *nf.* infusion
ingeniar: *v.* to think up; contrive; to use one's creative ability
ingeniarse: *vr.* to figure out a way to do something
ingeniería: *nf.* engineering

ingeniero;-a: *nmf.* engineer
ingenio: *nm.* talent; wit; talented person; creative ability
ingenioso: *aj.* clever
ingenuidad: *nf.* honesty and sincerity; naiveté
ingenuo: *aj.* honest; sincere; naïve
ingerir: *vt.* to ingest
ingle: *nf.* groin
inglés -sa: *aj.* English
ingobernable: *aj.* ungovernable
ingratamente: *av.* ungratefully
ingratitud: *nf.* ingratitude
ingrato: *aj.* ungrateful
ingravidez: *nf.* weightlessness
ingrávido: *aj.* weightless
ingresado: *aj.* entered; enrolled
ingresar: *vi.* to enter; to become a member of; to deposit
ingreso: *nm.* deposit
inhábil: *aj.* unable; unskillful; tactless
inhabilidad: *nf.* inability
inhabilitación: *nf.* preventing someone from exercising a right or privilege
inhabilitar: *vt.* to disable; disqualify; to become disqualified; to prevent
inhabitable: *aj.* uninhabitable
inhabitado: *aj.* uninhabited; vacant
inhóspito: *aj.* inhospitable
iniciación: *nf.* initiation
iniciado: *aj.* initiated
iniciador;-a: *nmf.* initiator
inicial: *nf.* initial; first letter of a name
iniciar: *vt.* to initiate; to begin; to be initiated
iniciativa: *nf.* initiative
inicio: *nm.* beginning
inimaginable: *aj.* unimaginable
ininteligible: *aj.* unintelligible
ininterrumpidamente: *av.* uninterruptedly

ininterrumpido: *aj.* uninterrupted
injertar: *vt.* to graft
injuria: *nf.* insult; offense
injuriar: *vt.* to offend; to insult; to injure
injurioso: *aj.* offensive
injustamente: *av.* unjustly
injusticia: *nf.* injustice
injustificable: *aj.* unjustifiable
injustificadamente: *av.* unjustifiably
injustificado: *aj.* unjustified
injusto: *aj.* unjust
inmadurez: *nf.* immaturity
inmaduro: *aj.* immature
inmaterial: *aj.* immaterial
inmediaciones: *nm.* pl immediate surroundings
inmediatamente: *av.* immediately
inmediato: *aj.* immediate
inmejorable: *aj.* not improvable
inmemorial: *aj.* immemorial
inmensamente: *av.* immensely
inmensidad: *nf.* immensity
inmenso: *aj.* immense
inmerecidamente: *av.* undeservedly
inmerecido: *aj.* unmerited; undeserved
inmiscuir: *vt.* to mix; *ovr.* to interfere
inmobiliaria: *nf.* house construction company
inmobiliario: *aj.* pertaining to real estate
inmodestamente: *av.* immodestly
inmodestia: *nf.* immodesty
inmodesto: *aj.* immodest
inmolar: *vt.* to immolate; *vr.* to sac-rifice oneself
inmoral: *aj.* immoral
inmoralidad: *nf.* immorality
inmoralmente: *av.* immorally
inmortal: *aj.* immortal
inmortal: *nmf.* an immortal
inmortalidad: *nf.* immortality

inmortalizar: *vt.* to immortalize
inmortalizarse: *vr.* to be immortalized
inmotivado: *aj.* unmotivated
inmovible: *aj.* immovable
inmóvil: *aj.* immobile
inmovilidad: *nf.* immovability
inmovilización: *nf.* immobilization
inmovilizado: *aj.* immobilized; not moving
inmovilizar: *vt.* to immobilize; to become immobilized
inmueble: *nm.* property which cannot be moved
inmundicia: *nf.* dirt; fifth; filthiness
inmundo -da: *aj.* dirty; filthy; unclean
inmutar: *vt.* to change; alter
innato: *aj.* innate
innecesariamente: *av.* unnecessarily
innecesario: *aj.* unnecessary
innegable: *aj.* undeniable
innombrable: ajunspeakable
innominado: *aj.* unnamed
innovación: *nf.* innovation
innovador: *aj.* innovative
innovador;-a: *nmf.* innovator
innovar: *vt.* to innovate
innumerable: *aj.* innumerable
inocencia: *nf.* innocence
inocente: *nm.* innocent; someone without malice (e.g.; a child)
inocente: *aj.* innocent
inocentón: *aj.* very good; ingenuous
inofensivo: *aj.* inoffensive
inolvidable: *aj.* unforgettable
inoperable: *aj.* inoperable
inoportunamente: *av.* inopportunely
inoportuno: *aj.* inopportune
inorgánico: *aj.* inorganic
inquebrantable: *aj.* unbreakable
inquietante: *aj.* upsetting; worrisome
inquietar: *vt.* to disquiet; disturb; to worry; to be anxious; to upset

inquietarse: *vr.* to become upset
inquieto: *aj.* upset
inquietud: *nf.* anxiety; worry
inquilino -na: *nmf.* tenant
insalubre: *aj.* unhealthy
insalubridad: *nf.* poor health
insano: *aj.* insane
insatisfacción: *nf.* dissatisfaction
insatisfactorio: *aj.* unsatisfactory
insatisfecho: *aj.* unsatisfied
inscribir: *vt.* to inscribe; to register (on a record)
inscribirse: *vr.* to be inscribed; to enroll; to enlist
inscripción: *nf.* inscription; enrollment
inscrito: *aj.* inscribed; enrolled
insecticida: *aj.* insecticidal
insecticida: *nf.* insecticide
insectívoro: *aj.* insect-eating
insecto: *nm.* insect
inseguridad: *nf.* insecurity
inseguro: *aj.* insecure
inseminación: *nf.* insemination
inseminar: *vt.* to inseminate
insensatez: *nf.* senselessness
insensato: *aj.* senseless
insensibilidad: *nf.* insensibility
insensibilizar: *vt.* to desensitize
insensibilizarse: *vr.* to become desensitized
insensible: *aj.* unfeeling
inseparable: *aj.* inseparable
inseparablemente: *av.* inseparably
insertar: *vt.* to insert
inservible: *aj.* unusable
insigne: *aj.* illustrious; eminent; important; valued; celebrated
insignia: *nf.* insignia
insignificancia: *nf.* insignificance
insignificante: *aj.* insignificant
insinuación: *nf.* insinuation
insinuante: *aj.* insinuating; suggestive

insinuar: *vt.* to insinuate; hint; suggest
insistencia: *nf.* insistence
insistente: *aj.* insistent
insistentemente: *av.* insistently
insistir: *v.* to insist
insociable: *aj.* unsociable
insolación: *nf.* over-exposure to the sun
insólito -ta: *aj.* unusual
insoluble: *aj.* insoluble
insomnio: *nm.* insomnia; sleeplessness
insonorización: *nf.* soundproofing
insonorizado: *aj.* soundproof
insonorizar: *vt.* to soundproof
insonoro: *aj.* pleasant sounding
insoportable: *aj.* intolerable
insospechado: *aj.* unsuspected
insostenible: *aj.* unsustainable
inspeccionar: *vt.* to inspect; oversee
inspiración: *nf.* inspiration
inspirado: *aj.* inspired
inspirador: *aj.* inspiring
inspirar: *vt.* to inspire; inhale; breathe in; to inspire
instalación: *nf.* installation
instalador;-a: *nmf.* installer
instalar: *vt.* to install; induct
instalarse: *v.* to be installed
instantáneamente: *av.* instantaneously
instantáneo: *aj.* instantaneous
instante: *nm.* instant; moment
instaurar: *vt.* to restore; re-establish
instintivamente: *av.* instinctively
instintivo: *aj.* instinctive
instinto: *nm.* instinct
institución: *nf.* institution; pl. institutes
institucional: *aj.* institutional
institucionalizado: *aj.* institutionalized
institucionalizar: *vt.* to

institutionalize
instituido: *aj.* instituted
instituir: *vt.* to institute; establish
instituto: *nm.* institute
institutriz: *nf.* private teacher (woman)
instrucción: *nf.* instruction
instructivo: *aj.* instructive
instructor;-a: *nmf.* instructor
instruido: *aj.* instructed
instruir: *vt.* to instruct; teach; to drill; to inform; to learn
instrumentación: *nf.* instrumentation
instrumental: *aj.* instrumental
instrumental: *nm.* instruments or tools of a profession
instrumentista: *nmf.* person who plays a musical instrument; surgical assistant
instrumento: *nm.* instrument
insubordinación: *nf.* insubordination
insubordinado: *aj.* insubordinate
insubordinado;-a: *nmf.* an insubordinate person
insubordinar: *vt.* to disobey
insubordinarse: *vr.* to become insubordinate
insustancial: *aj.* insubstantial substantial;
insubstituible: *aj.* not substitutable sustituible;
insuficiencia: *nf.* insufficiency
insuficiente: *aj.* insufficient
insular: *aj.* insular
insultante: *aj.* insulting
insultar: *vt.* to insult
insulto: *nm.* insult
insumergible: *aj.* unsinkable
insuperable: *aj.* unconquerable; invincible
insustancialidad: *nf.* insubstantiality
intachable: *aj.* blameless; faultless
integral: 1. *aj.* integral; 2. *nf.* integral (math)

íntegramente: *av.* completely
integrante: *aj.* integral; integral part of a group
integrar: *vt.* to integrate; compose; form
integrarse: *vr.* to become integrated
integridad: *nf.* integrity; wholeness; integrity; honesty
integro -a: *aj.* integral; whole; entire; honest; upright
intelecto: *nm.* intellect
intelectual: 1. *aj.* intellectual; 2. *nmf.* intellectual
intelectualidad: *nf.* intelligentsia
intelectualismo: *nm.* intellectualism
inteligencia: *nf.* intelligence; intellect; mind
inteligente: *aj.* intelligent; clever
inteligible: *aj.* intelligible
intemperie: *nf.* outdoors
intempestivo: *aj.* inopportune; not at the right time
intención: *nf.* intention
intencionadamente: *av.* intentionally
intencionado: *aj.* intentioned
intencional: *aj.* intentional
intensidad: *nf.* intensity
intensificación: *nf.* intensification
intensificar: *vt.* to intensify
intensificarse: *v..* to become intensified
intensivo: *aj.* intensive
intenso: *aj.* intense
intentar: *vt.* to try; attempt; to intend; mean
intento: *nm.* attempt; try
intentona: *nf.* rash attempt
interacción: *nf.* interaction
intercambiable: *aj.* exchangeable
intercambiar: *vt.* to exchange
intercambio: *nm.* exchange
interceder: *vi.* to intercede
interceptar: *vt.* to intercept

intercomunicación: *nf.* intercommunication
intercomunicador: *nm.* intercom
interdecir: *vt.* to interdict
interdependencia: *nf.* interdependence
interdicción: *nf.* interdiction
interdicto: *nm.* interdict
interés: *nm.* interest
interesado: *aj.* interested
interesante: *aj.* interesting
interesar: *vt.* to interest; to concern
interesarse: *vr.* to become interested
interfono: *nm.* intercom
intergubernamental: *aj.* intergovernmental
interino -na: *aj.* provisional; temporary
interior: 1. *aj.* interior; 2. *nm.* interior
interioridad: *nf.* quality of the interior
interioridades: *nmf.* intimacies
interiorizarse: *vr.* to study a subject carefully
intermediar: *vi.* to be in the mid-dle; to mediate
intermediario: 1. *aj.* intermediary; 2. *nm.* intermediary
intermediario;-a: *nmf.* intermediary
intermedio: *aj.* intermediate
interminable: *aj.* interminable
internacional: *aj.* international
internacionalismo: *nm.* internationalism
internacionalizar: *vt.* to internationalize
internacionalizarse: *vr.* to become internationalized
internacionalmente: *av.* internationally
internamiento: *nm.* internment
internar: *vt.* to intern; to penetrate; to go deeply into

internista: 1. *aj.* internist; 2 *nmf.* internist.

interno -na: *aj.* internal; interior; boarding student

interplanetario: *aj.* interplanetary

interponer: *vt.* to interpose; place between

interponerse: *vr.* to interpose oneself; to put oneself between others

interposición: *nf.* interposition

interpretación: *nf.* interpretation

interpretar: *vt.* to interpret

intérprete: *nmf.* interpreter

interrogación: *nf.* interrogation

interrogador;-a: *nmf.* interrogator

interrogante: *aj.* interrogating

interrogante: *nm.* unknown

interrogar: *vt.* to interrogate

interrogativo: *aj.* interrogative

interrogatorio: *nm.* interrogatory; series of questions

interrumpir: *vt.* to interrupt; suspend; *ovr.* to be interrupted

interrupción: *nf.* interruption

interruptor: *nm.* interrupter; something or someone that interrupts

intersección: *nf.* intersection

interurbano: *aj.* inter-urban

intervención: *nf.* intervention

intervencionismo: *nm.* interventionism

intervencionista: 1. *aj.* interventionist; 2. *nmf.* interventionist

intervenir: *vi.* to intervene

intimar: *vt.* to intimate; notify; *vi.* to become intimate

intimidación: *nf.* intimidation

intimidad: *nf.* intimate friendship; intimacy

intimidades: *nmf.* family secrets

intimidar: *vt.* to intimidate; to daunt; to become intimidated

intimidarse: *vr.* to be intimidated

íntimo: *aj.* intimate

intitular: *vt.* to give a title to

intocable: 1. *aj.* untouchable; 2. *nmf.* untouchable

intolerable: *aj.* intolerable

intolerancia: *nf.* intolerance

intolerante: 1. *aj.* intolerant ; 2. *nmf.* intolerant

intoxicar: *vt.* to poison; to be poisoned

intramuros: *av.* intramural

intramuscular: *aj.* intramuscular; within the muscle

intranquilidad: *nf.* anxiety

intranquilizar: *vt.* to make nervous

intranquilizarse: *vr.* to become nervous

intranquilo: *aj.* anxious

intransitable: *aj.* impassable

intransitivo: *aj.* intransitive

intratable: *aj.* unsociable; hard to deal with

intravenoso: *aj.* intravenous

intrigar: *vi.* to intrigue; plot; scheme

intrincado -da: *aj.* intricate

introducción: *nf.* introduction; preliminary step

introducir: *vt.* to introduce; to insert; *ovr.* to introduce oneself

introducirse: *vr.* to enter; to become involved

introductor: *aj.* introductory

introductor;-a: *nmf.* introducer

intuición: *nf.* intuition

intuir: *vt.* to intuit; to know by intuition

intuitivamente: *av.* intuitively

intuitivo: *aj.* intuitive

inundar: *vt.* to inundate; to flood; to overflow

inusitado -da: *aj.* unusual

inútil: *aj.* useless

inutilidad: *nf.* uselessness

inutilizar: *vt.* to render useless; *ovr.*

to become useless
inútilmente: *av.* uselessly
invadir: *vt.* to invade
invalidación: *nf.* annulment
invalidar: *vt.* to invalidate
invalidez: *nf.* invalidity
inválido: *aj.* invalid; handicapped
invariabilidad: *nf.* invariability; unchanging
invariable: *aj.* invariable
invasión: *nf.* invasion
invasor;-a: *nmf.* invader
invencible: *aj.* invincible
invención: *nf.* invention
inventar: *vt.* to invent; contrive
inventiva: *nf.* inventiveness
inventivo: *aj.* inventive
invento: *nm.* invention
inventor;-a: *nmf.* inventor
invernal: *aj.* winter
invernar: *vi.* to spend the winter
inverosímil: *aj.* unbelievable
inversión: *nf.* investment; inversion
inversionista: *nmf.* investor
invertido: *aj.* invested; inverted
invertir: *vt.* to invest; to invert
investigación: *nf.* investigation
investigador: *aj.* investigating
investigar: *vt.* to investigate; inquire into
invidente: *aj.* blind
invidente: *nmf.* blind person
invierno: *nm.* winter
inviolabilidad: *nf.* inviolability
inviolable: *aj.* inviolable
inviolado: *aj.* inviolate
invisible: *aj.* invisible
invitación: *nf.* invitation
invitado;-a: *nmf.* invited guest
invitante: *aj.* inviting
invitar: *vt.* to invite
invocar: *vt.* to invoke; call upon
involuntario: *aj.* involuntary
inyección: *nf.* injection

ir: *vi.* to go proceed
ira: *nf.* anger; wrath
iracundo: *aj.* easily angered
iris: *nm.* iris; arco iris; rainbow
ironía: *nf.* irony
irónico: *aj.* ironic
ironizar: *vt.* to use irony
irradiación: *nf.* irradiation
irradiar: *vt.* to irradiate
irrazonable: *aj.* unreasonable
irreal: *aj.* unreal
irrealidad: *nf.* unreality
irrealizable: *aj.* unrealizable; unachievable
irreconocible: *aj.* unrecognizable
irreducible: *aj.* irreducible
irreflexión: *nf.* lack of reflexion
irreflexivo: *aj.* without reflection
irregular: *aj.* irregular
irregularidad: *nf.* irregularity
irremediable: *aj.* irremediable
irremediablemente: *av.* hopelessly
irremplazable: *aj.* irreplaceable
irreparable: *aj.* irreparable
irreprochable: *aj.* irreproachable
irresistible: *aj.* irresistible
irresoluto: *aj.* irresolute
irrespetuoso: *aj.* disrespectful
irrespirable: *aj.* unbreathable; suffocating
irresponsabilidad: *nf.* irresponsibility
irresponsable: *aj.* irresponsible
irresponsable: *nmf.* irresponsible person
irreversible: *aj.* irreversible
irrisorio: *aj.* laughable; ridiculous
irritabilidad: *nf.* irritability
irritable: *aj.* irritable
irritación: *nf.* irritation
irritante: *aj.* irritating
irritar: *vt.* to irritate; to anger; to annoy
irritarse: *vr.* to become irritated

irrompible: *aj.* unbreakable
irse: *vi.* to go away; to leave
isla: *nf.* island; isle
isleño;-a: *nmf.* islander
islote: *nf.* isolated rock that protrudes from the sea
islote: *nm.* small desert island
itinerante: *aj.* itinerant
itinerario: m. itinerary; route; timetable; programme
izar: *vt.* to hoist
izquierda: *nf.* left
izquierdismo: *nm.* political leftism
izquierdista: *aj.* leftist
izquierdo -da: *aj.* left

J

jabalí: *nm.* wild boar
jabón: *nm.* soap
jabonado: *nmf.* the act of putting soap on something
jabonar: *vt.* to soap. Jaca; *nf.* Cob
jaboncillo: *nm.* a small piece of soap; tailor's soap
jabonera: *nf.* soap dish
jabonoso: *aj.* soapy
jaleo: *nm.* noise; trouble; work
jamás: adv. never; ever
jamón: *nm.* ham
jaque: *nm.* check
jaqueca: *nf.* headache
jarabe: *nm.* syrup. jarana *nf.* con. fun
jardín: *nm.* garden
jardinería: *nf.* the art of gardening
jardinero;-a: *nmf.* gardener
jarra: *nf.* jar; jug
jarro: *nm.* pitcher; jug
jarrón: *nm.* vase

jaula: *nf.* cage; crate. jazmin *nm.* jasmine
jefa: *nf.* female boss; chief; or manager
jefatura: *nf.* leadership; management group; position of leadership
jefe: *nm.* boss; chief; manager; leader
jerarquía: *nf.* hierarchy
jerez: *nm.* sherry
jeringuilla: *nf.* syringe
jeroglífico -ca: *aj.* Hieroglyphic
Jesucristo: *nm.* Jesus Christ
Jesuita: 1. *aj.* Jesuit ; 2. *nmf.* Jesuit
Jesús: *nm.* Jesus
jinete: *nm.* horse man; rider
jinetear: *vt.* to mount a horse
jornada: *nf.* a day of work
jornal: *nm.* salary; wage
jornalero;-a: *nmf.* worker
joven: 1. *aj.* young; *nm.* youth; *nf.* girl; 2. *nmf.* young man or woman
jovencito;-a: 1. *aj.* very-young; teenage; 2. *nmf.* very young man or woman; teenager
jovial: *aj.* jovial; cheery
Joya: *nf.* jewel; piece of jewelry
joyería: *nmf.* jewelry store
joyero: *nm.* jewelry box
jubilación: *nf.* retirement; jubilation
jubilado: 1. *aj.* retired ; 2. *nmf.* retired person
jubilar (se): *vt.* (r) to retire
jubileo: *nm.* jubilee
júbilo: *nm.* rejoicing
jubiloso: *aj.* rejoicing
judaico: *aj.* Judaic
judaísmo: *nm.* Judaism
judaizar: *vt.* to convert to Judaism
judeocristiano: *aj.* Judeo-Christian
judería: *nf.* Jewry
judicial: *aj.* judicial; legal
judío: 1. *aj.* Jewish; 2. *nm.* Jewish; *nf.* Jewess

juego: *nm.* play; playing; game; cards; set
juerga: *nf.* con. carousal; spree
jueves: *nm.* Thursday
juez: *nm.* judge
jugada: *nf.* one play in a game
jugador;-a: *nmf.* player
jugar: *vt.* to play; to gamble; to stake
jugo: *nm.* juice; gravy
juguete: *nm.* toy; plaything
juguetear: *vi.* to do something for fun
juguetería: *nf.* toy store
juguetón: *nm.* overly playful
juicio: *nm.* judgment; considered opinion; trial
juicioso: *aj.* just; judicious
julio: *nm.* July
jumento: *nm.* ass; donkey
junio: *nm.* June
junta: *nf.* meeting
juntar: *vt.* to join; to unite; to gather
juntarse: *vr.* to become joined to
junto: *aj.* together
juntura: *nf.* area where two pieces are joined together
jura: *nf.* oath
jurado: 1. *aj.* jury; 2 *nm.* jury
juramentado: *aj.* sworn
juramentarse: *vr.* to take an oath
juramento: *nm.* oath; curse
jurar: *vt.* to swear
jurídico: *aj.* related to law
jurisconsulto: *nmf.* a person knowledgeable in law
jurisdicción: *nf.* jurisdiction
jurisdiccional: *aj.* jurisdictional
jurisperito: *nmf.* specialist in legal matters
jurisprudencia: *nf.* jurisprudence
jurista: *nmf.* jurist
justicia: *nf.* justice
justiciero: *aj.* exaggeratingly strict; following justice to the extreme

justificable: *aj.* justifiable
justificación: *nf.* justification
justificado: *aj.* justified
justificante: *aj.* justifying; proving
justificar: *vt.* to justify
justificarse: *vr.* to justify oneself
justo: 1. *aj.* just; 2. *nmf.* just person
juvenil: *aj.* youth; related to youth
juventud: *nf.* youth
juzgado: 1. *aj.* judged; 2. *nm.* court of justice
juzgar: *vt.* to judge; to give an opinion

K

kilo: *nm.* kilogram; kilo
kilociclo: *nm.* kilocycle
kilogramo: *nm.* kilogram
kilolitro: *nm.* kiloliter
kilometraje: *nm.* distance in kilometers
kilométrico ;-a: *aj.* kilometric; long; measuring in kilometers
kilómetro: *nm.* kilometer
kilovatio: *nm.* kilowatt
kiosco: *nm.* kiosk

L

labial: *aj.* labial
labio: *nm.* lip; labium
labiodental: *aj.* labiodental
labor: *nf.* labor; work; farm work;

farming; needlework
laborable: *aj.* workable
laboral: *aj.* work
laborar: *vt.* to work
laboratorio: *nm.* laboratory
laboriosidad: *nf.* laboriousness
laborioso: *aj.* laborious
labrado -da: *aj.* worked; wrought;
nm. working; carving
labrador: *nm.* agricultural worker
labranza: *nf.* agricultural cultivation
labrar: *vt.* to work; to carve; to
plough
labriego;-a: *nmf.* agricultural worker
lacrar: *vt.* to seal (with wax)
lacrimal: *aj.* lachrymal
lacrimógeno: *aj.* tear-provoking
lácteo -tea: *aj.* lacteous; milky
ladera: *nf.* slope; hillside
lado: *nm.* side; direction
ladrador: *aj.* barking
ladrar: *vt.* to bark
ladrillo: *nm.* brick
ladrón; na: *nm.* thief; burglar
ladronera: *nf.* thieves hideout
ladronzuelo;-a: *nmf.* little thief
lago: *nm.* lake
lágrima: *nf.* tear; drop
lagrimal: *nm.* tear duct
lagrimear: *vt.* to tear
lagrimeo: *nm.* tearing
laguna: *nf.* lagoon; pond; gap
llamar: *v.* to call
lamentable: *aj.* lamentable
lamentoso *aj.* making sorry
lamentablemente: *av.* lamentably
lamentación: *nf.* lamentation
lamentar: *vt.* to lament
lamentarse: *vr.* to be sorry
lamento: *nm.* lament
lámpara: *nf.* lamp; light; grease spot;
oil spot
lámpara: *nf.* lamp
lana: *nf.* wool

lance: *nm.* casting of a net when
fishing
lancha: *nf.* barge; gig long-boat
lanchero: *nmf.* boat owner or skipper
langosta: *nf.* locust; lobster
lanza: *nf.* lance; pike; spear
lanzacohetes: *nm.* rocket launcher
lanzada: *nf.* hit with a lance
lanzador;-a: *nmf.* pitcher
lanzagranadas: *nm.* grenade
launcher
lanzallamas: *nm.* flame-thrower
lanzamiento: *nm.* pitch; throw
lanzar: *vt.* to launch; to hurl; to
throw
lapicero: *nm.* pencil holder;
mechanical pencil
lápida: *nf.* tablet; tombstone
lápiz: *nm.* pencil; lápiz de labios;
lipstick
largo -ga: 1. *aj.* long; generous;
abundant; 2. *nm.* length
largometraje: *nm.* long film
largura: *nf.* length
laringe: *nf.* larynx
lástima: *nf.* pity
lastimado: *aj.* hurt
lastimadura: *nf.* wound
lastimar: *vt.* to hurt
lastimarse: *vr.* to hurt oneself
lastimero: *aj.* painful
lastimoso: *aj.* hurtful; pain-causing
lata: *nf.* tin plate; tin can
lateral: *aj.* lateral
latido: *nm.* beating
latigazo: *nm.* lash; stroke
latín: *nm.* Latin
latinidad: *nf.* Latin culture
latinismo: *nm.* Latinism
latinizar: *vt.* to Latinize a word
latino: *aj.* Latino
latir: *vt.* to beat; palpitate
latón: *nm.* brass
lava: *nf.* lava

lavable: *aj.* washable
lavabo: *nm.* washstand; wash-room; lavatory
lavacoches: *nmf.* car washer
lavada: *nf.* washing
lavadero: *nm.* washboard
lavado: *aj.* washed
lavado: *nm.* washing
lavadora: *nf.* washing machine
lavamanos: *nm.* sink
lavandera: *nf.* laundress; laundry-woman
lavandería: *nf.* laundromat
lavandero: *nmf.* person who washes clothes
lavaojos: *nm.* container for washing out the eyes
lavaplatos: *nm.* dishwasher
lavar: *vt.* to wash
lavarse: *vr.* to wash oneself
lavativa: *nf.* enema; colonic irrigation
lavatorio: *nm.* lavatory
lavavajillas: *nm.* dishwasher
lazar: *vt.* to lasso
lazo: *nm.* knot; bow; tie
leal: *aj.* loyal
lealtad: *nf.* loyalty
lección: *nf.* lesson
lechazo: *nm.* sucking lamb
leche: *nf.* milk
milklechada: *nf.* whitewash
lechería: *nf.* dairy store
lechero: *aj.* milk-producing
lecho: *nm.* bed; couch
lechoso: *aj.* milky; milk-like
lechuga: *nf.* lettuce
lector -ra: 1. *aj.* reading; reader; lector; 2. *nmf.* reader
lectura: *nf.* reading
leer: *vt.* to read
legal: *aj.* legal
legalidad: *nf.* legality
legalismo: *nm.* legalism

legalista: *nmf.* legalist
legalización: *nf.* legalization
legalizar: *vt.* to legalize
legalmente: *av.* legally
legaña: *nf.* (Path.) blearieye
legible: *aj.* readable
legión: *nf.* legion
legionario: 1. *aj.* legionary; 2. *nm.* legionary
legitimar: *vt.* to legitimize
legitimidad: *nf.* authenticity
legítimo: *aj.* legitimate
legua: *nf.* league
legumbre: *nf.* legume
leído: *aj.* read
lejanía: *nf.* far distance
lejano: *aj.* distant
lejía: *nf.* lye; bleaching
lejísimos: *av.* very far away
lejos: *av.* far away
leña: *nf.* firewood;
lencería: *nf.* linen goods
lengua: *nf.* tongue; language
lenguaje: *nm.* language
lengüetada: *nm.* a lick
lentamente: *av.* slowly
lente: *nmf.* lens; pl. spectacles; glasses
lentitud: *nf.* slowness
lento -ta: *aj.* slow; heavy
Leo: *nm.* Leo
león: *nm.* lion
leona: *nf.* lioness
leonera: *nf.* lion cage
leopardo: *nm.* leopard
les: *prom. pers.* (to) them; (ta) you
lesión: *nf.* lesion; wound
lesionado: 1. *aj.* wounded; 2. *nmf.* wounded person
lesionar: *vt.* to hurt; injure
lesionarse: *vr.* to become wounded
lesivo: *aj.* wounding; injuring
leso: *aj.* injured; used in law referring to an injured party

letra: *nf.* letter
letrado: 1. *aj.* literate; 2. *nmf.* literate person
letrero: *nm.* label; sign; placard
levadizo: *aj.* able to raise; often said of drawbridges
levadura: *nf.* yeast; ferment
levantada: *nf.* act of getting out of bed
levantador;-a de pesas: *nmf.* weightlifter
levantamiento: *nm.* the raising
levantar: *vt.* to raise; to lift; to clear (the table); to weigh (anchor)
levantarse: *vr.* to get up
léxico: *nm.* lexicon; vocabulary
ley: *nf.* law; loyalty; norm; standard
leyenda: *nf.* legend; inscription
liar: *vt.* to tie; bind; to tie up; to roll
liberación: *nf.* liberation
liberado: *aj.* liberated
liberador;-a: *nmf.* liberator
liberal: 1. *aj.* liberal; generous; 2. *nm.* liberal
liberalidad: *nf.* liberality
liberalismo: *nm.* liberalism
liberalización: *nf.* liberalization
liberalizar: *vt.* to liberalize
liberalmente: *av.* liberally
liberar: *vt.* to free
liberarse: *vr.* to become liberated
librería: *nf.* bookstore; bookshop
libertad: *nf.* liberty; freedom
libertador;-a: *nmf.* liberator of a nation
libertar: *vt.* to liberate; to set free
libertario: 1. *aj.* libertarian; 2. *nmf.* libertarian
libertinaje: *nm.* licentiousness
libertino: 1. *aj.* libertine; 2. *nmf.* libertine
libra: *nf.* pound
libranza: *nf.* draft; bill of exchange
librar: *vt.* to free; to save; spare; to

join (battle)
libre: *aj.* free; vacant
librecambio: *nm.* free trade
librecambista: 1. *aj.* free-trading; 2. *nmf.* free-trader
librepensador: 1. *aj.* free-thinking; 2. *nmf.* free-thinker
librepensamiento: *nm.* free thinking; free thought
librería: *nf.* bookstore
librero: *nm.* bookcase
libreta: *nf.* notebook; loaf of bread
libro: *nm.* book
licencia: *nf.* license
licenciado: *aj.* certified; licensed
licenciado -da: *nm.* graduated; certified professional
licenciar: *vt.* to license; to discharge
licenciarse: *vr.* to become certified or licensed
licenciatura: *nf.* licensure
licencioso: *aj.* licentious
liceo: *nm.* lyceum
lícito: *aj.* licit
licor: *nm.* liquor; spirits
licorera: *nf.* decanter
licorería: *nf.* liquor store
licuado: *nm.* milkshake-like drink
licuar: *vt.* to liquefy
licuarse: *vr.* to become liquefied
líder: *nm.* leader
lidiar: *vt.* to fight; to face up
liebre: *nf.* hare
lienzo: *nm.* linen; linen cloth
ligado: *aj.* tied
ligado: *nm.* a tie in music; tied notes
ligadura: *nf.* action of tying
ligamento: *nm.* ligament
ligar: *vt.* to tie; bind; to alloy; to join
ligarse: *vr.* to become tied
ligeramente: *av.* lightly
ligereza: *nf.* lightness
ligero -ra: *aj.* light; fast; slight; simply

lijar: *vt.* to sand
lila: *nf.* lilac
lima: *nf.* file
limar: *vt.* to file; to polish
limero: *nm.* lime seller
limitación: *nf.* limitation
limitado: *aj.* limited
limitar: *vt.* to limit; to restrict
limitarse: *vr.* to limit oneself
límite: *nm.* limit
limón: *nm.* lemon; lemon tree
limonada: *nf.* lemonade
limonero: 1. *aj.* lemon; 2. *nm.* lemon seller
limosna: *nf.* alms
limpiabotas: *nm.* bootblack
limpiachimeneas: *nm.* chimney-sweep
limpiador: *nm.* rag
limpiaparabrisas: *nm.* windshield wipers
limpiar: *vt.* to clean; to cleanse
limpiarse: *vr.* to clean oneself
limpieza: *nf.* cleaning
limpio -pia: *aj.* clean; neat; chaste; clear; free
linaje: *nm.* lineage; class
lindamente: *av.* prettily; in a wonderful way
lindar: *vt.* to border on
linde: *nmf.* property line
lindeza: *nf.* prettiness; handsomeness; wonderfulness
lindo: *aj.* pretty; handsome; wonderful
línea: *nf.* line
lineal: *aj.* linear
lingual: *aj.* lingual
lingüista: *nmf.* linguist
lingüística: *nf.* linguistics
liquidación: *nf.* liquidation
liquidado: *aj.* liquidated
liquidar: *vt.* to liquidate
liquidez: *nf.* liquidity

líquido: 1. *aj.* liquid; 2. *nm.* liquid
lírica: *nf.* a musical
lírico: *aj.* lyrical
lirio: *nm.* lily
lisiar: *vt.* to hurt; cripple; *vr.* to become crippled
liso -sa: *aj.* smooth; even; plain; unadorned
lista: *nf.* list
listo -ta: *aj.* ready; prepared
listón: *nm.* tape; ribbon; strip (of wood)
literal: *aj.* literal
literalmente: *av.* literally
literario: *aj.* literary
literato; -a: *nmf.* writer
literatura: *nf.* literature
litigio: *nm.* lawsuit; litigation
litro: *nm.* liter
liviandad: *nf.* lightness (weight)
liviano: *aj.* light (weight)
lívido -da: *aj.* livid
llaga: *nf.* ulcer; sore
llama: *nf.* flame; blaze
llamada: *nf.* call; sign; signal
llamado: *aj.* called
llamador: *nm.* doorbell
llamamiento: *nm.* calling
llamar: *vt.* to call; to summon
llamarada: *nf.* flare-up
llamarada: *nf.* sudden bursts of flame
llamarse: *vr.* to call oneself
llanero;-a: *nmf.* ranger; one who lives on a plain
llano: 1. *nm.* plain; flatland; 2. *aj.* smooth; even; level; plain; clear; evident
llanto: *nm.* weeping; crying
llanura: *nf.* smoothness; evenness; plain
llave: *nf.* key; wrench; tap; faucet
llavero: *nm.* keeper of the keys; key ring

llegada: *nf.* arrival
llegar: *vi.* to arrive; to happen; to reach; to amount to
llenar: *vt.* to fill; to fulfill; to satisfy; fill up; become full
llenarse: *vr.* to become full
lleno: *aj.* full
llevadero -ra: *aj.* bearable; toler-able
llevar: *vt.* to carry; to take; to lead; to yield; to keep
llorar: *vt.* to weep; *vi.* to weep; cry
lloriquear: *vi.* to whine; to cry without reason or only for attention
lloriqueo: *nm.* whining; crying for attention only
lloro: *nm.* crying
llorón: *aj.* frequently crying
lloroso: *aj.* tearful
llover: *vt.* to rain; to leak
llovizna: *nf.* light rain; sprinkling
lloviznar: *vi.* to drizzle; to rain lightly; to sprinkle
lluvia: *nf.* rain
lluvioso: *aj.* rainy
lo: art. def; neut. the; him; it
lobo: *nm.* wolf
local: *aj.* local; *nm.* rooms; quarters; locale; place
localidad: *nf.* locality
localización: *nf.* localization
localizar: *vt.* to localize; to find
locatario;-a: *nmf.* tenant
loción: *nf.* wash; lotion
loco: *aj.* crazy
locomoción: *nf.* locomotion
locomotor: *aj.* locomotive
locomotora: *nf.* locomotive
locura: *nf.* madness; insanity
locutor -tora: *nmf.* announcer; speaker
lodo: *nm.* mud
lograr: *vt.* to get; obtain; to produce
lógica: *nf.* logic
lógicamente: *av.* logically

lógico: 1. *aj.* logical; 2. *nmf.* logician
logrado: *aj.* accomplished; achieved
lograr: *vt.* to achieve; to reach a goal
lograrse: *vr.* to accomplish
logro: *nm.* accomplishment
lúgubre: *aj.* dismal; gloomy; dark
lombriz: *nf.* worm; earthworm
lomo: *nm.* back
longaniza: *nf.* pork sausage
longitud: *nf.* length; longitude
longitudinal: *aj.* longitudinal
longitudinalmente: *av.* longitudinally
lonja: *nf.* exchange; market
lúpulo: *nm.* hop
loquero;-a: *nmf.* caretaker of people who are mentally ill
loro: *nm.* parrot
losa: *nf.* slab; flagstone
lote: *nm.* lot; share
lotería: *nf.* lottery
loza: *nf.* earthenware; crockery
lubricar: *vt.* to lubricate
lucha: *nf.* fight; struggle; quarrel
luchador: 1. *aj.* struggling; 2. *nmf.* struggler; fighter
luchar: *vi.* to fight; to struggle; to quarrel
lucidez: *nf.* lucidity; clarity
lúcido: *aj.* radiating; shining; lucid; clear
luciente: *aj.* shiny; bright
luciérnaga: *nf.* firefly
lucimiento: *nm.* shining; brilliance
lucir: *vt.* to radiate; to shine
lucirse: *vr.* to be a shining example; to be brilliant; to dress sharply
lucrar: *v.* to profit; to get money
luego: adv. soon; at once; desde luego; of course; right away; hasta luego; see you
lugar: *nm.* place; position; spot; seat
lujo: *nm.* luxury
lujosamente: *av.* luxuriously

lujoso: *aj.* luxurious
lumbre: *nf.* fire; light
lumbrera: *nf.* flame
luminaria: *nf.* lighting
luminiscencia: *nf.* luminescence
luminiscente: *aj.* luminescent
luminosidad: *nf.* luminosity
luminoso: *aj.* luminous
luna: *nm.* moon; mirror
lunar: *nm.* round mark on the skin; mole; beauty mark
lunático: 1. *aj.* lunatic; crazy; 2. *nmf.* lunatic
lunes: *nm.* Monday
lupa: *nf.* magnifying glass
lustrar: *vt.* to shine something
lustre: *nm.* the act of shining of something
luto: *nm.* mourning; sorrow
luz: *nm.* light; opening; pl. enlighten-ment

M

macabro -bra: *aj.* macabre
macarrón: *nm.* macaroni; macaroon
maceta: *nf.* plant pot
machacar: *vt.* to pound; crush; bruise; drum; *vi.* to importune
machete: *nm.* cutlass
macroeconomía: *nf.* macroeconomics
madeja: *nf.* hank (or) skein; lock of hair
madera: *nf.* wood; timber
maderable: *aj.* timber-yielding
maderaje: *nm.* woodwork
maderería: *nf.* woodworking shop or store
maderero;-a: *nmf.* woodworker

madero: *nf.* log
madrastra: *nf.* step-mother
madraza: *nf.* over-protective mother
madre: *nf.* mother; generatrix; nun
madreperla: *nf.* mother-of-pearl
madrina: *nf.* godmother; sponsor
madrugada: *nf.* midnight to sunrise
madrugador: *aj.* early-morning rising
madrugar: *vi.* to rise early; to get up early
maduración: *nf.* maturation
madurar: *vt.* to ripen; mature; to season
madurez: *nf.* maturity
maduro: *aj.* mature
maestra: *nf.* teacher; instructress
maestría: *nf.* master's degree
maestro -tra: 1. *aj.* masterly; main; 2. *nm.* master; teacher
magisterio: *nm.* profession of teaching
magistral: *aj.* pertaining to teaching
magnetófono: *nm.* tape recorder
magnificar: *vt.* to laud or praise
magnificencia: *nf.* magnificence
magnífico: *aj.* magnificent
magnitud: *nf.* magnitude
magno: *aj.* great; extraordinary maintaining health
mago -ga: *nm.* magician
magulladura: *nf.* bruising; contusion
magullar: *vt.* to bruise; to mangle
maicena: *nf.* corn starch
maíz: *nm.* corn
maizal: *nm.* cornfield
majestad: *nf.* majesty
majestuosidad: *nf.* majesty
majestuoso: *aj.* majestic
majo: 1. *aj.* showy; 2. *nm.* dandy; sickness; ache
mal: *aj.* bad
malacostumbrado: *aj.* having the bad habit of

malacostumbrar: *v.* to develop a bad habit

malamente: *av.* badly

malandanza: *nf.* misfortune

malandrín: 1. *aj.* criminal; 2. *nmf.* scoundrel

malasombra: *nmf.* person with brusque or poor manners

malbaratar: *vt.* to sell below cost or value

malcarado: *aj.* irritable; with an angry-looking face

malcasado: *aj.* separated or divorced

malcomer: *vi.* to eat poorly

malcriado: *aj.* spoiled

malcriar: *vt.* to spoil

maldad: *nf.* evil

maldecido: *aj.* cursed

maldecir: *vt.* to damn; curse; accurse

maldiciente: *aj.* cursing

maldición: *nf.* curse

maldito: *aj.* cursed; damned

maleante: *aj.* immoral; criminal

maleante: *nmf.* fugitive from the law; rogue; immoral person

malear: *vt.* to pervert; corrupt; to forge

malearse: *vr.* to damage or ruin oneself

maledicencia: *nf.* cursing

maleducado: *aj.* rude

maleficio: *nm.* curse; spell

maléfico: *aj.* damaging

malentendido: *nm.* misunderstanding

malestar: *nm.* feeling of illness

maleta: *nf.* valise; suit-case

malevolencia: *nf.* malevolence

malévolo: *aj.* malevolent

malformación: *nf.* malformation

malgastador: *aj.* misspending

malgastador;-a: *nmf.* spendthrift

malgastar: *vt.* to misspend; waste; squander

malhablado;-a: *nmf.* blasphemer; shameless person

malhadado: *aj.* unfortunate person

malhechor: *aj.* delinquent

malhechor;-a: *nmf.* criminal

malherir: *vt.* to hurt badly

malhumor: *nm.* bad mood

malhumorado: *aj.* in a bad mood

malhumorar: *vt.* to put someone in a bad mood

malhumorarse: *vr.* to be in a bad mood

malicia: *nf.* malice

maliciar: *vt.* to damage; to ruin

malicioso: *aj.* malicious

malignidad: *nf.* malignity

maligno: *aj.* malignant

malintencionado: *aj.* ill-intentioned

malmirado: *aj.* badly thought of

malo: *aj.* bad

malogrado: *aj.* failed

malograr: *vt.* to lose; waste; miss; to fall through

malograrse: *vr.* to fail to accomplish

maloliente: *aj.* bad-smelling

malparado -da: *aj.* damaged

malpensado: *aj.* bad or evil thinking

malpensado;-a: *aj.* pessimist

malquerencia: *nf.* ill-will

malquerer: *vt.* to wish evil on someone

malsano: *aj.* unhealthy

malsonante: *aj.* bad-sounding; unpleasant sounding

maltratar: *vt.* to mishandle; abuse; to spoil

maltrato: *nm.* mistreatment

maltrecho: *aj.* unkempt

malva: *nf.* mallow

malvado: *aj.* evil

malvado;-a: *mnf* evildoer

malvender: *vt.* to sell below cost or value

malversación: *nf.* misappropriation of funds
malversador: 1. *aj.* fraudulent; embezzling; 2. *nmf.* embezzler
malversar: *vt.* to embezzle
malvivir: *vi.* to be needy; to live under difficult circumstances
mamá: *nf.* mom; mother
mamada: *nf.* sucking of the breast
mamar: *vt.* to suckle; to drink from breast or bottle
mamario: *aj.* mammary
mañana: *nf.* morning; tomorrow;
mañanero: *aj.* early morning
mañanita: *nf.* early morning
manantial: *aj.* flowing; *nm.* waterspring; fountain
manar: *vi.* to spring from; flow
mancha: *nf.* stain
manchado: *aj.* stained
manchar: *vt.* to stain; spot; dirty
mancharse: *vr.* to become stained
manchón: *nm.* big stain
mancilla: *nf.* dishonor
mancillado: *aj.* dirty; with stains; dishonored
mancillar: *vt.* to stain; to dishonor
mancillarse: *vr.* to become stained; to become dishonored
mancomunar: *vt.* to associate or place two people together for a purpose
mancomunarse: *vr.* to be grouped; associated; or placed together for a common purpose
mancomunidad: *nf.* grouping or associating of people for a common purpose
mandado: *nm.* grocery shopping
mandamiento: *nm.* commandment
mandar: *vt. & vi.* to command; to govern; boss; dictate; lead
mandatario;-a: *nmf.* governor
mandato: *nm.* mandate

mandíbula: *nf.* jawbone
mandil: *nm.* apron
mando: *nm.* authority
mandón: 1. *aj.* bossy; 2. nmf bossy person
manejabilidad: *nf.* manageability
manejable: *aj.* manageable
manejar: *vt.* to manage; to drive
manejarse: *vr.* to manage oneself
manejo: *nm.* managing; driving
manera: *nf.* manner; way
manga: *nf.* sleeve; waterspout; breath of ship's beam
mango: *nm.* handle of a tool
manía: *nf.* mania
maníaco: *aj.* maniacal
maníaco;-a: *nmf.* maniac
maniaco depresivo: *aj.* manic-depressive
manicomio: *nm.* madhouse
manicura: *nf.* manicure
manicuro;-a: *nmf.* manicurist
manifestación: *nf.* demonstration; declaration
manifestador: *aj.* demonstrating
manifestante: *nmf.* demonstrator
manifestar: *vt.* to manifest; to show
manifestarse: *vr.* to manifest oneself; to show oneself
manifiesto: *aj.* manifest; evident
manifiesto: *nm.* manifesto
manija: *nf.* tool handle; furniture handles
manilargo: *aj.* with long hands
manilla: *nf.* bracelet; handle
maniobra: *nf.* handiwork; stratagem
maniobrabilidad: *nf.* maneuverability
maniobrable: *aj.* maneuverable
maniobrar: *vt.* to maneuver
manipulación: *nf.* manipulation
manipulador: *aj.* manipulating
manipular: *vt.* to manipulate; handle
manipuleo: *nm.* manipulation

mano: *nf.* hand
manojo: *nm.* handful; parcel; bunch
manopla: *nf.* mitten
manoseado: *aj.* over-handled
manosear: *vt.* to finger; to put one's hands in something; to paw
manoseo: *nm.* fingering; picking with hands or fingers (e.g.; food); pawing
manotazo: *nm.* hit with the hand
manotear: *vti.* to flail; to gesticulate
manoteo: *nm.* exaggerated gesture; flailing
manso -sa: *aj.* tame; domestic
manta: *nf.* blanket
mantel: *nm.* tablecloth
mantelería: *nf.* table linen
manteleta: *nf.* cape for covering the shoulders
mantener: *vt.* to maintain
mantenerse: *vr.* to maintain oneself; to keep on
mantenido: *aj.* maintained
mantenimiento: *nm.* maintenance
mantequilla: *nf.* butter
mantilla: *nf.* saddlecloth; scarf
manto: *nm.* cover
mantón: *nm.* shawl
manual: 1. *aj.* manual;2. *nm.* manual
manubrio: *nm.* handle
manufactura: *nf.* manufacture
manufacturado: *aj.* manufactured
manufacturar: *vt.* to manufacture
manufacturero: *aj.* manufacturing
manuscrito: 1. *aj.* manuscript; 2. *nm.* manuscript
manutención: *nf.* maintaining; maintenance
manzana: *nf.* apple; block
mapa: *nm.* map; chart
máquina: *nf.* machine
maquinación: *nf.* machination; intrigue; conspiracy
maquinal: *aj.* mechanical

maquinar: *vt.* to work with a machine; to conspire
maquinaria: *nf.* machinery
maquinismo: *nm.* mechanization process in general
maquinista: *nmf.* machinist
maquinización: *nf.* mechanization
maquinizar: *vt.* to mechanize
mar: *nmf.* sea; ocean
maravilla: *nf.* marvel
maravillar: *v.* to be marvelous
maravillarse: *vr.* to be surprised or amazed
maravillosamente: *av.* marvelously
maravilloso: *aj.* marvelous
marca: *nf.* mark; stamp; sign; character
marcadamente: *av.* markedly
marcado: *aj.* marked
marcador: 1. *aj.* marking; useful for marking; 2. *nm.* marker; scoreboard
marcapasos: *nm.* heart pacemaker
marcar: *vt.* to mark
marchan: *nf.* march
marchar: *vi.* to march; to run (machine); to be on the move
marcharse: *vr.* to go away
marchitar: *vt.* to wither; fade
marco: *nm.* frame
marea: *nf.* tide
mareado: *aj.* dizzy
mareaje: *nm.* art of navigation
mareante: *aj.* dizzying
marear: *vt.* to make dizzy
marearse: *vr.* to become dizzy
marejada: *nf.* high sea; swell
maremoto: *nm.* earthquake under the ocean floor
mareo: *nm.* dizziness
marfil: *nm.* ivory
margen: *nmf.* margin (river) side; border; edge
marginal: *aj.* marginal; pertaining to the margin or edge of something

marginar: *vt.* to put margins
Maria: *nf.* Mary
marido: *nm.* husband
marina: *nf.* navy; coast
marinería: *nf.* seamanship; profession of a sailor
marinero: *aj.* naval; navy
marino;-a: *nmf.* marine
marioneta: *nf.* puppet
mariposa: *nf.* butterfly
marisco: *nm.* seafood
marisquería: *nf.* seafood store
marital: *aj.* marital
marítimo: *aj.* maritime
mármol: *nm.* marble
marmolería: *nf.* workshop where marble is worked; large amount of marble
marmolista: *nmf.* one who works with marble
marmóreo: *aj.* marble; of marble
marrón: *aj.* brown
martes: *nm.* Tuesday
martillar; martillear: *vt.* to hammer
martillazo: *nm.* hit with a hammer
martilleo: *nm.* hammering
martillo: *nm.* hammer
martinete: *nm.* mallet
mártir: *nmf.* martyr
martirio: *nm.* martyrdom
martirizador: *aj.* martyring; torturing
martirizador;-a: *mnf* one who tortures or does the killing of a martyr
martirizar: *vt.* to martyr; to torture
marzo: *nm.* March
mas: *adv.* more; most; plus; longer; rather
mas: *conj.* But
masa: *nf.* mass; dough
masaje: *nm.* massage
mascar: *vt.* to chew; *con.* to mumble; to mutter

masilla: *nf.* putty
matachín: *nm.* butcher
matadero: *nm.* slaughterhouse
matador: *nm.* killer; matador; bullfighter
matamoscas: *nm.* flyswatter
matanza: *nf.* massacre; slaughter
matar: *vt.* to kill
matarratas: *nm.* rat poison
matarse: *vr.* to kill oneself; to commit suicide
matasanos: *nmf.* quack
matasellos: *nm.* stamp used to cancel stamps; postmark
matemática: *nf.* mathematics
matemáticamente: *av.* mathematically
matemático: 1. *aj.* mathematical; 2. *nm.* mathematics
matemático;-a: *nm.* mathematician
materia: *nf.* matter; stuff; material; subject
material: 1. *nm.* material; 2. *aj.* material
materialidad: *nf.* materiality
materialismo: *nm.* materialism
materialista: 1. *aj.* materialistic; 2. *nm.* materialistic person
materialización: *nf.* materialization
materializar: *vt.* to materialize; to become real
maternal: *aj.* maternal
maternidad: *nf.* maternity
materno: *aj.* maternal
matinal: *aj.* morning
matiz: *nm.* hue; shade
matización: *nf.* combining of colors
matizar: *vt.* to combine colors
matriarcado: *nm.* matriarchy
matriarcal: *aj.* matriarchal
matricida: *nmf.* murderer of one's mother
matricidio: *nm.* matricide
matricula: *nf.* register; roll;

matriculation
matriculación: *nf.* matriculation;
registration
matricular: *vt.* to matriculate; to
enroll; to register
matricularse: *vr.* to be matriculated;
to be enrolled
matrimonial: *aj.* matrimonial
matrimonio: *nm.* matrimony;
marriage
matriz: *nf.* womb; uterus;
headquarters
máxima: *nf.* maxim; precept
máximo: 1. *aj.* maximum; 2. *nm.*
maximum
mayo: *nm.* May
mayonesa: *nf.* mayonnaise
mayor: *aj.* older; bigger
mayoral: *nm.* shepherd; one who
looks after a flock
mayorazgo: *nm.* primogeniture;
rights of the firstborn
mayordomo: *nm.* butler
mayoría: *nf.* majority
mayorista: *nmf.* wholesaler
mayoritario: *aj.* majority
mayúscula: *nf.* capital letter
mazmorra: *nf.* dungeon
mazo: *nm.* mallet; maul; bunch
mear: *vt.* to urinate
mecánica: *nf.* mechanic
mecánico: *aj.* mechanical
mecanismo: *nmf.* mechanism
mecanización: *nf.* mechanization
mecanizar: *vt.* to mechanize
mecanografía: *nf.* typing
mecanografiar: *vt.* to type on a
typewriter
mecanógrafo; a: *nmf.* typist
mecer: *vt.* to stir; to shake; to swing;
to rock
mecha: *nf.* wick; fuse; match; tin-der
mechero: *nm.* burner; lighter
medalla: *nm.* medal

medallista: *nmf.* medalist
medallón: *nm.* medallion
media: *nf.* stocking
mediación: *nf.* mediation
mediado: *aj.* half-full
mediador;-a: *nmf.* mediator
medialuna: *nf.* half-moon shaped
object
mediana: *nf.* medium
medianero: *aj.* intervening; middle;
dividing
medianía: *nf.* medium position
mediano: *aj.* medium
medianoche: *nf.* midnight
mediante: *prep.* through; by way of
mediar: *vi.* to be or get halfway; to
be half over; to mediate
medicación: *nf.* medication
medicamento: *nm.* medicine
medicamentoso: *aj.* medicinal
medicar: *vt.* to medicate
medicarse: *vr.* to be medicated
medicina: *nf.* medicine
medicinal: *aj.* medicinal
medicinar: *vt.* to medicate
medición: *nf.* measuring;
measurement
médico -ca: *aj.* medical; *nm.* doctor
medida: *nf.* measure; measurement
medidor: *aj.* measuring
medieval: *aj.* medieval
medievalismo: *nm.* medievalism
medievalista: *nmf.* medievalist
medievo: *nm.* Middle Ages
medio: 1. *aj.* half; middle; 2. *av.* half;
partly
mediocre: *aj.* mediocre
mediocridad: *nf.* mediocrity
mediodía: *nm.* noon; mid-day; south
mediodía: *nf.* noon
Medir: *vt.* to measure; to scan
(verse); *vi.* to be moderate
meditabundo: *aj.* thoughtful
meditación: *nf.* meditation

meditar: *vti.* to meditate
meditativo: *aj.* meditative
medroso: *aj.* causing fear; provoking fear
Médula: *nf.* marrow
medular: *aj.* pertaining to marrow or pith
megafonía: *nf.* Megaphone; speaker
megáfono: *nm.* megaphone
Mejilla: *nf.* check
mejor: 1. *aj.* better; best; 2. adv. better; best; rather
mejora: *nf.* improvement
mejorable: *aj.* improvable
mejoramiento: *nm.* improvement
mejorar: *vt.* to make better; to improve; to mend
mejorarse: *vr.* to improve oneself; to become improved
Mejoría: *nf.* improvement
Melado: *aj.* honey-colored
Melancolía: *nf.* melancholy
melancólico;-a: *nmf.* person suffering from melancholy
Melaza: *nf.* molasses
Melcocha: *nf.* honey-like paste made of sugar
Melena: *nf.* long lock of hair; long hair; loose hair
Mella: *nf.* nick; dent; gap; hollow; harm
mellizo –za: 1. *aj.* twin; 2. *nmf.* twin
melocotón: *nm.* peach
melosidad: *nf.* sweetness
meloso: *aj.* honey-like
membrete: *nm.* letterhead; heading. *nm.* quince
memorable: *aj.* memorable
memorándum: *nm.* memorandum
memoria: *nf.* memory
memorial: *nm.* memorial
memorión: *aj.* possessing an excellent memory
memorización: *nf.* memorization

memorizar: *vt.* to memorize
amenazante: *aj.* threatening
mención: *nf.* mention
mencionado: *aj.* mentioned
mencionar: *vt.* to mention
mendicidad: *nf.* begging
mendigar: *vti.* to beg
mendigo;-a: *nmf.* beggar
menear: *vt.* to stir; to shake; to wage
menguar: *vt.* to lessen; diminish; to wane; to fall
meñique: *aj.* little; *nm.* little finger
menor: 1. *aj.* less; smaller; younger; least; smallest; youngest; 2. *nmf.* minor; younger
menos: 1. *aj.* minus (sign); 2. *av.* less; fewer; least; lowest
menoscabar: *vt.* to discredit
menoscabo: *nm.* discrediting
menospreciable: *aj.* contemptible; despicable
menospreciar: *vt.* to disdain; to scorn; to despise
menosprecio: *nm.* disdain; scorn
mensaje: *nm.* message
mensajero: *aj.* pertaining to messages
mensual: *aj.* monthly
menta: *nf.* mint
mental: *aj.* mental
mentalidad: *nf.* mentality
mentalmente: *av.* mentally
mente: *nf.* mind
mentecato: *aj.* foolish
mentecato;-a: *nmf.* fool; idiot
mentir: *vi.* to lie; to be false
mentira: *nf.* lie
mentiroso -sa: 1. *aj.* lying; liar; 2. *nmf.* liar
menudillo: *nm.* pl. giblets
menudo -da: *aj.* small; slight; minute
meollo: *nm.* marrow; essence
mercadear: *vi.* to buy or sell; to participate in a market

mercader: *nmf.* merchant
mercadería: *nf.* participation in a market
mercado: *nm.* market
mercadotecnia: *nf.* marketing
mercancía: *nf.* merchandise
mercante: *aj.* merchant
mercantil: *aj.* mercantile
mercantilismo: *nm.* mercantilism
mercantilista: 1. *aj.* mercantilist; 2. *nmf.* mercantilist
merecedor: *aj.* meriting; deserving
merecer: *vt.* to deserve; to merit; to be worth
merecerse: *vr.* to be deserving of
merecidamente: *av.* deservedly
merecido: *aj.* merited; deserved
merecimiento: *nm.* condition of being deserving
merendar: *vt.* to lunch; to have afternoon tea; *vi.* to lunch
meridiano: 1. *aj.* meridian; 2.*nm.* meridian
meridional: *aj.* southern
merienda: *nf.* lunch; snack; afternoon tea; picnic
mérito: *nm.* merit
meritocracia: *nf.* meritocracy
meritorio: *aj.* meritorious
merluza: *nf.* hake
mermelada: *nf.* marmalade; jam
mero -ra: *aj.* mere
mes: *nm.* month
mesa: *nf.* table; desk
mesilla: *nf.* small table
meta: *nf.* goal; limit; purpose
metal: *nm.* metal; brass; latten
metálico: *aj.* metallic
metalista: *nmf.* metal worker
metalización: *nf.* covering with metal
metalizar: *vt.* to cover something in metal
metaloide: *nm.* metalloid

metalurgia: *nf.* metallurgy
metalúrgico: *aj.* metallurgic; pertaining to metallurgy
meter: *vt.* to insert
meterse: *vr.* to insert oneself; to go inside
metódico: *aj.* methodical
metodizar: *vt.* to methodize; to systematize
método: *nm.* method; system
metodología: *nf.* methodology
metodológico: *aj.* methodological
metralla: *nf.* grapeshot; shrapnel balls
métrica: *aj.* metric
metro: *nm.* meter
metrónomo: *nm.* metronome
metrópoli: *nf.* metropolis
metropolitano: *aj.* metropolitan
mezcla: *nf.* mixture
mezcladora: *nf.* mixing machine; mixer
mezclar: *vt.* to mix; *vr.* to mix; to mingle
mezclarse: *vr.* to be mixed; to be involved
mezcolanza: *nf.* strange mixture
mezquita: *nf.* mosque
mi: *aj.* my; *nm.* mi
mí: *pron* me
microbiología: *nf.* microbiology
microbiológico: *aj.* microbiological
micrófono: *nm.* microphone
microorganismo: *nm.* micro-organism
microtecnología: *nf.* micro technology
mieditis: *nf.* fear
miedo: *nm.* fear; dread
miedoso: *aj.* fearful; afraid
miel: *nf.* honey
miembro: *nm.* member; limb
mientras: 1. *aj.* while; 2. *conj.* while
miércoles: *nm.* Wednesday

mies: *nf.* grain; cereal; harvest time
miga: *nf.* bit; crumb
mil: 1. *aj.* thousand; 2. *nm.* thousand
milagro: *nm.* miracle
milagroso: *aj.* miraculous
milenario: 1. *aj.* millennial; 2. *nm.* millennium
milésimo: *aj.* thousandth
miliciana: *nf.* woman soldier in the militia
miliciano: *aj.* pertaining to the militia
miliciano: *nm.* soldier in the militia
miligramo: *nm.* milligram
mililitro: *nm.* milliliter
milímetro: *nm.* millimeter
militancia: *nf.* militancy
militante: 1. *aj.* militant; 2. *nmf.* militant
militar: *aj.* military
militar: *nm.* soldier
militar: *vi.* to serve in the military
militarismo: *nm.* militarism
militarista: 1. *aj.* militarist; 2. m*nf.* militarist
militarización: *nf.* militarization
militarizar: *vt.* to militarize
milla: *nf.* mile
millar: *nm.* group or package of one thousand
millón: *nm.* million
millonada: *nf.* several million
millonario: 1. *aj.* millionaire; 2. *nmf.* millionaire
millonésimo: *aj.* millionth
mimar: *vt.* to pet; fondle
mimbre: *nmf.* Wicker
mina: *nf.* mine
minador: *aj.* mining
minar: *vt.* to mine; to undermine; to consume; *vi.* to mine
mineral: 1. *aj.* mineral; 2. *nm.* mineral
mineralización: *nf.* mineralization

mineralizar: *vt.* to mineralize
mineralizarse: *vr.* to become mineralized
mineralogía: *nf.* mineralogy
mineralógico: *aj.* mineralogical
minería: *nf.* mining
minero; -a: *nmf.* miner
miniatura: *nf.* miniature
miniaturista: *nmf.* miniaturist
miniaturizar: *vt.* to miniaturize
minifalda: *nf.* mini-skirt
mínima- a: *nmf.* smallest; least
minimizar: *vt.* to diminish
mínimo: *aj.* least; slightest; minimum; tiny bit minimal
mínimo: *nm.* minimum
ministerial: *aj.* ministerial
ministerio: *nm.* ministry
ministro: *nm.* minister
minucia: *nf.* minutiae
minuciosidad: *nf.* meticulousness
minucioso: *aj.* meticulous
minúscula: *nf.* lower-case letter
minúsculo: *aj.* tiny
minusválido: *aj.* handicapped
minutero: *nm.* minute hand
minuto: *nm.* minute
mío; mía: *aj.* poss. mine; of mine; *pron.* poss. mine
miope: *aj.* myopic; shortsighted; *nm.* myope
mira: *nf.* sight of a gun or instrument
mirada: *nf.* look
mirado: *aj.* observed
mirador: *nm.* lookout
miramiento: *nm.* examination; respectful dealings
mirar: *vt.* to look at; to watch; to contemplate; to consider carefully
mirarse: *vr.* to look at oneself; to see oneself
mirón: 1. *aj.* curious; 2. *nmf.* curious person
misa: *nf.* mass

misal: *nm.* annual liturgical book of masses; missal
miserable: *aj.* wretched; vile; wicked; wretch
miseria: *nf.* misery
misericordia: *nf.* mercy; compassion
misericordioso: *aj.* merciful
mísero: *aj.* poor; unfortunate; wretched; vile
misión: *nf.* mission
misionero: 1. *aj.* missionary; 2. *nmf.* missionary
mismo; ma: 1. *aj.* same; own; very; self; 2. *pron.* same; own; very; self
misterio: *nm.* mystery
misterioso: *aj.* mysterious
mística: *nf.* mysticism
misticismo: *nm.* mysticism
místico: 1. *aj.* mystical; 2. *nmf.* mystic
mistificación: *nf.* mystification
mistificar: *vt.* to mystify
mitad: *nf.* half; middle
mítico: *aj.* mythical
mitigar: *vt.* to mitigate
mito: *nm.* myth
mitología: *nf.* mythology
mitológico: *aj.* mythological
mixto: 1. *aj* mixed; 2. *nm.* mixture
mixtura: *nf.* mixture
mobiliario: *nm.* stage set; furniture
mocedad: *nf.* youth
mocerío: *nm.* young people
mochila: *nf.* knapsack; backpack
moco: *nm.* mocus; snuff (of candlewick)
moda: *nf.* fashion; custom
modal: *aj.* pertaining to manners or customs; pertaining to grammatical modes
modales: *nm. pl.* behavioral norms; manners
modalidad: *nf.* modality; form; manner

modelado: *nm.* model building process; clay or wax model
modelador: *aj.* modeling; shaping
modelar: *vt.* to model; to form; shape
modelarse: *vr.* to model oneself
modelista: *nmf.* model designer; mold maker
modelo: 1. *aj.* model; 2. *nmf.* model
modernamente: *av.* modernly
modernidad: *nf.* modernity
modernismo: *nm.* modernism
modernista: *aj.* modern; fashionable
modernista: *nmf.* modernist
modernización: *nf.* modernization
modernizar: *vt.* to modernize
modernizarse: *vr.* to become modernized
moderno: *aj.* modern
modestia: *nf.* modesty
modesto: 1. *aj.* modest; 2. *nmf.* modest person
modificable: *aj.* modifiable
modificación: *nf.* modification
modificador: *aj.* modifying
modificar: *vt.* to modify
modismo: *nm.* idiom
modista: *nf.* dressmaker; modiste
modo: *nm.* manner; way; custom
modoso: *aj.* civilized; well-behaved
mofar: *vi.* to scoff; jeer; mock
mojado -da: *aj.* wet; *nmf.* wetting
mojar: *vt.* to wet; to drench; to moisten
moldear: *vt.* to mould; to cast
moledor: *nm.* cylinder used for crushing
moler: *vt.* to grind; to mill; to tire out
molestar: *vt.* to bother
molestarse: *vr.* to be bothered
molestia: *nf.* annoyance
molesto: *aj.* bothersome; annoying; annoyed; bothered
molido -da: *aj.* worn out; exhausted;

milled
molienda: *nf.* milling
molinero: *aj.* pertaining to mills or with milling
molinero;-a: *nmf.* mill worker
molinete: *nm.* small or toy mill or windmill
molinillo: *nm.* hand mill
molino: *nm.* mill
molleja: *nf.* gizzard; sweetbread
molturación: *nf.* milling or crushing process
molturar: *vt.* to mill; to crush into powder
momentáneo: *aj.* momentary
momento: *nm.* moment
momia: *nf.* mummy
monacato: *nm.* monastic order
monaguillo: *nm.* assistant to a priest
monarca: *nm.* monarch
monarquía: *nf.* monarchy
monárquico: *aj.* monarchic
monárquico;-a: *nmf.* monarchist
monarquismo: *nm.* monarchism
monasterio: *nm.* monastery
monástico: *aj.* monastic
mondar: *vt.* to clean; to prune; to peel; to hull
moneda: *nf.* money; coin
monedero: *nm.* moneybag; coin purse
monetario: *aj.* monetary
monetarismo: *nm.* monetarism
monetarista: *nmf.* monetarist
monja: *nf.* nun
monje: *nm.* monk; anchorite
monjil: *aj.* pertaining to nuns
monotonía: *nf.* monotone
monótono: *aj.* monotonous
monstruo: 1. *aj.* monster; 2. *nm.* monster
monstruosidad: *nf.* monstrosity
monstruoso: *aj.* monstrous
monta: *nf.* mounting

montacargas: *nm.* freight elevator; lift
montado: *aj.* mounted
montadura: *nf.* saddle
montaje: *nm.* mounting; assembly
montaña: *nf.* mountain
montañero;-a: *nmf.* mountaineer; mountain climber
montañés: *aj.* relating to mountains
montañés: *nmf.* mountain man or woman
montañismo: *nm.* mountaineering; mountain climbing
montañoso: *aj.* mountainous
montar: *vt.* to mount; to climb
montarse: *vr.* to mount
monte: *nm.* mount; mountain
montículo: *nm.* small mountain
montón: *nm.* pile; heap; crowd
montura: *nf.* mount; animal one mounts
monumental: *aj.* monumental
monumento: *nm.* monument
morada: *nf.* house; residence
morado -a: *aj.* mauve; dark violet
morador;-a: *nmf.* inhabitant; resident
moral: 1. *aj.* amoral; moral; 2. *nf.* moral
moraleja: *nf.* moral of a story
moralidad: *nf.* morality
moralismo: *nm.* moralism
moralista: *nmf.* moralist
moralización: *nf.* moralization
moralizar: *vt.* to moralize
morar: *vi.* to live; dwell
mordaza: *nf.* gag
mordedor: *aj.* biting
mordedura: *nf.* biting
morder: *vt.* to bite; to eat away; to gossip about
morderse: *vr.* to bite oneself
mordida: *nf.* bite; bribe
mordisco: *nm.* nibble

mordisquear: *vt.* to nibble
moreno -na: *aj.* brown
morfinómano -a: *nm.* drug addict
morir: *vi.* to die; to be dying
morirse: *vr.* to die; to be dying to
morro: *nm.* know
mortadela: *nf.* luncheon meat
mortaja: *nf.* shroud
mortal: 1. *aj.* mortal; 2. *nmf.* mortal
mortalidad: *nf.* mortality
mortero: *nm.* mortar
mortífero: *aj.* deadly; lethal
mortificar: *vt.* to mortify
mortificarse: *vr.* to be mortified
mortuorio: *aj.* mortuary
mosca: *nf.* fly; con. money
mostaza: *nf.* mustard
mosto: *nm.* grape juice
mostrador: *nm.* showcase
mostrador -ra: *aj.* showing; pointing
mostrar: *vt.* to show; prove
mostrarse: *vr.* to show oneself
mote: *nm.* nickname
motivación: *nf.* motivation
motivar: *vt.* to motivate; cause
motivo: *nm.* reason
moto: *nm.* motorcycle
motocarro: *nm.* three-wheeled motorcycle
motocicleta: *nf.* motorcycle
motociclismo: *nm.* motorcycling
motociclista: *nmf.* motorcyclist
motocross: *inn.* motocross
motocultivo: *nm.* mechanized agriculture
motonáutica: *nf.* motorboat racing
motonáutico: *aj.* pertaining to motorboat racing
motonave: *nf.* motorboat; motorized boat or ship
motor: 1. *nm.* motor; engine; 2. *aj.* motor
motora: *nf.* small boat with a motor
motorismo: *nm.* motorized sport

motorista: *nmf.* motorist
motorizado: *aj.* motorized
motorizar: *vt.* to motorize
motorizarse: *vr.* to become motorized
motosierra: *nf.* chainsaw
movedizo: *aj.* movable; easily moved; unstable
mover: *vt.* to move; to stir
moverse: *vr.* to move oneself
movible: *aj.* movable
movido: *aj.* moved
móvil: *aj.* mobile
movilidad: *nf.* mobility
movilización: *nf.* mobilization
movilizar: *vt.* to mobilize
movimiento: *nm.* movement
moza: *nf.* servant; maid
mozalbete: *nm.* young servant or boy
mozo: *nm.* servant; entry-level worker; boy
muchacha: *nf.* girl; wench
muchachada: *nf.* group of boys or girls
muchachería: *nf.* group of boys or girls; especially a rebellious group; immature behavior appropriate to boys or girls
muchacho;-a n: *nf.* young man or woman
muchedumbre: *nf.* crowd; group of many people
muchísimo: *aj.* very much
mucho: 1. *aj.* a lot of; much; 2. *av.* much; 3. pro. a lot
muda: *nf.* change of clothes
mudable: *aj.* changeable; transformable; variable
mudanza: *nf.* move to another residence
mudar: *vti.* to change or transform; to lose one's baby teeth
mudarse: *vr.* to move to another residence

mudez: *nf.* muteness
mudo: 1. *aj.* dumb; silent; mute; 2. *nmf.* mute
mueble: *aj.* movable; referring to an object
mueble: *nm.* piece of furniture; furnishing
muela: *nf.* millstone; grindstone; back tooth
muelle: *aj.* soft; easy; *nm.* spring; pier
muerte: *nf.* death; murder
muerto: 1. *aj.* dead; 2. *nmf.* dead person
muestra: *nf.* sample; specimen
muestrario: *nm.* sales catalog
muestreo: *nm.* sampling; analytic sampling
mujer: *nf.* woman; wife
mujeriego: *nm.* philanderer
mujerío: *nm.* group of women
mujerona: *nf.* large woman
mujerzuela: *nf.* bad woman; prostitute
mula: *nf.* mule; she-mule
muleta: *nf.* cruth; red cloth
mulo: *nm.* mule
multa: *nf.* fine
multidireccional: *aj.* multi-directional
multilateral: *aj.* multilateral
multinacional: *aj.* multinational
múltiple: *aj.* multiple
multiplicable: *aj.* multipliable
multiplicación: *nf.* multiplication
multiplicador: *nm.* multiplier; factor in multiplication
multiplicando: *nm.* multiplicand; factor in multiplication
multiplicar: *vt.* to multiply
multiplicarse: *vr.* to be multiplied
multiplicidad: *nf.* multiplicity
múltiplo: 1. *aj.* multiple; 2 *nm.* multiple.

mundano: 1. *aj.* worldly; 2. *nmf.* worldly person
mundial: *aj.* world
mundial: *nm.* world championship
mundialmente: *av.* world-wide
mundillo: *nm.* one's personal world of acquaintances
mundo: *nm.* world
muñeco -a: *nm.* wrist; doll; puppet
muñequera: *nf.* wristband
municipal: *aj.* municipal
municipalidad: *nf.* municipality
municipalizar: *vt.* to convert a private service to a municipal service
municipio: *nm.* municipality; city
mural: 1. *aj.* mural; pertaining to walls; 2. *nm.* mural
muralla: *nf.* wall; rampart
muro: *nm.* wall
muscular: *aj.* muscular; pertaining to muscles
musculatura: *nf.* musculature
músculo: *nm.* muscle
musculoso: *aj.* muscular; having a lot of muscles
museo: *nm.* museum
museología: *nf.* study of museums
música: *nf.* music
musical: 1. *aj.* musical; 2. *nm.* musical
musicalidad: *nf.* musicality
músico;-a: *nmf.* musician
musicología: *nf.* musicology
musicólogo;-a: *nmf.* musicologist
muslo: *nm.* thigh
mutilar: *vt.* to mutilate; to cripple
mutismo: *nm.* deliberate silence; intentional silence; forced silence
mutualidad: *nf.* mutuality
mutualista: *aj.* pertaining to mutuality
mutualista: *nmf.* member of a mutual aid organization
mutuo: *aj.* mutual

muy: ad*v.* very; very much

N

nácar: *nm.* nacre
nacer: *vi.* to be born; to arise
nacido: 1. *aj.* newborn; 2. *nm.* a newborn
naciente: *aj.* new; recent
nacimiento: *nm.* birth; origin; crib
nación: *nf.* nation; country
nacional: *aj.* national
nacionalidad: *nf.* nationality
nacionalismo: *nm.* nationalism
nacionalista: 1. *aj.* nationalist; 2. *nmf.* nationalist
nacionalización: *nf.* nationalization
nacionalizar: *vt.* to nationalize
nacionalizarse: *vr.* to become nationalized
nacionalsocialismo: *nm.* national socialism
nada: *nf.* nothingness; *pron.* indef. nothing
nadador;-a: *nmf.* swimmer
nadar: *vi.* to swim
nadie: *nm.* nobody
nalga: *nf.* buttock; rump
nana: *nf.* lullaby
naranja: *nf.* orange
narigón;-a: *nmf.* big-nosed person
nariz: *nf.* nose
narración: *nm.* narration
narrador;-a: *nmf.* narrator
narrar: *vt.* to narrate; tell
narrativa: 1. *nf.* narrative; 2. *aj.* narrative
nata: *nf.* cream; elite

natación: *nf.* swimming
natal: *aj.* native
natalicio: *aj.* pertaining to a date of birth
natalicio: *nm.* date of birth
natalidad: *nf.* birth rate
natillas: *nf.* pi custard
natividad: *nf.* birth; nativity
nativo: *aj.* native
nato: *aj.* in-born; birth
natura: *nf.* nature
natural: 1. *aj.* natural; 2. *nmf.* natural
naturaleza: *nf.* nature; disposition
naturalidad: *nf.* the quality of acting naturally or normally
naturalismo: *nm.* naturalism
naturalista: *nmf.* natural scientist
naturalización: *nf.* naturalization
naturalizar: *vt.* to naturalize
naturalizarse: *vr.* to become naturalized
naturalmente: *av.* naturally
naufragar: *vi.* to be wrecked to sink; to be shipwrecked
naufragio: *nm.* shipwreck
náufrago: 1. *aj.* shipwrecked; 2. *nmf.* shipwrecked person
náusea: *nf.* nausea; sea sickness
nauseabundo: *aj.* nausea-provoking
náutica: *nf.* the art of navigation
náutico: *aj.* nautical
navaja: *nf.* folding knife; navaja de afeitar; razor
naval: *aj.* naval
nave: *nf.* ship; vessel; nave
navegabilidad: *nf.* navigability
navegable: *aj.* navigable
navegación: *nf.* navigation
navegante: *nmf.* navigator
navegar: *vt.* to navigate; to sail
Navidad: *nf.* Christmas
naviero;-a: 1. *aj.* naval; 2. *nmf.* seaman
navío: *nm.* a very large ship

neblina: *nf.* mist; haze; fog
nebulosa: *nf.* nebula
nebulosidad: *nf.* cloudiness
nebuloso: *aj.* misty; foggy
necedad: *nf.* foolishness
necesario: *aj.* necessary
necesidad: *nm.* necessity
necesitado: *aj.* needy
necesitar: *vt.* to require; to need
necio: 1. *aj.* foolish; 2. *nm.* fool
nefasto -ta: *aj.* ominous; fatal
negación: *nf.* negation; denial
negado: *aj.* denied
negar: *vt.* to deny; to refuse; *vi.* to deny
negativa: *nf.* a negative charge
negativismo: *nm.* negativism
negativo: *aj.* negative; pessimistic
negociable: *aj.* negotiable
negociación: *nf.* negotiation
negociado: *nm.* department; bureau
negociante: *nmf.* negotiator; businessman; or businesswoman
negociar: *vt.* to negotiate; to trade
negocio: *nm.* business
negrear: *vt.* to become black; to exploit a subordinate; to treat a subordinate cruelly
negrero: *aj.* pertaining to black slavery; may be used to mean inhumane or cruel
negrero;-a: *nmf.* one who exploits subordinates; one who treats his subordinates cruelly
negro: 1. *aj.* black; 2. *nm.* black
negroide: *aj.* Negroid
negrura: *nf.* blackness
negruzco: *aj.* very dark; almost black
nene: *nm.* con. baby; child
neoclasicismo: *nm.* neoclassicism
neoclásico: *aj.* neoclassic
neoclásico;-a: *nmf.* neoclassicist
neorrealismo: *nm.* neo-realism
nervio: *nm.* nerve; vigor; strength

nerviosidad: *nf.* nervousness
nervioso: *aj.* nervous
nervudo: *aj.* sinewy
neto -ta: *aj.* pure; neat
neumático -ca: *aj.* pneumatic
neurología: *nf.* neurology
neurólogo;-a: *nmf.* neurologist
neurona: *nf.* neuron
neurosis: *nf.* neurosis
neurótico: *aj.* neurotic
neutralizar: *vt.* to neutralize
nevado -da: *aj.* snow-covered; *nf.* snow fall
nevar: *vi.* to snow
nevera: *nf.* refrigerator; ice box
nevisca: *nf.* snow flurry
neviscar: *vi.* to snow lightly
ni: *conj.* neither; nor
nido: *nm.* nest; home
niebla: *nf.* misty cloud or fog
nieto;-a: *nmf.* grandchild
nieve: *nf.* snow; ice cream
inimitable: *aj.* inimitable
niñada: *nf.* a childish action
niñera: *nf.* nanny
niñez: 1. *nf.* childhood aniñado; 2. *aj.* childlike
ninguno -na: *aj.* indef. no not any
niño -ña: *aj. nmf.* child
niquelar: *vt.* to nickel-plate
nitidez: *nf.* brightness; clearness; brilliance
nivel: *nm.* level
nivelación: *nf.* leveling
nivelador: *aj.* leveling
nivelador;-a: *nmf.* bulldozer
nivelar: *vt.* to level
níveo: *aj.* snowy-white
inumerablemente: *av.* innumerably
noble: *aj.* noble
noble: *nmf.* nobleman
nobleza: *nf.* nobility
noche: *nf.* night
nochebuena: *nf.* Christmas Eve

noctámbulo;-a: *nmf.* night person; night owl
nocturno: *aj.* nocturnal
nogal: *nm.* walnut tree
nogalina: *nf.* walnut color extracted from walnut shell
nogueral: *nm.* walnut orchard
nómada: *aj. nmf.* nomad
nombrado: *aj.* named
nombramiento: *nm.* the naming of someone to a position
nombrar: *vt.* to name; to appoint; to mention
nombre: *nm.* name
nomenclatura: *nf.* nomenclature
nómina: *nf.* list; pay roll
nominación: *nf.* nomination
nominal: *aj.* nominal
nominar: *vt.* to nominate
nominativo: *nm.* nominative case
nono -na: *aj.* ninth
noria: *nf.* chain pump; water-wheel
norma: *nf.* norm; standard
norte: *nm.* north
nos: *pron.* us
nosotros: pron we; us
nota: *nf.* note; mark; bill
notable: *aj.* notable
notar: *vt.* to note; to notice; to criticize
notaría: *nf.* notary
noticia: *nf.* news; notion
notición: *nf.* news flash; special news update
notificación: *nf.* notification
notificar: *vt.* to notify; inform
notoriedad: *nf.* notoriety
notorio: *aj.* noticeable; well-known
novatada: *nf.* initiation
novato -ta: *aj. nmf.* beginner
novecientos: 1. *aj.* nine-hundred; 2. *nm.* nine hundred
novedad: *nf.* novelty
novedoso: *aj.* new and different

novela: *nf.* novel; soap opera
novelar: *vt.* to novelize; to make into a novel
novelero: *aj.* soap-opera loving
novelesco: *aj.* pertaining to novels or soap operas
novelista: *nmf.* novelist
novelística: *nf.* novels or soap operas in general; novels or soap operas considered as a group telenovela
novelístico: *aj.* pertaining to novels or soap operas
noveno: 1. *aj.* ninth; 2. *nm.* one-ninth (fraction)
noventa: 1. *aj.* ninety; 2. *nm.* ninety
novia: *nf.* fiancée; bride; girl friend
noviazgo: *nm.* courtship
noviembre: *nm.* November
novio: *nm.* groom; boyfriend
nubarrón: *nm.* a big dark cloud
nube: *nf.* cloud
nublado: *nm.* (figurative) dark cloud (of life)
nublado: *aj.* cloudy
nublar: *v.* to get cloudy
nublarse: *vr.* to become cloudy
nubosidad: *nf.* cloudiness
nuboso: *aj.* cloudy
nuca: *nf.* part of the neck at the base of the skull; nape
nuclear: *aj.* nuclear
núcleo: *nm.* nucleus
nudismo: *nm.* nudism
nudista: 1. *aj.* nudist; 2. *nmf.* nudist
nudo: *nm.* knot; tie
nuera: *nf.* daughter-in-law
nuestro;-a: *aj.* our
nueva: *nf.* the latest news
Nuevamente: *av.* newly
Nueve: 1. *aj.* nine; 2. *nm.* nine
Nuevo: *aj.* new
Numeración: *nf.* numbering
Numerador: *nm.* numerator
Numeral: 1. *aj.* numeral; 2. *nm.*

numeral
Numerar: *vt.* to number
Numérico: *aj.* numeric
Número: *nm.* number
Numeroso: *aj.* numerous
Nunca: adv. Never
Nupcias: *nf. pl.* nuptials; marriage
Nutrición: *nf.* nutrition
Nutrido: *aj.* nourished; filled with
Nutrir: *vt.* to nourish
nutritivo: *aj.* nutritious

O

obedecer: *vt.* to obey
obediencia: *nf.* obedience
obediente: *aj.* obedient
obelisco: *nm.* obelisk
obertura: *nf.* overture
obispada: *nm.* bishopric
obispado: *nm.* office of the bishop
obispo: *nm.* bishop
objeción: *nf.* objection
objetante: *aj.* objecting
objetar: *vt.* to object
objetividad: *nf.* objectivity
objetivo: 1. *aj.* objective; 2. *nm.* objective
objeto: *nm.* object; purpose; aim
objetor: *nmf.* one who objects; objector
obligación: *nm.* obligation
obligado: *aj.* obligated
obligar: *vt.* to obligate; to oblige; to force; to compel
obligarse: *vr.* to obligate oneself; to become obligated
obligatorio: *aj.* obligatory

obra: *nf.* work; building
obrar: *vt.* to work (metal; wood; etc.)
obrerismo: *nm.* worker class; proletariat
obrero: 1. *aj.* working; referring to people; 2. *nmf.* worker
oscuro: *aj.* dark
obsequiar: *vt.* to give presents; flatter; to present; to court
observable: *aj.* observable
observación: *nf.* observation
observador: 1. *aj.* observing; 2. *nmf.* observer
observancia: *nf.* observance
observar: *vt.* to observe; to notice; to obey
observatorio: *nm.* observatory
obsesión: *nf.* obsession
obsesionar: *vt.* to obsess
obsesionarse: *vr.* to become obsessed
obsesivo: *aj.* obsessive
obseso: 1. *aj.* obsessed; 2. *nmf.* obsessive person
obstaculizar: *vt.* to block; to obstruct
obstáculo: *nm.* obstacle
obstinación: *nf.* obstinacy
obstinado: *aj.* obstinate
obstinarse: *vr.* to become obstinate
obstrucción: *nf.* obstruction
obstruir: *vt.* to obstruct; block
obstruirse: *vr.* to become
obtención: *nf.* obtaining
obtener: *vt.* to obtain; get acquire
oca: *nf.* goose
ocasión: *nf.* occasion; opportunity; occasion; chance
ocasional: *aj.* occasional
ocasionar: *vt.* to cause or bring about
ocaso: *nm.* sundown
occidental: *aj.* western
occidentalizar: *vt.* to westernize
occidente: *nm.* west
ochenta: *aj.* eighty
ocho: 1. *nm.* eight; 2. *aj.* eight

ochocientos: 1. *aj.* eight hundred; 2. *nm.* eight hundred
ocio: *nm.* free-time activity; leisure time activity; idleness
ociosidad: *nf.* unemployment
ocioso; -a: 1. *nmf.* unemployed person; 2. *aj.* unemployed
octagonal: *aj.* octagonal
octágono: *nm.* octagon
octanaje: *nm.* level of octane
octano: *nm.* octane
octava: *nf.* octave
octavo: *nm.* one-eighth (fraction)
octogenario: 1. *aj.* octogenarian; 2. *nmf.* eighty-year-old person
octosílabo: 1. *aj.* eight-syllable; 2. *nm.* eight-syllable word or verse
octubre: *nm.* October
ocular: *aj.* ocular
ocultar: *vt.* to hide; to conceal
ocultarse: *vr.* to become hidden or concealed
ocultismo: *nm.* occult
ocultista: 1. *aj.* pertaining to the occult; 2. *nmf.* one who practices arts of the occult
oculto: *aj.* belonging to the shadows; shadowed
ocupación: *nf.* occupation
ocupado: *aj.* busy
ocupante: *nmf.* occupant
ocupar: *vt.* to occupy
ocuparse: *vr.* to busy oneself
ocurrencia: *nf.* an idea; a sudden thought
ocurrente: *aj.* witty
ocurrir: *vi.* to occur; to happen
ocurrirse: *vr.* to occur to oneself; to think of
odiar: *vt.* to hate; detest
odio: *nm.* hate
odioso: *aj.* hateful
odontología: *nf.* dentistry
odontológico: *aj.* dental

odontólogo; -a: *nmf.* dentist
oeste: *nm.* west
ofender: *vt.* to offend
ofenderse: *vr.* to become offended
ofensa: *nf.* offense; insult
ofensivo-a: 1. *nf.* offensive; 2. *aj.* offensive
ofensor; -a: *nmf.* offender
oferta: *nf.* offer
oficio: *nm.* office; occupation
oficial: 1. *aj.* official; 2. *nm.* official
oficializar: *vt.* to make official
oficiar: *vt.* to officiate
oficina: *nf.* office
oficinista: *nmf.* office-worker
oficio: *nm.* official
oficioso: *aj.* officious
ofrecer: *vt.* to offer
ofrecerse: *vr.* to offer oneself
ofrecimiento: *nm.* offer
ofrenda: *nf.* offering of money
ofrendar: *vt.* to make an offering
oídas: *av.* by way of the grapevine
oído: *nm.* ear; especially the inner ear
de
oír: *vt.* to hear
ojear: *vt.* to eye; stare at
ojera: *nf.* dark mark under the eyes
ojeroso: *aj.* having dark marks under the eyes
ojival: *aj.* ogival; gothic
ojo: *nm.* eye
ola: *nf.* wave
oleada: *nf.* big wave
oleaje: *nm.* waves in succession; swell
óleo: *nm.* holy oil; oil painting
oler: *vt.* to smell; to sniff; *vi.* to smell
olfatear: *vt.* to sniff
olfateo: *nm.* sniffing
olfato: *nm.* sense of smell
oliva: *nf.* olive
oliváceo: *aj.* olive-colored
olivar: *nm.* olive orchard
olivarero; -a: *nmf.* olive farmer

olivicultura: *nf.* technique of harvesting olives
olivo: *nm.* olive tree
olla: *nf.* pot; kettle; stew
olmo: *nm.* elm tree
olor: *nm.* smell; odor
oloroso: *aj.* smelly; strong-smelling
olvidadizo: *aj.* forgetful
olvidado: *aj.* forgotten
olvidar: *vt.* to forget (in general)
olvidarse: *vr.* to be forgotten; to forget
olvido: *nm.* the forgotten
ombligo: *nm.* umbilicus; center
omitir: *vt.* to omit
omnipotencia: *nf.* omnipotence
omnipotente: *aj.* all-powerful
omnipresencia: *nf.* omnipresence
omnipresente: *aj.* omnipresent
once: *aj.* eleven
onda: *nm.* wave
ondear: *vt.* to make waves
ondulación: *nm.* curliness
ondulado: *aj.* curly; wavy
ondulante: *aj.* waving
ondular: *vt.* to make hair curly or wavy
ondulatorio: *aj.* wave-propagating
onza: *nf.* ounce
opacidad: *nf.* opaqueness
opaco: *aj.* opaque
operable: *aj.* operable
operación: *nf.* operation
operacional: *aj.* operational
operado: 1. *aj.* operated on; referring to a patient; 2. *nmf.* person who is operated on
operador; -a: *nmf.* operator; surgeon
operante: *aj.* operating
operar: *vt.* to operate
operario; -a: *nmf.* worker that operates a machine
operarse: *vr.* to be operated on
operativo: *aj.* operative
opinable: *aj.* debatable

opinar: *vi.* to opine; to give an opinion
opinión: *nm.* opinion
oponente: 1. *aj.* opposing; 2. *nmf.* opponent
oponer: *vt.* to oppose
oponerse: *vr.* to be opposed
oportunamente: *av.* opportunely
oportunidad: *nf.* opportunity
oportunismo: *nm.* opportunism
oportunista: *nmf.* opportunist
oportuno: *aj.* opportune
oposición: *nf.* opposition
opositor; -a: *nmf.* opponent
opresión: *nf.* oppression
opresivo: *aj.* oppressive
opresor; -a: *nmf.* oppressor
oprimido: *aj.* oppressed
oprimir: *vt.* to oppress
optimismo: *nmf.* optimism
optimista: *nmf.* optimist
óptimo: *aj.* optimal
opuesto: *pp.* of opener; *aj.* adverse
oración: *nf.* prayer
oráculo: *nm.* oracle
orador; -a: *nmf.* orator; speaker
oral: *aj.* oral
orar: *vi.* to pray
oratoria: *nf.* oratory; art of speaking in public
orbe: *nm.* orb
órbita: *nf.* orbit
orbital: *aj.* orbital
orden: *nm.* order
ordenación: *nf.* ordination
ordenado: *aj.* well-ordered
ordenamiento: *nm.* an ordering
ordenanza: *nm.* command
ordenar: *vt.* to place in order; to order
ordinario: *aj.* ordinary
oreja: *nm.* ear
orejear: *vi.* to move the ears; as done by animals
orejera: *nf.* ear-coving on some hats
orejón; -a: 1. *aj.* disobedient; 2. *nmf.*

person with big ears
orejudo: *aj.* large-eared
orgánico: *aj.* organic
organillero; -a: *nmf.* player of a small portable piano
organillo: *nm.* small portable piano
organismo: *nm.* organism
organista: *nmf.* organist
organización: *nf.* organization
organizado: *aj.* organized
organizador; -a: *nmf.* organizer
organizar: *vt.* to organize
organizarse: *vr.* to organize oneself
órgano: *nm.* organ
orgullo: *nm.* pride
orgulloso: *aj.* prideful
orientación: *nf.* orientation
orientador; -a: *nmf.* guide
oriental: *aj.* eastern
oriental: *nmf.* Oriental person
orientar: *vt.* to orient
orientarse: *vr.* to orient oneself
oriente: *nm.* the east
origen: *nm.* origin; birth
original: 1. *aj.* original; 2. *nmf.* an original
originalidad: *nf.* originality
originar: *vt.* to originate; to initiate
originario: *aj.* original
originarse: *vr.* to originate; to come from
ornamentación: *nf.* ornamentation
ornamental: *aj.* ornamental
ornamentar: *vt.* to decorate; to adorn; to beautify
ornamento: *nm.* ornament
ornato: *nm.* ornament
oscuramente; obscuramente: *av.* obscurely oscuro;
oscurecer; obscurecer: *vt.* to darken
oscurecerse; obscurecerse: *vr.* to become dark
oscurecimiento: *nm.* the coming of darkness

oscuridad: *nf.* darkness
ostensible: *aj.* ostensible; apparently
ostentación: *nf.* ostentation
ostentar: *vt.* to show off
ostentoso: *aj.* ostentatious
otoñal: *aj.* autumn; fall
otoño: *nm.* autumn; fall
otorgamiento: *nm.* conceding or allowing a request
otorgante: *nmf.* person who concedes or allows
otorgar: *vt.* to concede; allow in a formal sense
oval: *aj.* oval
óvalo: *nm.* oval
ovario: *nm.* ovary
ovular: *aj.* pertaining to oval shaped objects
ovular: *vi.* to ovulate
óvulo: *nm.* ovule
oyente: *nmf.* hearing

P

paciencia: *nf.* patience
paciente: 1. *nmf.* patient; 2. *aj.* patient
pacientemente: *av.* patiently
pacificación: *nf.* pacification
pacificador: *aj.* pacifying
pacificador; -a: *nmf.* peacemaker
pacificar: *vt.* to pacify
pacificarse: *vr.* to be pacified
pacífico: *aj.* pacific
pacifismo: *nm.* pacifism
pacifista: 1. *aj.* pacifist; 2. *nmf.* pacifist
pactar: *vi.* to make an agreement; to pact; stipulate

pacto: *nm.* agreement
padecer: *vt.* to suffer from
padecimiento: *nm.* suffering
padrastro: *nm.* stepfather
padre: *nm.* father
padrenuestro: *nm.* prayer "our Father"
padrinazgo: *nm.* act of being a godfather
padrino: *nm.* godfather; sponsor
padrón: *nm.* poll; census
paga: *nf.* payment of wages; salary
pagable: *aj.* payable
pagadero: *aj.* to be paid
pagado: *aj.* paid
pagador; -a: *nmf.* payer
pagar: *vt.* to pay
pagaré: *nm.* paper which notes a debt
página: *nf.* page
paginación: *nm.* pagination
paginar: *vt.* to paginate
pago: *nm.* payment
país: *nm.* country
paisaje: *nm.* countryside; landscape
paisanaje: *nm.* fellow countrymen
paisano; -a: *nmf.* countryman
paja: *nf.* straw; padding (in writing)
pájara: *nf.* female bird
pajarear: *vi.* to hunt birds; to wander
pajarera: *nf.* large birdcage
pajarería: *nf.* flock or multitude of birds
pajarero; -a: *nmf.* person who cares for or sells birds
pájaro: *nm.* bird; crafty fellow
pajarraco: *nm.* ugly bird
pala: *nf.* shovel; racket
palabra: *nf.* word
palabrear: *vt.* to chat
palabreja: *nf.* strange or ugly word
palabrota: *nf.* expletive or blasphemous word
palacete: *nm.* small palace; mansion
palacio: *nm.* palace
paladear: *vt.* to taste; to relish

palanca: *nf.* lever; pole; bar
palangana: *nf.* washbowl
palanqueta: *nf.* small lever; crowbar
palco: *nm.* box (theatre)
paleta: *nf.* small shovel; fire shovel
paliar: *vt.* to palliate
palidecer: *vi.* to become pale
palidez: *nf.* paleness
pálido: *aj.* pale
palillo: *nm.* toothpick
paliza: *nf.* beating
palma: *nm.* palm of the hand; palm tree
palmada: *nf.* soft slap
palmar: *nm.* grove of palm trees
palmeado: *aj.* palm-shaped
palmear: *vt.* to pat; to applaud
palmera: *nf.* palm tree
palmetazo: *nm.* hard slap
palmo: *nm.* hand (measurement)
palmotear: *vt.* to pat
palmoteo: *nm.* patting
palo: *nm.* long stick or handle
paloma: *nf.* dove
palomar: *nm.* place where doves live
palomilla: *nf.* small dove
palomina: *nf.* dove droppings
palomino: *nm.* young dove
palomo: *nm.* male dove
palpable: *aj.* palpable
palpación: *nf.* groping; feeling with the palm
palpar: *vt.* to touch with the palm
palpitación: *nf.* palpitation
palpitante: *aj.* palpitating
palpitar: *vi.* to palpitate
pamplina: *nf. con.* nonsense; trifle
pan: *nm.* bread
panadería: *nf.* bakery
panadero; -a: *nmf.* baker
panal: *nm.* honeycomb
pañal: *mpl.* swaddling clothes
panecillo: *nm.* small loaf of bread
panera: *nf.* bread basket or box

panificación: *nf.* making of bread
panificadora: *nf.* bakery
panificar: *vt.* to make bread
paño: *nm.* woolen fabric
pañoleta: *nf.* scarf for hair
panorama: *nm.* panorama
panorámico: *aj.* panoramic
pantalla: *nf.* lamp shade; screen
pantalón: *nm.* pants
pantalonera: *nf.* sweatpants
pantalonero; -a: *nmf.* tailor who makes pants
pantano: *nm.* dam
pantorrilla: *nf.* calf
pañuelo: *nm.* handkerchief
panza: *nf.* paunch; belly
papa: *nm.* father; dad; pope
papado: *nm.* term of papal governing
papal: *aj.* papal
papalote: *nm.* paper kite
papel: *nm.* paper; part; role; pl. documents
papeleo: *nm.* red tape; paperwork
papelera: *nf.* wastepaper basket; paper industry
papelería: *nf.* stationery store
papelero: *aj.* pertaining to paper
papeleta: *nf.* report card
papiro: *nm.* papyrus
papista: *nmf.* papist
paquete: *nm.* parcel; packet
par: 1. *nm.* pair; even number; 2. *aj.* even (numbers)
para: *prep.* to; for; towards
parabién: *nm.* congratulation
parabrisa: *nm.* windshield
paracaídas: *nm.* parachute
paracaidismo: *nm.* parachuting
paracaidista: *nmf.* parachutist
parachoques: *nm.* bumper
parada: *nm.* stop; bus stop
paradero: *nf.* rest stop; whereabouts
paradisíaco: *aj.* paradisiacal; pertaining to paradise

parado; -a: 1. *nmf.* unemployed worker. 2. *aj.* stopped; not working; standing still
paradoja: *nf.* paradox
paradójico: *aj.* paradoxical
paraestatal: *aj.* semi-official
parafrasear: *vt.* to paraphrase
paráfrasis: *nf.* paraphrase
paraguas: *nm.* umbrella
paragüero: *nm.* umbrella stand
paraíso: *nm.* paradise
paralelamente: *av.* parallel
paralelas: *nmf.* parallel bars used in gymnastics
paralelismo: *nm.* parallelism
paralelo: 1. *aj.* parallel. 2. *nm.* parallel; latitude line
paralelogramo: *nm.* parallelogram
parálisis: *nm.* paralysis
paralítico; -a: *nmf.* paralytic. 2. *aj.* paralytic
paralización: *nf.* paralysis
paralizador: *aj.* paralyzing
paralizante: *aj.* paralyzing
paralizar: *vt.* to paralyze
paralizarse: *v.* to become paralyzed
parámetro: *nm.* parameter
paramilitar: *aj.* paramilitary
páramo: *nm.* high barren plain; moor
parangón: *nm.* comparison
paraninfo: *nm.* assembly hall; auditorium
Paraplejia; paraplejía: *nf.* paraplegia
parapléjico; -a: *nmf.* paraplegic. 2. *aj.* paraplegic
parar: *v.* to stop; to fix (attention). to stop
pararrayo: *nm.* lightning rod
pararse: *vr.* to stop oneself; to stand up
parasicológico: *aj.* Para psychological
parasicólogo; -a: *nmf.* parapsychologist
parasitología: *nf.* parapsychology
parasol: *nm.* umbrella used to protect

from sunlight
parcela: *nf.* plot; piece of ground; lot
parcial: *aj.* partial
parcialidad: *nf.* partiality
parcialmente: *av.* partially
parco; a: *aj.* frugal; sparing
Pardal: *aj. nm.* sparrow
pardo; da: *aj.* brown; dark; cloudy; grayish
Pardusco; parduzco: *aj.* somewhat grayish
parecer: *nm.* opinion
parecer: *vt.* to seem; to look like
parecerse: *vr.* to look like each other
parecido: 1. *aj.* similar to; alike; like. 2. *nm.* similarity
pared: *nf.* wall
paredón: *nm.* firing squad wall
pareja: *nf.* pair; couple
parejo: *aj.* even
parentela: *nf.* kinsfolk; relations
parentesco: *nm.* family relationship
paridad: *nf.* parity
pariente: *nmf.* relative
parir: *vt.* to give birth
parlamentar: *v.* to talk; chat
parlamentario; -a: *nmf.* parliamentarian. 2. *aj.* parliamentarian
parlamento: *nm.* parliament
parlanchín: *aj. con.* chattering
parlante: *nmf.* speaker
parlar: *vt.* to talk
parlotear: *vi.* to talk
parloteo: *nm.* informal chat
paro: *nm.* work stoppage; strike
parpadear: *vi.* to blink; to wink
párpado: *nm.* eyelid
parrafada: *nf. con.* talk; chat
parrilla: *nf.* grill; grate; grating
parroquia: *nf.* parish; clientele; customers
parroquia: *nf.* parish
parroquial: *aj.* parochial
parroquiano; -a: *nmf.* parishioner

parte: *nf.* part; share; side
partera: *nf.* midwife
partición: *nf.* partition
participación: *nf.* participation
participante: *aj.* participating
participante: *nmf.* participant
participar: *vt.* to communicate; to inform; *vi.* to participate
participar: *vi.* to participate
partícipe: *aj.* participating; sharing
partícipe: *nmf.* participant
partícula: *nf.* particle
particular: *aj.* particular; private
particular: *nm.* specific detail
particularidad: *nf.* particularity
particularizar: *vt.* to specify
particularizarse: *vr.* to distinguish oneself
particularmente: *av.* particularly
partidario: *aj.* factional
partidario; ria: n. partisan; follower
partidismo: *nm.* factionalism
partidista: *aj.* factional
partido: *aj.* split
partido: *nm.* party; match or game
partir: *vt.* to cut into pieces; to depart
partirse: *vr.* to be cut into pieces
partitura: *nf.* score
parto: *nm.* childbirth
párvulo: *nmf.* child
pasa: *aj.* dried
pasada: *nf.* place for passing; passing
pasadero: *aj.* passable
pasadizo: *nm.* passageway; secret passage
pasado: 1. *aj.* past; 2. *nm.* past
pasador: *nm.* smuggler; hairpin
pasaje: *nm.* passage
pasajero; -a: 1. *nmf.* passenger; 2. *aj.* passenger
pasamano: *nm.* handrail
pasaporte: *nm.* passport
pasar: *vt.* to pass
pasarela: *nf.* fashion

pasatiempo: *nm.* pastime
pascua: *nf.* Passover; Easter
pase: *nm.* pass
paseante: *nmf.* passerby
pasear: *vt.* to go for a walk or a ride
pasearse: *vr.* to be going for a walk; to take a trip
paseo: *nm.* walk; excursion
pasillo: *nm.* passage; corridor; hallway
pasión: *nf.* passion
pasional: *aj.* pertaining to passion
pasmo: *nm.* astonishment; wonder
paso: *nm.* step; pace; passing; measure
pasta: *nf.* paste; dough; pie crust; pasta
pastar: *vi.* to graze in a pasture
pastel: *nm.* cake
pastelería: *nf.* pastry shop
pastelero; -a: *nmf.* cake maker or seller
pastilla: *nf.* tablet
pastizal: *nm.* pasture
pasto: *nm.* grass
pastor: *nm.* pastor; elder; bishop; shepherd
pastoral: *aj.* pastoral
pastorear: *vt.* to shepherd
pastoreo: *nm.* shepherding
pastoril: *aj.* pastoral
pastoso: *aj.* pasty
pata: *nf.* paw; hoof; leg
patada: *nf.* forceful kick
patalear: *vi.* to hick; to stamp
patalear: *vt.* to repeatedly kick
pataleo: *nm.* repeated kicking
patán: *aj.* churlish; simpleton
patata: *nf.* potato
patear: *vt. con.* to trample on; tread on; to kick
patente: *aj.* patent; clear
paternal: *aj.* paternal
paternalismo: *nm.* paternalism
paternalista: *aj.* paternalistic
paternidad: *nf.* paternity
paterno: *aj.* paternal
patíbulo: *nm.* scaffold

patinar: *vi.* to skate; to skill
patio: *nm.* patio; court; yard; pit
patizambo: *aj.* bowlegged
pato: 1. *nm.* duck; drake; pagar el pato; 2. *con.* to be the scapegoat
patria: *nf.* country; mother country; fatherland; native country
patriarca: *nm.* patriarch
patriarcado: *nm.* term of patriarchal governing
patriarcal: *aj.* patriarchal
patriarcal : patriarchy
patrimonial: *aj.* patrimonial
patrimonio: *nm.* patrimony
patriota: *nmf.* patriot
patriótico: *aj.* patriotic
patriotismo: *nm.* patriotism
patrocinador; -a: *nmf.* sponsor; patron
patrocinar: *vt.* to sponsor
patrocinio: *nm.* sponsoring
patrón; -a: *nmf.* employer
patronal: *aj.* pertaining to the employer
patronato: *nm.* association for charity or mutual benefit
patrono; a: *nmf.* sponsor; protector; landlord
pausa: *nf.* pause
pausado: *aj.* paused
pauta: *nf.* guide lines
pavimentar: *vt.* to pave
pavo: *nm.* turkey
pavor: *nm.* horror; fear
pavoroso : *adj.* horrifying; frightening
paz: *nf.* peace
peaje: *nm.* toll
peatón: *nm.* pedestrian
pecado: *nm.* sin
pecador: *aj.* sinful (people)
pecador; -a: *nm.* sinner
pecaminoso: *aj.* pertaining to sin or sinners
pecar: *vi.* to sin
pecera: *nf.* fish globe; fish bowl

pechera: *nf.* top front part of overalls
pechero: *nm.* bib
pecho: *nm.* chest; breast; tomar a pecho; to take to heart
pechuga: *nf.* breast of an animal
pectoral: *aj.* pectoral
pecuario; a: *aj.* pertaining to cattle
peculiar: *aj.* peculiar
peculiaridad: *nf.* peculiarity
pedagogía: *nf.* pedagogy
pedagógico: *aj.* pedagogic
pedagogo; -a: *nmf.* pedagogue; teacher
pedal: *nm.* pedal; treadle
pedalear: *vt.* to pedal
pedaleo: *nm.* pedaling
pedazo: *nm.* piece
pedernal: *nm.* flint
pedestal: *nm.* pedestal
pedestre: *aj.* pertaining to the foot
pedida: *nf.* petition
pedido: *nm.* order; request
pedir: *vt.* to ask (favor)
pedrada: *nf.* throwing of a rock
pedregal: *nm.* rock floor
pedregoso: *aj.* rocky
pedrera: *nf.* rock quarry
pedrería: *nf.* group of precious stones
pedrisco: *nm.* small avalanche; rock slide; shower of stones; hailstones; hailstorm
pedrusco: *nm.* rock used for sculpting
pegadizo: *aj.* sticky
pegado: *aj.* stuck; attached
pegajoso: *aj.* sticky
pegamento: *nm.* glue
pegar: *vt.* to hit; to stick; to glue
pegarse: *vr.* to become stuck
peinado: *nm.* hairstyle
peinador; -a: *nmf.* hair stylist
peinar: *vt.* to comb; or. to comb one's hair
peinarse: *vr.* to comb one's hair
peine: *nm.* comb
peineta: *nf.* ornamental comb

pelado; da: *aj.* bare; bald; barren
peldaño: *nm.* step
pelea: *nf.* fight
peleado: *aj.* fighting
peleador: *aj.* aggressive; easily provoked to fight
pelear: *vi.* to fight; to quarrel; to struggle
pelearse: *vr.* to fight each other
peleonero; peleón: *nmf.* fighter
peletería: *nf.* furrier
peliagudo; da: *aj. con.* arduous; ticklish
peligrar: *vi.* to be in danger
peligro: *nm.* danger; risk; corer
peligrosidad: *nf.* dangerousness
peligroso: *aj.* dangerous
pelirroja -ja: *aj.* red-haired; red-headed
pellejo: *nm.* skin of an animal
pellejudo: *aj.* having a lot of skin
pellizcar: *vt.* to pinch; to nip
pelma: *nmf. con.* lump; poke; sluggard
pelo: *nm.* hair
pelón; -a: *nmf.* bald person
pelota: *nf.* ball
pelotera: *nf. con.* brawl; row
pelotón: *nm.* platoon; main body
peluca: *nf.* wig
peludo: *aj.* hairy
peluquería: *nf.* barbershop; hair salon
peluquero; -a: *nmf.* hair stylist; barber
peluquín: *nm.* toupee
pelusa: *nf.* down; *con.* jealousy
pena: *nf.* pity; grief; fine; punishment
peña: *nf.* loose rock
pena : *nf.* embarrassment; shame; penalty
penado; -a: *nmf.* inmate
penal: *aj.* penal
penalidad: *nf.* penalty; troublesome work
penalista: *nmf.* lawyer who specializes in criminal cases

penalización: *nf.* penalization
penalizar: *vt.* to penalize
penalti: *nm.* penalty kick in soccer
penar: *vt.* to punish; *vi.* to suffer
peñasco: *nm.* large loose rock
pendant; colgante: *aj.* earring (hanging)
pendencia: *nf.* dispute; quarrel
pender: *vt.* to hang
pendiente: *nm.* errand; pending task;
pene: *nm.* penis
penetrabilidad: *nf.* penetrability
penetrable: *aj.* penetrable
penetración: *nf.* penetration
penetrante: *aj.* penetrating
penetrar: *vt.* to penetrate; to break into; to see through (someone's intentions)
península: *nf.* peninsula
peninsular: *aj.* peninsular
penitencia: *nf.* penitence
penitenciaría: *nf.* penitentiary; prison
penitenciario: *aj.* penitentiary
penitente: 1. *aj.* penitent; 2. *nmf.* penitent
peñón: *nm.* large steep rock
penoso: *aj.* shy; timid; embarrassing
penoso -sa: *aj.* arduous; difficult
pensado: *aj.* thought
pensador; -a: *nmf.* thinker
pensamiento: *nm.* thought
pensar: *vt.* to think
pensativo: *aj.* pensive; thoughtful
pensión: *nf.* pension
pensionado; -a: 1. *nmf.* retired person; 2. *aj.* retired; receiving a pension
pensionista: *nmf.* person who receives a pension
penúltimo; -a: 1. *nmf.* the penultimate; the next-to last; 2. *aj.* penultimate; next-to-last
penumbra: *nf.* penumbra; shade
peón: *nm.* worker; laborer; pawn (chess)

peor: *aj.* worse; worst
pepita: *nf.* pip; melon seed
pequeñez: *nf.* smallness
pequeño; -a: *nmf.* small person; little one; term of endearment
percance: *nm.* mischance
percatar: *vi.* to think; to be aware of
percepción: *nf.* perception
perceptible: *aj.* perceptible
perceptivo: *aj.* perceptive
perchero: *nm.* rack
percibir: *vt.* to perceive
perdedor; -a: *nmf.* loser
perder: *vt.* to lose
perderse: *vr.* to become lost; to miss
perdición: *nf.* perdition
pérdida: *nf.* loss
perdidamente: *av.* completely; blindly
perdido: *aj.* lost
perdón: *nm.* pardon
perdonable: *aj.* pardonable
perdonar: *vt.* to pardon; forgive; to excuse
perdurable: *aj.* lasting
perdurablemente: *av.* eternally
perdurar: *vi.* to endure; to last
perecedero: *aj.* perishable
perecer: *vi.* to perish
peregrinación: *nf.* pilgrimage
peregrinaje: *nf.* pilgrimage
peregrinar: *vi.* to make a pilgrimage; to make a journey
peregrino; na: 1. *aj.* rare; strange; singular; 2. *mnf.* pilgrim
peregrino; -a: *nmf.* pilgrim
perennal: *aj.* perennial
perenne: *aj.* perennial
perennidad: *nf.* perpetuity
pereza: *nf.* laziness; sloth
perezosamente: *av.* lazily
perezoso: *aj.* lazy
perfección: *nf.* perfection
perfeccionamiento: *nm.* perfecting
perfeccionar: *vt.* to perfect

perfeccionismo: *nm.* perfectionism
perfeccionista: *nmf.* perfectionist
perfectamente: *av.* perfectly
perfectibilidad: *nf.* perfectibility
perfectible: *aj.* perfectible
perfectivo: *aj.* perfective
perfecto: *aj.* perfect
perfil: *nm.* profile
perfilado: *aj.* profiled
perfilar: *vt.* to draw a profile
perfilarse: *vr.* to show one's profile (figurative)
perforación: *nf.* perforation; drilling
perforador: *nm.* drill; person who drills holes
perforadora: *nf.* hole punch
perforar: *vt.* to perforate; to drill
perfumador: *nm.* perfume bottle
perfumar: *vt.* to put perfume on something
perfumarse: *vr.* to put perfume on oneself
perfume: *nm.* perfume
perfumería: *nf.* perfume store
perfumista: *nmf.* person who makes or sells perfume
pericia: *nf.* skill; expertness
perillán; llana: *aj.* rascally
periódico: *aj.* periodic
periódico: *nm.* newspaper
periodismo: *nm.* journalism
periodista: *nmf.* newspaper reporter
periodístico: *aj.* pertaining to newspapers or journalism
peritaje: *nm.* expert report
perito; ta: 1. *aj.* skilled; skillful; *nm.* expert; 2. *nmf.* expert
perjudicar: *vt.* to harm; damage
perjurar: *vi.* to commit perjury; to swear
perjurio: *nm.* perjury
perjuro; -a: *nmf.* perjurer
perla: *nf.* pearl; de perlas; pat
perlado: *aj.* pearl-colored; pearl-

shaped; having pearls
permanecer: *vi.* to stay; remain
permanencia: *nf.* permanence
permanente: 1. *aj.* permanent; 2. *nm.* permanent (hairstyle)
permanentemente: *av.* permanently
permisible: *aj.* permissible
permisión: *nf.* permission
permisivo: *aj.* permissive
permiso: *nm.* permission; permit
permiso de conducir: driver's license
permitido: *aj.* permitted
permitir: *vt.* to permit; to allow; r. to be permitted; to allow oneself
permitirse: *vr.* to be permitted
permutar: *vt.* to interchange; to barter; to permute
pernera: *nf.* leg (of trousers)
pernoctar: *vi.* to spend the night
pero: *conj.* but
perpetuación: *nf.* perpetuation
perpetuamente: *av.* perpetually
perpetuar: *vt.* to perpetuate
perpetuarse: *vr.* to be perpetuated
perpetuidad: *nf.* perpetuity
perpetuo: *aj.* perpetual
perplejidad: *nf.* perplexity
perplejo: *aj.* perplexed
perra: *nf.* female dog
perrera: *nf.* dog pound
perrero: *nm.* dog catcher
perro -rra: *nm.* dog; a otro perro con ese hueso; tell that to the marines
perruno: *aj.* pertaining to dogs
persecución: *nf.* persecution
persecutorio: *aj.* persecuting
perseguidor; -a: *nmf.* pursuer
perseguir: *vt.* to pursue; to perse-cute
perseverar: *vi.* to persevere; to insist
persiana: *nf.* window blinds
persignar: r. to cross oneself; make the sign of the cross
persistencia: *nf.* persistence
persistente: *aj.* persistent

persistir: *vi.* to persist
persona: *nf.* person
personaje: *nm.* celebrity; famous person
personal: 1. *aj.* personal; 2. *nm.* personnel
personalidad: *nf.* personality
personalizar: *vt.* to personalize
personalmente: *av.* personally
personificación: *nf.* personification
personificar: *vt.* to personify
perspectivo; va: 1. *aj.* perspective; 2. *nf.* perspective; outlook
persuadir: *vt.* to persuade; to become persuaded; to get convinced
pertenecer: *vi.* to belong to
perteneciente: *aj.* belonging; pertaining
pertenencia: *nf.* belonging; possession
perturbar: *vt.* to perturb; to disturb; to *conf*use
pervertir: *vt.* to pervert; r. to become perverted (see ir; sentir)
pesa: *nf.* weight (gym)
pesacartas: *nm.* postal scale
pesada: *nf.* weight; weighing
pesadez: *nf.* heaviness
pesadilla: *nf.* nightmare
pesado; da: *aj.* heavy; clumsy
pesadumbre: *nf.* affliction
pésame: *nm.* expression of condolence
pesar: *nm.* problem
pesar: *vi.* to weigh
pesarse: *vr.* to weigh oneself
pesca: *nf.* fishing
pescadería: *nf.* fish market
pescadero; -a: *nmf.* fishmonger
pescado: *nm.* fish (caught)
pescador; -a: *nmf.* fisherman
pescar: *vt.* to fish; to catch; to angle
pescuezo: *nm.* neck
pésimamente: *av.* very badly
pesimismo: *nm.* pessimism
pesimista: *nmf.* pessimist

pésimo: *aj.* very bad
peso: *nm.* weight; burden; load
pesquera: *nf.* place for fishing
pesquero: *aj.* pertaining to fish; fishing
pesquero: *nm.* fishing boat
pesquisa: *nf.* inquiry; search
pestaña: *nf.* eyelash
pestañear: *vi.* to move the eyelashes
pestañeo: *nm.* moving of eyelashes
pestañita: *nf.* nap
pestillo: *nm.* bolt; door latch
petardo: *nm.* bomb; fraud
petición: *nf.* petition
peticionario; -a: *nmf.* petitioner
peto: *nm.* breastplate
pétreo: *aj.* rock-like; of rock; stony (also figurative)
petrificación: *nf.* petrifaction
petrificado: *aj.* petrified
petrificar: *vt.* to petrify
petrificarse: *vr.* to be petrified
petróleo: *nm.* petroleum; oil
petrolero: *nm.* oil tanker
petrolífero: *aj.* oil-producing
petroquímica: *nf.* petrochemistry
petroquímico: *aj.* petrochemical
pez: *nm.* fish
pezuña: *nf.* hoof
piadoso: *aj.* pious pío
píamente: *av.* piously
pianísimo: *av.* very quietly
pianista: *nmf.* pianist
pianístico: *aj.* pertaining to the piano
piano: *nm.* piano
pianoforte: *nm.* piano
pianola: *nf.* player piano
piar: *vi.* to peep
pica: *nf.* pike
picado: *aj.* bitten; stung; chopped; piqued
picadura: *nf.* biting; stinging; bite; sting
picaflor: *nm.* hummingbird
picajoso: *aj.* hypersensitive

picajoso; -a: *nmf.* hypersensitive person
picante: *aj.* biting; stinging; hot (seasoning)
picapedrero: *nm.* rock sculptor
picaporte: *nm.* door catch
picar: *v.* to bite; to sting; to chop
picardía: *nf.* knavery; crookedness
picazón: *nm.* itch; itching
pico: *nm.* beak; peak
picor: *nm.* bothersome burning or stinging sensation
picotada: *nf.* forceful hit with a beak
picotazo: *nm.* forceful hit with a beak
picotear: *vt.* to be pecking
picoteo: *nm.* pecking
picudo; da: *aj.* beaked; pointed
pie: *nm.* foot
piedad: *nf.* piety
piedra: *nf.* rock
piel: *nm.* skin
pienso: *nm.* feed
pierna: *nf.* leg
pijama: *nm.* pyjamas
pila: *nf.* pile; battery; pool of stored water
pilar: *nm.* basin; bowl; pillar
píldora: *nf.* pill
pillaje: *nm.* pillage; plunder
pillar: *vt.* to pillage; plunder
pilotar; pilotear: *vt.* to pilot
piloto: 1. *aj.* pilot; 2. *nmf.* pilot
pimentón: *nm.* red pepper powder; paprika
pimiento: *nm.* red-pepper
pina: *nf.* pine cone; pineap-ple
piña: *nf.* pineapple
pinar: *nm.* pine grove
pincel: *nm.* brush
pinchar: *vt.* to prick; puncture; to stir up; provoke
pineda: *nf.* pine grove
pingüe: *aj.* oily; greasy; rich; abundant
pino; na: *aj. nm.* (Bat.) pine-tree

piñón: *nm.* pine nut
pinta: *nf.* stain
pintado: *aj.* painted; with makeup
pintar: *vt.* to paint; to put on makeup
pintarrajar: *vt.* to paint carelessly
pintarrajearse: *vr.* to put on makeup poorly or carelessly
pintarse: *vr.* to put makeup on oneself
pinto: *aj.* spotted
pintor; -a: *nmf.* painter
pintoresco: *aj.* picturesque
pintura: *nf.* painting
piojo: *nm.* louse
pipa: *nf.* pipe; wine cask
piquera: *nf.* cell in a beehive
piqueta: *nf.* pickax
piquete: *nm.* sharp jab; stake; picket
piragua: *nf.* canoe
pirámide: *nf.* pyramid
piropear: *vt.* to flirt
piropo: *nm.* flirtatious compliment
pisada: *nf.* step
pisapapeles: *nm.* paperweight
pisar: *vt.* to step on; to walk on
piscina: *nf.* swimming pool
piso: *nm.* floor; story; flat; apartment
pisotear: *vt.* to trample; to step on repeatedly
pisotón: *nm.* hard stamping with the foot
pista: *nf.* track; clue
pistola: *nf.* pistol
pistolera: *nf.* holster
pistolero: *nm.* pistol shooter; gu*nf.*ighter
pistoletazo: *nm.* pistol shot; hit with the butt of a gun
pitillo: *nm.* cigarette
pito: *nm.* whistle; horn
pizarra: *nf.* slate; blackboard
placa: *nf.* plate; insignia
placer: *nm.* pleasure; *vt.* to please
placidez: *nf.* placidity; calmness; tranquility

plácido: *aj.* placid; calm; tranquil
plaga: *nf.* plague; pest
plagar: *vt.* to plague; infest; r. to become plagued
plan: *nm.* plan; scheme
planchar: *vt.* to iron; to press
plane: *nm.* plant; floor; plane
planeado: *aj.* planned
planear: *vt.* to plan
planeta: *nf.* planet
planetario: 1. *aj.* planetary; 2. *nm.* planetarium
planificación: *nf.* planning
planificar: *vt.* to plan
plano: *nm.* plane; plan; map
planta: *nf.* plant
plantación: *nf.* plantation
plantado: *aj.* planted
plantar: *vt.* to plant
plantarse: *vr.* to be planted
plantear: *vt.* to organize or form plans
plantío: *nm.* planting; field of planted vegetables
plata: *nf.* silver; money
plataforma: *nf.* platform
plátano: *nm.* banana
plateado: *aj.* plated; silver-colored
plateado: *nm.* plated silver; plating of silver
platear: *vt.* to plate with silver
platería: *nf.* silversmith's shop; silversmithing; silverware
platero; -a: *nmf.* silversmith
plática: *nf.* talk; chat; homily
platillo: *nm.* dish
plato: *nm.* dish; plate; course (at meals)
playa: *nf.* beach
playera: *nf.* tee shirt
playero: *aj.* pertaining to the beach
plaza: *nf.* plaza; town square
plazo: *nm.* term; time; limit
plazoleta: *nf.* small plaza; town square
plazuela: *nf.* plaza; town square
plebe: *nf.* plebeians; commoners

plebeyo: *aj.* plebeian; common
plegable: *aj.* able to be folded
plegado: *aj.* folded; rolled-up
plegar: *vt.* to fold; to roll up
plegarse: *vr.* to be folded; to be rolled up
pleitista; -a: *nmf.* person who is always looking for a fight
pleito: *nm.* fight; argument
plenilunio: *nm.* full-moon
plenitud: *nf.* fullness
pleno: *aj.* full
pliego: *nm.* sheet; folder
pliegue: *nm.* fold; pleat
plomo: *nm.* lead
pluma: *nf.* pen; feather
plumaje: *nm.* plumage
plumazo: *nm.* hit with a pen
plumero: *nm.* feather duster
plumón: *nm.* color marker
plumoso: *aj.* feathery
pluriempleo: *nm.* moonlighting
plurilingüe: *aj.* multi-lingual
púa: *nf.* sharp point; barb; quill
población: *nf.* population
poblado: *aj.* populated
poblador; -a: *nmf.* person who lives in a town
poblar: *vt.* to populate
poblarse: *vr.* to become populated
pobre: *aj.* poor
pobre: *nmf.* poor person
pobreza: *nf.* poverty
poco: *av.* little; few
poda: *nf.* pruning
podadera: *nf.* pruning scissors; pruning knife
podar: *vt.* to prune; to trim
poder: *nm.* power
poder: *vt.* to be able to
poderío: *nm.* authority; power
poderoso; sa: *aj.* powerful; mighty; wealthy
poema: *nf.* poem

poesía: *nf.* poetry
poeta: *nm.* poet
poético: *aj.* poetic
poetisa: *nf.* poetess
polémica: *nf.* polemic; controversy
polémico: *aj.* polemic; polemical; controversial
polemista: *nmf.* person who engages in discussing controversy
polemizar: *vt.* to engage in a discussion over a controversial matter
policía: *nf.* police; policeman; policewoman
policiaco; policíaco: *aj.* pertaining to police
polideportivo: *nm.* sport facility
polilla: *nf.* moth; car-pet moth
polio: *nm.* children
político: *aj.* political
politiquear: *vt.* to engage in politics
politizar: *vt.* to politicize
póliza: *nf.* check; draft; constract; tax stamp
polla: *nf.* young hen
pollera: *nf.* chicken coop
pollero; -a: *nmf.* chicken farmer or merchant
pollito; -a: *nmf.* chick
pollo: *nm.* chicken
polluelo; -a: *nmf.* chick
polo: *nm.* support; pole
polvareda: *nf.* "rain" of dust
polvera: *nf.* talc or powder container
polvo: *nm.* dust
pólvora: *nf.* gunpowder
polvoriento: *aj.* very dusty
polvorín: *nm.* fine powder; fine gunpowder
pómulo: *nm.* cheekbone
ponderar: *vt.* to weigh; to ponder; to exaggerate
ponencia: *nf.* proposal; paper; report
ponente: *nmf.* speaker
poner: *vt.* to put

populachería: *nf.* local fame or popularity (pejorative)
populachero: *aj.* pertaining to town or people of a town (pejorative)
populacho: *nm.* town; people of a town (pejorative)
popular: *aj.* popular
popularidad: *nf.* popularity
popularizar: *vt.* to popularize
popularmente: *av.* popularly
populista: 1. *aj.* populist; 2. *nmf.* populist
populoso: *aj.* populous
por: *prep.* by; through; for the sake of; in place of; out of
porcelana: *nf.* porcelain
porcentaje: *nm.* percentage
porcentual: *aj.* percentage
pordiosero -ra: *nmf.* beggar
pormenor: *nm.* detail
pormenorizar: *vt.* to describe in detail
porque: *conj.* because
porqué: *nm. con.* why; reason
porrazo: *nm.* blow
portaaviones: *nf.* aircraft carrier
portada: *nf.* front; facade; title page
portador: *aj.* carrying
portador; -a: *nmf.* carrier
portaequipajes: *nm.* luggage compartment
portafolios: *nm.* portfolio
portal: *nm.* vestibule; entrance hall; porch
portalámparas: *nm.* socket
portamonedas: *nm.* coin purse or container
portaobjetos: *nm.* microscope slide
portar (se): *vt* to carry
portátil: *aj.* portable
portavoz: *nmf.* announcer; spokesman
portazo: *nm.* door slam
portento: *nm.* portent
portentoso: *aj.* portentous
portería: *nf.* soccer goal

portero; -a: *nmf.* goalie; goalkeeper in soccer; doorman
pórtico: *nm.* portico; porch
portuario: *aj.* pertaining to a port
porvenir: *nm.* future
pos: *prep.* after; behind
posada: *nf.* inn; boarding house
posadero; -a: *nmf.* innkeeper
poseedor; -a: *nmf.* possessor
poseer: *vt.* to own; to possess; to hold
poseído: *aj.* possessed
posesión: *nf.* possession
posesionar: *vt.* to take possession of
posesivo: *aj.* possessive
posibilidad: *nf.* possibility
posibilitar: *vt.* to make possible
posible: *aj.* possible
posiblemente: *av.* possibly
posición: *nf.* position
positivamente: *av.* positively
positivismo: *nm.* positivism
positivo: *aj.* positive
positivo; -a: *nmf.* positive person
poso: *nm.* sediment; dregs
posponer: *vt.* to postpone
postal: *aj.* postal; *nf.* postcard
poste: *nm.* post; pole; pillar
posteridad: *nf.* posterity
posterior: *aj.* posterior; back; rear
posterioridad: *nf.* posteriority
posteriormente: *av.* subsequently
postgraduado: *aj.* post-graduate
postigo: *nm.* wicket; shutter
postizo; za: *aj.* false; artificial; *nm.* switch
postoperatorio: *aj.* post-operative
postrar: *vt.* to prostrate
postre: *aj.* last; final
postre: *nm.* dessert
postrero: *aj.* following; next; yet-to-come
póstumo; ma: *aj.* posthumous
potable: *aj.* potable; drinkable
potaje: *nm.* stew; medley

potencia: *nf.* potency; power
potencial: 1. *aj.* potential; 2. *nm.* power
potencialidad: *nf.* potential
potencialmente: *av.* potentially
potenciar: *vt.* to give power to
potentado; -a: *nmf.* rich or powerful person
potente: *aj.* potent
potestad: *nf.* power; dominion; authority
poto: *av.* little; few
potro -tra: *nmf.* colt; young horse; rack
poza: *nf.* spring
pozal: *nm.* pail; bucket
pozo: *nm.* well
práctica: *nf.* practice
practicable: *aj.* practicable
prácticamente: *av.* practically
practicante: *nmf.* medical intern
practicar: *vt.* to practice
práctico: *aj.* practical
pradera: *nf.* large meadow
prado: *nm.* meadow
precalentamiento: *nm.* preheating
precalentar: *vt.* to preheat
precaución: *nf.* precaution
precaver: *vt.* to try; to prevent; to prepare
precaverse: *vr.* to be prepared
precavido: *aj.* prepared
precedencia: *nf.* precedence
precedente: *aj.* preceding
precedente: *nm.* precedent
preceder: *vt.* to precede; go before
preces: *nf.* pl. prayers
precio: *nm.* price; value; cost
preciosidad: *nf.* preciousness; beauty
precioso: *aj.* precious
precipitación: *nf.* precipitation
precipitadamente: *av.* precipitately; hurried
precipitado: *aj.* precipitated
precipitar: *vt.* to precipitate; to rush

precipitarse: *vr.* to be in a hurry; to be rushed
precisamente: *av.* precisely
precisar: *vt.* to explain carefully or precisely
precisión: *nf.* precision
preciso: *aj.* precise
preconcebido: *aj.* preconceived
preconcepción: *nf.* preconception
precoz: *aj.* precocious; premature
predecir: *vt.* to predict; foretell
prédica: *nf.* sermon
predicación: *nf.* sermon
predicado: *nm.* predicate
predicador; -a: *nmf.* preacher
predicar: *vt.* to preach
predicción: *nf.* prediction
predilección: *nf.* predilection
predilecto: *aj.* favorite; preferred
predisponer: *vt.* to predispose
predisposición: *nf.* predisposition
predispuesto: *aj.* predisposed
predominación: *nf.* predomination
predominante: *aj.* predominant
predominar: *vt.* to predominate; to over-rule
predominio: *nm.* predominance
preeminencia: *nf.* preeminence
preeminente: *aj.* preeminent
preescolar: *aj.* preschool
preestablecer: *vt.* to pre-establish
preestablecido: *aj.* preestablished
preexistencia: *nf.* preexistence
preexistir: *vi.* to preexist
prefabricación: *nf.* prefabrication
prefabricado: *aj.* prefabricated
prefabricar: *vt.* to prefabricate
preferencia: *nf.* preference
preferente: *aj.* preferable
preferentemente: *av.* preferably
preferible: *aj.* preferable
preferido: *aj.* preferred
preferir: *vt.* to prefer
prefijar: *vt.* to establish ahead of time

prefijo: *inn.* prefix
perforar: *vt.* to perforate; drill
pregón: *nm.* public announcement
pregonar: *vt.* to proclaim; to bring to public notice
pregonar: *vt.* to announce publicly in streets; on buses; in malls; etc
pregonero: *nm.* announcer in streets; on buses; in malls; etc
pregunta: *nf.* question
preguntar: *vt.* to ask (question)
preguntarse: *vr.* to ask oneself (question); to wonder
preguntón: *aj.* asking many questions; overly curious
prehistoria: *nf.* pre-history
prehistórico: *aj.* pre-historic
prematrimonial: *aj.* premarital
prematuro; ra: *aj.* premature
premeditación: *nf.* premeditation
premeditadamente: *av.* premeditatedly
premeditado: *aj.* premeditated
premiado: *aj.* prize-winning
premiar: *vt.* to reward; to give a prize
premio: *nm.* prize
prenatal: *aj.* prenatal
prendedor: *nm.* switch; ignition switch; ornamental pin
prender: *vt.* to seize; grasp; to catch; *vi.* to catch; to take root; to set fire
prender: *vt.* to turn on; to pin
prendido: *aj.* turned on; pinned
prensa: *nf.* press
prensado: *aj.* pressed
prensar: *vt.* to press
preocupación: *nf.* worry
preocupado: *aj.* worried
preocupar: *vt.* to cause concern or worry
preocuparse: *vr.* to worry
preparación: *nf.* preparation
preparado: *aj.* prepared
preparador; -a: *nmf.* preparer

preparar: *vt.* to prepare
prepararse: *vr.* to prepare oneself; to be preparing
preparativo: *nm.* preparation
preparatorio: *aj.* preparatory
prepotencia: *nf.* great power
prepotente: *aj.* abusive of power
prerrequisito: *nm.* prerequisite
presa: *nf.* dike; dam; seizure
prescindible: *aj.* dispensable
prescindir: *vt.* to omit
prescribir: *vt.* to prescribe
prescripción: *nf.* prescription
preselección: *nf.* preselection
preseleccionar: *vt.* to pre-select
presencia: *nf.* presence
presenciar: *vt.* to witness; to be present at
presentable: *aj.* presentable
presentación: *nf.* presentation
presentador; -a: *nmf.* presenter
presentar: *vt.* to present; to introduce
presentarse: *vr.* to present oneself; to introduce oneself
presente: 1. *aj.* present; 2. *nm.* present (time); present (gift)
presentimiento: *nm.* feeling about the future
presentir: *vt.* to have a feeling about the future
preservar: *vt.* to preserve; keep
presidencia: *nf.* presidency
presidencial: *aj.* presidential
presidente; -a: *nmf.* president; chairman
presidiario: *nm.* convict
presidir: *vt.* to preside
presión: *nf.* pressure
presionar: *vt.* to pressure
prestación: *nf.* lending
prestaciones: *nmf.* benefits
prestado: *aj.* lent; borrowed
prestamista: *nmf.* lender
préstamo: *nm.* loan

prestar: *vt.* to lend
prestarse: *vr.* to volunteer
prestatario; -a: *nmf.* borrower
prestigio: *nm.* prestige
prestigioso: *aj.* prestigious
presumible: *aj.* presumable
presumir: *vi.* to show conceit or excessive pride
presunción: *nf.* presumption
presuntamente: *av.* presumably; supposedly
presunto: *aj.* supposed
presuntuosidad: *nf.* presumptuousness
presuntuoso: *aj.* presumptuous
presuponer: *vt.* to presuppose
presupuestar: *vt.* to make a budget
presupuestario: *aj.* pertaining to a budget
presupuesto: 1. *aj.* presupposed; 2. *nm.* budget
pretencioso: *aj.* pretentious
pretender: *vt.* to pretend to; to try; to aspire
pretendido: *aj.* courted
pretendiente: *aj.* courting
pretensión: *nf.* pretension; aspiration
prevalecer: *vi.* to prevail
prevaleciente: *aj.* prevailing
prevención: *nf.* prevention
prevenir: *vt.* to prevent
preventivo: *aj.* preventive
prever: *vt.* to foresee
previamente: *av.* previously
previo: *aj.* previous
previsible: *aj.* foreseeable
previsión: *nf.* foresight
previsor: *aj.* farsighted
previsto: *aj.* foreseen
primario; ria: *aj.* primary; chief
primavera: *nf.* spring (season)
primaveral: *aj.* spring; pertaining to spring (season)
primer: *aj.* form of primero; first
primeriza: *nf.* first-time mother

primerizo; -a: 1. *nmf.* novice; 2. *aj.* novice
primero; ra: *aj.* first; former
primogénito; ta: *nmf.* first-born
primo -ma: *nmf.* cousin
princesa: *nf.* princess
principado: *nm.* principality
principal: *aj.* principal
príncipe: *nm.* prince
principesco: *aj.* pertaining to princes
principio: *nm.* star; beginning; principle
prior: *nm.* prior
prisa: *nf.* hurry; haste; urgency
prisión: *nf.* prison
prisionero; -a: *nmf.* prisoner
privación: *nf.* privation
privar: *vt.* to deprive; in to be in vogue; to be in favor
privarse: *vr.* to deprive oneself
privilegiado: *aj.* privileged
privilegio: *nm.* privilege
proa: *nf.* prow
probabilidad: *nf.* probability
probable: *aj.* probable
probado: *aj.* proven
probador: *nm.* dressing room for trying on clothes
probar: *vt.* to prove; to test; to try; to taste; to fit; to try
probeta: *nf.* test tube
problema: *nf.* problem
problemático: *aj.* problematic; problematical
procedencia: *nf.* origin; source
procedente: *aj.* originating in
proceder: *nm.* behavior
proceder: *vi.* to proceed
procedimiento: *nm.* procedure
procesado: *aj.* processed
procesamiento: *nm.* processing; prosecution
procesar: *vt.* to sue; to indict; to process; to prosecute

procesión: *nf.* procession
procesional: *aj.* processional
proceso: *nm.* process
proclama: *nf.* proclamation
proclamación: *nf.* proclamation
proclamar: *vt.* to proclaim
procreación: *nf.* procreation
procreador: 1. *aj.* procreative; 2. *nmf.* procreator
procrear: *vt.* to procreate; breed
procuración: *nf.* procurement
procurador: *nm.* solicitor; attorney
procurar: *vt.* to try; to get
prodigio: *nm.* prodigy; supernatural phenomenon
prodigiosamente: *av.* prodigiously
prodigioso: *aj.* prodigious
pródigo; ga: *nf.* prodigal
producción: *nf.* production
producir: *vt.* to produce; to yield; to cause
producirse: *vr.* to be produced
productividad: *nf.* productivity
productivo: *aj.* productive
producto: *nm.* product
productor; -a: *nmf.* producer
productora: *nf.* film production company
profecía: *nf.* prophecy
proferir: *vt.* to utter; to say; to express
profesar: *vt.* to profess; to take religious vows
profesión: *nf.* profession
profesional: 1. *aj.* professional; 2. *nmf.* professional
profesionalidad: *nf.* professionalism
profesionalismo: *nm.* professionalism
profesionalizar: *vt.* to make professional; to perform at a professional level
profesionalmente: *av.* professionally
profesor -ra: *n.* teacher; professor
profesorado: *nm.* professorship; teaching profession

profeta: *nm.* prophet
profético: *aj.* prophetic
profetizar: *vt.* to prophecy; foretell
prófugo; ga: *aj.* fugitive
profundamente: *av.* profoundly
profundidad: *nf.* profundity; depths
profundizar: *vt.* to deepen; *vi.* to go deep into
profundo: *aj.* profound; deep
programa: *nf.* program
programable: *aj.* programmable
programador; -a: *nmf.* programmer
programar: *vt.* to program
programático: *aj.* pertaining to a program
progresar: *vi.* to progress
progresión: *nf.* progression
progresismo: *nm.* progressivism
progresista: 1. *aj.* progressive; 2. *nmf.* progressive
progresivamente: *av.* progressively
progresivo: *aj.* progressive
progreso: *nm.* progress
prohibición: *nf.* prohibition
prohibicionista: *nmf.* prohibitionist
prohibir: *vt.* to prohibit; to forbid
prohibitivo: *aj.* prohibitive
prohijar: *vt.* to adopt a child
prójimo: *nm.* neighbor
proletario; ria: *nm.* proletarian
prolongación: *nf.* prolongation; extension
prolongadamente: *av.* extensively
prolongado: *aj.* prolonged
prolongamiento: *nm.* prolonging
prolongar: *vt.* to prolong; to extend; *or.* to extend
prolongarse: *vr.* to be prolonged
promesa: *nf.* promise
prometedor: *aj.* promising
prometer: *vt.* to promise
prometerse: *vr.* to make a promise
prometido: *aj.* engaged
prometido; -a: *nmf.* fiancé; fiancée

promotor; ra: *nmf.* promoter
promover: *vt.* to promote; raise; cause
promulgar: *vt.* to promulgate issue
pronombre: *nm.* pronoun
pronto: *av.* soon
pronto; ta: *aj.* quick; prompt; ready
pronunciación: *nf.* pronunciation
pronunciado: *aj.* pronounced
pronunciamiento: *nm.* pronouncement
pronunciar: *vt.* to pronounce; *or.* to rebel; revolt
pronunciar: *vt.* to pronounce
pronunciarse: *vr.* to pronounce one's opinion
propaganda: *nf.* advertisement; propaganda
propagar: *vt.* to propagate
propagarse: *vr.* to propagate; to be propagated
propiedad: *nf.* property; ownership; propiedad literaria; copyright
propina: *nf.* tip; fee
propio; pia: *aj.* proper; suitable; peculiar; himself; herself; etc.
proponer: *vt.* to propose
proponerse: *vr.* to propose to oneself; to intend
proporcionar: *vt.* to proportion; to provide; supply
propuesta: *nf.* proposal; suggestion
prorrogar: *vt.* to prorogue
prosa: *nf.* -prose
proscribir: *vt.* to proscribe; to prohibit
proseguir: *vt.* to proceed
prosperar: *vt.* to prospect
protagonista: *adj.* protagonista
protagonista: *nmf.* protagonist
protección: *nf.* protection
proteccionismo: *nm.* protectionism
proteccionista: 1. *aj.* protectionist; 2. *nmf.* protectionist
protector: *aj.* protecting
protector; ra: 1. *aj.* protective;

1. *nmf.* protector
protectorado: *nm.* protectorate
proteger: *vt.* to protect; to shelter
protegido: *aj.* protected
protesta: *nf.* protest
protestante: 1. aj protestant;
2. *nmf.* protestant
protestantismo: *nm.* Protestantism
protestar: *vt.* to protest
provecho: *nm.* advantage; benefit;
profit; gain
provechosamente: *av.* beneficially
provechoso: *aj.* good; useful;
beneficial
proveedor -ra: *nmf.* supplier; provider;
purveyor
proveer: *vt.* to provide; furnish
proveniente: *aj.* proceeding (from);
originating (in)
provenir: *vi.* to come; originate
providencia: *nf.* Providence
providencial: *aj.* providential
providencialmente: *av.* providentially
próvido: *aj.* prepared
provincia: *nf.* province
provincial: *aj.* provincial
provincianismo: *nm.* provincialism
provinciano: *aj.* pertaining to a
province
provisión: *nf.* provision
provisional: *aj.* provisional
provisionalmente: *av.* provisionally
provisiones: *nmf.* provisions
provista: *nf.* foreseen circumstance
provisto: *aj.* foreseen
provocación: *nf.* provocation
provocado: *aj.* provoked
provocador; -a: *nmf.* provoker
provocante: *aj.* provoking
provocar: *vt.* to provoke; to incite; to
tempt
provocativo: *aj.* provocative
proximidad: *nf.* proximity
próximo; ma: *aj.* next; near

proyección: *nf.* projection
proyectar: *vt.* to project
proyectarse: *vr.* to cast a silhouette
proyectil: *nm.* projectile
proyectista: *nmf.* person who works on
projects
proyecto: *nm.* project
proyector: *nm.* projector
prudencia: *nf.* prudence
prudencial: *aj.* prudential
prudencialmente: *av.* prudentially
prudente: *aj.* prudent
prudentemente: *av.* prudently
prueba: *nf.* proof; trial; test;
examination
psicoanálisis: *nm.* psychoanalysis
psicoanalista: *nmf.* psychoanalyst
psicoanalizar: *vt.* to psychoanalyze
psicodélico; sicodélico: *aj.* psychedelic
psicodrama: *nf.* psycho-drama
psicología: *nf.* psychology
psicológico: 1. *aj.* psychological; 2.
nmf. psychologist
psiconeurosis: *nf.* neurosis
psicópata: *nmf.* psychopath
psicopático; sicopático: *aj.*
psychopathic
sicopatología: *nf.* psychopathology
psicosis: *nf.* psychosis
psicosomático; sicosomático: *aj.*
psychosomatic
psicoterapeuta; sicoterapeuta: *nmf.*
psychotherapist
psicoterapia: *nf.* psychotherapy
psique: *nf.* psyche
psiquiatra; siquiatra: *nmf.*
psychiatrist
publicable: *aj.* publishable
publicación: *aj.* publication
públicamente: *av.* publicly
publicar: *vt.* to publish
publicidad: *nf.* publicity; advertising
publicista: *nmf.* publicist; newspaper
or magazine writer

publicitario: *aj.* publishing
público-ca: 1. *aj.* public; 2. *nm.* public
puchero: *nm.* pot; kettle
púdico: *aj.* shameful; modest; reserved; decent
pudor: *nm.* shame; modesty; reserve
pudoroso: *aj.* having shame; modesty; reserve
pudrir: *vt.* to rot; putrefy
pueblerino: *aj.* from a small town
pueblo: *nm.* town; townspeople
puente: *nm.* bridge; deck
pueril: *aj.* childlike in action or word
puerilidad: *nf.* childlike action or word
puerta: *nf.* door; gate
puerto: *nm.* port; harbor; pass; haven
pues: *adv.* then; well; yes
puesta: *nf.* setting
puesto: *aj.* placed
puesto: *nm.* post; position
púgil: *nm.* fighter; boxer
pugna: *nf.* fight; dispute
pugnar: *vi.* to fight; to engage in a dispute
pujar: *vt.* to push; to raise; *vi.* to struggle
pulga: *nf.* flea
pulgada: *nf.* inch
pulgar: *nm.* thumb
pulido; da: *aj.* pretty; neat
pulpo: *nm.* octopus
pulsar: *vt.* to feel or take the pulse of
pulsera: *nf.* bracelet
puñado: *nm.* handful
puñal: *nm.* dagger
puñalada: *nf.* stab with a dagger
puñetazo: *nm.* hit with the fist
puño: *nm.* fist; blow; cuff
punta: *nf.* point; end of a piece of yarn; string; hair; etc
punteado: *nm.* making of dots
puntear: *vt.* to make dots
puntería: *nf.* aim
puntero: *nm.* pointer

puntiagudo: *aj.* sharp; pointed; with a sharp point
puntilla: *nf.* brad; finishing nail
punto: *nm.* point; dot; loop; jot; mote; fig. point
puntual: *aj.* punctual
puntualizar: *vt.* to fix in the memory; to enumerate
pupitre: *nm.* desk
pureza: *nf.* purity
purga: *nf.* laxative; purging
purgante: *aj.* purging
purgante: *nm.* medicinal substance prepared to help with purging the stomach and intestinal tract
purgar: *vt.* to purge; to purify; refine; to expiate
purgatorio: *nm.* purgatory
purificación: *nf.* purification
purificador: *aj.* purifying
purificar: *vt.* to purify
purista: *nmf.* purist
puritanismo: *nm.* Puritanism
puritano: *aj.* puritanical
puritano; -a: *nmf.* Puritan
puro: *aj.* pure

Q

que: 1. *aj.* and pron. rel. that; which; who; 2. *adv.* than; 3. *conj.* that; for; because
quebrada: *nf.* break or crack in something
quebradizo: *aj.* easily broken
quebrado: *aj.* broken
quebrado: *nm.* fraction
quebradura: *nf.* break or crack in something
quebrantado: *aj.* broken-hearted or

broken in spirit

quebrantador: *aj.* heart-breaking

quebrantamiento: *nm.* the act of breaking physical objects; conceptual objects; laws; etc. quebrantado

quebrantaolas: *nm.* breakwater

quebrantar: *vt.* to break; to twist; to crush

quebrantarse: *vr.* to become broken

quebranto: *nm.* the act of breaking down or causing discouragement or pain

quebrar: *vt.* to break; to twist; to crush; *vi.* to fail

quebrarse: *vr.* to become broken

quedar: *vi.* to remain; to stay; to be left; agree on

quehacer: *nm.* work; task

queja: *nf.* complaint

quejar: *vt.* to complain; lament; to whine

quejarse: *vr.* to complain; to groan

quejido: *nm.* whine or groan

quejumbroso: *aj.* complaining

quema: *nf.* fire; burning

quemado: *aj.* burned; burnt

quemadura: *nf.* burn; scald

quemar: *vt.* to burn; to scald; to parch

quemarse: *vr.* to burn oneself or itself

quemazón: *nf.* unbearable heat; also; the burning down

querella: *nf.* complaint; quarrel; dispute

querer: *nm.* love; affection; will; *vt.* to wish; want; desire; to like; to love

querer: 1. *nm.* to want; to love; 2. *vt.* to want; to love

querido -da: 1. *aj.* dear; beloved; mistress; 2. *nmf.* beloved

queso: *nm.* cheese

quicio: *nm.* pivot hole; hinge

quién: *pron.* *int.* and *rel.* who; whom

quién: *pron.* who when used in a question

quienquiera: *pron.* anyone; anybody; *pron.* whoever; whichever

quieto: *aj.* calm; quiet

quietud: *nf.* calmness; quiet; stillness

quilla: *nf.* keel

química: *nf.* chemistry

químico -ca: 1. *aj.* chemical; *nm.* chemist; 2. *nmf.* chemist

quimioterapia: *nf.* chemotherapy

quincalla: *nf.* hardware; costume jewelry

quince: 1. *aj.* fifteen; 2. *nm.* fifteen

quinceañero a: *nmf.* fifteen-year-old boy or girl

quincena: *nf.* fifteen days; one-half month; fortnight; two-weeks

quincenal: *aj.* semi-monthly; every fifteen days

quincuagenario: *aj.* fifty-year-old

quincuagenario; -a: *nmf.* fifty-year-old person

quincuagésimo: *aj.* fiftieth

quinientos: 1. *aj.* five-hundred; 2. *nm.* five hundred

quinqué: *nm.* oil lamp

quinquenal: *aj.* five-year

quinquenio: *nm.* five-year term; a period of five years

quintacolumnista: *nmf.* member of a fifth column

quinteto: *nm.* a musical group of five people

quintillizo; -a: *nmf.* quintuplet

quinto: 1. *aj.* fifth; 2. *nm.* one-fifth (fraction)

quiosco: *nm.* kiosk

quirófano: *nm.* operating room; operating theatre

quitaesmalte: *nm.* fingernail polish remover

quitamanchas: *nm.* stain remover

quitanieve: *nm.* snowplow

quitanieves: *nm.* snow plow

quitar: *vt.* to remove

quitarse: *vr.* to remove from oneself; to take off

quitasol: *nm.* umbrella used to protect from sunlight

quizá; quizás: *adv.* maybe; perhaps

R

rábano: *nm.* radish
rabí: *nm.* rabbi
rabia: *nf.* anger; rage
rabiar: *vt.* to anger
rábico: *aj.* rabies
rabieta: *nf.* tantrum
rabioso: *aj.* rabid
rabo: *nm.* tail
racha: *nf.* squall; *con.* streak
racial: *aj.* racial
racimo: *nm.* bunch; cluster
raciocinio: *nm.* argument; reasoning
radar: *nm.* radar
radiación: *nf.* radiation
radiactividad: *nf.* radioactivity
radiactivo: *aj.* radioactive
radiador: *nm.* radiator
radiante: *aj.* radiant
radiar: *vi.* to radiate
radical: 1. *aj.* radical; 2. *nm.* radical
radicalismo: *nm.* radicalism
radicalizarse: *vr.* to become radical
radicalmente: *av.* radically
radio: *nm.* radio
radioactividad: *nf.* radioactivity
radioactivo: *aj.* radioactive
radioaficionado; -a: *nmf.* fan of radio
radiodifusión: *nf.* radio broadcasting
radioescucha: *nmf.* radio listener
radiografía: *nf.* radiography
radiografiar: *vt.* to give an x-ray

radiología: *nf.* radiology
radiólogo; -a: *nmf.* radiologist
radiómetro: *nm.* radiometer
radiorreceptor: *nf.* radio receiver
radioteléfono: *nm.* radio telephone
radiotelegrafista: *nmf.* radio telegrapher
radiotelescopio: *nm.* radio telescope
radioterapia: *nf.* radio therapy
radiotransmisión: *nf.* radio transmission
radiotransmisor: *nm.* radio transmitter
radioyente: *nm.* radio listener
raíz: *nf.* root; origin
rajar: *vt.* to split; to cleave; to crack
rallar: *vt.* to grate; *con.* to grate on
rama: *nf.* branch; department
ramaje: *nm.* collection of bouquets or branches; bouquets or branches in general
ramal: *nm.* strand; branch line
rambla: *nf.* dry ravine; tenter; boulevard
ramera: *nf.* whore; strumpet
ramificar: *vt.* to ramify; to spread out
ramo: *nm.* branch; cluster; bough; bouquet
rampa: *nf.* ramp; gradient
rana: *nf.* frog
rancidez: *nf.* rancidness
ranciedad: *nf.* rancidness
rancio: *aj.* rancid
ranura: *nf.* groove; slot
rapacidad: *nf.* rapaciousness
rapaz: *aj.* rapacious
rapaz: *nf.* bird of prey; robber
rape: *nm.* al rape; crew cut
rápidamente: *av.* rapidly
rapidez: *nf.* rapidity; speed
rápido: 1. *aj.* rapid; 2. *nm.* rapid (river)
rápido: *av.* rapidly
raposo: *nm.* male fox; *con.* fox
raptar: *vt.* to abduct; to kidnap
raqueta: *nf.* racket

raramente: *av.* rarely
rareza: *nf.* rareness
raro; ra: *aj.* rare; odd; uncommon; querer
ras; a ras de: *nm.* even with
rascacielos: *nm.* skyscraper
rasgar: *vt.* to tear; to rip; to become torn
rasguño: *nm.* scratch
raspar: *vt.* to scrape; scrape off; to scratch
rastreador: *nm.* investigator; one who can read signs or clues
rastrear: *vt.* to trail; to track; to trace; *vi.* to rake; to drag
rastreo: *nm.* act of searching for clues or following signs
rastrillo: *nm.* rake
rastro: *nm.* sign; footprint; mark
rastrojo: *nm.* what is left over after the harvest
rasurar: *vt.* to shave
rata: *nf.* rat
ratificar: *vt.* to ratify
ratón: *n.* mouse
raya: *nf.* stripe; stroke; dash; parting (hair); rayfish; boundary.
raya: *nf.* line
rayado: 1. *aj.* lined; crossed-out; 2. *nm.* lined
rayar: *vt.* to rule; to line; to stripe; to scratch; score; *vi.* to border; to begin; arise
rayar: *vt.* to shine with rays (dawn); to draw lines
rayo: *nm.* ray; beam; lightning thunderbolt
raza: *nf.* race; breed; quality
razón: *nf.* reason; right; account; story
razonable: *aj.* reasonable; fair
razonablemente: *av.* reasonably
razonado: *aj.* reasoned
razonamiento: *nm.* reasoning
razonar: *vt.* to reason; to think

reabrir: *vt.* to reopen
reabrirse: *vr.* to be reopened
reacción: *nf.* reaction
reaccionar: *vi.* to react
reaccionario; -a: 1. *nmf.* reactionary; 2. *aj.* reactionary
reacio-cia: *aj.* obstinate; stubborn; reluctant
reacondicionar: *vt.* to make ready for use once again
reactivar: *vt.* to reactivate
reactivo: *aj.* reactive
reactor: *nm.* reactor
readaptación: *nf.* the act of adapting to a situation or circumstance again
readaptar: *vt.* to adapt again
readaptarse: *vr.* to become adapted again to
readmisión: *nf.* readmission
readmitir: *vt.* to readmit
reafirmación: *nf.* reaffirmation
reafirmar: *vt.* to reaffirm
reagrupación: *nf.* regrouping
reagrupamiento: *nm.* regrouping process
reajustar: *vt.* to readjust
reajuste: *nm.* readjustment
real: *aj.* real
realce: *nm.* splendor
realeza: *nf.* royalty
realidad: *nf.* reality
realismo: *nm.* realism
realista: *nmf.* realist
realizable: *aj.* realizable; achievable
realización: *nf.* realization; achieving of a goal
realizador; -a: *nmf.* producer or director of film or television
realizar: *vt.* to realize a goal; to make real or achieve a goal or objective
realizarse: *vr.* to become or develop into something
realmente: *av.* really
realzar: *vt.* to elevate the quality; to

enhance
reanimación: *nf.* reanimation
reanimar: *vt.* to reanimate; revive
reanimarse: *vr.* to be reanimated
reaparecer: *vi.* to reappear
reaparición: *nf.* reappearance
reapertura: *nf.* reopening
reaprovisionar: *vt.* to restock
provisions
rearmar: *vt.* to rearm
rearmarse: *vr.* to become rearmed
rearme: *nm.* rearmament
reavivar: *vt.* to restimulate; to
reawaken; to bring something back to
life
rebaja: *nf.* rebate; reduction; sale
rebajado: *aj.* lowered; often in price
rebajar: *vt.* to lower; to diminish; to
relax; to become relaxed
rebajarse: *vr.* to humble oneself
rebanada: *nf.* slice; piece
rebaño: *nm.* flock; herd
rebelarse: *vr.* to rebel
rebelde: *aj.* rebellious
rebelde: *nmf.* rebel
rebeldía: *nf.* rebellion
rebelión: *nm.* rebellion
reblandecer: *vt.* to soften (situation)
reblandecerse: *vr.* to become soft
reblandecimiento: *nm.* the act of
softening (situation)
rebosar: *vi.* to overflow; run over; to
overflow with; burst with
rebrotar: *vi.* to sprout a branch; to
revive
rebusca: *nf.* act of looking for
something again
rebuscar: *vt.* to look for again
recadero -ra: *nm.* messenger; *nm.*
errand boy; errand girl
recaer: *vi.* to suffer a relapse (illness)
recaída: *nf.* relapse
recalentar: *vt.* to heat up; to warm up;
to reheat

recámara: *nf.* bedroom
recambiar: *vt.* to move or change
again
recambio: *vt.* spare part
recapacitar: *vi.* to reflect; to think over
recarga: *nf.* recharging
recargable: *aj.* rechargeable
recargado: *aj.* recharged
recargar: *vt.* to overload; to
overcharge; to increase; to overwork
recargo: *nm.* extra charge or fee;
surcharge; penalty
recaudación: *nf.* tax collecting; sum
collected
recaudar: *vt.* to gather; collect
recelar: *vt.* to be suspicious
recelo: *nm.* suspicion
receloso: *aj.* suspicious
recepción: *nf.* reception admission
recepcionista: *nmf.* receptionist
receptividad: *nf.* receptivity
receptivo: *aj.* receptive
receptor: *nm.* electrical receiver
receta: *nf.* recipe; prescription
recetar: *vt.* to write a prescription; to
prescribe
recetario: *nm.* recipe book
rechace: *nm.* rebound of a missed shot
in sport
rechazar: *vt.* to repel; repulse; reject;
refuse
rechazo: *nm.* rejection
rechiflar: *vi.* to whistle insistently
recibidor: *nm.* entry room
recibimiento: *nm.* celebration of
arrival
recibir: *vt.* to receive; to welcome; or.
to be received; be admitted
recibo: *nm.* receipt
reciclado: *aj.* recycled
reciclaje: *nm.* recycling
reciclar: *vt.* to recycle
recién: *adv.* recently; just; newly
reciente: *aj.* recent

recientemente: *av.* recently
recipiente: *nm.* container; vessel
recitar: *vt.* to recite; declaim
reclamación: *nf.* complaint
reclamar: *vt.* to claim; demand; to complaint
reclinar: *vt.* to recline; to lean
recluir: *vt.* to seclude; shut in; to imprison; r. to go into seclusion
recluta: *nf.* recruiting; levy *nm.* recruit
recobrar: *vt.* to recover
recogedor: *nm.* dustpan
recogepelotas: *nmf.* ball boy or girl
recoger: *vt.* to pick up; to gather; to harvest; to collect; fetch; r. to take shelter; take refuge;
recogerse: *vr.* to retire for the evening or go home
recogida: *nf.* the act of gathering up and putting things in place
recogido: *aj.* collected; gathered and put in place
recogimiento: *nm.* collection
recolección: *nf.* recollection
recolectar: *vt.* to collect
recomendable: *aj.* recommendable
recomendación: *nf.* recommendation
recomendado: *aj.* recommended
recomendar: *vt.* to recommend
recomenzar: *vt.* to recommence; to begin again
recompensa: *nf.* reward
recompensar: *vt.* to recompense; reward
reconciliar: *vt.* to reconcile
reconocer: *vt.* to recognize; to admit; to inspect
reconocible: *aj.* recognizable
reconocimiento: *nm.* recognition
reconquista: *nf.* reconquest
reconquistar: *vt.* to reconquer
reconsiderar: *vt.* to reconsider
reconstituir: *vt.* to reconstitute
reconstituyente: *nm.* medicinal

substance which revitalizes
reconstrucción: *nf.* reconstruction
reconstruir: *vt.* to rebuild; to reconstruct
recontar: *vt.* to recount
reconversión: *nf.* reconversion
reconvertir: *vt.* to reconvert
recopilar: *vt.* to compile
record: *nm.* record
récord: 1. *aj.* record; 2. nm record best mark
recordar: *vt.* to remember; to remind
recordatorio: *nm.* reminder; memo
recorrer: *vt.* to cross; to traverse; to go over (or) through; to run over
recorrido: *nm.* journey; trip; distance to be covered
recortado: *aj.* cut with attention to detail
recortar: *vt.* to trim; cut off; to cut out
recorte: *nm.* detailed cutting
recostar: *vt.* to recline; to lean against
recreación: *nf.* recreation
recrear: *vt.* to recreate; amuse; enjoy
recrearse: *vr.* to recreate; to enjoy oneself
recreativo: *aj.* enjoyable
recreo: *nm.* recreation; recess
recriminación: *nf.* recrimination
recriminar: *vt.* to recriminate
recta: *nf.* straight line
rectangular: *aj.* rectangular
rectángulo: *nm.* rectangle
rectificable: *aj.* rectifiable
rectificación: *nf.* rectification
rectificador: *nmf.* verifier; person who verifies
rectificar: *vt.* to rectify; amend.
rectilíneo: *aj.* straight; in or following a straight line
rectitud: *nf.* rectitude; proper behavior
recto: 1. *nm.* rectum; 2. *aj.* straight; right
rector; -a: *nmf.* rector

rectorado: *nm.* rectorate
rectoral: *aj.* relating to the rector or rectorate
rectoría: *nf.* rectorate
recuadro: *nm.* box or framed part of a document (in newspaper; form; advertisement)
recubrimiento: *nm.* re-covering
recubrir: *vt.* to recover
recuento: *nm.* recount
recuerdo: *nm.* memory; remembrance;-souvenir
recuperar: *vt.* to recuperate; recover; regain
recurrente: *aj.* appearing before a judge for recourse
recurrible: *aj.* appealable; having recourse
recurrir: *vi.* to appear before a judge as a recourse
recurso: *nm.* recourse; resource
red: *nf.* net; network
redacción: *nf.* editing; editing
redactar: *vt.* to edit; to write up; to word
redactor; -a: *nmf.* editor
redada: *nf.* catch
redención: *nf.* redemption
redentor; -a: *nmf.* redeemer
redil: *nm.* sheepfold
redimible: *aj.* redeemable
redimir: *vt.* to redeem
redimirse: *vr.* to be redeemed; to redeem oneself
redistribución: *nf.* redistribution
redistribuir: *vt.* to redistribute
redoblar: *vt.* to redouble
redoble: *nm.* redoubling
redondear: *vt.* to make round
redondearse: *vr.* to be round
redondel: *nm. con.* circle; arena
redondez: *nf.* roundness
redondo-de: *aj.* round
reducción: *nf.* reduction

reduce: *vt.* to rebate; to deflate; or. to stoop; to humble oneself; to become deflated
reducido: *aj.* reduced
reducir: *vt.* to reduce; abridge; *conf.*ine
reductible: *aj.* reducible
reedición: *nf.* republication
reedificación: *nf.* rebuilding
reedificar: *vt.* to build up again; to rebuild
reeditar: *vt.* to republish
reeducación: *nf.* reeducation
reeducar: *vt.* to reeducate
reelección: *nf.* reelection
reelecto: *aj.* reelected
reelegir: *vt.* to reelect
reembolsable: *aj.* reimbursable
reembolsar: *vt.* to reimburse
reembolsarse: *vr.* to become reimbursed
reembolso: *nm.* reimbursement
reemplazable: *aj.* replaceable
reemplazar: *vt.* to replace; to act as substitute
reemplazo: *nm.* replacement
reencarnación: *nf.* reincarnation carnal
reencarnarse: *vr.* to be reincarnated
reencontrarse: *vr.* to meet up with again
reencuentro: *nm.* to encounter again
reestructuración: *nf.* restructuring
reestructurar: *vt.* to restructure
reexportar: *vt.* to reexport
referencia: *nf.* reference
referéndum: *nm.* referendum
referente: *aj.* concerning
referir: *vt.* to refer
referirse: *vr.* to be referring to
refinado: *aj.* refined
refinado: *nm.* refining
refinamiento: *nm.* refined quality of a person or business
refinar: *vt.* to refine or purify
refinarse: *vr.* to become refined

refinería: *nf.* refinery
reflectante: *aj.* reflecting
reflectar: *vi.* to reflect
reflector: *nm.* reflector
reflejar: *vt.* to reflect
reflejarse: *vr.* to be reflected
reflejo: 1. *aj.* reflected; 2. *nm.* reflection; reflex
reflexión: *nf.* reflection (thought)
reflexionar: *vt.* to reflect; to think over
reflexivo: *aj.* with reflection; reflective; reflexive (grammar)
reflujo: *nm.* ebbing; ebb tide
reforma: *nf.* reform
reformación: *nf.* reformation
reformador: *aj.* reforming
reformar: *vt.* to reform
reformarse: *vr.* to become reformed; to reform oneself
reformatorio: *nm.* reformatory; reform school
reformismo: *nm.* reformism
reformista: *nmf.* reformer
reforzado: *aj.* reinforced
reforzar: *vt.* to reinforce; to strengthen
refrán: *nm.* proverb; saying
refrenar: *vt.* to rein; curb; to check; to restrain
refrescante: *aj.* refreshing
refrescar: *vt.* to refresh; to cool; *vi.* to cool off; get cooler
refrescarse: *vr.* to become refreshed
refresco: *nm.* soda; soft drink
refrigeración: *nf.* refrigeration; air conditioning
refrigerador: *nm.* refrigerator
refrigerar: *vt.* to cool; to refrigerate; to refresh
refuerzo: *nm.* reinforcement

refugiado; -a: 1. *nmf.* refugee; 2. *aj.* refugee
refugiar: *vt.* to shelter; or. to take refuge

refugiarse: *vr.* to take refuge
refugio: *nm.* refuge
refulgencia: *nf.* radiance
refulgente: *aj.* radiant
refulgir: *vi.* to glitter or shine
refundición: *nf.* refounding of metals
refundir: *vt.* to refound or remelt metals
refutar: *vt.* to refute
regadera: *nf.* the shower
regadío: *aj.* cultivatable
regalado: *aj.* given as a gift
regalar: *vt.* to give; to present; to regale
regalo: *nm.* gift; present; joy
regar: *vt.* to water; sprinkle; to irri-gate
regencia: *nf.* regency
regenerar: *vt.* to regenerate; to revive
regenta: *nf.* wife of the regent
regentar: *vt.* to direct; to manage
regente: *aj.* ruling
regente: *nm.* regent
regicidio: *nm.* murder of a regent or prince
regidor; -a: *nmf.* member of a governing council
régimen: *nm.* regimen
regimiento: *nm.* regiment
regio: *aj.* related to the king; luxurious
región: *nf.* region
regional: *aj.* regional
regionalismo: *nm.* regionalism
regionalista: *nmf.* regionalist
regionalmente: *av.* regionally
regir: *vt.* to rule; govern; to control
registrado: *aj.* registered
registrador; -a: *nmf.* registrar
registradora: *nf.* cash register
registrar: *vt.* to examine; to inspect; to register
registrarse: *vr.* to be registered
registro: *nm.* registration caja
regla: *nf.* rule; ruler
reglamentación: *nf.* regulation of

something
reglamentar: *vt.* to impose a law
reglamentario: *aj.* required by regulation
reglamento: *nm.* regulation; constitution
regocijar: *vt.* to cheer
regocijarse: *vr.* to rejoice; to be rejoicing
regocijo: *nm.* rejoicing
regresar: *vi.* to return
regresión: *nf.* regression
regresivo: *aj.* returning
regreso: *nm.* return
regulable: *aj.* adjustable
regulación: *nf.* regulation
regular: *aj.* regular
regularidad: *nf.* regularity
regularización: *nf.* regularization
regularizar: *vt.* to regularize
regularmente: *av.* regularly
regusto: *nm.* after-taste
rehabilitar: *vt.* rehabilitate
rehabilitarse: *vr.* to become rehabilitated
rehacer: *vt.* to redo
rehacerse: *vr.* to become redone or remade
rehuir: *vt.* to shrink from; *vi.* to avoid
rehusar: *vt.* to refuse; turn down
reimportar: *vt.* to reimport
reimpresión: *nf.* reprint
reimprimir: *vt.* to reprint
reina: *nf.* queen; queen bee
reinado: *nf.* reign
reinante: *aj.* reigning
reinar: *vi.* to reign
reincorporación: *nf.* reincorporation
reincorporar: *vt.* to reincorporate
reincorporarse: *vr.* to sit up or stand up again
reingresar: *vt.* to reenter
reingreso: *nm.* reentry
reino: *nm.* kingdom; reign

reintegración: *nf.* reintegration
reintegrar: *vt.* to restore; *r.* to reintegrate; to recover
reintegrarse: *vr.* to become healthy; to recuperate
reintegro: *nm.* return of an investment (esp. lottery ticket); return of an overpayment
reír: *vt.* to laugh at (or) over; *vi.* to laugh; or. to laugh at
reírse: *vr.* to be laughing
reja: *nf.* grate; grating; plowshare; rail
rejilla: *nf.* grill of a window or duct system
rejuvenecedor: *aj.* rejuvenating
rejuvenecer: *vt.* to rejuvenate
rejuvenecerse: *vr.* to become rejuvenated
rejuvenecimiento: *nm.* rejuvenation
relación: *nf.* relation
relacionado: *aj.* related
relacionar: *vt.* to relate; to connect
relacionarse: *vr.* to be related to
relámpago: *nm.* lightning
relampagueante: *aj.* lit up by lightning
relampaguear: *vt.* to light up with lightning
relampagueo: *nm.* lighting up of the sky by lightning
relanzamiento: *nm.* re-throwing lanza *nf.* lance
relatar: *vt.* to relate; to report
relatividad: *nf.* relativity
relativismo: *nm.* relativism
relativista: *nmf.* relativist
relativo: *aj.* relative
relato: *nm.* narrative; stop
releer: *vt.* to re-read
relevo: *nm.* relief
relieve: *nm.* relief; prominence
religión: *nf.* religion
religiosamente: *av.* religiously
religiosidad: *nf.* religiousness
religioso; -a: *aj.* religious

reliquia: *nf.* relic; trace; vestige
rellenar: *vt.* to refill; to fill up (bricks); to stuff
relleno: *aj.* refilled
reloj: *nm.* watch; clock
relojería: *nf.* clock shop
relojero; -a: *nmf.* watchmaker; watch repairman; or watch salesman
reluciente: *aj.* very shiny; resplendent
relucir: *vi.* to shine; glow
relumbrar: *vi.* to give off an excessive amount of light
relumbrón: *nm.* sudden intense flash of light
remangar: *vt.* to pull up sleeves
remar: *nm.* to row
remarcable: *aj.* remarkable
remarcar: *vt.* to mark again; to radial; to remark
remediable: *aj.* remediable
remediar: *vt.* to remediate
remedio: *nm.* remedy; help; recourse
remembranza: *nf.* remembrance
rememoración: *nf.* formal remembering
rememorar: *vt.* to remember
remendar: *vt.* to mend; patch
remesa: *nf.* remittance; shipment
remirar: *vt.* to review carefully
remisión: *nf.* remission; pardon
remite: *nm.* sender's name and address or other details
remitente: *aj.* remittent; *nm.* sender
remitente: *nmf.* sender
remitir: *vt.* to remit; to forward
remitirse: *vr.* to use something to back up one's word
remo: *nm.* oar
remodelación: *nf.* remodeling
remodelar: *vt.* to remodel
remojar: *vt.* to soak; to steep
remolcar: *vt.* to tow
remolque: *nm.* towing
remontar: *vr.* to remount

remover: *vt.* to remove; to disturb; move away
renacer: *vi.* to be reborn; to bloom again
renacimiento: *nm.* rebirth
Renacimiento: *nm.* Renaissance
rencilla: *nf.* dispute or argument resulting in ill-will
rencilloso: *aj.* argumentative
rencor: *nm.* rancor
rencoroso: *aj.* rancorous
rendición: *nf.* surrender
rendido: *aj.* fatigued
rendimiento: *nm.* fatigue
rendir: *vt.* to conquer; to subdue; to exhaust
rendirse: *vr.* to surrender oneself
renegado; -a: 1. *nm.* renegade; 2. *aj.* renegade
renegar: *vi.* to have a fit; to forcefully refuse
renegrido: *aj.* very black
renglón: *nm.* line
reñido: *aj.* competitive
reniego: *nm.* forceful ill-mannered refusal often using foul language
reñir: *vt.* to scold; *vi.* quarrel; wrangle; to fight
renombre: *nm.* renown
renovable: *aj.* renewable
renovación: *nf.* renovation
renovar: *vt.* to renovate; *or.* to renew
renovarse: *v.* to become renewed
renta: *nf.* rent; annuity; income
rentabilidad: *nf.* profitability
rentable: *aj.* profitable
rentar: *vt.* to rent
rentero; -a: *nmf.* landlord or landlady
rentista: *nmf.* one who earns his living through rentals
renuevo: *nm.* renewal
renuncia: *nf.* resignation
renunciar: *vt.* to renounce; to resign
reordenar: *vt.* to re-order

reorganización: *nm.* re-organization
reorganizador: *aj.* reorganized
reorganizador; -a: *nmf.* reorganizer
reorganizar: *vt.* to reorganize
reparable: *aj.* reparable
reparación: *nf.* repair
reparar: *vt.* to repair; to mend; to notice
repartición: *nf.* distribution
repartidor; -a: *nmf.* distributor
repartir: *vt.* to distribute; to deliver
reparto: *nm.* distribution
repasar: *vt.* to repass; to retrace; to revise; to mend
repaso: *nm.* review
repatriación: *nf.* repatriation
repatriado: *aj.* repatriated
repatriado; -a: *nmf.* repatriate
repatriar: *vt.* to repatriate
repeler: *vt.* to repel
repente (de repente): *av.* suddenly
repentinamente: *av.* suddenly
repentino: *aj.* sudden
repercusión: *nf.* repercussion
repercutir: *vi.* to rebound
repetición: *nf.* repetition
repetidamente: *av.* repeatedly
repetido: *aj.* repeated
repetidor: *nm.* electronic repeater
repetidor; -a: *nmf.* student who is repeating a class or grade
repetir: *vt.* to repeat
repetirse: *vr.* to be repeated; to repeat oneself
repintar: *vt.* to repaint
repintarse: *vr.* to put on too much makeup; to reapply makeup
replantar: *vt.* to replant
replantear: *vt.* to reorganize or redo plans
replantearse: *vr.* to reorganize one's plans
replegar: *vt.* to fold up with many folds; to retreat

replegarse: *vr.* to be folded up with many folds
repleto; ta: *aj.* replete; full
réplica: *nf.* replica
replicar: *vt.* to argue against; *vi.* to argue back
repliegue: *nm.* military retreat; double fold or pleat
repoblación: *nf.* repopulation
repoblar: *vt.* to repopulate; to afforest
reponer: *vt.* to replace
reponerse: *vr.* to recover
reportaje: *nm.* reporting
reportar: *vt.* to report
reportero; -a: *nmf.* reporter
reposacabezas: *nm.* headrest
reposado: *aj.* quiet; rested
reposapiés: *nm.* footrest
reposar: *vi.* to repose; to rest
reposarse: *vr.* to be resting or in a state of repose
reposo: *nm.* repose; rest
repostería: *nf.* dessert shop
repostero; -a: *nmf.* dessert maker or seller
represa: *nf.* small dam
representación: *nf.* representation
representante: *nmf.* representative
representar: *vt.* to represent; to appear to be; to perform
representativo: *aj.* representative
represión: *nf.* repression
represivo: *aj.* repressive
reprimido: *aj.* repressed
reprobación: *nf.* failure
reprobado: *aj.* failed
reprobar: *vt.* to fail; to give a failing grade to; to reprove
reprochable: *aj.* reproachable
reprochador: *aj.* reproaching
reprochar: *vt.* to reproach
reproche: *nm.* reproach
reproducción: *nf.* reproduction
reproducir: *vt.* to reproduce

reproducirse: *vr.* to reproduce; to procreate
reproductor: *aj.* reproducing; reproductive
república: *nf.* republic
republicanismo: *nm.* republicanism
republicano; -a: 1. *nmf.* republican; 2. *aj.* republican
repuesto: *nm.* stock; supply
repugnancia: *nf.* repugnance
repugnante: *aj.* repugnant
repugnar: *vt.* to conflict with; to loathe; *vi.* to be repugnant
repulsión: *nf.* repulsion
repulsivo: *aj.* repulsive
reputación: *nf.* reputation
reputado: *aj.* reputed
requemado: *aj.* re-burned
requemar: *vt.* to burn again; to parch; to overcook
requemarse: *vr.* literally; to re-burn oneself or itself; (figurative) to do something quickly
requerimiento: *nm.* requirement
requerir: *vt.* to require
requisito: *nm.* requisite
res: *nf.* head of cattle; beat
resaltar: *vt.* to emphasize or to call attention to something
resalto: *nm.* emphasizing; calling attention
resbaladizo: *aj.* slippery
resbalar: *vi.* to slip; to slide
resbalón: *nm.* slip or slide
resbaloso: *aj.* slippery
rescatar: *vt.* to ransom; to rescue
resecarse: *vr.* to dry out
reseco: *aj.* dried-out
resentido; -a: 1. *nmf.* resentful person; 2. *aj.* resentful
resentimiento: *nm.* resentment
resentir: *r.* to become weakened; to be resentful
resentirse: *vr.* to resent

reserva: *nf.* reserve; reservation
reservado: *aj.* reserved; discreet
reservar: *vt.* to reserve; to put aside; to conceal
reservarse: *vr.* to be reserved
reservista: *nmf.* member of military reserve
resfriado: *aj.* chilled; with a cold
resfriado: *nm.* a cold or chill
resfriar: *vt.* to cool or chill
resfriarse: *vr.* to catch cold
resfrío: *nm.* a cold or chill
resguardar: *vt.* to protect or defend something
resguardarse: *vr.* to protect or defend oneself
resguardo: *nm.* defense; protection; voucher
residencia: *nf.* residence; residency
residencial: *aj.* residential
residente: 1. *aj.* resident; 2. *nmf.* resident
residir: *vi.* to reside
resignación: *nf.* resignation
resignadamente: *av.* resignedly
resignado: *aj.* resigned
resignar: *vt.* to resign; to submit
resignarse: *vr.* to be resigned to
resistencia: *nf.* resistance
resistente: *aj.* resistant
resistir: *vt.* to resist; to bear; to stand
resistirse: *vr.* to resist
resolución: *nf.* resolution
resolver: *vt.* to resolve; to solve
resolverse: *vr.* to be resolved
resonancia: *nf.* resonance
resonante: *aj.* resonant
resonar: *vi.* to resonate
resoplido: *nm.* the act of being out of tune
respaldar: *vt.* to endorse; to back
respaldarse: *vr.* to be helped (by) or protected (by)
respaldo: *nm.* economic backing; hard-

copy; back of a chair; couch; etc
respectar: *vt.* to have to do with
respectivamente: *av.* respectively
respectivo: *aj.* respective
respecto; a: *nm.* with respect to
respetabilidad: *nf.* respectability
respetable: *aj.* respectable
respetar: *vt.* to respect; reverence
respeto: *nm.* respect
respetuoso: *aj.* respectful
respiración: *nf.* respiration
respiradero: *nm.* ventilator; vent
respirar: *vi.* to breathe
respiratorio: *aj.* respiratory
respiro: *nm.* breath
resplandecer: *vi.* to shine; to give off light
resplandeciente: *aj.* shiny or bright
resplandor: *nm.* brilliance; radiance; glare
responder: *vt.* to respond
respondón: *nmf.* back talker
responsabilidad: *nf.* responsibility
responsabilizar: *vt.* to make responsible for
responsabilizarse: *vr.* to take responsibility for
responsable: *aj.* responsible
respuesta: *nf.* answer; response
resquebrajar: *vt.* to crack
resquebrajarse: *vr.* to become cracked
resta: *nf.* subtraction
restablecer: *vt.* to reestablish; r. to recover; to get better
restablecimiento: *nm.* reestablishment
restante: *aj.* leftover
restar: *vt.* to subtract; to reduce
restauración: *nf.* restoration
restaurador; -a: *nmf.* specialist in
restaurante: *nm.* restaurant
restaurar: *vt.* to restore
resto: *nm.* the rest; the remainder
restregar: *vt.* to rub
restringir: *vt.* to restrict

resuelto: *aj.* resolute
resulta: *nf.* result
resultado: *nm.* result
resultante: *aj.* resulting
resultar: *vi.* to result in
resumen: *nm.* summary; resume
resumir: *vt.* to sum up; summarize; to resume
retablo: *nm.* altarpiece; retable
retaguardia: *nf.* rear guard
retal: *nm.* remnant; piece
retardado: *aj.* late; behind schedule
retardar: *vt.* to delay
retardarse: *vr.* to be delayed
retardo: *nm.* tardy
retemblar: *vi.* to repeatedly tremble
retén: *nm.* reserve emergency personnel; military reserve
retención: *nf.* retention
retener: *vt.* to retain; keep; withhold
retenerse: *vr.* to restrain oneself
retentiva: *nf.* retentiveness
retentivo: *aj.* retentive
retirada: *nf.* military retreat; retiring (for the evening)
retirado: *aj.* retired; distant
retirar: *vt.* to retire; to withdraw; to take away
retirarse: *vr.* to go to bed for the evening
retiro: *nm.* retiring for the evening; retreat for prayer; meditation or study
reto: *nm.* challenge
retocar: *vt.* to retouch
retoque: *nm.* touching up; finishing touch
retorcer: *vt.* to twist; r. to twist; to writhe
retorcerse: *vr.* to writhe with laughter or pain
retorcido: *aj.* twisted
retorcimiento: *nm.* twisting
retórica: *nf.* rhetoric
retórico: *aj.* rhetorical

retornable: *aj.* returnable
retornar: *vt.* to return; give back; to return; go back
retorno: *nm.* return; turnaround (on highway; street; etc.)
retractar: *vt.* to retract; withdraw
retrasado: *aj.* late; behind schedule; behind (clock or watch)
retrasado; -a: *nmf.* slow learner
retrasar: *vt.* to delay; retard; to put off; to set (or) turn back (a watch); *vi.* to be slow; r. to be late
retrasarse: *vr.* to be late
retraso: *nm.* turning back of a clock; delay
retratado: *aj.* photographed or painted in portrait form
retratar: *vt.* to portray; to make a portrait (or) photograph; r. to have a photograph taken
retratarse: *vr.* to have one's portrait made or taken
retratista: *nmf.* portrait painter or photographer
retrato: *nm.* portrait
retrete: *nm.* toilet; water closet
retroacción: *nf.* retroactive action
retroactivo: *aj.* retroactive
retroceder: *vi.* to recede; to go back
retroceso: inn. going back; backing up
retrovisor: *nm.* rear view mirror
reunión: *nf.* meeting
reunir: *vt.* to join; unite
reunirse: *vr.* to meet; to be reunited
revalidación: *nf.* evaluation
revalidar: *vt.* to *conf.*irm; to transfer credits from a university
revelación: *nf.* revelation
revelado: *aj.* developed; revealed
revelador; -a: *nmf.* film developer
revelar: *vt.* to reveal; to develop
revendedor; -a: *nmf.* reseller
revender: *vt.* to resell
reventa: *nf.* resale; retail

reventón : *aj.* bursting; *nm.* burst
reverdecer: *vt.* to turn green again
reversible: *aj.* reversible
reversión: *nf.* reversion
reverso: *nm.* back side; reverse
revertir: *vi.* to revert
revés: *nm.* back; reverse
revestir: *v.* to put on a cloak; robe; armor
revisar: *vt.* to revise; review; check
revisión: *nf.* revision
revisionismo: *nm.* revisionism
revisionista: 1. *aj.* revisionist; 2. *nmf.* revisionist
revisor; -a: *nmf.* ticket inspector
revista: *nf.* review; inspection; magazine
revistar: *vt.* to review the troops
revistero: run magazine holder
revitalizar: *vt.* to revitalize
revivificar: *vt.* to reanimate; to restrengthen
revivir: *vt.* to revive
revolcar: *vt.* to knock down; to roll over; or. to wallow
revolotear: *vt.* to twirl in the air
revoloteo: *nm.* twirling
revoltijo: *nm.* disorganized mess
revoltoso: *aj.* turbulent; mischievous
revolución: *nf.* revolution
revolucionar: *vt.* to revolt; to revolutionize
revolucionario; -a: 1. *nmf.* revolutionary; 2. *aj.* revolutionary
revolver: *vt.* to stir; to disturb
revólver: *nm.* revolver; pistol
revuelo: *nm.* second flight of a bird
revuelta: *nf.* disorder of people
revuelto: *aj.* scrambled; mixed-up; disorganized
rey: *nm.* king
rezar: *vt.* to pray; to say
rezo: *Nm.* prayer using repetition of words

rezumar: *vt.* to ooze
ría: *nf.* estuary; ria; inlet
riachuelo: *Nm.* small river
ribera: *nf.* bank; shore; riverside
ricamente: *av.* richly
rico; ca: *aj.* rich; delicious
ridiculez: *nf.* ridiculousness
ridiculizar: *vt.* to ridicule
ridículo: *aj.* ridiculous
riego: *nm.* irrigation; watering
rienda: *nf.* rein
riesgo: *nm.* risk; danger
rifa: *nf.* raffle; fight
rifle: *nm.* rifle
rigidez: *nf.* rigidity
rígido: *aj.* rigid
rigor: *nm.* rigor; severity; harshness;
strictness
rigurosamente: *av.* rigorously
rigurosidad: *nf.* rigorousness
riguroso: *aj.* rigorous
rimar: *vt.* to rhyme
riña: *nf.* fight; quarrel; dispute
rincón: *nm.* corner
rinconera: *nf.* corner piece of furniture
río: *nm.* river
riqueza: *nf.* riches
risa: *nf.* laughter
risible: *aj.* laugh provoking
risita: *nf.* chuckle
risotada: *nf.* loud and strong laughter
risueño: *aj.* cheerful
rítmico: *aj.* rhythmic
ritmo: *nm.* rhythm
rival: 1. *aj.* rival; 2. *nmf.* rival
rivalidad: *nf.* rivalry
rivalizar: *vt.* to rival
rivera: *nf.* creek
robar: *vt.* to rob; to steal
roble: *nm.* oak tree
robo: *nm.* robbery
robustecer: *vt.* to make strong; to become strong
robustecer: *vt.* to make robust or

stronger
robustecerse: *vr.* to become more robust or stronger
robustecimiento: *nm.* act of becoming more robust
robustez: *nf.* robustness
robusto: *aj.* robust
roca: *nf.* rock
roce: *nm.* rubbing; friction
rociar: *vt.* to sprinkle; to spray
rocío: *nm.* dew; sprinkling
rocoso: *aj.* rocky
rodada: *nf.* wheel rut
rodado: *aj.* with wheels
rodaja: *nf.* disk; small wheel; slice
rodaje: *nm.* wheels in general
rodamiento: *nm.* rolling
rodante: *aj.* rolling
rodar: *vt.* to roll; to film; to screen
rodear: *vt.* to surround; go around
rodeo: *nm.* rodeo; act of surrounding or encircling
rodilla: *nf.* knee
rodillada: *nf.* a hit with the knee
rodillazo: *nm.* a hit with the knee
rodillera: *nf.* knee protectors or knee guards
rodillo: *nm.* roller
roedor: *nm.* rodent
roer: *vt.* to gnaw
rojear: *vi.* to show a red coloring
rojez: *nf.* redness
rojizo: *aj.* reddish
rojo: 1. *aj.* red; 2. *nm.* red
rollo: *nm.* roll; roller
Roma: *nf.* Rome
romance: 1. *aj.* romance; 2. *nm.* romance
románico: *aj.* Romanesque
romano; -a: 1. *nmf.* Roman; 2. *aj.* Roman
romanticismo: *nm.* romanticism
romántico; -a: 1. *nmf.* romantic; 2. *aj.* romantic

romería: *nf.* pilgrimage; gathering at a shrine
rompecabezas: *nm.* riddle; puzzle
rompecorazones: *nmf.* heartbreaker
rompehielos: *nm.* ship made for sailing in icy waters
rompeolas: *nm.* breakwater; part of a boat that hits the waves
romper: *vt.* to break; to tear; to smash; to burst open
romperse: *vr.* to become torn or broken
rompible: *aj.* breakable
rompimiento: *nm.* break-up; breaking
ron: *nm.* rum
roncar: *vi.* to snore; to roar
ronda: *nf.* rounds of vigilance
rondalla: *nf.* vocal and instrumental musical group
rondar: *vt.* to make rounds; to court a woman
ropa: *nf.* clothes
ropaje: *nm.* garments
ropavejero; -a: *nmf.* used clothing merchant
ropero: *nm.* closet; wardrobe
rosa: 1. *aj.* rose; 2. *nf.* rose
rosáceo: *aj.* rose-colored; rosy
rosado: 1. *aj.* rose; 2. *nm.* rose color
rosal: *nm.* rose bush
rosaleda: *nf.* rose garden
rostro: *nm.* beak
rostro: *nm.* face
roto; ta: *aj.* broken; torn; ragged
rotulación: *nf.* action of putting up an announcement on a sign
rotulador; -a: *nmf.* sign maker or painter
rotular: *vt.* to put up an announcement on a sign
rótulo: *nm.* announcement on a sign
rozadura: *nf.* from rubbing
rozamiento: *nm.* rubbing; friction
rozar: *vt.* to touch lightly; to brush

against; to give a rash to by rubbing
rozarse: to develop a rash from rubbing
rubí: *nm.* ruby
rubio: 1. *aj.* blond; 2. *nm.* blond
rubor: *nm.* blush; rouge
ruborizar: *vt.* to cause to blush
ruborizarse: *vr.* to blush
rueda: *nf.* wheel; ring
ruido: *nm.* noise
ruidoso: *aj.* noisy
ruin: *aj.* base; mean; vile; puny; *nm.* scoundrel
ruina: *nf.* ruin
ruinoso: *aj.* ruinous
rumor: *nm.* rumor
rumorearse: *vr.* to be rumored
rumoroso: *aj.* murmuring

S

sábado: *nm.* Saturday; Sabbath
sábana: *nf.* sheet
sabático: *aj.* sabbatical
sabatino: *aj.* Saturday; Sabbath
sabedor: *aj.* knowing
sabelotodo: *nmf.* know-it-all
saber: *nm.* knowledge; learning
saber: *vt.* to know; to be able to
sabido: *aj.* known; well-known
sabiduría: *nf.* wisdom
sabiendas (a): *av.* knowing full well
sabihondo; -a; sabiondo; -a: *nmf.* presumptuous person
sabio; bia: *aj.* wise; *nmf.* wise man; scientist
sabiondo; -a: *nmf.* know-it-all
sabiondo; sabihondo: *aj.* literally; deep with knowledge; pejoratively;

presumptuous
sable: *nm.* saber
sabor: *nm.* flavor; taste
saborear: *vt.* to savor
saboreo: *nm.* savoring
sabroso; sa: *aj.* tasty; delicious
sabrosura: *nf.* deliciousness
sacaclavos: *nm.* nail remover
sacacorchos: *nm.* corkscrew
sacamuelas: *nmf.* informal term for dentist
sacapuntas: *nm.* pencil sharpener
sacar: *vt.* to take out; to serve; in sport
sacarse: *v.* to get oneself out
sacerdocio: *nm.* priesthood
sacerdotal: *aj.* pertaining to priests and priesthood
sacerdote: *nm.* priest
sacerdotisa: *nf.* priestess
saciar: *vt.* to satiate; get enough; satisfy
saco: *nm.* sack; bag
sacralizar: *vt.* to consecrate; to sanctify
sacramental: *aj.* sacramental
sacramentar: *vt.* to offer a sacrament
sacramento: *nm.* sacrament
sacrificado: *aj.* sacrificed
sacrificar: *vt.* to sacrifice
sacrificarse: *vr.* to sacrifice oneself
sacrificio: *nm.* sacrifice
sacrilegio: *nm.* sacrilege
sacrílego: *aj.* sacrilegious
sacristía: *nf.* sacristy
sacro; cra: *aj.* sacred; holy
sacrosanto: *aj.* sacrosanct
sacudida: *nf.* shaking
sacudidor: *nm.* tool for cleaning dust; duster
sacudir: *vt.* to shake; to jar; to beat; to shake
sacudirse: *vr.* to be shaking
sagaz: *aj.* sagacious; clever
sagrado: *aj.* sacred
sahumar: *vt.* to burn incense; to burn a scented candle

sahumerio: *nm.* the act of burning incense
sal: *nf.* salt; charm; grace
sala: *nf.* hall; drawing room; living room; parlor
saladero: *nm.* place for salting fish
salado: *aj.* salted
saladura: *nf.* salting
salar: *vt.* to salt; to season
salarial: *aj.* pertaining to a salary
salario: *nm.* salary
salazón: *nm.* salting of meats
salchicha: *nf.* sausage
salchichón: *nm.* sausage
saldar: *vt.* to make the final payment
saldo: *nm.* settlement; liquidation; salary
salero: *nm.* saltshaker
salida: *nf.* exit
salido: *aj.* protruding beyond the normal
saliente: *aj.* protruding; projecting
saliente: *nm.* protrusion
salífero: *aj.* salty
salina: *nf.* salt mine
salinidad: *nf.* salinity
salino: *aj.* saline
salitre: *nm.* salt that remains after one sweats
saliva: *nf.* saliva
salmo: *nm.* psalm
salmuera: *nf.* salty water
salobre: *aj.* salty
salón: *nm.* lounge; saloon
salpicar: *vt.* to splash
salpimentar: *vt.* to salt and pepper something
salsa: *nf.* salsa; sauce
saltador; -a: *nmf.* acrobat; high jumper
saltamontes: *nm.* grasshopper
saltaojos: *nm.* peony
saltar: *vt.* to jump; to spring; to come off
saltarín: *aj.* bouncing

saltarse: *v.* to skip over or to jump over; to omit
saltear: *vt.* to attack; to hold up
saltimbanqui: *nmf.* circus acrobat
salto: *nm.* jump; leap; bound
salubre: *aj.* healthy
salubridad: *nf.* healthiness
salud: *nf.* health; welfare
saludable: *aj.* healthy
saludar: *vt.* to greet; salute
saludo: *nm.* salute; greeting
salvable: *aj.* savable; rescuable; able to be saved
salvación: *nf.* salvation
salvador; -a: *nmf.* savior
salvaguardar: *vt.* to protect; to safeguard
salvaguardia: *nf.* safeguard; protection; *nm.* bodyguard
salvajada: *nf.* savagery
salvaje: *aj.* savage; wild
salvajismo: *nm.* savagery
salvamanteles: *nm.* placemat
salvamento: *nm.* deliverance; refuge
salvar: *vt.* to save
salvarse: *vr.* to save oneself; to be saved
salvavidas: *nm.* lifeguard
salvedad: *nf.* qualification
salvo: *aj.* safe
salvoconducto: *nm.* safe conduct
sanable: *aj.* curable
sanador: *aj.* healing; curative
sanar: *vt.* to heal
sanatorio: *nm.* restroom; bathroom
sancionar: *vt.* to sanction; ratify; to fine
sandalia: *nf.* sandal
saneado: *aj.* cleaned-up; disinfected
sanear: *vt.* to clean up; to disinfect
sangrante: *aj.* bleeding
sangrar: *vt.* to bleed; to tap. sangre
sangrarse: *vr.* to bleed; to be bleeding
sangre: *nf.* blood

sangría: *nf.* red wine
sangriento: *aj.* bloody; bloodstained
sanguijuela: *nf.* leech
sanguinario: *aj.* cruel
sanguíneo: *aj.* pertaining to blood
sanguinolento: *aj.* bloody; bloodstained
sanidad: *nf.* healthiness
sanitario: *aj.* sanitary; clean
sano; na: *aj.* healthy; healthful; salutary; right; sane
santateresa: *nf.* praying mantis
santero: *aj.* saint-worshiping; image-worshiping
santidad: *nf.* sanctity
santificación: *nf.* sanctification
santificar: *vt.* to sanctify
santiguar: *vt.* to make the sign of the cross
santiguarse: *vr.* to make the sign of the cross on self
santísimo: 1. *aj.* most holy; 2. *nm.* Most Holy; God; Christ
santo; -a: 1. *nmf.* saint; 2. *aj.* holy
santoral: *nm.* book of the saints
santuario: *nm.* sanctuary
santurrón: *aj.* hypocritical
santurronería: *nf.* sanctimoniousness
sapiencia: *nf.* wisdom
sapiente: *aj.* wise
sapo: *nm.* toad
saque: *nm.* service in sport
saquear: *vt.* to sack; to plunder
sarampión: *nm.* measles. sastre
satirizar: *vt.* satirize
satisfacción: *nf.* satisfaction
satisfacer: *vt.* to satisfy
satisfacerse: *vr.* to be satisfied
satisfactorio: *aj.* satisfactory
satisfecho: *aj.* satisfied
saturar: *vt.* to saturate; to fill
savia: *nf.* sap
saviour; savior: *nm.* Savior
sazón: *nf.* season

sazonar: *vt.* to ripen; to mature; to season; flavor
seca: *nf.* drought
secadero: *nm.* place for drying
secador: *nm.* dryer; hairdryer
secadora: *nf.* dryer
secano: *nm.* dry agricultural land
secante: *aj.* drying
secante: *nm.* blotting paper
secar: *vt.* to dry; or. to dry; to get dry
secarse: *vr.* to become dry; to dry out
sección: *nf.* section
seccionar: *vt.* to divide into sections
seco: *aj.* dry
secreta: *nf.* secret police
secretaría: *nf.* secretary
secretariado: *nm.* secretariat
secretario; -a: 1. *nmf.* secretary; 2. *aj.* secretary
secretear: *vi.* to secret; to tell secrets to one another
secreteo: *nm.* act of telling secrets to one another
secreter: *nm.* small desk with small drawers
secreto: 1. *aj.* secret; 2. *nm.* secret
secta: *nf.* sect
sector: *nm.* sector
secuela: *nf.* long-term consequence
secuencia: *nf.* sequence
secuencial: *aj.* sequential
secular: *aj.* secular
secularizar: *vt.* to secularize
secundar: *vt.* to second a motion; to help
secundario: *aj.* secondary
sed: *nf.* thirst
seda: *nf.* silk
sedal: *nm.* fishing line
sedero: *aj.* of silk
sediento: *aj.* thirsty
sedoso: *aj.* silky
seducción: *nf.* seduction
seducir: *vt.* to tempt; to seduce; to

captivate
seductor; -a: *nmf.* seducer
seguida: *nf.* act of following
seguido; da: *aj.* continued; successive; straight; in a row
seguidor; -a: *nmf.* follower
seguimiento: *nm.* pursuit
seguir: *vt.* to continue; to follow
segundero: *nm.* second hand on a clock
segundo; da: *aj.* second
segundón: *nm.* child who is not the firstborn
seguramente: *av.* surely
seguridad: *nf.* security; surety
seguro: *aj.* sure; secure; safe
seguro: *av.* sure
seguro: *nm.* lock; insurance
seis: 1. *aj.* six; 2. *nm.* six
seiscientos: 1. *aj.* six-hundred; 2. *nm.* six hundred
selección: *nf.* selection; all-star team
seleccionador; -a: *nmf.* selector
seleccionar: *vt.* to select
selectividad: *nf.* selectivity
selectivo: *aj.* selective
selecto: *aj.* select
sellador: *aj.* sealing
sellar: *vt.* to seal; to stamp
sello: *nm.* seal; stamp
selva: *nf.* forest; woods
semáforo: *nm.* traffic lights
semana: *nf.* week
semanal: *aj.* weekly
semanario: *aj.* weekly
semblante: *nm.* facial expression
semblanza: *nf.* literary self-portrait
sembrado: *nm.* field for planting seeds
sembrador; -a: *nmf.* person who plants seeds
sembradora: *nf.* machine for planting seeds
semejante: *aj.* like; similar
semejanza: *nf.* similarity

semen: *nm.* semen
semental: *nm.* male animal used for breeding
sementera: *nf.* planted field
semicircular: *aj.* semicircular
semicírculo: *nm.* semicircle
semiconsciente: *aj.* semiconscious
semidesierto: *aj.* semi-desert
semidesnudo: *aj.* semi-nude; semi-naked
semidiós; -a: *nmf.* demigod
semifinal: *aj.* semifinal
semifinalista: *nmf.* semifinalist
semilla: *nf.* seed
semillero: *nm.* temporary planter
seminal: *aj.* seminal
semiprecioso: *aj.* semi-precious
semitono: *nm.* half-tone
sempiterno: *aj.* eternal
seña: *nf.* sign
señal: *nf.* sign; mark; landmark
señalado: *aj.* signaled; aforementioned
señalar: *vt.* to mark; to show; to indicate
señalarse: *vr.* to distinguish oneself
señalización: *nf.* placement of signs
señalizar: *vt.* to place signs
sencillez: *nf.* simplicity
sencillo: *aj.* simple
sendero: *nf.* path; footpath
seno: *nm.* bosom; breast; womb; asylum; refuge
señor; ra: *nm.* sir; mister; gentleman; lord; master; owner
señora: *nf.* married woman; madam; Mrs.
señorear: *vt.* to rule
señoría: *nf.* lordship; formal courtesy
señorial: *aj.* noble; majestic
señorío: *nm.* dominion
señorita: *nf.* unmarried woman; Miss
señoriíto: *nm.* son of a noble
señorón; -a: *nmf.* big shot
sensación: *nf.* sensation

sensacional: *aj.* sensational
sensacionalismo: *nm.* sensationalism
sensacionalista: 1. *aj.* sensationalist; 2. *nmf.* sensationalist
sensatez: *nf.* common sense
sensato: *aj.* sensible
sensibilidad: *nf.* sensibility; sensitivity
sensibilización: *nf.* sensitization
sensibilizar: *vt.* to sensitize
sensible: *aj.* touchy; easily irritated
sensiblería: *nf.* feigned sensitivity; hypocrisy
sensitivo: *aj.* sensitive
sensorio: *aj.* sensory; pertaining to physical senses
sensual: 1. *aj.* sensual; 2. *nmf.* sensualist
sensualidad: *nf.* sensuality
sentada: *nf.* sitting
sentado; da: *aj.* seated; established
sentar: *vt.* to seat; to suit; fit
sentarse: *vr.* to be seated
sentencia: *nf.* sentence
sentenciado: *aj.* sentenced
sentenciar: *vt.* to sentence; to condemn
sentido: *aj.* feeling; touchy; easily irritated
sentido: *nm.* meaning; sense
sentimental: 1. *aj.* sentimental; 2. *nmf.* sentimental person
sentimentalismo: *nm.* sentimentalism
sentimiento: *nm.* feeling
sentir: *nm.* feeling; opinion; judgment
sentir: *vt.* to feel
sentirse: *vr.* to be feeling
separable: *aj.* separable
separación: *nf.* separation
separado: *aj.* separated
separador: *nm.* bookmark
separar: *vt.* to separate; to dismiss; to detach
separarse: *vr.* to separate oneself; to become separated
separatismo: *nm.* separatism

separatista: 1. *aj.* separatist; 2. *nmf.* separatist
sepelio: *nm.* burial
septiembre: *nm.* September
séptimo: *aj.* seventh
septuagenario; -a: *nmf.* seventy year old person
septuagésimo: *aj.* seventieth
sepulcral: *aj.* pertaining to a sepulcher
sepulcro: *nm.* sepulcher; grave
sepultar: *vt.* to entomb; to bury
sepultura: *nf.* tomb; grave
sepulturero-a: *nmf.* cemetery worker who performs the burial
sequía: *nf.* drought
ser: *nm.* being; essence
ser: *vi.* to be
serenar: *vt.* to calm; to fall (dew)
serenarse: *vr.* to calm oneself; to become calm
serenata: *nf.* serenade
serenidad: *nf.* serenity
sereno: *aj.* serene
serial: 1. *aj.* serial; 2. *nm.* television or radio series
seriar: *vt.* to make a series; to serialize
serie: *nf.* series
serpentear: *vt.* to wind
serpenteo: *nm.* winding
serpentín: *nm.* coil
serpentina: *nf.* streamer
serpiente: *nf.* serpent
serranía: *nf.* mountainous area
serrano; -a: *nmf.* highlander
serrar: *vt.* to saw
serrería: *nf.* sawmill
serrucho: *nm.* handsaw
servible: *aj.* usable
servicial: *aj.* helpful
servicio: *nm.* service
servidor; -a: *nmf.* server
servidumbre: *nf.* group of servants
servilismo: *nm.* servility
servilleta: *nf.* napkin (table)

servilletero: *nm.* napkin holder
servir: *vt.* to serve
servirse: *vr.* to serve oneself
sesenta: *aj.* sixty
sesentavo: *aj.* sixtieth
sesentón: *aj.* sixty-year old
sesentón; -a: *nmf.* person in his sixties
seso: *nm.* brain
seta: *nf.* mushroom
setecientos: *aj.* seven hundred
setenta: *aj.* seventy
setentavo: *aj.* seventieth
setentón; -a: *nmf.* person in his seventies
seto: *nm.* fence; hedge
severidad: *nf.* severity
severo: *aj.* severe
sexagenario; -a: *nmf.* sixty year old
sexagésimo: *aj.* sixtieth
sexismo: *nm.* sexism
sexista: *aj.* sexist
sexo: *nm.* sex
sexología: *nf.* sexology
sexólogo; -a: *nmf.* sexologist
sexto: *aj.* sixth
séxtuplo: 1. *aj.* sextuplet; 2. *nm.* sextuplet
sexual: *aj.* sexual
sexualidad: *nf.* sexuality
sexualmente: *av.* sexually
sexy: *aj.* sexy
si: 1. *conj.* if; whether; 2. *adv.* yes
siembra: *nf.* planting; sowing
siempre: *av.* always
siempreviva: *nf.* perennial plant
sien: *nf.* temple
sierra: *nf.* mountain; saw
siervo -va: *nmf.* slave; humble servant
siesta: *nmf.* siesta
siete: 1. *nm.* seven; 2. *aj.* seven
sietemesino: *aj.* born prematurely
sigla: *nf.* initial
siglo: *nm.* century
signar: *vt.* to sign; to make the sign of

the cross
signarse: *vr.* to make the sign of the cross over oneself
signatario; -a: 1. *nmf.* signatory; 2. *aj.* signatory
signatura: *nf.* signature
significación: *nf.* meaning
significado: *aj.* distinguished; well-known
significante: *aj.* significant
significar: *vt.* to mean
significativamente: *av.* significantly
significativo: *aj.* well-explained; clear; meaningful
signo: *nm.* sign
siguiente: *aj.* following; next
sílaba: *nf.* syllable
silbar: *vt.* to whistle; to blow; to hiss
silenciador: *nm.* silencer
silenciar: *vt.* to silence
silencio: *nm.* silence
silencioso: *aj.* silent
silla: *nf.* chair
sillín: *nm.* bicycle or motorcycle seat
sillón: *nm.* large comfortable chair or couch
silueta: *nf.* silhouette; profile
simbiosis: *nf.* symbiosis
simbólico: *aj.* symbolic
simbolismo: *nm.* symbolism
simbolista: *aj.* symbolic
simbolizar: *vt.* to symbolize
símbolo: *nm.* symbol
simetría: *nf.* symmetry
simétrico: *aj.* symmetrical
simiente: *nf.* seed
similar: *aj.* similar
similitud: *nf.* similarity
simpatía: *nf.* sympathy; congeniality
simpático: *aj.* sympathetic; pleasant
simpatizante: *aj.* sympathizing
simpatizante: *nmf.* sympathizer; one who sympathizes
simpatizar: *vi.* to sympathize

simple: *aj.* simple
simplemente: *av.* simply
simpleza: *nf.* foolishness
simplicidad: *nf.* simplicity
simplificación: *nf.* simplification
simplificar: *vt.* to simplify
simplismo: *nm.* simplicity
simplista: *aj.* simplistic
simplón; -a: 1. *nmf.* simpleton; 2. *aj.* very silly or foolish
simulación: *nf.* simulation
simulacro: *nm.* practice exercise; simulation
simulado: *aj.* simulated
simular: *vt.* to simulate
sin: *prep.* without
sinceramente: *av.* sincerely
sincerarse: *vr.* to be sincere
sinceridad: *nf.* sincerity
sincero -ra: *aj.* sincere; frank; true
sincronía: *nf.* synchrony
sincrónico: *aj.* synchronous
sincronización: *nf.* synchronization
sincronizar: *vt.* to synchronize
sindicación: *nf.* syndication
sindical: *aj.* union-related
sindicalismo: inn unionism
sindicalista: *aj.* pertaining to unionism
sindicalista: *nmf.* unionist
sindicar: *vt.* to form a union
sindicarse: *vr.* to become part of a union
sindicato: *nm.* union
síndico: *nm.* union representative
sinfín: *nm.* something endless; countless number
singular: *aj.* singular; unique; peculiar
singular: *nm.* grammatical term meaning one
singularidad: *nf.* singular quality; uniqueness; individuality; distinct quality
singularizar: *vt.* to single out
singularizarse: *vr.* to be distinguished

singularmente: *av.* singularly
siniestro; tra: 1. *aj.* sinister; 2. *nm.* disaster
sinnúmero: *nm.* without number; countless
sinónimo; ma: 1. *aj.* synonymous; 2. *nm.* synonym
sinrazón: *nf.* unreasonableness
síntesis: *nf.* synthesis
sintético: *aj.* synthetic
sintetizador: *nm.* synthesizer
sintetizar: *vt.* to synthesize
síntoma: *nm.* symptom
sintomático: *aj.* symptomatic
sintonía: *nf.* symphony
sintonización: *nf.* tuning
sintonizador: *nm.* tuner knob
sintonizar: *vt.* to tune into a radio station
sinvergüenza: *nmf.* person who is brazen
siquiera: ad*v.* at least; *conj.* although; even though
sirena: *nf.* mermaid; siren
sirviente; -a: *nmf.* servant
sistema: *nf.* system
sistemático: *aj.* systematic
sistematizar: *vt.* to systematize
sitiar: *vt.* to surround; besiege
sitio: *nm.* site
situación: *nf.* situation
situado: *aj.* situated
situar: *vt.* to situate; to place; locate
situarse: *vr.* to situate oneself; to be situated
soberbia: *nf.* feeling of superiority
soberbiamente: *av.* in a manner displaying a feeling of superiority
soberbio: *aj.* dominated by a feeling of superiority; overly proud
sobornar: *vt.* to bribe; to suborn.
sobra: *nf.* leftovers; extra; excess
sobradamente: *av.* excessively; extremely

sobrado: *aj.* excessive
sobrante: 1. *aj.* extra; leftover; excess; 2. *nm.* leftovers; extra; excess
sobrar: *vt.* to exceed; surpass
sobre: 1. *nm.* envelope; 2. *prep.* on; upon; above; about;
sobreabundancia: *nf.* overabundance
sobreabundar: *vi.* to abound greatly
sobrealimentación: *nf.* overeating
sobrealimentado: *aj.* overfed
sobrealimentar: *vt.* to overeat
sobrecalentar: *vt.* to overheat
sobrecalentarse: *vr.* to be overheated
sobrecarga: *nf.* surcharge
sobrecargar: *vt.* to overload; to overburden
sobrecargarse: *vr.* to become overcharged with energy
sobrecargo: *nm.* overload
sobrecogedor: *aj.* surprising
sobrecoger: *vt.* to take by surprise
sobrecogerse: *vr.* to be taken by surprise
sobrecubierta: *nf.* second lid; dust jacket
sobredicho: *aj.* aforementioned; aforesaid
sobredorar: *vt.* to plate with gold
sobreexceder: *vt.* to exceed
sobreexcitación: *nf.* overexcitement
sobrexcitar: *vt.* to overexcite
sobreexcitarse: *vr.* to become overexcited
sobreexponer: *vt.* to overexpose
sobreexposición: *nf.* overexposure
sobregirar: *vt.* to over-extend one's credit
sobrehilado: *aj.* zigzagged
sobrehilar: *vt.* to zigzag stitch
sobrehumano: *aj.* super-human
sobreimpresión: *nf.* superimposing of film
sobrellevar: *vt.* to put up with; to tolerate

sobremanera: *av.* excessively
sobremesa: *nf.* after-dinner conversation
sobrenadar: *vi.* to float
sobrenatural: *aj.* supernatural
sobrenombre: *nm.* nickname
sobrentender: *vt.* to understand through context
sobrentenderse: *vr.* to be understood through context
sobrepaga: *nf.* bonus
sobrepasar: *vt.* to excel
sobrepeso: *nm.* excess weight
sobreponer: *vt.* to superimpose; to overlap
sobreponerse: *vr.* to overcome
sobreproducción: *nf.* overproduction
sobrepuesto: *aj.* superimposed; overlapping
sobresaliente: *aj.* remarkable; outstanding
sobresalir: *vi.* to protrude; to stand out from the rest
sobresaltar: *vt.* to assail; to rush upon; to frighten; *r.* to be frightened; be startled
sobresaltarse: *vr.* to be scared
sobresalto: *nm.* surprise; fright
sobrestimar: *vt.* to overestimate
sobresueldo: *nm.* extra income
sobrevenir: *vt.* to overcome
sobreviviente: *nmf.* survivor
sobrevivir: *vi.* to survive
sobrevolar: *vt.* to fly over something
sobriedad: *nf.* sobriety
sobrina: *nf.* niece
sobrino: *nm.* nephew
sobrio: *aj.* sober
socarrón: *nf.* sly; cunning; shrewd
socavar: *vt.* to dig under; to undermine
sociabilidad: *nf.* sociability
sociable: *aj.* sociable
social: *aj.* social
socialdemocracia: *nf.* social democracy
socialdemócrata: *nmf.* social democrat
socialismo: *nm.* socialism
socialista: 1. *aj.* socialist; 2. *nmf.* socialist
socialización: *nf.* socialization
socializar: *vt.* to socialize
socialmente: *av.* socially
sociedad: *nf.* society
socio -cia: *mnf.* partner; member; shareholder; associate
socioeconómico: *aj.* socioeconomic
sociología: *nf.* sociology
sociológico: 1. *aj.* sociological; 2. *nmf.* sociologist
socorrer: *vt.* to help
socorrido: *aj.* available to offer emergency response
socorrismo: *nm.* emergency help
socorrista: *nmf.* paramedic; rescue worker
socorro: *nm.* help
sofá: *nm.* sofa
sol: *nm.* sun
solamente: *av.* only
solana: *nf.* area unprotected from the sun
solano: *aj.* warm and suffocating; relating to an east wind
solapa: *nf.* lapel
solar: 1. *aj.* solar; 2. *nm.* lot; plot; ground
soldadesca: *nf.* troop of soldiers
soldadesco: *aj.* pertaining to soldiers
soldado: *nm.* soldier
soldar: *vt.* to solder
soleado: *aj.* sunny
solear: *vt.* to sun
solearse: *vr.* to bask in sunlight
soledad: *nf.* loneliness
solemne: *aj.* solemn
solemnidad: *nf.* solemnity
solemnizar: *vt.* to solemnize
soler: *vi.* to be accustomed to

solfear: *vt.* to solfa
solicitación: *nf.* solicitation; application
solicitador; -a: *nmf.* solicitor
solicitante: *nmf.* applicant
solicitar: *vt.* to solicit; to woo; to court; to apply
solícito: *aj.* available to help; solicitous
solicitud: *nf.* solicitude; willingness to help; application
solidaridad: *nf.* solidarity
solidario: *aj.* pertaining to solidarity
solidarizar: *vt.* to act with solidarity
solidarizarse: *vr.* to be acting with solidarity
solidez: *nf.* solidness
solidificación: *nf.* solidification
solidificar: *vt.* to solidify
solidificarse: *vr.* to become solidified
sólido: 1. *aj.* solid; 2. *nm.* solid
solista: *nmf.* soloist
sollozar: *vi.* to sob
sollozo: *nm.* sob
solo: *nm.* solo (music)
sólo: 1. *av.* only; 2. *aj.* only; along
solomillo: *nm.* sirloin
soltar: *vt.* to let go; to let loose; to free
soltero: 1. *aj.* bachelor; 2. *nm.* bachelor
solterón: *nm.* conf.irmed bachelor; mature bachelor
solterona: *nf.* spinster; mature unmarried woman
soltura: *nf.* ease of expression
solubilidad: *nf.* solubility
soluble: *aj.* soluble
solución: *nf.* solution
solucionar: *vt.* to solve
solventar: *vt.* to solve a complicated problem; to become solvent
solvente: 1. *aj.* solvent; 2. *nm.* solvent
sombra: *nf.* shade; shadow
sombreado: *nm.* shading
sombrear: *vt.* to cover with shade
sombrera: *nf.* hatbox

sombrerería: *nf.* hat store
sombrerero; -a: *nmf.* hat maker
sombrero: *nm.* hat
sombrilla: *nf.* parasol; umbrella for sun; sunshade
sombrío: *aj.* shadowy; gloomy
someter: *vt.* to submit
someterse: *vr.* to submit oneself
sometimiento: *nm.* submission
somier: *nm.* spring mattress
son: *nm.* pleasant sound; especially a musical sound
soñado: *aj.* dreamed of; well-known; frequently heard
soñador; -a: *nmf.* dreamer
sonaja: *nf.* baby's rattle
sonajero: *nm.* child's rattle
sonámbulo; -a: *nmf.* sleepwalker
soñar: *vt.* to dream; to sound
sónar: *nm.* sonar
soñarrera: *nf.* act of dreaming frequently
sonata: *nf.* sonata
sonatina: *nf.* short sonata
sónico: *aj.* sonic
sonido: *nm.* sound
soñoliento: *aj.* sleepy
sonorización: *nf.* placing of a sound track to a film
sonorizar: *vt.* to add the sound track to a film
sonoro: *aj.* sonorous; sounding; able to sound
sonreír: *vi.* to smile
sonreírse: *vr.* to be smiling
sonriente: *aj.* smiling
sonrisa: *nf.* smile
sonrojar: *vt.* to cause to blush
sonrojarse: *vr.* to blush
sonrojo: *nm.* blushing
sonrosado: *aj.* rose-colored; referring to skin
sonrosar: *v.* to lightly blush
sonsonete: *nm.* rhythmic sound

sopa: *nf.* soup
sopar: *vt.* to dip bread in a soup
sopear: *vt.* to scoop soup with a tortilla
sopera: *nf.* pot for making soup
sopero: *aj.* snoppy
sopesar: *vt.* to weigh in one's hand
soplado: *nm.* intestinal gas
soplador: *nm.* glass blowing apparatus
soplar: *vt.* to blow
soplarse: *vr.* to be blown (glass)
soplete: *nm.* welding torch
soplido: *nm.* brusque blowing sound
soplo: *nm.* blowing
soplón; -a: *nmf.* prompter in theater
soportable: *aj.* tolerable
soportar: *vt.* to support; bear; to suffer
soporte: *nm.* toleration
sordera: *nf.* deafness
sordina: *nf.* mute; in music
sordo: *aj.* deaf
sordomudez: *nf.* deaf-muteness
sordomudo: *aj.* deaf-mute
sorprendente: *aj.* surprising
sorprender: *vt.* to surprise
sorprenderse: *vr.* to be surprised
sorpresa: *nf.* surprise
sorpresivo: *aj.* surprise; surprising
sortija: *nf.* ring; curl
sosegado: *aj.* calm
sosegador: *aj.* calming
sosegar: *vt.* to calm
sosegarse: *vr.* to become calm
sosiego: *nm.* sense of calm
sospecha: *nf.* suspicion
sospechar: *vt.* to suspect
sospechosamente: *av.* suspiciously
sospechoso: *aj.* suspected
sospechoso; -a: *nmf.* suspect
sostén: *nm.* bra; support
sostener: *vt.* to support; hold up; sustain
sostenerse: *vr.* to maintain balance; to sustain oneself
sostenido: *aj.* sustained

sostenimiento: *nm.* sustenance
sotechado: *nm.* thatched roof; temporary roof
suave: *aj.* smooth; soft; gentle
suavemente: *av.* softly
suavidad: *nf.* softness
suavizante: *nm.* softener
suavizar: *vt.* to make soft or smooth
subalimentación: *nf.* malnutrition
subalimentado: *aj.* underfed
subarrendamiento: *nm.* subletting
subarrendar: *vt.* to sublet
subarrendatario; -a: *nmf.* tenant of sublet property
subatómico: *aj.* subatomic
subcampeón: *nm.* runner-up; second place winner
subcomisión: *nm.* subcommittee
subconciencia: *nf.* subconscious
subconsciente: *aj.* subconscious
subcontrato: *nm.* subcontract
subdelegación: *nf.* sub delegation
subdelegado: *aj.* sub delegated
subdelegar: *vt.* to sub delegate
subdesarrollado: *aj.* underdeveloped
subdesarrollo: *nm.* underdevelopment
subdirector; -a: *nmf.* sub-director
súbdito -ta: *nmf.* subject
subdividir: *vt.* to subdivide
subdivisión: *nf.* subdivision
subempleo: *nm.* underemployment
subespecie: *nf.* subspecies
subestimar: *vt.* to underestimate
subfusil: *nm.* submachine gun
subgénero: *nm.* sub-genus
subida: *nf.* going up; rise
subido: *aj.* strong (smell); dark (color); elevated; raised
subir: *vt.* to go up; to get on; to board
subirse a: *vt.* to go up; to get on; to board
subjefe; -a: *nmf.* assistant manager; supervisor
sublevación: *nf.* rebellion

sublevamiento: *nm.* rebellion
sublevar: *vt.* to incite to rebellion; to revolt; to disgust
sublevarse: *vr.* to be rebellious
sublimado: *aj.* exalted
sublimar: *vt.* to exalt
sublime: *aj.* sublime
submarinismo: *nm.* submarine technology
submarinista: *nmf.* submarine sailor
submarino: *aj.* submarine
submarino: *nm.* submarine
submarino; na: *nm.* submarine
suboficial: *nm.* person below the rank of officer
subordinación: *nf.* subordination
subordinado; -a: 1. *nmf.* subordinate; 2. *aj.* subordinate
subordinar: *vt.* to subordinate
subordinarse: *vr.* to subordinate oneself
subproducto: *nm.* by-product
subrayar: *vt.* to highlight; to underline
subscribir; suscribir: *vt.* to subscribe
subsecretaría: *nf.* office of undersecretary
subsecretario; -a: *nmf.* undersecretary
subsiguiente: *aj.* subsequent
subsistencia: *nf.* subsistence
subsistente: *aj.* subsistent
subsistir: *vi.* to subsist
substancial: *aj.* substantial
substitución: *nf.* substitution insustituible
substituible: *aj.* substitutable
substituir; sustituir: *vt.* to substitute; replace
substraer: *vt.* to subtract; deduct; or. to elude; evade
subsuelo: *nm.* subsoil
subteniente: *nm.* subtenant
subterráneo: *aj.* subterranean
subterráneo: *nm.* tunnel or cave beneath the surface of the earth

subtitular: *vt.* to subtitle; to give a subtitle to (a book)
subtítulo: *nm.* subtitle
suburbano: *aj.* suburban
suburbano: *nm.* one who lives in a suburb
suburbio: *nm.* suburb
subvalorar: *vt.* to under-value
subyacente: *aj.* lying beneath something else
suceder: *vi.* to happen; to occur
sucesión: *nf.* succession
sucesivamente: *av.* successively
sucesivo: *aj.* successive
suceso: *nm.* event; happening; occurrence
sucesor; -a: *nmf.* successor
suciedad: *nf.* dirtiness; rubbish
sucursal: *nf.* branch
sudar: *vt.* to sweat
sudoeste: *aj.* southwest
sudor: *nm.* sweat
suegra: *nf.* mother-in-law
suegro: *nm.* father-in-law
suela: *nf.* sole
sueldo: *nm.* salary; pay
suelo: *nm.* ground; soil; floor; pavement
suelto: *aj.* loose
sueño: *nm.* sleep; dream
suerte: *nf.* luck; fortune; chance; kind; sort; way
suficiencia: *nf.* sufficiency
suficiente: *aj.* sufficient
suficientemente: *av.* sufficiently
sufijo: *nm.* suffix
sufragar: *vt.* to help; support
sufrir: *vt.* to provide; furnish; to produce
sugerencia: *nf.* suggestion (counsel)
sugerente: *aj.* suggestive
sugeridor: *aj.* suggesting
sugerir: *vt.* to suggest
sugestión: *nf.* suggestion

sugestionable: *aj.* influenced easily
sugestionar: *vt.* to provoke through the power of suggestion
sugestivo: *aj.* suggestive
suicida: *nmf.* suicide victim
suicidarse: *vr.* to commit suicide
suicidio: *nm.* suicide
sujeción: *nf.* subjection
sujetador: *nm.* fastener; brass
sujetapapeles: *nm.* paper clip
sujetar: *vt.* to subject; to fasten
sujetarse: *vr.* to subject oneself; to be subjected to
sujeto: *aj.* subjected
sujeto: *nm.* subject; person
suma: *nf.* addition; amount; sum
sumadora: *nf.* adding machine
sumamente: *av.* greatly
sumando: *nm.* addend
sumar: *vt.* to add; to sum
sumarse: *vr.* to be added to; to unite with
sumergible: *aj.* submergible
sumergido: *aj.* submerged
sumergir: *vt.* to submerge
sumergirse: *vr.* to submerge oneself
sumir: *vt.* to submerge something; to sink
sumirse: *vr.* to be sinking
sumiso; sa: *aj.* submissive; humble
sumo; ma: *aj.* high; great; supreme
superabundante: *aj.* very abundant
superabundar: *vi.* to super-abound; overflow
superación: *nf.* improvement
superar: *vt.* to overcome; to surpass
superarse: *vr.* to succeed; to achieve one's goals
supercarburante: *nm.* high-octane fuel
superconductividad: *nf.* superconductivity
superconductor: *nm.* superconductor
superdesarrollado: *aj.* overdeveloped

superdesarrollo: *nm.* overdevelopment
superdotado: *aj.* very gifted; very talented
superestructura: *nf.* superstructure
superficial: *aj.* superficial
superficialidad: *nf.* superficiality
superficie: *nf.* surface; area
superfino: *aj.* very fine
superfluidad: *nf.* superfluity
superhombre: *nm.* superman
superior; -a: 1. *nmf.* superior; 2. *aj.* superior
superiora: *nf.* mother superior in a convent
superioridad: *nf.* superiority
supermercado: *nm.* supermarket
supermujer: *nf.* superwoman
superpetrolero: *nm.* supertanker
superpoblación: *nf.* overpopulation
superpoblado: *aj.* overpopulated
superproducción: *nf.* overproduction
supersecreto: *aj.* super-secret
supersónico: *aj.* supersonic
superstición: *nf.* superstition
supersticioso: *aj.* superstitious
supervalorar: *vt.* to over-value
supervisar: *vt.* to supervise
supervisión: *nf.* supervision
supervisor; -a: *nmf.* supervisor
supervivencia: *nf.* survival
superviviente: *aj.* surviving
suplencia: *nf.* substitution; replacing
suplente: *nmf.* replacement; substitute
súplica: *nf.* supplication
suplicante: *nmf.* one who pleads
suplicar: *vt.* to supplicate; implore; beg; play
suplir: *vt.* to substitute for; to replace; to supply; provide
suponer: *vt.* to suppose
suposición: *nf.* supposition
supremacía: *nf.* supremacy
supremo: *aj.* supreme

supresión: *nf.* suppression
suprimir: *vt.* to suppress; cut out
supuesto: *aj.* supposed; *nm* .
supposition
sur: *nm.* south
surcado: *aj.* filled with ruts or furrows
surtir to stock
surcar: *vt.* to make ruts or furrows
surco: *nm.* rut or furrow
sureño: *aj.* southern
sureste; sudeste: *nm.* southeast
suroeste; sudoeste: *nm.* southwest
surrealismo: *nm.* surrealism
surrealista: *aj.* surrealistic
surtido: *aj.* well-stocked
surtido: *nm.* stock
surtir: *vt.* to stock
susceptibilidad: *nf.* susceptibility
susceptible: *aj.* susceptible
suscitar: *vt.* to cause or provoke
suscribir; subscribir: *vt.* to subscribe
to an opinion
suscribirse; subscribirse: *vr.* to
subscribe to a publication or club
suscripción; subscripción: *nf.*
subscription
suscrito; subscrito: *aj.* subscribed
susodicho: *aj.* aforesaid; above
mentioned
suspender: *vt.* to suspend
suspensión: *nf.* suspension
suspensivo: *aj.* suspensive
suspenso: *nm.* suspense
suspicacia: *nf.* suspiciousness
suspicaz: *aj.* suspicious
suspirar: *vt.* to exhale; to sigh
suspiro: *nm.* sigh; breath
sustancia; substancia: *nf.* substance
insubstantial
sustanciar; substanciar: *vt.* to
substantiate
sustancioso; substancioso: *aj.*
substantial; valuable
sustantivo; substantivo: *aj.*

substantive sustentar to sustain
sustentación: *nf.* sustaining
sustentar: *vt.* to sustain; support
sustentarse: *vr.* to be sustained
sustento: *nm.* sustenance
sustituir; substituir: *vt.* to substitute
sustituto; -a; substituto; -a: *nmf.*
substitute
susto: *nm.* scare; fright
susurrar: *vi.* to whisper; to murmur; to
hum
sutil: *aj.* subtle; keen
sutileza: *nf.* subtlety
sutilizar: *vt.* to refine the details
sutilmente: *av.* subtly
suyo; ya: *aj.* and pron. poss. his; hers;
yours; theirs; its; one's

T

tabacalero; -a: *nmf.* tobacco farmer or
seller
tabaco: *nm.* tobacco; tobacco de polvo;
snuff
tabaquera: *nf.* snuff box; case for
tobacco
tabaquismo: *nm.* illness caused by the
use of tobacco
taberna: *nf.* tavern; pub
tabique: *nm.* thin wall
tabla: *nf.* board; table; butcher shop
tablear: *vt.* to make wooden planks
tablero: *nm.* board; panel; bulletin
board
tableta: *nf.* tablet
tablilla: *nf.* small plank or board
tablón: *nm.* thick plank or board
taburete: *nm.* stool
tacaño; ña: *aj.* stingy; cunning

tachar: *vt.* to erase; to strike out; to censure
táctil: *aj.* tactile
tacto: *nm.* sense of touch
tajada: *nf.* cut; slice
tajo: *nm.* cut; trench
tal: 1. *aj.* indef. such; 2. *pron.* indef. so-and-so; 3. *adv.* so
taladrar: *vt.* to bore; drill
talar: *vt.* to fell
talega: *nf.* bag; sack
talento: *nm.* talent
talentoso: *aj.* talented
talla: *nf.* cut; carving; height; stature; size
tallado: *aj.* carved
tallado: *nm.* action of engraving
tallador; -a: *nmf.* engraver
tallar: *vt.* to carve; to engrave; to cut
talle: *nm.* shape; figure
taller: *nm.* shop; workshop; atelier; studio
tallo: *nm.* stalk
talludo: *aj.* long-stemmed tapar to cover; to put a lid on
talonario: *nm.* receipt book
tamaño; na: 1. *aj.* such a big; 2. *nm.* Size
también: *adv.* also; too
tambor: *nm.* drum
tamizar: *vt.* to sieve
tampoco: *adv.* neither; not either; nor
tantear: *vt.* to compare; to size up; to test
tapa: *nf.* lid; cover
tapabocas: *nm.* surgical mask; gag
tapadera: *nf.* lid; cover; cap
tapado: *aj.* covered
tapar: *vt.* to cover up; to conceal
taparrabos: *nm.* loin cloth
taparse: *vr.* to cover oneself
tapete: *nm.* rug; card table
tapia: *nf.* adobe brick
tapiar: *vt.* to enclose using adobe brick

tapicería: *nf.* tapestry; upholstery
taquilla: *nf.* triangular kerchief
tara: *nf.* tare; defect
tardanza: *nf.* late arrival; lateness
tardar: *vi.* to be long; to be late; a más tardar; at the latest
tarde: *adv.* late; too late
tarde: *nf.* afternoon
tardío: *aj.* delayed
tardo: *aj.* slow
tarea: *nf.* homework; assignment; work
tarifa: *nf.* tariff; price list; rate; fare
tarima: *nf.* stand; platform
tarjeta: *nf.* card
tarro: *nm.* jar
tarta: *nf.* tart; pan
tartamudo; da: 1. *aj.* stuttering; stammering; 2. *nmf.* stutterer; stammerer
tasa: *nf.* measure; estimate
tasar: *vt.* to appraise; to regulate
tatarabuela: *nf.* great-great-grandmother
tatarabuelo: *nm.* great-great-grandfather
tataranieto; -a: *nmf.* great-great-grandchild
tatuaje: *nm.* tattoo; tattooing
tauromaquia: *nf.* bullfighting
taxi: *nm.* taxi; cab
taza: *nf.* cup
tazón: *nm.* bowl
té: *nm.* tea; drink
teatral: *aj.* of the theater; theatrical
teatro: *nm.* theater
techado; a: *aj.* roofed
techar: *vt.* to put a roof on
techo: *nm.* ceiling; roof; shelter
tecla: *nf.* key
técnica: *nf.* technique
tecnicismo: *nm.* technical term
técnico: 1. *aj.* technical; 2. *nmf.* technician

tecnicolor: *nm.* technicolor
tecnología: *nf.* technology
tecnológico: *aj.* technological
teja: *nf.* roofing tile; shovel hat
tejado: *nm.* roof or ceiling
tejamaní: *nm.* roofing tile
tejar: *vt.* to put a roof on
tejedor; -a: *nmf.* one who knits; weaver
tejer: *vt.* to knit; to weave
tejido: *nm.* weave; texture
tela: *nf.* cloth; fabric
telar: *nm.* weaving machine; loom
telaraña: *nf.* spider web; cobweb
tele: *nf.* television
telecabina: *nf.* car or cabin suspended from an aerial wire
telecomunicación: *nf.* telecommunication
telediario: *nm.* daily television news bulletin
teledirigido: *aj.* remote-controlled
teledirigir: *vt.* to operate by remote control
telefax: *nm.* fax machine
teleférico: *nm.* aerial tramway; sky cable car
telefilm; telefilme: *nm.* film made for television
telefonear: *vt.* to telephone
telefonía: *nf.* telephony
telefónico: *aj.* telephonic
telefonista: *nmf.* telephone operator
teléfono: *nm.* telephone
telegrafía: *nf.* telegraphy
telegrafiar: *vt.* to telegraph
telegráficamente: *av.* telegraphically
telegráfico: *aj.* telegraphic
telegrafista: *nmf.* telegrapher
telégrafo: *nm.* telegraph
telegrama: *nf.* telegram
telemando: *nm.* remote control system
telenovela: *nf.* soap opera
teleobjetivo: *nm.* telephoto lens

telepatía: *nf.* telepathy
telepáticamente: *av.* telepathically
telepático: *aj.* telepathic
telequinesia: *nf.* telekinesis
telescópico: *aj.* telescopic
telescopio: *nm.* telescope
telesilla: *nf.* ski lift chair
telespectador; -a: *nmf.* member of a television audience
telesquí: *nm.* ski lift
teletipo: *nm.* teletype machine
televidente: *nmf.* television watcher
televisar: *vt.* to televise
televisión: *nf.* television
televisivo: *aj.* television
televisor: *nm.* television
telón: *nm.* curtain
tema: *nf.* theme; subject
temario: *nm.* list of subjects
temática: *nf.* overall theme
temático: *aj.* thematic
temblar: *vt.* to temper; to soften; to tremble
temblón: *aj.* trembling
temblor: *nm.* earthquake
tembloroso: *aj.* trembling temer to fear
temer: *vt.* to fear
temeroso: *aj.* fearful
temerse: *vr.* to be afraid; to suspect
temible: *aj.* fearsome
temor: *nm.* fear; dread
temperamental: *aj.* temperamental
temperamento: *nm.* temperament
temperancia: *nf.* temperance
temperar: *vt.* to temper
temperatura: *nf.* temperature
tempestad: *nf.* storm; tempest
tempestuoso: *aj.* tempestuous
templo: *nm.* temple; church
temporada: *nf.* season; period
temporal: 1. *aj.* temporary; provisional; 2. *nmf.* temporary worker; seasonal employee
temprano: *av.* early

tenacidad: *nf.* tenacity
tenaz: *aj.* tenacious
tenazas: *nf.* pl tongs
tendencia: *nf.* tendency
tendencioso: *aj.* tendentious
tender: *vt.* to spread out; to hang; to tend to
tenderete: *nm.* provisional store as in a flea market
tendero; -a: *nmf.* storekeeper; shopkeeper
tenderse: *vr.* to stretch out
tendido: *aj.* spread out; hanging
tenebrosidad: *nf.* darkness
tenebroso: *aj.* dark; full of darkness
tenedor: *nm.* fork; holder
tenencia: *nf.* possession
tener: *vt.* to have; to keep; to own; to possess
teniente: *nm.* tenant
teñir: *vt.* to dye; to stain; to tinger
tenis: *nm.* (sport) tennis
tenorio: *nm.* lady-killer
tenso; sa: *aj.* tense; tight; stiff
tentación: *nf.* temptation
tentador: *aj.* tempting
tentar: *vt.* to touch; to try; to tempt; to attempt
teorema: *nf.* theorem
teoría: *nf.* theory
teórico: *aj.* theoretical
teorizar: *vt.* to theorize
tercera: *nf.* third
tercermundista: *aj.* third-world
tercero: *aj.* third
terciar: *vt.* to divide into thirds
terciario: *aj.* tertiary tierra
tercio; cia: *aj.* third
terciopelo: *nm.* velvet
tergiversar: *vt.* to twist; to distort
terminación: *nf.* termination
terminado: *aj.* finished
terminal: 1. *aj.* terminal; 2. *nf.* terminal
terminante: *aj.* definite; unarguable; decisive
terminantemente: *av.* definitely; unarguably; decisively
terminar: *vt.* to terminate; to end; to finish; to terminate
terminarse: *vr.* to be finished
término: *nm.* term; end
termo: *nm.* thermos bottle; flask
termómetro: *nm.* thermometer
ternera: *nf.* calf; veal
terracota: *nf.* terra-cotta; earthen color
terraplén: *nm.* rampart; bank
terráqueo: *aj.* of planet earth;
terrateniente: *nmf.* landowner
terraza: *nf.* terrace
terregoso: *aj.* dusty
terremoto: n earthquake
terrenal: *aj.* terrestrial
terreno: 1. *nm.* terrain; 2. *aj.* terrestrial
terrestre: *aj.* terrestrial
terrícola: *nmf.* human being; earthling
territorial: *aj.* territorial
territorio: *nm.* territory
terrón: *nm.* dirt clod; lump
terror: *nm.* terror
terrorífico: *aj.* full of terror
terrorismo: *nm.* terrorism
terrorista: *nmf.* terrorist
terroso: *aj.* dirt-like; dusty
terruño: *nm.* dirt clod; little country
terso: *aj.* smooth
tersura: *nf.* smoothness
tertulia: *nf.* party; cirde
tesis: *nf.* thesis; theme
tesorería: *nf.* treasury
tesorero; -a: *nm.* treasurer
tesoro: *nm.* treasure
testamentaría: *nf.* execution of a will
testamentario: *aj.* relating to a will
testamentario; -a: *nmf.* beneficiaries of a will
testamento: *nm.* testament; will
testar: *vi.* to make a will
testificar: *vt.* to testify; to act as a

witness
testigo: *nmf.* witness
testimonial: *aj.* testimonial texto text
testimoniar: *vt.* to give testimony
testimonio: *nm.* testimony
teta: *nf.* breast; nipple
tetera: *nf.* teapot; teakettle
texto: *nm.* text
textual: *aj.* textual
tez: *nf.* complexion; facial skin
tía: *nf.* aunt
tiburón: *nm.* shark
tiempo: *nm.* time; season
tienda: *nf.* store; tent
tierno; na: *aj.* tender; soft; delicate
tierra: *nf.* earth; ground; land; country; soil
tieso; sa: *aj.* stiff; tight; tense
tiesto: *nm.* flowerpot
tijera: *nf.* scissors; shears
tila: *nf.* linden tree
timar: *vt.* to cheat; trick
timbre: *nm.* seal; stamp
timidez: n timidity
tímido: *aj.* timid; shy
timo: *nm.* theft; swindle
timón: *nm.* beam; helm
tímpano: *nm.* eardrum
tinaja: *nf.* large earthen jar
tinieblas: *nf.* darkness
tino: *nm.* aim
tinta: *nf.* ink
tintar: *vt.* to ink
tinte: *nm.* dye
tintero: *nm.* ink bottle
tinto: *aj.* dark red
tintura: *nf.* dyeing
tío: *nm.* uncle
típico: *aj.* typical
tipificación: *nf.* classification by type
tipificar: *v.* to typify
tira: *nf.* strip
tirabuzón: *nm.* corkscrew; curl
tirador: *nm.* gun shooter; thrower;

drawer
tiranía: *nf.* tyranny
tiránico: *aj.* tyrannical
tiranización: *nf.* tyrannizing
tiranizar: *vt.* to tyrannize
tirano; a: *nmf.* tyrant
tirar: *vt.* to throw; to cast; to shoot; to fire
tiritar: *vi.* to shiver
tiro: *nm.* shot; range; draft
tirotear: *vt.* to shoot bullets into the air
tirotearse: *vr.* to be shooting bullets into the air
tiroteo: *nm.* exchange of gu*nf.*ire
titubear: *vi.* to stagger; totter; to stammer
titulación: *nf.* act of entitling
titulado: *aj.* licensed; titled
titular: 1. *aj.* titular official; 2. *nm.* bearer; holder
titular: *vt.* to title something
título: *nm.* title
tiza: *nf.* chalk
toalla: *nf.* towel
tobillo: *nm.* ankle
tobogán: *nm.* slide
tocadiscos: *nm.* record player
tocador: *nm.* boudoir
tocar: *vt.* to feel; to touch; to ring; to touch
tocino: *nm.* the white of the bacon; bacon
todavía: *av.* still; vet
todo: *pron.* all
todopoderoso: *aj.* all-powerful
tolerable: *aj.* tolerable
tolerado: *aj.* tolerated
tolerancia: *nf.* tolerance
tolerar: *vt.* to tolerate; to bear; to suffer; to endure
toma: *nf.* dose; electrical outlet
tomadura: *nf.* taking
tomar: *vt.* to take; to get; to seize
tomarse: *v.* to drink

tomate: *nm.* tomato
tomavistas: *nm.* motion picture
tomillo: *nm.* thyme
tomo: *nm.* volume
tonada: *nf.* tune; melody
tonadilla: *nf.* short song; musical interlude
tonalidad: *nf.* tonality
tonel: *nm.* cask; barrel
tonelada: *nf.* ton
tonelaje: *nm.* tonnage
tónico: 1. *aj.* tonic; 2. *nf.* tonic
tonificante: *aj.* invigorating
tonificar: *vt.* to tone up
tono: *nm.* tone
tontada: *nf.* foolish or silly act
tontear: *vi.* to do a foolish thing
tontería: *nf.* foolish or silly act
tonto: *aj.* foolish; silly
topo: *nm.* mole
toque: *nm.* touch; knock; beat
torcedura: *nf.* twisting
torcer: *vt.* to twist
torcerse: *vr.* to lose one's way
torcido: *aj.* twisted
torear: *vt.* to fight; *vi.* to fight bulls
toreo: *nm.* bullfighting
torero: *aj.* bullfighting
tormenta: *nf.* storm; tempest
tormento: *nm.* torment; torture
tormentoso: *aj.* stormy
tornado: *nm.* tornado
tornar: *vr.* to turn
tornarse: *vr.* to return; to turn (change)
tornasol: *nm.* su*nf.*lower plant
torneado: *aj.* lathed
tornear: *vt.* to turn in a lathe
tornero; -a: *nmf.* lathe or turntable operator
tornillo: *nm.* screw; vice
torniquete: *nm.* tourniquet
torno: *nm.* turntable; lathe
toro: *nm.* bull
torpe: *aj.* physically or mentally

uncoordinated
torpeza: *nf.* lack of coordination; lack of physical or mental dexterity
torre: *nf.* tower; watchtower
torrencial: *aj.* torrential
torrente: *nm.* torrent
torrente sanguíneo: *nm.* blood circulation
torreón: *nm.* big tower
torrero: *nm.* lighthouse keeper
torreta: *nf.* turret
torta: *nf.* cake; *con.* slap
tortilla: *nf.* omelet
torturar: *vt.* to torture; to torment
toser: *vi.* to cough
tostar: *vt.* to toast; to roast; to tan
total: 1. *aj.* total; 2. *nm.* total
total: *av.* total
totalidad: *nf.* totality
totalitario: *aj.* totalitarian
totalitarismo: *nm.* totalitarianism
totalizar: *vt.* to total
trabajado: *aj.* work
trabajador; -a: *nmf.* worker
trabajar: *vt.* to work; to till (the soil)
trabajoso: *aj.* hard-working
traca: *nf.* string of firecrackers
trace: *aj.* thirteen
tradición: *nf.* tradition
tradicional: *aj.* traditional
tradicionalismo: *nm.* traditionalism
tradicionalista: *aj.* traditionalistic
traducción: *nf.* translation
traducir: *vt.* to translate
traductor; -a: *nmf.* translator
traer: *vt.* to bring; to carry; to cause
traficar in: to traffic; deal; trade
tragadero: *nm.* pharynx
tragaluz: *nm.* skylight; bull's eye
tragaperras: *nm. con.* slot machine
tragar: *vt.* to swallow; to gulp
tragarse: *vr.* to be swallowed up by earth or water
tragedia: *nf.* tragedy

trágico: *aj.* tragic
tragicomedia: *nf.* tragic comedy
tragicómico: *aj.* tragicomic
trago: *nm.* swallow; gulp; *con.* misfortune
tragón; -a: *nmf.* a big eater
traición: *nf.* betrayal
traicionar: *vt.* to betray
traicionero: *aj.* betraying
traidor; -a: *nmf.* traitor
traje: *nm.* suit trama plot
trajearse: *vr.* to wear a suit
trajín: *nm.* carrying; going and coming
trama: *nf.* plot tranquilo tranquil
tramar: *vt.* to weave; to plot; to scheme
tramo: *nm.* tract; stretch; flight
trampa: *nf.* trap; snare; pitfall; foul play
trampolín: *nm.* spring board
tranquilidad: *nf.* tranquility
tranquilizador: *aj.* calming; tranquilizing
tranquilizante: *nm.* sedative; tranquilizer
tranquilizar: *vt.* to tranquilize; to calm
tranquilizarse: *vr.* to become calm; to calm down (oneself)
tranquilo: *aj.* tranquil; quiet
transacción: *nf.* transaction
transbordar: *vt.* to change planes; trains; ships
transbordo; trasbordo: *nm.* the act of changing planes; trains; etc. while on a trip
transcontinental: *aj.* transcontinental
transcribir: *vt.* to transcribe
trascripción; transcripción: *nf.* transcription
transcurrir: *vi.* to pass
transcurso: *nm.* passage (of time); period (of time)
transeúnte: 1. *aj.* transient; 2. *nmf.* transient; passer-by

transexual: *aj.* transsexual
transexualismo: *nm.* transsexualism
transferir: *vt.* to transfer
transformable: *aj.* transformable
transformación: *nf.* transformation
transformador: *nm.* transformer
transformar: *vt.* to transform; to change
transformarse: *vr.* to become transformed
transformista: *nmf.* quick-change artist
transigir: *vt.* to settle; to compromise
transitable: *aj.* passable
transitado: *aj.* frequently traveled
transitar: *vi.* to travel; journey; to pass by; to pass through
transitivo: *aj.* transitive
tránsito: *nm.* traffic cop; traffic
transitorio: *aj.* transitory
transmitir: *vt.* to transmit; forward
transparencia: *nf.* transparency
transparentar: *vt.* to make transparent
transparentarse: *vr.* to be transparent
transparente: *aj.* transparent
transpirar: *vt.* to transpire
transplantar: *vt.* to transplant
transplante: *nm.* transplant
transponer: *vt.* to transpose
transponerse: *vr.* to be behind something
transportador: *aj.* transporting
transportar: *vt.* to transport
transportarse: *vr.* to be transported
transporte: *nm.* transport
transportista: *nmf.* transportation worker
transposición: *nf.* transposition
tranvía: *nf.* streetcar
tranviario: *aj.* relating to streetcars
trapo: *nm.* rag
trasero; ra: 1. *aj.* back; 2. *nm.* buttock; rump; bottom
trasladar: *vt.* to transfer

trasladarse: *vr.* to move from one place to another
traslado: *nm.* moving from one place to another
traslucirse: *vr.* to be semi-transparent
trasluz: *nm.* light that shines through something transparent
trasnochador; -a: *nmf.* person who stays up all night
trasnochar: *vt.* to be up all night; *vi.* to spend the night
traspapelado: *aj.* mixed in with a pile of papers
traspapelar: *vt.* to misplace a piece of paper
traspapelarse: *vr.* to be misplaced (piece of paper)
traspasar: *vt.* to cross; cross over; to pierce
traspaso: *nm.* trespass
trasplantar: *vt.* to transplant
trasplantarse: *vr.* to be transplanted
traste: *nm.* fret
trastienda: *nf.* back shop
trastornado: *aj.* ill for having lost one's common sense or reason
trastornar: *vt.* to cause physical or mental disorder
trastornarse: *vr.* to lose one's common sense or reason
trastorno: *nm.* loss of common sense or reason
tratado: *nm.* treaty
tratamiento: *nm.* treatment
tratar: *vt.* to try; to treat
tratarse: *vr.* to be treated; to get along with each other
trato: *nm.* relationship
través: *prep.* through; across; misfortune; mishap
travesaño: *nm.* crosspiece or crossbar
travesía: *nf.* cross street or road; crossing
trayecto: *nm.* journey; passage; path

trayectoria: *nf.* trajectory
traza: *nf.* design of a project
trazado: *nm.* act of designing a project; plan or project
trazar: *vt.* to plan; design
trazo: *nm.* line in a drawing
trébol: *nm.* clover; trefoil; shamrock
trece: 1. *aj.* thirteen; 2. *nm.* thirteen
treceavo: *aj.* thirteenth
trecho: *nm.* stretch
tregua: *nf.* truce; letup
treinta: 1. *aj.* thirty; 2. *nm.* thirty
treintavo: *aj.* thirtieth
treintena: *nf.* a group of thirty
tren: *nm.* train; outfit
trenza: *nf.* braid; plait
trepador: *aj.* climbing
trepar: *vt.* to climb without a ladder
tres: *aj.* three
trescientos: *aj.* three-hundred
tresillo: *nm.* three-player card game
triangular: *aj.* triangular
triángulo: *nm.* triangle
tribunal: *nm.* court; bar
tributación: *nf.* act of paying a tribute
tributar: *vt.* to give tribute; to pay
tributario: *aj.* tributary; tribute-paying
tributo: *nm.* tribute
triciclo: *nm.* tricycle
trigo: *nm.* wheat
trillar: *vt.* to thresh
trimestre: *nm.* term
trinchar: *vt.* to carve; to slice
trino: 1. *aj.* trinal; three fold; 2. *nm.* rill; warble
tripa: *nf.* gut; intestine
triple: *aj.* triple
tripulación: *nf.* crew
tripular: *vt.* to man (ship)
triste: *aj.* sad; sorrowful
tristeza: *nf.* sadness
triturar: *vt.* to triturate; to mash; grind
triunfador; -a: *nmf.* conqueror
triunfal: *aj.* triumphant

triunfar: *vi.* to triumph
triunfo: *nm.* triumph
trofeo: *nm.* trophy
tromba: *nf.* column; avalanche; water-sport
trompo: *nm.* top
tronchar: *vt.* to chop off; to break off
tronco: *nm.* trunk; stalk
trono: *nm.* throne
tropa: *nf.* troop; flock; troops
tropezar: *vt.* to hit; to strike; to stumble
tropezarse: *vr.* to trip
tropezón: *nm.* trip or fall
tropiezo: *nm.* stumbling block
trozo: *nm.* piece; bit; fragment
trucha: *nf.* trout
trueno: *nm.* thunder
tu: pron. pers. you
tuba: *nf.* tuba
tubería: *nf.* piping; pipes
tubo: *nm.* tube; pipe
tubular: *aj.* tubular
tuerca: *nf.* nut
tuerto; ta: *aj.* one-eyed person
tufo: *nm.* fume; vapor
tumba: *nf.* grave; tomb
tumbar: *vt.* to knock down; or. *con.* to lie down
tundir: *vt.* to shear (cloth); *con.* to beat
túnel: *nm.* tunnel
turba: *nf.* disorderly crowd
turbación: *nf.* disturbance; chaos
turbado: *aj.* disturbed
turbador: *aj.* disturbing
turbar: *vt.* to disturb; upset; trouble
turbarse: *vr.* to be disturbed
turbina: *nf.* turbine
turbio: *aj.* turbid
turbonada: *nf.* small lightning and thunder storm
turborreactor: *nm.* turbine engine
turbulencia: *nf.* turbulence
turbulento: *aj.* turbulent

turismo: *nm.* tourism
turista: *nmf.* tourist
turístico: *aj.* touristic; tourist; touristy
turnar: *vi.* to alternate
turno: *nm.* turn; shift
tutor -ra: *nm.* guardian; protector; tuter
tuyo; ya: *aj.* pron. poss. yours

U

ubicación: *nf.* location; situation
ubicar: *vt.* to place; locate
ulcera: *nf.* ulcer
ulterior: *aj.* ulterior; farther; subsequent
ulteriormente: *av.* subsequently
últimamente: *av.* 700 recently; lately
ultimar: *vt.* to end; finish; to conclude
ultimátum: *nm.* ultimatum
último: *aj.* last; latest
ultraderecha: *nf.* ultra-right
ultraderechista: *aj.* ultra-right wing
ultraderechista: *nmf.* ultra-right winger
ultrajar: *vt.* to outrage
ultramar: *nm.* overseas
ultramarino: *aj.* overseas
ultramoderno: *aj.* ultramodern
ultrasónico: *aj.* ultrasonic
ultrasonido: *nm.* ultrasound
ultratumba: *av.* beyond the tomb
ultravioleta: *aj.* ultraviolet virgen virgin
uno; una: 1. *art.* indef. a; an; 2. *aj.* one (numeral)
umbral: *nm.* threshold
un: *aj.* one
uña: *nf.* fingernail or toenail

unánime: *aj.* unanimous
unanimidad: *nf.* unanimity
unción: *nf.* unction
undécimo: *aj.* eleventh
undécimo: *nm.* one-eleventh (fraction)
uñero: *nm.* ingrown nail
ungir: *vt.* to anoint; consecrate
unicameral: *aj.* unicameral
unicelular: *aj.* unicellular
único: *aj.* only; unique
unicolor: *aj.* of one color
unicornio: *nm.* unicorn
unidad: *nf.* unity; unit
unidireccional: *aj.* one-directional
unido: *aj.* united
unificación: *nf.* unification
unificador;-a: *nmf.* unifier; one who unifies
unificar: *vt.* to unify; to unite
uniformado: *aj.* uniformed
uniformar: *vt.* to make uniform
uniforme: 1. *aj.* uniform; 2. *nm.* uniform
uniformidad: *nf.* uniform
unigénito: *aj.* only-begotten
unilateral: *aj.* unilateral
unión: *nf.* union
unir: *vt.* to unite; to join
unirse: *vr.* to become united with; to become joined to
unisexo: *aj.* unisex
unísono: *nm.* unison
unitario: *aj.* unitary; per unit
universal: *aj.* universal
universalidad: *nf.* universality
universalización: *nf.* generalization
universalizar: *vt.* to generalize uno;-a pron one
universitario: *aj.* university
universitario;-a: *nmf.* professor or student in a university
universo: *nm.* universe; earth
uno: *aj.* one
untar: *vt.* to anoint; to smear; grease

unto: *nm.* grease; fat
uralita: *nf.* asbestos
uranio: *nm.* uranium
urbanidad: *nf.* urbanity; good-manners; civility
urbanismo: *nm.* city planning
urbanización: *nf.* urbanization
urbanizar: *vt.* to urbanize
urbano: *aj.* urban
urbe: *nf.* well-populated city; big city; metropolis
urgencia: *nf.* urgency; emergency
urgente: *aj.* urgent
urgentemente: *av.* urgently
urgir: *vi.* to be urgent
urna: *nf.* urn; ballot box
usado –da: *aj.* used
usar: *vt.* to use or to wear
uso: *nm.* use; custom; habit; practice
usted: pron. you
usuario;-a: *nmf.* one who uses
usurpar: *vt.* usurp
utensilio: *nm.* utensil
útil: *aj.* useful
útil: *nm.* use
utilerla: *nf.* collection of stage props
utilidad: *nf.* utility; usefulness; profit from a business
utilitarismo: *nm.* utilitarianism
utilizable: *aj.* utilizable
utilización: *nf.* utilization
utilizar: *vt.* to utilize
uva: *nf.* grape

V

vaca: *nf.* cow; beef
vacación: *nf.* vacation
vacante: 1. *aj.* vacant; 2. *nf.* vacancy
vaciado: *nm.* plaster cast
vaciar: *vt.* to drain; to empty
vaciarse: v. to become empty
vacilación: *nf.* vacillation
vacilante: *aj.* vacillating
vacilar: *vi.* to vacillate
vacío: *aj.* empty
vacuo: *aj.* vacuous
vagabundear: *vi.* to live the life of a vagabond
vagabundeo: *nm.* the life of a vagabond
vagabundo;-a: 1. *nmf.* vagabond; 2. *aj.* vagabond
vagancia: *nf.* vagrancy
vagar: *vi.* to wander aimlessly
vago: *aj.* vague
vago;-a: *nmf.* vagrant; idler
vagón: *nm.* wagon
vaguear: *vi.* to wander around
vaguedad: *nf.* vagueness; ambiguity
vaho: *nm.* vapor; fume
vaivén: *nm.* coming and going
vale: *nm.* bond; receipt; voucher
valentía: *nf.* courage; bravery
valentón;-a: *aj.* pretentious; arrogant
valentonada: *nf.* pretentious act
valer: *nm.* worth; merit
valer: *vi.* to be worth
valeroso: *aj.* courageous; brave
validar: *vt.* to validate
validez: *nf.* validity
válido –da: *aj.* valid; strong
valiente: *aj.* courageous; brave
valientemente: *av.* courageously; valiantly

valija: *nf.* valise; bag
valioso: *aj.* valuable
valla: *nf.* fence; barricade
valle: *nm.* valley; vale
valor: *nm.* courage; bravery; value; worth
valoración: *nf.* determination of price; appraisal; valuation
valorar: *vt.* to value
valorizar: *vt.* to value or appreciate; to evaluate
valuar: *vt.* to value; to appraise
válvula: *nf.* valve
vanagloria: *nf.* vainglory
vanagloriar: *vr.* to boast
vanagloriarse: *vr.* to brag or boast
vanguardia: *nf.* vanguard
vanguardismo: *nm.* tendency to be at the cutting edge in arts and letters
vanguardista: *nmf.* person who is at the cutting edge
vanidad: *nf.* vanity
vanidoso: *aj.* very vain
vano: *aj.* vain
vapor: *nm.* vapor
vaporización: *nf.* vaporization
vaporizador: *nm.* vaporizer
vaporizar: *vt.* to vaporize
vaporizarse: *vr.* to be vaporized
vaporoso: *aj.* vapor-producing; vaporous
vaquero: *nm.* cowboy
vara: *nf.* twig; stick
variabilidad: *nf.* variability; changing
variable: 1. *aj.* variable; 2. *nf.* variable
variación: *nf.* variation
variado: *aj.* varied
variante: *nf.* variant; version
variar: *vt.* to vary; to change
variedad: *nf.* variety
varilla: *nf.* rod; twig; wand
vario: *aj.* different; diverse
varón: *nm.* man
varonil: *aj.* relating to man or men

vasija: *nf.* small container; jar
vaso: *nm.* glass
vastedad: *nf.* vastness
vasto: *aj.* vast
vaticinar: *vt.* to prophesy
vecindad: *nf.* apartments or houses sharing common facilities
vecindario: *nm.* apartments or houses sharing common facilities
vecino;-a: 1. *aj.* neighboring; 2. *nmf.* neighbor
veda: *nf.* prohibition
vedar: *vt.* to forbid; prohibit
vega: *nf.* fertile plain
vegetación: *nf.* vegetation
vegetal: 1. *aj.* plant; 2. *nm.* plant
vegetar: *vi.* to vegetate
vegetarianismo: *nm.* vegetarianism
vegetariano;-a: 1. *nmf.* vegetarian; 2. *aj.* vegetarian
vegetativo: *aj.* vegetative
vehemencia: *nf.* vehemence
vehemente: *aj.* vehement
vehículo: *nm.* vehicle
veintavo: *nm.* one-twentieth (fraction)
veinte: 1. *aj.* twenty; 2. *nm.* twenty
veintena: *nf.* collection of twenty; score
vejez: *nf.* old age
vejiga: *nf.* bladder
vela: *nf.* wakefulness; candle; sail
velado: *aj.* veiled; blurred
velador: *nm.* night watchman
velar: *vt.* to keep watch late at night; to veil or to conceal
velatorio: *nm.* place where the body of the deceased is presented for viewing
velero: *nmf.* candle merchant; sail maker; sailboat
vello: *nm.* down
velo: *nm.* veil
velocidad: *nf.* velocity; speed
velocímetro: *nm.* speedometer
velódromo: *nm.* velodrome

vena: *nf.* vein
vencedor: *nmf.* conqueror
vencer: *vt.* to conquer
vencido: *aj.* conquered
vendaje: *nm.* bandage
vendaval: *nm.* strong wind
vendedor;-a: *nmf.* salesman; seller
vender: *vt.* to sell; in. to sell; or. to sell oneself
venderse: *vr.* to be sold
vendible: *aj.* saleable
vendido: *aj.* sold
veneno: *nm.* venom; poison
venenoso: *aj.* venomous; poisonous
venerable: *aj.* venerable
veneración: *nf.* veneration
venerar: *vt.* to venerate; to worship
vengador: *aj.* avenging
vengador;-a: *nmf.* avenger
venganza: *nf.* revenge
vengar: *vt.* to avenge; or. to take revenge
vengarse: *vr.* to avenge oneself
vengativo: *aj.* vengeful
venida: *nf.* coming
venidero; ra: *aj.* coming; future
venir: *vi.* to come
venirse: *vr.* to be coming
venoso: *aj.* venous; pertaining to veins
venta: *nf.* sale
ventaja: *nf.* advantage; profit
ventajista: *nmf.* person who takes advantage of a situation in a selfish way
ventajoso: *aj.* advantageous
ventana: *nf.* window
ventanal: *nm.* very large window
ventanilla: *nf.* small window
ventarrón: *nm.* strong wind
ventilación: *nf.* ventilation
ventilador: *nm.* fan; ventilator
ventilar: *vt.* to ventilate; to do
ventilarse: *vr.* to become ventilated
ventoso: *aj.* windy

ventura: *nf.* happiness; luck; good fortune
venturoso: *aj.* fortunate; happy
ver: *nm.* sense of sight
ver: *vt.* to see
veracidad: *nf.* veracity
veranear: *vi.* to spend the summer
veraneo: *nm.* summer holidays
veraniego: *aj.* summer
verano: *nm.* summer
veras: *fpl.* truth; de veras; in truth
veraz: *aj.* true; sincere
verbo: *nm.* verb; the word
verdad: *nf.* truth
verdaderamente: *av.* truly
verdadero –ra: *aj.* true
verde: 1. *aj.* green; 2. *nm.* .green
verdear: *vi.* to turn green
verdor: *nm.* deep green color of plants
verdoso: *aj.* greenish
verdulería: *nf.* vegetable store
verdulero;-a: *nmf.* greengrocer
verdura: *nf.* vegetable
verdusco: *aj.* greenish
verge: *nm.* borde; margen
vergonzoso: *aj.* shameful; causing shame
vergüenza: *nf.* shame; bashfulness; shyness
verídico: *aj.* true; real
verificación: *nf.* verification
verificador;-a: *nmf.* verifier
verificar: *vt.* to verify
verificarse: *vr.* to become verified
verja: *nf.* grate; iron
verosímil: *aj.* believable; probable
versado: *aj.* well-versed
versar: *vi.* to turn around
verse: *vr.* to look; to appear
versículo: *nm.* verse of scripture
versificar: *vt.* to write verse
verso: *nm.* verse
vertedero: *nm.* trash bin or container
verter: *vt.* to pour; in. to flow; or. to urn

verterse: *vr.* to be poured
vertical: *aj.* vertical
vértice: *nm.* vertex
vertiginoso: *aj.* vertiginous
vértigo: *nm.* vertigo; dizziness
vestíbulo: *nm.* vestibule hall
vestido: *nm.* clothing; costume; dress
vestido: *aj.* dressed
vestidura: *nf.* dress
vestimenta: *nf.* vestments
vestir: *vt.* to dress
vestirse: *vr.* to dress oneself; to get dressed
vestuario: *nm.* clothing; wardrobe
vetar: *vt.* to veto
veto: *nm.* veto
vez: *nf.* time; turn
vía: *nf.* way; route; railroad tracks
viajante: *nmf.* traveler
viajar: *vi.* to travel
viaje: *nm.* trip
viajero;-a: *nmf.* traveler
vianda: *nf.* viand; food
viario: *aj.* relating to railroad tracks; relating to routes
víbora: *nf.* viper
vibración: *nf.* vibration
vibrador: *nm.* vibrator
vibrante: *aj.* vibrating; vibrant
vibrar: *vt.* to vibratevirgen
vibratorio: *aj.* capable of vibrating
vicealmirante: *nm.* vice-admiral
vicepresidencia: *nf.* vice presidency
vicepresidente;-a: *nmf.* vice president
vicesecretario;-a: *nmf.* assistant secretary
viciado: *aj.* corrupted
viciar: *vt.* to corrupt; to pervert
viciarse: *vr.* to be corrupted
vicio: *nm.* vice
vicioso: *aj.* vicious
victima: *nf.* victim
victoriosamente: *av.* victoriously

victorioso: *aj.* victorious vida life
vida: *nf.* life
vidente: 1. *aj.* seeing; 2. *nm.* prophet; seer
videoclub: *nm.* video rental store
videojuego: *nm.* video game
vidriado: *nm.* technique of glazing
vidriar: *vt.* to glaze
vidriarse: *vr.* to be glazed
vidriería: *nf.* glass shop
vidriero;-a: *nm.* person who works with glass
vidrio: *nm.* glass
vidrioso: *aj.* glass-like; glassy
vieja: *nf.* old woman; informally; a wife
viejo: *aj.* old
viejo: *nm.* old man; informally; a husband
viejo –ja: *aj.* old; ancient; *nm.* old man
viento: *nm.* wind; air
viernes: *nm.* Friday
vigencia: *nf.* valid status
vigente: *aj.* valid
vigía: *nmf.* security guard; watchman
vigilancia: *nf.* vigilance
vigilante: 1. *aj.* vigilant; 2. *nmf.* security guard
vigilar: *vt.* to watch over; to watch
vigilia: *nf.* vigil
vigor: *nm.* vigor
vigorizador: *aj.* invigorating
vigorizante: *aj.* invigorating
vigorizar: *vt.* to invigorate
vigoroso: *aj.* vigorous
villa: *nf.* town
villancico: *nm.* carol
viña: *nf.* vine; vineyard
viñador;-a: *nmf.* winegrower
vinagre: *nm.* vinegar
vinagrera: *nf.* vinegar bottle
vinagrero;-a: *nmf.* person who makes or sells vinegar
vinagreta: *nf.* sauce made with oil;

onions and vinegar
vinajera: *nf.* burette; cruel
vinatero;-a: *nmf.* wine merchant
vincular: *vt.* to entail
viñedo: *nm.* vineyard
vinícola: *aj.* relating to the making of wine
vinicultura: *nf.* winemaking
vinificación: *nf.* process of winemaking
vino: *nm.* wine
vinoso: *aj.* wine-like
violación: *nf.* violation; rape
violador;-a: *nmf.* violator; rapist
violar: *vt.* to violate; to rape
violas: *vt.* to violate; to trespass
violencia: *nf.* violence
violentamente: *av.* violently
violentar: *vt.* to force open; to do violence to
violentarse: *vr.* to become violent
violeta: 1. *aj.* violet; 2. *nf.* violet (flower); violet (color)
violetera: *nf.* florist that sells only violets
viraje: *nm.* turn; change of direction
virgen: 1. *aj.* virgin; 2. *nmf.* virgin
virginal: *aj.* virginal
virginidad: *nf.* virginity
virgo: *nm.* Virgo
viril: *aj.* virile
virilidad: *nf.* virility; manliness
virreina: *nf.* wife of the viceroy
virreinato: *nm.* position or office of viceroy
virrey: *nm.* viceroy
virtud: *nf.* virtue
virtuosidad: *nf.* virtuosity
virtuoso: *aj.* virtuous
virus: *nm.* virus
visibilidad: *nf.* visibility
visible: *aj.* visible
visiblemente: *av.* visibly
visión: *nf.* vision

visionario; -a: *nmf.* visionary
visita: *nf.* visit; visitor
visitación: *nf.* visitation
visitador: *aj.* visiting
visitador;-a: *nmf.* visitor; inspector
visitante: *aj.* visitor
visitar: *vt.* to visit; to call
vislumbrar: *vt.* to glimpse; to barely see
vislumbre: *nf.* glimpse; glimmer of light
víspera: *nf.* eve of an event vista sight
vista: *nf.* sight
vistazo: *nm.* a quick glance
visto –ta: *aj.* evident; obvious
vistoso: *aj.* captivating for its visual characteristics
visual: *aj.* visual
visualizar: *vt.* to visualize
vital: *aj.* vital
vitalicio: *aj.* lifelong
vitalicio –cia: *aj.* lifetime
vitalidad: *nf.* vitality; health
vitalizar: *vt.* to vitalize
vitamina: *nf.* vitamin
vitaminado: *aj.* vitamin-enriched
vitamínico: *aj.* vitamin-rich
vitrina: *nf.* glass show-case
viudez: *nf.* widowhood
viudo: *aj.* widow
viudo; da: *aj.* widowed
viudo;-a: *nmf.* widower; widow
viva: int. long live!
vivacidad: *nf.* vividness
vivamente: *av.* with intensity
vivaracho: *aj.* very awake; fun person;
vivaz: *aj.* vigorous; sharp; intelligent
vivencia: *nf.* life experience
víveres: *nm.* pl provisions
vivero: *nm.* nursery
viveza: *nf.* brightness of colors; eyes; and ideas
vívido: *aj.* vivid
vividor;-a: *nmf.* someone who lives

life at the expense of others
vivienda: *nf.* place where one lives; house
viviente: *aj.* living
vivificante: *aj.* animating; strengthening; encouraging
vivificar: *vt.* to animate; to encourage; to strengthen
vivir: *vt.* to live; to live in
vivo: *aj.* alive
vivo: *nmf.* living creature
vizconde: *nm.* viscount
vizcondesa: *nf.* viscountess
vocablo: *nm.* word; term
vocabulario: *nm.* vocabulary
vocación: *nf.* vocation; calling
vocacional: *aj.* vocational
vocal: *aj.* vocal
vocal: *nmf.* voting member of a committee
vocalismo: *nm.* vowel system
vocalista: *nmf.* vocalist
vocalización: *nf.* vocalization
vocalizar: *vt.* to vocalize
voceador: *aj.* announcing
voceador;-a: *nmf.* announcer; one who sells newspapers in the street
vocear: *vt.* to talk through a loudspeaker or megaphone
vocerío: *nm.* loud talking; especially of a crowd
vocero;-a: *nmf.* announcer; one who sells newspapers in the street
vociferador: *aj.* boasting
vociferante: *aj.* boasting
vociferar: *vt.* to vociferate
volador: *nm.* flyer person
volandas: *av.* in the air
volante: *nm.* flyer
volar: *vi.* to fly
volcar: *vt.* to upset
volear: *vt.* to volley
voleibol: *nm.* volleyball
voleo: *nm.* volley

voltear: *vt.* to turn around; to upset; to roll over
voltereta: *nf.* flip; somersault
volumen: *nm.* volume
voluminoso: *aj.* voluminous
voluntad: *nf.* will; determination
voluntariamente: *av.* voluntarily
voluntario: *aj.* voluntary
voluntario;-a: *nmf.* volunteer
voluntarioso: *aj.* strong-willed; self-willed
voluptuosidad: *nf.* voluptuousness
voluptuoso: *aj.* voluptuous
volver: *vt.* to return; to go back
volverse: *vr.* to be returning; to be going back
vos: *pron. pers.* you
vosotros –tras: *pron. pers.* you
votación: *nf.* voting
votante: *nmf.* voter
votar: *vt.* to vote; to vow
voto: *nm.* vote
voz: *nf.* voice
vozarrón: *nm.* a deep voice
vuelco: *nm.* upset; overturning
vuelo: *nm.* flight
vuelta: *nf.* lap
vulgar: *aj.* vulgar
vulgaridad: *nf.* vulgarity
vulgarismo: *nm.* vulgarism
vulgarización: *nf.* vulgarization
vulgarizar: *vt.* to vulgarize
vulgarizarse: *vr.* to be vulgar
vulgarmente: *av.* vulgarly
vulnerar: *vt.* to harm; injure

Y

yacente: *aj.* lying down
yacer: *vi.* to be lying down; to remain lying down; refer to the sick or the dead
yacimiento: *nm.* a bed of rock
yanqui: *aj.* Yankee
yarda: *nf.* yard
yate: *nm.* yacht
yegua: *nf.* mare
yelmo: *nm.* helmet
yema: *nf.* yolk; bud
yerno: *nm.* son-in-law
yerro: *nm.* error; mistake
yesca: *nf.* tinder
yesería: *nf.* place where plaster is processed or sold
yesero;-a: *nmf.* one who works with plaster
yeso: *nm.* gypsum; plaster
yesoso: *aj.* having the texture of plaster
rodilla
yo: *pron. pers.* 1
yuxtaponer: *vt.* to juxtapose
yuxtaposición: *nf.* juxtaposition
yuxtapuesto: *aj.* juxtaposed

Z

zafiro: *nm.* sapphire
zagal: *nm.* youth; shepherd's helper
zagala: *nf.* shepherdess
zaguán: *nm.* vestibule; entrance
zalamero; ra: 1. *aj.* flatterer; 2. *nmf.* flatterer
zamarra: *nf.* shepherd's sheepskin jacket

zanahoria: *nf.* carrot
zanca: *nf.* long leg
zángano: *nm.* drone
zanja: *nf.* ditch; trench
zanjar: *vt.* to dig a ditch (or) ditch-es in
zapapico: *nm.* pickax
zapata: *nf.* brake shoe
zapatazo: *nm.* kick
zapateado: *nm.* tap-dance
zapatear: *vt.* to tap with the sole of the shoe; to tap dance
zapateo: *nm.* foot-tapping
zapatería: *nf.* shoe store
zapatería: *nf.* shoe's shop
zapatero;-a: *nmf.* shoemaker; cobbler; shoe repairman
zapatilla: *nf.* slipper
zapatilla: *nf.* a fine shoe; woman's dress-shoe; ballet slipper
zapato: *nm.* shoe
zapatón: *nm.* big shoe; rain boot
zarandear: *vt.* to sift; to screen
zarpar: *vt.* to weigh
zarzuela: *nf.* zarzuela; musical comedy
zócalo: *nm.* socle; pediment
zona: *nf.* zone
zorro: *nm.* male fox
zozobra: *nf.* the act of becoming shipwrecked
zumo: *nm.* juice
zumbar: *vi.* to buzz; to hum
zumbido: *nm.* buzz; hum
zurcir: *vt.* to darn